W9-ACO-175

Nor Is It Over Yet

Nor Is It Over Yet

Florida in the Era of Reconstruction

1863–1877

Jerrell H. Shofner

A University of Florida Book

The University Presses of Florida
Gainesville / 1974

Library of Congress Cataloging in Publication Data

Shofner, Jerrell H. 1929–
Nor is it over yet; Florida in the era of Reconstruction, 1863–1877.

Bibliography: p.
1. Reconstruction—Florida. 2. Florida—Politics and government—1865–1950. I. Title.
F316.S56 975.9'06 70–186325
ISBN 0–8130–0353–9

PRINTED BY THE ROSE PRINTING COMPANY, INCORPORATED
TALLAHASSEE, FLORIDA

Preface

Perhaps the problems of the historian's craft are most acute in studying the period of the American Reconstruction. Historians deal with evidence about facts rather than with undisputed facts themselves. They are required to evaluate existing evidence and choose between conflicting sources of information. If they are obliged to deal with incomplete records, they also face the sheer magnitude of the human past. Most historians must limit their topics in space and time, yet when part of the story is lifted out of context for analysis and discussion, the author tampers with the shape of the past. The beginning and ending which he gives his period may not have been recognized by contemporaries. Historians must also recognize the possibility that their judgment may be influenced by their own angle of vision toward the topic under study. Whether or not I have dealt adequately with them, these limitations have been imposed on me, as on all historians practicing their craft, by the nature of my topic and the results of my research.

In limiting my study to the period from 1863 to 1877, I have accepted the term "Reconstruction" to mean an epoch which followed the Civil War. This implies a beginning and ending which were more sudden and substantive than was actually the case, but the celebrated Hayes-Tilden election controversy and the withdrawal of Federal troops in 1877 comprised an event too dramatic to be overlooked by historians. Still, those major turning points overshadow a continuity of social, economic, and even political affairs which was at least as significant as the political change. In Florida the continuity was much greater than the change.

The problem of periodization is slight, however, when compared to that of interpreting the existing evidence and evaluating the events of the period. Almost everyone who has even the slightest knowledge of the past has his own ideas about what happened after the Civil War. And, since the problems of that period are still unsettled in American society, people often judge historical works on the subject by the extent to which they confirm existing notions. On January 3, 1971, in the *Tallahassee Democrat,* a capable journalist described the inauguration of Reuben Askew as the first time "since the carpetbaggers packed up and headed north" that the change of leadership in Tallahassee has been "quite so complete." The newspaperman thus innocently re-inforced one of the most durable myths about the Reconstruction. Although historical scholarship of the past thirty years has done much to revise earlier interpretations, most Floridians today, whatever their origin, still believe that policy-makers between 1868 and 1877 were "carpetbaggers" who "packed up and headed north" when George F. Drew "redeemed" Florida from them in 1877.

One of the reasons for the persistence of that interpretation is that able scholarship around 1900 produced books which re-inforced contemporary popular belief and political campaign oratory about the nature of Reconstruction. One of the best of those writers was William Watson Davis, a native of West Florida, whose *Civil War and Reconstruction in Florida* was first published in 1913. Writing under the direction of William Archibald Dunning of Columbia University, he produced a scholarly monograph based on massive research of the records available at the time and interviews with people who lived during the Reconstruction era, including William D. Bloxham. From his own viewpoint, Davis was eminently fair in dealing with the events of Reconstruction, but the viewpoint from which he examined the evidence affected his conclusions.

Just as Davis and others who wrote at the time re-inforced existing popular beliefs about Reconstruction, they were themselves influenced by those beliefs. Interviewing Bloxham, by that time an elder statesman who had twice been governor after battling the Republicans during Reconstruction, Davis lent a receptive ear to the admirable old man. Yet Bloxham could scarcely be called impartial. Editorial statements of the *Tallahassee Floridian,* edited by Charles E. Dyke, the mastermind of Democratic strategy during Reconstruction, were also accepted without the caution necessary in dealing with inspired sources. Davis was not consciously unfair. Quite the contrary: he was a historian of considerable ability who prided himself on his scholarly detachment. But speaking of conservative white resistance to Negro suffrage, he wrote, "And in this contest for a very necessary supremacy many a foul crime was committed by white against black. Innocent people suffered. There is no mercy and scant justice in social adjustment. The Negro was first freed, then enfranchised, then launched in practical politics, and then mercilessly beaten into reasonable subjection" (1964 reprint, p. 586). At the risk of committing what David Donald has recently called "historical cannibalism" (*Charles Sumner and the Rights of Man* [New York, 1970], p. xii), I suggest that Davis' examination of the evidence about Reconstruction was influenced by a priori attitudes about his subject. There were others at the time who thought the "subjection" quite unreasonable.

In an excellent introduction to the 1964 reprint of Davis' *Civil War and Reconstruction in Florida,* Fletcher M. Green defended the author as a fair-minded scholar who acknowledged his prejudices and criticized white Floridians when they erred. Green cited the same statement quoted above to prove his point. But my own point is that Davis, because he wrote in the context of his time, did not question whether that "very necessary supremacy" justified "many a foul crime," let alone whether it was "necessary." Elsewhere Green credited Davis with impartiality on the question of Republican corruption and excessive indebtedness: "Davis noted that [the debt] had increased under the Radical Republican administration from $523,856.95 in 1868 to $5,620,809.55 in 1874, nearly 900 percent, but he remarked that 'a public debt . . . is not in itself necessarily indicative of bad government' " (Davis, p. xli). Green did not know that Davis used sources which led him to exaggerate the 1874 debt by $4 million. The actual increase was nearer 300 per cent (see chapter 15).

While acknowledging agreement with Green that Davis was a competent scholar, I believe that his interpretations are misleading. They have contributed to the enduring popular belief that "carpetbaggers" and "scalawags" dominated Florida by manipulating black voters, and that they were ousted by an aroused native population in 1876, after which they departed and the state began to prosper. Davis' concentration on political affairs and his conclusion of the book with the 1876 election dispute strengthen the interpretation.

Some of Davis' sources are no longer available. Bloxham and others who were interviewed have died, and some documents have been misplaced or destroyed. But a large volume of new material has since become available, especially in the Library of Congress and the National Archives. Recent scholarship and personal beliefs about the abilities and inalienable rights of people involved in the post–Civil War controversies make my viewpoint vastly different from that of Davis. Throughout this book I have used the new material that is available. It seems that there were many more shadings of opinion and conduct than Davis' categories implied. People were concerned with many things other than the struggle between contending political groups. For that matter, the contending groups were amorphous. The problems of earning a living consumed at least as much energy as those of maintaining a particular political party in power. The men who made policy prior to 1877 were not all Republicans, and all Republicans did not seek the same goals. Certainly they were not all "carpetbaggers" who "headed north" in 1877. Governor O. B. Hart was born in Jacksonville and died in office. Governor Harrison Reed's trip to Florida was one way: he died in the state in the 1890s; his grandson died there in 1970. Marcellus L. Stearns accepted a Federal appointment outside Florida in 1877, but he maintained a home at Quincy for many years. Other Republicans lived out their days as transplanted Floridians just as did thousands of apolitical immigrants during the period and just as hundreds of thousands have since.

This study begins with the Florida response to Lincoln's Reconstruction plan during the war and ends with the inauguration of Governor Drew in 1877. The organization is basically chronological, but there are topical chapters which describe events in the state other than the central political struggle. Where they seemed appropriate, conclusions have been drawn at the ends of chapters and in a brief concluding chapter. Where the interpretive differences seemed significant, issue has been taken with Davis and others. But the purpose is not to quarrel with earlier historians; rather it is to try to rediscover the past.

I wish to express my appreciation for assistance furnished by the staffs of the Florida State University Library; the Florida State Library; the Flowers Collecton at Duke University; the Federal Records Center, East Point, Georgia; the Manuscript Division of the Library of Congress; the National Archives; the New York Public Library; the P. K. Yonge Library of Florida History, University of Florida; and the Southern Historical Collection at the University of North Carolina at Chapel Hill. I am also indebted to Mrs. Leroy Collins for permitting me to use the Richard Keith Call Papers in the Southern Historical Collection.

I was assisted in my research by a grant from the Graduate Research Council of the Florida State University.

I wish to thank Professor Samuel Proctor of the University of Florida for reading the manuscript and for permitting me to use portions of two articles previously published in the *Florida Historical Quarterly*. I am also grateful to my colleague Professor Joe M. Richardson for reading the manuscript. I am especially indebted to Professor William W. Rogers of the Florida State University who has given assistance and encouragement in many ways over the years.

Publication of this book was assisted by the American Council of Learned Societies under a grant from the Andrew W. Mellon Foundation.

J.H.S

Contents

1. If That Scheme Fails, I Have Another 1
2. The Place Beset with Yankees 17
3. In the Hands of the White Race 31
4. Discrimination upon the Soundest Principles 46
5. I Fear You Have Hercules' Task 59
6. Custom Has Become the Law 81
7. No Road Is in Condition To Pay Cash 108
8. It Is Not Considered Disgraceful To Work 123
9. Gradually We Learned How To Manage 141
10. There Is Some Political Excitement Here 157
11. Radicalism Has Been Sent Howling 177
12. Reed Has Been Abused and Slandered and Tormented 198
13. Assassination Is Not a Pleasant Fate 225
14. A Combination To Promote Our State Interest 243
15. A Northern City in a Southern Latitude 258
16. Political Smoke Is Like the Pitch Pine Smoke 275
17. The Muddy Pool of Florida Politics 288
18. To Give the Lost Cause a Union Flavor 300

19. One Might Decide the Other Way with Perfect Fairness 314
20. The Matter before the Supreme Court 328
21. We Have Lost the State for a Long, Long Time 340
Notes 345
Bibliography 385
Index 393

1

If That Scheme Fails, I Have Another

When Confederate forces in Florida surrendered in May 1865 and national attention turned from war to rebuilding a nation, there had already been major efforts to establish a loyal government in the state. Wartime reconstruction activities were motivated by desire to defeat the Confederacy as much as by desire to restore Florida to the Union, but they caused problems, identified issues and personalities, and began shaping political factions which influenced postwar affairs.

Floridians had never been united on the secession or subsequent support of the Confederacy. A majority favored secession in January 1861, but a significant minority did not. Many of those who were opposed remained Unionists throughout the Civil War, and their Unionism was manifested in various ways. Richard Keith Call opposed secession until his death, serving as an example for some Unionists who remained quietly at home in Confederate towns. Such a man was Ethelred Philips, a doctor at Marianna, who declared that "secession is the greatest act of folly and crime that ever disgraced the earth," but was able to live without disturbance to his person or property. Perhaps his advanced age and his sons' Confederate service spared him. Not so fortunate was John S. Sammis of Jacksonville, who lobbied in Tallahassee against secession. When he refused to buy $10,000 worth of Confederate bonds his property was confiscated. He fled the state, returning as a staunch Unionist in East Florida as soon as the area was occupied. He claimed to have lost $75,000 in property to Confederate confiscation.[1]

David S. Walker, subsequently a state governor, represented a different opposition. When Florida seceded, Walker accepted a civil position in the government but made no military contribution. Joseph B. Roulhac opposed secession, but later served in the army and ran for the Confederate Congress in 1863. Some fled to avoid military service or personal injury. Samuel Walker moved to Key West for the duration. Others escaped without incident to Jacksonville, Fernandina, St. Augustine, and the North. C. P. Chaires of Leon County was cutting timber at Cedar Key when Confederate officials ordered all civilians out of the area. He returned to his Leon County plantation and lived without incident until 1865.[2]

Most of the secession opponents seem to have followed the examples of Walker and Roulhac, participating to some degree in Confederate activities, but several hundred either ran across the Union lines or remained passively at home.

There were other Floridians who opposed the Confederacy. Some yeoman white Floridians felt little commitment to the Confederate cause and when the conscription laws forced them into the army, more than 2,000 deserted. State and Confederate policy as well as the diminishing hopes of military victory increased the desire to desert. Some left the ranks when letters from home indicated the desperate needs of their dependents. A few were infuriated when the Confederate government's efforts to suppress Union guerillas along the coast resulted in their homes being burned and their families being herded into a stockade in Tallahassee. The desertion rate was a serious factor by mid-1863. Whether the deserter was an incipient Unionist from the outset or simply a disillusioned Confederate soldier, his defection affected his position in Florida after the war. W. W. Strickland of Taylor County, leader of a guerilla band called the Royal Rangers, is illustrative. He had deserted the Confederate army and formed a band which raided plantations and furnished food and military intelligence to Union blockaders on the Gulf Coast. He wrote a pursuing Confederate commander that he and his men were willing to accept amnesty and raise stock for the Confederacy, but they would not again serve in its army.[3]

By 1864, guerilla bands were roaming almost at will from Jackson County to the coast and along it through Taylor, Lafayette, and Levy counties to Tampa Bay. The sheriff of Jackson County declared the deserters so numerous that he could not enforce the laws against them. Governor Milton said the Washington County sheriff was in league with deserters. In a two-day period in January 1864, fifty-nine men deserted a company at Marianna, allegedly because they had not been paid for seven months. During the same period Levy County slaveholders were evacuating the county because deserters were driving off their slaves.[4]

The two regiments of Union Florida Cavalry drew many of their recruits from the deserters and declared Union sympathizers, some of whom had lost property under the Confederate sequestration acts or had been punished for refusing the loyalty oath. Commanded by Lieutenant Colonel Eugene Kielmansegge and Major Edmund C. Weeks, the two units had about 1,200 men and engaged the Confederates repeatedly along the Gulf Coast from Tampa Bay to St. Marks.[5] Their efforts to regain confiscated property and to find a place in Florida communities populated predominantly by ex-Confederates added to the complexities of Reconstruction after the war.

Although Florida was strategically and physically peripheral to the Civil War, the Union coastal blockade and the occupation of key ports contributed to events which shaped postwar issues. Key West was never relinquished by United States authorities. Fernandina, Jacksonville, St. Augustine, Cedar Key, Apalachicola, and Pensacola were taken early in the war and, except for Cedar Key and Jacksonville, remained continuously in Union hands. Jacksonville was occupied repeatedly, with Union troops remaining after December 1863. Confederate citizens had to decide whether to evacuate or to remain and try to protect their property. If they evacuated, their property was subject to the whims of a hostile government. If they remained, their lives were in danger and they risked being denounced as Union sympathizers by those who departed. Many who remained in the ports became Unionists but others did not. Most were distrusted and criticized by one or both sides after the war.

Fernandina, Jacksonville, St. Augustine, and Key West were centers of wartime Reconstruction efforts. Unionists from the interior fled to these towns while Confederate sympathizers evacuated them in large numbers. Both governments enacted legislation to dispose of the evacuees' property, which led to years of bitterness and confusion when the war ended. The vagaries of United States military policy, especially in the frequent evacuations of Jacksonville, sorely tried the Unionists' loyalty.

The Florida Unionists were joined and usually overshadowed in the occupied cities by United States officials, most of whom found sufficient time away from their duties to pursue several schemes for restoring Florida to the Union either with or without slavery. With so many conflicting ideas emanating from Washington on the nature and goals of the war, it was natural that these men held differing views about the proper policies to pursue. Although they failed to restore Florida before the war ended, the activities of these wartime Unionists influenced Reconstruction politics and society.

When Union troops invaded East Florida in 1862, proposals for establishing a loyal government soon followed. Fernandina was occupied in early March just as the last train of evacuees crossed the bridge from Amelia Island to the mainland. Only a few inhabitants remained to welcome the arriving troops. St. Augustine offered no resistance, and some of its inhabitants even staged a welcoming ceremony.

Occupation of Jacksonville in mid-March brought on a premature restoration effort. Chaired by Vermont-born Calvin L. Robinson, who had arrived in Jacksonville in 1857, a meeting of loyal citizens was held on March 20, 1862. Others present included Philip Fraser of Elizabeth, New Jersey, and Jacksonville, and John S. Sammis, O. L. Keene, Paran Moody, and John W. Price, all substantial citizens and longtime Jacksonville residents. The group protested any state's authority to abrogate the rights of United States citizens, denied the propriety of secession, and proclaimed Florida an integral part of the Union. When the Union invasion force left Jacksonville a few days later, those who had proclaimed their Unionism deemed it expedient to accompany the departing troops. Most of them continued to work for a restored government from Washington, New York, or Fernandina.[6]

While Sammis, Fraser, Robinson, and Moody were attending meetings and passing resolutions in New York and Washington calling for official support of a loyal Florida government, a Fernandina resident wrote that East Floridians were opposed to formation of such a government unless it could be protected by at least 5,000 troops. He thought it imperative that the national government keep its promises to Union men in the future, noting that twenty good citizens of Jacksonville were in danger of the "halter or assassination" for having participated in the Union movement which had collapsed with the army's withdrawal.[7]

In the northern cities, the expatriate Florida Unionists gained additional supporters. Lyman D. Stickney, who was to become a proponent of Secretary of Treasury Salmon P. Chase in his bid for the 1864 presidential nomination, and Harrison Reed, Stickney's principal adversary, became prominent in wartime Florida. Stickney was an opportunist about whom few were indifferent. He ingratiated himself with those who could help him and impugned the motives of his detractors, who usually responded in kind. He had first appeared in Tallahassee during the secession convention, ostensibly representing a group which desired a land grant on which to settle a colony of free laborers. After obtaining two townships in South Florida at five cents an acre, he formed a partnership with James Evans of Fort Myers who proved to be a smuggler of African slaves into the United States.[8] Stickney dissolved his partnership with Evans and next turned up in Washington where he joined the expatriate Florida Unionists. Under the direct tax act of June 7, 1862, Secretary Chase appointed him to the direct tax commission in Florida, where the peripatetic Stickney identified with advocates of a restored loyal government.

Harrison Reed had been a newspaper editor in Wisconsin for more than twenty years and had influential connections in the Republican party. Governor Louis P. Harvey and numerous Wisconsin legislators wrote President Lincoln that Reed was "a man of ability, of strict and unimpeachable moral character, and a Republican of the right sort." In addition, Senator James R. Doolittle and thirty-two other senators and representatives notified Lincoln of their esteem for Reed.[9] He was made a member of the direct tax commission along with Stickney, and John Sammis of Jacksonville filled the third seat. Although the official and unofficial acts of the commission and its members were to complicate Florida politics and property titles long after the agency was abolished in 1867, its official mission was simple enough. As a device for acquiring title to property of Confederates, the earlier confiscation acts involved a lengthy legal process. The direct tax act was much more effective: it provided for assessment of property and notification through newspaper advertising of the taxes due. If the taxes were not paid—which was difficult for Confederates who owned abandoned property in Union-held territory—the commission was empowered to sell the real estate to the highest bidder at an auction.

Establishment of the tax commission temporarily revived the plan of New England abolitionist Eli Thayer to destroy the Confederate hold on Florida by settling 20,000 soldier-farmers there. A member of the New England Emigrant Aid Company, formerly active in Kansas, Thayer planned to raise an army to oust the Confederates, settle in Florida, and restore it to the Union as a free state. President Lincoln had never been enthusiastic about the plan, but for a while in 1862 Stickney worked with Thayer. In December Stickney petitioned for the New Englander's appointment as military governor "with authority to raise 20,000 or more emigrants, who will reside permanently in that state and become citizens thereof." Some congressional Radicals supported Thayer's plan, but its implication of confiscation, resettlement, and permanent subjection were opposed to Lincoln's moderate ideas of nation rebuilding. No action was taken and Stickney launched another scheme before Thayer's idea was decently interred, but colonization in Florida remained appealing to abolitionists.[10]

Recognizing that the tax commission could only be effective in Union-occupied territory, Stickney undertook to expand the Florida beachhead. Having met General Rufus Saxton, an abolition-minded commander at Beaufort, South Carolina, he learned that Colonel Thomas W. Higginson's Negro regiment was comparatively unemployed while preparations were underway for an assault on Charleston. Higginson's troops had just returned from a successful pillaging expedition up the St. Mary's River and were anxious for more action. As Higginson put it, "My chief aim . . . was to get the men into action, and . . . [Stickney's was] to get them into Florida." General David Hunter agreed to the expedition, and Higginson's black troops, less than 1,000 strong, arrived at Jacksonville on March 10, 1863, accompanied by the tax commissioner. While Higginson raided up the St. Johns River, Stickney tried to obtain re-inforcements so that Jacksonville could be occupied permanently. He failed because Hunter needed the Negro regiment for renewed activity in South Carolina. On March 29, the Union troops set fire to Jacksonville and sailed down the river, leaving the city in flames.[11]

Undaunted by the unexpected interruption, Stickney revealed new plans to Secretary Chase, carefully cultivating his superior's well-known ideas about southern slavery. He wanted to open the port of Fernandina because it was easy to defend and would be a good place for "contrabands" to come and find employment as the lumber industry revived. He would use the direct tax law to restore civil authority in Florida by having the commission acquire all real property and lease it out to loyal people. His plan required military and naval assistance to drive out Confederates, and General Saxton had already given hearty approval. If Chase could persuade the War Department to furnish military assistance, Stickney promised to make Florida a free state within the year.[12]

The commissioners had arrived in Fernandina in January 1863, but Stickney spent most of his time between Washington, Hilton Head, and Beaufort trying to obtain support for his political-military campaign. He spent no time with the other commissioners assessing property and preparing for a sale. As a result, he was soon at odds with Reed and Sammis over the legality and desirability of a sale which the two had announced for June 1863. They had assessed the Fernandina property and advertised the amount of taxes due. That property upon which taxes remained unpaid was auctioned on June 15, despite Stickney's protests that the sale was irregular. His opposition may have been motivated by private arrangements made on a recent trip to New York. Most of Fernandina was owned by the Florida Railroad Company, about $750,000 of whose stock was held by Marshall O. Roberts, a New York financier. Only about one-fourth of the company stock was owned by David L. Yulee and other Confederates, the remainder belonging to Roberts and other New Yorkers still loyal to the United States. Unwilling to see the railroad company's land sold for unpaid taxes, Roberts paid Stickney a $500 retainer to represent his interests in Fernandina.[13]

Stickney demanded the sale be voided and a subsequent investigation revealed irregularities. The sale netted only about $10,608. There were few qualified purchasers and most of them had agreed before the sale not to bid against each other. For example, Joseph Finegan's house, valued at $3,500, was sold for $25 to Chloe Merrick of Syracuse, New York, who converted it into an orphanage for Negro children. Miss Merrick later married Harrison Reed, a balding middle-aged widower with full, black beard and steel-rimmed glasses, who had brought two grown sons with him to Florida. Several hundred lots were sold at nominal prices to Negroes, and Reed readily acknowledged that, although "the sale was conducted strictly in accord with the law . . . the freedmen were generally allowed by the people to purchase the buildings occupied by them without competition."[14] Neither Reed nor Sammis saw any conflict of interest in their own purchases of lots at the sale.

Stickney was not alone in his criticisms. H. H. Helper (General Saxton's superintendent of freedmen at Fernandina and brother of Hinton R. Helper who had written *The Impending Crisis*) accused Reed and Sammis of cheating the freedmen in the sale. Sammis was highly critical of Reed. An investigator, Austin Smith, concluded that violations were not willful and that the sale should be allowed to stand except for the lots purchased by the commissioners. But Chase voided the sale on October 22, 1863. Both Sammis and Reed were removed. Reed defended himself to Chase, noting that he had assisted nearly 5,000 freedmen to find homes and provided an orphan asylum, and that "While I was doing this I was constantly at my post, while my malicious assailant was almost constantly absent." Eli Thayer volunteered his opinion that "the removal of Mr. Reed was an injury to the public interest but by no means so great an injury as the . . . retention of Mr. Stickney." Others agreed. William Marvin, United States judge at Key West and later Florida's postwar provisional governor, also condemned Stickney. But there were others who applauded him and called his opponents "rebels" or "copperheads."[15]

Stickney did not allow his battle with the other commissioners to interfere with his most ambitious undertaking. Still hoping to use the tax commission as his instrument to "weed out rebellion," he sought military support to expand his area of operation. On his return voyage to Florida in December 1863, Stickney conferred with General Quincy A. Gillmore at Beaufort about using Negro troops to reconquer Florida. When Gillmore proved receptive, Stickney enthusiastically inquired of Chase, "Can you not influence Mr. Stanton to direct Gillmore to employ the Negro troops in the department against the Florida rebels? The time is most favorable."[16]

At that time Stickney envisioned calling a constitutional convention and changing the state's fundamental law by abolishing slavery and making all residents voters without reference to race or duration of residence. Chase was considering challenging Lincoln for the 1864 presidential nomination and the ambitious tax commissioner's schemes coincided with both his convictions and his personal interest. Secretary Chase gained another supporter at Key West about the same time. Homer G. Plantz arrived there in November 1863 to serve as district attorney for the southern judicial district. Plantz was a loyal Chase advocate and became a great admirer of Lyman Stickney. The district attorney supported the convention plan and kept Chase abreast of the Key West political climate.[17]

At Stickney's urging, a Union meeting was held at St. Augustine on December 19. After he called the meeting to order, D. R. Dunham was elected chairman with C. L. Robinson and G. N. Papy as secretaries. Others present were Philip Fraser, William Alsop, Homer G. Plantz, W. C. Morrill, Charles Howe, Bartolo Oliveros, and Samuel Walker. They approved a series of resolutions disavowing the existing rebellion, calling for immediate reorganization of a loyal state government, declaring the secession null and void and slavery outlawed, announcing their intention to reorganize Florida under the United States Constitution, and inviting the participation of all loyal citizens who would take an oath of future allegiance. A convention was called to meet at St. Augustine on March 1, 1864, to amend the state constitution according to these resolutions.[18]

On December 8, 1863, Lincoln issued his Proclamation of Amnesty and Reconstruction. It offered amnesty to any Southerner who would take an oath of future loyalty to the United States. Whenever a number of persons in a state equal to 10 per cent of the voters in the 1860 election had taken the oath, Lincoln was willing to recognize a government which they organized. Although Stickney had not anticipated the necessity of enrolling over a thousand loyal citizens, he readily adapted to this condition when it became clear that Lincoln was directly interested in the state. Repeating his request for a revenue cutter, he told Chase that with it he could easily collect enough voters to recognize Florida according to the president's plan. He even claimed that the St. Augustine meeting was in response to the December 8 proclamation. An amused young Union officer, observing Stickney's machinations, wrote a farcical account of the affair in which he had Stickney say, "the immense population of scared crackers in this district must be prepared to swallow my politics. . . . If that scheme fails, I have another."[19]

Chase complied with Stickney's appeal of December 11, and on December 22 General Gillmore was authorized to invade Florida. About this time Lincoln become involved in Florida activities. Stickney hedged his position with Lincoln by suggesting to John Hay that he come to Florida to assist in political reorganization and be the state's congressman.[20] Hay, who had visited Florida the year before, was interested and spoke to Lincoln. The president soon commissioned Hay to go South and enroll the requisite 10 per cent of Florida's 1860 voters. He then wrote Gillmore, "I understand an effort is being made by some worthy gentlemen to reconstruct a loyal state government in Florida. Florida is in your department and it is not unlikely that you may be there in person. I have . . . sent [Mr. Hay] to you with some blank books . . . to aid in the reconstruction. . . . It is desirable for all to cooperate, but if irreconcilable differences of opinion shall arise, you are master. I wish the thing done in the most speedy way possible, so that, when done, it lies within the range of the late proclamation on the subject. . . ."[21]

Gillmore was in Florida when he received Lincoln's letter, had already conferred with Stickney, and promised hearty support of Major Hay's mission. Although Stickney would probably have preferred to proceed without the president's emissary, he gave neither the general nor Hay cause for concern. Instead, as he explained, "I have not opposed [Major Hay], but rather moulded his views in harmony with my own."[22] Of course, their purposes were not mutually exclusive. Both Lincoln and Chase favored the acquisition of Confederate territory and restoration of state governments as serving the national interest. There is no reason to believe that Stickney was any less anxious than they to see the nation preserved, but if he were able to enhance the political fortunes of Secretary Chase and to serve his own interests at the same time, the tax commissioner was too astute to pass up the opportunity.

Stickney and General Gillmore discussed the military expedition and apparently became close allies. Stickney told Chase that "Gillmore is very gracious, I feel sure he will do all he consistently can. . . . He has given me very strong evidence indeed that he's your friend." And Gillmore was impressed, too. Before Hay arrived in Florida, the general informed Secretary Stanton and General Halleck that he was going to occupy the west bank of the St. Johns River. When he was reminded that this area had but small military significance, Gillmore explained that it was the richest area of the country and he intended to bring out of it cotton, lumber, turpentine, and, perhaps, some Negro recruits. He also intended to restore Florida to the Union. On January 31, he ordered Hay to proceed according to the president's proclamation.[23]

When the military expedition reached Jacksonville in early February, Stickney and Hay seemed to be working well together. On February 5, Stickney was "convinced of the ease with which Florida can be restored to the Union. . . . To enroll 1,100 voters under the Union Constitution of Florida can be done very quickly." To assure Chase, the writer added, "I have lately been occupied in organizing a free State league, or if you please, a Chase league, it will work to a charm."[24] Apparently influenced by Stickney's conversation as well as his own observations Hay sent a perceptive report to Lincoln three days later:

> I found among the few leading men I have met, a most gratifying unanimity of sentiment. Those who have been formerly classed as Conservative are willing to accept readily the accomplished events of the war and to come back at once, while those of more radical views whom, we had reason to fear would rather embarrass us, are heartily in favor of your plan as exhibited in the case of Louisiana and Arkansas. There is no opposition to be apprehended from either native Unionists or "treasury agents."
>
> The people are ignorant and apathetic. They seem to know nothing and care nothing about the matter. They have vague objections to being shot and having their houses burned, but don't know why it is done. They will be very glad to see a government strong enough to protect them against these every day incidents of the last two years.
>
> I have the best assurances that we will get the tenth required, although so large a portion of the rebel population is in the army and so many of the loyal people, refugees in the North, that the state is well-nigh depopulated. We will have almost a clean slate to begin with. . . .[25]

Both men had overestimated the number of citizens in Union-occupied Florida willing to take the requisite oath. Some Confederate prisoners were only too willing to do so, but many others had seen the United States army come and go too many times to risk being left behind again at the mercy of General Joseph Finegan's forces after having sworn allegiance to the United States. What chance there was for obtaining the necessary signatures depended on the expansion of Union lines to the west. General Truman Seymour landed at Jacksonville on February 7 with about 5,000 men. This force, with some smaller units from Fernandina, moved through the area, fighting successful engagements as far west as Baldwin and Sanderson. Gillmore left Jacksonville for Hilton Head on February 15, after a strategy conference with Seymour. He understood that Seymour would establish a defensive line in the area of Baldwin, the railroad junction west of Jacksonville. There was no plan for further penetration.

At about this time, Stickney and Hay changed their optimistic estimate of the political situation. On February 16, Stickney wrote that he and Hay agreed that the president's plan for reconstructing Florida would fail. Hay intended to try enrolling the requisite 1,100 voters, but if he failed the young major had agreed to go back to Washington and ask Lincoln to accept Stickney's original plan of restoration, which, as already noted, was more radical than Lincoln's ideas.[26] Although the Olustee disaster on February 20 became symbolic of the failure of the 10 per cent plan, its demise had already been predicted four days earlier.

It is well known that General Joseph Finegan's Confederate force met General Seymour's Union troops at Olustee near Lake City and severely defeated them in a battle which inflicted many Union casualties and gave Florida its single major engagement of the Civil War. Neither is it a revelation that this victory was especially satisfying to the Confederate soldiers because they were mostly from Florida and Georgia, while many of Seymour's troops were Negroes. But there is a great mystery as to why Seymour was at Olustee. On February 11 he said that the Suwannee railroad bridge was not worth taking, that a movement on Lake City was inadvisable, that the Floridians had no particular desire to come back into the Union at that time, and that such a move was opposed to sound strategy. On the fourteenth he and Gillmore had discussed the defensive positions along the Baldwin line. Then, two days later, Seymour reported to Gillmore that the Suwannee bridge was vital, that the people of Florida were tired of war and, if kindly treated, would soon be ready to return to the Union. He also said he was proceeding west to the Suwannee River. Gillmore was shocked at Seymour's conflicting views and especially at the misunderstanding of his orders.[27] He tried to countermand Seymour's orders, but the Battle of Olustee occurred before his message reached the field.

The Lincoln administration was severely criticized for the abortive Florida campaign. Most caustic was the *New York Herald*'s accusation that "brigades of our brave armies are sent into rebellious states to water with their precious blood the soil that may produce Presidential votes. Let the Presidential squabble end." John Hay was angered by the manner in which the press handled his mission, but when he returned to Washington in March, John G. Nicolay noted his arrival after "having had rather an agreeable trip down south."[28] Stickney admitted that the military disaster was serious, but he was scarcely upset because the blame was laid on General Seymour, a racial and political conservative opposed to Chase, and it ended the Lincoln-Hay efforts to reconstruct according to the 10 per cent plan.

In retrospect, it seems that Stickney's Florida career crested with the Olustee battle, but he remained optimistic for a while that Lincoln would support his earlier plan. Even before the battle he had concluded that the 10 per cent plan would not suit his purposes. Instead of an electorate of ex-Confederates who had taken amnesty oaths, he still preferred to hold a convention with selected delegates and alter the state constitution by abolishing slavery and enfranchising every adult male without regard to residence. With such a fundamental law and with the ports of Fernandina, Jacksonville, and St. Augustine opened to northern immigrants, Stickney pledged to make Florida "as bright a star as shines in freedom's constellation." He had long believed in the encouragement of immigrants to Florida. The tax commission would still be beneficial because those who were loyal could retain their estates, while the "incorrigably rebellious" could be deprived of their property.[29] Of course, such a program never had a chance with Lincoln. Stickney's dilemma in 1864 was not unlike the problem which would face the nation after 1865. A plan which was radical enough to have a chance of success was too radical to win support from the chief executive.

Stickney was disappointed when Salmon Chase withdrew from the presidential nomination race in March 1864, but he had more immediate problems. Reed and Sammis, whose removal from the tax commission he had successfully sought, had built up enough evidence for an investigation of his conduct with that agency. His business partner, C. L. Robinson, had dissolved the partnership because of distaste for Stickney's business ethics. Worst of all, several Unionists were challenging his leadership in public affairs. One minor irritation came from Orloff M. Dorman, a paymaster in the army at Hilton Head, who had lived in Jacksonville for about twenty-five years prior to his departure with the Union troops in 1862. Dorman sought and received an opportunity to return to Jacksonville with Seymour in February 1864, and was soon being denounced by Stickney as "the worst copperhead in the country." It was the conservative Unionists, Dorman, S. L. Burritt of Jacksonville, and others like them, who had given Stickney cause for alarm over the 10 per cent plan. Dorman never had much influence after his return in 1864, but his kind of Unionism worried Stickney. Like many other wartime Unionists of Florida, Dorman later became a bitter critic of the United States government during Reconstruction. After Andrew Johnson failed to distinguish between loyal and disloyal Southerners and after Congress enfranchised Negroes, he and many like him felt betrayed.[30]

There were also problems at Key West. Isolated from the rest of Florida, the Unionists there were suspicious of each other and often ignorant of events elsewhere. Homer Plantz, former personal secretary to Chase, remained loyal to his former boss and admired "Judge" Stickney long after other Floridians became disenchanted with him. But Plantz saw firsthand the problems of Unionism in Key West and reported the situation to Chase. He had arrived at his new station only after a journey through

Havana, Cuba. Fernandina and St. Augustine were accessible from Key West only by way of Hilton Head or New York. This isolation, according to Plantz, caused a deadening political apathy. He sarcastically observed that there were none but Union men on the island: "From the delegate to the Florida convention who voted for secession, to the 'Conks' who purchase prize vessels and sell them in Havana and Nassau as blockade runners—all are Union men." None of them supported the administration or opposed slavery. Even the military commander there had suppressed an antislavery newspaper and refused to allow it to resume publication.[31]

Neither was Plantz satisfied with Federal officials on the island. District Judge William Marvin had resigned because of ill health in 1863 after thirty years on the bench. Because the load of admiralty cases in the district was so heavy, William J. Boynton had soon replaced him. Plantz said that Boynton had arrived at Key West a Radical but had gone so far native that he was hopelessly in the hands of "copperheads." He thought Boynton favored slavery. Stickney had earlier assessed Boynton as opposed to equality before the law for blacks and in favor of their removal from the United States. Even so, when Boynton became gravely ill Plantz lamented that, if he died, he would probably be replaced by Marvin who wanted the judgeship back. The district attorney thought his return would be a calamity for Union men because the secessionists would unite solidly behind the former judge.[32] He was probably right.

Despite the gloomy picture, Plantz and other Key West Unionists had attended the December meeting at St. Augustine, and at a local meeting in January, Plantz won endorsement of the Hay-Stickney-Gillmore restoration plan. However, after the Olustee defeat and the abandonment of the 10 per cent plan, serious opposition to Stickney's radical plan developed on the island. The leader was Samuel G. Walker who had left mainland Florida to avoid Confederate laws. He condemned Stickney as the "leading spirit in a political plot . . . to foist upon the small reclaimed portions of Florida an over hasty reorganization of the State government contrary to the will of the people." Walker and his followers argued that Florida's sparse population in 1860 had been so severely depleted by "rebel conscription" and the devastation of war that it should be left under military occupation until immigration could replace the lost population. They accused Stickney of conspiring to hold a convention without even a pretense of an election and with no effort to make it representative of even the small Union-occupied portion of Florida. Finding Stickney "unfit for his office," they asked the Commissioner of Internal Revenue to remove him.[33]

Stickney continued to enjoy the support and confidence of Homer Plantz who was elated when the tax commissioner visited him in March

1864 to confer about Federal appointments. But the meeting was to be of little practical significance. While Plantz was at the Republican convention in Baltimore in June, yellow fever struck Key West. As a newcomer to the island Plantz was too vulnerable to the disease and could not risk a return until the end of the year.[34]

After the Key West conference, Stickney advised Chase against appointing C. L. Robinson as tax assessor because his "recent acts satisfy me that he is politically unstable." This signaled the defection of an important ally. Robinson's disapproval of Stickney's business conduct may have been the reason for the dissolution of their partnership, but they became political opponents at about the same time. Robinson, like most Unionists during the Civil War, had his detractors. Stickney had not disapproved of him until he began pursuing a separate political path, but some of the military officers in Fernandina thought Robinson an opportunist who had knowingly profited from his association with the tax commissioners. O. M. Dorman in his diary accused Robinson of being a Unionist only when the troops were in East Florida and of being a Confederate collaborator the rest of the time.[35] Charges were hurled indiscriminantly during the war and for years afterward, and no one was ever able to devise a suitable standard for judging loyalty under these circumstances—certainly not the United States government which solved the dilemma by treating all southerners alike after the war. Despite Stickney's disapproval, Robinson remained a respected and influential Republican and a constructive citizen of Jacksonville until his death some twenty-five years later.

The Stickney-Robinson split led to a general realignment between Lincoln and Chase supporters among the Florida Unionists. The Robinson faction met at Jacksonville on May 24 and named a slate of delegates to the Baltimore Republican convention to be held on June 7: Robinson, Buckingham Smith, John W. Price, John S. Sammis, Philip Fraser, and Paran Moody, all residents of Florida except Fraser who still kept a home in New Jersey.[36] Stickney had been dealt a serious blow: all the delegates were Lincoln supporters and Sammis and Robinson were his personal enemies. Although the Stickney group named a slate of delegates to the convention, the Robinson delegation was seated. Florida was not allowed a vote in the proceedings, but Robinson was given a seat on the Union Republican National Committee.

While the political and military efforts at Reconstruction were in progress, the dispute among the tax commissioners continued. Sammis was replaced by William Alsop, a Florida resident with Radical convictions whose appointment was supported by Stickney and Philip Fraser. However, Reed's replacement was Austin Smith, whose investigation of the June tax sale had shown that there was insufficient cause for setting the sale aside. There was no continuity on the commission, and most of the members were frequently under attack from various groups. Even Stickney was ultimately indicted for presenting false vouchers for payment, an act which was disclosed in the investigation he instigated against Reed. A true bill was found, but the disposition of the case is not recorded.[37]

When the June 1863 sale was set aside, the purchasers were given back their money and a new sale was held in Fernandina between December 24, 1864, and February 20, 1865.[38] These two sales involved hundreds of purchasers, many of whom had little knowledge of the laws, and caused considerable confusion regarding titles. The situation became much more complicated when the war ended and ex-Confederates began returning to their homes. Another sale was held at St. Augustine from December 21–28, 1863, with proceeds of about $19,000. At these sales a large number of improved and unimproved tracts, formerly owned by Confederates, were sold to redeem unpaid United States taxes. The purchasers were Unionists, both Negro and white.

Although there was some Confederate property disposed of by United States marshals under the confiscation acts, that sold by the direct tax commission constituted the majority of the property, other than slaves, taken from Confederates. Some of it was acquired by the United States government and leased to private citizens by the tax commission; some of it was purchased by large operators; but most of it went to poor Negroes or whites, some of the latter having already lost property to the Confederacy because they remained loyal to the United States government. When the national government reversed itself and permitted former owners to redeem the property sold for taxes, endless litigation and strife resulted.

The war was grinding to a close. Union military action, whether its goals were military or political, encouraged Negroes to escape to Union lines. They began collecting in the east coast towns, especially Fernandina and Jacksonville. General Saxton appointed superintendents to look after them. H. H. Helper at Fernandina and N. C. Dennett at Jacksonville were both involved in this difficult task before the war ended. Each of them met resistance. Helper left Florida after he was dismissed because of his troubles with Harrison Reed and John Sammis over the 1863 tax sale. Dennett was active in the early days of Reconstruction, although he had problems with the military commanders and his services were refused by the Freedmen's Bureau.[39]

Some positive accomplishments of the war years formed a small basis on which those concerned with the freedmen's well-being could build after the war. A school was operating at St. Augustine in 1863. The orphan asylum of which Reed had boasted was organized by Miss Chloe Merrick in 1864. The National Freedmen's Relief Assocation had sent a few teachers to Florida by 1865. The *Fernandina Peninsula* claimed for that city two schools with three hundred students. Esther Hawks, who later made Florida her home, taught in Jacksonville in 1864, although she had trouble keeping any other teachers to help her manage more than one hundred children. Perhaps more important for the future was the difficulty she encountered in keeping children in school. In February 1864, many white children of Jacksonville attended with the blacks, but gradually they dropped out. After six weeks only one white child remained. The last mother to take her child out told Mrs. Hawks that she would be glad to have her offspring in school, but the neighbors "make so much fuss" she had to give in.[40]

By the end of the war none of the efforts to restore a civil government in the state had succeeded, but the issue had been raised and many Unionists had identified the kind of government they wished to see. Although they continued to fluctuate in response to changing news from Washington, these individuals provided a vague basis for political action during Reconstruction. The tax commission had started a program which gave land to a small number of freedmen, but the policy was reversed, causing endless complications in later years. There was scarcely a beginning in the area of freedmen's affairs during their transition from slavery to freedom, but even the little that was done demonstrated the difficulties that lay ahead.

2

The Place Beset with Yankees

"Johnston surrendered to Sherman which winds up our cause," wrote John A. L'Engle on May 3, 1865. Five days earlier, Major General Sam Jones had proclaimed, "Unclear reports coming out of Virginia indicate a reverse, but not so large as that of Vicksburg," and commanded all his Confederate troops in Florida to stand firm. Even then Jones was discussing surrender terms with General Israel Vogdes, the United States commander at Jacksonville. Open peace meetings were being held in Florida's capital city, soldiers were reporting "demoralization" in Confederate camps, and Governor John Milton committed suicide.[1]

But confusion was not confined to the Confederate side. General Vogdes, sympathetic with the political and racial radicals in East Florida, planned to accept the surrender of Confederate forces in the state. He was in the Department of the South, commanded by Major General Quincy A. Gillmore at Hilton Head, South Carolina, whose territory extended westward to the Apalachicola River in Florida. But Major General James H. Wilson, a fast-riding young cavalry commander from another command, had led his forces through Alabama late in the war, arriving at Macon, Georgia, as hostilities ended. He dispatched General Edward McCook with six companies to Tallahassee. Vogdes considered this unnecessary interference, but it was McCook who accepted the surrender of 8,000 Confederates in Florida. Beginning on the tenth of May, 6,000 men were paroled at Tallahassee and the remainder at various smaller stations.

With all the speed and grace of a bulldozer, the Confederate military force and the civil government of Florida were dismantled in the spring of 1865. The change was more drastic than that of 1861, because this time the state government was abolished and the nation had no plans for replacing it. President Lincoln's death left the United States without a leader until Andrew Johnson could familiarize himself with the pressing problems he had inherited. Meanwhile, many matters demanded immediate attention. Policy decisions devolved upon military field commanders. Sometimes they made decisions which were countermanded; sometimes they paused and awaited instructions. In either case there was delay, uncertainty, and anxiety.

The civil officials of Florida assumed the initiative. Acting Governor Abraham K. Allison, who had acceded to the office when Governor Milton died, called a special legislative session and a gubernatorial election, and appointed a five-member commission to go to Washington and negotiate with the United States government. His action is indicative of the way Florida leaders understood state government and its relation to the United States. Firmly committed to the theory that secession was a legitimate prerogative of a state, these men had taken Florida out of the Union in 1861. Now the Confederacy was gone and they conceived of the state as still existing and free to form a new relationship with the United States, just as it had done in 1845. These Floridians did not fully understand that many Northerners regarded secession and military opposition to the United States as treason.

When Allison requested passports for his delegation to Washington, General McCook asked his superior for instructions. General Wilson ordered him not to recognize the "so-called Governor" and to arrest Allison if he continued to act as a civil official.[2] On May 14 Gillmore declared the acts of the Florida governor null and void, and on May 24 martial law was proclaimed. Allison was arrested and jailed at Fort Pulaski, Georgia, and the Confederate state government of Florida was replaced by the Union army. Local officials were asked to continue in their positions.

Arrested with Allison were Florida's former United States Senators, David L. Yulee and Stephen R. Mallory, and John H. Gee of Gadsden County. Gee had been warden of a Confederate prison in North Carolina.[3] There was some northern sentiment for pressing treason charges against these and other Confederate leaders, but within a few months all were released. There was no punishment of Floridians for wartime acts. The men who surrendered to McCook were generously treated and quickly paroled. Officers retained side arms and mounts; privates kept their horses if they had them. Some Floridians lamented the loss of stores of food and equipment in warehouses, but the Union troops had arrived so quickly that the supplies could not be distributed. By authority of a captured property act, cotton belonging to the Confederacy was confiscated along with all other Confederate property which could be identified.[4] Efforts to claim the cotton led to some dishonesty on the part of treasury agents and Southerners who handled it at transportation centers. Antipathy was created by overzealous agents who broadly interpreted Confederate ownership and took cotton belonging to private owners.

In time the majority of white Floridians, some of whom had not even supported the Confederacy, rallied to the "Lost Cause" which glorified the Southerners' wartime sacrifices, exaggerated in memory the desirable qualities of society in the "Old South" while de-emphasizing its seamier aspects, and condemned perpetrators of "Reconstruction" for ravaging a helpless population. Although the anti-northern sentiment upon which the legend of the "Lost Cause" has thrived was developed more in response to what happened after 1865 than during the war itself, the severity of the combat-related losses was no myth. With a white population in 1860 of only 77,747, Florida sent more than 15,000 men into the Confederate armies. More than 5,000 of them had died of battle wounds or disease by 1865. Numerous others suffered crippling physical wounds, and no one knows how many were disabled by mental disorders. These casualties constituted a liability in lost manpower and generated persistent hostility toward the United States.

The matter was complicated by more than 1,200 Floridians who had served in various Union military units, especially the First and Second Florida Cavalry Regiments which were mustered out at Tallahassee in late 1865. Although they, too, had suffered battle casualties, the future was affected more by the treatment that they and their families had suffered at the hands of the Confederates during the war. When these Union veterans and their Confederate counterparts came back to the same communities, wartime antipathies often continued. There were also more than 1,000 Negro Floridians who served in the Union army. Casualty figures are unavailable, but some lost their lives in civil strife as well as in combat. A permanent reminder to Floridians of the costs of the war, the Negro soldiers were frequently singled out for harsh treatment. One of many such cases occurred in the Ocala area near the end of the war. Some Negro soldiers were captured, burned to death, and beheaded, and their heads were thrown into a well, allegedly because they were recruiting other Negroes for the Union army.[5]

There was property damage, but much of the loss of wealth was in the form of depreciated property values and repudiated securities. The greatest loss of private wealth resulted from emancipation. Even the conservative estimates by congressional investigating committees valued the slave property at about $22 million.[6] As devastating as this was to plantation balance sheets, there was the compensating gain of more than 62,000 freedmen, many of whom augmented the free labor force. These freedmen provided low-cost labor for the same planters and capitalists who had lost their capital investments in slaves.

The value of other property was reduced by nearly half. Of an estimated value in 1860 of $47 million, about $25 million remained in 1865. The loss of capital in repudiated bonds and treasury notes hampered economic recovery. There was some military damage to railroads, port facilities, and private property which contributed to the decline, but it was limited by the small size and number of military engagements in the state. Cedar Key and Jacksonville suffered the greatest physical damage from military action, yet both towns were booming soon after the war. Jacksonville, which was nearly destroyed by the repeated invasions and evacuations of both armies, had an especially rapid economic revival. Apalachicola, St. Marks, and Newport, with varying degrees of war damage, never recovered their prewar importance, but this was due to postwar changes in trade routes caused by railroad building, not to wartime destruction. One Floridian boasted that "the State as a whole suffered less than any of the other states."[7]

The real destruction in the economic sphere resulted from the utter exhaustion of the economy and the disappearance of necessary capital. The collapse of the monetary system, price fluctuation, scarcity of goods, decay of internal transportation, and drastic alteration of the agricultural system all combined to create an economic stalemate. Political stability and an inflationary economic policy were necessary for recovery, but the immediate future held political indecision approaching chaos and a rigidly deflationary financial policy, a large part of which was aimed directly at punishing the South. Congress enacted a tax on cotton which remained in force through 1868 and siphoned $918,945 out of Florida. The loss equaled nearly half the state debt at its highest point during Reconstruction.[8] This tax angered many Unionists who were beginning to resent a national policy which subjected them to the same punishment as their Confederate neighbors. It seemed poor compensation for the sacrifices they had made as Union loyalists in Confederate Florida during the war.

Most of the native Unionists were white supremacists and were angered by the presence of Negro troops, who constituted a majority of the occupation forces. Ethelred Philips of Marianna, who had denounced secession and praised William T. Sherman's march through Georgia, was incensed at the prospect of Negro occupation. "We have had a garrison of fifty New York troops here for more than a month," he wrote, "and the Captain has been of great use to us in making the negroes stay home . . . but now he is to be superceded by a gang of 200 negroes which we dread very much." Expressing hope that the state would soon pass laws to protect the interests of the white population, he cautioned, "If they do not . . . I do apprehend much trouble and feel sure thefts and insolence will make it necessary to kill many." Feeling certain the two races could never live together as free men, he contemplated going to California "where the negro is not and never will be."[9]

Few ex-Confederates were as harsh towards blacks or the United States government as Unionist Philips, but a number of them were unwilling to accept the changes they anticipated. Philips wrote of many Jackson County people deranged by inability to adjust. "Nor is it over yet," he predicted. R. E. Durr of Quincy, overcome by shock at the loss of his slaves, took a lesson from Governor Milton and shot himself with a Maynard rifle. F. F. L'Engle hoped that the "power struggle" in Washington following Lincoln's assassination would produce "anarchy in Yankeedom" and make possible Southern independence. If that did not happen, then "let us seek asylum in another land where the hated name of Yankee will not be breathed except to deride and defy them." Arriving at Madison in late June, he found the "place beset with Yankees" and would not go outside because the sight of them upset him.[10]

One reason for L'Engle's visit to Madison was to complete plans for settling a colony in Brazil. He and others had formed the Florida Emigration Society and planned to embark in February or March of 1866. Among his associates were John C. McGehee of Madison, presiding officer of the 1861 secession convention; Benjamin F. Whitner of Madison, prominent planter and surveyor; J. Wales Baker, former Confederate Congressman; Daniel Ladd, founder and leading merchant of Newport and one of the most stubborn opponents of secession in the 1861 convention; Reverend William Eppes; Vans Randel; Albert Dozier; J. E. Buckman; John L. Miller; and George A. Croom of Leon County.[11] Also expected to join them were John L'Engle, Lewis Fleming, and J. J. Daniel of Jacksonville. Edward M. L'Engle was asked to join Benjamin Whitner as a commissioner to Brazil to make the necessary arrangements. When L'Engle declined, J. J. Daniel agreed to go.

According to F. F. L'Engle, most of those named were disposing of their Florida interests and were not planting crops in order to be prepared to leave the next year. He said that "if the Yankees do not strip us any further of property we will be able to command large means and will perhaps buy a steamer." Soon he had located a steamer which could be chartered for $1,500. The estimated cost of transportation and three months' subsistence was about $65 per person. He concluded that most of the men interested in the society were financially well equipped to defray costs of the move. Complaining that his wife was having a hard time in

Florida with only one servant, L'Engle said, "I will buy two or three in Brazil and hold them as long as the abolition spirit will allow me."[12]

But while making extensive plans to leave, L'Engle was also completing a contract to cut crossties for the military custodians of the Pensacola and Georgia Railroad between Madison and Lake City. J. J. Daniel and B. F. Whitner finally started for Brazil on their advance trip, but the journey was never completed because delays had made it impossible for the colony to settle in time to make a crop in 1866. Whitner and his family left Madison County and moved to the unsettled portion of South Florida. Others from the plantation counties followed his lead. Some Floridians went to Brazil, usually with Alabama groups,[13] but most of them had second thoughts. Even as they planned their departure, L'Engle and others were looking for opportunities in the state. In addition to L'Engle's contract with the railroad, J. J. Daniel bought a sawmill which he planned to operate with free Negro labor.

If the actions of the former Confederates seemed contradictory and confused, so were most of the complicated events and expectations of that spring. Although Andrew Johnson's wartime speeches had misled many people, few could have been more wrong than one of his admirers at Key West. In a wide-ranging letter, L. C. Man reported Key West as a town of about 3,500 inhabitants of all colors, some of whom had been loyal to the Union, but larger numbers of whom had been either actively or passively on the side of rebellion. So far he had corroborative evidence. But he went on to praise the president's willingness to recognize blacks as voting citizens, condemn General McCook for paroling former Confederates on condition that they conform to existing laws, and then conclude with the caution that "it is important to the success of your administration that no even apparent support should be given to slavery by generals in command."[14] If Johnson ever read the letter, he must have been surprised to see his views so interpreted. As with many Florida Unionists, Johnson's antipathy for Confederate leaders was not accompanied by any desire to elevate freedmen to the status of voting citizens.

General Vogdes traveled to Tallahassee from Jacksonville in late May and sent Chief Justice Chase an incisive evaluation of Florida's society. Since Vogdes was sympathetic with the Radical position of Chase, his analysis, with its cautious suggestion of a moderate policy toward ex-Confederates, is important. He divided Floridians into four categories: the wealthy and best-educated whites, the partially educated whites (the hostile class), the poor whites, and the Negroes. He believed that the wealthy group was resigned to immediate emancipation, though a few nourished hopes that unsolved difficulties would compel the national government to accept some kind of apprentice system. Having lost their slaves, these people had nothing but their lands and some cotton: they were afraid both would be confiscated, leaving them in poverty. Vogdes saw opportunity in this. If these formerly wealthy Floridians were permitted to keep their property, he thought they would "acquiesce in any policy the government may adopt." Most of this class saw the possibility of recovery as dependent on peace and hard work, and they were anxious to begin.

As for the partially educated class and the women, the general believed them still hostile to the government. In this second group he put nearly all the subordinate officers of the Confederate army. "They seem to set no value on the title of American citizen, pretend to despise the government and occasionally express a desire to expatriate themselves," he wrote. "Here is the hotbed in which treason will be forged and from which it may spread to others." These Floridians were restless and potential troublemakers: "They are the real authors of the rebellion and would not hesitate if a future opportunity offers to renew it. . . . They are not and will not be good citizens and in any other country would be placed under surveillance."

He thought the poorer class to be genuinely tired of the war and anxious to return home. They were hostile to both planters and Negroes. In intelligence and education they were barely ahead of the blacks.

These judgments of white Floridians determined Vogdes' actions in his own sphere of responsibility and his suggestions to his superiors. He declined the oath of allegiance to paroled prisoners because, if any opposition to the government developed, he expected its warmest support among them. Beyond that he was concerned with encouraging industry, trade, and the supremacy of the law. With reference to the formerly wealthy Floridians, Vogdes suggested that the United States government should give "liberal construction to the Confiscation Act" in order to exempt from it all who wanted to be loyal. By the time he wrote, sales under the act had already been suspended. He suggested restraining the "hostile class" by denying them the right to vote, because while "they are not the majority . . . [they are] very active, bold and unscrupulous." He considered the other two classes of whites either tired or indifferent and believed that power was certain to pass into the hands of the hostile class.

Arriving at this grim and ultimately correct conclusion, Vogdes saw only one way to counter the "hostile secession element." Although he had originally opposed it and still saw many difficulties in its execution, the general thought that Negro suffrage was the only hope for preventing a return to power of the secessionists. He had little confidence in the quality of the Negro electorate but was certain that the blacks "will not want for advisers" and their votes could always be counted for the Union and liberty.[15]

Vogdes had divided Floridians and predicted their future actions with almost prophetic accuracy. He also identified the dilemma of the national leaders whose responsibility it was to rebuild the nation. In suggesting that Floridians be permitted to accept amnesty and retain their nonslave property and that Negroes be enfranchised, he was calling for two measures which were ultimately taken. Yet most historians agree that Reconstruction measures failed to achieve the desired goals. Even had his third suggestion of repression of the "hostile class" been undertaken, it is doubtful that the outcome would have been much different, at least as long as thoughts about Union occupation were in terms of months rather than years.

Many wealthy Floridians uttered statements bearing out Vogdes' estimate of them. Former Confederate Secretary of the Navy Stephen R. Mallory favored gradual enfranchisement of Negroes, a few at first with the number expanding in time. But in a classical understatement Mallory declared, "The negroes' present and future I do not regard as questions of much difficulty." W. O. Girardeau of Leon County, with more realism, thought it useless to argue over emancipation, but felt that it had nevertheless caused a social and political condition which required the most thoughtful legislation. As long as the two races coexisted on the same soil, their interests were mutual, and there was not only a duty but a necessity to protect freedmen in their new rights and to assist them in becoming better members of society. But Girardeau was no better equipped than anyone else to supply specific proposals. He believed the Negroes should be given such rights as were consistent with the safety of government and society, but that immediate universal suffrage would be harmful.[16]

William F. Robertson, also of Leon County, challenged fellow Floridians to "show to the North and to the whole civilized world, who have clamored against slavery and heaped so much abuse on us for years, that we can live in honor and prosperity without riding the eternal negro; that notwithstanding such losses as history has never before recorded, we have that recuperative energy within that will lead us to the proud position of a prosperous and happy people." Another writer appealed to economic motives, arguing that prosperity was dependent upon a reliable labor supply. Negroes were human beings possessing rights and constituting an element of Florida society which was bound to have some influence. "We should feel kindly toward them, but not just for moral duty. . . . Owners of the soil must treat the negroes the same way that they would white employees."[17]

These few samplings of opinion show some of the conflicting assessments of the situation in Florida at the end of the war. People with differing backgrounds agreed with each other at times while those with similar backgrounds were often in conflict. Although they had widely varying views on solutions, they generally agreed about what the problems were. Florida society required rebuilding, the economy needed reviving, and alterations of the laws were necessary to provide for 62,000 new citizens who had previously been the property of other citizens. Several basic decisions had to be made before Floridians could make necessary reforms, and most of those decisions had to be made outside the state. Time elapsed before national policy on Reconstruction was formulated. Meanwhile life in the state continued and local military commanders and civilian leaders worked out problems as they arose, depending upon their respective abilities and attitudes and the needs of the moment.

Aside from getting Confederate soldiers back to their homes, no problem was so urgent as the need to get the 1865 crop planted. Places needed to be found for the freedmen, but a harvest in 1865 was essential to avoid starvation during the winter. It was late in the planting season when the surrender occurred. The Freedmen's Bureau in Florida consisted of agents at Jacksonville, St. Augustine, and Fernandina, all responsible to the assistant commissioner of South Carolina. An assistant commissioner for Florida did not arrive until September of 1865. Even then he thought that rations should be issued only in emergency conditions because easy access to rations might discourage initiative.

When General Gillmore announced in late May that the slaves had been emancipated, many were already away from the plantation, either because they had chosen to escape to Union lines or because the plantations had ceased to function for one reason or another. As word of emancipation spread, others left the land and went into the towns. But by far the largest number remained working the plantations as they always had. The impulse to roam lasted only about two months before most of the wanderers began returning to the plantations. Unfortunately, they had been furnished free transportation when they left and the return often required some time.[18]

Numerous planters handled the transition from slavery to free labor as it was done at "Pine Tucky" in western Jefferson County. The owner called the former slaves together, explained the change, and offered to hire them for wages. He paid $10 per month for males and $6 for females and he furnished their rations.[19] Wages varied widely, but these are near the averages. Many planters were without funds for a money wage or felt the Negroes would not be dependable if paid by the month, so they arranged to share the crop. Shortly after the war ended, General Vogdes ordered planters to make contracts with their former slaves, but he offered no guidelines. The result was that some planters gave half the crop while others paid almost nothing. The Freedmen's Bureau later abrogated many of the worst contracts, but others remained in force because they were never reported.

On July 3, 1865, from Florida District Headquarters at Tallahassee General John Newton issued a comprehensive regulation of labor relations. His purpose was to preserve order, reduce vagrancy, and promote the well-being of the community until permanent regulations were established by higher authorities. Newton recognized only free labor except in cases of criminal punishment. He urged freedmen to remain on the plantations. Landowners were prohibited from turning away without cause any freedmen who had formerly lived on their land. Newton recommended written labor contracts be made and a copy filed with the provost marshal or local military commander. If there was no formal contract, the same authorities were responsible for adjudicating disputes which arose. Planters were required to continue supporting aged and infirm freedmen and small children. Military commanders were instructed to discourage vagrancy by returning Negroes to their former homes or finding work for them on railroads or other jobs. General Newton asked planters and other employers to deal justly with the freedmen, who were in turn asked to fulfill their obligations. When a contract was deemed unjust, the officials reviewing it were empowered to replace it. Newton thought the laborers should receive one-fourth of the crop and this figure became the standard. If a laborer quit one employer to take another job, the new employer was obliged to support the laborer's family.[20]

Major General John G. Foster continued Newton's policies when he assumed command in Florida in early August.[21] Thus, while the Confederate military and the state government were being disestablished, plantation life continued with some emergency adjustments according to guidelines laid down by the Union army. This was more than a temporary arrangement. The efforts of planters, freedmen, and Union officers to meet the needs of 1865 were the origin of the free labor system which, with its tenancy, sharecropping, crop liens, ruinous credit arrangements, and one-crop concentration, plagued the agricultural areas of Florida for decades afterward.

Efforts to keep them down on the farm did not entirely solve the problems of migrants and the concentration of unemployed Negroes in the towns. Some of those who left the plantations decided for their own reasons not to return. Others simply had nowhere to go. Near Fernandina, it was impractical for Negroes to stay on the land because most of the owners were gone. The land had been sold at least once during the direct tax sales and it was not being farmed in 1865.[22] The problem was complicated in Fernandina and Jacksonville because these were transportation centers, and many Negroes, dislocated by the war, were stranded in those towns with no way to get home. Of about 1,000 in Fernandina, one-third were from Jacksonville and the rest from Georgia. Some itinerants in Jacksonville were from South Carolina and a few from as far away as Virginia. Florida Negroes outside the state had obtained free military transportation back to Jacksonville and were stranded there by destitution and a transportation shortage. Military authorities in both towns sought permission to transport them home at government expense, but approval was slow. These waiting people increased the number of idle Negroes in the towns. Many Unionists with Radical sentiments were also in these towns, and most of the racial strife in Florida during the immediate postwar period occurred there.

As noted elsewhere, the Union army confiscated quantities of arms, equipment, and food, and treasury agents gathered up cotton which belonged to the Confederate government. The United States government also took over and operated for a time most of the railroads and telegraph lines in the state. Because this property was usually privately owned, its seizure was sometimes effected through legal process. The United States district attorney obtained authority from the court and the marshal seized the property. Marshal Joseph Remington supervised operation of the railroad from Fernandina to Cedar Key for a short period.[23] The government made some repairs so the roads could be used for moving troops and supplies. When the railroads were returned to the owners, the repairs were a gratuitous benefit, but it had been decided that both the repairs and the early return were in the common interests of the railroads, the state, and the United States government.

The Florida Railroad Company was also involved as a major landowner in the complicated confiscations of individual parcels of land and improved property. Sales under the direct tax act were suspended when the war ended, although the tax was collected for a few more months. Property had also been seized from Confederate owners—including John P. Sanderson, David L. Yulee, Joseph Finegan, Archibald H. Cole, Theodore Hartridge, Lewis I. Fleming, A. S. Baldwin, George R. Fairbanks, and Daniel G. Ambler—under the confiscation acts, but this also stopped in the spring of 1865.[24] The transactions undertaken in accordance with both laws left such confusion over land titles that courts, military authorities, and local officials were almost overwhelmed.

While a few national leaders, notably Thaddeus Stevens, thought that large-scale confiscation of land from Confederates should be undertaken to provide lands for the freedmen, this was too radical a measure for most northern leaders. Some agreed with General Vogdes that if wealthy planters were permitted to keep their property, they would form a nucleus of loyal Union supporters in the South. As a result, some of the land sold under the direct tax act was returned to its original owners through a redemption clause in the law and through regular litigation. Many parcels taken under the confiscation acts were returned by the courts. Some of the litigation lasted several years, but numerous claims were settled in favor of original owners at the 1866 session of United States District Judge Philip Fraser's court at St. Augustine. Usually the land was returned on grounds that title to the property was held by the wife who was not disloyal or that the person involved was adjudged disloyal through circumstances rather than choice. As a result of this turnabout by the national government, most of the confiscated land was returned and the land which remained available for settlement by freedmen was mainly that which the United States government had acquired at the tax sales. The tax commissioners and later the Freedmen's Bureau agents placed Negroes in possession of the land for their use as long as the United States held it.[25] The property and its occupants were a subject of controversy in East Florida for many years after the war.

One of the first duties of the Freedmen's Bureau when it began operating in Florida was to take over all abandoned and confiscated land held by the military but not needed for military purposes. Its agents were instructed to return the property to original owners as soon as they made proper application for it. The only land excluded, other than that necessary for military purposes, was that which had been bought by the United States or was owned by men not yet pardoned.[26] The bureau restored hundreds of parcels of property to original owners at Jacksonville, Apalachicola, Pensacola, and elsewhere. In this way numerous ex-Confederates had their property restored without litigation.

Although some Radicals both in Florida and in Congress deplored the policy, United States District Attorney Nathaniel Usher explained the reason for it. He admitted that some former owners had been ordinary rebels who used their property to aid the rebellion. Some had been cruel enemies of the government and their neighbors loyal to it. All the condemned property was inside Union lines and the owners could have protected it merely by staying home. Instead they followed the rebel army, left their homes, and were suffering from their own actions. Their property had been rightfully taken, but Usher saw no reason why Floridians should suffer merely because a small portion of the state had been occupied by Union troops: "*If they lose their property, then all rebel property ought to be seized.*"[27] That was exactly what many Florida Unionists thought should have happened.

Within a year after hostilities ceased, some bureau agents were reporting that all property in their districts had been restored to original owners, although in a few cases restorations were delayed. Recalcitrance of Union officers was not the only reason for the delay. General Seymour at Pensacola reported property held by the bureau in 1867 which was not rented and therefore was not producing any revenue. As long as the property was in bureau hands, the city of Pensacola could not tax it. The owners were not anxious to apply for its return and Seymour was unable to rid himself of it.[28]

Some unused church buildings were being used as schools in the East Florida towns when the war ended. When ex-Confederates returned, church congregations soon began to ask for their buildings back. Some tension arose between local commanders and the citizenry, but the churches were retained until school was dismissed for the summer of 1866. Some Union officers felt that the congregations were more concerned with getting Negroes out of their churches than with having a place to worship. The schools were in session only five days a week and the buildings had always been available on Sundays. In Fernandina, Captain Thomas Leddy said the Methodists had no minister and that the Baptist congregation consisted of two families, also without a minister. Only the Episcopal and Presbyterian churches were used for schools and they had always been available for Sunday worship, but the people were unwilling to hold services in buildings shared with Negroes. General Oliver O. Howard authorized retention of the churches until other arrangements could be made, and they were returned to their trustees in June 1866.[29]

Even as Floridians were returning home from the war and with Union military units still occupying the state, there were indications that business and trade would revive despite the uncertain political climate, limited communications and transportation, and depressed conditions. The plantations were partially operating in 1865. Although they needed supplies and lacked funds, they were expecting a crop in the fall. This was a starting point, and merchants were soon advertising goods recently received from New York and New Orleans.

Commission merchants opened warehouses and offices in Florida port towns with connections in New Orleans, New York, England, and Europe. By July 1865, Joseph Remington, former United States marshal in North Florida, was advertising his Jacksonville commission and forwarding enterprise. He was shipping cotton to New York and had arrangements with the treasury agent in Jacksonville to weigh the cotton and collect the tax. Bruce, Morgan, and Company opened a commission house at Apalachicola with connections in both New York and Liverpool. The Southern Export and Import Company, capitalized at $100,000, offered to make advances to planters on cotton and other products which were consigned to its Liverpool agents. The company was willing to advance up to half the value of cotton in gold or its currency equivalent. It also solicited orders for goods from merchants and planters. A few Floridians successfully collected on investments they had made before the war in both southern and northern enterprises.[30]

The lumber industry was also reviving. Some impetus came from the military officials operating railroads. F. F. L'Engle and his associates cut railroad crossties for the Pensacola and Georgia Railroad while it was still under Union management. Companies were already cutting and shipping timber at Milton and Pensacola. A load of lumber left Jacksonville for Rio de Janeiro less than sixty days after McCook arrived in Tallahassee. C. P. Chaires, a Leon County Unionist who had been driven from Cedar Key by Confederate authorities during the war, was back in business in 1865. John McKay of Tampa purchased a steamer in New York, named it the *Governor Marvin,* and converted it into a cattle boat for the trade between Tampa and Havana. Cattle sales to Cuba stimulated grazing activities in South Florida and gradually brought much-needed capital into the state. The *Governor Marvin* and other steamers engaged in the coastal trade often benefited from contracts with the Union military force in the state. At Ocala, Robert W. Bullock reported a wide range of activities including a successful mercantile business, a profitable plantation he had rented, a cedar-cutting enterprise, and a contract to haul logs for another cedar company. At Lake City there were "good signs of prosperity, trade is opening actively in East and middle Florida."[31]

The end was also a beginning. Amid the turmoil of a government falling, an army breaking up, and soldiers returning home, there was the constructive activity of people engaged in the basic pursuit of earning a living. Some Floridians were unwilling to accept the changes wrought by war and defeat, but many others were facing the future. General Vogdes perceptively identified the major groups of Florida society and correctly evaluated their attitudes. He also identified the major issues to be met. His suggestions were as sound as was possible, but their contradictions were too obvious. There seems to have been a brief opportunity in 1865 when national leadership could have won approval by some of the major segments of Florida society for a Reconstruction program. But any policy chosen would have alienated important groups. A united government in Washington might have carried out Vogdes' moderate policy of appealing to the wealthy planting class, or his radical suggestion of Negro enfranchisement. But even a united government could not do both and the Washington government was not in a position to implement any program effectively. As a result both the moderate and the radical ideas were attempted, and neither succeeded.

3

In the Hands of the White Race

When Andrew Johnson became President of the United States in April 1865, some Radical Republicans in Congress were unable to contain their exultation. Abraham Lincoln's 10 per cent plan for Reconstruction with its offer of amnesty had never been acceptable to them. Johnson's hostility toward Confederate leaders was well known, and Radicals thought his accession removed an important obstacle to their postwar goals. Their initial enthusiasm for Johnson was short lived, however, for his disapproval of aristocratic Southerners was not accompanied by any desire to use national authority to alter the southern social hierarchy. President Johnson readily accepted the abolition of slavery which had been accomplished by Lincoln's proclamation and military action. While he desired positive evidence that the restored southern governments were being supported by loyal men, he was unwilling to use executive authority to guarantee Negro equality. As Johnson's Reconstruction plan unfolded, Radical enthusiasm turned to disappointment and finally to bitter opposition. The disagreement between the chief executive and important Radical Republican congressmen had tragic consequences for Florida and the nation.

On May 29, 1865, Johnson issued two proclamations which reflected his acceptance of Lincoln's mild plan for Reconstruction. He offered amnesty with restoration of property, except slaves, to most former Confederates who would take an oath of future loyalty to the United States. High Confederate officials and persons whose taxable property was valued at $20,000 or more were not included in the general amnesty, but they were encouraged to apply personally to the president for individual pardons.[1]

Another proclamation of the same date named William H. Holden as provisional governor of North Carolina with power to supervise reorganization of the state government. Disregarding Lincoln's 10 per cent formula, Johnson assumed that a majority of white males in each southern state would take oaths of future allegiance. The provisional governor was to register them as voters and call an election for delegates to a constitutional convention. The convention was expected to declare secession null and void, repudiate state debts incurred in support of the Confederacy, abolish slavery, and recognize all United States laws passed since 1860. Although he later modestly suggested to the Mississippi convention that it consider enfranchising some Negroes, Johnson left the question of suffrage qualifications entirely to the state conventions. When the constitution was ratified by a general election, the state would be ready to elect its officials and United States congressmen. As soon as the newly elected state legislature met and ratified the Thirteenth Amendment, Johnson would consider Reconstruction accomplished. So far as he was concerned, the state would then be ready to have its representatives seated in Congress and the Union would be restored. A proclamation of July 13 extended this plan to Florida.

President Lincoln had still been considering a final plan of Reconstruction when he was assassinated. Moreover, he had always left open the door to a joint presidential and congressional supervision. Johnson made up his mind by May 1865 and stuck doggedly to his program as enunciated in the North Carolina proclamation. With an interim of six months before Congress met, he had decided to complete restoration unilaterally by executive initiative.

The presidential plan had a mixed reception in Florida. Many native Unionists found it acceptable as did most former Confederates. But numerous Unionists, some natives of the state and others recently from the North, denounced the Johnson plan. Adolphus Mot—mayor of Fernandina, clerk of the direct tax commission, and a pronounced Radical closely identified with Chief Justice Salmon P. Chase—thought the president's proclamation stood in the path of future history "like a sphinx at the gate of Thebes, offering problems to be solved, enigmas and secrets to be devined."[2] What form of republican government by the votes of which loyal citizens, he asked? Was the freedman a citizen who would be permitted to vote? "Will oath and testimony make southern men loyal? Should reconstruction be left at the hands of prejudiced southern men? What 'form' of government can be expected, but the C.S.A. pattern?"

Touring Florida in late May, Chief Justice Chase helped nurture the idea that the president might favor punitive measures against ex-Confederates. Well known for his views on punishment of southern leaders and the related subject of Negro suffrage, Chase told the Key West Unionists that he and the president were in perfect accord. At Fernandina, Chase's friends had begun organizing Negroes for political participation. They reasoned that they could permit Negro voting in local elections and the Supreme Court would uphold their action because there was no authority for denying suffrage to citizens. Just before Chase arrived, an election was held in Fernandina in which both blacks and whites voted. Chase was pleased that he arrived just in time to administer the oath of office to Adolphus Mot who was elected mayor at what must have been the first Florida election in which Negroes participated.[3]

Rumors of the election and the continuing close friendship manifested between Chase and Lyman D. Stickney when the former arrived at Fernandina provoked Harrison Reed, the former tax commissioner. Reed had since been appointed postal agent for Florida and Georgia by Postmaster General Montgomery Blair. He wrote Blair that the Chase machine was being revived in Florida by use of national government patronage to the disadvantage of loyal resident white citizens. "There is a loyal element here which deserves notice," Reed declared, "but thus far every appointee is from abroad."[4] Although Stickney's radicalism was changing at the time of the president's proclamations, he was still allied with Chase and those opposed to Reconstruction along the lines the Chief Executive was adopting. Reed, on the other hand, accepted Johnson's policies in 1865 and remained a moderate even after the Reconstruction Acts of 1867.

The Radical Unionists in Florida, who could be counted in the dozens rather than the hundreds, generally disliked Johnson's reorganization plan, but few were so outspokenly opposed as Mayor Mot. At the same time many expressions of enthusiastic approval were heard. A representative example was a petition from twenty-three Hillsborough County residents, among whom were both former Union soldiers and former Confederates: "We rejoice in the restoration of peace. . . . Give us a provisional governor under whose administration Florida may be conducted into the Loyal line on the North Carolina plan."[5] It is unlikely that the petitioners understood what the North Carolina plan entailed. Another man who misunderstood the president's intentions was J. George Harris, a serious candidate for the provisional governorship, strongly recommended for the post by his Key West friends. Harris' own letter to the president may have unwittingly damaged his chances for appointment. He wrote: "Your North Carolina plan of restoration is admirable. The civil and military authorities are kept in the appropriate spheres—distinct and yet coordinate and cooperative under your command. Honor and gratitude to you for the wisdom, justice, and mercy, displayed in your late proclamation of Amnesty. It saves us. It is a perfect safeguard against the preponderance of rebellious influences at the polls." On solid ground so far, Harris warmed to his subject and added that "I have not feared negro suffrage, for the freedmen are loyal. I have feared universal amnesty for there are thousands of unrepenting rebels who still talk defiantly in our midst."[6]

Although the president had indicated a desire to appoint a native Floridian as provisional governor, it was soon clear that the favored candidate was William Marvin. Marvin was a native of New York and was first sent to Key West as a district attorney by Andrew Jackson in 1836. He became a judge in 1839 and decided many admiralty cases, gaining recognition as an authority on admiralty law. Over the years he built up favorable acquaintances with the New York City merchants and insurance executives with whom he dealt. He resigned his judgeship in 1863 and was living in New York when his name was first mentioned for the governorship of Florida in 1865.

Marvin had opposed the doctrine of secession and run as a pro-Union candidate for the 1861 secession convention, losing by a narrow margin. His Unionism was unquestionable, but his racial conservatism alienated some northern Unionists who came to Florida during the war. When he resigned his judgeship Marvin explained that ill health rendered him unable to cope with the heavy docket of prize cases resulting from the successful blockade of the southern coast, but he was also having an altercation with General David Hunter, the Union commander of the area. Disagreeing with Hunter's racial policies, Marvin had joined others in openly criticizing the general. A command reorganization in March 1863 separated Key West from Hunter's command, ending his plans to arrest the judge and send him north under guard. Hunter was convinced that Marvin actively sympathized with the "rebellion" and remained on the bench only because he could serve the Confederacy better under "the violated sanctity of the U.S. ermine."[7] Hunter's charges were exaggerated, but it was well known in Florida that Judge Marvin had little desire to alter the state's social structure.

Marvin and Lyman Stickney had also been enemies since 1863, and that erstwhile Radical entered the field against the judge's candidacy. "I am recently from Tallahassee," Stickney wrote. "Passing over the state I learned to my regret that the prominent proslavery men, the active rebels during the rebellion are with great unanimity in favor of Judge Marvin. He would reconstruct the State antagonistic to the administration." That he was correct about Marvin's suitability to the administration may be doubted, but Stickney correctly analyzed the attitudes of numerous ex-Confederates. Several of them petitioned the president for Marvin's appointment. David S. Walker and a delegation of former slaveholders went to Washington to present Marvin's case in person.[8]

Perhaps most informative of all was the letter of Stephen R. Mallory who was unable to go to Washington because of his incarceration at Fort Pulaski, Georgia, for having served the Confederacy as its secretary of the navy. Mallory wrote his former senatorial colleague William H. Seward that Marvin was peculiarly well fitted for the position of provisional governor. He was an able lawyer; long a resident of the state; thoroughly familiar with its institutions, laws, resources, interests, and leading men; and had been a Free Soil Democrat. In addition to this vigorous support from the former slaveholding, ex-Confederate portion of Florida citizenry, Judge Marvin was also recommended by several New York businessmen who knew him from his days on the bench. Harrison Reed, by this time thoroughly identified with Montgomery Blair and the conservative element of Johnson advisers, also suggested that Marvin would be a good appointee, adding, "for God's sake don't let the President send any man in Chase's interest."[9]

Judge Philip Fraser was probably the most important figure in the Marvin camp. Originally affiliated with C. L. Robinson, Lyman Stickney, and other wartime Unionists, Fraser broke with them on the question of a provisional governor. Fraser had suggested the Marvin appointment both to the judge and to Johnson administration officials. Marvin demurred in a lengthy letter which he authorized Fraser to use any way he saw fit. Marvin's brother wrote Seward that the former judge would not seek the office but would accept it if offered. He also encouraged the recommendations which came from the New Yorkers.[10]

Stickney and Robinson had parted company over the 1864 Union Republican convention, and they had personal differences as well, but they apparently collaborated to oppose the judge. A telegram from Robinson on July 3 announced a delegation of Unionists bound for Washington and asked that the appointment be delayed until it arrived. On July 9, Stickney wrote warning against Marvin's appointment until the Florida men had reached Washington and submitted the name of a northern man for the office. Whether this delegation was backing Robinson is not clear, although he had been recommended by others.[11] Their mission failed: President Johnson named William Marvin as provisional governor of Florida on July 13, 1865. His instructions were similar to those given William Holden in North Carolina. The appointment was praised by ex-Confederates and by those Unionists who favored a moderate or conservative racial policy. The Radical Unionists denounced it.

While Johnson was developing his Reconstruction policy and naming officials, the army finally clarified its command structure in the South. The conflict between General Israel Vogdes at Jacksonville and General Edward McCook at Tallahassee was settled by placing Florida in the Department of the South for a brief period. For the first time Key West and the Dry Tortugas were joined with mainland Florida in one military district. Brigadier General John Newton was placed in command. In late June another significant change occurred. The Division of the Gulf was created with Major General Philip H. Sheridan commanding at New Orleans. The Department of Florida was included in this division with Brevet Major General John G. Foster commanding. Newton remained in Florida for a while as commander of a subdistrict under Foster.[12]

Provisional Governor Marvin and General Foster traveled to Florida together. In lengthy discussions of the tasks before them, which both realized would require cooperation between civil and military authorities, a mutual respect had developed. Foster was an engineering officer and an 1846 West Point graduate. He was not politically involved except to the extent necessitated by his Florida assignment. As a loyal Union officer, he was determined to carry out the policies of the United States government as he understood them, but he was dispassionately fair in doing so. Before going to Florida he had expressed the belief that it would be necessary to have troops in the South for a long time.[13] When he arrived in the state, he saw little to alter his opinion but was encouraged by what he regarded as a willingness to cooperate on the part of influential Floridians. But, as time passed and the presidential-congressional conflict continued, Foster became more pessimistic. He finally left the state in late 1866, disappointed over the prospect of rebuilding a loyal society and government in Florida under the national policy existing at that time.

That Foster ultimately despaired of achieving his goals seems even more tragic when one recognizes the modesty of his views at the outset. After learning of Marvin's conservative views on Reconstruction, the general wrote cheerfully that the provisional governor was an excellent man with whom it would be easy to work. And General Foster was always solicitous of the sensitivity of native Floridians on racial matters. His requests for troop replacements always specified white troops because of the hostility to the presence of Negro soldiers in the interior of the state.[14] It is natural for soldiers to think in terms of procedure and the execution of orders from higher authority with the least possible disturbance. While many of the generals in Florida from David Hunter to Israel Vogdes had executed their orders with a view to achieving substantive political and racial ends, Foster apparently limited himself to the narrower role. If this estimate of Foster is correct, his praise of Marvin is understandable.

Provisional Governor Marvin willingly cooperated with Foster. He recognized the military government as the only one existing in Florida until a constitutional covention could be held and a new state government organized.[15] In return Marvin received assistance from the military commander in his gubernatorial duties. Upon arrival in the state, the new governor addressed the people, explaining his authority and objectives. The president had appointed him to aid the loyal people of Florida in organizing a government. Until that was done, it was the duty of military authorities to preserve the peace and protect the rights of persons and property. The military commander had agreed to retain in office all judicial and administrative officials whose performance of duty was necessary for ordinary business. If there should be any doubt concerning the validity of their actions in the interim period, the legislature could later remove the uncertainty by law.

Marvin reminded Floridians that slavery had ceased to exist and could not be revived. Every voter for delegates to the forthcoming convention, by taking the amnesty oath, swore to support the freedom of former slaves. But the freedom he referred to was that of a citizen of the United States quietly enjoying full constitutional guarantees. It did not necessarily include the voting privilege, which was a proper subject to be discussed and decided by the convention. The governor concluded his address with an optimistic but ambiguous proclamation that, "upon establishment of a republican form of state government . . . there will no longer exist any impediment in the way of restoring the state to its proper constitutional relations to the government of the United States."[16]

Marvin spoke in every portion of the state, explaining to white audiences the necessity of nullifying secession, abolishing slavery, repudiating state debts incurred in support of the war, recognizing United States laws, and admitting Negroes as witnesses in judicial proceedings. He continually reminded his listeners that they need not enfranchise Negroes in order to meet the president's requirements for restoration to the Union. On August 23, he called for an election of convention delegates to be held on October 10.[17] Only loyal men were permitted to participate. In order to be registered, potential voters had to be adult, white males who had lived in the state one year and the county in which registered at least six months. Evidence of loyalty entailed acceptance of the amnesty oath or a special pardon from the president. Because of the absence of mail facilities, General Foster agreed to assist in distributing poll books to the judges of probate throughout the state. The judges were to establish precincts and appoint three inspectors at each. Foster agreed to receive the election returns and transport them to Governor Marvin after the balloting. He was also willing to provide transportation for delegates from all the distant port cities in the state to the port nearest Tallahassee.

To make it as convenient as possible for "well disposed persons" to demonstrate their loyalty and vote, Marvin authorized all election inspectors to administer the amnesty oath at the polls at election time. They were warned not to permit anyone to vote who had not taken the oath.[18] On election day, 1,470 persons were administered the oath at the polls. During the registration period, military authorities administered 7,042 oaths to potential voters. Thus there were 8,512 Floridians, nearly 60 per cent of the 14,347 who had voted in 1860, eligible to participate in the 1865 election. Of the 8,512 registered, 6,707—nearly 47 per cent of the 1860 voters—cast ballots in 1865.[19]

The provisional governor spoke to many audiences of both black and white men before the election. His tone was conciliatory, and he called for restraint on the part of all. Acceptance of the president's conditions was reasonable and necessary for readmission, he told the whites. But he made equally clear to them that the Negroes had no reason to expect more than the president's minimum demands. Although he spoke to several Negro gatherings, Marvin's speech to a crowd of about 1,000 at Marianna on September 19 was the most comprehensive and certainly received the greatest national attention. His paternalistic tone was similar to that of many Florida aristocrats who had formerly owned slaves. It had been a white man's war, he said, the Negroes had had nothing to do with it. "Neither Northern or Southern white men when it began intended what has happened. So you are not indebted for your freedom to either side. You should be thankful to God. I know the Northerner from head to foot, and tell you that the Southern man is your best friend." While encouraging blacks to remain on the plantations, the governor lamented, "I as Governor stand here and tell you you are free, but you will not believe it, saying you still work for the same man as before. I know too that on 1 January next you will leave your old homes and drift about the country from plantation to plantation, looking for freedom." But he advised them not to flock to the towns where there were no jobs. They should remain on the land and make contracts with their former masters.

The Negro soldiers who first occupied Florida came from South Carolina where they had seen Negroes being given land to farm near Port Royal. Some had also observed a small number receiving plots which the United States government had acquired at the tax sales in Fernandina. These soldiers, with perhaps some encouragement from a few Radical Unionists, were apparently the major vehicle of the widely circulated rumor that on January 1, 1866, Negroes would be given land and equipment confiscated from their former masters. Marvin sought to dispel that fiction: "Do not believe the story about free land and mules, for it is not true. The President will not give you one foot of land, nor a mule, nor hog, nor cow, not even a knife and fork or spoon." He reasoned with the Negroes that they should accept the windfall of freedom and work to improve themselves: "You must not think because you are as free as the white people, that you are their equal; because you are not. [Before equality is realized] you will have to be able to write a book, build a railroad, a steam engine, a steamboat and a thousand other things you know nothing of."[20]

One Marianna Negro, if present at the meeting, may have been amused by the speech. Elijah Williams, a Jackson County freedman, was then preparing an application for a patent on his invention of a large propeller for boats used in shallow water. The patent was issued in April 1867. Not only was Williams intelligent and creative enough to see the advantage of his device over the old poling method, but after developing it before the war, he was astute enough to keep quiet about it until he was freed. But the governor was not acquainted with ingenuity on the part of plantation Negroes, and the advice which he gave them was apparently sincere. As nearly as can be determined, his speeches in that town and elsewhere were well received by the Negroes who heard him. At least, when the Marianna meeting was broken up by a torrential afternoon rainstorm, the crowd reassembled afterward to hear the remainder of the governor's speech.[21]

There was reason for optimism among white Floridians when the constitutional convention met on October 25, 1865, to revise the state constitution to conform with recent social and political changes and the president's requirements. The *Tallahassee Floridian*, edited by Charles E. Dyke who had edited the *Floridian and Journal* for years before joining the Confederate army as a captain of artillery, applauded Marvin's efforts and called on the people to reorganize the state government immediately. The existing condition of uncertainty was damaging the state because "capital will not come unless protected by a sound government."[22]

The 6,707 people who voted on October 10 sent fifty-six delegates to Tallahassee. They represented every Florida county, none of which had more than four delegates. Harrison Reed, former tax commissioner, current postal agent, and editor of the *Jacksonville Florida Times*, thought that the prospects of a satisfactory state reorganization were bright indeed because of the quality of the delegates. Reed pronounced E. D. Tracy of Nassau County, who presided over the convention, a sound man and a safe legislator. He called Judge Thomas Baltzell of Leon County "something of a politician" but a statesman of ability, and Judge D. P. Hogue, also of Leon, an able man. Reed also had high praise for George Troup Maxwell, saying that he had fought to preserve slavery but now accepted the fact that it was gone and was working for the future. "Such 'rebels' will make faithful citizens," wrote the future Republican governor of Florida.[23] There were a few Unionists in the convention, and at least one had served in the United States army, but the overwhelming majority were from backgrounds similar to those of these delegates that Reed singled out for praise.

Marvin's address to the convention was an elaboration of his August 3 proclamation. Slavery was gone and it was necessary to define in the constitution the civil rights and political privileges of the freedmen: "The governing power is in the hands of the white race, but the colored race is to be free and the government is to be administered in such a manner as not to infringe on that freedom." After extensive admonition that freedom did not include participation in politics, Marvin told the delegates that they must decide whether to give Negroes the vote. He then suggested that if the convention abolished slavery and provided guarantees for protection of the freedmen, the Congress would hardly refuse admission to the state's senators and representatives. That there might be no doubt as to his meaning, Marvin admitted that he could see no good in conferring the vote on freedmen since neither race was prepared for so radical a change.[24]

Marvin may have been correct at the time about congressional intentions, but with so narrow a charge from the provisional governor representing the national administration, the convention acted with reluctance in meeting even the minimal demands he made on it. Whether the convention's reluctance, together with the discriminatory laws of the first legislature, were enough to alter congressional willingness to seat Florida's representatives is doubtful, but the position of the congressional minority which was calling for additional guarantees to protect freedmen before restoring the Southern states to the Union was clearly strengthened.

The governor asked little enough. He wanted the constitution worded so as to prohibit racial discrimination by the courts or the legislature: "I think a clause may be so drawn as to accomplish this object, and at the same time exclude the colored people from any participation in the affairs of government." He specifically called for an ordinance declaring Negroes competent as witnesses in cases involving Negroes only. He also thought that a law making vagrancy punishable by temporary involuntary servitude was a necessary stimulant to Negro initiative.[25] Noting that favorable action by only two more state legislatures was necessary for ratification of the Thirteenth Amendment, Marvin thought it desirable for the convention to call on the legislature to approve it.

He concluded his address with a statement of the limited role he envisioned for Negro citizens and a prophetic warning of the consequences of denying the civil rights he called for: "What their condition as a race may be at the end of . . . 100 years, I do not think any person . . . [can] predict. But we may . . . hope . . . they will progress and improve in intelligence and civilization, and become, not many years hence, the best free agricultural peasantry, for our soil and climate, that the world has ever seen. . . . But, if denied equality and justice, industry will be, to them no more profitable than idleness. Discontent will prevail, and in the end the peace of society [will] be disturbed and the welfare of the state seriously affected."[26] The *Floridian* seconded the governor's remarks with glowing paternalism. Of course, freedom did not include political participation, "but as the disability rests on the ground of general incapacity, the more solemn the appeal to the ruling class to see that those whom God has made their inferiors, shall not suffer from the misfortune."[27]

Marvin undoubtedly had the best intentions, and from his viewpoint, acquired during a lifetime in the pre-1860 South, what he was suggesting was a radical innovation for Florida. Yet, he held out the promise that if the state leadership would accept these conditions, Florida would be restored to its previous relationship to the Union with most of its political and social structure intact. The delegates and their constituents decided they could meet the minimum demands of presidential Reconstruction. When they adjourned, they felt they had done this. Then, when Congress refused to seat their representatives, Floridians felt that the national government was not living up to its part of a bargain. There was scarce justification for this attitude, but it existed nevertheless and became a factor in Reconstruction politics.

In complying with the president's plan, the convention unanimously annulled the secession ordinance and, by a less impressive vote of twenty to fourteen, abolished slavery and involuntary servitude except as punishment for crime. A major obstacle developed when the finance committee reported its resolution regarding state debts. The cause of controversy was $1,857,269.99 worth of outstanding Florida treasury notes. The committee recommended their redemption by the issuance of state bonds at the rate of ten cents on the dollar. Many delegates thought this proper because the state's integrity was involved and because many Floridians had already lost heavy investments in now worthless Confederate bonds and notes. Unable to agree, the convention voted to submit the question to the people. By a vote of twenty-five to twenty-one it was decided that at the first gubernatorial election the people could vote to "pay" or "repudiate" the treasury notes. Just before adjournment the convention was informed that President Johnson required total and unequivocal repudiation of the state debt as a condition precedent to readmission. By a hurried vote of thirty-three to nine the state was relieved of responsibility for the treasury notes.[28]

In other actions the convention limited suffrage, political office, and jury duty to white men. In a special ordinance to be effective until the legislature could act, it authorized the arrest, on complaint of any civil official, of "strolling and wandering" persons. These vagrants could be punished by fines not exceeding $500 or could be sold for periods not to exceed one year.[29] Negroes were permitted to testify in cases involving blacks only, but the legislature was empowered to change this provision if it chose. In apportioning legislative representation, the convention retained the antebellum three-fifths formula of counting Negroes.

A resolution of the convention called on President Johnson to pardon Jefferson Davis and release from incarceration former Florida Senators David L. Yulee and Stephen R. Mallory as well as former Acting Governor A. K. Allison.[30] Another resolution urged Governor Marvin to exert every effort to have Negro occupation troops removed from posts in the interior of Florida. The presence of black soldiers in the inland towns had been especially vexing to white citizens. They argued that Negro soldiers were a disruptive element because of their own conduct and their influence on freedmen in general, but most of the whites resented the presence of the blacks as a reminder of their recent military defeat.[31] The resolution was unnecessary since the army was removing Negro troops to the ports or discharging them outright as rapidly as white replacements could be obtained.

The convention authorized the provisional governor to raise a state militia. Unwilling to be protected by Negro soldiers, native Floridians wanted a white militia because they felt it necessary to control the freedmen. There was no evidence that Negroes were contemplating violence and most of those who had wandered from the plantations in the spring were back home by fall, but rumors were circulating that the freedmen would leave their old habitats around Christmas of 1865 in a general and violent uprising. Apparently the rumor stemmed from several factors. The rumored division of the plantations at the rate of forty acres for each freedman was supposed to occur on Christmas. Adding to the apprehension was a much-publicized letter, evidently forged by a white person, which threatened a general uprising growing out of disappointment when the land was not divided.[32] The rumors and the longstanding white dread of Negro insurrections led to the desire for a white state militia.

No one in a responsible position in Florida gave credence to the rumors, but General Howard had suggested extra patrols to quiet the anxieties of the whites. Thomas W. Osborn, head of the Freedmen's Bureau, discounted the need for them, but both Foster and Newton complied with General Howard's suggestion. A few investigations were made of publicized Negro gatherings during the holidays. L. M. Hobbs, a Freedmen's

Bureau official, rode out to the Frederick R. Cotten plantation near Lake Iamonia in northern Leon County where a Christmas meeting was scheduled. They had planned to have a Christmas sermon but had canceled it because Cotten objected.[33]

As was often the case, preventive action by the whites during the Christmas episode was enough to provoke violence from all but the most docile people. D. C. Hawkins of Chattahoochee visited nearby Negro families and seized their firearms, promising to return them after Christmas. By June 30, 1866, the weapons had still not been returned. Furthermore, some Negroes in that area were being turned off the land at Christmas without compensation and no civil official would hear their complaints. In Quincy, Probate Judge E. C. Love, who was also the Freedmen's Bureau agent, closed the combination barroom and drygoods store of Robert Hall, an enterprising freedman, for a week after Christmas. When Hall complained, Love explained that he had closed all liquor establishments on Christmas but had refused to permit Hall to reopen during the critical week because as a freedman he could not command enough respect to keep order in his place in case of a disturbance. Despite the fears and precautions of the whites, no violence occurred.[34]

Governor Marvin complied with the request for a militia. On November 21, he called for its organization. General Foster approved the action, but subsequently obtained Governor David S. Walker's promise that if the militia had to be called, it would be under the command of the United States officer from the nearest post. Even with this limitation, few Unionists, ex-Confederates, or Negroes could have missed the symbolism when J. J. Dickison, a hero for his wartime guerilla raids against Union forces in Florida, was named militia commander of a large area in north-central Florida with power to appoint subordinate officers.[35]

The convention also called on the governor to authorize all civil officials who had been in office before May 1865 to resume their duties. Marvin first obtained General Foster's approval and on November 10 restored civil authority. In most cases he simply directed former civil officials to function as they had in the past. Until further notice, however, the military commander retained exclusive jurisdiction over offenses committed by his own troops and in the trial of all cases of murder, manslaughter, arson, and rape. All lesser crimes were to be handled by civil courts. Emphasizing that the proclamation required the approval of the military commander, Marvin exhorted judges, justices of the peace, sheriffs, and constables to be vigilant but also to cooperate with the military authorities. On December 1, President Johnson restored habeas corpus privileges in the state.[36]

Governor Marvin was also asked to appoint three men to report to the next general assembly on amendments necessary to make the laws conform with the amended constitution with special reference to Negroes. He subsequently named Charles H. Dupont of Gadsden County, former supreme court justice and soon to be named to the same bench by Governor Walker; Anderson J. Peeler of Leon County, a prominent ex-Confederate and an unreconstructed rebel who denounced the president's plan as unconstitutional while praising the institution of slavery; and Mariano D. Papy of Leon County, a former Confederate of much milder demeanor.[37]

A general election for state officials and a congressman was called for November 29. After hearing Governor Marvin praise its actions, the convention adjourned sine die on November 7. Governor Marvin reported to the president with satisfaction that the convention had annulled the secession ordinance, abolished slavery, declared inhabitants free without distinction of color, and permitted Negroes to testify in cases involving their own race.[38]

The convention had done, often with outspoken reluctance, exactly what the president required as minimum conditions for readmission. It had also left room for the forthcoming legislature to distinguish between black and white citizens, and Marvin had appointed a committee whose majority was disposed to do so. The equivocal action of the convention had raised suspicion among some Northerners as to the adequacy of the president's requirements. The president was often in contact with Governor Marvin and his successor, David Walker, yet he apparently gave them no indication that the state's limited accommodation to the postwar situation was unacceptable to him. His program for Reconstruction encouraged Floridians in their belief that the state was a continuing sovereign entity which had left the Union intact in 1861 and was free to return to it equally intact after meeting certain conditions. A bargain had been struck by the state and the United States. The state had fulfilled its part of the agreement. From their point of view, the Floridians had made sweeping changes in the state's legal structure to conform with changes resulting from war and emancipation. "We did all the U.S., acting through its President, asked of us, but do not have our rights," Governor Walker later complained.[39] That any responsible national leaders could legitimately ask for more was beyond their understanding. Governor Marvin's speeches had encouraged the delegates and other Floridians in their convictions.

Noting the eagerness with which Floridians looked to the convention as a necessary step toward immediate restoration, Assistant Commissioner Osborn wrote, "There appears to be on the part of every citizen of the state a firm belief that after the meeting of the convention, and that of Congress that the state will at once resume its proper relation in the

General Government—the military force will be withdrawn and the negroes will be again in their power to do with as they may see fit."[40] This was no suspicious Radical writing. Osborn's moderate views early won him social acceptance by upper-class Tallahasseeans while he was assistant commissioner, and he was the law and business partner of McQueen McIntosh, the most outspoken advocate of immediate secession at the 1861 convention. Osborn was more optimistic after the convention adjourned, reporting in November that "bitter feeling is dying away and will finally give way . . . providing . . . that our laws have sufficient character to maintain equal rights of freedmen before the law."[41] The accuracy of Osborn's speculations cannot be ascertained because it was precisely the absence of clearly stated national laws and evenhanded enforcement of them which led to confusion and uncertainty in the months following the convention.

4

Discrimination upon the Soundest Principles

The choice of state officials under the revised constitution evoked less interest than the earlier election of convention delegates. Florida had over 8,500 potential voters and about 6,700 had voted on October 10, yet fewer than 6,000 went to the polls on November 29. David Walker ran unopposed for governor, receiving all but eight of the votes cast. He was a former Whig, an unsuccessful Know-Nothing candidate for governor in 1856, a former state senator, and an opponent of secession who had reluctantly gone with the state out of the Union. He had not served in the Confederate army but was a judge during the war. W. W. J. Kelley of Pensacola defeated Thaddeus A. McDonell of Gainesville for lieutenant governor. Another former Whig, Ferdinand McLeod of west Florida, was elected to Congress. He had been in the Confederate army, and there was doubt as to his eligibility to take the oath of office. Other state officials elected were Secretary of State B. F. Allen, Attorney General John B. Galbraith, Comptroller L. G. Pyles, and Treasurer C. H. Austin. Most of the legislators, as well as the executive officers, were former slaveholders and ex-Confederates. In a widely publicized speech in the United States Senate, Charles Sumner read a letter from Florida denouncing the state for electing "rebels": "The Legislature are 4/5ths rebel officers, from B/Gen. Joseph Finegan down to a corporal. . . . The people of Florida are more hostile than they ever have been. They were surrendered too soon." The *Tallahassee Floridian* challenged this estimate, arguing that only thirteen representatives and seven senators were former Confederate officers, making a total of twenty out of eighty-eight assemblymen.[1] More than that number had served in the Confederate army in some capacity. Regardless of which estimate was most accurate, the majority of legislators were no more willing to enact a program which would appeal to Charles Sumner than had been the recently adjourned constitutional convention, in which many of them sat as delegates.

When the general assembly convened on December 18, every facet of public policy required its attention. But two issues were paramount: the relation of the state to the United States government and the alteration of the state laws to conform to the amended constitution. Because of its urgency the latter problem consumed most of the time and effort of the session. With a handful of exceptions, including former Union Captain James D. Green of Manatee County, the legislators were in broad agreement about the changes in Florida laws necessitated by emancipation and President Johnson's Reconstruction plan. Whether Whig or Democrat before 1860, whether Unionist or secessionist in 1861, most of the members favored legislation which distinguished between black and white citizens. Most of them also agreed with the work of the constitutional convention and with Governor Marvin's limited recommendations upon which it had acted.

Governor Walker, with a paternalism common to many upper-class white Floridians, put the need for discrimination in the kindest terms: "It is not their fault they are free—they had nothing to do with it. . . . But they are free. They are no longer our contented and happy slaves, with an abundant supply of food and clothing for themselves and families and the intelligence of a superior race to look ahead and make all necessary arrangements for their comfort. They are now a discontented and unhappy people . . . and doomed to untold sufferings and ultimate extinction, unless we intervene for their protection and preservation." The governor anticipated a move already gaining support to encourage immigration of foreign white laborers on the theory that Negroes would not work under a free labor system. "We must remember," Walker said, "that these black people are natives of this country and have a pre-emption to be recipients of whatever favors we may have to bestow." Walker considered this a magnanimous position for he quickly added that it was well known that black laborers could not do as much work as white ones: "We know that they cannot do it. . . . Our fathers of 1783 knew that it takes five black men to do the work of three white ones." Calling on the assembly to provide laws protecting the Negroes in their new condition, he added that white Floridians could never accede to the demand for Negro suffrage, but he did not believe there would be such a demand since so few northern states allowed it.[2]

Walker had no doubt that his position was fair. His outlook had been formed during a lifetime as a member of a slave-owning class which had developed an extensive legal and ideological framework for racial slavery. Negro slavery had developed in colonial America because it was practical. Slavery was a widely accepted institution in the seventeenth century; the blacks were suited to working conditions in the colonies, and there was an available supply of Negroes. After the institution was established, an elaborate justification for it evolved. By the time Florida became a United States territory, racial slavery was justified on the ground that Negroes were so inferior to other races that legal servitude was their natural condition. The belief carried over and included free Negroes, whose presence in a society where racial slavery was so important was a nuisance and a potential threat. All of the slaveholding states developed legal slave codes and extensive regulations of free Negroes as well. The environmental conditions of slavery—prohibition of education, menial labor, lack of opportunity to develop family relations—re-inforced the belief in the Negroes' inherent inferiority. When the slaves were emancipated, many Floridians who considered themselves decent people also believed that whites and blacks could not live as free and equal citizens in an open society. Many accepted the abolition of slavery and were still concerned about how to adjust the state laws to meet the president's demands and at the same time salvage a system under which the whites with their responsibilities to the blacks, and Negroes with their natural limitations, could live.[3]

In retrospect one is compelled to ask why, if Negroes were naturally inferior, was it necessary to develop an extensive legal code to make them so? But that question was not raised in 1865. Florida had had a slave code as well as regulations of free blacks, parts of which had become unconstitutional. The assembly had to decide how much change was necessary to comply with constitutional requirements and how much of the regulatory system could be salvaged to avoid further disruption of society. Most legislators were also influenced by their strict constitutional views regarding national-state relations. They believed that the states had definite rights which would not be breached, even after military defeat. One of these was the right to regulate domestic institutions, into which category fell laws relating to blacks, either slave or free. The national government had no right to interfere with legislation in this area and many of them resented even President Johnson's mild demands. Given the gravity of the problem and the limitations imposed by their constitutional theory, it is not surprising that the action of the Florida legislative body appeared defiant and inadequate to northern Radicals who had good reason to watch the South closely on this issue.

The idea that Negroes would not work as free laborers was widespread, although large numbers of planters seemed to wish them well. One bureau official reported that the planters in his area were willing to try the free system, but "they regard it as an experiment." Others wanted to make the system work by passing laws to insure that Negroes would be available as laborers. A mass meeting in Jefferson County called for legislation providing for just and equitable contracts between landholders and laborers, but it also condemned anyone who rented land and mules to black tenants. The *Monticello Family Friend* agreed that renting land to Negroes was wrong since it would "ruin the negro and injure the industrial and financial prospects of the South." Negroes were bound "by an enactment of nature" to till the soil for the white man.[4] But the natural law did not lessen the need for man-made legislation.

In addition to the racial and legal attitudes of the legislators and the requirements laid down by President Johnson, there were other important influences on the legislative decisions of 1865–66. Orders which had the effect of laws regulating white employer–Negro laborer relations had been issued by the military occupation forces since the previous spring and by the Freedmen's Bureau since September. Begun by occupation commanders and continued by the bureau, the policy of encouraging written contracts between the parties according to guidelines laid down and supervised by the bureau agents influenced the legislators' thinking.

The very presence of the military force was a factor, but there was more to it than that. Both General Foster and Colonel Osborn were on good relations with Governor Marvin, Governor Walker, and other Floridians. They both agreed with native whites that all parties would be best served if the Negroes continued as agricultural laborers, even remaining, wherever possible, on the same plantations where they had been slaves. The Union officers differed with the Floridians, however, in their understanding of the scope of the Negroes' civil rights. Osborn was especially interested in labor relations, education, and the criminal code. By ordinary lobbying techniques he helped shape the laws relating to education. Failing to obtain desired changes in the proposed criminal laws, he mitigated their effect by more direct pressure. Both Osborn and Foster held moderate views on racial relations and both restrained themselves from interference in many cases where the actions of whites were questionable. They followed this policy knowing that the military units would one day be withdrawn and the Negroes left to fend for themselves. Neither wished to antagonize the whites while they were in Florida so as to invite retaliation when they were gone. At the same time they were unwilling to accept flagrant discrimination. When a commander at St. Augustine became so anxious to avoid racial conflict that he ordered Negroes to give whites the inside of the sidewalk when they met, Osborn quickly obtained a cancellation of the order.[5]

The question of corporal punishment caused the most disagreement between Colonel Osborn and the assembly, and military examples probably influenced the legislators to some extent even in this matter. On October 29, while the constitutional convention was in session, the commander of the Third United States Colored Troops at Jacksonville tied a Negro soldier up by the thumbs as punishment for misbehavior. Other soldiers tried to release him, but the colonel shot the first three men who moved, killing two of them. Fourteen men were tried for mutiny by courts-martial. Six were executed by a firing squad, six were imprisoned, and two were acquitted.[6] This does not justify the assembly's rationale for discrimination as its members wrote it into Florida law, but it may have led them to believe that the army would approve corporal punishment.

Another factor which should have influenced the Florida general assembly, but which seems to have been ignored, was the manifestation of northern dissatisfaction with legislation in other southern states. By late December, when the Florida assembly met, the Mississippi and South Carolina legislatures had already completed sessions at which both passed laws harshly distinguishing between blacks and whites. These early "black codes" brought a rash of criticism from northern newspapers and public speakers. Southerners were warned that the northern people would accept nothing less than equal protection of black citizens. The comparatively few Radicals who were demanding Negro suffrage at this time were joined by others who, while unwilling to go so far as enfranchisement, expected an effort made in good faith by southern states to guarantee civil rights of freedmen. All the states except Florida whose legislatures met after the criticism was expressed adopted milder "black codes" than those of Mississippi and South Carolina. In contrast, the Florida laws were as harsh as either of the earlier ones, and the debates surrounding their adoption suggested belligerence and defiance.

A committee on Federal relations, headed by G. Troup Maxwell of Leon County, prefaced its report with comments on "the contest now being waged by the radicals in Congress against the policy and plan of restoration . . . recommended and inaugurated by President A. Johnson." It was a contest between "confiscation and execution" on the one hand and "wisdom and clemency" on the other. The hope of a nation was centered in President Johnson, the great breakwater against which a bloody-minded, diabolical radicalism raged. Johnson was standing valiantly over a brave people to protect them from "the radical wolves and hyenas who would suck their life blood and revel at the repast."[7] Northern moderates found little encouragement in such words and it is no wonder that Charles Sumner chose Senator-elect Marvin's subsequent request to be seated in the Senate as a focal point for an assault on unrepentant Southerners.[8] While it appears that most Floridians cared little about northern public opinion, the general assembly's action regarding race relations seems to defy the longstanding belief in southern political acumen and leadership.

The special committee appointed by Marvin to recommend statutory amendments to the general assembly was largely responsible for the defiant tone and harsh substance of the Florida "black code." C. H. Dupont signed the majority report, but it was primarily the work of A. J. Peeler, who thought Johnson's entire Reconstruction plan an unconstitutional incursion on the rights of the state. Mariano D. Papy, the third member, refused to sign the majority report and called on the assembly to correct its errors. Although it suggested limiting such power to exceptional cases, the committee "strenuously assert[ed]" the general assembly's authority to discriminate. The power to discriminate between the two races had always been exercised without stint by the states of the Union, including those of New England. The Dred Scott case proved that Negroes were not citizens and that Congress was incapable of supplying a remedy. Although slavery had been abolished, the act of emancipation alone made no social, legal, or political changes in the status of Negroes who were already free. And, the committee concluded, "freedmen" occupied no higher position in the scale of rights and privileges than did the "free negro." For that matter, they saw very little wrong with the system of slavery as it existed in Florida, except for the deleterious consequences of a lack of marriage requirements. The committee recommended preserving insofar as possible the beneficial features of the "benign, but much abused and greatly misunderstood institution of slavery."[9] At most the freedman should be placed in no higher legal position than that of the antebellum free Negro.

Despite Governor Marvin's caution that the state's domestic affairs would be reviewed by Congress unless the assembly accepted the freedom of Negroes and gave them equal protection of person and property, the legislators followed the committee recommendations closely.[10] There was no single set of laws comprising the "black code." It was enacted piecemeal as part of several legislative acts dealing with labor contracts, vagrancy, apprenticeship, marriage, taxation, the judicial system, and crime and punishment. Collectively, these laws accomplished the goals stated in the committee report.

"An act in relation to contracts of persons of Color" drew heavily from the system already implemented by the military commanders and Freedmen's Bureau, but the assembly added some innovations. Contracts were required to be in writing and witnessed by two white persons. If Negroes broke their contracts, they could be punished as common vagrants by being whipped, placed in the pillory, imprisoned, or sold for as long as a year. They could be convicted of breaking the contract if found guilty of "willful disobedience, wanton impudence, disrespect to the employer, failure to perform assigned work, or abandonment of the premises." If the employer broke the contract, the laborer could seek redress in the courts. That the Negroes' access to legal counsel was severely limited by lack of knowledge or funds was not considered the fault of the lawmakers. The Florida attorney general declared the law unconstitutional, but the next session of the assembly rewrote it so as to apply to both races in occupations limited almost entirely to Negroes.[11]

A crop lien law was passed which had the effect of keeping tenants on the land. A landowner was empowered to seek a writ placing a lien on crops grown on rented land if the rent was not paid within ten days of the due date.[12] If a tenant failed to pay out at year's end, the lien could be extended to the next year's crop and he could be legally held on the land. While it attracted little attention at the time, the law became more important as Negroes began to rent land. In time it contributed to an agricultural system which kept many Negroes in economic bondage for decades after the Civil War.

"An act to punish vagrants and vagabonds" was similar to the special ordinance that had been passed by the constitutional convention. It allowed a convicted vagrant to post bond as a guarantee of good behavior for the following year. If no bond was posted, the vagrant could be punished by the pillory, the whip, prison, or by being sold for his labor for one year. The *Tallahassee Floridian* applauded the vagrancy law as a good way to discourage Negroes from coming into the towns. The Freedmen's Bureau also showed little patience with vagrants. Colonel Osborn sent agents to Jacksonville and Fernandina to round up unemployed Negroes and place them on plantations where there was a demand for labor. In the spring of 1866, some Negroes gathered in Monticello and refused to work. The military commander there was authorized to arrest them and work them on the public roads until they changed their minds. "This procedure has worked well in Jacksonville. The vagrants disappear when they find the military after them," the order read.[13]

An extensive revenue law contained provisions for a five-mill tax on real property and a capitation tax of three dollars on every male between twenty-one and fifty-five years of age. The head tax was difficult for the Negroes to pay. If they became delinquent, they could be arrested and sold for their labor in an amount sufficient to liquidate the debt and all expenses incurred. Another law defined a Negro as any person with one-eighth or more Negro blood. This definition was necessary to the enforcement of several acts aimed at separating the races. Both blacks and whites were prohibited from intruding on meetings of the other race or from entering segregated railway cars. Penalties of fines, imprisonment, whipping, or the pillory were provided for violators of both races. A school law, which will be discussed later, provided separate schools for Negroes. Marriages between Negro men and white women were prohibited. White violators of the enactment could be fined $1,000, jailed for three months, or both. Besides a fine of $1,000, Negroes could be made to stand in the pillory for one hour, be administered thirty-nine lashes, or both.[14]

The prohibition of intermarriage caused less criticism than a law intended to correct a problem growing out of the slave system. "An act to establish and enforce the marriage relations between persons of color" gave all Negro couples living together nine months in which to decide whether they wished to continue their relationship. If so, they were to be legally married. There had been little recognition of monogamous marriages of Negroes during slavery; slaves had often had their mates chosen for them or arbitrarily separated from them, and no stigma was attached to indiscriminant cohabitation of slaves. Accustomed as they were to their experiences during slavery, it is little wonder that Negroes did not immediately adopt the white moral code. Many couples were married under the law, but bureau agents continued to complain of sexual promiscuity, although they noted marked improvement in time. Acceptance of a legally recognized system of monogamous marriages required time for people who had been denied the institution in the past. Yet as slow as their acceptance of the change was, it was a good deal more rapid than white acceptance of civil rights changes of the same period.

The marriage law was enforced, and many indictments were brought against Negroes who had not been married in the prescribed time. When the next assembly convened in late 1866, Governor Walker recommended an extension because freedmen had not learned of the requirement soon enough to act on it. "We must live down the false and slanderous stories which are circulated against us on this subject," he said. By statute the assembly declared all Negroes living as husband and wife to be legally married and all indictments for unlawful cohabitation dismissed.[15]

"An act in relation to apprentices" empowered courts to apprentice the children of vagrants or paupers to persons who could supervise their activities, provide for them, and teach them a trade.[16] A number of children were apprenticed, and disputes arose between parents and those to whom they were apprenticed. The bureau held that normally freedmen should have authority over their children, but there were still questions of paternity as well as ability to care for the children.

The "act in relation to judicial proceedings" and the one "prescribing additional penalties for the commission of offenses against the state, and for other purposes" evoked considerable discussion, although only a few members opposed them and no ameliorating amendments were made to the original bills. The special committee lamented the loss of the excellent institutions which had existed on each plantation for punishment of those minor offenses to which Negroes were addicted. Now that these offenses had to be handled by the courts, the committee recognized that the circuit courts were too limited in capacity to handle the increased volume of minor offenses. It recommended as a solution the establishment of a criminal court in each county. The assembly responded with a law providing these courts. They were soon handling cases and their judicial standards caused great controversy between state officials and bureau personnel, an issue which will be pursued in a later chapter. Another provision of the law was based on the committee recommendation that "whenever a crime be punishable by fine and imprisonment we add an alternative of the pillory for an hour or whipping up to thirty-nine lashes or both at the discretion of the jury." This discrimination was "founded upon the soundest principles of State policy, growing out of the difference that exists in social and political status of the two races. To degrade a white man by punishment, is to make a bad member of society and a dangerous political agent. To fine and imprison a colored man in his present pecuniary condition is to punish the State instead of the individual."[17] Eminently practical on its face, the recommendation was hardly calculated to please northern Radicals who were watching the South for signs that Negroes were not receiving equal treatment.

Crimes were enumerated and assigned penalties of fine or imprisonment, and the pillory or whipping could be substituted. The death penalty was provided for those found guilty of inciting insurrection, raping a white female, or administering poison. Burglary was punishable by death, a fine not exceeding $1,000, or a public whipping and the pillory. Some of the crimes punishable by fines, imprisonment, or whipping and the pillory included malicious trespass, buying or selling cotton without evidence of ownership, and defacement of public or private property. Punishment by whipping or the pillory was provided for willfully killing or injuring another's livestock, hunting with a gun on another's property, or unauthorized use of a horse whether in the employ of the owner or not.[18]

All antebellum laws applying exclusively to slaves and free Negroes were repealed except one which prevented their migration into the state. Negroes were specifically denied the right to carry firearms, bowie knives, dirks, or swords without a license from the probate judge. The fine was forfeiture of the weapon and a whipping, the pillory, or both. This latter provision reflected the apprehension about Negro insurrections carried over from slavery times and exaggerated by the persistent rumors of trouble during the Christmas holiday period. Just as the whites wanted a reliable militia, they wanted to prevent the Negroes from acquiring guns and the right to carry them.

Colonel Osborn protested the discriminatory acts of the assembly. He wrote Governor Marvin that "standing in the pillory" and "whipping" were repugnant to civilized people. He also thought it wrong to inflict the death penalty on a Negro or mulatto for raping a white female since the same penalty was not required for white persons. The requirement of a bond for Negroes to possess firearms he also condemned. All this "partial legislation" was in conflict with the instructions under which the assembly had been allowed to meet. Since Marvin had suggested the unequal treatment, Osborn did not expect his warning to be heeded. He asked General Howard for instructions and was told not to acknowledge corporal punishment: "No distinction in punishment on account of race may be tolerated in this country," the commissioner said.[19]

When Osborn communicated these instructions to Governor Walker, the chief executive responded equivocally. Asserting that the law inflicted corporal punishment on both blacks and whites, he wanted to know if General Howard intended to intervene to protect blacks even though whites were obligated to suffer the penalty. The issue continued during most of 1866. Osborn intervened to stop the whippings when he could, but he acted through personal contact with the governor or between bureau officials and local civil officers as individual cases arose.[20] A general order was issued prohibiting corporal punishment, but it was revoked in May 1866 when the governor proclaimed that whipping would be used only as "absolutely necessary."[21]

For a time in this period, an agreement existed between the state administration and the military that all Negroes sentenced to be whipped or placed in the pillory would be turned over to the nearest military post where imprisonment would be substituted at the rate of one day at hard labor for each lash and one day for each two minutes in the pillory.[22] Some whippings occurred in 1866 but the government apparently tried to avoid them. Osborn was dissatisfied with the situation, but there was little more that he could do without a much clearer policy from Washington than that which existed in 1866.

It was still an intolerable situation, and both Osborn and his successor refused to accept it. In April 1866, Osborn recommended that the idle United States arsenal at Chattahoochee be turned over to the state as a penitentiary. With the treasury empty, this seemed to be the only way the state could abolish the "cruel punishment we abhor," Osborn wrote. When General Foster became assistant commissioner he also promoted this idea, and Governor Walker agreed that if the United States would give the arsenal to the state, he would attempt to bring an end to whipping and the pillory as punishment for crime. But when the next session of the assembly received the bill to abolish corporal punishment, it was tabled without action. Foster declared, "This terminates my desire to give them the arsenal."[23]

A similar situation arose over the firearms law. Because of Osborn's complaints, Governor Walker asked for the opinion of Attorney General John B. Galbraith who promptly declared the law unconstitutional. Osborn reported with satisfaction that he had won his point by this approach and had avoided a military-civil conflict. The law was still enforced by some local officials, but upon complaint of the bureau, Governor Walker intervened and nullified their actions. This was unsatisfactory because cases were not always reported. The next assembly stubbornly refused to abolish the law even after the attorney general's opinion and Governor Walker's statement that it was not being enforced.[24]

Just as emancipation had destroyed the law enforcement capability of the plantations, it had abolished the institution which had previously cared for indigents. When the legislature took up a proposal to make children of elderly and infirm Negroes responsible for their welfare, Colonel Osborn protested that the state would have to assume responsibility for indigents. Walker also suggested that emancipation may have necessitated state care for the poor. Both were ignored and "an act to require the children of destitute persons to provide for the support of such persons" became law. Individuals responsible under the law for parental care were subject to garnishment of their salaries if they refused to comply.[25]

The *Floridian* boasted that Florida was the only "rebel" state to make a provision for Negro education. Actually the state enacted a discriminatory Negro education law, but the initiative for it came from the Freedmen's Bureau. Both Colonel Osborn and Chaplain Hobbs claimed authorship of the bill, although Osborn said the original draft was mutilated and weakened by amendments. Both bureau men proposed segregated schools to be operated at no expense to the state. Osborn added the enticement that, by assuming the initiative in this important matter, white Floridians would have control over the freedmen's education. Most of the public commentary at the time indicated willingness of whites to establish Negro schools as long as they were staffed by local personnel. The assembly passed a law providing for separate Negro schools to be financed by a one-dollar tax on each adult Negro male for that specific purpose. The levy was in addition to all other taxes. Other revenue was to come from an annual license required of all white teachers who taught in the Negro schools. The latter provision was intended as a barrier to northern white teachers.[26] Practical though it was, the role of the bureau officials in recommending such a narrow Negro educational policy encouraged Florida legislators in their belief that their accomplishments were acceptable to the United States government.

On December 29, the assembly ratified the Thirteenth Amendment and elected United States senators. Wilkinson Call, an outspoken ex-Confederate who advocated acceptance of the president's plan only as a necessity, and J. Patton Anderson, a former Confederate general, were the leading candidates for the first seat. Call was elected on the second ballot. For the second seat, the major contenders were Benjamin D. Wright, J. J. Finley, and Edward Hopkins. All were former Confederates, although Hopkins had been the 1860 Constitutional Union condidate for governor. None of them received a majority and Governor Marvin was nominated as a compromise candidate. He was elected on the ninth ballot.[27]

The two senators-elect and congressman-elect Ferdinand McLeod presented themselves for seating in Congress and were denied seats along with other southern states' representatives until the Joint Committee of Fifteen on Reconstruction could investigate conditions in Florida and the South generally. They were never seated, but both senators-elect remained in Washington as lobbyists for Florida during the following weeks.

Governor Marvin performed the duties with which he was charged but failed to accomplish the state's readmission. His failure was due to factors largely beyond his control. On the one hand, President Johnson's plan for a quick, executive Reconstruction was doomed because it did not satisfy important congressional leaders in either substance or method. Some were angered by his refusal to include Congress in his planning, others because he did not envision Negro suffrage. But, most important, his plan did not satisfy the majority of congressmen because it provided inadequate security for the newly acquired rights of freedmen.[28] Although most congressmen and their constituencies in the 1860s accepted more or less consciously the principle of white supremacy, many still desired assurances that Negroes would be protected from arbitrary treatment.

Marvin shared some of the blame. His narrow charge to the people of Florida, to the constitutional conventon, and to the assembly had convinced a receptive audience that readmission could be accomplished with comparatively small concessions on the part of the former ruling class. Because of his position and the Floridians' reluctance to give up any more than absolutely necessary, the convention delegates and subsequent legislators argued at length before making even the minimal concessions expected by the president. Their reluctance, often approaching defiance, aided the Radicals in delaying readmission of the southern states until a program could be worked out demanding much more than Johnson had. Marvin's role as provisional governor was at least partially responsible for his failure to be seated as a senator from Florida. He had also encouraged the state's assembly to enact the laws which became known as Florida's "black code."

Many of the men who enacted the "black code" firmly believed that the United States government had no legal right to intervene in the affairs of the state, and many congressmen agreed with them. Yet Florida's legislators made so few concessions that the congressmen reluctantly set aside their own constitutional views in order to prevent what they considered an even greater wrong. Perhaps it was never in the power of Governor Marvin or the Floridians to prevent the subsequent intercession of Congress, but even if it had been their actions could not have been more self-defeating.

5

I Fear You Have Hercules' Task

The Bureau of Refugees, Freedmen, and Abandoned Lands was created by Congress on March 3, 1865, to last one year during which it was to control all matters relating to refugees and freedmen, provide emergency relief for them, and administer the confiscated and abandoned lands held in the South by the United States government. The agency was placed in the War Department. Two months later General Oliver Otis Howard was appointed commissioner of the bureau, a position he held until the organization's dissolution. The bureau had broadly defined powers but little financial support initially. Still, Howard envisioned it as a vehicle for guiding people just freed from slavery through the difficult process of adjusting to their new places in a free society: furnishing emergency subsistence, securing equal treatment before the law, developing a system of compensated labor in place of slavery, and providing the opportunity for education. Although President Johnson's opposition soon prevented it, Howard also thought of the bureau as the instrument through which Negroes could acquire land on which to sustain themselves. Because its resources were inadequate, the bureau was dependent on the northern benevolent associations, and Howard always cooperated closely with them. The magnitude of Howard's undertaking was summed up by his old army friend, William T. Sherman, who wrote that "I hardly know whether to congratulate you or not . . . I cannot imagine that matters . . . could be put in more charitable and more conscientious hands. So far as man can do, I believe you will, but I fear you have Hercules' task."[1]

It soon became clear that the bureau's mission could not be completed in one year. It was equally clear that its very existence was controversial. With responsibility for the affairs of freedmen in a society which at worst denied their right to freedom and at best still believed them inherently inferior beings unfit for full citizenship, the bureau was bound to stir opposition. As President Johnson's personal convictions and public acts identified him more clearly with conservative southern whites in early 1866, a growing number of congressmen became convinced that the term of the bureau had to be extended. After a major battle between the two branches of government, including a presidential veto, the life of the Freedmen's Bureau was extended for two more years in July 1866, and again for one additional year in July 1868. When Republican administrations assumed power in most southern states, many persons believed the bureau had served its purpose. Except for its educational activities and the payment of bounties to qualified Negro veterans of the United States Army, the agency came to an end on January 1, 1869. Within two more years it had completely ceased to function in Florida.

For the important positions of assistant commissioners in the various states, Howard selected men with whom he was personally acquainted, usually having served with them during the war. But financial difficulties, presidential opposition, and the bureau's close relationship to the army both in command structure and field responsibility caused frequent changes of personnel. General Rufus Saxton, already involved in freedmen's affairs in the Department of the South, was made assistant commissioner for South Carolina, Georgia, and Florida. The area proved too large for him to administer and was divided into three separate districts. In September 1865, Brevet Colonel Thomas W. Osborn of the First New York Artillery, who had served under Howard in the West and also campaigned in Florida with the 24th Massachusetts Infantry, became assistant commissioner for the state with headquarters at Tallahassee. Although state-wide organization of the bureau in Florida began only with Osborn's arrival in September, the agency had already been operating on a limited scale in the Jacksonville area during the summer of 1865.

After Congress extended the bureau's mandate, Major General John G. Foster, military commander of the Department of Florida, assumed the additional duty of assistant commissioner in June 1866. The combining of the bureau and the military had been proposed by General U. S. Grant in late 1865 and recommended by the Steedman-Fullerton report in early 1866. The change was praised by the local press in Florida. Colonel Osborn acted as an inspector until he was discharged in August 1866. Remaining in Florida, he became an important Republican politician. General Foster, whose administration was praised by conservative Floridians, became disillusioned because of his lack of authority and the Southerners' reluctance to give Negroes equal treatment before the law. He left Florida in December 1866 at his own request. Colonel John T. Sprague, whose long acquaintance with Florida since the years of the Second Seminole War made him highly acceptable to native whites, became military commander and assistant commissioner of the bureau. Sprague soon moved the bureau headquarters to St. Augustine where he had made his permanent home. When the agency's functions were restricted to education and bounty-paying in late 1868, Lieutenant Colonel George W. Gile replaced Sprague as head of the bureau and remained until its activities in Florida ended.[2]

During its existence in Florida, the Freedmen's Bureau enjoyed the anomaly of having its assistant commissioners praised and accepted socially by native whites while it was denounced as an institution.[3] Its critics never admitted that it performed a worthwhile service which benefited white Florida planters at least as much as it did blacks, without tampering with the state's social or economic structure. Its agents were generally able, honest, and fair, although some were more exuberant than others as they tried to carry out their duties in the face of bitter personal hostility and flagrant violations of due process of law. The Florida Bureau received an excellent commentary on its performance when the Steedman-Fullerton investigation failed to find any wrongdoing.[4] The two generals were sent by President Johnson specifically to build a case against the bureau, and although they found some ammunition for the president elsewhere, their report on Florida was favorable. While the bureau agents tried to force native whites to make and honor equitable contracts with the freedmen and to afford them equal treatment in the courts, they also required the freedmen to fulfill their contractual obligations. No agent encouraged indolence with unnecessary issues of rations, and freedmen who broke their contracts were arrested and returned to work.

It appears that the agents with the worst reputations among native whites were those located in counties where treatment of freedmen by whites was worst. They do not all deserve the reputation of transitory carpetbaggers which they have received from many writers. Two young bureau agents who became involved in the most acrimonious struggles with local white citizens in their districts were J. E. Quentin at Madison and A. B. Grumwell at Monticello. Yet when General Foster offered to reassign Quentin to Tallahassee because of hostility toward him in Madison, Quentin asked the general not to do it. Except for his association with the bureau, Quentin said, he had no trouble in his social relations. He had purchased a home in Madison and brought his mother to live with him. A transfer would work a hardship on him. Quentin remained at Madison. Grumwell remained in Monticello and became editor of a local newspaper after his association with the bureau ended.[5] Other agents remained in Florida, some of them becoming high public officials. The record of the bureau was not perfect; some discrepancies were uncovered. But they were exaggerated by a hostile population which also denied recognition of the bureau's valuable relief and educational activities and its role as a referee between laborers and employers in the emerging free labor system.

The Freedmen's Bureau bill empowered the commissioner to appropriate confiscated or abandoned land and rent it to refugees and freedmen in forty-acre plots for three-year terms. At the end of the term the land could be conveyed to the tenant upon payment of the assessed value of the property. General Howard tried to carry out the policy, and in June 1865 called upon the assistant commissioners to establish lists of lands which could be used according to his instructions. But he was never able to place many Negroes on abandoned lands. Andrew Johnson's amnesty plan offered restoration of property to ex-Confederates who would take an oath of future loyalty There were several weeks of confusion over the land matter in the summer of 1865, but when Provisional Governor Marvin arrived in Florida in August he stopped further confiscation of lands by the United States marshal. About the same time, President Johnson ordered Howard to return the land held by the bureau to all former owners who had been pardoned. Freedmen who were farming the restored lands were permitted to stay and reap their harvests, but some anxious Floridians tried to take the growing crops as well as the land. In this uncertain period while the president's policy was evolving, N. C. Dennett, Saxton's agent at Jacksonville, followed the general's orders to settle freedmen on United States land. He encountered resistance and hostility from returning ex-Confederates.[6]

When Osborn assumed duty as assistant commissioner in September, he decided to discontinue efforts to place freedmen on confiscated land. He also replaced Dennett and subsequently refused to consider him for another bureau position when Dennett returned to Florida as a cashier of the Freedmen's Savings Bank.[7] As a result of President Johnson's policy, Howard had little land for freedmen. In Florida a few gained possession of plots purchased by the United States at the Fernandina tax sales, but their number was small, and they encountered endless difficulties in retaining possession.

Colonel Osborn's problem was an extension of Howard's in Washington. How was he to carry out the bureau's responsibilities without funds and personnel? During his first months in the state, the bureau's only income was a little rent from property not yet returned to its original owners. He needed subassistant commissioners and agents for the districts of the state. With the exception of Jacksonville and Fernandina, there were no concentrations of Negroes in towns. Bureau agents often found themselves responsible for two, three, or even four large rural counties. With a small clerical staff at Tallahassee and fifteen to twenty-five agents in the field at various times, the Freedmen's Bureau was never the omnipotent force alleged by native Floridians. To enforce its orders, the bureau could use moral suasion, negotiation, legal process, and military power. Since the number of soldiers stationed in Florida was small and President Johnson disapproved bureau courts, agents usually had to rely on the first two methods. From April 1866 until civil government was fully restored in July 1868, the number of soldiers in Florida ranged between 1,067 and 1,524. One company at Key West, one at Pensacola harbor, and about 300 prison guards at Fort Jefferson in the Dry Tortugas were unavailable for assistance to bureau officials.[8]

When Osborn first arrived, the commanding officers of the military posts served as ex officio agents. Because of the heavy burden this placed on local commanders and the rapid turnover as military personnel were mustered out following the war, Howard suggested that state civil officials be appointed as bureau agents to supervise labor contracts. Both Colonel Osborn and General Foster thought it inadvisable to turn over control of the contracts to white Floridians. But when Howard visited Florida, Osborn relented and on November 15, 1865, ordered the judges of probate to administer bureau affairs within their civil jurisdictions. In the absence of the judge, the court clerk was authorized to act. In the large north-central counties the judges were empowered to appoint justices of the peace as assistants. All post commanders were ordered to turn over their bureau duties to the justices, who would then urge both planters and freedmen to make written contracts for 1866. If children could not be cared for by parents, the civil agent could apprentice them. They were also to see that vagrancy was punished only according to laws dealing with white vagrants. Corporal punishment was forbidden by Osborn except by authority of a court of law. General Howard subsequently ordered this provision changed to prohibit *all* corporal punishment. The similarity between these provisions and some of the laws discussed in the last chapter is readily apparent.[9]

The civil agents were informed that their authority was military insofar as they acted for the bureau. Some of the judges performed their duties more to Osborn's satisfaction than others. For example, Judge Robert W. Bullock, a Marion County planter and former Confederate who later became an active Conservative Democratic politician, executed his bureau duties with racial equity. J. C. Gardner of Alachua was reportedly "as little biased in his views" as any Floridian. J. B. Collins of Jefferson County was respected by both Osborn and the freedmen in the county. On the other hand, Osborn dismissed the judge of Sumter County for his harsh and unfair treatment of freedmen. Judge E. C. Love of Gadsden County allowed his racial feelings to affect his judgment both as a judge and as a bureau agent. Osborn was dissatisfied with him, but Love was not removed because Bureau Agent Marcellus L. Stearns, a Veterans Reserve Corps officer from Maine, declared him the best man available in the county. These judges were compensated for their bureau work on a fee basis. Many resigned as soon as replacements could be found.[10]

In early 1866, Osborn was able to make additional appointments of civil agents, some of whom were paid on a fee basis while others were given salaries. Several members of the Veterans Reserve Corps were employed as subassistant commissioners during the period, and upon their discharge on January 1, 1868, all were retained as civilian agents at $125 per month. When Foster replaced Osborn as assistant commissioner in June 1866, he reverted to the earlier policy of relying on military officers to carry out bureau duties wherever possible.[11] When the bureau began reducing its Florida activities in 1868, there were fifteen subassistant commissioners. Eight of them were army officers and seven were civilians who had once served in the army. In spite of the lack of continuity in personnel and organization and the small staff, the Freedmen's Bureau accomplished much during its brief stay in Florida. Yet it never attempted to alter the social strata of the state; bureau policy in Florida was based on the Southerners' view of freedmen as an agricultural labor force.

The bureau's immediate task was relief. Destitute freedmen and refugees had to be fed and sheltered. Closely associated with this high priority problem was the need to work out a system of gainful employment. Colonel Osborn continued the policy—initiated by the military commanders—of encouraging freedmen to stay on the plantations or to return to them. "I wish to discontinue so far as possible the Negroes collecting about the posts and also the impression that they will be fed," he wrote. He wished to keep the number of rations issued as small as humanity would permit. Provoked by what he regarded as professional ration-drawing among some freedmen, Osborn notified them that all ration issues would cease in Florida on December 1, 1865. When Howard telegraphed questioning whether Osborn had actually stopped issuing rations, the assistant commissioner explained that he had done so until inspectors could determine whether the practice was really necessary. When conservative Colonel John T. Sprague, military commander of East Florida, complained of Negroes suffering from hunger in Jacksonville, Osborn ordered the issue of limited rations only to freedmen in "dire circumstances," noting that there was a labor shortage on the plantations and many advertisements in the Jacksonville newspapers for workers: "it might be a little harsh to let men go hungry, but in the long run best for them that they learn to work."[12]

The approximately 20,000 rations issued each month during the winter of 1865–66 went to destitute freedmen and refugees in Jacksonville, St. Augustine, and Fernandina; to the Fernandina orphanage; the Jacksonville hospital; and to destitute families of white Union veterans in Hillsborough and Manatee counties. The ration problem was complicated by the concentration of stranded whites as well as blacks in the East Florida ports. Close coordination between the bureau and the army was required to get transportation for these persons both into and out of Florida. Meanwhile, they had to eat and there was "no way to live but theft and just day to day jobs as they can find." As these people were transported home, the number of ration recipients declined. Osborn ultimately sent agents into Jacksonville to round up remaining unemployed freedmen and have them escorted to the plantations by military guards.[13]

The assistant commissioners who succeeded Colonel Osborn continued his stringent ration policy. They provided rations when the 1867 cotton crop failed in many portions of the state and the Negroes received inadequate provisions from their labors, but these issues were closely connected with attempts to alter the contract labor system. Many planters and other observers were dissatisfied with sharecropping, and there was inadequate money for a wage system. Any freedman who could prove that he was farming at least ten acres of land could draw rations until his crop began to produce. The only other major issue of government rations went to individuals who took up land under the 1866 homestead act. They were supported until they could clear land and get their first crop ready for harvest. In both cases there were close supervision and accounting of rations. The goal was to keep freedmen from abject starvation while encouraging them to become self-supporting landowners or tenants. While in Florida, the bureau issued about 760,000 rations to destitute persons both black and white, orphans, old and infirm people, and prospective cultivators of the land.[14] A few cases of agents misappropriating rations were reported, but most criticisms of the bureau officials' honesty were invented or perpetuated by hostile Floridians after the agency ceased to exist.

The greatest single change in postwar society in Florida was the labor system. The issue of rations was an emergency measure necessary only to prevent starvation. A system of compensated labor had to be developed and implemented by planters skeptical of the Negroes' willingness to work without coercion and by Negroes inexperienced at managing their own economic affairs. When the bureau came to Florida, the written contract was already established by the military commanders as the basis for new labor arrangements. The bureau became supervisor and arbiter of the system in the transition period. Specific provisions were left to the contracting parties, although General John Newton's earlier suggestion of provisions and one-fourth of the crop as a reasonable remuneration for the freedmen was used as a guideline. Many of the contracts hastily drawn in 1865 were so unfair that it was deemed necessary to set them aside, but those that seemed reasonable, bureau officials simply observed to see that settlements were made according to the contracts.[15] Usually they acted only when complaints were initiated by one of the parties—and intercession was not always at the request of the freedmen. Planters often called on bureau officials to settle disagreements, especially when freedmen had been permitted to draw supplies on credit during the year and their debts consumed all or most of their shares of the crop.

Many freedmen worked without written contracts, especially in 1865. Where there was no written agreement and controversy occurred, bureau personnel applied General Newton's rule. Since it was the first time the contracts had been used, considerable latitude was permitted in settling up for 1865. Settlement was made easier by the good crop yield and high prices of that year, but military assistance was requested by some agents who encountered difficulties.[16] The problems increased the following years when crops failed and prices declined.

The rumors of "forty acres and a mule" for freedmen and possible violence around Christmas 1865 caused apprehension among planters and delays by some freedmen in making contracts for 1866. There were also planters who refused to put in crops because of skepticism about free Negro labor. But the successes of 1865 and the lack of an alternative induced most planters and freedmen to enter into contracts for the new crop year. Bureau personnel assisted in drawing up contracts and charged the planters a small fee for their services.[17] They permitted the law of supply and demand to set wages and other rates of compensation as long as the contracts seemed reasonable. Where monthly wages were paid, male laborers received from $10 to $12 per month and provisions, with some variations above and below these figures. Women were paid from $6 to $10 per month and provisions. Children received less. Since money was scarce, it was more common to pay in shares of the crop. The workers on shares received provisions and from one-fourth to one-third of the crop. Later, some who furnished their own provisions received one-half of the crop. Although there was a continuing labor shortage in Florida, remuneration for plantation work was inadequate for maintaining a household.[18] Both bureau agents and planters were irritated by a tendency among Negro women to remain at home rather than make contracts as field hands.

Some bureau agents found that Negroes preferred not to sign contracts because they were too reminiscent of the old slavery system. Others found that it was the planters who disliked written contracts. Where the share-crop system was used, it was common practice for the planters to permit freedmen to purchase goods on credit from a store operated on the plantation. Books were kept by the planter and cleared at the end of the year before a settlement was made on the crop. With unrestrained credit buying and high interest rates, many laborers ended up with nothing to show for a year of work. Even those receiving a monthly wage might make no discernible gain. When crops failed, as they did in 1867, workers wound up in debt at the end of the year, and the contract system was condemned by most parties to it. Many planters vowed not to plant again because the Negroes had not worked well. Some elected to bring in white laborers; others decided to lease their plantations either to large operators or in small plots. Freedmen disenchanted with the system tried to enter public lands under the homestead act or rent small plots rather than continue contracting. Others willing to make contracts preferred a monthly wage to a share of the crop.[19]

Contracts were usually made between a planter and a number of freedmen. For example, a bureau agent in Jackson County reported 116 contracts involving 600 laborers. A single Marion County contract included seventy laborers. Usually the contract ran from early in the year until after harvest time. The planter agreed to furnish land, implements, mules, provisions, and housing for the laborers and their families. The freedmen agreed to labor honestly from Monday morning until Saturday night unless time could be spared without injury to the crop. They also agreed to keep fences repaired and to care for the livestock on the plantation. Freedmen often agreed to go and come from the fields in groups. In most cases they were assessed fifty cents per day for time lost because of sickness. Failure to obey orders was usually cause for discharge with all services previously rendered going to the planter as a penalty. There were endless variations, but these contractual provisions are representative.[20]

Bureau agents were called upon by both planters and freedmen to enforce contracts during the crop year. Sometimes freedmen were forced to return and fulfill their agreement after leaving a plantation, and there were also cases of mistreatment of freedmen by planters.[21] But most complaints came at the end of the year over settlements. Agents tried to arbitrate disputes on the basis of the specific contracts in question, but they naturally tried to protect the freedmen from unfair applications of the contracts by the more experienced planters.

The contractual provisions opened opportunities for planters to take advantage of freedmen. While freedmen sometimes were remiss in fulfilling their obligations, especially in getting to work on time in the mornings, some planters interpreted the contracts to find causes for dismissal after crops were in the ground and most of the cultivating was completed. Agents frequently incurred the wrath of planters when interceding to correct abuses of this kind. Many planters understandably resented the mere presence of bureau agents who had authority to supervise contracts between themselves and freedmen whom they had once owned. When A. B. Grumwell, bureau agent for Jefferson County, impounded the cotton on the J. J. Pettus plantation until the owner agreed to settle with his contracted laborers, Pettus' son-in-law threatened to show him a "power behind the throne." But even Grumwell admitted that most of the planters were fair in their settlements with freedmen.[22]

The majority of freedmen worked on the plantations during the transitional period, but a sizeable number were engaged in other occupations. Bureau agents supervised contracts between lumber companies and freedmen in most parts of the state, but especially in Nassau County, along the St. Johns River, around Cedar Key, and in West Florida.[23] Laborers in the woods earned from $25 to $30 per month and provisions, although again there were exceptions.

All the railroads employed freedmen, but the Florida Railroad from Fernandina to Cedar Key was the largest single employer. The railroad wages were higher than farm work and usually somewhat lower than the lumber industry. Antipathy of employers toward bureau interference was just as intense as on the plantations. Bureau Agent William G. Vance was informed that the Atlantic and Gulf Railroad Company was discharging laborers before their contracts expired and claiming all prior labor without compensation as penalty for alleged contract violations. When Vance investigated, construction supervisor John C. Reynolds invited him to "Go to Hell," promising to make himself available if the agent wished to make a personal issue of it. Vance reported, "I have not. But, something ought to be done about it."[24]

Even problems encountered by house servants and hotel workers in collecting their wages came to the attention of bureau agents. Since the sums were so small that it was impractical to sue in civil courts, the agents interceded when possible to obtain equitable settlements.

It was sometimes necessary to send troops to assist bureau agents with recalcitrant contracting parties. Military force was used to capture and return freedmen who had broken their contracts as well as to encourage compliance by planters, but there was insufficient military manpower available for the purpose. Agents in all parts of the state complained that they were limited in ability to enforce contracts because force was sometimes the only remedy. And even military force was sometimes inadequate. A file of soldiers visited three plantations in Jackson County in late 1867 where complaints had been received from freedmen. At each place the corporal in charge was threatened with death if he set foot on the place. The planters declared they were southern gentlemen and "no damned Yankee government" could interfere with them. Because armed men were dug in behind the houses, the corporal withdrew without enforcing the contracts.[25]

Another problem was the failure of the civil courts established by the 1865–66 legislature to provide justice. Many freedmen were given harsh sentences and assessed large sums for court costs where they were alleged to have broken their contracts.[26] The failure of state courts necessitated the organization in late 1866 of bureau courts whose duty was to intercede in cases where freedmen could not get fair treatment. These bureau courts were disapproved by President Johnson, however, and only a few ever convened. In their absence the assistant commissioner instructed bureau agents in making contracts to insert a provision for arbitration of all disputes. Questions arising between contracting parties were to be decided by a three-man board composed of one member representing each side and the bureau agent whose decision was final.[27]

When the 1867 crop failed, both planters and freedmen looked for alternatives to the contract system. The bureau had already recognized that rations would have to be issued in 1868 simply to avoid wholesale starvation in areas where crops had failed. To make the most of the situation, Colonel Sprague authorized a weekly ration to all freedmen with at least ten acres of land under cultivation. The ration was a peck of corn and three pounds of bacon weekly for each adult, and half that amount for each child, until the next crop was harvested. In all the plantation counties—from Jackson near the Apalachicola River to Alachua and Marion in the center of the peninsula—freedmen rented plots of ten acres or more, usually agreeing to pay the rent in shares of the crop, but farming the land according to their own judgment. Thousands of rations were issued on Sprague's authority by agents who according to one report, carefully distinguished between the "industrious and idle, the deserving poor and the vicious poor."[28]

Although its role as arbiter of disputes caused much resentment and it was only partially successful in securing fair treatment for freedmen, the bureau nevertheless made an important contribution by supervising the contract system during a difficult period. The state press generally acknowledged the success of the free labor experiment. The bureau also helped to implant the sharecropping and crop lien system which bore heavily on everyone involved, especially the tenants, but this was not the fault of the agency. As Colonel Sprague observed in 1868, the products of Florida soil were insufficient to support a plantation system based on wage labor. Only subsistence farming was possible at the time: "Small farms will succeed in Florida, plantations are at an end." If Sprague was correct, there was no alternative to the system which emerged during and shortly after the tutelage of the bureau.[29]

The original idea of settling freedmen on confiscated and abandoned lands never materialized, but the bureau did encourage and assist a number of freedmen to acquire land of their own. The homestead act of 1866 opened for settlement public lands in several southern states including Florida. Freedmen and whites of unquestioned loyalty had exclusive rights to these lands until January 1867. Although both General Howard and Colonel Sprague doubted the wisdom of settling Negroes on their own uncleared homesteads, both supported the plan once the bill passed. For Sprague it was duty rather than conviction, however, for he wrote Howard that "the Negro cannot be colonized. He is incapable of providing for himself. Immediate contact with the white man is indispensable for his improvement and happiness."[30] Perhaps it was just as well for Florida freedmen that General Foster was still assistant commissioner for several months after the act passed.

As in the case of the tenant farmers the bureau issued rations to homesteaders to sustain them until crops could be made. Because it was difficult to locate public land to which a clear title could be given and because there was immense hostility from white citizens toward Negroes trying to settle, the bureau employed locating agents who surveyed the plots and helped freedmen file claims with the public land office. White resistance stemmed at least partially from the desire to keep Negroes available as a labor supply. There had been a labor shortage in Florida since the war ended, and, despite repeated assertions that Negroes would not work, planters had been bringing in large numbers of them from South Carolina and Georgia. But resistance to Negro landownership went beyond the desire to keep them as laborers. There was also opposition to them by communities where they wanted to settle. In Lafayette County, where Union sentiment was strong during the war and where the few who farmed employed even fewer laborers, ten Negroes intent on homesteading at Old Town Hammock were met on the road and laconically informed that Lafayette citizens had agreed to resist their entry. In Gadsden and Calhoun counties, whites refused to identify their property lines to Negroes desiring to occupy public land adjoining them and later refused to join fences with them.[31]

With assistance from several energetic locating agents such as Solomon

F. Halliday, who operated out of Newnansville in Alachua County, many freedmen took up eighty-acre homesteads under the 1866 law while the bureau was active in Florida. Although many of them failed to prove their claims and some of those who settled were white Union refugees, the General Land Office records show that 3,648 homesteads were located and filed with the Tallahassee land office between June 1866 and December 1868. A large majority of the claimants were Negroes. Without the government rations and assistance of the locating agents, many of them would never have been able to take up the land.

Blacks met resistance as long as A. B. Stonelake was register of public lands at Tallahassee. This enigmatic character—who at various times was connected with the Freedmen's Savings Bank and an agricultural society in which Governor David Walker was prominently involved—often used his official powers to favor ex-Confederates and their families when conflicts arose between them and freedmen. He was also either dishonest or grossly inefficient. In addition to the five-dollar fee required by the 1866 law for filing a claim, he assessed an additional two dollars which he called a surveying fee. Although it may have been a legitimate charge, many freedmen complained that they had paid the fee and never received credit for it. Stonelake ultimately resigned without adequately explaining his methods or the disposition of the receipts in question.[32]

Attempts to colonize Negroes in large groups also received bureau assistance, but none of them succeeded. Plans for colonizing the public domain of Florida dated from Eli Thayer's schemes of the early 1860s. Chaplain H. H. Moore of the 34th United States Colored Troops attempted to have the entire regiment discharged in Florida to homestead, but the plan failed, even though it had approval of the bureau and high military officials.[33] Two other schemes went beyond the planning stage and both received encouragement and material assistance from the bureau. The leaders of both had been in the South Carolina sea islands during the war when Negroes were being settled on confiscated lands.

General Ralph Ely brought about 1,000 Negroes to Volusia County in 1867 for settlement. The expedition was not well planned, however, and soon the freedmen were approaching starvation. It was the freedmen in this colony who had trouble with Stonelake at the land office. Their most pressing problem was immediate subsistence. Bureau provisions were made available to them as settlers on new lands, but the supplies were either inadequate or mishandled by Ely or his subordinates. Colonel Sprague heard complaints that the rations were being sold in a general store when they should have been given to the freedmen.[34]

William J. Purman was sent to investigate and found one of the few cases of bureau malfeasance which occurred in Florida. Observing of Ely's colony that "their condition is pitiable," Purman found evidence convincing him that the general had misused a portion of the government supplies. Apparently Ely was carrying on a planting operation in partnership with a black woman who was paying her hired hands with the rations. Some supplies had also been sold in a store in Port Orange managed by Dr. John Milton Hawks, the leader of another colonizing expedition in East Florida. Purman did not follow up on this lead, however, and remained exceptionally cordial with Hawks' wife, a popular young abolitionist teaching in a freedmen's school at Port Orange.[35]

In addition to the probable misappropriation of supplies, General Ely also had exacted ten dollars from each freedman transported to New Smyrna and permitted his clerk to assess them seventy cents. When the colony failed and they were forced to find employment elsewhere, none of the freedmen had their money returned. Nearly all of them made contracts with planters in Marion and Alachua counties where a labor shortage continued through 1867.[36]

Milton Hawks brought several hundred Negroes to Port Orange intending to provide work for them in his Florida Land and Lumber Company. Hoping to obtain a large land grant for the enterprise, Hawks purchased steam engines and other equipment for saw and grist mills with which he would feed his employees and cut lumber for the market. Minor assistance was furnished him by the bureau, but the company languished and the Negroes soon scattered. Some took up land as homesteaders, but most became laborers on plantations and in the lumber camps and sawmills along the St. Johns River. Hawks remained in Florida, but his equipment stood for years unused and slowly rusting at Port Orange.[37]

An enduring accomplishment of the Freedmen's Bureau in the state occurred in the area of Negro education. It not only established and operated schools, assisted the benevolent associations in their contributions to education, and encouraged the state to provide schools for Negroes while it was active, but it also left an operating school system, many school buildings, and a desire for learning in many Florida Negroes. Although the bureau was authorized little monetary support for education before July 1866, it was active before that date. General Howard and his Florida subordinates believed that education was the one thing which could eventually give Negroes lasting freedom. Official support of bureau educational efforts increased in July 1868 when Congress authorized continuation of its school activities until the state had provided an educational system. But appropriations for schools were always meager in comparison to what was accomplished.

Benevolent associations had preceded the bureau in educational activities in Florida, and General Howard wisely cooperated with them as much as possible. When the war ended teachers sent by the Freedmen's Aid Society were operating schools in Fernandina, Jacksonville, and St. Augustine. Miss Chloe Merrick had a school and orphanage in the former home of General Joseph Finegan at Fernandina and Esther Hawks was teaching school and dazzling young Union officers in Jacksonville. Soon after Colonel Osborn arrived in the state, the Freedmen's Aid Society and the National Freedmen's Relief Association were operating ten schools with nearly 2,000 pupils.[38] The two groups were later joined by the New England Freedmen's Union Commission and the American Missionary Association. Osborn appointed former chaplain H. H. Moore to supervise education, with instructions to cooperate closely with the benevolent societies. Without funds for education, the bureau relied on the societies to furnish teachers while it provided buildings for the schools, free transportation, some rations, and assistance in securing places for the teachers to live.

At first, schools were conducted in buildings abandoned by their owners or confiscated by United States authorities. Many church buildings were used. President Johnson's policy of returning property to former Confederates caused a shortage of buildings. By early 1866 congregations were returning to East Florida and demanding their churches back. Subsequent policy was to obtain and repair buildings at bureau expense or to encourage interested freedmen to construct them.

The argument over church buildings was just one manifestation of white Floridians' opposition to Negro schools, or at least to Negro schools taught by northern white instructors. Most of the commentary in the public press during the first year after the war indicated a willingness to accept Negro schools as long as the teachers were suitable. Several prominent Floridians urged that a program of education was necessary if the Negroes were to become a suitable source of free labor. Noting the freedmen's intense interest in education, not only for their offspring but for adults as well, a number of planters established schools on their plantations, perhaps out of a benevolent concern for their former slaves, but almost certainly to make their plantations more desirable as places to work. It may also have occurred to them that this was a way of seeing that Negroes were taught the proper things. The latter reason gains credibility when one considers the hostility of Florida communities toward northern white teachers in Negro schools. It was impossible for these teachers to find suitable lodging at prices they could manage. Nearly all local whites, especially the women, refused to associate with them. In Lake City, teachers drawing salaries of less than $20 per month were asked $30 per month for room and board at the only place in town which would even accept them. The bureau agent finally commandeered an old Confederate government building for their use, but the teachers left at the end of the school term and never returned.[39]

Since he was dependent on the overburdened benevolent societies for teachers, Colonel Osborn was anxious for the state government to provide support for freedmen's education. Recognizing the antipathy toward northern teachers, the Colonel was also aware of white refusal to mix with Negroes. When the Freedmen's Relief Commission sought to improve relations by inviting white children to its schools, Osborn advised that "there is no probability of poor white children attending the negro schools. . . . There is some feeling against introducing northern teachers under auspices of northern societies. I do not think the enmity would be removed by emphasizing that white children would also be welcome." Although several schools attended by blacks and whites together in the late 1860s proved Osborn partially wrong, it was easy to derive such an opinion from living in Florida in 1866, and Osborn capitalized on this racial feeling in his appeal for a state law on Negro education. Pointing out that it would enable native Floridians to control freedmen's education, he called for a law establishing a separate Negro school system to be financed at no cost to the state.[40] The legislators responded with the bill establishing separate Negro schools, discussed earlier.

Osborn believed it imperative to obtain legislation committing the state to Negro education at least in principle and felt that it could only be done on a segregated basis at no cost to the bankrupt treasury. But in recommending the system, he set one more precedent in which the bureau supported a racial policy acceptable to Southerners and opposed by northern Radicals who were increasingly apprehensive about developments in the South.

Although the initiative for the law came from the Freedmen's Bureau, the *Tallahassee Floridian* proudly proclaimed that Florida was the only "rebel" state to make any provision on this important subject. Actually that was all the state did. The school tax was collected but erroneously paid into the general revenue fund without any record. The governor later explained that this was a mistake but that nothing could be done about it since the money had been spent on other state expenses. In November 1866, General Foster wrote that "the state has a fine school law but has not yet spent one cent on the Freedmen's schools." The excellent law was implemented by the bureau which was paying for transportation of teachers and building repairs while the Negro parents were paying tuition for teachers' salaries. One observer thought it unjust that Negroes paid ordinary state taxes and an additional dollar for their separate schools only to have the extra money paid into the general revenue fund.[41]

The bureau and the state government cooperated on freedmen's education as much as possible. For more than a year the superintendent of freedmen's schools for the state was the same person who held the position with the bureau. In January 1866, Governor Walker had appointed L. M. Hobbs to the state position because of his work in drafting the school law. At that time H. H. Moore was the bureau superintendent of schools. When both men were mustered out of the service in the spring of 1866, E. B. Duncan replaced them and held the two appointments until May 1867. C. Thurston Chase held the joint position from that date until April 1868, when Colonel Sprague became dissatisfied with his performance.[42] Chase continued as state superintendent of freedmen's schools and became Governor Harrison Reed's first superintendent of public instruction in July 1868. Colonel George W. Gile was both assistant commissioner and superintendent of education for the bureau until its dissolution. While they lasted, the joint appointments facilitated cooperation between the Freedmen's Bureau and the conservative Walker administration.

Neither the state, the bureau, nor the benevolent societies had the resources to provide adequate facilities to accommodate all the Negroes who desired schools. The result was a wide variety of methods of establishing and maintaining schools and just as great a variety of instruction in them. The superintendents encouraged benevolent societies to send teachers to the state, assisted planters who showed interest in establishing schools on their plantations, and gave encouragement and assistance to the many local freedmen's groups formed to secure schools for their children and themselves. Under the state law anyone could start a school merely by employing a teacher and submitting his name to Tallahassee. The superintendent would make out the necessary teaching certificate and return it. Financing was by monthly tuition of one dollar per pupil according to the law, although orphans and destitute persons were supposed to be supported by a school fund.[43] In practice, financial arrangements varied widely. Some schools assessed pupils fifty cents per month and some towns and plantations provided free schools. But for most schools there was never enough money, and there was always a shortage of qualified teachers. Many who taught were scarcely better informed than their students, and the buildings were inadequate despite admirable fund-raising efforts by the freedmen.

Regardless of numerous examples to the contrary, white resistance to Negro schools continually caused problems. The most pervasive problem was social ostracism which was sometimes carried to violent extremes. Whites in Alachua County assaulted a Negro school where northern white teachers insisted on the right to have their students sing the patriotic

"Rally 'Round the Flag." Although their fourth generation descendants see the situation differently, these white Floridians thought it proper to suppress songs which they found offensive. Events in Jackson County were more serious: at Greenwood, a landowner refused to sell freedmen land for a church and school unless a guarantee was given that "no Yankees should ever be employed to preach or teach," and State Representative John M. Irvin denounced freedmen's schools before a crowd which threatened the bureau personnel. In Marianna, a white teacher was harassed in his efforts to conduct a night school for freedmen, and at Campbelltown a man who tried to start a freedmen's school was "hooted" out of town.[44]

The teachers varied in ability and training, but most were serious about their profession. Whether it was an ex-slave such as John Wallace, torn between his black identity and loyalty to his ex-Confederate benefactor, or a well-educated New England woman such as Mrs. Esther Hawks, teachers were usually interested in helping ignorant Negroes learn.[45]

The plight of George H. Braman, a white man who taught at Marianna, demonstrates the problems encountered by white teachers of Negroes in a community where attitudes were at best mixed regarding Negro education. Having opened his school for freedmen soon after the war, Braman was in Marianna when the first bureau agents arrived. White citizens of the town complained that he associated only with Negroes and lived in a black man's home. The accusations led E. B. Duncan to remove him as a teacher because his "associations have been . . . with the colored people which was at best very inexpedient." "A man should never sacrifice the dignity of his European blood," the superintendent of freedmen's schools later added. Duncan relented when he became convinced that Braman had made himself acceptable to the Marianna white community. About that time Charles M. Hamilton, bureau agent for Jackson County, denounced the teacher for being a charlatan intent on defrauding the freedmen and for becoming a "vigorous rebel." Hamilton issued an order relieving Braman from the school and commanding him to leave town as soon as possible.[46] Braman's was an unusual case because of the opposition from the bureau agent, but many teachers would have found some of his experiences familiar.

Enthusiasm for learning on the part of the blacks made up for many educational problems of the period. Teachers were impressed by the lengths to which parents and children went to acquire the rudiments of an education. Even reluctant conservatives were surprised by the zeal and progress of black students. Willingness of poor parents to pay as much as a dollar tuition per month to keep some of the schools going was eloquent testimony of the importance they attached to education.

When the 1868 Freedmen's Bureau extension bill passed and Colonel Gile assumed leadership of the Florida agency, there was more government money available for both building and rental of school houses. After March 1869, about seventy-five buildings, some of which were churches, were rented by the bureau for schools.[47] Gile was also authorized to assist in constructing buildings if communities would furnish a deed to a building site. Depending upon the size of the community, he was able to spend from $500 to $1,000 on a simple rectangular building and furniture. Such luxuries as blinds, paint, and plaster were usually not included. In most cases communities were able to pay a portion of the expense which amounted to a kind of matching fund. Sometimes communities volunteered labor as part of their contribution.

Although most requests for bureau building assistance were quite modest, there were exceptions. From Mandarin came Mrs. Harriet Beecher Stowe's plan for a structure which she believed befitted her community. Gile estimated the cost at $4,000 and rejected it, explaining that such an expenditure would deprive other communities of their share of the limited funds. Apparently the indomitable Mrs. Stowe persisted with her plan, for Gile ultimately compromised by authorizing $1,500 for the Mandarin school.[48]

As word of his building program circulated in 1869, Gile was deluged with requests for assistance. He tried to apportion his funds so they would be most beneficial, insisting that the schools he built be available for *all* citizens. Sometimes extenuating circumstances received consideration. Jackson County needed school buildings, but in 1869–70 the area was so torn by racial conflict that people were unable to obtain the necessary land and assistance for a school. Gile wrote that he was allowing for the "unsettled conditions of public affairs in your town" and was holding $1,000 for a building in Marianna. Although the Marianna situation did not improve appreciably before the bureau left Florida, Gile spent the money on a building there even though the community had not complied with the law.[49]

In his final report Colonel Gile said he had spent about $20,000 on the construction of 16 school buildings. There were then 137 schools in Florida, with the bureau furnishing 87 of the buildings. By that time Gile could justly claim that the bureau's activities had spurred the 1869 legislature to enact provisions for a state-supported school system. The bureau also established a system of schools which "if continued by state authorities will give Florida freedmen the rudiments of education." Although the benevolent societies were still active, county school boards were paying teachers in nearly every school.[50]

Yet much remained to be done. The quality of instruction was uneven where it was offered, and only a minority of school-age children were served by the schools. Only eighteen of thirty-nine counties had schools. Jefferson, one of the largest counties, had one; Leon had five.[51]

Colonel Gile became less pessimistic about Florida's ability to finance a school system, but he envisioned even greater problems. Ranging beyond his primary concern for Negro education, he argued that education of southern youth was too important to be left entirely to state or local influence. Hostility toward the general government pervaded the minds of many Southerners and found its way into literature and press in denunciations of the Lincoln government. Gile was afraid that this hostility would make a lasting impression on the minds of those who would control the future of the South. As a remedy, the Colonel recommended careful supervision of public schools as well as financial aid. He thought it especially important "that a carefully compiled history of the late war (political and military) in series suitable for the lower grades be published for use of southern schools."[52] Of course, there was no chance that Gile's recommendations could be followed, but he identified the avenue along which the South would ultimately win the peace after having lost the war.

The bureau was also concerned with public health and the maintenance of eleemosynary institutions. Miss Chloe Merrick's orphanage, maintained by the New York Branch of the Freedmen's Union Commission and the bureau at Fernandina, was forced to relocate when Joseph Finegan was permitted to redeem his home which they had been using. Colonel Osborn suggested its removal to Hilton Head, South Carolina, because Florida lacked a suitable site, but it was finally located at Magnolia on the St. Johns River where the bureau also maintained a hospital. A few orphans were cared for and taught until homes could be found for them. The Freedmen's Union Commission stopped supporting the orphanage in September 1867, and Assistant Commissioner Sprague advised Governor Walker that the state would have to take it over. The governor suggested that the state apprenticeship law be applied instead. In January 1868, Sprague recommended discontinuing the orphanage and apprenticing the twenty-six children. Some of the northern teachers in Florida were able to place a few in orphanages in their home states, but the others were apprenticed in Florida.[53]

With regard to medical care, Colonel Osborn's policy was to assist the aged and infirm and leave all other freedmen to provide for themselves. Only one small hospital was established at Jacksonville and later moved to Magnolia. Before admitting patients to the hospital, bureau agents first tried to place them with their families or even with neighbors who could be compelled to care for them. Only when no alternative existed were patients admitted to the hospital. This policy was necessary because the hospital's facilities were limited and it was probably wise because the bureau's tenure was uncertain. When the bureau ordered the Magnolia Hospital closed at the end of 1868, the few patients were ordered returned to the counties in which they had last resided. The county commissioners were then responsible for their care.[54]

Osborn and his successors did furnish some individual medical assistance, although it was usually aimed at the prevention of epidemics. When smallpox appeared in North Florida towns in 1865–66, the bureau hired physicians to vaccinate as many people as possible. Such preventive measures continued during the bureau's stay in the state.[55] Although some local authorities refused to accept responsibility for controlling epidemics among freedmen in their jurisdiction, there was usually cooperation between local white citizens and the bureau on this matter. Some communities had bureau medical officers assigned on a more permanent basis. In Marianna, Dr. John L. Finlayson served as doctor by day and taught adult freedmen at night. The freedmen at Lake City expressed their gratitude to the bureau for assigning Dr. Watson Porter to minister to their needs when the local doctors either could not or would not.[56]

The political activities of the Freedmen's Bureau and its individual members will be discussed more fully in another context, but it should be noted that when Congress enacted legislation extending political privileges to Negroes, bureau agents were responsible for informing the freedmen of their newly acquired rights and responsibilities. With an entirely different point of view, native white leaders also went among the freedmen advising them about political participation. Since some bureau agents became political candidates and nearly all of them advised support of the national Republican party, they were in direct competition with native whites for Negro political support. The whites had not accepted the validity of Negro suffrage and sought black support only because they felt it necessary to keep their society intact. When they failed to win the Negroes' allegiance, they blamed the bureau personnel. Although only a small percentage of the time and energy of bureau personnel was spent on politics, the fundamental nature of the struggle insured the calumny which was heaped on the agency by native whites during Reconstruction and by their historians afterward.

The legacy of the Freedmen's Bureau in Florida is anomalous. By the generations after the 1860s, it was widely regarded as a malevolent institution through which corrupt and self-seeking men worked their will on helpless native whites while a hostile national government looked on approvingly. This reputation was largely constructed after the bureau ceased to exist, as campaign material against Republican politicians, some of whom had been bureau agents. There is a remarkable difference between the latter-day reputation of the bureau and the warm approval enjoyed by its principal officers while it was in operation. Colonel Osborn, General Foster, and Colonel Sprague were repeatedly praised for fair administration. While some communities chafed at the presence of individual agents, at least as many others approved of the officials in their areas.

The bureau performed a useful service for the freedmen by furnishing emergency relief for the destitute, developing an educational system where none existed, and protecting Negroes as they became accustomed to freedom. But the agency never had power to obtain for them equal protection under the law and it did not leave them in a position to fend for themselves successfully. Its supervision of an evolving labor system was at least as helpful to planters as to black laborers, most of whom remained economically tied to land not their own.

6

Custom Has Become the Law

David S. Walker was elected governor of Florida under Andrew Johnson's plan of Reconstruction and served with varying authority from January 1866 to July 1868. Until March 1867, there was uncertainty and confusion over the extent of the governor's powers and his relationship to the military authorities in the state. In theory the governor was free to act in most matters and the state courts had jurisdiction in civil and most criminal cases, but both were ultimately subject to martial law which continued in force throughout the period. However, because of a continuing conflict between President Johnson and the congressional Radicals over control of Reconstruction policy, the practical situation was much more complicated. Floridians, believing the state a sovereign entity free to bargain, had complied with the president's minimum requirements and expected readmission as Governor Marvin had suggested. As the controversy over readmission developed in Washington, Florida civil officials adhered to President Johnson's pronouncements which reflected their own sentiments. Meanwhile, Congress provided additional authority for military commanders to protect the rights of freedmen.

Since directions from Washington conflicted, officials had to decide which should be heeded. Major General Foster, military commander and, after June 1866, assistant commissioner of the Freedmen's Bureau, was uncommitted in the executive-legislative struggle and was moderate on issues relating to freedmen. But he was determined to enforce the laws of the United States to the extent that he could decide what they were at a given time. Fnjoying good personal relations with Governor Walker and the respect and approval of many Floridians for his mild-mannered administration, Foster nevertheless often found himself in conflict with the governor and local officials because doubts about his authority stemmed from President Johnson's proclamations. Civil officials' resistance to martial law increased as military personnel at all levels became increasingly uncertain of their authority. The result was timid enforcement of the congressional enactments intended to protect the freedmen.

Factors other than race complicated law enforcement problems for Governor Walker and General Foster. Florida was still a frontier state whose population was scattered thinly over a large area served by few roads. There was dislocation caused by the war and people were still unaccustomed to new laws. Local tax collectors, for example, had difficulty assessing and collecting taxes from people who had so recently returned to making a living. Yet it was the racial change which was most troublesome and least amenable to solution, and which permeated almost every aspect of Florida society.

Even efforts to preserve the public health were aggravated by disputes arising from local citizens' resentment of military personnel who symbolized the Confederate defeat and the end of slavery. However, there was also extensive cooperation in this area between civil and military authorities. Local white leaders did cooperate with the Freedmen's Bureau to control epidemics of smallpox, cholera, and other contagious diseases. Both military commander and civil governor recognized the desirability of inspection and quarantine facilities in the ports to control yellow fever. General Grant ordered such a system and Foster implemented it in April 1866. Because the state's treasury was depleted, the army maintained most of the stations, although the civil government assisted when it could. By late 1866, St. Augustine and Jacksonville city governments had relieved the military quarantine personnel in their cities. Civilian doctors were hired by the army on contract and paid with proceeds from a three-dollar fee levied on each ship inspected.[1]

Several complaints were made about the inspections, usually alleging delays while awaiting the inspectors. The most adamant critic was Captain James Tucker of the *Sylvan Shore*: he wrote a letter threatening the bureau agent at Fernandina and refused to transport United States government freight unless he was exempted from the onerous inspection requirements. General Foster refused to exempt him on the ground that public health was paramount to the personal annoyance of one citizen.[2] Since Tucker was constantly embroiled with military and civil authorities and with individuals in the 1860s, his allegations may be discounted.

There was an outbreak of yellow fever at Key West in 1866 which was successfully contained, suggesting that the quarantine system was effective. Although Foster complained that the civil government was doing nothing to support the system, he admitted that its resources were inadequate. There was as much cooperation as friction resulting from public health regulation by the army.

The basic problem of both civil and military authorities, however, was how to achieve equal protection of the laws for freedmen and Unionists in a community where the majority opposed it. With acceptance of the reactionary Peeler-Dupont report as a guideline for reshaping laws relating to former slaves, the 1865–66 legislature demonstrated white Floridians' reluctance to depart any more than absolutely necessary from the social system supported by the old slave code. As the executive-legislative debate accelerated in Washington, Florida leaders found support for their racial and constitutional beliefs in the president's speeches and proclamations. When they enunciated their ideas of the sanctity of states' rights against national interference, these leaders encouraged Floridians to resist the unwelcome changes in their lives. Unwilling to recognize Negroes as free citizens imbued with civil rights, and hearing state leaders and the president denounce the military's presence in Florida as unconstitutional, Floridians from all walks of life, most of whom considered themselves entirely law-abiding, were encouraged to deny freedmen the rights of citizenship. Concomitantly, the Freedmen's Bureau and military personnel were charged with seeing that Negroes were afforded equal treatment before the law. Even with a united effort from Washington theirs was a formidable undertaking, for these are rights which can only be guaranteed by the community itself. With the divisions that existed in the national capital, it was impossible.

As mentioned earlier, Freedmen's Bureau Assistant Commissioner Thomas W. Osborn protested against certain laws enacted by the 1865–66 legislature and General Howard supported his position. By working patiently with Governor Walker, Osborn managed to obtain some modifications of the discriminatory laws without destroying working relations with the state administration. Corporal punishment of Negroes was never fully implemented because of the Osborn-Walker negotiations, although there were individual cases where it was applied by local officials. An indication of future difficulties on this point came from the Tallahassee *Floridian*; it approved the amicable settlement achieved by the colonel and the governor, but deplored the idea that the bureau had any right to interfere with state law enforcement. At least as late as February 1867, county criminal courts were still sentencing Negroes to corporal punishment. In Alachua County at that time, Daniel Baskins had to stand in the pillory for one hour each day for three days and Ben Simmons received twenty-five lashes on his bare back.[3]

Colonel Osborn also obtained from Attorney General John B. Galbraith a ruling that the law against Negroes carrying firearms without a license was unconstitutional. The governor notified local officials not to enforce the law, but several Negroes were arrested and their weapons confiscated. A group of Franklin County freedmen reported the problem to Osborn: "The civil authority in this county are taking away all the fire arms that is found in the hands of the Colored people. Thay do not only take our arms but they bring us before a Criminal Court and make us pay eight or ten dollars as cost of Court then we have to get two white men as Bail to appear in court in March. Sir we hope these are not the laws of the U.S. if thay are then we are werst than Slaves, houses are serched Day and Night. Peaceful persons put in jail if a gun is found in their house."[4] On a visit to Lafayette County in September 1866, General Foster discovered that the judge, clerk of the county court, and sheriff were requiring Negroes to license their arms. He asked Governor Walker to intervene but the chief executive did not do so. All the local officials were subsequently tried in the United States District Court under the Civil Rights Act of 1866.

Difficulty arose over the state law requiring Negro couples to separate or be legally married. The problem was settled by the 1866 legislature, but not before several individuals had been punished. There were also abuses of the contract law, the capitation tax, and the provision that persons unable to pay debts could be sold for labor to liquidate their debts.

Custom had to be overcome to achieve equal law enforcement. White Floridians had treated Negroes as property undeserving of the rights afforded citizens. Statutory enactments at Washington or Tallahassee could not immediately change the attitudes, as evidenced by the violence toward Negroes and the frequent refusal of law enforcement officials to arrest whites for offenses against freedmen. One discouraged bureau agent accurately described the problem; "the freed people are looked upon as an inferior and distinct race, and the difference which is made is almost as great as in other parts of the civilized world, the difference between man and beast. The white man expects strict obedience even in the face of the grossest insult with the calmness of a dumb brute."[5]

Without some such explanation, many of the violent acts committed in this period surpass understanding. A drunken white man put out a Negro's eye with a stick after having failed to thrust it down his throat, and yet he was walking the streets of Gainesville the following day unfettered by law enforcement officials. It is easier to understand that two Negroes were stabbed near Archer about the same time because they had served in the United States Army. Michael Young and Andrew Dutton, two young planters of Madison County, beat a Negro youth nearly to death, apparently because he was reluctant to make a contract with

Young. The Negro had refused because he was afraid of him.[6] These are examples of a widespread state of affairs in early 1866 which indicated a need for strong encouragement of law enforcement officials in the state by the national governments. Instead there was continual debate as to whether military officers had any authority at all in civil matters. There was too little attention given to the question of whether military intervention was needed or how to avoid it by removing the problem.

Military commissions met periodically and tried cases of serious crimes as they accumulated until April 2, 1866, when President Johnson's proclamation ended their jurisdiction. In obedience to the president, General Foster issued an order restoring civil law and giving the state courts full jurisdiction over all cases. The only exception involved specific cases wherein bureau agents and military commanders could submit evidence that the civil courts were not giving justice. Governor Walker exulted at this advance in the state's situation. Acknowledging Florida's indebtedness to Johnson for his "wise reconstruction policy," the governor declared that the president was in great difficulty because of it and needed the help of all Floridians. "We should do all we can to help him by keeping cool and quiet, obey the laws, and prove that we are worthy of freedom. . . . Every lawless act committed in our state will be viewed as showing that the President is wrong and his enemies right. . . . Let us see that the law is enforced and crime punished," the governor implored.[7] Walker reminded local officials that martial law was still in force and could be invoked if the commanding general felt it necessary.

General Foster was advised that the proclamation did not remove martial law, but that it was nevertheless inexpedient to employ military tribunals as long as justice could be obtained through civil process. After April 9, Foster permitted all cases to go before the civil courts and ordered his officers to watch the proceedings. Where injustice was obvious, they were to appeal to the next higher court in order to delay execution of the sentence until the case could be transferred to the United States court as provided by Congress. Where civil officials refused to make arrests of whites for higher crimes, the general made the necessary arrests and entered the cases directly in the United States court. The problem with this procedure was that the judge of the United States court in North Florida was absent from the state during most of the year. Judge Philip Fraser was a native of New Jersey, where he was residing in 1866 because of illness. This worked a hardship on anyone having business in the court, especially those who could not obtain equal treatment by the state courts. Foster implored the attorney general to intercede, only to be reminded that there was nothing an executive official could do to influence a judicial officer.[8]

Foster was satisfied with Governor Walker's cooperation during the first few weeks after the president's proclamation and was comparatively optimistic about the Florida situation. Admitting that there had been an increase of hostility against Union men and the United States among the "secessionists," caused by delay in readmitting the state to the Union, he thought most Floridians were law-abiding. He also though most state officials were fair and impartial, but that juries frequently were prejudiced in their decisions where whites opposed Negroes or secessionists opposed Unionists. In cases of this kind, he notified Governor Walker who had "in all cases acted firmly and justly and his action has thus far proved effective to preserve the rights of citizens." But the general also thought the military presence had been helpful to United States officials in protecting freedmen and Unionists and that occupation would be necessary for a long time before the changes being wrought in Florida were accepted. Foster even felt that "the better portion of the people" not only admitted the necessity of military occupation but preferred it as a deterrent to the "more lawless portion of the Community." He may have been correct, but, as he wrote, Senator-elect Wilkinson Call was complaining to General Grant that the "military authorities of Florida consider themselves obliged to all civil process from the State Courts," and asked the chief of staff to "withdraw from the military the authority to interfere with the ordinary course of the law."[9]

There were examples supporting Foster's evaluation. J. A. Remley, bureau agent in Marion County, also doubted that juries would give justice to freedmen where the Negroes were arrayed against whites, but he applauded Judge Robert W. Bullock as a fairminded man. Bullock settled many disputes by compromises, thus eliminating the costs of trials and the problem of prejudiced juries. When Freedman John Shade of Lake City was brought before the county criminal court in 1866 for killing a pig in 1861 while he was still a slave, both the governor and Circuit Judge Thomas T. Long came to his relief. E. R. Ives, the animal's owner, possessing a long memory and a meticulous desire for justice, filed a complaint which resulted in a conviction and a sentence of a $250 fine and $100 for costs. Upon notification by the bureau, Governor Walker unhesitatingly remitted the fine and the costs. Judge Long, however, thought the governor's intervention wrong and Shade's case appeared on his docket. Long reasoned that a freedman should be exempt from punishment for acts while he was a slave and wanted an acquittal rather than gubernatorial amnesty to become the precedent in such cases.[10]

When justices of the peace in several counties refused to act in criminal cases until freedmen paid their fees in advance, Governor Walker admonished them that their action was in violation of the law. Attorney

General Galbraith said such a procedure violated the state constitution. Walker asked bureau agents to bring such cases to his attention so that he could take action against offending officers, and Foster tried to encourage such state initiative. When Colonel L. L. Lulansky intervened in a dispute between employer and laborers at Pensacola in April, the general praised him for his vigilance but suggested that he not repeat it since "we will eventually leave and the planters will be the more revengeful for the restraint they are held in while we are here."[11]

It appears that Foster was too optimistic. A. B. Grumwell, bureau agent at Monticello, tried to follow instructions and settle disputes without recourse to the courts "but, when freed people come to me complaining of abuse with their clothes discolored with their blood and their persons bearing marks of violence . . . I feel that . . . justice should take hold of some." When a Jackson County Negro woman was beaten by John Bates, struck by his son, and bitten by their dog, the man and boy were tried in the county criminal court. The boy was acquitted and Bates was fined five cents and costs.[12]

In Hernando County, the court dealt harshly with freedmen in cases brought before it. Bureau agent William G. Vance was especially aroused when a freedman was sold for his labor for eleven months to pay a $40 debt. "Can they do that? I wish you would let me know," wrote the confused officer. The answer was "You can take no official action on sentences in civil courts, but you can use your influence to see that a fair trial is had." Seventeen-year-old Alfred Jefferson was convicted by the Bradford County criminal court of riding his employer's horse without permission. He was fined $200 which he did not have and was sold for his labor for three years to liquidate the debt. Allen Thomas purchased his services and was later brought before a bureau court for several severe beatings of the youngster. The bureau court was necessary because the county criminal court refused to act.[13]

In Alachua County a Negro girl accused Charles U. Taylor of striking her with a board. Three witnesses testified against Taylor, but he was acquitted. Then Taylor accused the girl of contract violation on grounds of insolence, the nature of which he did not specify. She was convicted and given ten lashes. In the same court, several freedmen sued their employers for contract violations and the whites won nearly all the cases. When this happened, the Negroes were assessed court costs which they were unable to pay. They were then hired out to work off the debt. The agent reporting these incidents thought justice somewhat too expensive for some parties. When the bureau agent in Alachua County tried to settle a contract between J. S. Stanley and his laborers, the planter questioned the agent's jurisdiction. Stanley's attorney argued that jurisdiction over all civil contracts had been transferred to the state courts by President Johnson's April 2 proclamation.[14] That was similar to saying that he did not intend to pay his hired hands as he had agreed.

Near Palatka, Milton Busby was tried for assaulting his wife and fined $106. Without funds to pay, he was auctioned off for one year and his services purchased by the county sheriff. Freedman George Scribner took a drifting log from the river and sold it to a mill. He was tried, convicted, and sold for forty days. The man who bought his labor immediately sublet him for about twice the fine paid, "thus making a game of speculation and 'reconstructing' the defunct system of slavery in another form," according to bureau agent W. L. Apthorp. In Columbia County, numerous freedmen were convicted of a variety of crimes, fined, and sold to the highest bidder to pay the fine. Two of them were convicted of stealing two boxes of dry goods from a boxcar and were fined $500 each. But there were few alternatives. While these harsh sentences were being meted out, Leon County Judge E. L. T. Blake was chastized by an irate citizen for not selling Negro Edward Thomas and for permitting him to languish four months in jail wasting taxpayers' money.[15]

Military-civil relations were strained when James Denton was arrested for shooting Alec Johnson, a Negro, at Micanopy on April 6. Denton rode into Johnson's yard and called him. Johnson came to the door, Denton thought him insolent, and killed him. Civil authorities failed to arrest Denton, and United States troops apprehended him on April 28. A mob confronted the soldiers in Gainesville and set the prisoner free. Some of them were arrested the following day, but others escaped. Because of the incident the local military commander arrested some of the town's prominent citizens and held them as hostages. This erroneous act was corrected but not before considerable hostility was engendered. The debacle was completed more than a year later in the Circuit Court of Eastern Florida presided over by Judge B. A. Putnam. Denton was convicted of manslaughter and sentenced to pay $225 court costs and serve one minute in jail.[16] Denton had eluded arrest for one entire year and only turned himself in to get a civil trial. He had heard that military trials were about to be re-instated under the 1867 Reconstruction laws.

A serious conflict between Walker and Foster occurred when Elias Earle, a prominent Alachua planter who had served in the Confederate army, was brought before the county criminal court for severely beating a freedman and was found not guilty. He then sued the freedman for trespassing on his property. Testimony showed that the man had attended a church service on Earle's plantation. He was found guilty and sentenced to pay a fine and costs. Unable to pay, he was held in jail. The governor was contacted and he called for the case records. Since no trial records were kept in the county court, they were composed from the clerk's memory. With the record, Walker received several affidavits alleging that General Foster was misinformed on the case and that the Negro in question was a notorious liar while Earle was above reproach.[17] The case ended only after a heated exchange between the two authorities, but Walker declined to intervene and the court decision stood.

Two Madison County cases finally forced a showdown in June. Frank Cheatham shot and killed freedman Simon Warren without provocation before three witnesses, all Negroes. Justice of the Peace Thomas Morris refused to arrest Cheatham because, according to him, there were no competent witnesses. Cheatham made an unhurried escape to Greenwood, South Carolina. Morris was arrested for neglecting his official duty and remanded to the United States district court, but the district attorney asked that he be tried by the state courts which also had jurisdiction. Whether Usher chose this remedy because of Judge Fraser's continued absence or to give the state every opportunity to provide justice is not clear. However, Morris was never tried by state authorities and his case was placed on the district court docket in late 1866.[18]

The Cheatham case was followed by a more flagrant abuse of justice. Shortly after General Foster issued his order restoring civil jurisdiction in all cases subject to review, two events occurred on the Hampton plantation. J. J. Hampton, a white man, provoked an argument with Jim Hampton, a Negro who worked for him. When the white man pulled a gun and then a knife, he was disarmed by the Negro in a rigorous scuffle. Jim Hampton was then arrested for assault and battery. The Hampton's Negro cook, Eliza, protested and was beaten over the head with a club by A. T. Hampton. The county criminal court presided over by Judge Joseph Tilman fined A. T. Hampton one dollar for the assault on Eliza. Jim Hampton was sentenced to thirty-nine lashes for assault despite evidence that he had been defending himself. The court refused to entertain a case against J. J. Hampton.

Lieutenant J. E. Quentin witnessed the proceedings and informed the civil officials that he intended to intervene. In a heated exchange the bureau agent was reminded that he had insufficient military force to prevent execution of the sentence. Jim Hampton was taken by a guard superior to Quentin's meager force to a room where the doors were barred and the sentence carried out. Quentin complained to Foster who contacted the governor. Citing the Madison County court's refusal to try J. J. Hampton, the difference between the one dollar fine and thirty-nine lashes, the insults to Quentin, and the hasty execution of the sentence, General Foster demanded an explanation from the governor. Because of the Hampton and Cheatham cases, Foster resumed the system of military arrests in Madison County and several other North Florida counties.[19]

This confrontation occurred in June 1866, before President Johnson's second proclamation restoring civil law. Walker was furious with Judge Tilman and the other Madison County officials. Demanding a record of the trials and an explanation, the governor asserted, "I have and claim the right to review, the prisoner has the right to appeal, but if corporal punishment is inflicted immediately, the accused is deprived of his constitutional rights." Furthermore, "as martial law still prevails in this state, it would certainly be better in all cases where a military officer officially forbids the execution of a sentence, to pause and refer the matter to me and let the case come before the commanding general. I have never yet failed to secure from the commanding general the removal of any improper interference." A month later three men at Apalachicola murdered a Florida Unionist and the local authorities refused to arrest them. The military commander arrested them and confined the men at Fort Pickens until the civil authorities should agree to try them. The counties where martial law was re-instated were Madison, Escambia, Santa Rosa, Levy, and Alachua.[20]

General Foster lamented to the governor that he was becoming doubtful of the state courts' impartial administration of justice. There was a growing apprehension among Negroes, Florida Unionists, and Northerners that they could not obtain justice, and the state courts had only themselves to blame. "I firmly believe," the general concluded, "that if the military power be withdrawn it will be followed by the exodus of a large portion of the Northern men, and capital, now seeking profitable settlement and investment in the state." Others besides military officials denounced court injustices. William S. Dilworth, county solicitor of Jefferson County and a former Confederate officer who had favored the radical secessionists in 1861, excoriated a criminal court jury in his county for failure to mete out impartial justice. "This thing has got to be stopped," he declared. The jurists were under oath to do justice and personal sympathies should not affect the verdict. The Negroes had the same rights before the law as whites and it was in the native whites' interest to give them justice and let them feel that it was available before civil tribunals. It was also necessary to show white people disposed to wrong Negroes that they would be punished.[21]

Dilworth probably spoke for many community leaders in the state, but he was one of the few who articulated his convictions. The president of the United States was giving the impression that there would be no national governmental interference in state civil affairs under any circumstances. By the time Dilworth addressed the Jefferson County jury in late September, the issue was becoming one of states' rights versus national interference rather than of the Florida judicial system's failure to provide for the redress of wrongs inflicted by whites against Negroes.

To discount charges against the county criminal courts, Governor Walker sent Foster controverting testimony. Judge Charles N. Jordan of Pensacola affirmed that blacks and whites were treated equally in his court, but "since the Freedmen's Bureau intervenes to inflict the punishment on freedmen they often get off with light punishment while whites suffer the full vengeance of the law." Alexander C. Blount, a wartime Unionist, said he had defended many freedmen in Jordan's court and saw no differences except in punishment as the judge had said. Referring to these letters, Governor Walker demanded that Foster stop bureau interference in affairs of the state courts.[22]

In July, James West, a prominent Madison County planter, was arrested by Negro soldiers late at night and taken to Madison. Lieutenant Quentin had probable cause for the arrest, but Walker complained bitterly that the insult of being "arrested by negroes . . . like a felon" was unnecessary. Walker insisted that the military should not have become involved because "the Courts of the Country were open to punish him and recourse there should have been taken."[23] The incident undoubtedly exacerbated the bad relations then existing in Madison County, but both Quentin and Foster had good reason to doubt that recourse to civil courts would have solved anything.

While the jurisdictional struggle continued, Governor Walker acted on the widespread belief that white Floridians should be armed to defend themselves in emergencies, and that emergencies could best be avoided by denying arms to Negroes. It will be recalled that whites were restive until Negro occupation troops were removed from interior posts. Soon after their removal, Governor Walker organized a state militia to which he appointed former Confederate officers, such as Captain J. J. Dickison, who was a hero only to the white ex-Confederates of Florida.[24]

About the same time Walker was forming the militia, a group of black and white citizens of Jacksonville petitioned for permission to form a volunteer militia company. When native whites protested, Foster was consulted and he contacted the governor. Foster reminded Walker of Attorney General Galbraith's opinion that Negroes could not be prevented from keeping arms, and of the state constitutional provision that "all the inhabitants of the State without distinction of color are free and shall enjoy the right of person and property without distinction of color." Although the militia act of January 1866 did not name Negroes as subject to duty, neither did it prohibit them from serving. Would the governor recognize the Jacksonville volunteer company? Walker replied that the militia law limited duty to "able bodied white men between the ages of

18 and 45" and was not required of "white males outside of those ages nor of colored men." Militia duty was regarded as distinct from the right to bear arms which all citizens possessed. Furthermore, another statute prohibited military organizations except those provided by law. Unwilling to authorize the company over the governor's opposition, Foster asked his superiors whether the 1866 civil rights act did not guarantee the right and whether he as commanding general could authorize the militia unit.[25] The company was never formed.

Whites were also apprehensive of events attracting large crowds of Negroes. Marianna whites protested an anticipated Fourth of July celebration. Ethelred Philips denounced bureau agent C. M. Hamilton as a "pest" who "put up the Negroes to celebrate the 4th inst as the anniversary of their freedom. . . . We are a little uneasy about it." Sheriff W. H. Kimball asked General Foster to stop it because carrying Abraham Lincoln's portrait in a parade was almost certain to cause violence. Hamilton called for additional troops to protect "the raising of the flag in Marianna on the 4th where whites have sworn to prevent it." Despite the apprehension, Foster approved the "innocent and proper" celebration on the "anniversary of our greatest national holiday" and refused to interfere. The celebration was attended by nearly 3,000 black and white people who enjoyed a barbecue without disturbance.[26]

Since General Foster was unwilling to permit Negro military activity without approval from either Governor Walker or his own military superiors, and the Negro gatherings were almost always peaceful, it is difficult to understand continuing charges from Florida whites. When General Sheridan tried to suppress the state militia, a furious Leon County planter fumed, "his order prohibits all Southern white men in other words Rebels from drilling at the same time allowing that privilege to loyal men (Negroes). They are drilling all over this country, except in this immediate neighborhood and they may be at it here for what I know. There is certainly great change in the negroes down here for the worse. . . . If there should be any disturbance down here the negroes will be killed up like sheep." Without regard to the several factual errors in Whitehead's fulminations, the contradiction between his evaluation of Negro military activities and the outcome of any possible encounter between Negroes and whites is significant. Bureau agent D. M. Hammond at Fernandina, where racial affairs were highly combustible during 1866–67, thought it "singular and significant that in all the affrays with Freedmen it seldom appears that a white man is hurt. If the Freedmen were organized armed turbulent and vindictive as some affect to believe it could not be so uniformly one sided in results."[27]

Two national events of August 1866—the National Union Convention at Philadelphia on the fourteenth and President Johnson's August 20 proclamation—had important repercussions in Florida. The convention caused white Floridians to hope that they could gain readmission and a solution to their problems through a political victory in November 1866. Senator James R. Doolittle of Wisconsin and other conservative Republicans tried to build a coalition with Democrats based on Lincoln's old wartime party headed by Andrew Johnson and dedicated to restoring the Union. Conservative white Floridians responded enthusiastically. Governor Walker saved the expense of a state convention by naming twenty-two Florida delegates to the Philadelphia meeting. All sections of the state and both Unionists and ex-Confederates were represented in the delegation. Although the convention was not all its northern proponents had hoped, its tone was pleasing to Floridians. Editor Charles E. Dyke of the *Floridian*, the state's most influential conservative newspaper, cautioned that Southerners should not criticize the Philadelphia convention, "for this just weakens conservatives and strengthens radicals. You are wrong if you think things can stay the same as now. . . . They will either get better or worse. If Johnson wins the 1866 elections we will have to bear grevious [*sic*] burdens of taxes but we can do it. But if the radicals win they will impose negro suffrage, military rule." If the latter occurred, Dyke thought it would be the "duty of a whole people to abandon a country which can no longer claim to be theirs."[28]

Meetings were held throughout Florida praising the National Union convention. Radical leaders countered with their own Northern and Southern Loyalists Convention at Philadelphia in early September. A group of Florida Unionists led by Ossian B. Hart of Jacksonville met in Tallahassee and named delegates to it. Conservative Floridians denounced them as "Unconstitutional Unionists."[29]

In early September, General Foster interpreted the renewed interest in politics as having a beneficent effect on native white Floridians: "Many of the most violent secessionists now declare [restoring the full Union of the States] to be their most ardent wish."[30]

Foster's optimism was short lived. After a bitter campaign in which President Johnson engaged his Radical opponents in a manner that discouraged his potential moderate supporters, Radical Republicans won a two-thirds majority of the seats in both congressional bodies. Having placed their hopes of early readmission and an end to national interference on Johnson's ability to maintain control of Reconstruction policy, the Floridians were disappointed at the election's outcome.

The disappointment was greater because of the heights to which hopes had been raised by Johnson's August 20 proclamation. It surpassed his April 2 pronouncement by declaring that "the said insurrection is at an end, and . . . peace, order and civil law now exist in and throughout the whole of the United States."[31] The proclamation probably had more to do with the improved attitudes of which Foster spoke than the political activities of the National Union party although the two complemented each other. The proclamation made a Johnson victory in November all the more desirable.

General Foster realized there was an adverse side to the proclamation, however, when Tallahassee Mayor Francis Eppes began arresting United States soldiers on the city's main street for violating a city ordinance against "fast riding." Foster informed Eppes that his men were not to be interrupted when performing their official duties. The mayor replied that he was only enforcing city ordinances, and while he regretted the collision between civil and military authority "the issue had better be made at once." "You misapprehend the importance of your position," the general replied, adding that martial law was still supreme in Florida. Ordering Mayor Eppes not to arrest his men, Foster assured him that any complaints against them would be investigated and punishment administered according to military law. Eppes persisted in his belief that martial law had been removed by Johnson's August 20 proclamation, but agreed to respect the general's orders "until they can be tested." Genuinely confused, the mayor reported the incident to Governor Walker and asked, "How can he [Foster] think martial law is still supreme?"

Although Foster had unhesitatingly assured Mayor Eppes and others that martial law was in effect, he was not sure himself what the recent proclamation meant: he asked General Sheridan, "Does it deprive me . . . of the supremacy of martial-law in cases of conflict between the authority of Acts of Congress and orders of my military superiors, and the State or Municipial [*sic*] authorities?"[32] Sheridan's reply was equivocal. He promised definite instructions as soon as he received them. A little later the *Floridian* published a United States attorney general's opinion that Johnson's proclamations guaranteed civil authorities immunity against military interference. "Nothing could be more explicit than this," the paper concluded. As a result of the altercation Foster discovered that Tallahassee ordinances required city officials to take a "Confederate States" oath and that they provided different penalties "on account of color or condition of servitude." The mayor was advised that a suit was being instituted in the U.S. court for violation of the civil rights law.[33]

Mistreatment of freedmen by whites and unfair administration of justice continued, and civil officials' resistance to bureau or military interference was noticably more adamant after the August 20 proclamation. Mayor Eppes' actions were exceptional only in that he confronted the commanding general rather than a subordinate officer at an outlying location. Jefferson County Judge M. H. Strain told a bureau agent, "I cannot recognize any authority above the Constitution and laws of the State of Florida and to them and them alone I must in my official capacity refer all my actions." Judges in Marion, Hernando, and Sumter counties echoed this statement.[34] In Monticello, a Negro boy was beaten by a white man; in mayor's court, the boy was fined five dollars for disturbing the peace. When bureau agent Grumwell complained, the mayor said civil law was restored and there was nothing the military could do about it.

In Jackson County, Mary Jane Baker, a Negro, tried to swear out a warrant against William Parker, a white man who had beaten her. The justice of the peace refused to act until she paid a six-dollar fee. Parker was then arrested, tried, and fined five dollars.[35] The advance payment was required despite the state attorney general's opinion, widely disseminated by the governor, that such a requirement violated state law. At Waukeenah, Jefferson County, Martha Richardson, a Negro, was ordered by Mrs. James Dewitt to wash clothes for her. The woman refused, saying that she was employed by her uncle as a nurse. On James Dewitt's testimony, she was convicted of vagrancy. Since she was not a vagrant, the Freedmen's Bureau agent contacted the judge who told him that, regardless of any injustice, he would neither set aside the sentence nor delay its execution because the military was without authority to intercede.

By fall of 1866 most bureau agents and military commanders observing local civil administration concluded that Negroes could not expect justice. Although there were many examples of judges and law enforcement officers trying to execute their duties impartially—just as there were examples to the contrary—nearly all observers felt that juries could not rid themselves of prejudice. In most cases they were simply unwilling to accept testimony of Negroes when it was contradictory to that of white men. And some cases were so complicated that justice would have been difficult even under ideal circumstances. The shooting of City Marshal Jesse Dickson at Quincy in September 1866 is an example. On September 28, Marshal Dickson fired three times at a Negro for reasons which were obscure. Thinking the shooting an unprovoked assault, the Negro gathered five friends the next day and engaged Dickson in a gun battle during which one of them was wounded and the marshal killed. They were arrested by a posse led by the former guerilla leader J. J. Dickison, who was living in Quincy at the time. All six men were tried for murder by the circuit court in Quincy where the white community was aroused against them and no lawyer would defend them. As bureau agent Marcellus L. Stearns observed, "that part, or all the culprits are guilty of a crime there can be no doubt, but what degree, is a question of law and justice." Doctor Charles A. Hentz, a Quincy native, concluded that "They got a fair trial, but were hung."[36]

White men who had opposed the Confederacy during the war or who spoke against Andrew Johnson's policies afterward were held in contempt equal to that felt toward Negroes and were often denied equal protection of the laws. Antipathy for Unionists was especially strong among ex-Confederates along the Gulf Coast from Taylor and Lafayette counties to Hillsborough and Manatee. In this sparsely settled region, neighbors had often served in opposing armies, plundered each other's property, and sometimes fought each other. Anger and bitterness did not abate with the end of hostilities. Most of the Unionists were just as anti-Negro as their ex-Confederate neighbors; they tended to blame Negroes for the suffering they had endured and often refused to allow freedmen to settle in their communities.[37] Despite their racial attitudes, the plight of Unionists during the Walker administration was similar to that of the blacks, and the problem was statewide.

A Nassau County Unionist who had deserted the Confederate army returned home in August 1866. He was recognized and shot by a former acquaintance, because "the feeling against such men by old rebels is intense." A widow with three children sought economic assistance from Judge E. C. Love of Quincy and was told to ask for it from her "deserter" friends who had caused the Confederate defeat. During the war Lemuel Wilson of Gainesville had been an outspoken Unionist. Threatened with bodily harm for his views, he had tried to secure a horse for transportation out of the area, but no one would sell him one. Believing his life in danger, he took a horse and fled to Jacksonville. He returned in October 1866 and was arrested and tried by the county criminal court for horse-stealing. Colonel Sprague was outraged, but at the time the Johnson administration had left him without recourse except to appeal the case in the United States court, which was not then in session. Wilson must have been relieved when Governor Walker issued an amnesty statement in January 1867 precluding prosecution in such cases.[38]

On a Jacksonville street the uninhibited proslavery filibusterer Henry Titus seriously wounded Myron S. Mickler, a former Union soldier, because the latter defended congressional policy in a discussion between the two men. Titus told the mayor's court, "I had a political discussion with this fellow. . . . he used some language that did not suit me and I knocked him in the head with my stick." Fined five dollars by the mayor's court, Titus appealed to the county court where a jury acquitted him.[39]

Judge Perry G. Wall, a long-time resident and respected citizen of Brooksville in Hernando County, was well known for his strong Unionist views during and after the war. Serving as a bureau agent, he was concerned at the plight of a Negro couple trying to comply with the state's marriage law. He performed the necessary ceremony for them. The sheriff arrested him on the ground that he had no authority for what he had done. Since military officials were aware of the hostility shown by ex-Confederates toward Unionists at Brooksville, they were afraid Wall would be sentenced to corporal punishment and the sentence executed before an appeal could be made. A ten-man detachment was sent to Brooksville with orders to take possession of the judge if such a sentence occurred. After considerable excitement he was convicted and fined one dollar. Freedmen's Bureau agent W. G. Vance, who witnessed the trial, thought that only the presence of the troops averted a harsh sentence.[40]

During the war Isham Johnson, a white Unionist of Hernando County who had once served in the territorial legislature, joined the United States Army and served along the Gulf Coast of Florida. After he participated in the destruction of salt stills belonging to Confederate citizens, his wife was driven out of the area and his property sequestered by the Confederate government. Penniless on his return after the war, Johnson had difficulty sustaining his family. Neighbors would not sell him corn at any price. Many unbranded cattle roamed the county at the time and Johnson killed and butchered what he believed to be one of them. But, finding an obscured brand on the carcass, he followed accepted practice in this range cattle country and called some neighbors to assess a just value which they set at six dollars. He then tendered that amount to F. Crichton of Bayport, owner of the animal. Crichton said no payment would suffice and that Johnson must be prosecuted.

Realizing the bitter feeling against him, Johnson left the county and his wife appealed to the bureau agent. Crichton, contacted by the commanding officer at Tampa, agreed to drop the case, but when Johnson returned home county solicitor S. Y. Finley brought him to trial. Johnson was fined $50 and assessed $150 court costs. Without funds, he was working off the fine at $3 a day repairing the county courthouse. Governor Walker took no action on General Foster's request that the fine be remitted, but Finley was indicted for trial by the United States court under the civil rights law.[41]

Because of many reports that justice was not being done in the state courts after military tribunals ceased in April 1866, General Howard ordered re-establishment of bureau courts on September 19. They were to be composed of three members—the bureau officer and one selected by each party to a dispute. They would have jurisdiction over civil cases involving freedmen where the amount did not exceed $300 and over all offenses by or against freedmen where punishment was no more than $100 fine or thirty days in jail. Court judgments could be enforced by military authority. Howard reasoned that the bureau existed by an act of Congress and, in matters relating to refugees, freedmen, and abandoned lands, its authority was paramount to and not subject to revision by state courts. Capital crimes, felonies, and questions of real estate titles were to be referred to either military commissions, the United States court, or the state court. Howard was making an interpretation of his authority which was then in dispute between Congress and the president. Three months after its issue, Howard's letter was disapproved by President Johnson "until further consideration." In the interim, bureau courts were convened in a few cases. Most Floridians argued that they were illegal after the August 20 presidential proclamation. But there was at least one exception in Hernando County where the freedmen were having riotous night gatherings and there was no civil court in session to punish them. White citizens there expressed gratitude to bureau agent Vance for convening a court to deal with them.[42]

Most of the business before the military courts, however, was directed toward the more pervasive problem of achieving justice for Negroes. These courts were used sparingly and only under close review by General Foster. A typical case involved Allen Thomas of Bradford County who had purchased Alfred Jefferson, the young Negro who had been sold for illegally using a horse. Thomas gave Jefferson a severe beating and threatened another if the boy reported him. When bureau agent F. E. Grossman learned of it, he ordered Thomas to desist and the beating was repeated as promised. The county court refused the case so a bureau court was convened. Thomas was convicted and fined $75 and $35 costs. Grossman was worried about the trial's legality; Thomas had appeared with two lawyers, and since there was no prosecutor, Grossman had prosecuted the case while also serving as a member of the court. Foster reviewed the case and approved the conviction despite the agent's acting as both prosecutor and judge.[43]

Although their use was limited, bureau courts and military tribunals for higher crimes continued until they were disapproved by the president in December 1866. Colonel John T. Sprague, who assumed command after Foster left and whose actions were usually approved by native Floridians, reflected on the military courts: "Where white men have not been punished by civil law for murder and abuse of freedmen, the military have exercised power with very doubtful authority, however, there was no alternative, unless the bureau agents submitted to abuse and disgrace. *This power will still be exercised* [italics mine]. I hope for some vigorous measure before long to insure protection to Union men, to the military, and to the freedmen, without which all exertions will be fruitless."[44] Three days later, the March 2 Reconstruction Act passed.

The clash of military and civil authorities was nowhere more acute than in Fernandina where property title disputes resulting from the wartime tax sales caused several confrontations. It will be recalled that some freedmen and white Unionists bought land at the tax sales while others rented land which the United States government had acquired at the sale. President Johnson's amnesty policy enabled original owners to redeem their land in some cases, but the policy was ambivalent and the process was extremely slow and complicated. Former Confederate owners who returned to Fernandina and found Negroes claiming their land were often too impatient to follow the cumbersome legal process of redemption, and they tried to oust the tax sale purchasers by force. With advice and leadership from Radical political leaders in the town, the tax sale purchasers resisted the former owners and called on the local military commander to protect them. Under the authority of a War Department circular of November 1865, the military commander protected the tax sale purchasers from eviction.[45]

As late as May 1866, General Grant reaffirmed his support of such a policy and declared that only the United States courts had jurisdiction in tax sale cases. General Foster accordingly ordered the Fernandina post commander to protect all loyal citizens from injury by writs from the state or municipal courts.[46] But Governor Walker, citing President Johnson's April proclamation ending the insurrection, insisted that Foster not only lacked authority to resist civil officials in the land title dispute but that he was obligated to use military force to oust the tax sale purchasers and put the redeemers in possession of the property. Ignoring some salient facts, the *Tallahassee Floridian* attributed the Fernandina troubles to "Northern radicals" who "encouraged the freedmen to band together to resist any attempt of the former owners of property to secure it back even though it was taken by a doubtful process." Hoping to avert violence, Foster and Walker visited Fernandina in June but there was little they could do as long as each disputant believed the law to be on his side.[47]

On August 19, about the time President Johnson issued his second proclamation restoring civil law, General Grant amended his earlier instructions and authorized the state courts to hear appeals regarding property sold for taxes.[48] The civil courts soon issued numerous writs of ejectment which the sheriff served against the tax sale purchasers. Foster was denied authority to intervene, but the matter was still unsettled because some purchasers appealed in the United States court, an act which Foster interpreted as a stay of proceedings. In these cases he was empowered to stop ejectments until the court had acted. Because the appeals process meant further delay, even this interference was unsatisfactory to the original owners. Complications also arose when tax sale purchasers occasionally resisted the sheriff. Attempting to preserve order and still comply with his restricted authority, Foster ordered the Fernandina commander to assist the sheriff in ejecting tax sale purchasers if called upon to do so but only after he had determined that the redemption was proper and no appeal was pending. But no military force was to be used to injure Union men claiming rights under United States law.[49]

The showdown at Fernandina occurred at about the same time that Foster's authority was being restricted in other matters. In October, the sheriff notified John Hubbard, a tax sale purchaser whose property had been redeemed by its original owner, that a writ of ejectment had been issued against him. Hubbard said he would resist it. The sheriff called on the military commander for assistance, alleging that a "riotous disturbance" was likely. The commander refused on the ground that he was required to remain neutral unless a disturbance occurred, after which he was obliged to stop it by arresting all parties. This answer angered Governor Walker who interpreted the military position as interfering with civil process. It was tantamount to saying that the sheriff could not execute his duties, the governor wrote, adding that "nothing can justify a military order to a civil officer to suspend the execution of civil process or be imprisoned, except the position that martial law is still the supreme law of this state. . . . My settled convictions are that Civil Law is supreme in the state, and that the military can only act when called to assist the civil." Walker demanded that Foster order the Fernandina commander to withdraw his "threats to arrest the sheriff," and to assist that official when called upon. If Foster was unwilling, Walker wanted to know immediately so he could telegraph the president and General Grant for instructions to avoid a collision and prevent bloodshed.[50] Without waiting for the general's reply, Walker asked President Johnson to intervene.

Foster disagreed with the governor and replied somewhat impatiently that the local commander's refusal to assist the sheriff was proper. Many times the state and municipal courts had acted contrary to United States law in tax sale cases and the officer was under strict orders not to move until he had determined whether the sheriff was acting properly. The governor was also mistaken in asserting that the military could only act to assist civil authorities. Both the Freedmen's Bureau Act and the 1866 Civil Rights Act empowered him to protect freedmen in the enjoyment of their civil rights until the state "shall have been restored, in its constitutional relations to the Government and *shall be duly represented in the Congress of the United States*" [original italics]. "The President's Proclamation to which you refer . . . cannot of course alter the effect of the above laws."[51]

Governor Walker won the round. Secretary of War Edwin M. Stanton asked Foster for an explanation of the problem, but without waiting for a reply ordered the general to "abstain from interference against Civil Process, or officers executing the same." After a supplementary directive from Stanton, Foster ordered the Fernandina commander to remain strictly neutral and "in no case will you use the U.S. troops in Civil matters except by Special Orders from these Hd Quarters." These instructions amounted to a complete reversal of Grant's May order to protect tax sale purchasers from acts of state officials.

By November 1866, General Foster was losing hope that he could work with civil authorities. He was alarmed by the continuing evidence of injustice in the local courts, the increasing resistance to military personnel manifested by state officials at all levels, the overwhelming endorsement of President Johnson and bitter denunciations of Radicals during and after the congressional election campaign, and the erosion of his authority by executive orders. His October report noted that newspapers were "bitter towards the political party called the Radicals and eulogistic of the conservative or as it is termed the Johnson party." He expressed surprise at recently disclosed "deep-seated hostility to Congress and to all Union men who are either denominated 'Yankees,' or, if from the South, 'Deserters.'" There had been threats that the state militia would resist if United States troops arrested anyone. Foster termed this mere bluster but indicative of prevailing attitudes. He thought that Floridians were so much influenced by the "late war" that either a strong military force with clear authority over state affairs must be maintained or "Civil and Military power [must] be given to unconditional Union men."[52] The general believed the increasing difficulty of his position was due to "the belief entertained by most of the officials and people of the State, that the civil functions of the State Government are entirely restored by the President's proclamation of August 20th, 1866, and that Federal jurisdiction over the affairs of the Freedmen and Refugees as provided for in the laws of Congress, is unconstitutional." As a natural consequence of this belief, whenever United States officers carried out their official duties, they were brought into popular disrepute by speeches and newspaper articles which stigmatized their acts as oppressive and illegal.[53]

Foster was especially chagrined at Governor Walker's address to the legislature in which he denounced the bureau courts and criticized the military commander for interfering in the internal affairs of the state. Especially vexing was the governor's assertion that "Orders of the Major General commanding were recently issued in Fernandina permitting no civil process to be executed, except such as should seem to him proper, and to arrest and confine the Sheriff in case of his attempting to execute his process after being commanded by the officer to desist."[54] The governor's message has been accepted by some historians as evidence of military abuse of Florida's citizens. That is unfortunate, since it appears from the events leading up to his address that he was incorrect with respect to military activities at Fernandina.

Disappointed by the intemperate tone of the governor's speech, Foster laconically concluded that "regarding the popular feeling in the State which is becoming more outspoken in the matter of State rights it [his speech] is not perhaps more than popular pressure demanded." Foster decided that affairs in Florida had degenerated so much that it was absolutely necessary that he receive more definite instructions as to his authority. Under the circumstances he requested and received relief from his assignment because of his wife's illness in Baltimore and "the truly uncomfortable fix in which the present instructions from Washington leaves all loyal unionists in the South."[55]

The 1866 legislature offered little cause for optimism. It made a few minor modifications of the discriminatory laws passed in the last session, but refused to repeal the law providing corporal punishment despite the attorney general's ruling that it was unconstitutional. Governor Walker admitted that the county criminal courts had not worked well but neither he nor the legislature knew what to do about them. The comptroller gave an estimate of state finances: total indebtedness was put at $638,759.87, of which $167,759.98 was in warrants issued by the Walker administration to meet operating expenses; the remainder was bonded indebtedness or overdue interest on it. Taxes due were expected to pay the warrants and a little more, but collections were poor.[56]

The most significant action of the legislature was rejection of the proposed Fourteenth Amendment. The amendment had become a major issue between the president and Radical Republicans in the 1866 election campaign. Its definition of United States citizenship and guarantee to those citizens of equal protection of the laws, its threatened reduction of congressional representation of all states which refused to enfranchise Negroes, and its exclusion of certain former Confederates from office-holding had become a kind of congressional Reconstruction program. President Johnson recommended that the southern states reject the amendment and Floridians vigorously endorsed his recommendation. When Judge Philip Fraser urged some Tallahassee citizens to support ratification, the *Floridian* cautioned that the amendment would not be the end of Reconstruction as promised but only the beginning. Admitting the gloomy aspect of politics, the paper saw no need to "demean ourselves . . . by ratifying the 14th amendment." Governor Walker also recommended rejection of the amendment, saying that Floridians could never accept

Negro suffrage. A legislative committee report opposing the amendment was accepted with little opposition.[57]

With a two-thirds majority of both congressional houses in December 1866, the Radical Republicans replaced President Johnson's Reconstruction policies with their own. The congressional Reconstruction provisions of March 1867 will be considered in another chapter, but it should be noted that they removed the uncertainty about military authority in Florida and other southern states.[58] The states were divided into military districts, each commanded by an army general. Florida was in the Third Military District, commanded by General John Pope. Colonel Sprague remained as commander of the Florida subdistrict and as assistant commissioner of the Freedmen's Bureau. Governor Walker retained his office, but from March 1867 until his replacement by another elected governor in July 1868, his official acts were subject to approval of the military commander. State courts remained open but their jurisdiction was shared by military tribunals.

Third Military District records for 1867 are filled with correspondence between Governor Walker and military officials dealing with appointments and removals of civil officials. Walker's recommendations were often approved, but the appointments were military. For example, when he asked the district chief of civil affairs who should commission a Middle Florida circuit judge, the answer was "the only commission he can receive is the order from these Headquarters."[59]

The jurisdictional dispute was removed, but whether freedmen and Unionists fared any better is questionable. Attitudes were not improved by alterations of congressional statutes. It was a long way from military headquarters to the scattered communities of Florida, and the approximately 1,100 troops in the state were divided into very small detachments. William G. Vance wrote from Brooksville in September 1867 that "Courts are governed by men who still believe in secession and state rights and let their prejudices rule their decisions." From August 1867 to October 1868, there were no criminal cases tried in Marion County because no lawyers or judges would comply with General Pope's order to practice before mixed or Negro juries.[60]

In September 1867, William S. Dilworth of Monticello repeated his earlier admonition that prejudicial decisions by juries would destroy the Negroes' confidence in the court system and aid Radicals in winning Negro support. But Dilworth's words were weakened by general knowledge that he had recommended and supervised the severe beating of Bob Hauptman by other freedmen two months earlier. At Brooksville, J. David Hope drove contracted laborers off his plantation without compensation because they marched in a Fourth of July parade "under the U.S. flag."

From Jackson County came the complaint that "The freedman's remedy is in the civil courts. That these are a mockery is known to every honest observer. The white man is fined five and the black men fifty for the same offense. The Union man is convicted on insufficient testimony and the rebel is acquitted in defiance of the strongest testimony." In the same county freedman Gilbert Walker was murdered by Hugh Parker, a white man, because the former did not pull his loaded wagon far enough off the road when the two met. In Ocala, freedmen were still being jailed on flimsy charges of contract violations, and the capitation tax was being enforced only against the blacks, many of whom were jailed for nonpayment. When in early 1868 a Hernando court permitted Adeline Frierson to collect wages from the employer of a Negro on the ground that she owned him, the judgment was set aside by the military commander.[61]

A military detachment went to Orange Springs, Marion County, to arrest James Gibbons, Thomas Smith, and James Denton for assaulting freedman Jack Danforth. Denton was the man formerly sentenced to one minute in prison for murder. An investigation showed that Orange Springs, a popular resort at the time, was continually terrorized by the three men and civil authorities were unable or unwilling to stop them. Bureau agent J. A. Remley said military authority alone would prevail there "until there is a complete revolution in the sentiments . . . of a large portion of the people."[62]

But law enforcement was not entirely a racial problem. When the 1867 crops failed, the Madison County bureau agent said people who would have honored their contracts were turned by necessity into "perfect swindlers and rascals," and there were just as many cases of whites versus whites as whites versus blacks. In the same county, Unionist William R. Cone sued another white man for breach of contract and the county court decided against him. The appeal was thrown out by the circuit court. Cone felt he had not been treated fairly, especially when the criminal court judge's son shot at him during the trial, was tried, found guilty, and fined one dollar. Military commanders tried to enforce the law against Negroes as well as against whites. When a band of armed freedmen created a major disturbance in Monticello, Colonel F. F. Flint chastized bureau agent Grumwell for his inability to arrest them. In Jackson County, agent Purman was outraged when freedman Archibald Hunter "committed a violent rape on a white woman" and "has eluded all pursuit." A military commission convened at Monticello and tried John Holmes for killing James Cooper. Both were Negroes.[63]

Law and order collapsed in Madison County when Frank Pope, a fifteen-year-old student at St. Johns Seminary, ordered his teacher, a man named Bristow, to get on his knees and ask the youth's pardon for an alleged affront. The teacher refused and was shot seven times. The county sheriff resigned rather than make an arrest, and County Judge John Anderson was arrested by military authorities for refusing to sign the warrant. The editor of the *Madison Messenger* resisted appeals to delete the story from his weekly paper. Bristow died a few days later and Pope went unmolested to Georgia; the Madison community required several weeks for recovery.[64]

Throughout Governor Walker's term, whether under President Johnson's program or the subsequent military phase of congressional Reconstruction, civil law was neither supreme nor effective. His term was a period of confusion, uncertainty, and conflicting authority. Florida society was disrupted, chaotic, and violent. This was due partially to frontier conditions and partially to dislocations resulting from the recent war, but the greatest single problem was racial. At the same time many Floridians of both races were never involved in violence. Bureau agents from all over the state reported that the violent were the exceptions, and that most people accepted the changed conditions of society without overt resistance. The problems developed when the few committed their misdeeds and the need arose for redress of grievances through the essential institution of civilized society—the court of law.

If most Floridians considered themselves law-abiding, why did the courts fail? "The fact is custom with them has become the law," wrote one of Florida's few Radicals,[65] and he was correct. It was one thing for a white man to make his personal decision to treat former slaves fairly, even benevolently, especially if he had been a slaveowner. It was quite a different matter to overcome a lifetime of conditioning to the belief that Negroes were inferior, with certain character deficiencies which impaired their reliability as witnesses. It had been customary to administer physical punishment to Negroes without recourse to law; suddenly it became a crime to inflict physical harm on a former slave and Negroes gained the right to contest white men's interpretations of agreements made between them. Many white men serving as civil officials were reluctant to arrest other white men for violence toward Negroes. When cases did come before the courts, jurors were unwilling to accept the Negroes' testimony against the white men's because they had grown up thinking that Negroes were unreliable and had no cause to dispute a white man.

That is what caused the bad image of the army during this period. The record indicates that the military commanders were restrained in exercising their powers, but it was the army's duty to oversee a change which Florida's white community regarded as unacceptable. Regardless of its restraint, the army's mere presence on such a mission rendered it intolerable.

It is not enough to conclude that a few whites were given to violence and tried to take advantage of the poorly informed freedmen. It is certainly true, and those individuals were alone responsible for their crimes, but the white society of Florida was to blame for refusing to hold them accountable. In fact, Florida society tended to prevent the law from operating against those individuals. The few Floridians who tried to administer the law impartially, or who dissented from the accepted racial view were ostracized by their communities and sometimes subjected to violence themselves. That is why it was so easy to deny justice to the Unionists. The Unionists, or "Deserters," had opposed the Confederacy and helped to cause the situation which existed after the war. Thus it was felt that they did not deserve equal treatment before the law.

The white Floridians' selective justice was understandable, but with such an attitude prevalent there was little likelihood that Negroes could be incorporated as free citizens into Florida society according to either President Johnson's plan or that of the Congressional Radicals. However, President Johnson would have negated any possibility had it existed. Just as the Floridians believed slavery was the natural condition of Negroes, they also believed that states had certain rights which the United States Constitution barred the central government from disturbing. Secession and military defeat had not altered this belief. President Johnson agreed with them, and when Congress passed the second Freedmen's Bureau Act and the Civil Rights Act in early 1866—both moderate measures intended to extend the rights of citizenship to Negroes—Johnson vetoed the bills in terminology which delighted the ex-Confederates of Florida and the South. His veto messages and the April 2 proclamation convinced many Floridians that military interference in state affairs was wrong, although Governor Walker continued his attempts to cooperate with the commanding general. Then the August 20 proclamation removed any lingering doubts. Johnson's proclamations and veto messages replaced the basic issue of how to achieve citizenship for Negroes with the more abstract question of states' rights versus national interference. Where Governor Walker had once worked with General Foster to correct blatant abuses by the state courts, he began answering Foster's requests for corrective actions by challenging the general's right to make the requests.

Johnson intended his proclamations to restrict military authority, and the army's actions were severely circumscribed after April 1866. But, because of the conflict between Congress and the president, high-ranking military officials tended to follow those instructions which seemed best to them insofar as the situation permitted. For example, the Freedmen's Bureau Act and the Civil Rights Act, both enacted over Johnson's vetoes, gave the military the authority to act; Johnson's proclamations took it away. General Howard followed the congressional line with his letter recreating the bureau courts in September, but Johnson was able to countermand it in December. Meanwhile, the military commanders continued to act according to the letter's instructions, and Florida leaders regarded their acts as unconstitutional.

Having placed all their hopes with the president, the Floridians accepted his advice and rejected the Fourteenth Amendment, even after his overwhelming defeat at the polls. By that time, in their minds, he represented constitutional government as opposed to a group of Radicals intent on destroying that system. Negro suffrage was something they could never accept, and a number of Floridians again talked of emigrating to Brazil, Mexico, Texas, or California. But the *Tallahassee Floridian,* admitting the political situation seemed gloomy, advised its readers not to pack their bags for departure just yet.[66] Congressional Reconstruction came after a long delay during which Floridians had been led to believe that readmission would be quick and painless. Both the delays and its threatened severity made it unwelcome. But, just as the *Floridian* suggested, white Floridians were equal to its challenge when it came.

7

No Road Is in Condition To Pay Cash

Florida's transportation and communications facilities suffered from the Civil War and considerable rebuilding was necessary to restore them, but wartime destruction was not the only cause of inadequate transportation. The state was a largely undeveloped, frontier area when the war began. With nearly 60,000 square miles of real estate and a population of about 140,000 mostly concentrated in the northern counties along the Alabama and Georgia boundaries, Florida had communities separated by expanses of unsettled but potentially productive land. Until the 1850s Floridians had depended upon water transportation to and from New Orleans on the Gulf, and to Savannah, Charleston, and New York on the Atlantic. Although water transportation would remain important throughout the nineteenth century, the state gradually turned toward use of the railroads for several reasons.

First, the entire nation was beginning to rely on railroads as the basis of a modern transportation system. Also, a productive population in the Florida hinterland could not be adequately served by water because the rivers either did not flow in the right places or were not accessible because of shallow outlets. Furthermore, until more powerful ships were developed, the narrow, windy passage around the tip of Florida was too dangerous for low-cost, dependable water transportation. Finally, Florida leaders grasped the significance of railroads in a developing state at a time when both national and state governments were receptive to their suggestions.

David L. Yulee of Fernandina, usually regarded as the prime mover behind Florida's internal improvement legislation, was in the United States Senate when the national government began providing public land to the states to be used as incentive for developing internal transportation facilities. Some of the land was made available to Florida. The United States government was also willing to make direct grants to companies in addition to those provided by the state. To take advantage of the land, the state enacted comprehensive legislation calling for an east-west railroad connecting Jacksonville and Pensacola, another between Fernandina and several points on the peninsular Gulf Coast, an inland waterway from the Amelia River to Biscayne Bay, and several lesser facilities, all to be supported by state aid. The land comprised an Internal Improvement Fund to be administered by a Board of Trustees composed of the governor and several cabinet members. The board could grant land and pledge state credit to support private construction projects which would serve the public interest. The land was to be turned over to the private firms in increments as portions of their projects were completed. The companies were permitted to issue $10,000 in bonds for each mile of roadbed as construction progressed and the state assumed responsibility for them if a company defaulted. The railroad companies had to agree, however, to keep up the interest on the bonds and pay to the fund an annual installment amounting to 1 per cent of the amount of the bonds as a sinking fund for their redemption. As a first mortgage holder of the company, the Internal Improvement Board could take over and sell the company's property if it defaulted on the interest or the sinking fund.[1]

Under this law, several firms undertook construction in the late 1850s. Counties and municipalities often sold bonds and used the proceeds to buy stock of incipient railroad companies. But money was still scarce, and some firms ultimately surrendered partial ownership and control of their roads to New York investors in return for financial assistance.[2] When the Civil War began, some of these roads had just been completed and were beginning to operate. Most prominent of them was the Florida Railroad from Fernandina to Cedar Key, a 155-mile line built and managed by David L. Yulee. It had been chartered to build from Fernandina to Tampa Bay with a branch line to Cedar Key, but the branch was built first and was completed in 1861. Two other lines were built as parts of the connecting link between Jacksonville and Pensacola. Abraham S. Baldwin and others began constructing the Florida, Atlantic and Gulf Central Railroad from Jacksonville to Lake City in the mid-1850s. After 1857, its president and major promoter was John P. Sanderson, a prominent Jacksonville lawyer who had settled there in 1850. Popularly known as the Central Railroad, it was completed in early 1860, connecting with the Florida Railroad at Baldwin and with the Pensacola and Georgia at

Lake City. The Pensacola and Georgia, managed by Edward Houstoun, was completed from Lake City to Quincy in late 1861. It had acquired the older and moderately successful Tallahassee Railroad, a line from Tallahassee to St. Marks, which linked the Pensacola and Georgia to the Gulf port.[3] Other roads completed before the war were the Alabama and Florida from Pensacola northward to the Alabama line and the St. Johns Railroad from Tocoi to St. Augustine.

These roads were built when transportation men were still thinking of them as adjuncts to water transportation. They were intended to connect interior producing areas of middle Florida and southwestern Georgia to ports served by steamship lines; the Alabama and Florida was to connect Pensacola with the southern Alabama hinterland. The builders also envisioned these lines as connecting links between Gulf ports–accessible to steamers from New Orleans, Galveston, and Latin America–and either Savannah, Fernandina, or Jacksonville on the Atlantic coast. The idea of complete rail service to northern markets gained strength only in the post–Civil War era. Edward Houstoun envisioned the Pensacola and Georgia line as a profitable enterprise serving middle Florida and south Georgia producers through Savannah. This made him a competitor of Sanderson and his associates who wanted the Florida, Atlantic and Gulf Central to provide service for the same area through Jacksonville. He was also a potential competitor of Yulee's Florida Railroad for the traffic between the Gulf and Atlantic steamers. Because middle Florida and south Georgia comprised an economic unit in this period, Houstoun had also to consider the Atlantic and Gulf Railroad built from Savannah to Thomasville, Georgia, by John Screven and operating by 1860. Houstoun and Screven had both common and competing interests. If they linked the Pensacola and Georgia to the Atlantic and Gulf, their common interests would be served. Whether by choice or circumstance, these two men tended to cooperate during the Reconstruction era. This placed them in the position of promoting Savannah at the expense of Jacksonville, but Houstoun also cooperated with the East Florida people and the Florida, Atlantic and Gulf Central. Yulee's company was more concerned with developing and serving the unsettled upper Florida peninsula and providing the land connection between the Gulf and Atlantic ports. Yulee was wary of the Pensacola and Georgia which desired to tap the Gulf to Atlantic trade, but that road gave him little concern because St. Marks' port facilities were inadequate and the railroad was unable to build another Gulf outlet during the Reconstruction period.[4] All the lines were still developing when the war began. They were heavily encumbered with debts, owed partially to state, county, and municipal governments which had strained their financial resources in order to obtain necessary transportation. In the 1860s the railroad managers were too concerned with immediate survival to worry much about long-range competition.

During the war most of the lines remained in private hands, but they were subjected to heavy use without adequate maintenance or replacement of worn equipment. The Florida Railroad terminal facilities and bridges at both Cedar Key and Fernandina were destroyed, the Florida, Atlantic and Gulf Central suffered heavy damage at Jacksonville, and both were damaged when United States troops destroyed the Baldwin junction. In addition, the Confederate government took up about twenty-five miles of rails from the Alabama and Florida and nearly the same amount from the Florida Railroad. The rolling stock and the tracks of all the lines were in dilapidated condition in 1865. With empty treasuries and interest payments overdue to the Internal Improvement Fund, the roads required major expenditures before they could provide essential service or earn a profit.

When Confederate forces surrendered, the United States Army seized some of the privately owned roads; others had been acquired under the confiscation acts. Confederate-owned roads were taken as captured property.[5] The government held some of the roads briefly, even making improvements, but returned the property to its owners as soon as possible. The army continued using the roads without compensation for several months.[6] The small amount of Confederate-owned railroad property was made available to the private owners at favorable terms in order to promote the state's economic recovery and provide transportation for the military forces.[7] Both the United States Army's cooperation and the railroads' poor conditions were illustrated in late 1865 when General Foster furnished Provisional Governor Marvin water transportation for election returns and delegates to the 1865 constitutional convention. He also briefly permitted government teams to haul privately owned cotton from the interior fields to Gulf ports.[8]

The railroad owners and managers needed all the help they could get. There were no immediate prospects of income. County governments, forced to levy taxes for liquidating prewar railroad bonds, sometimes sued the roads or their guarantor, the Internal Improvement Fund, but, as they still desired transportation, most of them were patient. Some even issued new bonds to support rebuilding after the war. The Internal Improvement Board was considerate of this fact even as it acted to protect the state's interest under the law. Sometimes the board foreclosed and sold roads or declared land grants void because the roads had defaulted on agreements. Federal land grants were sometimes revoked for the same reason. Individuals holding stocks and bonds also tried to protect their interests. The result was a series of complex financial transactions, reorganizations, and forced sales following the war. Most of the sales were friendly, however, and were often requested by the railroad managers themselves to facilitate reorganizations.[9]

Since capital was unavailable in the state and some of the companies had already received financial support from New York, the managers looked northward again in 1865. To enhance Edward Houstoun's chances of securing a loan for the Pensacola and Georgia, the national government dropped its confiscation suit against the road in August 1865. Houstoun had already bought new crossties in June and in November he purchased five engines and materials for boxcars. Daily trains were running from Quincy to Lake City by November.[10] But Houstoun failed to procure iron rails because cash was demanded in payment and "no road in the South [was] in condition just [then] to pay cash."[11] This deprived both the railroad and the state of a connection to Savannah. Throughout most of 1866, the "quickest and most direct route north" from Tallahassee was by rail to Quincy and then by hack to Albany, Georgia, where northbound trains were running.[12]

The Pensacola and Georgia had been connected with Savannah by rail during the war. The Atlantic and Gulf had built southward from Lawton, Georgia, to the Florida line to meet a road built by the Pensacola and Georgia from Live Oak. The latter company had been unable to obtain rails and, after much delay and endless litigation, the Confederate government took up about twenty-five miles of Florida Railroad track despite the adamant protests of David Yulee. When the war ended, Yulee demanded his iron back, and both the government and the Pensacola and Georgia agreed to its return. Houstoun was anxious to restore the connection and was encouraged to do so by middle Floridians whose principal newspaper assured Fernandina and Jacksonville that they would have nothing to fear from the Live Oak to Lawton line.[13] Jacksonville railroad men, merchants, and shippers disagreed with good reason. The *Savannah News and Herald* encouraged Savannah citizens to invest $75,000 in the connector, claiming it would draw to Savannah 50,000 bales of cotton from middle Florida and make the city the supply center for most of Florida's population. Atlantic and Gulf president John Screven added that "the most valuable part of the trade of Florida would tend to Savannah over this connection." Screven and Houstoun were successful. Praising the two men for raising money under the most difficult circumstances, the *Tallahassee Floridian* announced that trains would be passing over the restored line by October. As an afterthought, it added, "Of course, this will also benefit the East Florida ports, too," but it did not explain how. By October 22, 1866, the connector was completed as a part of the

Atlantic and Gulf Railroad and service began from Quincy and Tallahassee to Savannah.[14]

While they cooperated on the connector, the two companies were also competitors. The Atlantic and Gulf had already graded to Bainbridge and planned a line from there to St. Andrews Bay on the Florida Gulf Coast, "where a very important city is anticipated to spring up," according to an enthusiastic Marianna citizen.[15] The Pensacola and Georgia recognized the threat and was anxious to build westward at least to the Apalachicola River, but it was unable to finance any new construction. The St. Andrews Bay to Bainbridge line failed to materialize, however, and West Floridians despaired of a rail connection with the Atlantic through either Georgia or Florida. The failure inspired a serious movement for annexation of west Florida to Alabama in the late 1860s, and the threatened secession became a major factor behind Republican Governor Harrison Reed's attempts to secure a line to Pensacola. There was also an effort to build a line from Albany, Georgia, through Thomasville to Monticello, and another to draw south Georgia commerce to St. Marks by a Thomasville to Tallahassee road. Both failed for lack of financing.[16]

The Pensacola and Georgia was finally overwhelmed by financial difficulties. It earned a small gross profit between 1865 and 1868, but the surplus was insufficient to pay overdue interest on its bonds and the sinking fund installments required by state law. In January 1867 and again in January 1868, the Internal Improvement Board agreed to assist the road in paying back interest, but when the company was still unable to meet interest and sinking fund payments in early 1869, the board took over the road and sold it.[17] Even then it was a friendly sale arranged by Houstoun and George W. Swepson, a controversial North Carolina railroad promoter whose questionable Florida activities subsequently caused the Harrison Reed administration tremendous embarrassment.

The Florida, Atlantic and Gulf Central was even less successful than the Pensacola and Georgia in recovering from the war. First headed by Silas L. Niblack, then by Ferdinand McLeod, and finally by Franklin Dibble, it was unable to restore adequate service or pay its debts by 1867. Running sixty miles from Jacksonville to Lake City, the road depended on its relationship to the Pensacola and Georgia for financial success. The earliest of several attempts to join the two lines occurred after railroad personnel refused to transport Freedmen's Bureau supplies or General Foster's horse. Exasperated, the general seriously considered taking over the line and allowing the Pensacola and Georgia management to operate it. He finally dropped the matter, but the road soon encountered more serious difficulties. Like the Pensacola and Georgia, it asked for and received Internal Improvement Board assistance with its January 1867 interest payment. But when it failed to pay the required sinking fund installment, the road was advertised for sale on September 4, 1867. To avoid the sale John P. Sanderson and the road's new president, Franklin Dibble—a Jacksonville banker whose brother was an important New York financier—sought a consolidation with the Pensacola and Georgia. At the request of Wilkinson Call, attorney for the company, the sale was postponed and Edward Houstoun tentatively agreed to an informal combination of the two roads, but the terms apparently did not satisfy all parties. John Sanderson's law partner, Edward M. L'Engle, sought an injunction on behalf of George Swepson against the sale. The injunction was soon dissolved and the road was sold on March 4, 1868, to William E. Jackson and associates for $111,000.[18]

Houstoun, who was simultaneously negotiating with Swepson to sell his own railroad, emerged from the March sale in a strong position. He became Jackson's agent and also acted as agent for the Internal Improvement Board in handling the purchase arrangements. In July the Florida legislature incorporated the Florida Central Railroad Company with the same rights as the former Florida, Atlantic and Gulf Central Company. The new firm took over the former's property and George Swepson emerged as its principal stockholder. Houstoun had acted as his agent in buying the controlling interest. In August the Central Railroad was leased to the Pensacola and Georgia for ninety-nine years with the first year rent free.[19] In the reorganization Franklin Dibble was forced out of the road's management and spent the next several months maneuvering to regain control.

By late 1868 the combined Pensacola and Georgia and Florida Central seemed to be working out an adequate schedule of passenger, mail, and freight service from Quincy to Jacksonville with steamer connections from St. Marks to all points on the Gulf and with Brock's line of riverboats on the St. Johns. There was also a regular schedule to Savannah over the Live Oak to Lawton connector.[20] But Houstoun was still short of capital to pay his debts, and West Floridians were demanding a railroad through their section. With Governor Reed's administration under pressure to build the road westward or face the possibility of a secession movement, the Internal Improvement Board notified Houstoun that the road would be sold on March 20, 1869. With ample notice he worked out the arrangement with Swepson.

The Florida Railroad had suffered more physical damage during the war than the other roads and its recovery was hampered because its president was imprisoned after the war, as were other prominent Confederates. Before Yulee's release in early 1866, the New York owners had already begun rebuilding and reorganizing the road. Marshall O. Roberts, a major stockholder, had retained Lyman D. Stickney to protect the company's interest before the war ended. Although some of its Fernandina property was lost through direct tax sales and more was tied up in lengthy litigation, its owners were determined to put the road back in operation. Some of the New York investors tried to depose Yulee, but Edward N. Dickerson, their representative in Florida Railroad Company affairs, insisted that he be retained. Upon his release from prison, Yulee went to New York to obtain financing for the road's repair. Employing nearly 300 workers in 1866–67, the company rebuilt wharves, bridges, and other facilities at Fernandina and Cedar Key and repaired or replaced the track and roadbed along the line. The iron rails repossessed from the Live Oak to Lawton connector were replaced between Baldwin and Fernandina. Weekly service was restored from Baldwin to Cedar Key in July 1865, but the bridge to Amelia Island was not rebuilt until early 1867.[21]

As the repair work progressed, Yulee and the New York stockholders agreed on financial reorganization and the future control of the road. Yulee explained the company's status to the Internal Improvement Board, which ordered a sale for November 1, 1866, at Gainesville. The road was bought by Isaac K. Roberts who asked that the deed be made out to Edward N. Dickerson. Thus ownership of the road remained the same as before, but Dickerson became president and Yulee vice-president, with both to be active policy-makers. The sale removed the heavy debts of the company and permitted it to start again under the same management and ownership, at the expense of bona fide creditors. It also gave the dissatisfied creditors legal cause to demand redress from the Internal Improvement Board rather than from the company.[22]

At the sale several claims against the road were made public. The sale had brought 20 per cent of the amount of the road's outstanding first mortgage bonds and the proceeds were used to take up all the bonds held by individuals who would accept twenty cents on the dollar for them. Numerous bondholders refused to settle and several suits followed, but the most significant was the case of Francis Vose—of Vose, Livingston, and Company—an iron manufacturer who had sold rails to Yulee in the 1850s. Vose asked the United States court for an injunction prohibiting the Internal Improvement Board from granting or selling any state lands until he was paid the full face value and accrued interest of his bonds. He argued that the state lands had been pledged as security for the bonds and that there would be no way for him to satisfy his claim if the lands were sold. His reasoning was accepted but the injunction was not issued until 1871, during the Reed administration.[23] Meanwhile, the Florida Railroad Company offered to accept the bonds at face value for land it owned along the line.[24] While Conservative David Walker was in office, the

Internal Improvement Board remained free to dispose of public lands according to state law. About 750,000 acres were used to buy up the outstanding Florida Railroad first mortgage bonds or past due interest coupons. Nearly 250,000 acres went to Edward N. Dickerson for coupons he held. Many bondholders accepted the twenty cents on the dollar offer, some accepted land, and Vose's heirs were ultimately paid full face value and interest in cash. But a large number of bonds were still outstanding as late as 1882 and for a decade Florida had been prevented from using its lands to encourage internal improvement.[25]

Yulee had always been interested in developing the state by attracting settlers. With huge quantities of land along the railroad right-of-way, he and the other managers became large-scale real estate dealers. Unfortunately, they sold the land for as little as eighteen cents an acre and the road never earned a profit from serving the communities between Fernandina and Cedar Key. For a time, Yulee's goal of providing a land connection between steamship lines on the Gulf and those on the Atlantic was met. By 1868 the Florida Railroad was regularly connecting with the Alliance steamers at Cedar Key. The Alliance line ran five ships between Havana and New Orleans. From the latter the steamers brought syrup, sugar, hides, and bacon; from Havana, cigars and tobacco; and from Key West and Tampa Bay, long-staple cotton and sponges. The Cedar Key facility included a 500-foot dock, with a 400-foot warehouse. It extended over the water with a railroad trestle running along one side. The steamers pulled up on the other side. Freight from each carrier was unloaded, rolled across the warehouse, and loaded on the other side. In the late 1860s there were sometimes as many as five steamers waiting to unload. Three administrative officials were employed by the road at Cedar Key and several regular stevedores were paid $23 per month. Extra hands were paid fifteen cents an hour.[26]

Even the Gulf-to-Atlantic trade was insufficient for the road to earn a profit during Reconstruction. Often criticized for poor service and conservative management, the road made repairs only when absolutely necessary. But, unlike the other lines, the Florida Railroad did not increase its indebtedness during the period, and it was not constantly entangled in litigation and receiverships as they were. In 1872 the road became the Atlantic, Gulf and West India Transit Railway Company with Dickerson and Yulee still in control.[27]

Before the war the Alabama and Florida Railroad (of Florida) was completed from Pensacola to the Alabama line, a distance of about forty-five miles. About three miles south of Pollard, Alabama, it connected with the Alabama and Florida Railroad (of Alabama) which ran to Montgomery. The Alabama line remained essentially intact during the war, but the

Florida road lost its rolling stock and about twenty-six miles of rails to Confederate confiscation. Some of the iron was used on other roads deemed more useful by the Confederacy; about 500,000 pounds of the iron was used for armor on gun batteries in Mobile Bay.[28] The Confederate government gave a receipt for about eleven miles of the iron, with which O. M. Avery, president of the company, purchased staple goods. In 1865 the road had about 17 miles of track, 650 bales of cotton, and about $2,000 worth of sugar and syrup.

After the war, Avery began suits to recover the iron and obtained a loan in New York to rebuild. In early 1866 he obtained permission to remove the iron from the Mobile Bay batteries, but it had to be rolled before it could be used on the tracks.[29] One engine and eleven freight cars were purchased from the United States and rebuilding began. The New York loans were inadequate and work stalled in late 1866, except for a small grading crew under the supervision of Warren Q. Dow, a Pensacola surveyor. In November 1867, the company petitioned for and received a bankruptcy judgment. James W. Hall of Pensacola was assigned to manage the road's affairs under the judgment. The city of Pensacola owned five-sevenths of the company stock and was just as anxious after the war for rail connections with Montgomery as it had been before. It offered its 2,500 shares of stock as a bonus to anyone willing to reconstruct the road. Augustus E. Maxwell was appointed to notify the road's first mortgage bondholders in New York of the offer in the hope of additional aid.[30]

The road's financial future remained doubtful during 1867. Cornelius Vanderbilt was rumored to be interested, but the Alabama and Florida was finally sold on March 25, 1868, to Ruter, Millington and Company of Kentucky, who reorganized it as the Pensacola and Louisville Railroad Company. They paid $55,000 for the road and equipment. Dow estimated that the movable property was worth $250,000 but that company debts totaled more than $500,000. He pessimistically observed that the road could be placed in profitable operation if the buyers were prepared to invest one million dollars. Two shiploads of iron, another engine, and additional cars were brought in by late 1868. In February 1869 the track was usable to Molino Mills, twenty-three miles north of Pensacola.[31]

The Internal Improvement Act authorized use of public land to encourage inland water transportation as well as railroads. In 1866 Hubbard L. Hart—a northern capitalist who had settled in Palatka and invested in sawmills, hotels, and river steamers with which he had served the Confederacy—received a 40,000-acre grant for clearing a navigable channel in the Oklawaha River. Completed in June 1868, this project is a good example of the way the Internal Improvement Fund was supposed to work: Hart was enabled to extend his river steamer service into the

Oklawaha, and the state gained a transportation link between Jacksonville and the agriculturally productive Marion County area by way of the Oklawaha and St. Johns rivers. The land grant enabled Hart to defray his expenses and possibly make a profit by selling to settlers, whose immigration benefited the state by increasing its sparse population. Hart's steamers *Kate* and *Dictator* had been running between Palatka and Charleston since early 1866. Ocala citizens were happy to see water transportation coming near their city since they had previously been obliged to ride by hack to the Florida Railroad station at Gainesville. The boats on the Oklawaha—the *Lollie Boy, Silver Spring,* and *Oklawaha*—were built especially for that stream. They were boxlike vessels propelled by a small stern wheel recessed in the hull to protect it from snags.[32]

To obtain the inland waterway on the east coast mentioned in the 1855 legislation, the Internal Improvement Board sold the Florida Canal and Inland Transportation Company 250,000 acres at five cents per acre on condition that it complete the waterway from the Amelia River to Jupiter Inlet, using the St. Johns and other natural streams wherever possible.[33] This company failed but others took its place. The Internal Improvement Board also gave aid to a south Florida development project by William H. Gleason. He was from Wisconsin and later became a Republican politician. Florida conservatives then denounced him as a "carpetbagger," but prior to his political activism, Gleason had been praised as a man of vision and ability whose presence was welcome in the undeveloped state. The Walker administration granted him concessions identical to those which conservatives subsequently criticized when granted by Republicans. In 1865 Gleason made an extended tour of South Florida in the company of Colonel George F. Thompson, a Freedmen's Bureau agent who was looking for a satisfactory site to settle a Negro colony.[34] The settlement never materialized, but Gleason became interested in draining and developing swampland on the lower east coast. The board authorized him to drain the land east of Lake Okeechobee and southeast of the Everglades adjacent to the Caloosahatchie River. For every 50,000 cubic feet of ditch he dug, Gleason was permitted to buy 640 acres of land for forty dollars.

Floridians fortunate enough to be served by railroads or river boats in the hinterland were still dependent on ocean-going vessels for access to markets. The railroad companies, commission merchants, newspapers, and other interested parties encouraged new or established steamship companies to provide scheduled service to Florida ports, but it was several years before such a system was accomplished. Soon after the war, Samuel Swann wrote a Cuban business acquaintance that lumbermen at Cedar Key and along the Florida Railroad were anxious for ships to carry cargoes from that port to both New York and Havana. "If your vessels want freight you might send them to Cedar Key and be sure of a cargo of lumber," he said.[35] In 1865 the United States government was using several privately owned steamers. Although it continued leasing some of them, the army returned most to their owners. An example was the *Sylvan Shore* operated from Fernandina by Captain James W. Tucker. Available for charter to any port, he usually moved between Savannah, Fernandina, Jacksonville, and Picolata. The latter port was on the St. Johns, connecting with St. Augustine by way of an eighteen-mile stage line. The *Lizzie Baker, City Point,* and *Nick King* also operated on the same route, which was called the "Outside Line." It was discontinued about 1877 when the "Inside Line" was opened to Savannah, thus avoiding the open sea. In early 1866 Hubbard Hart put the *Kate* and *Dictator* on a schedule between Palatka and Charleston, serving all intermediate points. The *St. Mary* was retained by General Foster and operated as a government transport between St. Marks and New Orleans. The *Governor Marvin* was purchased by James McKay of Tampa for use as a cattle steamer between south Florida and Cuba, but in 1866 it was used mostly as a government vessel. Although the two steamers were primarily for government use, they accommodated the public by taking both passengers and cargo when no other transportation was available.[36]

By March 1866, a line of steamers was plying between New York and Apalachicola, with *Linda* and *Key West* leaving the latter port every two weeks. One-way passage was sixty dollars.[37] Apalachicola had a shallow harbor, but it was accessible by the Chattahoochee, Flint, and Apalachicola rivers far into southern Alabama and Georgia. Having been a major cotton shipping port before the war, the small town continued handling a large number of bales for a short while after 1865. By early 1867 river traffic had increased to four or five steamers making weekly trips to and from Apalachicola. The city was also trading with New Orleans. In February 1866, a group of Tallahassee and Quincy men organized the Florida Line and purchased the *J. L. Smallwood* in New York. It was to run regularly between St. Marks, Apalachicola, and New Orleans. However, within a year the line was operating entirely between New Orleans and Apalachicola because of the diminishing quantity of freight to and from St. Marks and the port's navigational inadequacies. St. Marks was then served by the *Spray,* a small steamer owned by Daniel Ladd of Newport, which met the Florida Line steamer at Apalachicola three times a month. Apalachicola's importance diminished after the Atlantic and Gulf Railroad connected Bainbridge, on the Flint River, with Savannah in 1867.[38]

By early 1867 the Alliance Line—also known as the Florida Mail Line because it had a government mail contract—was operating the S.S. *Alliance* on a monthly schedule, leaving New Orleans on the seventeenth and Key West on the second. Intermediate stops were Pensacola, Apalachicola, St. Marks, Cedar Key, and Tampa. By 1868 the bureau agent at Tampa reported two steamers stopping regularly each month and the anticipation of four more. There were also unscheduled schooners stopping there en route to both New Orleans and New York.[39] At the same time the agent was unable to obtain transportation to Brooksville in the interior except by the mail vehicle.

In 1867 the New York Steamship Company inaugurated service between New York and Fernandina. A little later two large lines began regular service to Key West. C. H. Mallory and Company had a mail contract for its New York and Key West Steamship Line which claimed to have two steamers a week stopping at the island city by 1871. The Clyde Line, also carrying mail, began stopping there about the same time on its run between New York and Galveston, Texas. Neither line stopped at Florida mainland ports until the 1880s.[40]

In the early years after the war, Florida was connected to Gulf and Atlantic market cities only by unscheduled steamer service, with a few exceptions. Schooners carried lumber and other cargo as well as passengers to many Western Hemisphere and European markets in addition to domestic cities.[41] Service was generally inadequate. The state population was too small and too widely scattered for private corporations to provide suitable service and earn a profit. The dangers of the passage through the Florida channel hampered ocean shipping. Wrecking remained a profitable enterprise at Key West throughout the Reconstruction era, and marine insurance was expensive. Ships in trouble were at the mercy of wreckers and judicial redress was difficult. So many residents of the south Florida judicial district were engaged in wrecking or some related field that it was nearly impossible to obtain impartial juries.[42]

Yulee's idea of a railroad portage across the peninsula was a sound one, and might have paid dividends had the Florida Railroad been able to expand its service and improve efficiency. In 1868 inland shippers on the road were having to wait for service because of "the scarcity of cars and the almost daily demand for them to transfer freight between the [Gulf and Atlantic] steamers."[43]

The United States government eventually provided navigational assistance and rescue stations along the Florida east coast, but little was done in the early postwar years. Two schooners loaded with oranges for Savannah were wrecked in 1868 at Mosquito Inlet because there was no lighthouse or channel marker. River and harbor improvements also lagged. Nothing was done about the hazardous St. Johns bar until after 1878.

Navigation into St. Augustine was a game of chance. The independently owned steamer *Cricket*, bound from New York to Key West and forced by a fuel shortage to stop at the ancient city, followed the buoys only to find that the channel had changed. The *Cricket* was wrecked and its captain lost $10,000. St. Augustine was usually approached by stage from Picolata during the period. St. Marks, the anticipated Gulf outlet for the Pensacola and Georgia Railroad, did not have enough water to be accessible by steamers. Even before the war, most ships approaching the port had been obliged to anchor at Spanish Hole and transfer cargoes to lighters. It also had unsatisfactory customs collectors for awhile. The problem became so acute in 1866 that shipowners were increasing freight rates to St. Marks and "it is almost impossible to get any vessel which has been here to return."[44] The problem included illegal fees and lengthy delays in entering and clearing. Similar conditions existed at Apalachicola.

Most Florida towns were connected with the rest of the world by telegraph service soon after the Civil War. In 1865 the telegraph lines had been seized and operated by the United States Military Telegraph, connecting north Florida towns as far west as Quincy with points in the United States and Canada. The army soon got out of the communications business and both private individuals and public officials sought to expand facilities. The 1865–66 legislature incorporated the International Ocean Telegraph Company to establish communications between Cuba and the mainland.[45] By August 1867, the company had installed a cable from Havana to Key West and a land line through Punta Rassa to Gainesville. From Gainesville the line was built on Florida Railroad right-of-way to Baldwin. From there it ran along the Florida, Atlantic and Gulf Central Railroad to Lake City where it connected with Western Union. There was a branch line to St. Augustine. The railroads furnished the right-of-way and free transportation for men and materials. In return they were allowed to send railroad messages without charge. The rights and privileges of the International Ocean Telegraph Company were acquired by the Peninsular Telegraph Company, a New York firm formed to build and operate a line from New York to Key West.[46] The change resulted in a suit by the Florida Railroad Company, but the court upheld the telegraph firm which continued operating in Florida.

When Harrison Reed was removed from the direct tax commission in 1863, he had been appointed by Postmaster General Montgomery Blair as a special postal officer with authority to re-establish mail service in Florida and Georgia. The position enabled the energetic Reed to build a wide and favorable acquaintance with conservative Floridians who appreciated the way he handled postal affairs. United States postage stamps were available in Quincy by May 1865, although many Florida towns had to wait slightly longer.[47] Reed's greatest problems were lack of transportation for the mail and too few men who could take the oath required of postmasters. He addressed the 1865–66 legislature, asking members to recommend suitable persons. Since so few men were available, he appointed many women. By July 1866, the conservative *Tallahassee Floridian* was congratulating Reed for opening fifty-eight post offices, including all the most important ones. He contracted with carriers between all the interior towns and along the coast. In addition to the steamers which carried mail between ports, he engaged stages, hack lines, and contract riders to supplement the railroads in the interior.[48]

Despite political confusion and financial stringency during the years between the end of the war and the inauguration of Republican Governor Harrison Reed in July 1868, transportation and communications facilities were restored to their prewar conditions and extended slightly. The Live Oak to Lawton railroad connection and telegraphic lines were added. Although water and rail transportation remained inadequate, much of Florida was sparsely settled. Extension of transportation facilities and settlement of south Florida were mutually dependent and both received the attention of state officials of all political persuasions for years. The Republican administrations were subsequently condemned by opposition politicians and historians for the way they handled public land and state aid to internal development, but most of their difficulties were inherited from the prewar period and the conservative administration of David Walker. Both sides made generous land grants to private railroad and canal companies, but the Vose injunction had grown out of transactions between the Internal Improvement Board and the Florida Railroad Company in 1866, long before the Republicans came to power. The activities of the Internal Improvement Board before and after July 1868 were similar whether it was staffed by Conservatives or Republicans.

8

It Is Not Considered Disgraceful To Work

The accommodation of plantation agriculture to a free labor system was probably the paramount problem facing Floridians after the Civil War, yet many individuals were not directly affected by the disappearance of slavery. Hundreds of Florida farmers after the war continued doing what they had always done, tilling the land with their own hands or perhaps with assistance from family members. The majority of slaveholders had also been obliged to work in the fields themselves. Before 1860, there were 6,396 farms and 5,152 slaveholders in the state. While 1,244 farmers had no slaves at all, another 3,368 had fewer than ten. There were 808 owners of more than 20 slaves, and only 205 had more than 50. More than half of all farms—3,514—were under 50 acres in size. Only 1,720 were larger than 100 acres, and those over 500 acres numbered 288. After the war the proportionate number of small farms increased. With about 10,000 farms in 1870, Florida had about 42,000 people engaged in agriculture. Nearly 12,000 of them were farmers, planters, or plantation managers. By 1870 about 30 per cent of Florida's total working population was employed outside agriculture, in manufacturing, trade, and transportation, or in professional and personal services.[1]

Though small in number, the 808 planters who had each owned 20 or more slaves played a significant role in postwar economic and social adjustments. Their slave property had accounted for nearly three of every five slaves in the state. Their actions after the war had a tremendous influence on the rest of society. Some believed that free Negroes would not work, and some threatened to either emigrate to South America or give up planting for other activities; but the majority seemed willing to try cultivating on a large scale using free labor, although they often regarded the undertaking as an experiment. With few alternatives available to them and encouraged by the military commanders, a number of planters contracted with their former slaves on the basis of monthly wages or shares of crops as soon as the war ended in 1865. Some crops were already in the ground when this occurred. Although some planters took advantage of the former slaves and the Freedmen's Bureau later set aside a few of the obviously unfair contracts, the system worked comparatively well and a good crop was made, amounting in volume to about half the annual prewar production. Poor transportation facilities to the port towns and bureaucratic delays from cotton tax collections were often forgotten because of the high prices in 1865. Merchants anxious to rebuild their businesses offered to handle the crops and advance credit until they were sold.[2]

Considerable distrust still existed between freedmen and planters at the end of 1865 and rumors of a violent uprising by the Negroes caused concern, but most white Floridians agreed with military officials who thought the rumors unfounded. Many planters advertised their lands for sale, others spoke of replacing blacks with Chinese or European laborers, and still others adamantly refused to contract with their former slaves. But, despite these exceptions, most men who needed hired labor realized that they would have to rely on freedmen. Under the supervision of the Freedmen's Bureau and with guidance from a contract labor law enacted by the state legislature, employers and employees made agreements for the 1866 crop year.

There were differing opinions among planters and laborers in various sections of the state about the desirability of wages as opposed to sharecropping. Because of the shortage of circulating currency, most of the contracts provided for compensating laborers with a share of the crop. The terms of these contracts varied, but workers usually received from a fourth to a third of the crop. Those who furnished their own provisions and equipment received more, but most depended on the planters for subsistence. At first most worked in gangs, a system which the blacks disliked because it resembled slavery and the planters found unsatisfactory because there was no way to distinguish between those who worked well and those who did not. Some contracting parties on both sides preferred a money wage, but even when that was the stipulated form of remuneration, payment was usually in goods drawn in advance from the planters' stores. A Marion County planter explained why he preferred the money wage. Paying his hands from $6 to $10 per month in goods from his store, he made 75 to 110 per cent profit on store items and "consequently my labor is much cheaper than those who give them an interest in the crop."[3]

The planters were usually too generous with credit from the stores whether they contracted on money wages or shares of the crop. While the Negroes worked well, nearly every observer noted that they had not yet learned to manage their meager resources. Instead of frugally managing their incomes, which even at best were inadequate to sustain a family, the freedmen tended to buy unnecessary items at high credit prices and have the purchases recorded on a credit ledger for future settlement. The ledger was the only record. Often the year-end settlements left them with no money or even with a debt to be carried over.[4]

Some planters showed a preference for the sharecrop system because it tended to keep the workers on the land until the crop was harvested. At the same time, there were cases of wage-paying employers who dismissed workers during the slack summer season, leaving them with no income.[5] In this transition period, the Freedmen's Bureau received complaints from both sides about labor contracts, and it intervened impartially to see that freedmen fulfilled their obligations and to prevent employers from taking advantage of them.

The good crop yields and high cotton prices of 1865 encouraged the planters to continue the free labor experiment, but, unfortunately, too many people turned to the single crop as their major source of income. Concentration on cotton as a cash crop was based on expectations of continuing high yields and prices. Desiring to increase profits by expanding cotton acreage in 1866, planters discovered that they faced a labor shortage. Most of the freedmen who left their homes when the war ended had returned by early 1866, but they were too few to meet the demand for field hands. Many Negro women decided to remain at home rather than work in the field as they had been compelled to do as slaves. Both planters and bureau agents decried their refusal to work for wages. A prominent Floridian, exasperated by the scarcity of workers, criticized the women for "playing lady."[6]

Florida planters met the labor shortage in two ways. Some called on their neighbors to agree not to rent lands to Negroes, leaving the freedmen no choice but to hire out. Planters from Jefferson, Columbia, Alachua, and Marion counties sent agents to South Carolina to recruit field hands. Agreements were made whereby the planters paid transportation costs for Negroes hired to work during the crop year. Several hundred Negroes were brought to Florida from South Carolina and Georgia. The 1866 Homestead Act attracted numerous others from the same areas. A colony of freedmen was brought by Milton Hawks in early 1867 for his Florida Land and Lumber Company. When the company failed most of the freedmen went to work on the cotton farms. Between four and five thousand Negroes came to Florida in 1866 and 1867. The labor supply was augmented by the immigration, but many immigrants and Florida freedmen took up homesteads. Complaints of labor shortages continued through the 1860s. Some Georgia and South Carolina planters expressed alarm that the exodus would leave them without enough laborers to cultivate their own land.[7]

The shortage of capital remained acute, but merchants in most interior towns and all ports made arrangements with New York or other mercantile and financial interests for supplies and outlets for cotton. The merchants, many of whom were planters themselves, sold goods on credit to planters and farmers, hoping for good crops and stable cotton prices. Cotton factors at Apalachicola, Tallahassee, Jacksonville, and Savannah offered to pay the federal cotton tax and advance credit against anticipated proceeds from cotton sales. They offered to ship to New York, New Orleans, Charleston, and Liverpool, although the majority shipped to New York. More than 100,000 bales of cotton were shipped through Apalachicola in 1866 and that port remained active for several more years, but the other three cities become more important as the Gulf port declined. St. Marks also declined after the Civil War. With rail connections to both Jacksonville and Savannah, Tallahassee merchants divided their economic loyalties between the two cities. Revenue collector Lemuel Wilson recognized the importance of Savannah to north Florida growers and merchants when he agreed to accept bonds for the federal cotton tax at Live Oak where the railroad connected with Savannah, as well as at St. Marks and Jacksonville.[8]

By the time planters began making labor contracts and arranging credit for the 1866 season, an elaborate credit system had developed, making planters and farmers, agricultural laborers, local merchants, port merchants, and New York financiers jointly and severally dependent on continued good crops and prices. When heavy rains and caterpillars damaged the crops of 1866 and 1867 and prices dropped, Florida merchants, planters, and laborers were adversely affected. Tightening credit strained the emerging system of free agricultural labor. When Congress passed the bankruptcy act on March 2, 1867, many Floridians took advantage of it.[9]

The plight of Adam Eichelberger, an Ocala merchant and Marion County planter, is indicative of the problem. Encouraged in 1865 by the high cotton prices, Eichelberger went into planting and merchandising on a large scale. Ocala was a favorable location since Marion County was one of the state's most populous and productive agricultural areas. Borrowing heavily in Charleston and New York, he planted large cotton and corn acreage and sold quantities of merchandise on credit to other planters who advanced provisions to their laborers. With only a partial crop and moderate cotton prices in 1866, Eichelberger made no profit, but his losses were minor. He also held notes, although they were temporarily uncollectible, from planters and laborers who had purchased provisions on credit. Viewing the 1866 situation as exceptional, Eichelberger and his customers—now his debtors—expected to recoup in 1867. He bought more provisions on credit and planted another crop while extending more credit to others.

For most Marion County planters and others throughout the state, the 1867 crop was a miserable failure, making it impossible for Eichelberger to collect on many of the notes he held at his store. With $100,000 due him, the Ocala merchant planned to make another crop and sell to other planters again in 1868, but he was unable to meet his own obligations to Cohen, Henckel and Company of Charleston, E. Simpson and Company of New York, and other wholesale merchants from whom he had purchased on credit. Although his debts and assets were roughly in balance in late 1867, Eichelberger had to meet his own notes while he could not collect the money owed him. It became necessary to seek an additional loan of $40,000 to meet the emergency. Explaining that he had enough corn and fodder, mules and wagons, and other equipment to make a crop, as well as a good stock of goods in his store, the beleaguered merchant needed to pay his matured mortgages and buy bacon for his workers. He was willing to pledge all the notes due him, his 1868 crop, and his property for a $40,000 loan but no one would loan him the money.

Eichelberger's lawyer said he had not expected a loan under the circumstances. The merchant was "in a bad box," unable to meet his payments, unable to collect money owed him, and the 1867 crop—still in the field—was too small to meet the overdue mortgages. With no money circulating in the county, the lawyer thought Eichelberger could not survive "unless his creditors are more generous than they should be." To protect himself as much as possible, Eichelberger sued on all his claims and sold his plantations, mules, and equipment. At the same time his creditors sued him and several judgments were outstanding against his assets in early 1868. With the situation unsatisfactory to all involved, a compromise was worked out whereby Eichelberger should carry on his business and continue to plant with all his earnings going to his creditors for the next three years. If his debts remained unpaid at that time, all his property was to be sold. Eichelberger was unable to overcome his difficulties and was a poor man by 1871.[10]

Marion County planter John Taylor had contracted with his laborers on a sharecrop basis and furnished them provisions on credit. After the 1867 crop failure he had trouble settling accounts with the freedmen who were worried about feeding themselves during the winter. Hard pressed himself to make ends meet, Taylor was adamant in forcing some of his workers to turn over his share of their potato crop.[11] At the end of the year they still owed him over $4,000, and he was reluctant to try borrowing for another crop the following year, although he was ultimately more successful than Eichelberger. Unlike many of his neighbors, Taylor believed in diversified farming. In addition to the usual cotton and corn, he grew potatoes, made sugar from his own cane, salted and pickled beef from his herds, and made wine. He was less vulnerable to the vagaries of the cotton market, but still suffered financal difficulty in the late 1860s.

Owning several plantations, Taylor tried to reduce his operations by selling or leasing parts of his land. No major sale was made, but he did lease a tract and took on a partner. S. A. McDowell of New York bought a half interest in Taylor's planting interests for $5,000 cash and a note for $11,000. When McDowell failed to meet his note, Taylor foreclosed. The New Yorker complained that Taylor had assured him the note could be repaid from profits earned: "He is robbing me," McDowell declared. Taylor also became displeased with Negro labor and the contract system and joined an unsuccessful movement to induce white laborers to Florida. He ultimately survived as a planter, however, by relying on the freedmen, sharecropping, and the crop lien.[12]

The financial problem was statewide. A struggling dry goods merchant gave up in Marianna after 1867 and moved to Jacksonville. He found no market for his wares in Jackson County because "every dollar the farmers had was used to buy provisions." Simon Katzenberg, a Madison County merchant, was equally hard pressed but tried to stay in business. With New York creditors pressing for payment, Katzenberg explained that he had plenty of notes secured by growing crops in 1867 to satisfy the claims against him, but until the crop was sold there was not enough money in Madison County to make a suit worthwhile. Apparently his logic was lost on some creditors. Carter, Kirkland and Company told their lawyer to collect if he could—"we will be willing to make him a bankrupt without a moment's hesitation."[13] Katzenberg's financial problems were compounded in 1868 when his store was burned, allegedly by arsonists who disagreed with his policy of selling goods to local Negroes.

Foreclosures were common after the 1867 crop failure, but creditors were often hesitant because forced sales offered poor prospects of satisfying their claims. A Tampa lawyer advised his client that there was scarcely enough cash "in this whole country" to settle half of his $6,000 claim against a local citizen. Similar warnings came from Hernando, Hamilton, and Madison counties. The Freedmen's Bureau agent in Madison County reported that several planters had lost $7,000 to $8,000 and merchants as much as $70,000 to $80,000. The problem was intensified because formerly high cotton prices and prospects of a good crop had led merchants and planters to be generous with credit. When the crops failed, the freedmen ended up in debt and planters and merchants lost their credit. With credit gone, planters were unable to hire and merchants could not advance loans locally for the next year's crop.[14]

Bureau agents castigated the credit system for its effect on the freedmen. Unaccustomed to planning ahead and finding planters "too liberal" with their advances, freedmen squandered their earnings on unnecessary items. Colonel Sprague, observing in early 1868 that many cotton planters were bankrupt, declared that Florida soil would not support a wage labor system. "Small farms will succeed in Florida, plantations are at an end," he predicted. As he closed his business in Savannah and departed for New York, an unsuccessful merchant wrote his Florida associate that "the south is down down, and I fear [it] will be a long time before she will get up again."[15]

A constant irritant in the plantation areas was the widespread larceny of livestock and crops, acknowledged as a problem by all observers. So many livestock were being shot in Jackson County, according to one report, that planters were selling off their cattle. "Every gun that is heard is the knell of some fat hog or cow," he complained. In Wakulla County people were discouraged about raising livestock because so many cattle were being shot. "Animals are stolen and stock killed with impunity," came a report from Alachua County. The bureau agent in Madison County declared, "Stealing is almost incredible. Stores are robbed and stock destroyed until it is almost impossible to keep anything." A. B. Grumwell, the Jefferson County agent, thought the constant stealing was a sad commentary on the freedmen. "A stray hog has a very small chance for his life," he wrote.[16]

Although some of the agents thought stealing was a habit forced on freedmen during slavery days when they had augmented their rations by pilfering, none condoned the practice. When thievery became a problem in Gadsden County, bureau agent Marcellus L. Stearns, a future Florida governor, "put a wholesome restraint upon it by arresting and bringing to justice two of the guilty parties." Stearns thought destitution and hunger were great causes of thievery among the freedmen. Colonel Sprague agreed. After the 1867 crop failure, he wrote, "the food is not in the country, nor is there money to buy it, and the result will be that the freedman, as well as the white man, will be driven to the necessity of stealing it. Cattle and hogs roam free and they will be killed indiscriminately and then will come strife. Law, under such circumstances is of no avail and hunger is more sagacious and vigilant than the authority of a military force, or the posse of the county sheriff." But the agents did not excuse perpetrators of these crimes for that reason. A. B. Grumwell thought the problem so serious that either a penitentiary had to be built or the whipping post used as a deterrent. He reported that some Jefferson County Negroes had resorted to whipping thieves themselves.[17]

A. W. Da Costa of Jacksonville, noting that petty thefts were so numerous that their punishment was burdening county governments, suggested that the bureau agents resort to summary justice. Other white Floridians were more direct. Some Jackson County planters lay in wait near a corn crib which had been visited several times during the night, ambushed a Negro thief, and killed him. This was not an isolated occurrence. The *Tallahassee Floridian* decried the stealing by Negroes, declaring "they ought to be killed."[18]

The freedmen had no monopoly on thievery, however. Livestock killing was quite common among poor whites, and some white merchants were willing to buy stolen goods. The bureau agent at Tampa complained that it was difficult to enforce the laws against thieves, while the white merchants who bought their goods made matters worse. There was a similar situation in Madison County where white men purchased small quantities of corn and cotton at low prices from freedmen, knowing it had been taken unlawfully. Often referred to as "deadfalls," these illicit merchants transacted their business at night. Traffic in stolen cotton was diminished by a Freedmen's Bureau order prohibiting the buying of loose cotton, but it was difficult to enforce. With cotton and corn disappearing from the fields and warehouses, Jefferson County planters protested against freedmen who stole goods and merchants who bought from them. They petitioned the bureau for aid, asking that military authorities be empowered to stop the petty larceny by regulating the "manner and time of trading" these staples. Agent Grumwell prohibited sales by freedmen between 6:00 P.M. and 6:00 A.M. and threatened to arrest and punish merchants and freedmen who violated the order. The state legislative enactment of a "sunset to sunrise" law was thus preceded by the bureau officials by nearly a decade. About the same time a Negro constable of Nassau County became a minor celebrity by apprehending a gang of freedmen who had been living at Traders' Hill, Georgia, and stealing Nassau County livestock for two years.[19]

After the bureau began furnishing rations in early 1868 to alleviate the suffering caused by the 1867 crop failure, the number of complaints about stealing abated somewhat, but the problem continued for years. Many planters gave up raising pork and beef. There were even cases of milk cows being shot in their pastures in daylight.[20] Stealing of cotton and cottonseed was so common that planters thought it defeated the crop lien system. A "sunset to sunrise" law was considered by the legislature several times, but opponents defeated the measure until early 1877.

Petty thievery, dissatisfaction with the gang labor system in the fields, and the credit crisis after 1867 caused more planters to consider seeking immigrant white labor. There had been mild interest in attracting Chinese or European workers since 1865. A group went North in December 1865 to hire 300 white workers, but only a few were brought to the state.[21] Most planters remained comparatively satisfied with the free Negro laborers and sought legislation to prevent their obtaining land and to regulate contracts between white planters and black workers. The black labor force was augmented by active recruiting from other states. But interest in immigrants increased in 1867, partially because of the economic difficulties already discussed and partially because of anger at Negroes who began participating in politics after congressional Reconstruction began.

C. H. Dupont of Quincy, state supreme court chief justice and coauthor of the "Black Code," was the leading advocate of immigrant labor. At his urging a planters' convention was held at Monticello in August 1867 to promote and coordinate a statewide immigration association. The Southern Land and Immigration Company, organized by Jesse T. Bernard and Governor D. S. Walker, sent United States Register of Lands A. B. Stonelake as its representative. The company offered to bring European laborers on order from planters at a charge of five dollars each plus expenses which they estimated at approximately thirty dollars. Bernard was developing his own steamship line from Savannah to Liverpool as part of his cotton factorage business and the labor importation was to be a sideline. Others were simply determined to "crowd out the nigger."[22] Numerous planters pledged not to hire any more Negroes and to help pay agents to bring in white workers.

Several immigration meetings were held in Marion County after the Monticello convention, and the planters there resolved to send for white immigrants "as the negroes have come short of our expectations." Bureau agent Jacob Remley was convinced that such action was political. Only when the Negroes began supporting Republican politicians did the planters become dissatisfied with their labor, he asserted. He was probably correct. A farmers' meeting, held in Jackson County about the same time, agreed to offer low wages to the Negroes for 1868. Their ultimatum offered $75 for first-class hands and $48 for second-class, or one-third of the crop with the laborers furnishing their own supplies. The Marianna newspaper urged "unemployment of freedpeople who persistently array themselves in hostility to the Southern whites."[23]

A few white laborers were brought to Florida in the 1860s, including about twenty Germans hired in New York by Marion County planters, but the move to replace Negroes failed. Dupont did not give up, however.

He formed the Agricultural and Immigration Association of Florida on December 1, 1867, and subsequently received encouragement from the Republican state administration. Intended to attract both laborers and independent landowners, the organization brought in a few groups of workers in the 1870s but was more important for attracting settlers who bought their own land.[24]

Land values were seriously depreciated during the 1860s, especially in the plantation area. It was estimated that the average value of all Florida land in 1866 was down 55 per cent from 1860. In the northern counties, values had diminished by 75 per cent as compared to about a 50 per cent decline in Alachua and its immediate vicinity. The overall decline was offset somewhat by a 33 per cent increase in prices along the St. Johns River where many northern settlers were buying and establishing citrus groves and vegetable farms after the war. A recent arrival from the North wrote that people settling in Volusia County had only minimal resources, although some had been wealthy before the war. He was elated that "it is not considered disgraceful to work here" and most people relied on their own labors.[25]

Settlers were encouraged by the success of Douglas Dummit who had settled years earlier on a strip of land between Indian River and Mosquito Lagoon. With nearby water protecting his groves from freezing, Dummit had developed a 1,700-acre orange grove and was reputedly marketing 2 million oranges annually by 1867. He supplied rootstock to the settlers who tried to emulate him. There were also settlers from north Florida counties, but not all of them succeeded. Charles Hentz retrospectively conceded that his move to east Florida had been a foolish one. With insufficient capital, he had settled on land too poor for gardening or oranges. He returned to his medical practice in Quincy. But the area grew: by October 1868, 17 white families and 9 Negro families had settled near Port Orange and were growing sugarcane, rice, sweet potatoes, corn, and garden vegetables. About 100 people were living at New Smyrna. Settlers on Lake Jesup had formed a local orange-growing association. Most of the land on the upper St. Johns was selling for about $15 per acre, but near Jacksonville W. H. Christy sold a sizeable tract for $100 per acre in 1868. A year earlier John P. Sanderson reportedly sold a plantation on the St. Johns for $25,000 cash.[26]

The Sanderson sale was exceptional. Although many small tracts were bought and sold during the period, few people had the wealth or desire to buy large plantations during the unsettled 1860s. Landownership, land management, and labor arrangements changed continually after 1865, but the greatest alterations occurred after the 1867 crop failure. The agricultural system which has prevailed in north Florida until the twentieth century was fairly fixed by the late 1860s. The average size of farms was reduced by half between 1860 and 1870, but most of the large plantations remained intact. Some changed hands and many were rented in small plots to individual tenants. The planters who sold to avoid the problems of the new labor arrangements found cash buyers scarce. One Marion County planter sold his plantation to the Negroes who had labored on it and accepted mortgages which they were to pay from their crops.[27]

Priced at ten dollars per acre or more, a plantation was beyond the means of most potential buyers. William H. Branch advertised his Leon County plantation for sale in early 1866, but his terms were fifteen dollars cash per acre. More than a year later, real estate brokers were trying to convince him to change his terms because they could find no purchaser able to pay such an amount. In 1870, Branch finally sold 1,250 acres including houses and improvements to Howard S. Case of Lancaster, Pennsylvania, for $10,500. Frederick R. Cotten had similar difficulty when his two adjoining plantations on Lake Iamonia were offered for sale. With 4,280 acres of good land, 40 mules, 10 yoke of oxen, 200 cattle, 300 hogs, and 50 sheep included, he asked $100,000 cash in currency. In March 1870, he sold about 2,200 acres to William R. Wilson for $6,500. George Noble Jones advertised El Destino Mills and 2,000 acres with livestock and equipment at an unspecified price; he would accept half in cash and the remainder in two annual installments at 7 per cent. No sale was made, and he leased 450 acres to David Harger of Chemonie Plantation for a nominal sum. The severity of the problem was emphasized by Leon County Sheriff Alvin B. Munger's purchase of 3,200 acres at a forced sale to satisfy a $3,900 judgment.[28]

A few northern investors bought plantations but many more leased them. Ten former Union army officers rented plantations in Leon County, and sixteen northern men became planters in Alachua. Marion and Nassau each had several northern planters and a few others were scattered through other agricultural counties. Major E. C. Weeks of the Florida Union Cavalry, subsequently denounced as a plundering "carpetbagger" because he became a Republican politician, leased the G. W. Parkhill plantation north of Tallahassee and farmed on a large scale. Leonard G. Dennis farmed on a more modest scale in Alachua County. Condemned by the local society and threatened by night-riding regulators, Dennis invested about $10,000, employed from eight to twelve hands, and raised cotton and corn.[29]

Most planters kept control of their land, but tenantry largely replaced the contracted gang labor system after 1867.[30] With both planters and laborers complaining of the labor system and with starvation threatening, the Freedmen's Bureau adopted a policy which offered relief and encouraged freedmen either to acquire land under the Homestead Act or to rent small acreages from planters and cultivate on their own responsibility. The bureau's circular number three offered rations to any freedman who homesteaded a tract or rented at least ten acres. The rations were to continue until the 1868 crop matured. Thousands of freedmen took advantage of the rations, most of them simply renting from the planters land which was already in cultivation. The annual rental, usually to be paid with a portion of the crop, was secured by a crop lien law which had already been enacted by the 1865 legislature. Some planters were relieved since they could avoid the problems of gang labor as well as the deficit financing of their crops, although most continued advancing credit to the freedmen for supplies during the crop year. Freedmen preferred tenantry because they could live on their land and manage their own affairs a little more than under the old system.[31]

Elsewhere it was noted that numerous white farmers worked their own lands with little or no hired labor and that homesteads were made available to both black and white potential farmers in 1866. The homestead act of June 1866, intended to encourage freedmen to settle on vacant lands, made available eighty acres of public land to anyone who could take the loyalty oath and pay a small fee (the oath requirement was dropped in 1868). Both blacks and whites took advantage of the law, although many others lacked the seven dollars required for fees and the provisions to sustain themselves until the land was cleared and crops made. The bureau offer of provisions enabled people to acquire land who otherwise would have been unable to do so. Through 1868, entries numbering 3,648 were made on United States land by both blacks and whites.[32]

Land was taken up in nearly every county, despite resistance to Negroes trying to settle in Jackson, Gadsden, Leon, and other north Florida areas. The whites there did not wish to have landowning Negroes as neighbors, preferring that they remain in the agricultural labor force. The bureau issue of rations was denounced by some planters as a "Radical plan" to further reduce the already scarce labor supply. But others thought that making supplies available to settlers was beneficial since it put into cultivation land which otherwise would have remained vacant. Most of the homesteads were in Alachua, Marion, Orange, St. Johns, Hernando, Levy, Hillsborough, and the sparsely settled counties near them.[33]

Difficulties arose when homesteaders were inadvertently placed on land belonging either to the state or the railroad companies, both of which were also enticing settlers with low-priced land. Most of the errors were corrected without difficulty, but serious conflicts arose over some 800,000 acres of public land sold by the Florida government while it was part of the Confederacy. Confederate Floridians had purchased land and improved it, but the United States did not recognize their titles. Bureau agents sometimes advised freedmen and Union refugees to file claims for the improved lands. A. B. Stonelake, Register of Land at Tallahassee, believed this unfair when it meant dispossession and eviction of families who had invested time and money in the property. The homestead act required prospective homesteaders to take the loyalty oath, but Stonelake argued that wives or widows of Confederates could legally do so. He was apparently correct. Many women were serving as postmistresses at the time because too few men could take the necessary oath. Stonelake tried to give occupants of land pre-emptive claims. Considerable confusion ensued, and Stonelake was severely condemned by the bureau agents for favoring ex-Confederates over people who had remained loyal to the United States, but some of the former were ultimately permitted to keep the disputed land. The Confederate government's wartime practice of confiscating property of Florida Unionists also caused trouble. Local prejudice against these people made it difficult for them to reclaim their property through the courts, engendering bitterness between neighbors and uncertainty over land titles.[34]

Sometimes titles were of the least concern for settlers. Many were near failure when the bureau began issuing rations in early 1868, and the crops that year were little better than the two previous years. Furthermore, many tracts selected were very poor for farming. Hundreds of claims continued to be staked out every year, but numerous older claims reverted to the government as homesteaders gave up. Still, the effort was not entirely a failure. By 1870 there were about 1,000 Negro landowners in Florida where there had been none five years earlier.[35] A few Negro farmers attracted attention with their successful cultivation of various crops. There were also more small-scale white landowners as a result of homesteading. Although Florida did not become a haven for small-scale farmers after the war and most Negroes continued to be agricultural laborers, there was an increase in the number of people who worked their land without supervision, either as tenants or owners.

In 1868 there remained in Florida 17,424,438 acres of United States land. Scattered throughout the state, most of it was in the lower peninsula and still unsurveyed. Eager to develop the area and to promote his own fortune, William H. Gleason had accompanied Freedmen's Bureau agent George F. Thompson on an exploring party in 1865. Most of the people he encountered were uneducated, unconcerned, and sometimes uninformed about the recently concluded war, earning their living mostly from the forests. They had no great love for the North, but had tolerance for Northerners. A number were cattle-raisers; some had large herds and earned a good living supplying beef on the hoof to the Spanish in Cuba.

The herdsmen lived as much as forty miles apart and were migratory in habit, following the cattle as they grazed on open range.[36]

Cattle had ranged the south Florida area before the Civil War and some great herds had been built up by the late 1860s. Orlando and Bartow were the principal communities of the cattle country while Punta Rassa, Tampa, and Snead's Point were the major ports where the Cuba-bound cattle boats loaded. A few shipments were also made from New Smyrna to the Bahamas. Cattle were driven overland from the Kissimmee Valley for Gulf Coast loading, fording the Caloosahatchie River near Labelle. Others crossed at Breniza Ferry.[37]

James McKay, Sr., of Tampa was a prominent advocate of the cattle industry. Soon after the war he purchased two steamers, the *Governor Marvin* and the *Southern Star*, to haul cattle to Cuba. Praising him for his leadership, the Tampa newspaper urged its readers to help build up the cattle trade with Cuba. If the project were not pushed vigorously, the paper warned, Floridians would lose out to the Texans who could ship cattle to Cuba cheaper. The Cuban market was uncertain, but the range cattle industry and Cuban trade continued in south Florida. Florida cattlemen gradually began supplying a considerable quantity of beef to the domestic market. A slaughterhouse was opened at Enterprise in the late 1860s and sold beef to communities on the St. Johns River. It also shipped beef in barrels to Savannah where it was declared superior to beef from New York's Fulton market.[38]

F. A. Hendry owned 25,000 animals, widely acknowledged as the largest herd in Florida, but the flamboyant Jacob Summerlin, a truly "rugged individual" in the frontier tradition, ran about 20,000 head and was a major supplier of the Cuban market. Others with large herds were John Widden, Joel Knight, William Alderman, Ziba King, William Whitaker, and William Curry. Robert W. Bullock of Ocala managed a large herd at Orlando. John A. Henderson formed a company of ten men, each of whom contributed 1,000 head of cattle, to ship from Tampa to Cuba.[39]

It is difficult to determine the volume of the Cuban cattle trade or the number of Floridians engaged in it, but records of shipments from Punta Rassa between July 1871 and July 1872 are helpful. Fifteen schooners and three steamers made 142 trips carrying 18,349 head of cattle valued at $301,846. There were 183 employees involved in the operation. The volume of business at Snead's Point and Tampa was probably comparable to it. There was an increase in the number of head sold to Cuba in the late 1860s because of the revolution there. Because the island's own beef production diminished, Cuban purchasers were paying $10–$14 per head for Florida cattle.[40]

With an abundance of pine, cypress, live oak, and cedar, Florida had a sizeable lumber industry. The prewar lumbering activity—located primarily in west Florida, Nassau County, and along the St. Johns River, and largely financed by northern capital—had been discontinued during the war. Most of the equipment had been destroyed or was badly deteriorated by 1865, but many companies returned after the war and new operators began lumbering operations. In addition to local sources, financing came from investors in the North, France, and England. Lumbering was carried on in seventeen counties but was most important in Escambia and Santa Rosa in the west, Nassau, Duval, and Bradford in the northeast, Madison and Alachua near the Suwannee River, Levy near Cedar Key, and Hillsborough near Tampa Bay. Lumber was sold locally to the railroads and for construction in the Florida towns; some was shipped to Cuba, Brazil, and Europe; but most of it went to ports along the Atlantic Coast of the United States. Schooners of both United States and foreign registry carried the lumber. Most sawmills were near waterways and sometimes ships could load in the rivers, but lumber was also hauled by water or rail to Jacksonville, Cedar Key, Pensacola, or Fernandina for loading. The Florida Railroad Company was largely dependent on the lumbermills along its track for cargo, and George F. Drew's mill at Ellaville, Madison County, was the largest customer of the Florida Central Railroad Company.[41]

Of the 4,291 workers engaged in manufacturing according to the 1870 census, about 1,000 worked in sawmills. More than 500 others were timber cutters or turpentine workers. There were only a few turpentine distilleries in Florida and probably fewer than 100 laborers were engaged in that activity. It was dangerous, difficult, and seasonal, but paid from $25 to $35 per month, better than any other unskilled job in the state. Gilbert H. Barnhill operated a distillery at Baldwin which employed twenty freedmen. He paid good wages but his business failed in 1867 and he had difficulty in settling his accounts. His distillery was mortgaged for $30,000 to Franklin Dibble of Jacksonville who foreclosed on him. Timber cutters made from $20 to $30 per month with the best pay being offered in the cedar swamps near Cedar Key. The lumber business generally prospered after the war despite slumps in 1867 and 1873.[42]

Both black and white men engaged in lumbering, but most of the unskilled laborers were Negroes. There were Negroes with skilled jobs in the sawmills alongside the whites, however. A few freedmen became landowners by working part time in the woods while putting in their crops. One group of freedmen asked the bureau agent in Marion County to assist them in purchasing a steam engine for a milling operation they planned, but their success or failure is unknown. Procedures for "getting out" the logs and turning them into marketable lumber remained fairly constant, although William Penny of Milton received a patent for an improved gang sawmill, which was more easily portable than those generally used at the time. Because some timbermen were careless about property lines when they were cutting logs, a few men were employed by both public and private owners to protect their timber from poachers.[43]

Eleven hundred Floridians were carpenters, joiners, and cabinetmakers. Brick works in Fernandina, Jacksonville, and Pensacola employed 16 men and 109 stonemasons used their products. Cotton and woolen mills employed 370 people, 313 were blacksmiths, 133 were wheelwrights, and 275 worked as tailors and seamstresses. There were 98 machinists, 92 millers, 69 shoemakers, and 63 butchers. In 1870 there were 284 cigarmakers and tobacco workers, all working in Key West. But at various times there had been cigar factories at Quincy, Tallahassee, and St. Augustine. Discharged Union soldiers of both races went into the cigar business at Quincy in 1866.[44] There were about 160 fishermen along the Gulf Coast, especially at Cedar Key, Tampa, Snead's Point (near present-day Bradenton), Fort Myers, and Charlotte Harbor. One reporter estimated that a good fisherman could make $600 per year at the latter place. At Indian River on the Atlantic Coast, Henry Titus and Dr. John Westcott, with some New York investors, formed the New York and Indian River Preserving Company and employed ten men to catch fish, turtles, and oysters. Their special interest was oysters preserved in cans. They shipped the canned oysters to Provost and Company of New Jersey. The venture failed because of expensive operating costs and a natural disaster which destroyed their ship. In most of these occupations both Negroes and whites were employed.[45]

Transportation and communications were sources of employment for more than 2,000 Floridians. Forty-five persons worked for the International Ocean Telegraph Company. More than 300 people were officials and employees of the railroad companies, and during most of the 1860s a number of laborers were employed in railroad construction. The Florida Railroad Company employed about 300, some of whom were skilled carpenters, in repairing the wharves in Fernandina and Cedar Key and railroad buildings along the line. The Atlantic and Gulf Central, Pensacola and Georgia, and the Alabama and Florida also employed construction workers. The roads paid higher wages than the agricultural employees received but less than those paid to timber cutters. Sometimes they paid by the day and there were frequent layoffs when jobs were completed, but the railroads, with a few exceptions, were reliable in meeting their payrolls.[46]

About 850 men were crew members of ships and riverboats. Most of the highly skilled positions were filled by white men and most of the deck hands were black, but there were exceptions. A few first mates and pilots on the St. Johns River were Negroes and at one time all the pilots on the Oklawaha River were black. There were also some Negro mates on ships working out of Fernandina. Several hundred people were employed as stevedores in the port cities. The stevedores were better organized than any other workers: at the Jacksonville port a ship's captain complained that he was not permitted to unload his own vessel because licensed stevedores were available to do the job. Their organization of a "workingman's association" at Pensacola in 1868 was praised by the local press as a necessity and a benefit to the community. At Fernandina they attempted an unsuccessful strike for better wages in late 1868. More than 1,000 freedmen were employed at the United States navy yard at Pensacola, mostly in unskilled jobs.[47]

About 1,500 persons were involved in the merchandising and financial aspects of commerce. They were merchants, clerks, salesmen, accountants, insurance agents, and a few bankers. There were seven Negro grocers in Tallahassee, one Negro storekeeper and saloon operator in Quincy, and several blacks who carried on "respectable places of business" in Pensacola.[48]

Of more than 10,000 persons who provided professional and personal services in 1870, nearly 9,000 were domestic servants, laborers, and laundresses. There were 248 physicians, 250 teachers, 197 clergymen, 149 lawyers, 367 government workers, and 398 soldiers.

The level of employment was not constant in the state. There were complaints of agricultural labor shortages in the early years and expressions of planter dissatisfaction with Negroes as free laborers. Yet planters actively recruited more Negro field hands. The contract system gradually gave way to a tenant system in which most Negroes rented land for an annual sum, usually payable at a fixed rate in cotton or other crops produced on the land. A crop lien made it possible for the landowner to collect his rent before other creditors. Supplies were usually bought on credit and the tenant often ended the year in debt. The debt carried over to the following year and tenants were tied to the land much as they had been during slavery. It was a vicious system which evolved out of the adversity of the postwar era and, while unsatisfactory, appears to have been unavoidable.

Florida was somewhat diversified in types of employment available, but agriculture remained by far the most important field of endeavor and it set the pattern for labor compensation in other areas. The lumber industry paid better, but it was seasonal as were the higher paying jobs in the turpentine camps and in railroad construction. The Florida population grew during the period and some capital was invested from outside the state, but the amount was inadequate for the needs of the impoverished state. Some Negroes and formerly landless whites became landowners, although others lost their land and a few sold out by choice. But there was no major alteration in landownership during the period. Negroes usually held the menial jobs while most of the skilled and managerial jobs were filled by whites. But there were Negroes who had skills and many of them had responsible jobs. In Jackson County a bureau agent reported that Negro carpenters, mechanics, blacksmiths, and masons were preferred to whites.[49]

The late 1860s was a transitional period for most Floridians. Circumstances caused by the war necessitated changes in the old economic system which established patterns affecting the lives of Floridians for decades. Yet, except for the decreasing importance of cotton in proportion to lumber and transportation as a source of employment, the emerging system was remarkably similar to that which had existed before 1860.

9

Gradually We Learned How To Manage

With nostalgic memories of their antebellum past and bitterness over its unwelcome disruption, some white Floridians had time only to "worship the Confederate dead and hate the Yankee living," but most "gradually . . . learned how to manage."[1] Most planter families complained of the loss of their servants and some women declared they were having to cook their own meals for the first time in their lives. Nearly all of those accustomed to domestic help managed to keep one or two employees, however, and a few continued to live in the grand style. The majority of white Floridians continued to do their own housework as they always had.

Despite complaints of abject poverty and scarcity of servants, there seems to have been an active social life almost immediately following the surrender, at least around Florida's capital city. Young people organized riding clubs, literary societies, and even card-playing groups, notwithstanding parental disapproval of the latter. One eligible young woman remarked that there had never been so much "marrying and giving in marriage" as in 1865.[2]

At Goodwood Plantation, Arvah Hopkins, a New York–born merchant who had adapted to Tallahassee society, held lavish parties at which Leon County's elite mingled with the soldiers of General Foster's command. Hopkins said it was merely good policy, but both sides seemed to have enjoyed themselves.[3] The Seventh United States Infantry band often furnished music for these events.

If they were occasionally remiss in their attitudes toward the "Yankee living," Floridians lost no time in honoring the fallen Confederates. By early 1866, *Fall of the Confederacy* was a bestseller in northern Florida and *The Land We Love,* a monthly magazine published by former General D. H. Hill, was selling well. Women's memorial associations were formed in nearly every community to account for the Confederate dead or missing and raise money for a suitable monument to "slain countrymen who died in the holiest of causes." Items were sent from all over the state for sale at a fair and festival held by the Tallahassee Ladies Memorial Association in December 1866. With brisk sales, contributions from such diverse persons as General William Bailey of Monticello and Madame Murat of Tallahassee, and music furnished by the Seventh Infantry band, the event cleared nearly $3,000. More controversial was a charity ball in February 1867. All three white Tallahassee ministers criticized it because dancing was a sin, but the women responded that their requests for contributions had been nearly ignored while the dance had raised $1,100. The monument fund was temporarily diverted when the women decided that destitute families of the deceased could better use the money.[4]

The churches underwent major changes after the war, but perhaps none so significant as the move of Negro members to separate churches. Although blacks continued to attend services with whites and separate congregations shared buildings for several years after the war, the majority of the freedmen soon joined all-Negro denominations. With rare exceptions churches were completely segregated by 1875. The blacks preferred the separation but whites often resented their withdrawal. Their churches became the central political, social, cultural, and recreational institution for the freedmen. Negro ministers were more influential than their white counterparts and churches seemed more important to blacks than to whites.

Negroes and whites had always attended the same churches, but the master-servant relationship had been carefully maintained. When the war ended, whites demonstrated their resentment of Negroes in their churches in any other than a subservient role. Presbyterians, Episcopalians, Methodists, and Baptists at Fernandina, Jacksonville, St. Augustine, or Palatka refused even to share their church buildings with Negro schools, though there was no scheduling conflict.[5] Unwilling to continue as inferior members of established churches, Negroes joined separate denominations as they organized in Florida shortly after the war.

Hardest hit of all in terms of membership losses was the Methodist Episcopal Church, South, 40 per cent of whose 19,000 members in 1862 were Negroes. By 1867 it had only 6,266 members, nearly all of whom were white. A reorganization in 1866 reduced the white membership by separating south Georgia from the Florida Conference. In 1869 Florida Methodists transferred their interests in Bainbridge Female College and Fletcher

Institute at Thomasville to their Georgia neighbors and established similar schools in Florida towns. Florida west of the Apalachicola River was part of an Alabama conference. Methodist ministers were moved frequently during the period and many communities were "supplied," meaning that laymen served in place of ordained ministers. At the several annual conferences held during the period, most districts reported progress in church attendance and Sunday schools, but there were a few complaints that religious life was "unsatisfactory in many spiritual ways," and that "people are luke-warm and back-slidden." If this meant Methodists did not always follow their pastors' instructions, it was perhaps just as well. When asked what to do about Negro soldiers foraging in northern Leon County in 1865, Simon P. Richardson told his congregation to "bushwhack them."[6]

The Methodist Episcopal Church, South, became officially segregated in 1870 when the Colored Methodist Episcopal Church was organized. At that time there were only a few hundred Negroes who transferred to the new church.[7] By then nearly all Negro Methodists had joined the African Methodist Episcopal Church or the African Methodist Episcopal Zion Church.

The African Methodist Episcopal Church was far more important than either of the other Negro Methodist groups. It came to Florida unofficially when Henry Call of Cottondale, who had found a church handbill on a battlefield while searching for the body of his master, organized a church with four members on his return to Florida. Its official beginning was in June 1865 when William G. Stewart, a one-armed, full-bearded ex-slave of John P. Sanderson, was sent to Florida and organized a church at Midway. Stewart became an influential Negro religious and political leader, serving several years as a Tallahassee postmaster. In February 1866, the much more aggressive Elder Charles H. Pearce, an impressive black man with an excellent speaking ability, arrived in Florida from his native Canada where he had been reared and educated as a free man. Usually referred to as "Bishop," although he never held the office, Pearce was the dominant personality in the AME Church in Florida. When an AME Conference was organized in the state in 1867, it reported 4,798 members. A year later John M. Brown became bishop of Florida, presiding over an organization which then had 8,000 members. In 1875, during the four-year term of Bishop Thomas D. Ward who had replaced Brown in 1872, the church claimed over 13,000 members. By that date the AME Church had expanded into south Florida. Thomas W. Long, an educated minister who named his son after Charles Sumner and subsequently served three terms in the state senate, established churches at Tampa, Key West, and other communities.[8]

As the Negroes withdrew from the Methodist Church and formed their own, church facilities were understandably denied them. At Ocala a Negro Sunday school of 150 members was discontinued when Methodist Minister M. A. Clouts, a Republican politician soon to become Marion County sheriff, denied use of his church building to the blacks when they formed a separate congregation. Many AME groups met in brush arbors during the summer and private homes in winter, but buildings were rapidly erected. Robert Meacham's church at Monticello had a building and about 100 members by late 1866. Funds for construction had been raised in part by a festival held by the blacks in honor of Monticello whites the previous spring. When the Florida Conference was organized in 1867 the AME Church claimed $12,884 worth of property.[9]

Its members avidly supported the AME Church. Regular services and periodic regional meetings were enthusiastically attended and observers were impressed by the exuberant participation of members and the length of the services. Frequent festivals were held such as the one in the state capital in June 1869, to which everyone was invited without racial distinction. The church became the focal point of its members' social life and of their efforts to provide themselves with welfare services and education.

In 1870 the AME leaders began planning for a college to "teach theology and classics and promote a liberal and complete education" for Negroes. Fund-raising was off to a promising beginning when Simon Conover contributed a wagon and team of mules, William H. Gleason donated 640 acres of Volusia County land, and Milton Littlefield gave $20,000 in state scrip and railroad bonds. Unfortunately, the latter gift was destroyed when a conflagration consumed "Bishop" Pearce's home. Land at Jacksonville was offered as a site, but church officials decided that Live Oak would be more centrally located. The legislature chartered Brown's Theological Institute in 1872 and the following year changed its name to Brown's University. Construction began in 1873 but the white treasurer absconded with the funds, creditors sued, and the project was sold to satisfy their judgments. The church moved its school site to Jacksonville, finally opening an institution in the 1880s which eventually became Edward Waters College.[10]

The Baptists, the second largest denomination in the state, experienced changes similar to those of the Methodists. Black and white congregations began meeting separately soon after the war. There were Baptist church buildings in most communities, several of which were shared for a while, but gradually Negro Baptists established their own facilities as well as separate organizations. In 1866 the white Baptists of Jacksonville paid the Negroes $400 for their interest in the property of Bethel Baptist Church.

When the blacks built their own church and kept the name, the whites changed their church's name to Tabernacle Baptist. There were several varieties of Baptists among both black and white Floridians. By 1867 Negro Baptists numbered 4,400 with twenty-one churches and eighteen ordained ministers. In 1869 fifteen of the Negro Baptist churches formed the Bethlehem Baptist Association.[11]

As with the Methodists, the whites wanted segregation within the church while the blacks desired complete separation. The church became the paramount institution in the lives of Negro Baptists, but white Baptists also took their religion seriously. Church attendance was regular and widespread, and the institution reinforced the social attitudes of the membership. When Jesse Goss of Ocala became an outspoken Radical and vigorous defender of Negroes against injustice, the local Baptists seriously considered ousting him; they finally yielded to the moderate counsel of John Taylor and a few other prominent members.[12]

Because of its formal liturgy and refusal to permit separate Negro congregations, the Protestant Episcopal Church had few black members, but its problems after the Civil War were many. Three churches were burned and one sold for debt during the war, and, of thirteen prewar parishes, all except those at Tallahassee and Monticello were disrupted by 1865. Bishop Francis Rutledge died in 1866, but not before he had successfully urged the diocese to rejoin the Protestant Episcopal Church in the United States of America. John Freeman Young was chosen to replace Rutledge (at an election attended by Colonel John T. Sprague as a delegate from St. Augustine, and Francis Eppes, the Tallahassee mayor who a few months earlier had clashed with Sprague's military predecessor). Young travelled the length and breadth of Florida during the Reconstruction era, rebuilding and extending the services of the church. In 1875 he established a Spanish language mission at Key West at the request of the many Cubans who had recently immigrated there. The first Negro church in the diocese was formed at Key West about the same time and flourished for a few years. Young found Episcopalians at Titusville and further south during his travels, but the only Episcopal church between Key West and Palatka was completed in 1873 at Sanford. Some members were happier than others to have Young visit their community. A Pensacola parishioner reported in 1869 that Bishop Young confirmed eighteen persons there and "made a sophomoric disquisition which had the virtue of brevity."[13]

Before Rutledge died he licensed William D. Scull to work exclusively with the freedmen. Scull, who noticed the propensity of Negroes to avoid association with whites, thought education was the answer to their problems. With small monetary aid from the Freedmen's Bureau and a building furnished by General Foster, he established a school at Midway which had as many as 126 pupils during its three-year existence. Scull enjoyed some success with his school, but failed to attract many blacks to the Episcopal Church services he conducted there. Forced to close his school for lack of funds in 1868, Scull remained at Midway as a minister, still convinced that education which had improved white men could also uplift the blacks.[14]

One of Bishop Young's favorite projects was the establishment of schools to provide high quality Christian education for white boys and girls. Four were established, at Pensacola, Tallahassee, Jacksonville, and Fernandina, during the 1860s. Most significant of the four was St. Mary's Priory, "a High School for Young Ladies," begun at Fernandina in 1868 with a $10,000 loan from Bishop Young and supervised by Owen P. Thackera, his archdeacon in east Florida. The school prospered for a few years, attracting students from outside the state. But with stiff competition from Roman Catholic schools, the depressed economic conditions after 1873, and an unfortunate change of headmistresses, St. Mary's Priory failed in 1874. Relocated at Jacksonville, the Episcopal girls' school finally survived as Bradford Institute.[15] St. John's Male Academy, founded at Jacksonville in 1869, lasted nearly a decade before it closed permanently. The Tallahassee school also failed, but the Episcopal high school in Pensacola endured under the careful management of the Reverend J. J. Scott.

The church felt financial adversity during most of the period but some of its rebuilding on the east coast received assistance from the tourists who were beginning to winter in Florida. A fair held in 1869 to help pay the St. Augustine church's debt was attended by many visiting Episcopalians who were "much better off than the natives in a pecuniary way." Guests at the St. James Hotel in Jacksonville contributed a large portion of the $17,000 collected for rebuilding St. John's Church.[16]

The Presbyterians were more fragmented after the war than any other denomination, except perhaps the Baptists. Steadfastly refusing to rejoin the Northern Presbyterian Church, the Southern Presbyterian Church of Florida was torn by doctrinal, jurisdictional, patriotic, and racial differences. Several white members refused to sit in churches where Negroes were also seated. The Presbytery of Florida made no effort to retain old or attract new Negro members. It had no Negro congregations and nearly all individual black members had left it by 1870, most of them going to the AME Church. The St. Augustine congregation was largely from the North and joined the Northern Presbyterians, as did most of the communicants in Jacksonville. A few Jacksonville members disagreed and formed a new church, but the pro-Northern group retained all the property. The Fernandina church was torn for several years by a disagreement over choice of a minister. Colonel William S. Dilworth, a prominent Monticello Presbyterian, was expelled from the church for "neglect of the ordinances and general unchristian conduct," and Ferdinand McLeod of Lake City, elected but not seated as a congressman in 1865, admitted that he was guilty of "too free use of ardent spirits." He was permitted to remain in the church, however. The Presbyterian churches west of the Apalachicola River were separated from the Florida Presbytery and remained attached to Alabama until after 1890.[17]

The Northern Presbyterian Church organized the East Florida Presbytery at Jacksonville in 1870 with four ministers, including the two at St. Augustine and Jacksonville, Jonathan C. Gibbs, the prominent Negro leader, and Calvin E. Stowe, husband of Harriet Beecher Stowe. Its membership was small and racially mixed, but its presence was not appreciated by the Florida Presbytery of the Southern Presbyterian Church.[18]

The Southern Presbyterians eventually adjusted some of their differences and began expanding into south Florida. Churches were established at Gainesville in 1867, Clearwater in 1868, Sumter County in 1869, Mellonville in 1870, and Orlando in 1876.[19] Several ministers were active in education, among them John DuBose, principal of the State Female Seminary in Tallahassee in 1866, William J. McCormick, a teacher at East Florida Seminary when it moved to Gainesville, and Solomon F. Halliday, a former Freedmen's Bureau agent who was Alachua County school superintendent.

Like the other denominations, the Roman Catholics of Florida were poorly equipped to meet their postwar problems. All of Florida east of the Apalachicola River was served by Bishop Augustin Verot from Savannah. West Florida was served by Bishop John Quinlan from Mobile. Quinlan helped Pensacola Catholics rebuild both of their destroyed churches by 1867, and in 1870 there were a parish school and an academy operated by the Sisters of the Holy Cross, with 100 pupils between them.[20]

Bishop Verot was anxious to reopen the Catholic schools in Florida and to extend their services to the freedmen in whose education he took a deep interest. The Sisters of Mercy announced the reopening of St. Mary's Academy in September 1866. Board and tuition were $200 per year and students were advised to bring $6 pocket money. Eight additional nuns were recruited by Verot in his native Le Puy, France. These Sisters of St. Joseph opened a free school for Negroes in 1867 at St. Augustine. Verot had personally taught them English in five months.[21] Other nuns from Le Puy arrived in the next two years and by 1868 the Sisters of St. Joseph had sixty Negro pupils at St. Augustine and a new school at Fernandina. Most of the support for these schools came from France.

Verot hoped to convert the freedmen and in the late 1860s there were about 600 Negro Catholics in east Florida, but most of them ultimately gravitated to the Negro churches. Although there were some cases of mixed attendance at Catholic services, most churches permitted Negroes only in separate galleries.[22]

Verot re-established the burned church in Jacksonville and re-opened two small ones in Fernandina. Having obtained a few more clergymen from France, Italy, and Canada, he was able to provide service for most communities, although priests were permanently located only at the three east coast towns and at Tallahassee, Palatka, and Key West. A school and convent were established at the latter town in 1868. The Sisters of Mercy started a new convent at Jacksonville in 1873 and opened an institution to care for aged and infirm whites. When he successfully sought a separate Diocese of St. Augustine in 1870, Verot became its first bishop, serving there until his death in 1876. The new Florida Diocese still did not extend west of the Apalachicola River.[23]

The problem of public welfare for indigents was new to Florida and complicated by racial animosity. Local government officials were responsible for this service but were both financially and emotionally unprepared to provide it. When an 1866 act provided funds to relieve disabled Confederate soldiers and their widows and orphans, a bureau agent commented hotly that "it will be remembered that both loyal and disloyal paid taxes during last year." Without the protection formerly furnished by the plantation owners or a substitute provided by government, freedmen formed mutual aid societies to care for their aged and infirm in most counties.[24]

Several of the societies had deposits in the Freedmen's Savings Bank, among them the Church Aid Society, Sons and Daughters of Bethlehem, Sisters' Beneficent Society, Sisters of Protection, and Board of Hope. The Negroes seem to have been ahead of the whites in providing for the indigent, but the Florida Mutual Relief Company was chartered by the 1869 legislature to provide for widows, orphans, and heirs of several of Leon County's most prominent families. A Workingman's Aid Society of Duval County tried and failed to obtain a charter in 1875. Historian Buckingham Smith bequeathed his large estate for the creation of an asylum for aged Negroes at St. Augustine.[25]

The Freedmen's Bureau and some churches advocated the temperance cause which was gaining support throughout the nation during the period. Commissioner Howard, an avid opponent of alcohol, encouraged his agents to start "Lincoln Temperance Societies" and they regularly reported their successes in doing so. According to the reports, freedmen joined by the hundreds and swore total abstinence. Several agents pointed out that the Negroes were less in need of temperance lessons than the whites, and some whites heartily agreed. The St. Augustine debating society aired the issue in July 1869, and in October the Grand Division, Sons of Temperance, State of Florida, held a well-attended session at Live Oak. When the organization held a quarterly meeting in Jacksonville in 1873, it discovered "whiskey mills so numerous . . . that, *pro rata* profits would not treat a sick cat." The Rev. Thomas A. Carruth, as president of the State Council of the Friends of Temperance, lectured across the state and formed subordinate councils in several towns.[26]

Entrepreneurs sometimes capitalized on the temperance movement. An 1873 state law repealing taxes on soda fountains was entitled "A Law to Promote Temperance." The Alhambra Restaurant, a "ladies and gents ice cream saloon," was advertised as a "Temperance Saloon" in Jacksonville. Some people were less serious about the matter than others. S. D. McConnell was amused that St. George Rogers, well known in Ocala for his excessive libation, had started a division of the Sons of Temperance, but with the "usual loophole of sickness . . . in the pledge," and subsequently complained of frequent illness. When the Sons of Temperance at Live Oak broke a lengthy deadlock over a basic doctrinal dispute by deciding that eggnog was not a beverage, the *Key West Dispatch* predicted a rapid increase in its membership.[27]

The secret fraternal orders which attracted so many Negroes and alarmed whites with their frequent night meetings will be discussed in the following chapter, but the freedmen were merely following an American tradition which their white neighbors seemed to have enjoyed. Many kinds of organizations were formed in the period and most of them met frequently. Their purposes were fraternal, professional, benevolent, or a combination of these. In 1869 the Grand Lodge of the Masonic Order of Florida held a four-day session at Tallahassee which was attended by representatives from nearly every white lodge in the state. There were also Negro Masonic lodges in Florida. The Independent Order of Oddfellows was organized at several locations. Although its appeal to Floridians was obviously limited, the Grand Army of the Republic formed a provisional department in the state in 1868. Lasting until 1875, it had three commanders: Charles Mundee, former adjutant to General Foster, followed by Congressman Charles M. Hamilton, and finally Horatio Jenkins.[28]

There were several county agricultural societies in the 1860s, but the farmers' major social organization was the National Grange of the Patrons of Husbandry which in 1873 authorized the Rev. Thomas A. Carruth to organize local granges in Florida. Five were established by September 1873 and Benjamin F. Wardlaw, a planter from Madison County, became president of the state grange. The organization was concerned not only with fellowship but also with improved farming methods. The *Florida Agriculturist* served as the official means of communication for the grange. The organization enjoyed some local successes but gradually atrophied in the late 1870s. In 1877 the *Florida Agriculturist* had more subscribers in California than in Florida.[29]

The local fire-fighting companies were both service and fraternal organizations, enjoying more successes in the latter function. During the Reconstruction era fire destroyed the Fernandina business district; most of the businesses in Monticello and Quincy; blocks of Pensacola houses and businesses; mercantile houses, hotels, homes, schools, and a cotton factory in Tallahassee; and valuable Jacksonville property. Insurance agencies were active, but most of the destruction was inadequately covered. The fire companies tried. When a downtown block of Pensacola caught fire the Hope Hook and Ladder Company "did valiant service although much damage was done," but the Germania Company was "helpless for want of water." The Vigilant Fire Company of Tallahassee, organized in 1867 after the Planter's Hotel burned, held a parade and demonstration in 1869 to show that it did not have the Germania Company's problem. Its engine, the "Florida," threw water fifty feet in the air—high enough to reach the tallest stores—but there were destructive fires after that date. The Mechanics and Steam Fire Engine Company of Jacksonville fought fires, but also found time to entertain visiting firemen from Savannah who subsequently reciprocated the hospitality. The Jacksonville company also formed an association to provide for sick and disabled members. The Aetna Steam Fire Company of the same city exchanged visits with the Vigilant Company of Augusta. Jacksonville's fire bell became a noted tourist attraction because of its unusual mounting on a dilapidated bacon box.[30]

By the time the state legislature enacted a law in 1869 providing for tax-supported free public schools, much had already been done by other agencies. The role of the Freedmen's Bureau in providing Negro education has been mentioned elsewhere. It will be recalled that the bureau worked closely with northern benevolent associations which provided teachers, while the bureau constructed or rented buildings and lent other assistance. The bureau had also encouraged the state to enact legislation providing for Negro education. When it ceased operating in Florida, the bureau left an embryonic school system supported partially by charity and partially by tuition. The state was at least legally obliged to collect a tax for Negro schools. The churches also established schools for both Negroes and whites. Private academies, mostly supported by tuition, had been established for white pupils in many communities. Although some of these academies remained private, most were merged into the public system in 1869. As soon as tuition charges were eliminated enrollment surged upward in almost every school.[31]

Delayed a year because of white legislators' insistence on a segregation clause, the 1869 school law permitted separate schools without requiring them. Since several schools accepted Peabody Fund assistance between 1869 and 1876, they were at least encouraged to provide equal access, but the state left the matter up to local boards.[32] The civil rights act prohibited segregation in schools financed by public funds, but like some of its other provisions this one was largely ignored. Blacks and whites did attend school together, but only in a few places. Distance and sparse population sometimes encouraged integration.

In an 1869 editorial, the *Tallahassee Floridian* described a school situation which is still unresolved a century later. To correct what it believed to be misunderstanding about the schools provided by the law, the paper explained that the Leon School Board, although headed by a Republican, intended to keep the schools separate in all except a few instances where the population was thinly settled. "A white school here, and a colored school there, etc. The board realizes that mixed schools are distasteful to whites and should not be desired by the colored people (and we believe are not)."[33]

The new school system was headed by a state superintendent of public instruction and a three-member board. The counties were denominated school districts with local superintendents and boards of public instruction. The county board selected trustees for each school and appointed teachers subject to the latter's approval. The state and counties were to finance the schools jointly. County commissioners could levy and collect a tax not exceeding 1 per cent of the assessed value of taxable property. A separate law called for a state tax of one mill on the dollar levied on all taxable property in the state. Schools were to receive the money according to a pro rata formula based on attendance.[34]

Although state financing was inadequate and many counties refused to levy enough local taxes, the school system began to take shape after 1869. By 1870 all counties except one had existing boards of instruction, and schools were organized in twenty-six of them. There were 250 schools with about 7,500 students in the system. In some of the fifteen counties which levied no school tax, private contributions authorized by the law were keeping schools open. By early 1872, only four counties were still without a school tax, and 14,000 pupils were taught in 331 schools during a four-and-a-half month term by teachers whose salaries averaged $30 per month. Admitting that most schools were still inadequate, Superintendent Jonathan C. Gibbs wrote in 1874 that Peabody Fund–supported institutions in thirteen towns across the state were serving as model schools. They were graded, had one teacher for every fifty pupils, held ten month sessions, and had average attendance of more than 80 per cent.[35]

By 1877 much still remained to be done. Financial support, textbooks, and physical facilities were inadequate and the approximately 32,000 pupils enrolled were only about half of the school-age population. Nevertheless, Florida had a durable school system and was committed to its continuation. Only a few high schools were operating by 1877, but Duval Graded High School for whites and Stanton Institute and Lincoln Academy for Negroes, in Jacksonville and Tallahassee respectively, were sound institutions which survived the years of stringent school support begun by the Drew administration in 1877.[36]

The "need for a normal school [was still] painfully apparent" in 1877, but there were attempts to provide higher education in the twelve years following the Civil War. Because of the railroad facilities and other inducements offered by the city of Gainesville, the East Florida Seminary was moved there from Ocala and reopened in 1866 with 100 pupils. The State Seminary West of the Suwannee was reopened with female and male departments in 1866, although the latter was called the Florida Collegiate and Military Institute. The *Floridian* encouraged people to support it "to prevent the youths of our state from being sent abroad to receive an education."[37] It closed in 1868 and opened again in 1869 as the West Florida Seminary. Both schools were incorporated into the state system as free schools under the 1869 law which called for a state university. In that year the East Florida Seminary had ninety students, about forty of whom were in the primary department and sustained by the county. The West Florida Seminary had a male department with seventy-three students and a female department with seventy-five. Sometimes controlled by the county boards and at other times directly by the state, the two schools were little more than high schools at the end of the Reconstruction era.[38]

The unsuccessful efforts of the AME Church to establish Brown's University have already been discussed. A State Agricultural College was chartered in 1870 to be partially financed by a 90,000-acre land grant from the United States government. The land was sold for $81,000 in 1872 and all but $1,000 was invested in 6 per cent Florida state bonds purchased at 80 cents on the dollar, but litigation over the constitutionality of the bonds held up further action on the school for two years. Meanwhile, the board of directors of the college rejected an Alachua County offer of $50,000 and a Florida Railroad offer of 10,000 acres of land to locate the school in Gainesville. Instead, the board agreed to build it at Eau Gallie, a Brevard County site which William H. Gleason hoped to develop into a town. When the legality of the bonds was established, construction began. In 1876 the board's report boasted a coquina rock building with ten rooms and a Professor A. G. Hill in charge of the grounds. A six-mile road was built, connecting the college building with Indian River and Lake Washington.[39]

The school never opened at Eau Gallie. It was moved to Lake City where it opened in 1884. More successful were efforts to establish Cookman Institute at Jacksonville to train Negro teachers and ministers. With assistance from the Freedmen's Aid Society of the Methodist Episcopal Church, it opened in 1872 under the supervision of Samuel Darnell, a white minister. By 1875 it had two teachers and fifty students, which exhausted its limited capacity. Fifty years later the institute was merged with another school at Daytona to become Bethune-Cookman College.[40]

For people who were economically devastated and politically oppressed, Floridians enjoyed a wide range of entertainments. Churches and schools of both races continually held fairs and festivals, strawberry and ice cream suppers, dramatic performances, and concerts to raise money for buildings, musical instruments, textbooks, and the myriad needs of these institutions. Despite heavy taxes levied on them by the state and county governments, traveling shows regularly crossed the state holding one-night stands at large and small communities alike. Dan Castello's Great Show and Moral Exhibition visited Florida for at least four consecutive years after the war. Tallahasseans acknowledged their enjoyment of his circus but complained that a performance before 2,000 people in 1865 took about $8,000 out of the community. They were glad to see Castello in 1867, however, because both performers and patrons were gathered in town just in time to fight a huge fire which destroyed the Pratorious and Clark clothing store and T. P. Tatum's drugstore. Castello's 1868 performance in Jacksonville was attended by 2,600 people and reporters heartily recommended it to others. Castello's competition was Stone, Rosston, and Murray's Mammoth Circus which boasted Professor Hutchinson's trained dogs, Dan Stone's comic mules, and Signor Ferdinand's aeronautic oscillation. They were followed in the 1870s by the Great Eastern Circus and James Robinson's Mammoth Circus. These shows delighted children and many adults, but were not always welcomed by businessmen. A railroad superintendent at Pensacola charged higher rates on circus trains and reported in 1873 that "one is threatening us."[41]

High license taxes ended Reynold's Gymnasium, a travelling acrobatic troup, in 1869. A Negro man with a picture exhibit became the object of official censorship in Monticello when the city marshall permitted him to show all his pictures except three. The objectionable pictures were a copy of the Proclamation of Emancipation, a portrait of Abraham Lincoln, and a scene depicting Negro soldiers capturing a cannon at Petersburg. No one objected to a group of Japanese jugglers who performed from

Quincy to Key West. Templeton's Opera Troup was also favorably received in several Florida communities.[42]

That Walter Scott's novels still appealed to Floridians was emphasized by the ring tournaments which continued to be held for a few years after the war. Having been held only in Tallahassee and Quincy before 1860, they were extended to Monticello, Madison, Ocala, Bartow, and Fort Myers before their demise about 1890. Part of the Southerners' penchant for heraldry, the tournaments involved an elaborate ceremony in which "knights" rode full-speed to impale on their lances a small ring hanging from a crossbar between two uprights. The person adjudged the winner had the right to crown his "lady" as the "queen of love and beauty." Sixteen adults from Leon, Gadsden, and Jefferson counties participated in such an event at Tallahassee in 1870. A St. Augustine "frolic" of 1873 included a regatta, tub races, sack races, and a greased pig chase. These games were often connected with May Day picnics and other appropriate gatherings. By offering reduced excursion fares, the railroads encouraged outings to the beaches, watering places, and sometimes simply to neighboring towns. Tallahasseans were grateful to the Pensacola and Georgia Railroad for providing round trip travel to St. Augustine for ten dollars.[43]

Some communities formed amateur bands and drama groups, while at least one debating society attracted considerable local attention. Debates at St. Augustine attacked such issues as women's suffrage, tax-supported schools, and United States recognition of revolutionary Cuba. The *Gainesville Alachua Citizen* expressed astonishment when 2,000 people, including numerous white women, attended the hanging of a Negro convicted of murder. Roller skating rinks were opened in several communities from Tallahassee to Key West and caused considerable excitement in the former city. Established on the second floor of a Tallahassee store building in 1873, the rink attracted large crowds, including a few blacks who were denied admission. After several tense days during which someone threw bricks through the windows and a suit under the new civil rights law was dismissed by a Negro judge, the proprietors opened a second rink for Negroes only.[44]

Baseball teams were organized in Tallahassee and Jacksonville in 1867, but the game began attracting real attention in the early 1870s. In 1874 the Monticello "Jeffersons" played the "Garden City" club of Tallahassee, while the Tallahassee "Grasshoppers" played the Jacksonville "Duvals." In 1876 "Hayes and Wheeler" teams played "Tilden and Hendricks" clubs. In both years the baseball games competed favorably for press coverage with exciting election campaigns.[45]

Some Floridians visited Saratoga and White Sulphur Springs while others toured Europe as they had before the war, but more vacationed at

Florida resorts. Wakulla Springs and Newport restored facilities after the war, but White Springs on the Suwannee attracted more attention because of a new hotel which had opened there in 1866. Green Cove Springs became a popular watering place, easily accessible by steamer from Jacksonville. Orange Springs in Marion County was popular among Floridians, too, but St. Augustine was the vacation site most frequently visited by residents. The railroads provided favorable rates and many middle Floridians took advantage of them during the hot summers.[46]

Aggressive Jacksonville leaders decided in 1873 that a state fair would benefit their city and the state. A committee was appointed to work with state officials and Florida's state fair was held in Jacksonville on February 22–25, 1876.[47] Its favorable reception by Floridians contrasted sharply with their non-support of the Philadelphia Centennial Exposition held in the same year to celebrate the one-hundredth anniversary of the Declaration of Independence.

Ellen Call Long, who was the daughter of former Whig leader Richard Keith Call and who agreed with him that the Union should never have been broken up, thought Florida's participation in the independence centennial celebration would help restore good feelings between the two sections long embittered over the Civil War and its aftermath. In a patriotic speech which received considerable attention in and out of the state, she suggested that Floridians involve themselves in the 1876 celebration. Shortly afterward she became Florida's corresponding secretary for the exposition.[48] Her duties were to arouse interest in fund-raising activities and to induce Floridians to enter items in an exhibit. Her accomplishments in the enterprise are indicative of the extent to which Floridians had ideologically rejoined the Union by 1876.

Her most enthusiastic supporter among the old Floridians was Joseph B. Browne, a Democratic political leader at Key West, who sponsored a "Grand Callico Ball" in that city which raised $155. Several Republicans, both politically active and otherwise, assisted her. Malachi Martin contributed some of the wine he was making at Chattahoochee with prison labor. Mrs. George W. Atwood and Mrs. Abijah Gilbert contributed preserved fruits and orange wine to the exhibit and raised $50 at a tea in St. Augustine. Mrs. R. B. Van Valkenberg raised $450 in Jacksonville with a "Martha Washington reception." But it was a different story with most of her lifelong friends and neighbors.[49]

Jesse T. Bernard, prominent Tallahassee lawyer, merchant, and local Democratic official, was unable to attend Mrs. Long's meetings because he was "so busy in court prosecuting our *colored friends* for stealing, etc." No one in Wakulla or Jefferson counties wished to enter anything in the exhibit. When Mrs. Long suggested a fund-raising "Mardi Gras" at

Quincy, a local friend replied that it was inappropriate because the Presbyterian Church was holding a protracted meeting, after which a long Methodist meeting and festival were planned. Since the Presbyterian ladies were preparing for a strawberry supper immediately after that, there was simply no time for the centennial. Edward A. Perry wrote from Pensacola that the women there were not interested in the affair. Mrs. David Yulee at Fernandina also declined to participate.[50]

Florida contributed $47.25 to the centennial building fund. The state exhibit was praised by several who saw it, but it was less than Ellen Call Long had hoped and it would have amounted to little without the participation of "carpetbaggers." The problem had been succinctly identified by Mrs. Long's Chattahoochee friend: Ida Wood wrote in 1872, "you have a good idea, but it would not work here. . . . I'm sorry your effort in behalf of our oppressed state has been abortive. . . . You know fifteen years bitter struggle has crushed nearly every spark of patriotism from the Southern breast . . . and it will be hard to bury the past."[51]

10

There Is Some Political Excitement Here

The struggle between President Johnson and Congress was decided in favor of the latter in 1866 when the voters returned more than a two-thirds majority of Republicans to both houses of the legislative branch. When Congress reconvened after the Christmas holidays, most Republicans were prepared to enact new legislation dealing with Reconstruction of the southern states, but they were not agreed on any particular plan. The legislation which finally passed in early 1867 was not written entirely by Radicals; it was the result of a compromise. Thaddeus Stevens introduced a bill which set off extensive debate in both houses. A Senate committee headed by John Sherman of Ohio was established in mid-February to work out an acceptable bill. The Sherman bill with minor amendments was accepted by both houses and became the First Reconstruction Act on March 2, 1867, after the anticipated veto was overcome.[1]

Floridians of all persuasions watched the debate over the "military bill." Conservatives praised President Johnson's veto of the District of Columbia suffrage bill which received extensive press coverage in January. Some thought there was a possibility that the Supreme Court's decision in *Ex Parte Milligan* might be applied against the Reconstruction Act. But many were already anticipating the reduction of the state to territorial status. They watched congressional developments with anxiety and foreboding.[2]

Florida Republicans thought Congress was moving too slowly and offered advice. C. L. Robinson, Florida's Union-Republican national committeeman, suggested that Congress should "make a 'clean sweep' of it—

disfranchise the guilty and enfranchise the deserving." He thought it unsafe to risk reconstruction with Union white men alone. Negro suffrage was imperative. Ossian B. Hart, one of the few native Unionists and former slaveholders who favored Negro suffrage, also called for disfranchising everyone involved in the rebellion and enfranchising all one-year residents including Negroes. A military governor supported by military force would be necessary, he said, admitting that there would be intense opposition from the "late rebels, but no more than they already feel toward the old flag." General Foster had resigned his command, arguing that under existing laws he had insufficient power to carry out his mission. He was succeeded by Colonel John Sprague, a conservative with close ties among Floridians, who also believed that increased power for military officials was necessary if Negroes and former Union men were to be protected in the state.[3]

The First Reconstruction Act declared that no legal governments existed in the ten southern states and divided the states into five military districts. The president was to appoint a general officer to command each district, supported by a military force. Major General John Pope was made commander of the Third Military District which comprised Florida, Alabama, and Georgia. Colonel Sprague continued in command of the Florida sub-district. The commander was responsible for protecting life and property and for enforcing peace and order until a republican state government could be re-established. He could retain civil officers or establish military courts at his discretion. If military courts were used, their power was paramount to that of state and local officials. The general was to see that accused persons were tried without undue delay and that reasonable sentences were administered. All death sentences were to be reviewed by the president.

The citizens of Florida and the other states had some control over the duration of military occupation. Elections were to be held for delegates to another constitutional convention in which all adult male residents were permitted to vote, except those disqualified for officeholding by the Fourteenth Amendment. When the delegates wrote a constitution extending voting rights to all male citizens regardless of race and that constitution was ratified by a majority of the registered voters, elections could be held for state officers and a congressman. After the legislature ratified the Fourteenth Amendment the state's representatives could be seated in Congress and the state would resume its normal relations with the Union. In the interim, the state government was subordinate to the authority of the United States.[4]

Floridians differed in their reactions to the military bill. Some agreed with the *Gainesville New Era* that the most dignified and wisest policy was "masterly inactivity" in political affairs. By doing nothing they could remain under military government which they preferred to accepting Negro suffrage. The *St. Augustine Examiner* thought that if the military bill went into effect Florida was fortunate to have Colonel Sprague at the reins of government. An Ocala lawyer thought "this is only the beginning of worse times. Congress intends to grind us as low as possible, and will do it."[5] A few Floridians thought they should wait until the Supreme Court declared the Reconstruction Act unconstitutional. Mississippi had entered suit to enjoin the United States from implementing the law, but most state leaders advised against waiting for the court's decision.

The influential *Tallahassee Floridian* put the problem in terms of alternatives. It admitted that the bill established a "provisional government." While it did not abolish existing governments it reduced them to "empty nothings." Governors remained in office but with little to do. "A military officer . . . is empowered to make of himself a Court, and by a simple order . . . he can constitute himself Judge, Jury, and Sheriff, and clerk." The paper did not advise its readers to do anything and it predicted that Southerners would do nothing under the military bill, but it cautioned them to be sure they understood what was involved: "If the South is *ever* to accept negro suffrage; if it is *ever* to reorganize its State governments under federal dictation; if it is *ever* to ratify the pending constitutional amendment as a condition of restoration, there are manifest advantages in not postponing til another year what they may be brought to do at last." The advantage of early admission was that Southerners could influence the 1868 election and bring a speedy end to military control.[6]

While Southerners debated whether to act, Congress removed the option. The Second Reconstruction Act of March 23 was passed, making the commanding generals responsible for voter registration to be completed by September 1. The act required that an oath be sworn by each potential voter; essentially it declared that he was eligible under the law. The commander was to appoint three-member boards in each election district to supervise registration and the forthcoming election. The convention was to have the same number of delegates as the most numerous legislative house in 1860. Delegates were to be apportioned according to the registration figures. An election was to be held at which the voters would elect delegates to a constitutional convention and at the same time vote on whether they wanted a convention to be held at all. If a majority of the registered voters favored a convention, the commander was to see that it met within sixty days.[7]

After the second bill passed almost all Conservative Floridians accepted Negro suffrage as inevitable and tried to turn it to their advantage.

Colonel Sprague observed to General Howard that the Negroes, with only a vague idea of their civic obligations, needed good advisers and that the planters were fulfilling this service well. The *Floridian* thought it of "paramount importance that perfect confidence shall exist between the Southern whites and freedmen. . . . No greater misfortune could befall the two classes than a feeling of antagonism."[8] From Washington where he had remained as a lobbyist, Senator-elect Wilkinson Call urged "submission to the terms imposed on us." He denounced the Reconstruction laws as unconstitutional, but argued that resistance would gain nothing: "I do not despair of the freedmen exercising, under your aid, and with your sympathy and encouragement, the suffrage in such a manner as at least not to cause any great detriment to the country. Let us, before pronouncing judgment on them, give them a fair trial. . . . They are bound to us by many ties of kindly association and of interest. . . ."[9]

At the same time a widely publicized meeting was held at Pensacola at which a crowd of both blacks and whites listened to speeches on military Reconstruction. Former Confederate Secretary of the Navy Stephen R. Mallory called on the whites to accept the Negroes as equal before the law and to help educate them for citizenship. He cautioned the Negroes to avoid secret political societies. J. D. Wolfe, formerly a Union officer in a Negro regiment, also spoke for a policy of moderation. They were followed by Hayes Satterwhite, an elderly ex-slave who had lived in Pensacola for forty years. He declared white Floridians his friends and advised Negroes not to destroy that friendship. These speeches received statewide press coverage and were quite satisfactory to Conservative whites, but it is doubtful that many Negroes outside Pensacola were influenced by them since they had been prohibited by law from learning to read. The message was carried to them, however, at numerous meetings addressed by nearly every prominent Conservative leader in the state. In Leon County Governor Walker, Anderson J. Peeler, D. P. Hogue, Mariano Papy, and McQueen McIntosh were prominent among the advocates of an alliance between former slaves and masters. This was repeated in every planting county. The *St. Augustine Examiner* argued that Negroes owed support to the ex-Confederates because they "owe their freedom *not* to the good wishes of the Republicans . . . *but to the hard fighting of the Confederates,* which compelled the Republicans to call on the blacks to help them."[10]

When the Negroes failed to recognize the debt and began listening to the Republicans, Conservative appeals were increasingly accompanied by threats. Posing the question of whether an alliance between freedmen and Republicans could "possibly promote the happiness and welfare of the colored people," the *Floridian* answered: "No, it will have the reverse effect. The cultivable lands belong to the so-called 'rebels,' and it is from these lands that sustenance is to be obtained for the blacks as well as the whites. But the latter are not absolutely dependent upon colored people for labor. They can send off for white people . . . and if necessity compels will divide their lands out among or lease them to white immigrants."[11]

While calling for a coalition of Negroes and Conservatives, white Floridians continued to protest the imposition of military Reconstruction. There were various interpretations of the first two Reconstruction acts and of the temporary disruptions as military authorities adjusted to the new command structure, so there was uncertainty and anxiety about the extent to which the state was affected by the new laws. On March 17, Colonel Sprague notified Jacksonville Mayor Holmes Steele that Negroes would have to be permitted to vote in the city elections on April 1. "Our people are not prepared for this sudden change, but . . . they bow an humble obedience," the *Examiner* lamented. A few days later Sprague ordered the election postponed indefinitely, following the order issued by General Pope as he assumed command of the Third Military District on April 1. According to the order there were to be no further elections until the registration of voters was completed as directed by the second Reconstruction Act. Yet a municipal election was held at Pensacola on April 1, with Negroes participating, and its results were apparently allowed to stand.[12] The Key West District was merged with the District of Florida under Colonel Sprague. He soon moved the headquarters of both the military and the Freedmen's Bureau from Tallahassee to St. Augustine.

Pope ordered that civil officials should continue in office until their terms expired as long as justice was impartially administered. The general expressed hope that he would not need to interfere with civil administration. All existing and future vacancies, however, were to be filled by military appointment. Florida newspapers praised the conservative tone of Pope's order and called on the people to cooperate with him. In the following fifteen months, Pope and his successor filled numerous vacancies by military orders, but they usually worked closely and harmoniously with Governor Walker. Most Floridians appointed to office by Third Military District orders were nominated by the governor or other civil officials. The general was obliged to remove about fifteen persons, including sheriffs, Gainesville city officials, and justices of the peace.[13]

Pope promised restraint in using military commissions as long as the civil courts protected the rights of persons and property without distinction. The circuit judges of the state held regularly scheduled sessions in April without interference. Most of the cases tried during the period of military control were handled by the state courts. On a few occasions military orders commuted the state court sentences of freedmen. Floridians resented the fact that their courts operated at the discretion of a superior military authority, and much of the animosity toward Reconstruction resulted from this "military domination." Its practical effect was negligible, however. There are no records of the exact number of Floridians tried by military authority, but in the entire district—Florida, Alabama, and Georgia—there were only thirty-two trials and fifteen convictions. Only one person's conviction was upheld by the reviewing authorities and he was not a Floridian.[14]

Pope's efforts to put Negroes on juries were more bitterly resented than any other action regarding the courts. In August 1867 he ordered jury lists to be made up exclusively of registered voters, thus excluding from the duty all who could not take the oath. The order was widely protested with the most serious resistance at Ocala. A jury of eight white and seven black men was summoned for the November session of the county criminal court. Judge James M. Wiggins commented on the novelty of Negro jurors in his opening remarks but said he was obligated to hold court. County solicitor S. D. McConnell protested that their presence violated the Florida constitution and offered his resignation. All attorneys except one refused to practice before the mixed jury. McConnell was dismissed as solicitor by military action and barred from practice in Marion County. Since another solicitor could not be found, court did not convene again for several months. While this disagreement stalemated the judicial process in Marion County, the first mixed grand jury in Florida was empaneled without incident at St. Augustine on December 9.[15]

Floridians had begun changing their favorable estimate of General Pope even before the jury controversy arose. His order prohibiting state officials from using "any influence whatever to . . . dissuade the people from taking an active part in reconstructing their State Governments" aroused hostility soon after he assumed command. But the act which brought the most violent response was Pope's issuance of General Order No. 49 just a few days before he ordered the regulation of juries. General Order No. 49 directed that all official announcements of state and local governing agencies had to be made in newspapers which did not oppose congressional Reconstruction. Although this impractical law made it impossible to meet legal requirements regarding posting notices of public action in newspapers of the affected area, it was the overt abridgement of a free press which was most resented. An order prohibiting the carrying of guns was issued in June. Although it seems to have been difficult to enforce, there were so many complaints about the law that it was reaffirmed in November.[16]

Pope's policies relating to voter registration and preparation for the constitutional convention—which became the general's most important responsibility after the March 23 Reconstruction Act—also caused bitter and sustained condemnation by local whites. The act prescribed the qualifications for registering and stipulated that local registration boards were to consist of three loyal citizens, but left other details to the commander's discretion. On April 8, General Pope divided Florida into nineteen election districts and directed Colonel Sprague to submit the names of three people in each district to become registrars and one man to become state supervisor. Ossian B. Hart was appointed to the state position, with responsibility for visiting the registration boards and making sure that potential voters were informed of their political rights and knew how to exercise them. Several weeks elapsed before the local boards were all appointed. The March 23 act required registrars to be eligible for office under the pending Fourteenth Amendment. Pope wanted them to be civilians if possible and each board was to have one Negro member. The latter was to be literate and if such a person was unavailable in a district he could be brought in from another. Compensation for their services was based on the number of voters registered; the rate ranged from thirteen to forty cents per person. It was impossible to find enough qualified civilians to serve, so Freedmen's Bureau agents were assigned to the boards in several districts. In July, Pope ordered all military officers and bureau agents to inspect registration activities and report their findings.[17] Both as registration board members and bureau officials, the agents advised freedmen about their political rights. White Floridians regarded this as one more unnecessary interference.

In a series of orders in late May and early June, General Pope issued instructions for the registrars. By handbills, letters, and notices posted in public places, the boards were to inform potential voters of their appointment and the functions they were to perform. Beginning on July 15, they were to visit every election precinct in their districts and remain as long as necessary to complete registration. Pope's instructions concerning persons to be registered and those to be excluded revealed the difficulties which all the military commanders faced in interpreting congressional intent on the subject. The law excluded from participation in the election all persons who had held state or national legislative, executive, or judicial offices and subsequently supported the Confederacy.[18]

The several military commanders, General Grant, and Attorney General Henry Stanberry all had differing ideas as to the meaning of the law. For example, some thought that persons who had been conscripted into the Confederate army should not be excluded from voting. Others thought that minor officeholders who had not taken an oath to support the United States and later supported the Confederacy might legitimately register. Pope tried to clarify the law with a statement that all persons who had held legislative, executive, or judicial offices under the state or national governments were prohibited. But if any person whom the local board thought disfranchised insisted, he could be permitted to take the oath and his case would be held for subsequent review. Each board was to keep a list of all excluded persons. On June 17, Pope instructed the boards not to register any former state or national officials who had subsequently supported the rebellion, including mayors of towns and justices of the peace. By the time this order was transmitted, Attorney General Stanberry had issued a series of interpretive statements which aroused suspicion among some congressmen that the Reconstruction acts required clarification. On July 2, 1867, a Third Reconstruction Act was passed. It gave commanders more precise authority to remove civil officials, but its significance was that it superseded Stanberry's interpretations and gave the registration boards power to deny registration to any persons they believed to be disfranchised. The boards could also revise registration lists by adding persons they deemed eligible and eliminating others they believed ineligible.[19]

Although some native whites were confused as to their eligibility to vote and most of them criticized the discretionary powers of the boards, registration progressed satisfactorily. Pope wanted the task completed by August 20, but a few rural counties had been delayed so Colonel Sprague was authorized to continue registration until September 20. On the latter date, 26,417 Floridians were on the lists: 15,237 Negroes and 11,180 whites. When the books were opened again on October 31 for five days, additional registrants raised the total to 28,003 but did not significantly alter the proportion of Negroes and whites.[20]

The Reconstruction acts required that Pope draw election districts on the basis of the registration lists of September 20, and order an election of forty-six delegates. He called the election for November 14–16, to be held in each county seat under the supervision of the registration boards. Election officials were instructed to publish notices of the election by the best available means. The voters would cast ballots for or against a constitutional convention and at the same time choose delegates. The convention was to be held only if a majority of the registered voters approved it. The limitation of only one precinct to a county was modified so that boards could designate more if they deemed it necessary to assure a full vote. Pope was condemned by native whites for gerrymandering the districts against them[21] and he did intend to favor those who supported the Reconstruction acts. The native Conservatives could scarcely have won a majority of convention delegates by any districting arrangement, but their minority membership might have been increased by a more equitable system.

Resentment of Pope's orders increased as native whites gradually realized that they were not winning the support of their former slaves. Failure to attract the Negroes should not have been surprising. The former masters were saying "we are your best friends" while denouncing the national government for forcing Negro suffrage upon them and threatening to import white laborers to replace the blacks unless the blacks supported the Conservatives. There were other people seeking the Negroes' support in early 1867 who had more to offer them. A number of Republicans from both North and South, predominantly but not exclusively white, were building a Florida party. All of them were referred to by Conservatives as "Radicals" but their political views varied widely. In a fluid political situation they were trying to build bases of power from which they might attain party leadership. The obvious place to look for votes was among the Negroes, but by no means were they all radical on racial issues. There were many possible coalitions among the various groups in Florida, and many were attempted with differing degrees of success. Some identifiable political groupings eventually emerged, but they were never clearly divided along racial lines and they were not static.

One of the important early political organizations was the Jacksonville Union-Republican Club which had its origins in the wartime efforts to form a Union government in Florida. This ideologically amorphous club was not large, but among its members were some of the most important Republicans of the era—including Ossian B. Hart and Harrison Reed, two of the three Republican governors of the period. Hart was a native Unionist and former slaveholder who had worked for readmission of the state under the Lincoln plan in 1864. Immediately after the war he favored Andrew Johnson's strict states' rights idea of Reconstruction, but he soon decided that Negro suffrage and military occupation were necessary for the building of a loyal Florida. Harrison Reed, a former direct tax commissioner, also participated in the 1864 movement. He was a conservative, however, and as Montgomery Blair's postal agent in the state he had become acquainted with many native whites while rebuilding the postal system. Reed favored compliance with the Reconstruction laws and partnership between government and private businessmen to develop Florida's economy. He was a former Wisconsin Whig who had joined the Republican party after the Kansas-Nebraska Act. Some of the other wartime Unionists who belonged to the organization were Paran Moody, Judge Philip Fraser, John S. Sammis, and Calvin L. Robinson.

Other leading members were Jonathan C. Greeley, George Peck, L. M. Latta, C. Slager, O. L. Keene, S. F. Dewey, N. C. Dennett, and S. N. Williams. Adonijah S. Welch, who became a United States senator, and Clayton A. Cowgill, later state comptroller, also belonged. There were at least two important Negro members: William Bradwell, a Jacksonville minister, and Jonathan C. Gibbs, a Dartmouth and Princeton educated minister who was Florida's most accomplished Negro political leader.[22] The Jacksonville club encouraged organization of Union-Republican clubs in other counties, sent speakers on tours across the state, and prepared for a state convention. It was committed to a policy of compliance with the Reconstruction laws and Hart became state supervisor of voter registration, but this did not prevent a major attempt to form a coalition with native white Conservatives.

Harrison Reed and David L. Yulee had become acquainted through mutual interests in expanding the railroad system of the underdeveloped state. After a discussion of a possible alliance between some native Floridians and the Union-Republican party, Reed asked Yulee to furnish a statement upon which he and his Conservative associates were willing to unite. The "platform" which Yulee presented was in general agreement with the Reconstruction acts. Promising to bring leading Floridians into a conference with the Union-Republicans to get the movement started, Yulee avowed his support for any policy which "can best and soonest heal the wounds of the past."[23]

The alliance was never completed. Jonathan C. Greeley, deputy collector of internal revenue at Jacksonville, introduced Yulee's platform to the club as a statement upon which "some leaders of the opposition" were willing to unite with the "loyal element" to implement congressional Reconstruction. After a bitter debate a decision on the matter was postponed. In a move which Reed termed a major blunder, Greeley also sought to make the club more attractive to Yulee by dropping the word "Republican" from its name. This proposal was defeated after Ossian Hart attacked it. Hart and others had agreed to exclude the word "Radical" from the party name, but thought Greeley's suggestion was going too far. The advocates of a coalition finally had to be satisfied with a resolution which merely offered a cordial welcome to all persons without distinction of race, color, or former political association. Even this mild statement was contrary to the spirit of the club's constitution which stated that leaders of the rebellion should be forever excluded from political power.[24]

Coordinate negotiations in Tallahassee also collapsed at about the same time. Thomas W. Osborn, former Freedmen's Bureau assistant commissioner, was working with the Jacksonville group to organize a state party. His views on Reconstruction were similar to Reed's. As head of the bureau he had been popular among Tallahassee Conservatives and was welcomed by them socially. He became the law partner and business associate of McQueen McIntosh, a former United States judge who had been a prominent secession leader. McIntosh, Governor Walker, and *Floridian* editor Charles E. Dyke—in whose clever political mind the coalition idea probably originated—conferred with Osborn about a mutually satisfactory plan. For a while prospects seemed bright, but Walker found that Osborn had been organizing Negro voters into secret societies. Since the secret meetings had been strongly opposed by all native whites who were trying to win the Negroes' allegiance, Walker was furious that his potential ally was partially responsible. "I fear there will be no cooperation," he wrote. A few weeks later Dyke lashed out against Osborn. "While he has been proposing to us the most conservative sentiments, he has been all the while deluding the negroes into joining secret leagues. . . . We have proof. . . . Reed is no better."[25] The editor failed to drive a wedge between conservative Republicans and those interested in Negro rights, but the differences within the developing party remained and he was much more successful in the early 1868 struggle over a constitution.

The secret meetings of Negroes which caused such acrimony between the negotiators had begun before the Reconstruction acts passed. They were initiated by Osborn because they were ideal for political education and for organizing a large potential electorate. The elaborate ceremony, secret signs and passwords, and discussions of free land and civil rights attracted and held the attention of many freedmen. But these societies, called Lincoln Brotherhoods, served a broader function for the Negroes, and they were opposed by white planters for other reasons, too. The old fear of a Negro insurrection was rekindled. At Ocala, bureau agent Jacob Remley received complaints from local whites that Negroes were holding secret military meetings in Long Swamp. Yet when Remley, the local military commander, and the county sheriff investigated, they found a group of blacks enjoying the mysteries of a secret organization whose purpose was religious worship and mutual assistance. The only military item was a signal drum. But, since the planters objected to their staying up so late at night, Remley ordered the Negroes to stop their meetings.[26]

White Monticello citizens became alarmed at the regular meetings of a Lincoln Brotherhood lodge in a local Negro church. By cleverly misinterpreting General Pope's order that public meetings were to be protected, the city mayor issued his own instructions that political meetings could only be held upon filing of prior notice, that the marshal was required to attend even though not a lodge member, and that anyone attending a meeting without prior notice would be arrested. Colonel Flint, who commanded ten middle Florida counties from Tallahassee, ordered discontinuance of armed, secret, night meetings and threatened to arrest anyone found carrying arms.[27]

The fear of armed Negroes probably resulted partially from part of the lodge ritual which involved guards challenging all who approached to show secret handshakes or to respond to passwords. The Negroes were attracted by the secrecy and ceremony just as were whites who belonged to similar organizations at the time. The Lincoln Brotherhood aroused interest and commanded good attendance. It provided a vehicle for informing Negroes about political issues and candidates. Its membership oath ended with the phrase "I will not vote for or assist . . . any person for any office who is not a brother of this league."[28] But the organization was not a violent threat to the safety of white Floridians, nor did it make Republicans of Negroes who otherwise would have supported the Conservatives. Most of them were already inclined to the Republican party and to Abraham Lincoln for reasons that were difficult for Floridians who had supported the Confederacy to overcome.

Native white Floridians then and afterward criticized the Freedmen's Bureau personnel for their political activity among the Negroes. Some of the agents—Marcellus L. Stearns, Charles M. Hamilton, and William J. Purman, for example—allied with Osborn and became prominent Republican leaders. Most of the agents and local military commanders responded to General Pope's encouragement and spoke to the freedmen about their political rights and responsibilities. But several agents talked in tones which should have delighted the Conservatives, advising blacks to attend fewer political meetings and spend more time with their crops. D. M. Hammond criticized Radical leaders at Fernandina who were arousing Negroes against their employers. J. H. Durkee, agent at Gainesville, told a crowd of blacks to "vote only for those you know to be good and true on the basis of their past lives. Avoid pettifogging politicians." At the same time the local post commander, Captain E. R. Ames, gave a speech which the Conservative newspaper endorsed as "filled with practical advice." The *Lake City Press* praised Colonel Sprague's speech at a Negro Baptist church. Sprague spoke to Negroes throughout the state, receiving general acclaim from local whites for his moderation. When freedmen marched to a Republican county convention at Brooksville armed with shotguns and muskets, agent William G. Vance ordered them to disarm and the blacks immediately complied. A. B. Grumwell emphatically denied that he had organized or even attended the Lincoln Brotherhood lodge in Monticello.[29]

Most Negroes ultimately gave their support neither to the Conservatives nor to Thomas Osborn. By late 1867 most blacks favored a small group of Radical Republicans who favored far more sweeping social and political changes then were contemplated either by the white Floridians or the Osborn-Reed Republicans. The Radicals countered the Lincoln Brotherhood lodges by organizing local Union League chapters. The league's leaders in Florida were Liberty Billings, Daniel Richards, and

William U. Saunders. Billings had remained in Fernandina after having served there as an officer in a Negro regiment. Formerly a chaplain, he had an acid-tongued, emotional speaking style which combined religious sermons and political orations to make him extremely appealing to black audiences. Richards, a tax commissioner until 1866, had left Fernandina after his removal from office, but returned when it became apparent that the Reconstruction laws would pass. He was accompanied by Saunders, an educated Negro from Baltimore. They had the blessing of the national Republican party to form Union League chapters. Saunders was president of the Florida League. A Union Club had been meeting regularly in Fernandina since March 1866. The league spread all over the plantation area and the three men were its most influential spokesmen, but Fernandina continued to be an important political base and Liberty Billings made his permanent home there.

The Union League in Florida was a secret society whose mystic ritual appealed to Negroes in much the same way as did the Lincoln Brotherhood, yet it soon surpassed the latter in size and importance. The difference between them was the emotional fervor with which Richards and Billings appealed to black audiences. Claiming no social distinctions between themselves and the blacks, the two men assaulted former slaveowners in violent speeches. White Floridians were accused of desiring to restore slavery if given the chance. A Republican victory was the only way to thwart them. To make this possible Negroes would have to become Republicans and support the party of Grant and Lincoln. To become Republicans they would have to join the Union League. Once they joined it, the leaders found it easy to keep the new voters aroused to support the party. After taking oaths to support the League, Negroes were told that failure to do so was a violation of their oath and a grave offense.

Native white Conservatives, conservative Republicans, and military officials alike denounced Billings, Richards, Saunders, and the Union League. Bureau agent Durkee thought the great majority of Negroes would be "controlled by the secret Republican Clubs" and he saw "great danger that the freedmen's vote will become a venal thing. . . ." Bureau inspector Sanno attacked them in his September 1867 report as detrimental to the state's agricultural interests: "By the formation of secret political organization, binding the freedmen to unity of action, the leaders are enabled to assemble at any time a large number of voters . . . nothing seems to be done but to exhibit the aggregate political strength of a certain faction of the dominant party. . . . Much bad counsel and advice has been given, tending towards an antagonism of races. . . . Freedmen are continually advised to trust no man . . . who does not subscribe to certain political tenets. In some of the sub-districts, if not all, the freedmen have been taught by designing demagogues to consider the chief magistrate and his councilors as traitors, who would fasten again upon them the bonds of slavery. . . ."[30]

The Union Club of St. Augustine corroborated Sanno's charges with a resolution that its fifty members would vote for no man who had voluntarily supported the Confederacy. From west Florida a bureau agent reported that the freedmen were almost unanimously Republican and any attempted defections were resisted with "a shower of the most bitter persecution." In Madison County they were also well organized. In Alachua County a freedman calling himself Dr. Mitchell stirred up some excitement by announcing a conservative ticket in opposition to the regular Republicans in the county, but after one mass meeting his movement collapsed.[31]

As the native whites saw their former slaves "arraying themselves for the Union and against traitors" as one observer phrased it, anger showed in their speeches and actions. Several whites warned of a Negro insurrection on July 4, but the day passed quietly throughout the state. There was a revival of emigration fever, with numerous whites threatening to move to British Honduras. S. M. Pyles of Jackson County organized a group which went to Brazil in April 1867. About seventy Floridians joined people from Alabama and Georgia and sailed some 300 strong from New York. At Waukeenah, Jefferson County, Anderson J. Peeler—who had earlier asked freedmen for their political support—delivered an attack on the Reconstruction acts and advised planters not to hire Negroes who belonged to the Union League. A Jackson County bureau agent reported the whites becoming more "desperate and reckless" as their political fortunes diminished. "The serious truth is that many localities in west Florida have not 'surrendered' to the U.S. Govt," he concluded. They were "overpowered but unconquered," said agent Grumwell at Monticello.[32]

While Dyke, Yulee, Walker, and other Conservatives were working for a coalition with conservative Republicans and some still hoped for the support of a majority of the freedmen, a St. Johns County Conservative convention was held at the St. Augustine city hall. Former Confederates were joined by former Unionists W. W. Van Ness and W. Howell Robinson in adopting a platform which recognized the rights of Negroes and called on everyone to work for Reconstruction. The St. Johns Conservatives urged other counties to organize and send delegates to a state convention. A Leon County Conservative convention on August 24 was attended by about 150 white and Negro delegates. They resolved to work for reorganization of the state and to accept the Reconstruction acts as final. Leon County Conservatives joined with those of St. Johns in calling for a state convention on September 25. Accordingly, a Constitutional Union Party convention met in Tallahassee with Negro and white delegates. Van Ness, a former Union army officer, became permanent chairman. William Archer Cocke of Monticello—a pro-Confederate Virginian who had lived in Florida since 1863 and been a circuit judge during the Walker administration—shared the vice-chairmanship with a black about whom nothing is known except that his last name was Simms. George W. Scott, a former Confederate officer and prominent Leon County merchant-planter, was made secretary with Robert Kent, a Negro, as assistant. Frederick R. Cotten, George W. Scott, and Green A. Chaires, all planters in Leon County, were named to the state executive committee. Other members were General Charles Mundee, who had been General Foster's adjutant general and later became the first chairman of the Grand Army of the Republic in Florida; W. Howell Robinson, a St. Johns County Unionist; and Robert Kent.[33]

The convention adopted a lengthy platform calling for abolition of the cotton tax, removal of the restriction against former Confederates who desired to settle under the 1866 Homestead Act, encouragement of immigration, support of schools, and acceptance of the Reconstruction acts as the final measures in restoring the Union. It also adopted a resolution that Florida citizens had "furled their flag" and laid down their arms to accept peace. They had given Negroes rights and witnessed them becoming good, honest workers under contracts. But "political demons, who traverse the land amidst the darkness of the night" were leading the ignorant Negro people astray with falsehoods. "Let it be impressed upon the freedmen that these secret leagues, managed by people who know them not, are but snares to delude and destroy them, while their true and only friend is the white race, to whom they formerly belonged, but now, under the sanction of god, are free." The resolution concluded with a promise to "our colored fellow citizens" that "we mingle our interest with his [*sic*], and the law that protects the one will necessarily protect the other."[34]

Despite optimistic expressions from some Conservatives the Constitutional Union convention failed. The Negroes who attended did not represent the majority of blacks. Attended by delegates from only five counties—St. Johns, Leon, Wakulla, Jefferson, and Columbia—it showed that most native whites were either indifferent about the election or had decided it was futile to participate in it. The problem was enunciated by Edward M. L'Engle of the Duval County Union Conservative Club, who also suggested a course of action which many Conservative Floridians followed in the 1867 election. Apathy of voters in Duval and Nassau counties and the adamant refusal of several prominent men in the latter to act at all were major reasons why the Duval Club had decided not to run candidates for delegates. "Our aim is to defeat the convention, we can not control it," L'Engle wrote. Since the constitutional convention could be held only if a majority of registered voters favored it, there was a possibility of preventing it if enough people refused to vote. Reasoning that a vote for delegates might be construed as a vote for the convention L'Engle and others thought it better not to vote at all. This plan originated with Wilkinson Call who in late June had still been calling on Floridians to accept the Reconstruction acts.[35]

As a result, in most counties no Conservative candidates entered the November contest. The change from initial acceptance of the Reconstruction acts by Conservatives in early spring to opposition in the fall resulted from their failure to either win Negro support or build a conservative coalition. When early elections in some northern states went against the congressional Radicals, Florida Conservatives hoped that defeat of the constitutional convention might bring about alteration of Reconstruction legislation.

Because of the partial Conservative boycott, the November election was primarily between the Republican factions. Factional membership fluctuated and some individuals remained more independent than others, but there were two identifiable groups of leaders as the election approached. Working through the Union League, Billings, Richards, and Saunders won over most of the Negroes with their emotional assaults on native whites and promises of a vastly improved future from the party of Grant and Lincoln. The Radical faction had several other prominent leaders, among them Jesse H. Goss, Eldridge L. Ware, Samuel Walker, J. C. Emerson, Adolphus Mot, Fred A. Dockray, William H. Christy, George W. Atwood, Charles H. Pearce, William Bradwell, and Jonathan C. Gibbs. Jesse H. Goss was a Marion County native who first joined the Confederacy in 1861 and then became a Unionist. After the war he was the spokesman for Negroes at Ocala, using his considerable legal talents to defend them in court. This cost him his social position in the white community and the local Baptist congregation tried to expel him. Goss was the Ocala law partner of Ossian B. Hart's Jacksonville firm.[36]

Eldridge L. Ware was a native white Radical at Key West and had been a consistent Unionist during and after the secession crisis. Samuel Walker had come to Florida in the late 1850s and spent the war years in exile at Key West. He was the major opponent in that city of Lyman Stickney's 1864 reorganizing scheme.[37] After the war he moved to Tampa and then Tallahassee, where he identified with the Negro wing of the Republican party and was elected mayor in 1874. J. C. Emerson was a white minister at Fernandina. A vigorous and effective stump speaker, he infuriated the whites of several north Florida towns where he spoke. Adolphus Mot was a well-educated French immigrant, formerly on the personal staff of Secretary of the Treasury Salmon P. Chase. Mot came to Fernandina to grow olives, served as clerk of the tax commission, and in 1865 was elected mayor in one of the first elections in the country at which Negroes were permitted to vote. Fred A. Dockray and his father, William P. Dockray, were both Federal officials in St. Augustine and Jacksonville. The younger Dockray was not pro-Negro and switched to another faction when it was personally beneficial to do so.

William H. Christy was editor of the *Jacksonville Florida Times*. He tried to obtain congressional patronage for his paper but was rebuffed in favor of the moderate *Florida Union*, at a time when Congress was ostensibly dominated by Radicals. George W. Atwood was a Northerner who served briefly on the tax commission before settling at St. Augustine where he gained a reputation for his orange groves and nursery stock.[38] Charles H. Pearce was an African Methodist Episcopal minister who came from Canada to organize the church in Florida. Known as "Bishop" he became one of the most influential Negroes in the state. William Bradwell was a militant Negro AME minister at Jacksonville who advocated separate schools for blacks. Jonathan C. Gibbs was a Presbyterian minister who came from New York to Florida during the 1867 election campaign. At first a member of the Jacksonville Union-Republican Club he was always somewhat aloof from factional identity. He was the best-qualified Negro in Florida and one of only two who held high office during the Reconstruction period.

The other Republican faction centered around the Jacksonville club. Although its members had varying ideas about major issues and the faction was only temporarily cohesive, it is best described as moderate. Its leaders were not radical advocates of Negro rights, but they accepted the Reconstruction acts as a proper plan on which to reorganize the state government, after which they were eager to develop the frontier area through a friendly alliance between public agencies and private corporations. On the latter point they were in complete agreement with native white Conservatives. In addition to Reed, Hart, and those mentioned earlier, moderate Republican leaders included Colonel F. W. Bardwell, a former Union officer from Massachusetts; Eleazer K. Foster of St. Johns who later became a Democrat; Alva A. Knight, a former Union officer and briefly an official of the Union League; and William H. Gleason, formerly of Wisconsin and closely acquainted with leading congressional Republicans. Gleason had received favorable consideration for his development projects from the Conservative Walker administration. Other moderates were Horatio Bisbee, Jr., Horatio Jenkins, Jr., and Leonard G. Dennis, all of the department of internal revenue, and Sherman Conant, clerk of the United States district court. Conant replaced Hart as chairman of the state Republican executive committee at the July convention.[39] Some of the moderates were native southern Unionists but most of them were from the North. Nearly all were or had been officers of the United States government.

There were other moderate Republicans closely associated with Thomas Osborn who joined the Hart-Reed faction. Some of the bureau agents in this group were David M. Hammond of Nassau County, Charles M. Hamilton and William J. Purman of Jackson, Marcellus L. Stearns of Gadsden, Malachi Martin and George B. Carse of Leon, J. H. Durkee of Alachua, and Andrew Mahoney of Columbia. All were northern men formerly of the Union army. Osborn was still working with the Lincoln Brotherhood during the spring and summer of 1867 and did not join with Hart and Reed until Billings and the Union League officials won the allegiance of the secret societies.

A struggle for control of party policy and leadership began when Hart, as chairman of the state Republican committee, called a convention to meet at Tallahassee on July 4. An early hint of trouble came when some Duval Republicans refused to support Hart's delegation to Tallahassee and named a contesting Billings slate. With delegates from thirty of thirty-nine counties attending, the convention opened with Harrison Reed as temporary chairman and Alva Knight as temporary secretary. A committee on organization presented a majority report naming Osborn as permanent chairman and a minority report naming Hart. Osborn was made chairman by a vote of twenty-eight to nineteen, but only after an angry debate in which sectionalism was made an issue. Billings said a southern man such as Hart could not be trusted by the Radicals. He also condemned Reed for not appointing more Negroes to committees. Reed retorted that he was suspect of anyone who was always "bowing and scraping to persons of that race."[40]

Daniel Richards introduced a series of Radical resolutions which were adopted. Colonel Sprague was censured for his moderate policy as commander.[41] Another resolution called for a stay of tax collections.[42] After the convention the Radicals continued criticizing the Hart-Reed faction as "Conservative-Republicans." Billings told a Jacksonville crowd that the United States Army in Florida favored a continuation of slavery. Jonathan Gibbs told them that southern men were untrustworthy. A visitor to Jacksonville during the period observed laconically that "there is some political excitement here."[43]

The moderate Republicans seem not to have realized the threat to their leadership implicit in these Radical activities. During the summer they referred to Union Republicans, Republicans, and Unionists as interchangeable terms and reported optimistically that the party was strong and united. C. D. Lincoln, a former Massachusetts citizen who had lived in Florida since 1856, noted what was happening. Condemning Billings for his attack on Hart, Lincoln thought it useless to pit Negroes against southern Republicans. It would have been far better for party leaders to recognize that Negroes were committed Republicans and spend their energy trying to attract southern Unionists' support than to struggle among themselves for control of the black voters.[44] That was exactly what the moderate Republicans began doing after they finally realized that the Negroes were drifting away from them and aligning with the Billings faction.

For the November election the Republican party selected slates of candidates calculated to satisfy all groups in the potential Republican electorate in the nineteen districts, although moderate whites received slightly more consideration than Negroes. The eleventh district (Alachua County) nominated W. K. Cessna, Horatio Jenkins, and Josiah T. Walls. Only the latter was a Negro. Jefferson County with a predominantly black population constituted the seventh district. Authorized to send four delegates, its Republican convention named John W. Powell, A. G. Bass, Robert Meacham, and Anthony Mills. The latter two were Negroes. Leon County, with an overwhelming Negro majority, comprised the sixth district with five delegates. Its nominees were T. W. Osborn, Charles H. Pearce, Joseph Oates, O. B. Armstrong, and John Wyatt. All were black except Osborn. But the major problem was the fourteenth district comprising Nassau, Duval, and St. Johns counties. The regular party nominated E. K. Foster, O. B. Hart, F. W. Bardwell, and John Gordon. Only Gordon, a Fernandina minister, was black. This was the district where Billings, Richards, Saunders, Gibbs, and Bradwell lived.[45]

When the regular Republican party overlooked the Radical leaders, the differences which had been developing since the July convention split the party. The Radicals held a mass meeting in Jacksonville and nominated a contesting slate which included Billings, Gibbs, Bradwell, and Dennett.[46] To be effective in the constitutional convention, it was imperative for the Radicals to have their most skilled leaders present. They erroneously expected N. C. Dennett to side with them. Since there were only four delegate positions in their own district, Saunders and Richards moved to Gadsden County and began campaigning there less than six weeks before the election.[47] A shocked and angry Marcellus L. Stearns—the local bureau agent and a moderate Republican candidate for the convention who had been confidently reporting a united party in his district—complained that Billings, Richards, and Saunders launched a speaking tour in October which destroyed bureau control over the freedmen. A rowdy meeting on October 26 had forced Stearns to arrest several people for disorderly conduct and carrying arms. To make matters worse, Saunders was circulating a petition among the blacks urging Stearns' removal as bureau agent. Stearns was afraid Saunders would succeed, "for he wields the rod of a despot over the 'Loyal League' and threatens all who oppose his wishes with immediate excommunication."[48] The removal effort failed, but all five Radical leaders were elected to the convention over their moderate opponents.

Only 14,503 ballots were cast in the November election, with all but 203 favoring a convention. With a total of 28,003 registered voters, the 14,300 pro-convention votes were a bare majority. In December, General Pope issued an order naming the 46 delegates who had been elected and calling for a convention in Tallahassee on January 20, 1868. About 1,220 whites voted for a convention and 203 opposed it. Of the 13,500 registered voters who did not cast ballots, 10,491 were white. Meade estimated that 350 white Floridians were disfranchised by the Reconstruction acts and 550 who were eligible failed to register. Most of the eligible whites were registered but they attempted to prevent a convention by remaining away from the polls. In Marion County, for example, 473 whites were registered but only 8 voted. Thus they left a clear field for the Republicans to elect the delegates. The native whites boycotted the elections and sent poll watchers to observe the ballot boxes, but they still complained that frauds were committed.[49] If so, only competing Republicans were affected in most cases. Only 2 Conservative delegates were elected while the other 44 delegates were Republicans. Eighteen of them were Negroes and the remaining 26 were from both northern and southern states.

Richards exulted in the election results. "The Radical team has triumphed. Billings, Saunders, and myself have literally created the Republican party in Florida and made a convention with two-thirds if not three-fourths our friends. . . . The Convention will be extremely Radical. We have secured the confidence of the masses so that we do not much fear opposition."[50] Richards exaggerated the dimensions of the victory, but the Radicals had good reason for optimism as they prepared for the January convention.

11

Radicalism Has Been Sent Howling

In late December, Major General Pope was replaced as Third Military District commander by Major General George G. Meade, whose views were closer to President Johnson's than to those of the congressional Radicals. Meade tended to interpret his duties and responsibilities more narrowly than Pope had done. Where Pope had given the impression that he was using military power to bring about specific goals, Meade was more concerned with preserving peace and order than with achieving any particular end. Since he was obliged to exercise his military authority with respect to the Tallahassee convention, Meade's assumption of command was significant in shaping the course of Reconstruction in Florida.

Criticism of Pope's handling of the registration and election of 1867 continued after he left. Native white Floridians asked Meade to set aside the election. United States Marshal Alexander Magruder, a native Florida Unionist, claimed to speak for many loyal men when he condemned the districting because it had attached small white-populated counties to large Negro-dominated counties to deprive the former of a voice in the convention. Magruder was also angry that non-residents had been permitted to become delegates. Hoping that something could be done to "keep the proposed mob of all colors out of our State Capitol," he said nearly all whites of the state regardless of party were willing "to do any thing and accept every thing, except the doctrine of full and complete equality of the negro with the white race."[1] Neither Meade nor any other authority responded to these requests.

Daniel Richards interpreted the change of military command as an indication of President Johnson's increasing ability to influence congressional Reconstruction through administrative policy, but he was still confident of controlling the convention. Believing that he and the congressional Radicals were in agreement, Richards thought that Johnson's activities should be resisted by hasty completion and ratification of the constitution. In Tallahassee, Richards and Billings became known as the "mule team." In order to facilitate caucuses of their faction and decrease the likelihood of wavering members going over to the opposition, the Radicals had rented a furnished house where they provided rooms and meals for "some 15 or 20" delegates. They also rented a buggy and a team of mules with which they met incoming trains and transported friendly delegates to their headquarters. "I have paid out my last dollar and expect to borrow if I can more money to be used for the same purpose"; Richards' financial plight should have warned him that he was not the principal instrument of congressional Radicals in Florida. Until November 1867, he and William U. Saunders had received financial support for their Union League activities from a Republican financial committee headed by Thomas L. Tullock. After General Thomas Conway—a Freedmen's Bureau official involved in Louisiana affairs—visited Florida during the fall election campaign and reported his observations to the national committee, Tullock stopped the funds.[2]

An even clearer indication of Richards' declining popularity in Washington came when Tullock began sending financial contributions to the Florida Republicans through Harrison Reed, who was already receiving aid from Andrew Johnson's postmaster general, Alexander W. Randall. Reed had protested the election of Richards and other "aliens and nonresidents of Florida" to the convention, and in July 1867 he had criticized the Republican state convention for "pandering" to Negroes.[3] Reed emerged during the constitutional convention as the dominant personality in the moderate Republican faction. Moderates received consideration in other instances where they competed with Radicals for national party support. An 1867 law authorized the clerk of the U.S. House of Representatives to select newspapers which would publish official notices. After lengthy correspondence, Edward McPherson awarded this important patronage to the moderate *Florida Union* edited by Edward M. Cheney, while the Florida Radicals favored Fred A. Dockray's *Florida Times*.[4] Either Radicalism meant different things in Washington and Tallahassee or Radical domination of Congress was less than absolute.

Despite their financial setbacks, neither Richards nor any of his associates seemed to doubt that their policy had the whole-hearted support of congressional Radicals. When the convention met on Monday, January 20, 1868, in the house of representatives of the state capitol, there seemed no obstacle in the way of rapidly completing a satisfactory constitution.

With twenty-nine of the forty-six delegates present, Charles H. Pearce was named temporary chairman. He appointed Saunders to head the committee on permanent organization and it appeared that the "mule team" had undisputed control of the convention.

The situation was complicated, however, when Saunders' committee reported Daniel Richards for permanent president. William J. Purman, Freedmen's Bureau agent and delegate from Jackson County, argued that Richards should not be seated because he was not a resident of the county from which he had been elected. In a long and excited debate the Radicals responded that there could be no question of the eligibility of those named on General Pope's order. Richards was finally allowed to take up the gavel. He named seventeen committees which began working on a constitution, but the moderates continued to obstruct and delay. The convention spent nearly two weeks quarreling over procedural matters, especially the question of delegate eligibility. Meanwhile, more delegates arrived until forty-one had been seated by February 1. Richards complained that the delay was disastrous to the Radicals. They were impoverished while their opponents were lavishing money on wavering delegates. "All of our delegates are poor," he lamented, "probably three-fourths of them had to borrow money to come here and . . . all those of easy virtue soon fall prey to these minions of the devil and A. Johnson who have plenty of money."[5]

Richards was not alone in accusing delegates of accepting bribes, but it is easy to exaggerate the problem. With both factions asking allegiance in the name of the same party and principles, some of the delegates saw little difference between them. A few switched sides during the struggle and it may have been for money as Richards suggested. Because the convention was so disorderly and some delegates lacked knowledge of parliamentary procedure, hostile observers criticized and lampooned its actions. The Conservative press had predicted that a deliberative body with Negro membership would fail and it reported the convention's activities to prove that it had been correct. John Wallace, a Negro page at the convention who later became critical of the Republicans, wrote in 1888 that most delegates were either grossly ignorant or dishonestly motivated. An able but hostile historian subsequently concluded that "enlightenment and honesty were more than balanced by stupidity and dishonesty." Solon Robinson, a *New York Tribune* reporter who sympathized with the blacks, disagreed in part. He expressed pleasant surprise at the parliamentary abilities of several black delegates but was disgusted at the antics of some of the whites. A series of biting articles in the *Tribune* won Robinson the animosity of the moderates.[6]

During the struggle for control of the convention the amorphous membership gradually aligned into two factions. Although the Radicals claimed the allegiance of most Negroes, the alignment was not entirely racial. Of the fifteen Negroes who sided with the Radicals, nine participated in the debates. Joseph Oates, Green Davidson, and John Wyatt were natives of Leon County. Davidson was a barber and Wyatt a minister. All three were able speakers, although Oates and Davidson often angered the whites with their emotional styles. Frederick Hill, a native of Gadsden County, also spoke on the floor. Robert Meacham was a mulatto native of Jefferson County whose father had been his owner. Working as a house slave, Meacham had acquired a decent education. After the war he was a minister in Jefferson County and became an important political leader there. William Bradwell was a northern minister who came to Jacksonville in 1865. Elected to the state senate in 1868, he apparently left the state after his term ended. Charles H. Pearce was a minister who became a major influence among Negroes throughout the state, especially in Leon County. The white Conservatives did all they could to discredit Pearce, but his position in the black community was unassailable.

Saunders has been identified as an immigrant from Baltimore and president of the Union League in Florida. Josiah T. Walls had come to Florida after serving as a first sergeant in the Union army. A man of considerable ability and moderate demeanor, he was elected to three terms in the United States Congress. The most accomplished man of either race in the convention was Jonathan C. Gibbs. Having failed to obtain a missionary assignment to Africa after seminary training at Princeton, he served his church at Troy, New York, for several years before coming to Florida in 1867. He later served as secretary of state and superintendent of public instruction.

In addition to Billings and Richards, five white delegates allied with the Radicals. They were A. G. Bass of Jefferson County, Eldridge L. Ware of Monroe, Jesse H. Goss of Marion, William R. Cone of Columbia, and John N. Krimminger of Lafayette. Goss subsequently became a circuit judge and Krimminger was a state senator before being assassinated in 1871.

Of the three Negroes who supported the moderates, only Emanuel Fortune was active on the floor. A speaker of considerable ability, Fortune was from Jackson County but had to leave his home during the racial violence there in 1869. His son was T. Thomas Fortune, who as an expatriate Floridian in New York in later years became an accomplished newspaper editor, literary figure, and member of the Afro-American League. There were seventeen whites who supported the moderate faction on the crucial votes. Several of them became political leaders during the

Republican era, notably George J. Alden of Escambia, later secretary of state; T. W. Osborn and Simon B. Conover, later United States senators; Horatio Jenkins who ultimately presided over the convention; and W. K. Cessna, later an influential state senator. Most important in the early sessions were William J. Purman, Lyman Rowley of Escambia, and E. D. House of Putnam, all of whom obstructed the convention's progress until the moderate faction gained enough support to challenge Richards' control.

Purman led the opposition which insisted that four Radical delegates were ineligible. Pearce was not a Florida resident and had allegedly sworn allegiance to the English crown in 1867. Purman claimed that Billings was a non-resident whose legal address was New Hampshire, which was especially remarkable since Billings had lived at Fernandina as long as Purman had been in Jackson County. Purman correctly argued that neither Saunders nor Richards were voters in Gadsden County from which they were elected. The Radicals continued to insist that General Pope's order was final authority on delegate eligibility. Since Richards was the presiding officer and the others constituted the committee on privileges and elections, Purman had a formidable task. Still, there were lengthy and disorderly debates between Purman, Rowley, and House on one side and Saunders, Davidson, and Gibbs on the other. Solon Robinson especially deplored House's conduct.[7] Tempers flared because the moderates, with little support among the delegates present, were simply trying to prevent the majority group from writing a constitution. Richards had trouble maintaining order on several occasions and even the sergeant-at-arms was sometimes unable to quiet the antagonists. Most of the missiles hurled across the assembly hall were verbal, but a few spittoons and chairs were also thrown. The galleries were packed and some observers were unable to restrain themselves from urging on their favorites. Great throngs also gathered outside the capitol and heard addresses from several speakers. Liberty Billings won the unabashed support of the crowd with his political-religious rhetoric.

Little was accomplished during the first two weeks of the convention. Only two of the seventeen committees reported. Jesse Goss obtained passage of an ordinance which suspended tax collections and the laws providing punishment for non-payment of taxes. This ordinance, which was promulgated as a military order, was intended to relieve Negroes who had been incarcerated for not paying the capitation tax. An abortive effort was made to obtain pay for the delegates, but General Meade ordered the state treasurer not to recognize any requisitions by the convention president without the general's specific approval.[8] This was a blow to the Billings-Richard faction whose delegates were hard pressed for funds.

Billings succeeded in tabling the question about the four disputed delegates, but it came up again when George J. Alden moved that John W. Butler of Santa Rosa County be seated in place of George W. Walker, a Conservative elected in the first district. Walker had refused to claim his seat, saying he had not campaigned for it. When General Meade informed them that there was no authority for compelling attendance, the moderates appealed to have the order modified to recognize Butler in Walker's place. The issue set off renewed debate between Purman and Saunders which caused Solon Robinson to compare the convention floor to a gladiatorial arena.[9]

If they could have seated Butler, the moderates would have had a majority of one. Osborn and Purman, as delegates in the convention, and Harrison Reed, as a lobbyist, were working diligently to take over the organization. Reed's major ally outside the body was William H. Gleason. Both had friends among the influential native Conservative leaders and personal contacts with important congressional Republicans. But before these connections could be of value, the moderates had to shape the state's fundamental law, and they could not do that as long as Daniel Richards presided. While Richards was complaining about the "minions of the devil" influencing his supporters, Reed and Gleason told Solon Robinson they had the power to reorganize the convention and intended to use it. Robinson reported that Billings and Richards were losing their fight and that the moderates "might make an acceptable constitution, but if they do I will hereafter believe in miracles."[10]

The struggle climaxed on January 31 when N. C. Dennett was called to Jacksonville because of an emergency. Billings seized the opportunity to settle the question about Butler and tabled the matter by a vote of twenty-one to twenty.[11] Realizing that the Billings-Richards group was still in control, a moderate delegate moved to adjourn until Tuesday, February 4. Some delegates misunderstood his motive and the motion carried. It was only a temporary respite for the moderates, however. After nearly two weeks of procedural debates, the Radicals still held a narrow majority, but when they assembled on Tuesday the entire opposition was absent. During the weekend the moderates had moved to Monticello to prevent a quorum in the convention. Since only forty-one delegates had been seated, the twenty-two remaining members decided they constituted a quorum and proceeded with the convention's business. They voted themselves a pay and mileage bill and completed a constitution in two days of secret sessions. The twenty-two delegates signed the document and dispatched it by messenger to General Meade in Atlanta. The convention then adjourned until February 15, awaiting the general's instructions.

The moderate Republican *Florida Union* and the Conservative press reported that the "factious minority" had acted without a quorum. The *New York Times* agreed. When the convention adjourned, the Radicals held a nominating convention. With about 1,500 persons present, speakers indicted the delegates who had deserted the convention. One Negro speaker called on the crowd to hang them. Billings was nominated for governor with Saunders for lieutenant governor. Jonathan Gibbs was the Radical candidate for Congress.[12]

The moderates returned to Tallahassee on Monday night, February 10, without notifying anyone of their return, entered the assembly hall about midnight, and by two o'clock in the morning had reorganized the convention. During their stay in Monticello they had augmented their strength with two delegates who had never attended the Tallahassee conclave. They were John L. Campbell, a Conservative from the second district in west Florida, and Washington Rogers, a Republican who subsequently held appointive offices. With twenty-two delegates, the moderates needed two more to make a quorum of the forty-six named on the original order. Two Negro delegates who had consistently acted with the Radicals were routed from their beds and brought to the assembly hall by Charles Hamilton. The accepted explanation of their willingness to heed Hamilton was that he had recently been a bureau agent and represented authority to the confused men. In the earlier sessions of the convention, Billings had reduced the likelihood of defection among his supporters by making inflammatory speeches to the crowds of freedmen outside the capitol. The delegates who lived among them were discouraged from changing sides by fear of physical violence. The effectiveness of this tactic was demonstrated the day after the midnight session. The two defecting delegates were assaulted on the street by the crowd and escaped only after one of them shot and wounded an assailant.[13]

At the midnight meeting, Richards was deposed and replaced by Horatio Jenkins. A new committee on privileges and elections assumed authority to rule on the eligibility of delegates and vacated the seats of Richards, Saunders, Pearce, and Billings. They were replaced by Marcellus L. Stearns and J. E. A. Davidson of Gadsden County, Richard Wells of Leon, and Ossian B. Hart of Duval.[14]

During the next few days both groups met, each claiming legitimacy. The moderates held the assembly hall while the Radicals met in a Negro church or on the public square. Billings and Richards realized they were at a disadvantage as long as their opponents occupied the hall, but they were unable to regain access. The freedmen were willing to take the building by force, but Governor Walker obtained a military guard from Colonel Flint to prevent forcible entry. Although Flint's use of troops to guard the assembly hall was beneficial to the moderates, General Meade otherwise tried to avoid involvement. He expressed regret over the situation and recommended that the factions come to terms, but denied that he had power to intervene. While Conservative newspapers were predicting that Meade would intervene in favor of the Radicals, Saunders called him a "scalawag" for aiding the moderates. Richards desperately called on Governor Walker to arrest the usurpers, but Walker declined to interfere, assuring Richards that order would be preserved. When Colonel Flint also refused to change his policy, Richards appealed to Meade.

By February 16, the Tallahassee situation had become incredible to the general. He telegraphed Flint, "Richards telegraphs he has been dispossessed of the hall . . . by a mob, and that the military is protecting the mob. I presume there is some error. . . . You will see that order is preserved."[15] Meanwhile Horatio Jenkins had proposed to Meade that both contending presidents resign so that a new election could be held. This plan appealed to Meade.[16] Arriving in Tallahassee on February 17, Meade accepted resignations from Richards and Jenkins and ordered all original delegates back into the convention where Colonel Sprague, in full dress uniform, temporarily presided at a session on the following day.

Meade's intervention had the effect of legitimizing the moderate takeover of the convention. Horatio Jenkins was again elected president of the convention by a vote of thirty-two to thirteen. The four "ineligible" delegates were ousted and their replacements seated. When the military officers left the hall, the reorganized convention went to work. A resolution passed declaring that there had been no quorum and no business transacted between February 4 and February 17. Osborn noted that J. Berrien Oliver, the Conservative editor of the *Tallahassee Sentinel*, had kept a record of the convention from January 20 to February 3, and the convention resolved to accept it as the official and only journal for the period. Another resolution censured the *New York Tribune* for "maliciously assaulting the private character and public conduct of a majority of the convention, and grossly misrepresenting proceedings and purposes of this body" and denied Solon Robinson further access to the convention. A bond issue was authorized to pay the convention costs and William H. Gleason was elected financial agent.[17]

After correcting the record to their satisfaction, the moderates adopted a second draft of the constitution on February 25, by a vote of twenty-eight to sixteen. After an ordinance was passed denying pay to those refusing to sign, nine more delegates affixed their signatures under protest. A hostile newspaper commented, "now that the 'Mule Team' has made its constitution, we have a second version, the 'Fishing Party.'" The moderate draft had been written during the week at Monticello and the moderates had conferred with two important Conservatives, Charles E.

Dyke and McQueen McIntosh. By including provisions which were desirable to the Conservatives, the moderates hoped to win their support or at least mitigate their opposition to the Reconstruction laws. Although few of them publicly supported the moderate Republican administration subsequently established, many native white Floridians admitted that "a strong [bid] was made for Conservative votes." Harrison Reed, who had played a key role in the moderate victory and was to benefit immensely from it, wrote Conservative David Yulee that "under our constitution the Judiciary and state officers will be appointed and the apportionment will prevent a Negro legislature." Ignoring the extralegal methods by which his faction gained control of the convention he also boasted that "the destructors have been overthrown and the state saved to 'law and order.' "[18]

Of the two drafts of the constitution presented for his transmission to the joint committee on Reconstruction, General Meade recommended the moderate one because it was signed by a majority of the convention. He had previously informed Richards of his willingness to accept the first document if two more signatures could be added to the twenty-two on it. The constitutional convention had been in session for more than a month and most of its time had been spent in the struggle between two factions for control of the new government. Yet either of the drafts would have made an acceptable constitution. They differed significantly in only three areas and in each the Monticello version reflected the influence of the Conservatives who had consulted with its drafters.[19] The Radical constitution made most state and county offices elective while the Monticello document created more offices and made them appointive by the governor. The latter provision would enable the governor to limit Negro officials in the black belt counties. The Radical draft excluded from suffrage all those who had held Federal offices and afterward engaged in rebellion, and required a lengthy loyalty oath barring from office everyone who had supported the Confederacy. The Monticello document was much milder on this point, omitting any reference to the rebellion and requiring a simple oath of future loyalty for officeholders.

Probably the most important difference was in apportioning representation. The Radical version provided representation in proportion to population, joining some small counties into districts with only one representative. The larger counties, most of which had Negro majorities, were given multiple representation according to their size. This was advantageous to the predominantly Negro counties. Leon County, for example, would have had seven representatives while Orange, Volusia, Brevard, and Dade shared one. Senate districting was comparable. The Monticello constitution modified equal numerical representation and provided that each county must have at least one representative and no county more than four. All earlier constitutions of the state had similar provisions. By this method, approximately one-third of the voters would be able to elect a majority of the lower house. With Negro voting strength concentrated in eight north-central counties, white control of the lower house would be assured as Harrison Reed had reported.[20]

Before an election could be held, the Congressional Committee on Reconstruction had to approve one of the proposed constitutions. Meade had forwarded both to Washington, but endorsed the moderate one. Both factions were well represented in the capital city. Richards, who was closely acquainted with Elihu B. Washburne of the Reconstruction committee, and Saunders both appeared in Washington and memorialized Congress with a caustic attack on the Monticello draft both for its pro-Conservative features and its method of adoption. Pearce and Bradwell both spent several weeks in Washington trying to obtain support for the Radical version. Calvin L. Robinson of Jacksonville, still the Florida member of the Republican national committee, was probably the most influential opponent of the Monticello constitution and he argued the Radical case before the joint committee. He said the moderate document was anti-Republican and would tend to give the state to the Democrats.[21] Judge Philip Fraser also favored the Radical version but did not go to Washington.

The moderate case was presented by George J. Alden, William H. Gleason, and Harrison Reed. They were far better acquainted with congressional and Republican party leaders than the Radicals, and their restrained arguments were apparently more effective than the acidic attacks of some of their opponents. Gleason was personally acquainted with several prominent Republicans, especially Benjamin F. Butler of Massachusetts, one of the Radical congressmen. Reed was on close terms with several men of varying political persuasions, including most of the Wisconsin delegation, and especially with conservative Republican Senator James R. Doolittle. Horatio Jenkins and John W. Butler also knew Ben Butler and, like Reed and Gleason, capitalized on their acquaintance to present the moderate case.[22] In April the joint committee, which historians have often credited or blamed for implementing "Radical Reconstruction," decided that only one constitution should be submitted to the people of Florida for approval. They chose the moderate document which met the minimum requirements of the Reconstruction acts and had the endorsement of General Meade.

This was the state's most liberal constitution up to that time. It extended equal rights to all men and guaranteed protection in their free exercise. Every male twenty-one and over could vote regardless of race, color, or previous condition. The state was obligated to provide a uniform system of free public instruction and institutions for the physically and mentally handicapped. The tax burden was to be uniform on all citizens. Its most objectionable features were the disproportionate representation and the excessive number of appointive offices controlled by the governor.[23]

The constitution created a strong governor who would hold office for four years and could succeed himself. He could call extra sessions of the legislature and had veto power subject to override by two-thirds majority of both houses. With senatorial confirmation he could appoint his seven administrative assistants, and in each county appoint an assessor of taxes, treasurer, surveyor, superintendent of common schools, and five county commissioners. The judicial article empowered him to appoint three supreme court justices for life or during good behavior; seven circuit judges for eight-year terms, and a judge, sheriff, clerk of the court, and sufficient justices of the peace in each county. The voters were to elect constables, but no other local officials. The party which elected the governor would have a powerful position in Reconstruction Florida.

Emulating the actions of the Radicals, the moderates held a nominating convention for state officers as soon as the convention adjourned. Harrison Reed was nominated for governor with William H. Gleason for lieutenant governor. Charles M. Hamilton was the candidate for Congress. In the ensuing campaign, this became the regular Republican ticket.[24]

Political alignments were complex and extremely fluid in the period between the convention's adjournment and the election which was scheduled for May 14–16. There were individuals or groups in both camps who were satisfied with the constitution, or at least willing to accept it as a basis from which to work for a better one. There were also many on both sides unalterably opposed to ratification. The Republican party was irreconcilably split between Radicals opposing the constitution and moderates supporting it. Solon Robinson, who sympathized with the Radicals, said the Reed-Gleason ticket was a conservative one, that the Negroes had been sold out, and that no confidence should be placed in the new Florida government. The Florida Conference of the AME Church criticized the moderate constitution because it was "framed under rebel auspices" and provided disproportionate representation favoring whites. George J. Alden, who chaired the apportionment committee, retorted that he did not believe "all the loyalty of the State was concentrated in the AME Church."[25]

Daniel Richards and Liberty Billings were the most vociferous opponents of the Monticello constitution. Incensed by the apportionment provisions and the failure to proscribe ex-Confederates, Richards accused Reed and Osborn of selling out to the "vilest rebels." He regarded the former Confederates as criminals and his sincere hatred was amplified by his defeat in the convention. He campaigned against the constitution, hoping to defeat it and secure appointment as provisional governor under continued military control. Billings also used invective, but his opposition was soon eliminated. Colonel Sprague became impatient with "itinerant declaimers who are opposed to ratification." He thought that Billings' speeches of "semi-religious character, interspersed with exciting political sentiments," were generating unnecessary hostility toward the freedmen which would invite retaliation as soon as the military forces were withdrawn.[26] Billings was arrested for making "incendiary speeches" and incarcerated at Fort Marion. The unfortunate Radical leader was held without charge for about two months and released only when the Third Military District relinquished full control of civil affairs in early July.

Even before the arrest, the Radicals had recognized their plight. William Saunders deserted to the moderates. Jesse H. Goss, once proclaimed the "sheet anchor" of the Radicals in the convention, also changed his allegiance, called on all Republicans to support Reed and the constitution, and announced his candidacy for the state senate. Jonathan C. Gibbs at first campaigned against Reed but soon decided it was fruitless and threw his considerable influence behind the moderates in April. Congressman Ben Butler even wrote an endorsement of the moderate constitution which Horatio Jenkins circulated in Florida during the campaign.[27]

Realizing they had little chance of winning, the Radicals put a new ticket in the field only as a rallying point for opposition to Reed's candidacy and ratification. Samuel Walker was the gubernatorial candidate with William H. Christy for lieutenant governor. Liberty Billings was the congressional candidate. Christy was then editing the *Florida Times* as the Radical organ, but it was soon discontinued for lack of funds. With Billings in jail and Richards firing off bitter memorials to members of Congress, Harrison Reed wrote prophetically that "the rascals die hard, but die they must."[28]

Many white Floridians whose sympathies were with the Conservative party were either indifferent or opposed to the constitution. Their leaders' attitudes fluctuated during and after the convention but many remained vigorously opposed to any collaboration with Republicans regardless of the concessions offered. A few influential persons, having obtained a constitution which was as favorable as they could reasonably expect, were willing to refrain from opposing it. Some Conservative newspapers endorsed it. The *Jacksonville Mercury* came out for Reed and the constitution, and the *Pensacola West Florida Commercial* agreed with prominent white citizens who commended the document. The *Quincy Commonwealth* said the constitution was a "sensible document" which deserved examination. In the *Floridian,* Dyke had persistently praised the moderates during and after the convention while criticizing the Radicals. But other Conservative papers were hostile to all Republicans—regardless of origin or color—and opposed anything they did. The *St. Augustine Examiner* was unequivocal: "This is a White Man's Government. Organize! Vote Against the Constitution."[29] The most extreme of all was the *Jacksonville East Floridian,* "A White Man's Paper," which called Dyke a Radical.

The Republican division caused a difference of opinion among Conservatives about whether or not to run candidates for state offices. Conservatives were also divided about the constitution, but the important leaders believed it acceptable. Governor Walker found it "a good one, the chief objection being negro suffrage." Edward M. L'Engle, a Duval County Conservative, said Florida was "fortunately rid of the worst elements of the convention, and the proposed constitution will if adopted not absolutely ruin us."[30] As often happened, Dyke stated the Conservative case best. Fearing that a Conservative state ticket in the election would force the Republicans to re-unite, Dyke complained that he had praised the moderates and criticized the Radicals in the *Floridian* for a purpose: "I labored night and day to produce the split in the convention and the fact that I did so intensified the hostility of the Billings wing against the Reed crowd and every word I say in disparagement of the one and praise of the other widens the breach. . . . we ought to feel grateful to Reed and Company for trying to break the power of such a dangerous faction as that headed by Billings and for forming a constitution so much more liberal than was expected. If Billings had succeeded he would have put political power in the hands of the negroes and we could not have lived here, but we can live here under the Reed constitution if it should be fastened on us and what is more we can control the legislature of the state and elect United States Senators." But he was afraid that few influential Conservatives "could be induced to coalesce with the moderate Republicans," because "the Radical split encourages them to run a whole ticket and carry all without a compromise." He warned, "I'm afraid we may lose all." Dyke preferred to leave the gubernatorial and ratification questions alone and concentrate on winning control of the legislature, but he reluctantly agreed to go along with the party.[31]

Dyke correctly estimated his partisans' attitudes. In spite of their recognition that many potential Conservative voters were apathetic, that others were uncertain as to whether they would be eligible to vote in time for the May election, and that it would be difficult to determine which local men were both eligible and willing to run for office, party leaders decided to name a ticket. They decided against a nominating convention for two reasons: first, Negroes would have to be excluded from attending and that would attract publicity and cause hostility, and, second, any overt Conservative political action might cause the Republicans to reassemble the convention and disfranchise "large classes of our people." Instead, they decided to communicate privately with "a few gentlemen" around the state and ask them "without even local publicity or notice of the movement" to represent their section at a meeting in Quincy on March 31. Each person was to bring a list of the politically eligible Conservatives who met the requirements specified in the proposed Fourteenth Amendment.[32]

The suggestion was favorably received in most sections. Stephen R. Mallory, Augustus E. Maxwell, and other Pensacola men agreed that prudence was necessary to avoid Republican retaliation, but they definitely favored entering Conservative candidates. Gadsden County Conservatives agreed to send representatives and support any policy "to prevent the inauguration of Radical rule . . . and defeat negro supremacy." From Putnam County came a promise to "fight to elect a conservative ticket and defeat the constitution." Jefferson County agreed to send delegates to Quincy, but it was split between those who favored an active campaign and others who thought it safer to do nothing. "The Radicals are so determined, even if the Conservatives won, it is doubtful the election would stand," they suggested. From Jackson County, an antebellum Whig stronghold, J. C. McLean and William D. Barnes thought it a good idea to run a Conservative ticket. The only problem they envisioned was "to reconcile the extreme Union element." It would be best, they suggested, to nominate men of the original Union party because many people were "dubious of any identified as Democrats or secessionists." From Marion County, Samuel St. George Rogers, S. D. McConnell, and Robert W. Bullock applauded the Quincy meeting and agreed to cooperate. Joseph Finegan reported Nassau County favorable to the plan but unable to send delegates. "Few good men here qualified to hold office and none anxious for it," he added. The kind of Conservative position which alarmed Dyke most was voiced from Tampa where John A. Henderson not only agreed to be at Quincy but was determined to "defeat the Constitution because it is bad, because it might be worse is no reason we should endorse it."[33]

The Quincy meeting produced a Conservative ticket, but there was scant optimism about the forthcoming election. Few desirable candidates were both eligible and willing to run. To attract a broad cross-section of Conservatives, the delegates nominated George W. Scott, a Tallahassee planter-merchant and former Confederate officer, for governor; Thomas W. White of Jackson County, a former Whig and wartime Unionist, for lieutenant governor; and John Friend, a Northerner with extreme states' rights views and a future Republican, for Congress. White embarrassed the Conservatives by declining the nomination after his name was circulated. After a brief but frantic search, James W. Hall of Pensacola, another former Whig, was named to replace him. Several party leaders tried to withdraw Friend's name and replace him with a moderate Republican, but J. Berrien Oliver prevented the maneuver by immediately publishing the Conservative ticket in the *Tallahassee Sentinel*.[34]

Both the moderate Republicans, when they were still hoping to win Conservative votes, and the Conservatives tried to obtain an extension of the election date to give more time for registration. General Meade declined the request but ordered the registration books to be reopened two weeks before the election, for five days. There was also an abortive attempt by some of the moderate Republicans to have O. B. Hart removed and replaced by Horatio Jenkins as state superintendent of registration. When Conservatives complained to both Sprague and Meade of anticipated frauds at the polls, Meade ordered military officers to supervise the election. He sent three additional companies of soldiers for the event.[35]

The remnants of the Radical group and the poorly organized Conservatives were not enough to allay moderate Republican optimism, but the latter took no chances. Having neutralized Billings and won the support of Gibbs, Goss, and Saunders, they still hoped to mitigate Conservative opposition if an outright coalition did not materialize. When the constitution proved inadequate as a basis for compromise, Reed offered to include Conservatives in his administration and to give them some local offices. Assistance came to the moderates from Colonel Sprague and some of the bureau agents who advised Negroes about exercising their votes. The national Republican party also furnished a little money to support the campaign for ratification. Milton S. Littlefield, a railroad promoter who was to figure largely in Florida affairs after 1868 and who often served as middleman between Republican political leaders and Conservative businessmen, arrived just before the election and assisted the Reed ticket.[36]

There was some violence in the campaign. Bureau agent D. M. Hammond complained that Fernandina Negroes were so aroused by Billings and Richards that they shouted down everyone who tried to speak for the constitution. Another agent said Leon County plantation work was neglected because three political parties were working in the county, but he thought peace would return "if the state was relieved of the presence of the political buzzards [Radicals] that are now hovering over it." At Ocala, Samuel St. George Rogers and thirty white men forced their way onto the speaker's platform at a Republican meeting. Rogers delivered an incendiary speech and bureau agent Remley intervened to stop it. On election day Rogers and his associates gathered in front of the poll and the local commander ordered them away. When Rogers refused he was arrested and jailed in Gainesville. Another Conservative shot and killed Dennis Lee, a Radical Negro leader in Marion County.[37]

In Monticello Negroes bombarded a Conservative speaker with bricks and a few shots were fired in return, but there were no casualties. The threats from both sides were potentially more serious. Several Republican candidates in Jefferson County received threatening letters signed "KKK." Later on someone left a sign on the Monticello post office door warning that if any Negroes were killed "we would not give much for the town and people." William Kirk, Republican editor of the *Observer*, and Stephen R. Mallory became involved in heated exchanges through the Pensacola newspapers. Kirk challenged the former Confederate secretary of the navy to a duel, but was arrested and jailed by the military commander. Four days later Kirk was discharged from Fort Barrancas and promptly sent Mallory another notice. Mallory accepted and they faced each other on May 12, at the cantonment near town. Just as the action was about to begin, the local constable arrived and arrested both men. A Conservative observer thought the constable's timely arrival resulted from Kirk's having warned him of the impending duel.[38]

With a few soldiers at every poll, the three-day election was comparatively peaceful. Even explosive Jackson County had a quiet election "except for one or two knock-downs outside of town." From Monticello, where there had been pre-election excitement, came a report of "a very quiet and fair election." The principal attempt at intimidation came from Negroes trying to prevent other blacks from voting Conservative, reported bureau agent Grumwell. An unfortunate shooting in Monticello after the election was not related to politics. When a deputy sheriff told an army corporal he would "blow his brains out," the enlisted man opened fire, wounding a man and young woman standing nearby. Both recovered but the corporal was arrested. Both Radicals and Conservatives complained that frauds had been committed by election officials. A lengthy investigation resulted in a report that it was impossible to ascertain the quantity of fraud.[39]

The election returns ultimately showed a majority in favor of the constitution; 14,520 to 9,491. Harrison Reed was elected governor with 14,170 votes. Scott, the Conservative, received 7,852 and Samuel Walker, the Radical, received 2,262. Almost every Conservative and Radical who voted opposed the constitution. The Radicals unrealistically clung to their hope that Congress would reject the constitution and continue military control, but Adolphus Mot of Fernandina was an exception. He wrote with resignation that he had "fought very hard to defeat Harrison Reed, with an unmanageable radical wing and a disorganized Democratic center, but the Post Office Department was too much for us." An elated moderate Republican of Pensacola chortled, "Radicalism has been sent howling from our midst."[40]

Without waiting for the necessary approval of its constitution and election, the new legislature organized in early June and Governor Reed was inaugurated. General Meade ordered Governor Walker not to surrender the government until he had authorization from military headquarters. Some Conservative legislators declined to attend the premature session, but in doing so they deprived themselves of a voice in the United States senatorial elections which were allowed to stand even though accomplished before civil government was officially restored.[41] Thomas W. Osborn was elected to the long term ending in March 1873. His service in behalf of the moderate constitution and ticket was rewarded by this position which enabled him to control federal patronage in the state. Adonijah S. Welch was elected to the short term ending in March 1869. Referred to by some as a "carpetbagger," Welch was from Michigan where he had been principal of a normal school for more than fifteen years. After coming to Florida, he was elected president of an agricultural college in Iowa, but declined and served his adopted state briefly as its United States senator.

Although many observers believed the move illegal, the legislature elected a third senator to succeed Welch when his term expired in early 1869. The man chosen was Abijah Gilbert, who was also a northern immigrant to St. Augustine. Gilbert had apparently contributed financially to the Republican campaign, but had not been active during the convention. He became a lifelong resident of the ancient city and his superb home and gardens became a tourist attraction. The *Ocala Banner* said, "he is no carpetbagger," and "we were lucky to get him."[42]

On June 25, Congress passed an omnibus act admitting Florida and five other southern states as soon as they had ratified the Fourteenth Amendment. Florida's congressman and senators were seated by July 2. On the same day Reed notified General Meade that the requirements of the omnibus act had been met, including ratification of the amendment. In a brief ceremony on July 4, Colonel Sprague relinquished control of the state to Governor Reed.[43]

Sprague was ordered to assemble his troops for garrison duty. There were protests from both Conservatives and Republicans against removing the troops. Sprague notified Commissioner Howard of the Freedmen's Bureau that military detachments were being withdrawn from the trouble spots and "freedmen left to the generosity of citizens for protection . . . much strife and contention may be anticipated . . . as nearly all the constables elected . . . are colored men." Howard responded that "technically,

. . . military authority has ceased. Practically, it will never do for any officer to leave . . . until some arrangement has been made." Some time was required for Reed to appoint the several hundred local officials throughout the state. As a result, the military removal left several communities administered by holdover officials who were expecting their replacements any moment. As the appointments were slowly made, the bureau agent at Ocala noted that "some of them are not of such a character to give much satisfaction either to the loyal or disloyal . . . [but] such is the wages of Rebellion."[44]

The protests over troop removal came to the attention of Secretary of War John M. Schofield who ordered a temporary suspension of Meade's reassignment orders. Meade acknowledged that his plan was distasteful to many people, but he argued that local officials and citizens had to become accustomed to doing without the military authorities. Meade thought it better to assemble the troops at rail centers, making them more readily available for deployment to trouble spots wherever they occurred. Troops were finally stationed at Jacksonville, St. Augustine, Tampa, Pensacola, Key West, and the Dry Tortugas.[45]

The constitution of 1868 and its unusual method of adoption had an important influence on Florida Reconstruction. Republican administration was not imposed on a helpless native white population as the popular legend described it for years afterward. Neither was it solely the work of Northerners who benevolently provided an egalitarian organic law to protect the newly freed Negroes. It was the product of a struggle between groups of men with widely differing interests. The struggle took place within the framework laid down by Congress, but there was ample room for compromise. The Radicals who had initially dominated the constitutional convention were unable to modify their demands for Negro equality and punishment of ex-Confederates, and they could not win without doing so. Native white Conservatives were not permitted much participation in the convention but they constituted the most vocal and economically powerful part of the population. They were unwilling to be subjected to domination by northern Radicals supported by Negro voters if there was an alternative. The pragmatic Republicans favored that wing of the party which wanted an alliance between government and business to develop raw frontier lands, while only a minority of leaders agreed with Thaddeus Stevens about rebuilding the South. While recognizing the need for protection of Negroes, they had little sympathy for racial equality. They recognized that a state government would have a better chance for success if it attracted the support, or at least neutralized the opposition, of the native leadership.

Harrison Reed, Ossian B. Hart, William H. Gleason, and Thomas W.

Osborn all had economic interests in common with such Conservatives as Governor Walker and David Yulee. With easy and familiar communications already established between them, they tried to work an acceptable compromise. It ultimately failed because the basic issue—what to do about freedmen who now had political power—could not be resolved, but this does not detract from the significance of the effort. Reed unblushingly admitted the priority of his commitment to Republican party principles when he told the 1869 legislature that "it was only as a Republican that I could get measures for the benefit of the State from the dominant party at Washington. We would have been paralyzed without it."[46]

The moderate Republicans, unable to gain control of the convention by ordinary parliamentary methods and unwilling to submit to the Radicals, resorted to extralegal tactics to capture the convention. They preferred collaboration with the Conservative leaders. Once the extreme Radicals were defeated they believed the Negroes would be without a policy or leaders. There would be time enough to win them over after a constitution was constructed which commanded peaceful acquiescence from powerful Floridians. They were proved correct when Saunders, Gibbs, and Goss deserted the Radical side and came over to Reed and the constitution.

No permanent coalition with Conservatives resulted, but members of both groups worked together when it benefited them mutually. The Conservatives' support of the moderates was important in their victory over the large Radical wing of the party. It was significant that Governor Walker asked for and received military guards for the convention hall to preserve order *after* the moderates had illegally gained possession of it. He got the troops because of his favorable relations with Colonels Flint and Sprague. General Meade was primarily concerned with maintaining order rather than promoting a particular social pattern. Impressed with the favorable relations between the moderates and local leaders, he pursued a policy which benefited them immensely. Having built a slight majority by attracting to their side the two Conservatives who had refused to attend the convention and by intimidating two Negro delegates into joining them, the moderates were in a strong position when Meade insisted on peaceful parliamentary procedure. Had he so insisted on January 31, the result would have been different. An intangible but crucial asset was Conservative willingness to limit campaign activity to vocal and editorial criticism in most cases. This was Conservative policy only because the moderate constitution was favorable enough and they wished to avoid the risk of having another convention which might draft a different one.

The joint committee of Congress on Reconstruction also aided the moderates. The differences between the two drafts of the constitution before it were significant enough that its rejection of the Radical document in favor of the moderate one raises a question about just how "Radical" the committee was on matters relating to Negro citizenship.[47] Radical Daniel Richards sought adoption of his version of the constitution through personal contacts with Elihu B. Washburne, a moderate member of the committee. Moderates Gleason and Jenkins worked for their constitution through Benjamin Butler, a reputed Radical. Meade's recommendation of the moderate document strictly on narrow procedural grounds should not have made the difference. Whatever its reasons, the joint committee's action helped take most of the "Radical" out of Reconstruction in Florida before the congressional plan was fully implemented.

The Conservatives gained more than they gave. The apportionment provision of the constitution assured them a number of legislative seats. With the party badly disorganized and many whites not yet participating in politics, the first legislature of 1868 had eight Conservatives to sixteen Republicans in the senate and fifteen Conservatives to thirty-seven Republicans in the lower house. Since there was too little time to disseminate the news and register the voters, the absence of proscription against ex-Confederates was too late for the May elections, but it enabled most whites to resume political activity immediately afterward if they wished. The extensive gubernatorial appointive power was beneficial as long as a Radical was not elected to the office.

When Harrison Reed was elected he named prominent Conservatives to cabinet positions. Robert H. Gamble became comptroller and James D. Westcott, Jr., became attorney general. Westcott was soon moved to the supreme court where he joined Ossian B. Hart and Edward M. Randall. The latter was the postmaster general's brother. His appointment was probably a recognition of gratitude for assistance from the post office department. Of the seven circuit judges, three—Thomas T. Long, William Archer Cocke, and Pleasant W. White—were Conservatives. Some county officials were Conservatives because qualified Republicans were sometimes not available.[48] While many whites refused to have anything to do with the "negro-carpetbag regime," others agreed with Enoch J. Vann who accepted a Madison County judgeship to keep it from a "miserable scalliwag carpetbag Radical."[49]

The moderate Republicans had hoped their overtures would provide the basis for a lasting cooperation with native white leaders. But the Conservatives did not view the mid-1868 situation as a compromise settlement within which a majority party might carry out policy with a minority party acting as a loyal opposition. Rather, they saw it as a partial victory from which they might work toward their ultimate goal which was to eject from their society and politics the unwelcome intruders and the unacceptable Negro voters. In appealing to the Conservatives the moderate Republicans resorted to destructive tactics which set an unfortunate precedent for their party. It was continually torn by intraparty strife which sapped its strength and prevented unity.

12

Reed Has Been Abused and Slandered and Tormented

When Republican Governor Harrison Reed left office in 1873 he was a poor man without a political future. Numerous Floridians believed him dishonest. Others, while not necessarily accepting the viewpoint, encouraged it because it enhanced their own positions. For the Republicans who persistently opposed him, the allegation made their own actions seem more legitimate. For the Democrats, it strengthened their claims that Republican administration was synonymous with public plunder and chicanery. The endless factional battling during his administration hurt the Republican party and the state, but Governor Reed does not bear the responsibility alone. Despite several instances of poor judgment and by modern standards even conflict of interest, Reed usually worked toward establishing a sound state government with financial responsibility and broad support from Floridians. As his former political enemy Daniel Richards phrased it, "he may be guilty . . . but look at the leprous hands upraised against him."[1]

Reed's attempt to establish a broad, bipartisan base for his administration by concessions to native white Conservatives contributed directly to the dissolution of the moderate coalition which had successfully opposed the Radicals during the convention. But the coalition also disintegrated because it had served its purpose. Individuals with new bases of power and personal aspirations disagreed over specific policies and personnel appointments even when they agreed on broad goals. Beginning with the first legislative session in 1868, Republican opposition to Governor Reed came from former allies. Although the opposing group was amorphous, it was led by Senator Osborn who built a strong power base with the federal patronage at his disposal.

Overtures to the Conservatives—or Conservative-Democrats as they were beginning to call themselves—failed to gain the support Reed desired. Having obtained all they could from the Republicans, most Democratic leaders determined to accept these constitutional and political concessions as a basis from which to launch an all-out attack on the majority party and the system which supported it. Former Governor David S. Walker, who personally opposed Reed, always tried to marshal Democratic votes against him regardless of the issue. Charles Dyke was hostile toward Republican policy after civil government was resumed. His *Floridian* was always available to dissident Republicans who wished to criticize their own party. There were other Democrats who disagreed with Walker and accepted Reed as the lesser evil so long as choices were between Republicans, but most of them opposed Republican administration and the Negro suffrage upon which it was based.

The inauguration of Governor Reed and convening of the first legislature in the summer of 1868 occurred in a tense political atmosphere. There was as much hope as belief in native white observers' prognoses of the new government's impending failure. Reports from outlying districts indicated a tenuous balance between order and anarchy. Implementation of the new constitution required much from both the executive and legislative branches and a considerable amount of restraint and patience from persons of all persuasions. More than 400 state and county offices had to be filled by Governor Reed who was obliged to rely on local advisers for recommendations about his appointments. The fundamental law called for new educational and welfare institutions to be established and financed. Law and order had to be extended and maintained as the United States forces turned over police functions to the civil government. Courts of law, greatly expanded during the Walker administration, required attention. The county criminal courts had not worked well, and the addition of Negroes to juries was not automatically accepted throughout the state.

With the state treasury almost depleted and tax collections suspended by the constitutional convention, the new administration had to rely on credit for immediate operating expenses while creating an extensive financial program to provide new services and finance old debts. The stay law was only temporary, but in agricultural Florida it would be late fall before crops were sold and money became available for tax collections. In the interim, scrip and warrants of indebtedness were issued and inevitably a multiple-price system followed. As it turned out, a comprehensive revenue law was not effective until June 1869. Reed told the first legislature that the new government could be carried on without increased taxes, but his calculations anticipated better tax revenues than were realized during the following years. The governor based his statements on an assumed increase in the evaluation of property to be achieved by a state board of equalization, but the legislature did not authorize one until 1871.[2]

In the interim, deficit financing was expensive. The Reed administration inherited a debt of about $523,000 from the Conservatives. Inadequate tax collections and credit financing increased the debt and caused financial uncertainty. Bond issues were difficult to negotiate because of the unsettled nature of state affairs and the fact that about $3 million worth of Florida bonds, issued between 1835 and 1860, had been repudiated or left delinquent.[3] Lack of cooperation within the administration also complicated financial matters. On one occasion, for example, the legislature authorized a $200,000 bond issue; the sale was to be handled by Comptroller Robert H. Gamble, a Democrat. Governor Reed located a buyer in New York and asked Gamble to release the bonds. Meanwhile, Senator Osborn, who was by then hostile to Reed, told Gamble he had arranged a more favorable sale. Gamble refused to send Reed the bonds only to be informed by the senator that it was too late to meet his buyer's terms. Neither Gamble nor Osborn was disappointed at Reed's discomfiture, but the debacle did not help the state. When Reed finally obtained the equalization act—which he hoped would raise the state property evaluation to $50 million—it was largely nullified by Gamble's instructions to tax collectors that they must accept owners' sworn evaluations without question.[4]

Democrats anxious to discredit the Republican administration often furnished New York newspapers with sensational reports of Florida's financial activities. The *New York Herald* once reported that the state was planning to repudiate its bonds. Both State Treasurer Simon B. Conover and Comptroller Gamble denied the allegation, but their answer appeared in state papers which did not circulate extensively among readers of the *New York Herald.* When the *New York World* accused Reed of issuing illegal bonds, even President Edward N. Dickerson of the Florida Railroad Company, whose business associates were Conservative-Democrats, defended the governor against these charges by Florida taxpayers who "naturally oppose all issues of bonds."[5]

Governor Reed received the most severe criticism of any individual for his handling of state money. Having borrowed on personal notes for governmental operating expenses when he first assumed office, he subsequently tried to separate his personal finances from the state's. His efforts became a major factor in the repeated attempts to impeach him.[6] Bonds of 1868 and 1869 could not be sold at prices stipulated by the legislature, which usually prohibited sale at less than seventy-five cents on the dollar. It became necessary to place the unsold bonds on deposit as collateral for loans to keep the government functioning. This hypothecation, as the procedure was called, netted about half or less of the face value of the bonds. Since interest was calculated on the face value of the securities, the state was paying dearly for its operating cash.

Taxation and governmental expenditures were the most persistent Democratic campaign issues during the Republican period. Tax rates rose and seemed exorbitant when compared with those of the prewar period, but comparisons usually ignored the new public services supported by the state. As the *Tallahassee Sentinel* put it, the Republicans spent money on education and replaced the "whipping post and pillory" with courts of law and a penitentiary. A seven mill state tax in 1869 was raised to nine in 1872. It had been five mills during the Walker administration. Both the 1869 and 1872 laws limited county taxes to one half the state tax.[7] Some counties—such as Duval, Columbia, Madison, Jefferson, and Leon—levied much more than that amount because they were obligated to pay off bonds issued in support of railroad construction before the war (when there were no Republicans in Florida).

Tax laws were difficult to enforce and the system of collection by local officials was unsatisfactory. With state certificates circulating at depreciated rates, collectors frequently received currency and then settled their treasury accounts with depreciated scrip, pocketing the difference. Since most of the state scrip was acceptable for taxes, it was bought and sold at prices set by supply and demand. Its value in terms of gold ranged between fifty and eighty cents during Reed's administration. In this situation it was impossible to determine the extent to which collectors were taking advantage of the state. The only solution was to put the state on a cash basis and that required time. In the interim, most Floridians were adversely affected by the lack of an adequate amount of stable circulating medium. Legislators grumbled in 1868 when their salaries were paid at the rate of 30 per cent in currency and the balance in state scrip.[8] By 1872 scrip was so low that Governor Reed complained of realizing only $1,000 from his $3,500 salary. The issue of scrip by private companies such as the Florida Railroad and the Drew and Bucki Lumber Company further complicated matters. Since the Florida Railroad redeemed in $100 lots only, those who received small quantities for wages were forced to buy only where the scrip was accepted.[9]

Tax valuations were incomplete and varied greatly in different counties. Although the results were disappointing to him, Reed's state equalization board eventually raised the total state property valuation from about

$30 million to $34 million.[10] The board was unpopular with taxpayers who thought that only the owner should declare the value of his property. The reasons for their feelings are clearer when one considers that some property owners were still declaring their plantations worth eighty cents an acre, the price they had paid for unimproved land years earlier. Those who complained of high millage rarely admitted that its yield of revenue was severely reduced by these valuations. Attacking the equalization board as well as the Reed administration, Democrats exaggerated the prevalent but incorrect opinion that a propertyless class was controlling a state government determined to extract all its expenses from unrepresented property owners.

Money remained scarce and property values depressed. Tax collection machinery gradually improved and the volume of forced tax sales increased in the plantation counties. Enraged to see Negro officials sometimes selling their lands for delinquent taxes, impoverished whites eagerly accepted Democratic charges of Republican extravagance. The *Tallahassee Floridian* alleged that the Reed administration had increased the state debt from $523,000 to $14,999,000 in 1870.[11] Actually the debt reached its highest level in 1873 when it was less than $1.9 million. The 1873 figure does not include bond issues authorized to aid railroad construction. Although one $4 million issue was sold, it never obligated the tax system and was secured by a mortgage on railroad property. After 1873 the second Republican administration gradually reduced the debt, capitalizing on groundwork laid by Governor Reed.

A bipartisan taxpayers' convention was held during the period, protesting high taxes and wasteful spending policies.[12] The delegates bitterly condemned the equalization board. They claimed it had raised valuations when property values were declining. Several counties were well represented at the meeting, but others seemed less concerned. Too few people realized or admitted that the tax base was small and that only a larger population and the sound financial policies suggested by the governor would distribute the burden less onerously. Economic difficulties could be alleviated by attracting immigration and settling the large undeveloped and unproductive areas of the state. Railroad companies and development agencies cooperated with Reed's immigration commissioner on this matter. With Commissioner John S. Adams mailing quantities of Florida promotional pamphlets all over the country, the state was already becoming the most advertised in the Union.[13]

Within a few months after the restoration of civil government, the vague factional alignments of the constitutional convention disintegrated. The frequent legislative sessions became scenes of continual debate and maneuvering between contending individuals and groups. Conflicting personal ambitions of Republican leaders and the willingness of the Democratic minority to embarrass the majority party were serious obstacles to constructive legislation, but there was another problem. Reed had tried to establish a predominantly white government to attract support from Conservative-Democrats, but there were also influential men of his own party who were confirmed white supremacists. Lieutenant Governor William H. Gleason, for example, wrote retrospectively that Negro legislators were ignorant and incompetent, and that as president of the senate he had refused to appoint a Negro to chair a committee—preferring the ardent Tampa Democrat, John A. Henderson, to head the judiciary committee. On the other hand, the Rev. Charles H. Pearce, an influential minister and member of the senate, was enunciating ideas in 1868 which many still consider radical over a century later. Freedmen's Bureau agent Malachi Martin was shocked by Pearce's remarks when asked to help obtain volunteer Negro labor to erect a school building. Pearce replied that there were thousands of dollars in the United States treasury put there by the uncompensated labor of freedmen. The least the government could do was to construct a school for Negroes who had worked without compensation for generations and were too poor to build their own.[14]

It would have been exceedingly difficult for Reed to have found a common denominator upon which these two men could agree, even without the problem of the Conservative-Democratic minority. When the legislature met in mid-1868, Negro leaders were already angry at the way they had been treated during the constitutional convention and election campaign, and they were alienated further during the session. The legislature passed a bill guaranteeing equal treatment of all citizens on railroad cars and other public conveyances. Reed vetoed it on the ground that the constitution already protected all classes against discrimination and that such a bill would cause a race war. Another measure authorizing legislators' full annual salaries for the period from June to December was also vetoed. Conservative-Democrats, who had been organizing to campaign for Democrat Horatio Seymour for president, were embittered by a law authorizing the legislature to cast the 1868 electoral votes. Reed and the Republican press defended the act as an economy measure, arguing that Florida had a Republican majority and the procedure simply saved the expense of an unnecessary election.[15]

On October 28, Reed aroused opposition from some moderate Republicans with whom he had formerly worked in harmony. Since it was necessary to elect a Congressman, he called an election for December 29. Several legislators had been appointed to other state offices without resigning from the legislature, and the constitution prohibited a person from concomitantly holding offices in more than one branch of state government. Reed declared ten senate and five house seats vacant for this reason and called for them to be filled in the December election.[16] Several of those affected had resigned but others had intended to hold both offices.

When the legislature met in November and cast the state's three electoral votes for Ulysses S. Grant and Schuyler Colfax, Reed declared the meeting a special session so the members could draw travel allowances. But when that body authorized its members both per diem and mileage, the governor vetoed the measure because they were only entitled to travel pay. Within hours, Horatio Jenkins—one of the senators whose seat had been vacated—appeared before the lower house and lodged five vague charges against the governor: lying, incompetence, embezzlement, corruption, and "declaring many legislative seats vacant."[17] John W. Butler of Santa Rosa, whose house seat was also affected, moved adoption of an impeachment resolution. Angered by Reed's vetoes and hurried into voting without deliberating the emotional charges, the house impeached Reed by a vote of twenty-five to six. A committee informed the senate of the action, promising to furnish charges and evidence later. Theorizing that they had removed Reed from office without having to try the case before the senate, the house leaders moved adjournment. The senate disagreed. Assuming that he was acting governor, Gleason adjourned the legislature under a constitutional provision for such situations, ostensibly postponing Reed's trial until the next legislative session.

Gleason, in collusion with Secretary of State George J. Alden (who possessed the state seal and who had also been removed from a senate seat), declared the governor suspended in accordance with the constitutional prescription for impeachments. Unwilling to be so easily dislodged, Governor Reed asked the supreme court for an advisory opinion as to whether he had actually been removed. The governor reasoned that since only twelve of the twenty-four senators were present when that body was notified of the impeachment and four of those had been removed by his October 28 proclamation, there had been no quorum present and no business transacted.[18] He then removed Alden from his administrative office and appointed Jonathan C. Gibbs as secretary of state. The appointment not only gave Reed an able and loyal cabinet member, but also improved his relations with Negro leaders.

Reed continued acting as governor with the aid of Gibbs, a new state seal which Reed had recently purchased, and a twenty-four hour guard around the executive office—maintained by Adjutant General George B. Carse, a United States Army captain on extended leave, and Leon County Sheriff Alvin B. Munger. Unable to occupy the governor's office, Gleason—with Alden and the old state seal—established his own office in the City

Hotel across the street from the capitol. A wag remarked that Florida, having had three United States senators since the past June, now had two governors. The affair had taken the state by surprise, but excitement was soon aroused. Although some Democrats were elated to see the opposition falling apart, many others agreed with responsible Republicans who expressed disgust at the debacle and its adverse effect on the state.[19]

On November 25, the supreme court unanimously upheld Reed's contention that he had not been legally removed from office. When Gleason continued his charade at the City Hotel, Reed launched an offensive with a quo warranto action, asking the lieutenant governor to show cause why he should not be ousted from office. Gleason had not met the constitutional requirement of three years residence prior to assuming office. Meanwhile, Adjutant General Carse was zealously protecting the governor. When Gleason entered the executive chamber to reclaim some personal papers from the safe, Carse pointed a loaded revolver at him and the lieutenant governor retreated without his documents. George Alden had taken some of Reed's papers when he left the capitol in November. Determined to retrieve them, Carse found Alden in a billiard hall and physically assaulted him. The exuberant official was indicted for his effort and later left Florida after a true bill was found against him.[20] Carse was soon elected to the New Jersey legislature where his direct methods continued to attract attention.

In mid-December the state court ousted Gleason from office. Failing to get his case into the United States court, he relinquished his claim to the governorship. After this "war of the factions," as one disgusted observer called it, the December 29 election was anticlimactic. Charles Hamilton was re-elected to Congress over Democrat William D. Barnes of Marianna and dissident Republican William Saunders. The legislative election gave the Conservative-Democrats one or two additional seats in each house, but several local districts renominated and elected the same men whom Reed had declared ineligible. Everyone expected the impeachment to be revived in the regular session convening in January 1869.[21]

When the legislature met, both houses recognized Reed as governor, but House Speaker Marcellus L. Stearns favored impeachment and appointed a seven-member committee to investigate charges against the governor The major charges were that Governor Reed had accepted a $500 bribe to appoint Leroy Ball as county court clerk, and had sold $6,948 worth of Virginia bonds for cash and paid the money into the treasury in scrip. Reed explained to the committee that he had been forced to pay official expenses out of his own pocket when the state was bankrupt and that the $500 had been tendered him for that purpose. Upon returning from New York, he had found that he was being maligned for selling offices and offered to return the money. He had received the $6,948 while in New York and used it to pay for state seals, engraving of bonds, and related official purchases, subsequently paying the money into the treasury "in the only way I could and which was perfectly reasonable." Horatio Jenkins, who had initiated the impeachment in November, told the committee in January that he had no evidence which would support the charges.[22]

By late January many legislators were anxious to dispose of the embarrassing impeachment affair. When Gleason resigned as senate president, he was replaced by John N. Krimminger, a conservative Republican of Lafayette County who opposed impeachment.[23] The investigating committee returned a majority report favoring impeachment and a minority report opposing it. Emanuel Fortune, a Negro Republican, offered a resolution that no evidence had been found to justify impeachment. H. S. Harmon, a Negro from Alachua County, wanted a stronger exoneration of the governor. The Democrats sought a statement which inferred guilt without actually bringing charges. James D. Green, a white Republican from Manatee County, wanted to censure Reed. Finally, Fortune's motion carried by forty-three to five.[24]

By the time Reed was exonerated, Senator Osborn was being blamed for inspiring the attack. It was no coincidence that all the impeachers were soon appointed to federal offices. Fred A. Dockray and Hiram Potter became customs collectors at Jacksonville and Pensacola respectively. Stearns became surveyor general in the Tallahassee land office. Sherman Conant was made deputy marshal for the northern district of Florida and assistant assessor of internal revenue. Leroy Ball was made clerk of the United States district court and deputy collector of internal revenue.[25]

Reed also used his patronage and "extensively weeded his garden," according to the *Tallahassee Sentinel.* Some of the prominent removals included Leroy Ball from his county court clerkship, and Sherman Conant and Horatio Jenkins from their county judgeships.[26] His appointment of Jonathan Gibbs to the cabinet was Reed's most significant personnel action in terms of improving political strength.

Another unusual action of the January session was the attempt to elect a new United States senator. Abijah Gilbert had been elected in July 1868 to fill the seat to be vacated by Adonijah S. Welch in March 1869. Several people, most of whom desired the office, considered Gilbert's election illegal. When the supreme court ousted him as lieutenant governor, Gleason began pondering his chances of replacing Gilbert. Daniel Richards, who had aided Reed in his impeachment fight, wanted the seat and thought the governor would assist him. Welch, the incumbent, also assisted Reed during his troubles in expectation of a reciprocal gesture for his re-election. After considerable public discussion of the subject, the legislature decided to elect a new senator, but Gleason, Richards, Welch, and several others were passed over. Ossian B. Hart was elected—Reed had appointed him to the state supreme court and he had supported the governor. With a certificate of election and an explanatory letter from Reed, Hart presented himself to the United States Senate. After its judiciary committee looked into the matter briefly, the Senate declared Gilbert entitled to the seat.[27] Hart remained on the supreme court.

Prominent Republicans expressed embarrassment over both the impeachment affair and the abortive senatorial election, but hoped for improved party unity in the future. However, one of the major programs of the Reed administration which had the support of most segments of the political spectrum caused continuing factional difficulties which damaged the Republican party as well as the reputations of individuals. The trouble arose over Reed's recommendation that the 1855 internal improvement program be completed. While most parties agreed on the necessity of state aid for the projects, Reed's enemies tried to impeach him again for his role in assisting the Jacksonville, Pensacola and Mobile Railroad Company to complete an east-west railroad across north Florida.

There were compelling reasons for the cross-Florida road in 1869. West Floridians felt cut off from the rest of the state and were asking to be detached from it and joined to Alabama, whose agreeable officials sent a commission to discuss the matter with Governor Reed. Reed told the January 1869 session that he understood the west Floridians' desire to be ceded and thought it could be abated by completion of a railroad connecting them with middle Florida. The west Florida agitation thus stimulated officials to greater effort to obtain the road. The *Pensacola Commercial* and the *Marianna Courier* favored annexation to Alabama, while most middle and east Florida papers opposed it. Dyke of the *Floridian* said the issue would not be settled until west Floridians had their railroad. He thought retention of the area was so important that the state should "contribute our means and credit to give them the railroad they demand. . . . we are prepared to favor extending any reasonable aid that may be necessary to accomplish this purpose."[28]

Negotiations between the two states continued during 1869. After the Alabama commission left Tallahassee, a Florida delegation went to Montgomery. Alabama offered to pay an indemnity to Florida for the loss of its panhandle and it was agreed to call an election. In December west Floridians approved the plan by a vote of 1,045 to 659, but by that time hopes were high for a railroad across the panhandle so the matter was dropped, to be revived again in 1873 when construction lagged.

With West Floridians clamoring for a railroad, and ambitious investors pressuring for state aid for their projects, Reed called a special session in June 1869. Another reason for the session was the annual appropriations bill. Having become something of a veto governor during the 1868 sessions, Reed also vetoed the 1869 appropriations bill because it lacked a governor's contingency fund and money for law enforcement. As will be seen in a subsequent chapter, the state had an overwhelming law enforcement problem when United States troops were withdrawn in 1868. The governor wanted a state police force to assist local officials until recent social, political, and legal innovations became generally accepted. Refusal of financing for the force was one more obstacle caused by the coalition between Reed's Republican opponents and Democrats anxious to discredit him and his party.

Reed's message to the special session explained that its purpose was to provide a uniform tax system, to provide for completion of a railroad to the state's western boundary, and to ratify the Fifteenth Amendment to the United States Constitution. The tax law was enacted and the governor was provided funds for his police force. The amendment was ratified without difficulty.[29] Although it was ultimately passed, the railroad bill required the most attention during the session.

In other comments, Reed reviewed Republican accomplishments up to mid-1869. The Chattahoochee arsenal, offered to the Walker administration in 1866 for a state prison, had been taken over by the state in 1868 and forty-two convicts were in confinement. An excellent public school law had been passed and one mill of the state tax was earmarked for it. However, Reed recommended that no money be appropriated for schools in 1869 since more time was required before any funds could be realized from the tax. Despite his previous opposition to public accommodations legislation, the governor seemed more aware of its necessity after he began appealing for Negro support in late 1868. Noting that some railroads were charging Negroes first class fares and denying them comparable accommodations, he recommended a law on the subject. One observer thought Negro legislators were willing to support a bill giving state aid for railroad construction only if the railroad companies gave them an "even chance for seats *in any of the cars*." A public accommodations bill was taken up during the session, but was killed by a tie vote in the house, with two Republicans voting against it and several others carefully absenting themselves from the floor. The measure passed in 1870, requiring first class accommodations for anyone who offered to pay first class fare.[30]

The governor also called for legislation to enforce quarantine regulations along the coast. Epidemics, especially of yellow fever, were a recurring problem in the port cities. Pensacola was hard hit in 1867; many people lost their lives and others fled. Shortly after the war the United

States Army had enforced quarantines in cooperation with port cities, but after it left there was no authority which could coordinate enforcement between ports. Each local government had its own regulations, but since the threat of epidemics was statewide there was need for an authority of similar dimension. Reed was unsuccessful on this matter as were all succeeding governors until 1889, after an 1888 epidemic had devastated Jacksonville and surrounding communities.[31]

Reed emphasized the need for transportation. He promised to cooperate in any way to achieve rail connections between existing roads and Tampa Bay, Charlotte Harbor, "and finally Key West," as well as between Jacksonville and St. Augustine. But most important of all, he said, was the road to Pensacola. Although he recommended great care to protect the state and its people against exorbitant charges, he thought a company should be incorporated and given aid to begin construction.[32]

George W. Swepson, a North Carolina railroad financier, and Franklin Dibble, a Jacksonville banker, had bought the Pensacola and Georgia Railroad (Lake City to Quincy) and the Tallahassee Railroad (Tallahassee to St. Marks) through a long series of complex financial transactions and some generous decisions by the Trustees of the Internal Improvement Fund. They sought an act of incorporation consolidating the two roads and another lending state aid for extending the line to Pensacola. There was bipartisan support for the project in and out of the legislature, but the bills encountered serious opposition. Strong argument against a line favoring Jacksonville came from advocates of Savannah and Fernandina, whose trade would be adversely affected. John Screven of the Atlantic and Gulf Railroad (Savannah to Bainbridge, connecting at Live Oak with the Pensacola and Georgia), who desired to build westward toward New Orleans, memorialized the legislature against the proposed legislation. Dilatory efforts almost stalled action and a group of railroad supporters threatened to filibuster the annual appropriations measure if the bills failed. Senator William Purman of Jackson County warned that if construction of the road through his section were delayed, he would work for annexation of West Florida to Alabama. A colleague retorted that this would be an easy way to dispose of Senator Purman.[33]

Swepson's persuasive associate, Milton S. Littlefield of New York, was lobbying for the measures. He had become acquainted with Governor Reed and other important Florida leaders when he served in the state during the war, and his "propensity for having a good time and cutting the swell" was becoming legendary.[34] Littlefield's lavish spending policies dazzled several legislators. Aided by Franklin Dibble and his brother Calvin Dibble, a New York investment banker, Littlefield overcame the opposition and two important bills passed the legislature by nearly unanimous votes. "An Act for the Relief of Franklin Dibble and Associates" merged the Pensacola and Georgia Railroad with the Tallahassee Railroad as the Tallahasee Railroad Company. More important was "An Act to Perfect the Public Works of the State," which created the Jacksonville, Pensacola and Mobile Railroad Company, with monopoly rights for twenty years to build a line from Quincy to Mobile, Alabama, and authorized it to consolidate with either or both of the roads between Jacksonville and Quincy if their stockholders approved. The governor was authorized to issue state bonds amounting to $14,000 per mile of the estimated length of the road and exchange them for an equal amount of company bonds in twenty mile increments as construction progressed. The exchange would give the state a statutory lien on all property of the new Tallahassee Railroad, to be cancelled by the same twenty mile increments. The company was authorized to sell the state bonds and use the proceeds for new construction. In effect, the state of Florida was lending its credit to the private corporation. If the company defaulted on its bonds, the state could foreclose on the property.[35]

Little notice has been given to a section of the act authorizing the same state benefits to the Florida Railroad Company, controlled by David L. Yulee. Yulee intended to take advantage of the law. Although they were never sold by the company, $1 million in state bonds were issued by Reed to be exchanged with the South Florida Railroad Company, a separate firm established by Yulee to build southward to Tampa.[36] Historians of the period have not denied that Conservative-Democrats were involved in the legislative activities which benefited the railroads, but they have inferred that "carpetbag" Republicans manipulated ignorant legislators into passing bills whose effect was to line their pockets at the taxpayers' expense. If there were frauds committed in this regard, the executive branch had essential assistance from the legislature, just as the Republicans had aid from the Democrats.

The law failed to satisfy Swepson, Littlefield, or the governor. The investors opposed the provisions creating a lien on existing property and they wanted all the bonds at once rather than in increments as construction progressed. Adverse publicity resulted from the special session, especially when the printed version of the Jacksonville, Pensacola and Mobile law omitted the lien clause. This caused rumors that Littlefield had bribed the clerk who handled the printing. There was also critical discussion of Swepson's financial activities in purchasing the Pensacola and Georgia. Because of the unfavorable publicity and his own doubts about the legality of such action, Reed refused to exchange the state bonds for railroad company bonds until Swepson could prove a clear title to the property, which the governor insisted must be pledged as security. A personal check for over $470,000 which Swepson had tendered as partial payment for the Pensacola and Georgia was still outstanding. The *Jacksonville Florida Union* and the *Tallahassee Floridian* favored the westward railroad, but applauded Reed for refusing to issue the bonds under the circumstances.[37]

At the January 1870 legislative session, Littlefield successfully lobbied for an amendment to the earlier law. Far more favorable to the new company than the 1869 act, it provided for exchange of bonds at the rate of $16,000 for each mile of track constructed west of Quincy as well as for 100 miles of the existing road east of that city.[38] This meant a larger number of bonds and less collateral for the state. Governor Reed still hesitated to exchange bonds because Swepson's check was not settled and he was reluctant to release the entire quantity of bonds before any construction was completed.[39] But the governor changed his mind when John P. Sanderson and Mariano D. Papy—both respected Conservative lawyers who had pecuniary interests in the transaction—advised him that he was authorized by the new law to exchange state bonds for similar securities of both the Jacksonville, Pensacola and Mobile and the Florida Central, even though the latter road was not mentioned in the legislation. On the strength of this unusual interpretation Reed agreed to release the bonds.

The railroad legislation of June 1869 and January 1870 brought on another disruptive factional battle between Senator Osborn and Governor Reed. In late January 1870, James D. Green of Manatee introduced a resolution in the assembly calling for a committee to investigate charges against the governor. The Green resolution was no surprise to most Republican party leaders, several of whom supported Reed during the affair. In late December, Congressman Charles Hamilton had warned the Grant administration that Senator Osborn and the handful of men who had brought on the 1868 impeachment effort were preparing for another one. To head it off, Hamilton called for the removal of Collector Fred A. Dockray, Collector Hiram Potter, Internal Revenue Assessor Lemuel Wilson, and Wilson's six assistants. Senator Gilbert wrote the president that he was afraid the "federal officeholders in Florida are pursuing a course which is endangering the Republican government in our state." J. S. Adams, commissioner of immigration and a respected Republican newspaperman, wrote that "Florida is in danger of passing from Republican to Democratic control."[40]

Edward M. Cheney, editor of the *Florida Union* and chairman of the Republican state executive committee, tried to forestall the public confrontation with a compromise committee, half of whose members were appointed by each side. He discharged the committee in disgust, however, when he found that the anti-Reed faction was also working out a coalition with Democrats to impeach the governor. Calling for removal of the few federal officials who were causing the problem, Cheney lamented that "our defeat and Reed's impeachment will be a democratic triumph." He saw the struggle as "the Republican party defending itself . . . against the federal officeholders and the democrats."[41]

When the Green resolution was approved by the house on January 21, Speaker Stearns appointed a committee to investigate charges. It reported a majority and minority report on February 4. Some of the charges were repetitions of those lodged against the governor earlier, but there were additions. He had allegedly spent $12,000 for militia weapons and charged the state $21,060. The most serious charge involved an amazingly candid letter to Reed, signed by George W. Swepson, explaining how the governor had agreed to call the 1869 special session for the purpose of incorporating the Jacksonville, Pensacola and Mobile Railroad Company for which he was to receive $12,500.[42] John Wallace, a member of the house who subsequently wrote a book in which he defended Reed, claimed the letter was false and had been obtained by Senator Osborn by threatening to use his power in the state legislature against the 1870 amendment to the railroad bill unless Swepson signed it. There is little doubt that Osborn would have done such a thing and Swepson's activities in Florida and North Carolina are persuasive that he would have unhesitatingly committed the forgery. At the same time, it is almost incredible that such a man would have gratuitously committed the agreement to writing.

Nevertheless, the majority report recommended impeachment. After a lively debate it was defeated and the minority report against impeachment, written by W. B. White of Clay County, was accepted by a vote of twenty-seven to twenty-two. Nearly all the Negroes supported Reed and most of the Democrats opposed him. The three Democrats who voted for Reed on this point were condemned by the Democratic press. The minority report said that instances of informal, irregular, and indiscreet conduct, especially regarding finances, had been committed by the governor, but "the evidence, when taken in connection with the attending difficulties of the governor, does not show any criminal intention whatever."[43]

After the attack on the governor failed, Circuit Judge J. T. Magbee, one of his close allies, was impeached on five flimsy charges for no apparent reason except to embarrass Reed. When the senate was notified of the impeachment, it resolved to try the judge at the next regular session in 1871.[44] Magbee was left to ponder his status until the next year when the impeachment was set aside without a trial. Meanwhile, his circuit was without benefit of a court of law.

Rumors of bribery surrounding the railroad bills, exacerbated by the abortive impeachment, resulted in several Leon County grand jury indictments. Having obtained the Freedmen's Savings Bank records of Milton Littlefield's account, the grand jury discovered that several checks had been paid to legislators. Littlefield was charged with two counts of bribery: for paying Harrison Reed $12,000 and John N. Krimminger $3,000 in connection with the 1870 amended railroad bill. The cases were continued several times and closed without action in November 1873. Charles Pearce, the Leon County Negro senator, was convicted of paying Frederick Hill $500 allegedly furnished by Littlefield to vote against Reed's impeachment. Hill testified against Pearce but was not himself tried. Judge Pleasant W. White, a Quincy native and former Confederate quartermaster in whose court Democrats and whites always had an advantage over Republicans and Negroes, presided over Pearce's trial. Krimminger was indicted for receiving $3,000 from Littlefield to support the amended bill. One indictment was quashed and another marked "dead docket" on November 6, 1871, after Krimminger was assassinated with a shotgun at his Lafayette County home by "parties unknown."[45]

A deposition by S. Stern, a Tallahassee merchant, alleged that Simon Katzenberg, white Republican senator from Madison County, received $2,000 from Littlefield. Another by Ozias Morgan, a white Republican who worked in the federal land office, said John Wallace, a Negro assemblyman from Leon County, also accepted a small sum.[46] It is impossible to determine whether any of these charges were true. There was no record showing what the checks had been paid for, and, except in the Pearce case, the court did not decide at the time. But the publicity the cases received, along with the impeachment debacle, was damaging to the incumbent political party, about which many Floridians were anxious to believe the worst. With the unfavorable publicity fresh in the memories of many voters, and with its governor, congressman, one United States senator, and the state executive committee chairman calling for dismissal of several federal officeholders whose actions were instigated by the other senator, the Republican party began planning for the 1870 election.

In addition to the legislative offices to be filled, a congressman and a lieutenant governor were to be elected. The Republican nominating convention revealed another problem with which the party had to deal. The party had ignored the Negroes for nominations to high offices in 1868. Since Reed had begun seeking their support with Gibbs' appointment to his cabinet, blacks had been learning how to trade on their political strength, or at least they were less tolerant of the white domination of the party. Samuel T. Day, a white doctor from Columbia County and a native Southerner who was aligned against Reed, was nominated for lieutenant governor. But Congressman Hamilton was by-passed for renomination in favor of Josiah T. Walls, an able Alachua County Negro who had been in the 1868 constitutional convention and the state legislature. Hamilton was made revenue collector at Key West.

Although their party was still poorly organized, the Democrats determined to capitalize on the favorable apportionment provided by the 1868 constitution and to capture the legislature while attempting to elect a congressman and a lieutenant governor. According to David Walker, they planned to elect an "honest" lieutenant governor and a legislative majority so they could impeach Reed and restore "home-rule."[47] For lieutenant governor they nominated William D. Bloxham, a popular young Leon County planter and former Confederate captain. Bloxham had all the credentials for appealing to the native white Conservative-Democrats, but he was also comparatively acceptable to some Leon County Negroes. Silas L. Niblack, a Columbia County lawyer and one-time railroad president, was nominated for Congress.

Several counties, especially Jackson and Columbia, were besieged by political and racial violence for a long period before the November 1870 election. There was more physical intimidation of Negro voters by native whites at that election than at any other during the period. Whether it was a coordinated policy directed by the state Conservative-Democratic committee may be doubted, but tactics were similar in several counties. And many Republicans, both before and after the election, thought it was a statewide plan. United States Marshal George Wentworth predicted large-scale intimidation in the counties with Negro majorities, but thought the "enforcement act" could be made effective in most cases. As for Columbia and Jackson counties, he obtained authorization from the United States attorney general to use extra funds for deputies.[48]

Although both parties waged extensive speaking campaigns, probably more votes were affected by election-day activities than by all the speeches. In Jackson County, James Coker—a white extremist who headed a night-riding regulator group—personally assaulted Negroes who approached the polls to vote. He was arrested and indicted but never convicted. In Gadsden County armed Conservatives, led by former acting governor A. K. Allison, formed a line in front of the polls to prevent Negroes from voting. Fortunately the only violence occurred when the sheriff was struck on the head with a cane, but the disturbance lasted until after sundown when the polls were closed. Many Negroes were prevented from voting and the large 1868 Republican majority in the county was nearly erased. Allison was ultimately convicted of violating federal laws and served six months in jail. Jefferson County Conservative William Bird waved a weapon menacingly in front of the Monticello polls to prevent Negroes from approaching them. When Negro Florida Senator Robert Meacham tried to reason with him, Bird threatened to shoot him. This disturbance also lasted most of the afternoon and many Negroes were left without a chance to vote when the polls closed. As in the Coker case, Bird was arrested and indicted but never convicted. About 1,000 shots were estimated to have been expended in Monticello that afternoon. The situation was complicated by the presence of a band of armed white Georgians and by the arms carried by numerous Negroes.[49]

Election officials had located most polling places in the towns so that voters could be better protected from intimidation, but this had the adverse effect of congregating large numbers of people from distant places and increasing the likelihood of physical confrontations. On the night before the election, J. J. Dickison, an ex-Confederate cavalry officer and guerilla leader, led a group of mounted men in a wild ride around the Madison County Court House. Many blacks left town without voting after this provocative demonstration. A similar group rode into Lake City, Columbia County, and shot up a group of Negroes as they emerged from a political rally in a church. The group was dispersed and several persons were wounded. Some of the prospective voters of Columbia County were thus discouraged from exercising the franchise. In a few cases the poll inspectors themselves prevented people from voting by pretending great difficulty in locating names on the registration lists and consuming time until the polls could close. Individuals were arrested and convicted for repeated voting. A standard fine was fifteen dollars and costs.[50] The Conservative-Democrats had no monopoly on repeated voting, nor were all the polling inspectors who practiced fraud and deceit Democrats. At Yellow Bluff precinct in Duval County the inspector permitted a Republican trio to empty the ballot box and insert new ballots to alter the result. But the Republicans resorted to their most questionable activities later in Tallahassee where they had a majority of the board of state canvassers.

Early returns from the chaotic election encouraged the Democratic press to claim a Bloxham victory. Niblack obtained an unofficial count from Tallahassee showing a Democratic majority of nearly four hundred but cautioned that "returns must go through the hands of the Radicals before the final count."[51] Under Florida law poll inspectors sent election tabulations to a county canvassing board of three men who compiled returns from the entire county. Their figures were transmitted to the state canvassing board, composed of the secretary of state as chairman, the comptroller, and the attorney general. In 1870 there were two Republicans—Gibbs and Almon R. Meek, who had replaced Westcott as attorney general—and Democrat Robert H. Gamble on the board. Returns from north Florida counties were soon sent to Tallahassee by rail, but transportation was slow from south Florida where Democrats were usually in the majority. When the board met on November 29, nine county returns were still missing. Hearing that the two Republicans planned to count and declare the results without waiting for the nine late counties, Bloxham obtained an injunction from Circuit Judge Pleasant W. White prohibiting the board from counting until all returns were in. In compliance with the injunction, the board adjourned until December 26.

Judge White was arrested on a federal court order for violating the enforcement act. He was later released on a $2,000 appearance bond and the case was never tried, but the arrest served its intended purpose. With White removed the board reconvened and, while the Democratic member protested vehemently, awarded the election to Republicans Day and Walls. Bloxham applied to the supreme court for a writ of mandamus requiring a recount to include the nine omitted counties. The 1871 legislature enacted a law abolishing the state canvassing board, and the court dismissed the suit because there was no longer a respondent who could be reached by judicial process. The persistent Bloxham then entered suit for a writ of quo warranto, asking Day to show cause why he should not be ousted. Bloxham won his case, but not until June 1872. Niblack also contested Walls' congressional seat and it was finally awarded to him by a congressional committee after the Negro had served nearly the entire term. Several state legislative seats were contested and the committees on privileges and elections ousted some members of both parties and seated their opponents.[52] When the contests were settled, there were thirteen Republicans and eleven Democrats in the senate; twenty-nine Republicans and twenty-one Democrats occupied the house. The Democrats had gained strength in the legislature as a result of the violent 1870 election.

When the original election results became known, Republican leaders realized that party harmony was essential to survival, but they disagreed on what action was necessary to solve their factional problems. Reed and his supporters thought the answer lay in removing the federal officers, but Osborn felt they must be retained. The destructive intraparty warfare continued and a disgusted partisan complained that the Republican "factions persecute each other more than they oppose the enemy."[53] The Florida situation must have perplexed Republicans in Washington. When the national administration finally removed collectors Potter and Dockray as requested by Governor Reed, the president was soon informed that he had made a mistake.[54]

Reed asked the internal revenue commissioner to remove Horatio Jenkins, Leonard G. Dennis, and William J. Purman, all of whom were state legislators. Reed was angered at Purman and Dennis, Republican leaders of Jackson and Alachua counties respectively, because of their attempted interference with his personnel appointments in their counties. But Horatio Jenkins pointed out that six senators and nine assemblymen held federal offices and if even a few of them chose to give up their state legislative positions and keep the national offices—the salary for which was paid in United States currency instead of depreciated scrip—Florida would go Democratic. Senator Osborn endorsed Jenkins' argument and added "as for Jenkins holding office as Collector and State Senator, we have very few able men. . . . We need his service in the federal job *and* in the state senate."[55] In the face of these explanations, Grant's cabinet officials moved cautiously in the matter. The Reed-Osborn rivalry continued to disrupt the party during the 1872 legislative session.

Since it was his last opportunity as governor to address the joint assembly in regular session, Reed used his annual message to review some of his accomplishments and some reasons why he had not been more successful. The circuit courts had been expanded to seven, and the thirty-nine county courts established by the Walker administration had been put into efficient operation. A state penitentiary had been established by converting the arsenal at Chattahoochee. Reed might have added, but did not, that the 1868 law establishing the state penitentiary also authorized the contracting of convict labor to private employers. Because of complaints of high costs of the prison, the Reed administration began in 1870 to lease prisoners to private contractors, thus originating the "convict-lease" system which lasted until 1923, when all its potential for human degradation was eventually realized.[56]

The 1869 school law had established a uniform, tax-supported public school system and a university. In 1872 Reed reported 331 free schools with 14,000 students. Plans were underway for an agricultural college. An immigration commission had been established which Reed credited with attracting new inhabitants. A state militia had been organized.[57]

Admitting that disorders almost serious enough to warrant martial law continued in Taylor and Lafayette counties, Reed asserted that his policy of restraint had gone far toward establishing peace and order in most areas of the state. With regard to railroad construction he reminded the legislature that he had been reluctant to advance state aid to the railroad companies, finally agreeing only because of the state's pressing need for transportation. Expressing disappointment that construction had not met expectations, he assured his listeners that the state's investment was still secure. Elsewhere he had recommended that the legislature prohibit the further lending of state credit to private corporations.

The governor also called attention to a "factious minority" of Republicans and Conservative-Democrats who almost destroyed his program aimed at placing the state in a sound financial position. He had repeatedly tried to replace the scrip system with cash. His difficulty with the legislature over the state board of equalization has been mentioned elsewhere. He also criticized the legislature for its refusal to tax corporations and criticized the tax assessors for their unwillingness to place the land of absentee owners on the tax rolls. While attempting to raise the tax base, he had also tried to increase the revenue from state bonds by funding the debt. A special session of 1870 had attempted to redeem the bonds then hypothecated at "an inconsiderable portion of their value," and had failed because of obstruction in the legislature. Another "funding bill" passed in 1871, but the bonds it authorized were not attractive enough to investors and had not accomplished their purpose. The state's financial transactions had also been hampered by reports, widely circulated in the North, that Florida's governor was a forger.[58]

Reed reserved his greatest wrath for "the combinations of speculators and political gamblers to destroy the credit of the state." They had reduced the value of scrip so much that he had only realized $1,000 from his annual salary of $3,500 and judges were at the starvation level. Implementation of the cash system was imperative.[59] Referring bitterly to the daily accusations of fraud, bribery, and corruption levelled at his administration by the Conservative-Democratic press, Reed reviewed the history of the state's indebtedness. A comptroller's report of 1861, he said, showed that between 1848 and 1860 there had been no accounts of how money was spent. "This was during the halycon days of peace, prosperity and harmony 'before the war.' There were no 'scalawags' or 'carpetbaggers,' or 'freedmen' to disturb the political sea," he chided. It had been necessary in 1866 to establish a commission to ascertain the amount of debt.

The 1867 comptroller's report showed $45,000 worth of bonds held by the internal improvement fund which were missing. Investigation showed that they had been paid out for interest on the bonds of the Pensacola and Georgia Railroad and the Florida, Atlantic and Gulf Central Railroad.[60] Just before the Walker administration left office it had turned over all its funds to Edward Houstoun, a Conservative-Democratic railroad man, and there had been no accounting of the money since. At the same time, Moses Taylor, a New York banker, held $4,230 due the internal improvement fund and refused to turn it over because of the "confused state of political affairs in the State." The state's political affairs were still unsatisfactory to the New Yorker four years later.

Reed claimed that, as of January 1872, the bonded and floating debt was $1,311,694.97. All but $240,000 of that was caused by governments prior to 1868. There was about $300,000 in uncollected taxes due the state. According to his figures, Reed claimed that his administration had not caused the state's financial plight, even with the opposition party doing its utmost to destroy investors' faith in the state's credit.[61]

The governor's figures were selected to give him the benefit of the doubt, but they were close enough to refute the Democratic charges of Republican extravagance. It was the antebellum regimes which went twelve years without accounting for their expenditures. And there was no exaggeration in the charge that Democrats were trying to destroy the state credit in order to oust the Republican government. A correspondent of the *Floridian* wrote: "No greater calamity could befall the State of Florida, while under the rule of its present carpetbag, scalawag officials, than to be placed in good financial credit. . . . Our only hope is in the State's utter financial bankruptcy; and Heaven grant that that may speedily come! On the other hand, establish for the State financial credit on Wall Street, and you give these foul harpies a life-tenure of these offices. . . . The temporal salvation of the tax payers is in having scrip low, so that they can buy it to pay taxes with, and in having the State's financial credit low so that Reed & Co. can't sell State bonds so as to raise money with which to perpetuate their hold on office."[62]

There were important Conservative-Democrats who disagreed with him, but many others, including Editor Dyke of the *Floridian*, did their best to effect the suggestion of this angry writer. The latter group was willing to destroy the economy of the state to rid itself of the Republican regime. This seems to negate their contemporary and subsequent denunciations of Republican Reconstruction on grounds of wastefulness, extravagance, and corruption. At the time they seemed willing to tolerate and even help induce wasteful financing if it could accomplish their goal of driving out Republicans, eliminating Negroes from political activity, and restoring white supremacy. They had predicted in advance that government based on Negro suffrage would fail, done all they could to sabotage the Republican administration, and finally congratulated themselves on how correct their predictions had been.

The Republicans seemed compelled to oblige the opposition party with their headline-attracting quarrels. Before Reed addressed the joint assembly, William K. Cessna, a white Republican from Alachua County, introduced a resolution calling for a committee to investigate "state officials" who had been connected with passage of the Jacksonville, Pensacola and Mobile Railroad legislation. Governor Reed was the only state official with whom Cessna was concerned. With only mild interest at first, the resolution was debated for several days and finally passed on January 9, 1872.[63] The investigating committee reported its findings on February 10. After serving on the committee which prepared articles of impeachment and signing its report, Republican John Wallace later claimed he never saw the document or any evidence on which it was based. There were twelve articles, the first six of which accused Reed of violating the state constitution and laws in 1870 and 1871 by the way he issued or attempted to issue state bonds in support of the Florida Central Railroad, the Jacksonville, Pensacola and Mobile, and the Florida Railroad. Article seven alleged a conspiracy in 1869 between Reed and Littlefield to embezzle $22,000 of state funds. Article eight accused him of accepting a bribe from Littlefield in 1871 amounting to $3,500. Article nine charged a conspiracy in 1868 and 1869 to defraud the state of $15,000 in the purchase of militia arms. Article ten charged the governor with accepting $1,140 in currency from Isaac K. Roberts in 1869 and paying scrip into the treasury. Article eleven charged a conspiracy in January 1872 to bribe a justice of the peace. Article twelve accused him of accepting $10,000 in 1871 for conveying internal improvement land to Aaron Barnett.[64]

The house of representatives voted uanimously for impeachment. After trying in every annual session during his term except 1871, the Osborn faction had finally suspended Reed. J.P.C. Emmons, a Jacksonville attorney who supported Reed during all his difficulties, wrote Conservative-Democrat Edward M. L'Engle that the unanimity of the action "indicates mutual party expectations." He condemned the Osborn group for bringing disaster to the Republican party. As Emmons wrote, House Speaker Stearns was securing pledges from twenty-four Republican representatives to vote for impeachment the next morning. He afterward approached former Governor Walker, whose personal distaste for Reed had caused him to work with the impeachers since 1868, assuring him that impeachment would succeed if about seventeen Democrats would support it. Several Democratic leaders had pledged to participate in no more impeachments, but Walker called a late-evening caucus and asked its support. George P. Raney and a few others who had tried to remove the governor in the past disagreed with Walker this time, but the former governor overcame their objections and almost all the house Democrats voted for impeachment the next day. Raney was unable to determine whether they exacted any terms for their votes, but one must admit that the serious charges against the governor may have convinced them that a trial was in order.[65]

The impeachment occurred on February 10, and the senate was notified of the action and furnished the articles against Reed. Day proclaimed himself governor on February 13, and Liberty Billings was elected president of the senate. In the interim some of the Democrats threatened to withdraw their support unless articles five and six were deleted. The articles in question named David Yulee as the intended recipient of $1 million in state bonds, which the governor allegedly attempted to issue in violation of the law. The impeachment managers—Fred Dockray, Horatio Jenkins, George E. Wentworth, Speaker Stearns, W. K. Cessna, and

Leonard G. Dennis were prominent among them—obligingly dropped the questioned articles and replaced them with four others which merely repeated some of the earlier allegations.[66] Their pliability is the more remarkable because Reed had just arranged on January 13 to exchange state bonds with Yulee for South Florida Railroad Company bonds.[67]

Apparently the impeachers were no more anxious to try the case in 1872 than they had been in 1868. A resolution of *sine die* adjournment on February 19 followed the impeachment resolution in the house, but no action was taken on it at the time. The senate opened as a court on February 14. J.P.C. Emmons, appearing as counsel for the governor, presented a denial of the charges. The impeachment managers asked the court to adjourn because they required considerable time to subpoena witnesses from New York and New Jersey. Noting the right of the accused to a speedy trial, they argued that "the rights of the people . . . are as important to be preserved and to be guarded as jealously as those of the citizen in his individual character. We, too, are anxious for a speedy trial. But, above all, we ask that justice shall be done."[68]

Without ruling on the request, the senate concurred with the resolution to adjourn on February 19 which had by then passed the house. The house vote was ten to nine—seven Republicans and three Democrats favored adjournment. On February 17 Reed's lawyer argued that adjournment would deny him a trial until after his term expired. Ignoring the argument, Horatio Jenkins moved to adjourn in accordance with the joint resolution. Democrat Alexander McCaskill offered a substitute motion to try the case. Finally, the question was called on the adjournment motion and it passed by ten to six. Seven Republicans and three Democrats voted for adjournment; four Democrats and two Republicans opposed.[69] It seemed that after nearly three years of factional warfare and four impeachment attempts, Osborn and his supporters had removed Reed from the governorship ten months before his term expired.

Those who dismissed Reed as a force in Florida politics as he departed the capital reckoned without considering how tenaciously he had held his office. Convinced that adjournment of his trial to an impossible date was tantamount to acquittal, Reed waited at his farm near Jacksonville and watched for an opportunity to put the question before the supreme court. When Day attended a Republican party meeting in Jacksonville in April, Reed returned to Tallahassee, issued a proclamation that he was still governor, made several administrative appointments, and declared Day's action unlawful.[70] He asked the supreme court for an opinion on his trial and then returned home to await developments. When Day heard what Reed had done, he became alarmed and acted hastily. Angered at Jonathan Gibbs for affixing the state seal to Reed's proclamations and afraid the court would agree with Reed, Acting Governor Day called the legislature into special session. He planned to call for Gibbs' impeachment and for further action against Reed if the court acted unfavorably. Although Chief Justice Randall agreed with Reed, Hart and Westcott gave the majority opinion of the court. They decided that the supreme court had no jurisdiction in the matter; only the senate could decide whether Reed had been acquitted by the adjournment. The two justices further held that Reed in his suspended status had no authority to ask the court for an opinion.[71]

Day and his allies realized their mistake. They had removed Reed and the court upheld them, but, by calling the session, Day had re-opened the question of whether Reed should have a trial. Democratic Senators John Henderson and John Crawford argued that the case should be decided. Republican Senators Purman, Wentworth, Dennis, and Jenkins fought for adjournment. Henderson and Crawford won and the trial resumed. A motion to acquit passed on May 6, by a vote of ten to seven. Six Democrats and four Republicans favored Reed; four Republicans and three Democrats opposed him.[72]

After Day's inauguration as lieutenant governor in early 1871, William Bloxham had continued his legal action to obtain the office. While Reed was fighting to retain the governorship, Bloxham's quo warranto case was nearing a decision. Many observers expected the court to oust Day and seat Bloxham. In that event Bloxham would have become governor if Reed had been permanently removed. Some writers have concluded that the Republicans closed ranks to support Reed against the threat of a Democrat filling the governor's office. Samuel Pasco, a Jefferson County lawyer and prominent state Democratic leader, wrote years later that "terms were made with Reed," implying that Reed's enemies voted for acquittal to prevent Bloxham's possible accession.[73] But a breakdown of the votes refutes this plausible, but erroneous, thesis. Reed was not acquitted by a coalition of the feuding Republican factions against their common enemy, the Democrats. Four Republicans opposed him to the last roll call, apparently willing to risk loss of the governship to the Democrats. Four others were absent on the crucial vote. Six Democratic senators preferred to keep Reed in office until his term expired. Bloxham won his case in early June and served the remaining seven months of the term.[74]

Before the last struggle over the governorship ended, both parties were already preparing for the 1872 election. Many Republicans admitted their record would work against them. Jonathan C. Greeley, Republican mayor of Jacksonville and a lawyer with important banking and railroad interests, wrote that if the "old order of things" was continued "we can say good bye to Republican rule in Florida." Alva A. Knight, an officer of a

Negro regiment during the war who had since won the respect of Conservative-Democratic lawyers in his new capacity as fourth circuit judge, acknowledged that "the government has been bad in the past," but thought there would be improvements. John S. Adams, an independent Republican, said "the constant struggle of the administration to sustain itself against Federal officeholders has demoralized the party."[75]

The contest for control of the state during the Reed administration was not only between Republicans and Democrats. It was first between two Republican factions whose differences had less to do with policy than with which Republicans would rule the state. The major leaders of both groups were moderate on questions relating to the status of freedmen, accepted prevailing attitudes of the era about government-private enterprise cooperation in developing internal improvements, and generally agreed with native white property owners about fiscal policy. The legislation which gave state aid to railroad construction firms was bipartisan and prominent Democrats were financially interested in the companies receiving aid. Reed's fiscal policy was conservative. With any help at all from his comptroller and the legislature he might have been able to implement the cash system and "pay as you go" financing which Floridians before and after him have regarded as the only sensible way to operate a state government.

Governor Reed became more willing to favor civil rights legislation after he vetoed the 1868 public accommodations bill, and the legislature required equal accommodations in railroad cars in 1870, but Negroes did not obtain suitable civil rights laws before 1873. Ironically, Negro leaders in 1872 blamed Senate President Liberty Billings, their one-time leader, for blocking a bill they believed would have given them civil rights protection.

The Negroes were never able to influence policy in proportion to their voting strength. Government during the Reconstruction era was largely by and for white men. Nevertheless, Negroes were not merely manipulated and ignored. They learned a great deal as they participated in the political process. Many of them became effective legislators, making important contributions in committees and on the floor. While some of them were venal, Negroes had no monopoly on the condition. Freedmen turned out in overwhelming numbers to vote in the face of dangerous obstacles. They welcomed their political rights and exercised them enthusiastically. In their party they bargained with more success as time passed. The change in Reed's attitudes toward Negro-advocated legislation in 1868 after he turned to Gibbs for support is indicative. So is Walls' nomination in 1870. And it will become clear that they were not ignored in the 1872 nominating convention.

Capitalizing on the concessions of the moderate framers of the constitution and Reed's appointive policy, the Conservative-Democrats played an increasingly influential role between 1868 and 1872, although they did not agree on much except opposition to Republican administration. But it was more than the Reed administration and the Republican majority that they opposed. They intended to overturn the system which made a Republican majority possible. In short, they wished to correct the one objectionable feature that Governor Walker had noted in the 1868 constitution—Negro suffrage.

Contrary to long-standing myths which have been perpetuated by state historians, white Floridians were never helpless under a corrupt government staffed with outsiders and supported by ignorant voters. Democrats were in a strong minority position in all branches and at all levels of government from the beginning of Republican administration in 1868. They bargained for concessions with considerable success during the period. Whether they were scheming behind closed doors with moderate Republicans to thwart the Radicals and establish a white government during the constitutional convention, resisting unfavorable legislation by dilatory tactics in the legislature, joining an alienated Republican group to impeach the governor, or terrorizing Negro voters in the north-central counties as will be demonstrated, they were a limiting factor on Republican policy-makers.

The Democrats of the 1870s and afterward might well have been grateful to Reed and the Republicans who were in power during this difficult transitional period. Any leadership would have had trouble rebuilding a depressed economy and maintaining order during such attempted social transformation. The Democrats were able to participate actively in the process, reap the long-term benefits of Republican measures, and then blame the opposition party for all that was wrong. There was Democratic campaign material for years to come.

13

Assassination Is Not a Pleasant Fate

Law enforcement was the most difficult problem confronting the civil administrations of Florida and the United States after 1868. Spokesmen of nearly every group in the state regretted the withdrawal of military troops, Bureau agent A. B. Grumwell stated the problem succinctly: "If the military power is withdrawn, no safety will be had for those identified with reconstruction, as it is believed that once Northern men are gotten rid of it will be easy to terrorize and control the freedmen. . . . assassination is not a pleasant fate to look forward to and the great number of victims in the South already slain shows great probability of more being added."[1] Calling for immediate legislative authority for a 200-man mounted police force and rapid organization of a state militia, Governor Reed joined the legislature in urging that military forces remain deployed throughout the state. State Treasurer Simon B. Conover, Republican national committeeman, warned that "the Rebels are thoroughly organized and are using every means to intimidate and prevent the loyal people black and white from . . . exercise of their political rights."[2]

At the same time the conservative *St. Augustine Examiner* complained that withdrawal of the army left Floridians "to the tender mercies of the gentlemen now assembled at Tallahassee." Some native whites also petitioned for retention of the troops, expressing fears of the Negro population and a Republican governor with a secret police force, but others were more self-reliant. When Reed purchased 2,000 stands of arms for the militia, local regulators in collusion with railroad personnel entered the arms-bearing cars on the line from Jacksonville, destroyed the weapons, and scattered the pieces along the track in Madison County.[3]

General Meade defended the troop withdrawal because those "who have been depending on troops for the preservation of order" needed to begin relying on civil authority. But a few weeks later the general concluded that civil government could not stand without military aid. Several companies of the Seventh Infantry were redeployed. Two companies were stationed at Jacksonville and small detachments went to Fernandina, Marianna, Tallahassee, Gainesville, and St. Augustine. In his annual report a few weeks later, Assistant Commissioner George W. Gile of the Freedmen's Bureau reported the state peaceful enough for the withdrawal of his agents. His optimism was premature, but there were few troops in Florida after 1868. The army's presence was made known at several trouble spots, but the Republican administration was usually obliged to rely on its own limited resources. During the period of greatest disorder the number of troops in the state ranged from 354 to 453.[4]

Many crimes and acts of violence in Reconstruction Florida were unrelated to politics and race, and many racial problems had nothing to do with politics. It was a frontier area where people were quick to defend themselves against wrongs, actual or imagined. Communities were separated by miles of unsettled territory, transportation and communication were limited, long coastlines were broken by countless bays and stream outlets, and there were few law enforcement officials. It was easy to ignore laws which were new, unfamiliar, and lightly regarded. During the period there was rampant smuggling of taxable goods, gun-running, counterfeiting, poaching on government timber land, and official malfeasance. There were also violent acts committed in anger without premeditation. But the most pervasive and difficult law enforcement problem was the violence inflicted on Negroes and white Republicans by native white Floridians to suppress political activity.

Even with his extensive appointive powers, Governor Reed was only partially able to protect individuals from violence. Thwarted by the destruction of the militia weapons, he exercised great caution in declaring martial law, usually trying instead to compromise with local leaders in troublesome communities. The state courts were not much more successful in obtaining convictions after 1868 than they had been before. With prevailing opinion favorable to local whites who committed violence against Negroes and white Republicans, sheriffs were often unable or unwilling to make arrests. If arrests were made it was difficult to obtain convictions because the juries sympathized with the accused. Grand juries often returned verdicts of "shot by persons unknown," and petit juries refused to convict even if the case came to trial.

There was relatively less violence in the southern and western counties where Negroes comprised a smaller portion of the population. Perhaps that was because Conservative-Democrats could exercise control without it. In Leon County, where the capital was located and the Negro population was overwhelming, "Bishop" Pearce reported conditions as safe as in Massachusetts. But in most of the large counties near the Georgia line, populated by numerous blacks as well as whites, racial strife was bitter, violent, and continuous. Republicans exaggerated the atrocities for their own purposes, but even a casual examination of the evidence shows that violence against Negroes and white Republicans was committed by native whites on an organized basis in several counties.[5]

The Democratic press usually attributed violent acts to personal differences, scoffing at the idea that organized regulator groups existed. In November 1871, the *Tallahassee Weekly Floridian* chided E. G. Johnson, Columbia County Republican leader, when he published a threatening letter he had received. Editor Dyke disdainfully wrote, "the letter has all the earmarks of fraud. Persons who propose assassination or violence are not fools enough to write such stuff as Johnson parades before the public." Johnson, a state senator, was finally gunned down from ambush in 1875. There is a striking difference in Democratic commentary on the subject in the years after the Republican party was vanquished and Negroes were driven out of politics. Francis P. Fleming, Democratic governor from 1889 to 1893, wrote retrospectively that "the Ku Klux Klan investigations showed a bloody chapter [of Florida history] but none of the silent empire was caught." Klan members, he thought, fought well against great odds. He then related with telling familiarity an incident in which regulators caught several Negroes and summarily executed them for alleged crimes.[6]

In several counties secret regulator groups calling themselves Young Men's Democratic Clubs were organized to use terroristic methods against Negroes and white Republicans. The clubs were similar throughout the state and their constitutions, organizations, and activities were the same as those attributed to the Ku Klux Klan. Their purpose was to suppress Negro political activity.[7] Many acts of violence were committed at night by bands of hooded men; others occurred in daylight without attempts at disguise. In either case the victims were often able to identify attackers. Arrests or convictions under state law were rare, but Congress enacted legislation prohibiting these violations of civil rights. Several cases were pursued successfully in the United States courts.

In Madison County a regulator group, composed primarily of young men, sent threatening letters to the bureau agent and to freedmen during the 1868 election. Next came night visits of hooded riders who shot up the town and stoned several houses. Then two Negroes were killed about eight miles from Madison. When a coroner's jury declared that they were shot for stealing corn by parties unknown, bureau agent J. E. Quentin asked how information about the theft was furnished. About a week later, two more Negroes were shot, one in his front yard and the other on his way home from church. Quentin found that a regulator group headed by Emanuel Williams and Henry Rye had rounded up about twelve black men at the latter's home and ordered them out of the county within six days. The two men shot, Ned Harrison and Sam Tillman, had remained beyond the deadline. B. F. Tidwell—a Confederate veteran who became a Republican after the war and was appointed Madison County sheriff by Governor Reed—testified that twenty murders, almost all involving Negro victims, were committed in the county between 1868 and 1871 by men riding disguised at night. Simon Katzenberg and David Montgomery, both Republican officials and keepers of stores where blacks obtained credit, had trouble with arson. Montgomery's store was burned to the ground. In neighboring Jefferson County, Edward C. Henry reported that his house, which the attackers thought he still occupied, had been burned merely because he was a Republican. In Alachua County, Republican leader Leonard G. Dennis was repeatedly warned by letters signed "K. K. K." that he was marked for assassination, but he was never harmed. Sixteen other persons, most of them black, were not so lucky. Reporting renewed activity of the "old regulating companies" around Newnansville, Solomon F. Halliday remarked that "it is very singular that poor young men who never owned a slave" were most aggressive against Negroes.[8]

At least ten persons were murdered in Hamilton County between 1868 and 1871, although the regulators in the area were from both sides of the state line. After 1870 the Department of Justice established a small secret service headed by H. C. Whitley to gather evidence against regulators. When Edward Thompson was beaten to death and his wife severely beaten near the Georgia line, one of Whitley's agents found an eye-witness willing to testify. Eleven Hamilton County residents were arrested and several of them were eventually convicted.[9] Columbia County, the scene of sixteen murders between 1868 and 1871, was more turbulent than most counties during the entire Reconstruction period. From the ambush shooting of a fourteen-year-old girl at a candy pull in April 1869 to the midnight killing of Senator Elisha G. Johnson in mid-1875, the county was almost continually beset by violence. When Sheriff Robert Martin went into the country near Lake City on official business, he was captured by a group of armed, masked men. Threatening him with violent reprisal if he refused, they offered to release him if he would resign his office. The sheriff's office was soon vacant. Most of the Negroes killed in Columbia were politically active, but several were killed for no apparent reason. In 1870 a white Republican was killed after refusing to leave his party.

About the same time, Andrew Mahoney, a former Freedmen's Bureau agent and incumbent legislator, was killed. In 1871 an African Methodist Episcopal minister was forced to abandon his school in the county.[10]

The "Lake City Outrage" of 1873 was atypical, but it contributed to the county's turbulence. Warren S. Bush, a county native and nominal Republican after 1869, had served as tax collector since 1871 and was elected to the state legislature in 1872. Angered by some of Governor Hart's political appointments in 1873, Bush and some of his friends shot up the houses of the county officials and ran the postmaster out of town. When Bush and two associates were indicted by a county grand jury and bound over for trial in the United States court, they threatened witnesses who then became afraid to testify. Postmaster W. W. Moore even recommended Bush for a collectorship at Cedar Key, hoping to get him out of the county. Acquitted by the state court, the three men were tried under the Enforcement Act, only to have the case continued and ultimately quashed. Military forces patrolled Lake City for several weeks during the affair. Meanwhile it was discovered that Bush had embezzled about $24,000 of state and county funds while serving as tax collector. His arrest for embezzlement came shortly after his appointment as Cedar Key collector.[11]

Most of the violence in Marion County was overt and spontaneous, even though it resulted from similar racial and political attitudes. A prominent Negro Republican leader, Dennis Lee, was killed in a confrontation with a Conservative-Democrat, but the offense was called justifiable homicide. Four Negroes were killed in late 1868 for stealing and one was shot down in his doorway. Mixed juries brought in verdicts of justifiable homicide, but two cases were so outrageous that the local bureau agent predicted retaliation.[12]

S. D. McConnell of Marion wrote that "Clouts, our scalawag sheriff, shot Jess Dupree and tried to shoot Bob Young. His conduct was outrageous." This report lends support to the long-accepted interpretation that "scalawag" and "carpetbag" officials mistreated well-meaning local citizens. But bureau agent Jacob Remley reported additional details: Dupree, while intoxicated, rode his horse through the court house hall, cursing the sheriff and county judge; Robert Young was arrested for trying to help Dupree's escape by throwing sand in the sheriff's eyes.[13] If one accepts the latter and more objective account, the sheriff's actions do not seem so "outrageous."

When a Negro was seriously wounded while allegedly stealing cotton in 1869, Robert Bullock, a prominent Conservative-Democratic politician, reported that "the Radicals seem bloodthirsty" against the man who did the shooting. He apparently saw no anomaly when he added that "the new man Russell is ranting and ought by all means to be killed." Bullock had other unusual ideas about law and order. In early 1870 a Negro officer broke up a fight in Ocala between a white man and another black man. Bullock thought the officer's interference unwarranted and grabbed him by the throat, shook him, and "tried to break his head with a stick." When another Negro peace officer tried to arrest Bullock, the latter put a knife to his throat. By that time armed whites and blacks were facing each other menacingly in the street, but there was no further violence and Bullock went free.[14]

In Clay County, Samuel and Hannah Tutson were flagrantly assaulted and brutally beaten by some white men, including a deputy sheriff, who were trying to drive them from the land they were legally homesteading. After being tried and acquitted in state court, six of the men were arrested by Marshal Sherman Conant and four were convicted of assault in federal court. R. W. Cone, a native of Baker County, and his wife were severely beaten by three men because Cone served on the jury which convicted A. K. Allison for his role in the 1870 election. These men were also arrested by Conant and convicted.[15]

Gadsden County had a mixed record. Allison and his followers had created a major disturbance at the polls in 1870. A county judge and sheriff, both state legislators, were assassinated and several Negroes were assaulted between 1868 and 1871. Yet, Malachi Martin, prison warden at Chattahoochee and an active Republican, was on good relations with some Democrats in the community, exchanging addresses of "Johnny Reb" and "Yank" in good humor. They were good enough friends to warn Martin on several occasions when their local acquaintances planned violence against him.[16]

In 1869 the United States troops stationed at Jacksonville, presumably to allay violence, engaged in a bloody riot with local Negroes. One soldier was killed. Under official orders the soldiers invaded the Negro section of town, killing several inhabitants and arresting several others. In Suwannee County a band of whites, usually under the influence of liquor, terrorized the community of Live Oak for several weeks. They whipped two men and three women and branded one man on both cheeks and the forehead. A man and his wife and children were all beaten. One woman and one man were killed. When a courageous Negro, Doc Rountree, identified twelve of the men, the constable managed to arrest them. After all the Live Oak lawyers refused to prosecute them, state attorney C. R. King was brought in from Lake City. Governor Reed joined him there and peace was worked out by compromise.[17]

Lingering antipathy between Unionists and ex-Confederates in Taylor and Lafayette counties precipitated several violent outbreaks. At Governor Reed's request thirty United States soldiers were stationed in Lafayette County during the spring of 1871. The problem did not abate, however, and by the end of that year eight Republicans had been assassinated there, including John N. Krimminger, one-time president of the state senate.[18]

While it was difficult to protect Negroes in any area of the state and the disregard of their rights and lives was brutal in many areas, Jackson County was by far the most violent, suffered the greatest loss of life, and remained least amenable to peaceful solution of its difficulties by the Reed administration. A wealthy agricultural county and Whig stronghold before 1860, Jackson County had a Negro majority but the white minority was large. Many in Jackson had been Unionists, and numerous deserters from the Confederate army congregated there during the war. Considerable bitterness had been engendered by an 1864 Union raid on Marianna which resulted in loss of life and property. Jackson County Unionists were angered by President Johnson's policy which failed to distinguish between themselves and former Confederates concerning property rights.[19] Both former Unionists and former Confederates resented the post-war role of freedmen. Into this potentially explosive situation came Charles M. Hamilton and William J. Purman—both young, enthusiastic, strong-willed former Union officers—as bureau agents to supervise freedmen's affairs. Their efforts to establish schools for Negroes and their careful watch over labor contracts were deeply resented by local whites who had their own ideas about who should oversee Negro affairs. When the blacks were enfranchised, both Hamilton and Purman instructed them on the exercise of political rights. When Hamilton was elected to Congress and Purman to the state senate, the partially restrained anger of local whites erupted in an episode of violence which became known as "the Jackson County War."

Much of the trouble was caused by a band of night-riding regulators composed of younger members of the planting class. Many were former Whigs and some had been Unionists, but after the war they joined their old political enemies, the Democrats, to suppress Negro political participation and restore a racial and social order that both sides considered essential.[20] Many observers thought James Coker was the group's leader. Some believed that older planters acted as advisers, but others believed they were merely intimidated by the younger men. Whatever the case, the group's activities were an acceleration of what had been happening in Jackson County since the war. In June 1868, for example, there were three cases of violence unrelated to political intimidation. A transient white man named Lot Wood killed and mutilated James Donald, an aged freedman. Just across the line in Washington County, James Bellamy, a young Negro, was tied to an anchor and dragged under water until his tormenters tired of their sport and hanged him. Near Marianna, John Pitts shot three Negro women for drawing water from a well on his farm which had been used by the neighborhood for years. When a planter was wounded and his foreman later killed in the fall of 1868, the shooting was blamed on Negro laborers who allegedly disagreed about a labor contract.[21]

In late February 1869, Purman and Dr. John L. Finlayson—a quiet native Floridian who had formerly worked with the Freedmen's Bureau before becoming circuit court clerk of the county—were crossing a Marianna street when they were struck by a shotgun blast. Purman was shot in the neck and Finlayson died instantly. A group of prominent Marianna citizens drew up a resolution condemning the act, but asserting their agreement with Major Purman that it stemmed from personal rather than political motivation. Purman retorted from his hospital bed that the attack was entirely political and the committee had misrepresented his opinion. After the shooting Purman returned only once to the county—which he represented in the state senate—and then had to be escorted out of town by a group of older citizens to prevent another attempt on his life. Governor Reed offered a $2,000 reward for apprehension of Finlayson's murderer.[22]

A reign of terror began in Marianna in late September 1869. On the twenty-eighth some Negroes were having a picnic when a shot fired from ambush killed Wyatt Scurlock and a child he was holding. Columbus Sullivan, a Negro minister, was shot to death the next day. The first shooting was believed to have been an abortive attack on Constable Calvin Rogers, who had infuriated local whites. On October 1 James Coker, usually regarded as the regulators' leader, was conversing with James F. McClellan, a prominent planter, and his attractive daughter on the porch of Mrs. Attaway's boarding house. Shots, probably intended for Coker, rang out across the street; Miss McClellan fell dead and her father was seriously wounded. Coker was not hit. The next day, while ostensibly searching for Calvin Rogers whom they blamed for the shooting, Coker and his associates killed Oscar Granberry. Oscar Nichols escaped their bullets at the time, but was killed along with his wife and child a few days later. Rogers was finally killed, also. Marianna was virtually besieged by the regulators who were riding in daylight without disguise. While most citizens were intimidated into silence, Samuel Fleishman, a Jewish merchant and twenty-year resident of the county, denounced the violence and the men responsible for it. Fleishman was a Republican official and was disliked for advancing credit to Negroes. He had left Marianna during the war because of his Unionism, but had returned in 1865. Ordered from town by the regulators for his outspoken remarks, he refused to leave his family and business. He was taken forcibly to the Georgia line and told never to return to Marianna. A few days later his bullet-punctured body was found in the road leading back to town.[23]

Purman and other Republican leaders demanded that Governor Reed declare martial law, but he refused.[24] Reed later argued that compliance with the request would have caused a race war. He asked for and received a small detachment of United States soldiers for temporary duty in Marianna. Meanwhile, the governor sent a delegation to confer with local leaders about how to maintain peace. It was agreed that Thomas West, a local man, should become sheriff. The governor hoped that the military detachment and his conciliatory appointive policy would ameliorate the tension.

The governor was wrong. Sheriff West's life was so frequently threatened that he was afraid to serve a process outside the town. After being severely beaten by a group of his erstwhile neighbors, West resigned in March 1871. When the sheriff resigned, county clerk J. Q. Dickinson, formerly of Vermont, was the only white Republican official remaining in Jackson County. He had not yielded even to the most extreme pressure and had repeatedly angered local whites by his lucid reporting of county affairs and his insistence on issuing warrants against law violators. Antipathy toward him increased because he participated in forced sales of tax-delinquent property and had even acquired nearly 2,000 acres of the land for himself. On March 31, 1871, John R. Ely, a prominent landowner, threatened tax collector Homer Bryan if he did not cease advertising an impending forced sale of Ely's property. Ely also threatened Dickinson for assisting Bryan. Five days later Dickinson, who had frequently predicted his early demise, was shotgunned on Marianna's main street. His body was shot again at close range with a pistol, but there were no witnesses to the shooting. Although Ely was a suspect, no arrest was ever made. The *Floridian* and other Democratic papers alleged that the killer was a Negro intent on robbery.[25]

Richard Pooser, Calvin Rogers' replacement as constable, left the county along with Homer Bryan, the tax collector. Emanuel Fortune, although still in the legislature from Jackson County, moved permanently to Jacksonville. A white legislator elected as a Republican resigned to protect himself against threatened assassination. When a congressional committee investigated violence in Florida a few months later, a perplexed congressman asked a witness why Governor Reed could not control affairs in Jackson County if he had the power to appoint the officials. Marcellus L. Stearns, a future governor, answered that the officials would be killed as fast as they could be appointed unless the local populace approved the appointments. In June the governor told an African Methodist Episcopal Church convention that he was paralyzed and without power to protect "loyal people of the counties" such as Jackson.[26]

At the same time he sent J. S. Adams and John Westcott to Jackson County to discuss a settlement. They were given a list of persons whose appointments to county offices would be acceptable. From the list Reed appointed Charles W. Davis as county clerk and F. M. G. Carter as sheriff. A small detachment of United States troops remained for several weeks. The governor later claimed that the situation improved, but killing continued in the county. Secretary of State Jonathan C. Gibbs told the congressional committee that between 1868 and 1871 deaths from the political and racial strife numbered 153, a figure comparable to estimates of most observers on both sides. Richard Pooser, Homer Bryan, and three other Negroes who had fled the county protested that Gibbs' figures were incomplete. They named thirteen other persons who had been killed or wounded between July and October 1871 and described the circumstances of each. Daniel Gillis of nearby Orange Hill, less concerned about the atrocities, wrote that the governor had sent some "yankees" to Marianna "to proclaim peace I suppose as there was some killing down near that place a short time ago. It seems that the people will kill about Marianna occasionally."[27]

After the congressional investigation and additional legislation authorizing national protection of civil rights, night-riding activities diminished markedly and violence abated throughout the state, although it never ceased. Governor Reed claimed that his restraint in using force was responsible for the improvement. But by the end of 1871, Democrats had gained control of some of the troubled counties, thus removing a major cause of dissatisfaction. With strong Negro and white Republican leaders eliminated, there was less need for violence as a political weapon. The threat of United States court action also had a restraining effect. About thirty-eight violations of the Enforcement Acts involving more than 100 persons were brought before the court. Six decisions resulted in convictions of about twenty persons.[28]

Violence toward Negroes and Republican officials also occurred outside the plantation counties. When a Negro constable in Pensacola tried to arrest a local white man in 1868, the latter shot him three times. The man was respected by his neighbors and their comments on the affair reflect more opposition to Negro officials than aversion to the shooting. Pent-up anger at Cedar Key resulted in violence against United States officials and talk of "cleaning out the Yankee, nigger-loving set" when troops were first removed. Continued bad feeling caused confrontations between national and municipal authorities. Collector Isodore Blumenthal was arrested for violating municipal quarantine regulations while carrying out his official responsibility of entering and clearing vessels. Fined fifty dollars in police court, Blumenthal was forced to bear the expense of an appeal before the sentence was overturned. The aggressive Cedar Key mayor also levied an income tax on the postmaster's salary and threatened to take his property if it were not paid.[29]

The reluctance to accept Negro testimony, as manifested in the criminal courts before 1868, was only a short step from the proposition that guilty Negroes did not deserve trials. Mob lynchings of blacks accused of crime soon followed. When Jesse Dupree's wife was murdered near Ocala in 1868, a Negro suspect was beaten until he confessed. He was hanged by the mob.[30] Other lynchings of both blacks and whites accused of rape, murder, and "notorious" acts occurred in the 1870s.

It was considered tantamount to inviting violence for blacks to enter Sumter County on official business, but factors other than race were sometimes present in other south Florida localities.[31] When Negro laborers were taken to Sanford, Orange County, to clear orange grove land, local "crackers" attacked their camp and wounded one man. But they were as angry at having been fired from the job themselves as they were at Negroes living in the area. When the raid was repeated a few nights later, the foreman posted a reward and called for a grand jury investigation. The night attacks stopped; the Negroes completed the job and left. Nearly two years later another group was brought in for similar work. A band of whites warned them that they must leave or be shot. Two left and the others reluctantly remained. Meanwhile, the employer had learned that the sheriff was party to the first incident. The employer explained to the sheriff that he intended to report the names of those involved in the earlier episode to the United States commissioner at Jacksonville if further trouble occurred. The Negroes were not molested again.[32] In nearby Volusia County, only whites were involved when Daniel Clifton burned Elias Yulee's house and dug up his orange trees. Clifton had been living in the house rent-free and resented Yulee's decision to begin charging forty dollars annual rent.[33] Seven white men flogged a Dr. Lindley to death at Lake George in 1876. When the Volusia County sheriff failed to act, Marshal Conant arrested them for civil rights violations.[34]

In 1870 a disgusted observer wrote that "Pensacola seems to be improving. Ruter was burned out, young Hutchens was killed, old man Ford blew his brains out, and another man was badly cut by a desperado named Kelly, who is supposed to have had his skull fractured. All within 24 hours."[35] When a dispute developed between rival labor groups there, perhaps it was only natural that the aggrieved parties resorted to violence. By 1873 a large volume of lumber was being shipped from Pensacola and the British were vitally interested in the business as investors and purchasers. Although by no means a strong union, the Workingmen's Association had been organized at Pensacola in 1868 by the local stevedores, nearly all of whom were Negroes. Because of the British interest in West Florida, many Canadian lumberjacks and laborers were coming to the area during the busy winter months which was the slack season in the northern woods. The Pensacola stevedores resented their competition and by early 1873—led by a white customs house employee named Callahan—had demonstrated their feelings in several minor attacks on small groups of Canadians. On January 6, 1873, the local workers, armed with pistols and clubs, took over the town and drove the British subjects out or into hiding. They ransacked every hotel and most of the private houses in Pensacola, forcing all occupants out into the streets for identification. The stevedores literally occupied the town. Ironically, Callahan's house was burned along with some others on the block and he was the only serious casualty in the affair.[36] The British consul protested, but the mayor and city police were completely helpless and refused to interfere. Finally, a detachment was sent from the United States navy yard and a measure of order was restored on January 7. During the following weeks, the Negro stevedores prevented several ships from being loaded. The sheriff and the United States marshal tried to arrange a compromise, but the local men refused to consider their overtures. With the British embassy politely but firmly requesting that its subjects be protected and allowed to pursue their trade, Secretary of State Hamilton Fish did what he could, but he and the attorney general agreed that it was a state matter. The return of hot weather finally settled the matter as the Canadians left west Florida.[37]

Key West Negroes had a similar problem. Blacks from the Bahamas came to Key West and worked for lower wages than the local residents, causing several disturbances in 1873 and 1874. During the 1874 political campaign the local laborers decided that an election-day assault on their competitors could be disguised as political antipathy. During a parade on the appointed day they fired pistols near a wagon carrying a Negro band. The bandsmen overturned the wagon as they looked for cover and a street brawl followed involving guns, clubs, and knives. School children were sent home and the mayor called for United States soldiers. After several hours, order was restored but four men had been wounded and one killed. Although the riot was attributed to Reconstruction politics, economic competition between rival groups was the real cause.[38]

While it was the most serious law enforcement problem confronting state authorities, violent crime consumed only a portion of the energies of United States officials after 1868. Perhaps smuggling received as much attention as any other single problem. The plethora of taxes enacted during the Civil War continued for years afterward. As a result, the smuggling of cigars and whiskey was a comparatively lucrative enterprise, and control became more difficult as more and more scheduled and unscheduled trips were made between Cuba and Florida port towns. To overworked treasury agents it often seemed that all the fishermen, spongers, and wreckers, and most of the ship crews on the Gulf Coast, were engaged in illicit trade. No stigma was attached to smuggling, plans for which were openly discussed. Most boat operators considered it easy to elude customs officials. The only major deterrent was mutual distrust. A frustrated agent reported "Yellow fever raging at Key West, quarantines up along the coast. It is better at stopping smuggling than I am."[39]

Smuggling in small quantities was carried on at every port by crew members who hid packages throughout their ships. The cigars and liquor were usually taken inland and sold at places where customs officials seldom visited, but there were many variations. At Tampa, James McKay was suspected of unloading the *Governor Marvin* at the mouth of Tampa Bay before the customs officer boarded.[40] Cedar Key was the center of smuggling activities because its water was deep enough for ships to dock at the wharf which connected to a railroad. Illegal goods often came there on New Orleans, Florida, and Havana Steamship Company vessels. Packages were tied to buoys to be picked up later by the oyster fishermen, but sometimes even this ruse was unnecessary. Since the water was shallow near Cedar Key, a ship often had to remain two days because of the tides. The customs officer tried to have someone on board the whole time, but frequently there were two or more steamers in port and his staff was inadequate to handle them. At other times illegal packages were unloaded without detection merely because the fishing boats raced out to meet incoming steamers ahead of the revenue boat. The problem was compounded because S. N. Marks, the New Orleans, Florida, and Havana Company manager, was sympathetic with the smugglers. A Florida Railroad freight agent at Cedar Key also cooperated with them. When agents were too persistent their lives were endangered. Arriving at Tampa in early 1868, special agent A. Leib found his partner, Harry Jenks, stabbed nearly to death.[41]

Despite the obstacles, several convictions were obtained. By 1873 a merchant who preferred untaxed Cuban cigars wrote his lawyer that it was unsafe to send them through Cedar Key because "the Customs House folks at that place are 'shure shots.' "[42]

A large smuggling operation was carried on at Jacksonville by Pedro Bettelini and John B. Togni, two leading merchants and hotel owners whose popular restaurant was an excellent outlet for contraband wines.

They ran a bark, probably of French registry, between Jacksonville and Le Havre. In collusion with collector Fred A. Dockray—Senator Osborn's appointee who had worked so hard to impeach Governor Reed—the two businessmen were unloading their taxable cargo before entering the port. When one of the river pilots became angry at Bettelini and Togni, treasury agent M. H. Hale obtained evidence against them. Bettelini was convicted of falsifying records to avoid paying duty. Dockray had also marked "paid" on shipments and permitted the merchants to credit the amount to his personal account at their store.[43]

An ensuing investigation revealed that Dockray had also permitted $7,500 worth of Jacksonville, Pensacola and Mobile Railroad Company iron to enter without duty, costing the government about $2,280 in revenue. The United States finally obtained a judgment against Dockray which was paid by his bondsmen. The former collector could not be reached at the time because he was in prison at Valencia, Spain.[44]

In May 1873, Jacksonville citizens were alarmed to hear that the post office had been robbed. The affair was shrouded in mystery, but after a few weeks there was even more surprise when Morris H. Alberger, ex-Senator Osborn's former secretary and an incorporator of the Great Southern Railway, was arrested and arraigned before the United States commissioner. The case against him was lost, however, because United States Attorney J. B. C. Drew "mislaid" the papers relating to it and later dropped the charges over the adamant protests of the postal investigator.[45] There were several post office robberies during the period, especially at Gulf towns, but none so bizarre as the one at Jacksonville.

Since 1866 there had been counterfeit United States currency and coin turning up at Key West. It was also discovered that counterfeit United States coins, especially dimes, were circulating extensively in Cuba in the early 1870s. Acting on a report from former Lieutenant Governor William Gleason who lived in the area, agent Washington Rogers found a camp on the Miami River near Biscayne Bay where Cubans were doing the counterfeiting. The money was apparently distributed in mainland Florida by way of an old road running from Biscayne Bay to Indian River and by boat to Key West and Cuba. The counterfeiters were not apprehended, but several Floridians were arrested for dealing in their product.[46]

The Cuban revolution of 1868 caused two problems: numerous Cubans came to Key West, increasing law enforcement problems there, and gun-running became an attractive enterprise, violating the United States neutrality laws. The steamer *Henry Burden*, a United States vessel, and the British *Salvador* carried guns and troops to Cuba, but it was the Cuban steamer *Lillian* which caused the most excitement. In 1869 the *Lillian* and two other Cuban vessels were transporting guns and artillery from Cedar Key to Cuba. In October a steamer from New York was discovered unloading 200 men and supplies of arms at Fernandina for transportation to Cedar Key over the Florida Railroad. While United States officials were asking for instructions from the secretary of state, the *Lillian* sailed with its illegal cargo. Marshals arrived too late, finding that the soldiers had been treated most hospitably by Cedar Key residents.[47]

Because many Cuban refugees and immigrants were residing at Key West in 1869, there was also strong sympathy in that city for the revolution. The immigrants themselves were divided between supporters of the revolution and those who favored Spain. In July and October 1869 there had been riots resulting in several arrests for disturbing the peace. After the latter a celebration was planned in support of the revolution, bringing vehement protests from the Spanish consul. Local authorities refused to intervene and the event passed without incident. But the peace was threatened again in January 1870 when Don Gonzalo Castanon, editor of the *Havana Voz de Cuba,* and a group of Spaniards debarked from their ship to be immediately confronted by a crowd of angry Cubans. Several people were arrested and the affair was believed over. Then on January 31, two days later, a wild gunfight occurred in Castanon's hotel and he was killed. The army garrison at Fort Taylor sent a detachment at the mayor's request and order was restored. Stephen R. Mallory took charge of the body and escorted it back to Havana. Excitement gradually subsided but there were occasional attacks on the Spanish consulate and continued confrontations between hostile groups of Cubans.[48]

Because of the strong current and dangerous submerged reefs of the narrow Florida Straits, wrecking had long been important at Key West. Although regulated by law and custom, the industry was plagued by criminals whose activities were difficult to control. Wreckers and ship masters sometimes colluded to defraud maritime insurance companies, although improved insurance regulations reduced that problem. But there were still many wrecks from storms and faulty navigation. Masters were sometimes charged exorbitant rates under threat of being left to break up on the reefs. Others were threatened with death if they refused to abandon their vessels so they could be plundered. William H. Hunt, a large landowner and mail contractor at Miami, had his mail boat forcibly detained for several days to prevent word of wrecking activities from spreading to Key West. Dishonest wreckers sometimes burned remains of wrecks to prevent other ships from being warned of the location of dangerous reefs. It was difficult to obtain convictions against transgressors. Juries in the southern district of Florida were drawn largely from persons engaged in the business and they were reluctant to convict each other. Some relief was furnished by houses of refuge built during the period along the coast, but the ultimate solution came with larger and more powerful vessels and better navigational aids. The wrecking business, both legal and otherwise, was diminishing in importance as the Reconstruction period ended.[49]

Officials were unable to deal effectively with the problem of poaching on government timber land. The vast timber lands of the state were beginning to be worked on a large scale, and a ready market was available for logs regardless of their origin. The government had few officials to control poaching, and the penalties were so slight that the risk of apprehension was not a serious deterrent. A General Land Office circular of 1855 empowered local registers and receivers of land to employ deputy timber agents for brief periods when spoliation of the public lands was suspected.[50] The agents were empowered to confiscate the lumber or naval stores illegally taken but since they rarely had the means to move them, they usually compromised with the guilty parties.

One of the large-scale transgressors was George F. Nutter and Brother, a Madison County company which supplied lumber to the Drew and Bucki mills at Ellaville. Although they cut from government lands, the Nutter brothers also defrauded the government by hiring Negroes to apply for homesteads, none of which had any improvements made on them. By 1873 they had totally cleared a three-by-ten-mile belt in Hamilton County along the Suwannee River, a slightly smaller area in Madison County, and several hundred acres in Suwannee County. The matter was reported to the land office by irate citizens who thought the exploitation was destroying a major immigration attraction.[51] Another case involved the Cuba Tie Company, financed by J. J. Philbrick, a leading Key West businessman and longtime British consul at the island town. The company had a contract with Cubans to furnish railroad ties which it cut from both government land and fraudulently acquired homesteads. H. S. Harmon, an Alachua County Negro politician then working as a customs official at Tampa, was employed as timber agent to stop the depredations. After seizing several stacks of ties along the Hillsborough River, he was resisted by John A. Henderson, attorney for the company, but the court refused to accept the lawyer's reasoning. Then Philbrick appeared in person on a boat from Key West and threatened to use his considerable influence to have Harmon fired from the customs house if he persisted. Harmon persisted, and although the government realized very little from the sale of the ties, the company was served notice that it would be watched in the future.[52]

Other poachers were found operating on a large scale along the St. Johns River at Palatka, near the Halifax River in Volusia County, at several Nassau County locations, in Duval and Clay counties, and near

Cedar Key.[53] Military force was used in several cases involving physical resistance to the agents' attempted seizures. The results were disappointing, however, because District Attorney Horatio Bisbee dropped the charges on the ground that resistance in such cases was not a punishable offense. Although the timber agents in effect exacted small fines from many poachers when they accepted compromise settlements, the government received comparatively little compensation for the vast spoliation of timber land. In 1877 the land office at Gainesville reported that no timber agents had been employed since 1875.

Much of the crime in Reconstruction Florida was like that of any other period. People disagreed and sometimes the result was violence. Officials occasionally used their offices for personal aggrandizement. Stealing from the government, whether by cutting its timber or evading its tax laws, was somehow regarded as less reprehensible than other forms of theft. None of these distinguish the era from any other. Law enforcement in a free society is based on the assumption that the laws are accepted by a large majority of the population. Most people did not vent their anger in violence. Most officers were not corrupt. And even those who evaded the revenue laws and disregarded property lines in the pine forests were a small portion of society.

Such was not the case with respect to the violence committed against blacks and white Republicans. An overwhelming number of white Floridians opposed the legislation imposed by the United States government extending civil and political rights to Negroes. There had always been many whites who violently hated the freedmen and felt justified in attacking them at will. At the same time a portion of the influential planting class wished the free Negroes well in a paternalistic way. But even the latter group resented Negro participation in political affairs, especially since the blacks supported the Republican party. When the influential planting class decided that it was necessary to drive freedmen out of politics even if physical intimidation were required, it approved the worst deeds of the basest elements of white society. Once white supremacy became a goal paramount to human life there was no limit to the violence committed to achieve and perpetuate it. William Watson Davis, whose history of the period was decidedly sympathetic with the whites, admitted that "in this contest for a very necessary supremacy many a foul crime was committed by white against black. Innocent people suffered."[54] Davis was correct, but the matter did not end there. Once the deeds were done, it became necessary to justify them. Physical violence against Negroes and the justification for it fed on each other. Floridians already believed that Negroes were inferior and that the national government had exceeded its authority in trying to make voting citizens out of them. They believed that the whole Reconstruction effort was unconstitutional, wrong, and doomed to fail. Therefore, they felt that the trauma of the period had been unnecessarily perpetrated on a helpless population who understood the situation much better than the distant Washington government. When Negroes were finally driven out of politics, the Republican party practically disappeared and the national government backed away from its attempt to achieve Negro equality. White Floridians convinced themselves that this was proof that they had been right, but it also meant that they could never admit that the killing had been wrong. The era of Democratic solidarity in the state was based partially on the assumption that white supremacy was a principle worth preserving. Its correlative was continued violent suppression of Negroes and a determination that the national government never be permitted to interfere with the state's internal affairs, as whites interpreted them.

14

A Combination To Promote Our State Interest

When Governor Harrison Reed was inaugurated in 1868, Florida railroads were still hampered by lack of sufficient capital either to place existing lines on a sound basis or to build needed new roads. Reed, a typical ex-Whig, regarded completion of an adequate transportation system as an end worthy of any assistance the state could furnish, just as had the Conservative administration before him. In an early speech he outlined a comprehensive program aimed at completing a system which would bind the state together and encourage settlement of the extensive Florida hinterland. The major points of his program included railroad connections across the peninsula from Fernandina to several Gulf points and from Jacksonville to Pensacola, and an inland waterway from the Amelia River to Biscayne Bay. This would have finished the program begun in 1855 under the guidance of David Yulee and advocated by every administration since that time. But Governor Reed was also a fiscal conservative who recommended great care in preparing any legislation lending state credit to private corporations. Reluctantly recognizing the need for such legislation, he suggested limiting it to projects which would complete the railroads from Jacksonville to Pensacola and from Fernandina to Tampa and Charlotte Harbor.

Once committed to the policy, the governor used his considerable powers to see it through. Because the most ambitious and most urgent of the several projects—the Jacksonville, Pensacola and Mobile Railroad—ultimately failed (after becoming embroiled in questionable financial manipulations promptly dubbed the "Swepson-Littlefield Fraud"), the Reed administration received severe contemporary criticism and adverse historical judgment for its role in promoting internal improvements. The episode was cited as one more example of the waste, corruption, and inefficiency of the Republican—or "carpetbagger"—governments of the Reconstruction era. Critics have neglected to add that it was also a Republican administration which, between 1873 and 1875, enacted legislation and obtained ratification of a constitutional amendment prohibiting the use of state credit to aid private corporations.

While it is undeniable that public resources were badly used in internal improvement matters and that Republican officials as well as private individuals were involved, it is proper to point out that Reed tried to protect the state even though he believed that completion of the railroads was a goal which made the risks worth taking. The principle of government aid to private internal improvement companies was well-established at the time, and both state and national authorities were similarly engaged in granting aid throughout the United States. Furthermore, the Internal Improvement Fund of Florida was already being used for the purpose under legislation enacted in 1855. The fund's trustees had paid the debts of Florida's three major railroads during Governor Walker's administration, and before Reed's inauguration negotiations were already in progress between native Florida Conservative railroad men and George W. Swepson to obtain the latter's financial assistance.

Governor Reed and his associates were in agreement with Conservative-Democrats about railroad policy. Swepson of North Carolina and his flamboyant and charming associate, Milton S. Littlefield, were guilty of unethical practices and their railroad ventures failed because of wasteful financing and poor management. Yet their methods were patterned after most of the railroad financing of post–Civil War America. Their schemes failed and became known as the "notorious Swepson-Littlefield fraud," but if they had succeeded the two would probably have been applauded as great developers of Florida. Regardless of such speculation, neither Reed nor the Republican party bears all the blame for what happened. Numerous prominent Conservative-Democrats were connected with railroad schemes as owners, directors, managers, lawyers, receivers, and bondholders. They competed and collaborated with Republicans in the legislature and courts as well as the bond markets and business offices. And it was Conservative-Democrat Edward Houstoun, the richest citizen of Tallahassee immediately after the war, who was responsible for introducing Swepson to Florida.

In February 1869, Houstoun, president of the Pensacola and Georgia (Lake City to Quincy), wrote John P. Sanderson, a Conservative Jacksonville lawyer vitally interested in the Florida Central Railroad (Jacksonville to Lake City), that he was "about to complete a combination to promote our state interest": finishing construction of the railroad from Quincy to the Apalachicola River and beyond to Pensacola. "I think I have succeeded in forming a strong combination. Mr. Swepson's associates are the strongest capitalists [in New York] as well as North Carolina," he wrote, adding that they expected the state to aid construction in every possible way *"which I have pledged her to do"*[1] [italics added].

As previously discussed, Houstoun was instrumental in reorganizing the Florida, Atlantic and Gulf Central as the Florida Central Railroad, a change which forced Franklin Dibble out of the road's management and left Swepson as the major stockholder. On Swepson's behalf, Houstoun had purchased about four-fifths of the Central's $550,000 outstanding stock in the open market. The Florida Central was then leased to the Pensacola and Georgia. But Houstoun was unable to put the combined operation on firm financial footing, and the Internal Improvement Board ordered the Pensacola and Georgia sold on March 20, 1869. Acting as Swepson's agent, Houstoun purchased the company's outstanding bonds at thirty to thirty-five cents on the dollar to be used to pay for the road at the approaching sale. Houstoun argued that the sale was beneficial to the state since it would relieve the fund of much of its liability by permitting retirement of the bonds it received as purchase money.[2]

The impending sale was advertised as a cash transaction, but the trustees held a special meeting one hour before the road was offered for bidding and decided to accept either cash or its "appropriate equivalent." The change was intended to enable Swepson to buy the road with $807,600 worth of first mortgage bonds of the Pensacola and Georgia and $153,000 worth of Tallahassee Railroad securities, purchased at depreciated prices by Houstoun during the past several months. They agreed that the bonds should be accepted only at face value. Franklin Dibble foiled the plan by offering the high bid of $1,200,000 for the Pensacola and Georgia and $195,000 for the Tallahassee Railroad. Possessing neither sufficient cash nor securities to cover the amount, Dibble argued that he should be given time to obtain bonds because he had not had notice of the last minute change in terms of the sale. The trustees agreed and appointed a receiver to operate the road until the transaction was completed.[3]

Dibble and Swepson came to terms, and the two turned over to the trustees the $960,700 worth of bonds at nearly face value as part payment. The remainder of the purchase price was covered by a personal check from Swepson for $470,065. All parties to the transaction knew the check was not negotiable, but it was supposed to be settled as soon as the new company could be formed and negotiate a bond issue. At a New York meeting on April 22, the Internal Improvement Fund trustees deeded the roads to Swepson.[4]

These high-handed proceedings left several stockholders dissatisfied at the way they had been ignored when the roads were sold. Many individual stockholders complained and several filed suits. Jefferson County protested the sale with a suit which was ultimately withdrawn in 1870. Columbia County brought a similar suit against the Florida Central, alleging fraud in the sale of that road in 1868. Judge Alva A. Knight placed both roads in the hands of receivers, but the state supreme court overruled him and returned the roads to Swepson. The United States government also sued the Pensacola and Georgia for unpaid taxes and won a $16,000 judgment that eventually resulted in a forced sale of some railroad property.[5] Jacksonville authorities also considered court action to recover investments made in the old roads.

However, when Swepson threatened to give up the Florida venture because of these legal difficulties, the Jacksonville Board of Trade met to hear John P. Sanderson argue the advantages of retaining outside capital in the state. He said that Swepson intended to build a railroad across Florida and connect it to a direct steamship line to New York. He had also applied for a charter for a national bank in the city. Three hundred workers were already grading the twenty-one miles between Quincy and River Junction on the Apalachicola. Completion of that construction alone would bring thousands of bales of cotton to Jacksonville from the river. Furthermore, if Swepson sold out, the buyer would be Edward Houstoun, meaning that Savannah would get the business of middle Florida. Sanderson cautioned that Franklin Dibble and his associates could not finish the road because the necessary capital was just not in the state.[6] Sanderson asked Jacksonville businessmen to encourage Swepson by investing in his proposed bank. S. N. Williams added, "Don't kill the goose that lays the golden egg." He felt that Jacksonville should forget the financial sacrifice and just use the road. Edward L'Engle endorsed Swepson as an honorable gentleman who acted in good faith and had millions to invest. Lewis I. Fleming, another prominent Conservative lawyer, said care should be exercised that Jacksonville did not lose out to Savannah.[7]

But there was disagreement. The mayor thought the city should sue to recover its investment. James M. Baker and Wilkinson Call expressed doubt as to Swepson's integrity and ability. But when these two men decided to sue Swepson to collect the city's investment as a matter of "abstract justice," the *Union* chided them to "let us have peace, and railroads, and steamships, and let such a costly article as abstract justice take care of itself."[8]

Embroiled in litigation over their financial manipulations from the inception of the enterprise, the new owners of the railroad lines sought legislation authorizing them to consolidate their holdings and granting state aid for construction of a line west of Quincy. The result was the series of laws enacted at the special session of 1869 and the regular session of 1870 which was discussed in chapter 12.[9]

Swepson and Littlefield had intended to incorporate both of the lines between Jacksonville and Quincy into their new company. In May 1870 the new Tallahassee Railroad (Lake City to Quincy and Tallahassee to St. Marks) was merged with the Jacksonville, Pensacola and Mobile. Littlefield became president, Sanderson was vice-president, and Mariano Papy was company attorney.[10] The Florida Central (Lake City to Jacksonville) remained separate from the new company, but Littlefield was able to control it because Swepson owned a majority of its stock.

On June 2, 1870, Reed exchanged $3 million worth of state bonds for a similar amount of Jacksonville, Pensacola and Mobile securities and $1 million worth for Florida Central bonds. The exchange was made in New York where it was hoped that state bonds could be sold. David Yulee launched an attack on the legality of the $4 million issue which eventually precluded its sale in the United States. Charles Dyke, whose *Floridian* supported the railroad legislation even after the 1870 amendment, became hostile to the bond exchange about the time Yulee corresponded with him on the subject. Two weeks after Swepson and Littlefield obtained possession of the state bonds, the *New York World* carried a telegram warning investors not to buy the bonds because Floridians would not support them.[11] Denied a New York market, the two men looked for buyers in Europe.

At about the same time, information became available indicating that Wilkinson Call was right and Sanderson and L'Engle were wrong about Swepson. The North Carolinian had been president of the Western Division of the Western North Carolina Railroad Company, whose intended construction funds he had used to invest in Florida. The money Edward Houstoun had used to buy stocks and bonds of the Florida roads in 1868–69 had been the proceeds from North Carolina bonds sold for railroad building. Having discovered the embezzlement, a North Carolina legislative committee—chaired by Nicholas W. Woodfin—tried to recover the money invested in Florida. Swepson retired to Canada for awhile, but at a meeting in April 1870—before Governor Reed issued the Florida bonds—Littlefield convinced Woodfin that he should permit completion of the Florida transaction.[12] Littlefield agreed to restore some of the misappropriated North Carolina funds by paying Woodfin one-half the proceeds from the Florida securities.

When the *New York World* article ruined chances of a market in that city, Littlefield placed $3 million worth of bonds representing the Jacksonville, Pensacola and Mobile with S. W. Hopkins and Company of

London. While that company was negotiating a sale, Woodfin appeared in London and announced that neither Littlefield nor Hopkins had a right to the bonds they were selling; that Governor Reed, the secretary of state, and the chief justice of Florida "could all be bought for $10,000"; and that he intended to attach the bonds as soon as they were presented for sale. In sheer disbelief, Hopkins wrote that the "consummate blockhead" saw no damage in his talk. "We must get him out of London. It is impossible to stop his talking," Hopkins decided.[13] In fact, Woodfin was not Hopkins' greatest obstacle. Englishmen who held Florida territorial bonds that had been repudiated in the 1840s brought pressure to collect on their investments before any more Florida bonds were handled on the London exchange.

When the London sale failed the securities were finally sold to a Dutch syndicate. Governor Reed perhaps aided the sale by his statement, backed by a state supreme court opinion, that the bonds were a legitimate obligation of Florida. He said no tax had been levied to pay the interest merely because that was supposed to come from interest paid to the state by the company on its own bonds held as security. About $2,966,000 worth of bonds were sold at about seventy cents on the dollar. Slightly more than half of the proceeds was paid to Hopkins and Company for expenses and commissions. Swepson and Littlefield realized about $900,000 and nearly two-thirds of this went for their expenses incurred in Florida and North Carolina. Only a little over $300,000 was used for railroad construction and purchase of equipment.[14]

The $1 million worth of bonds exchanged for Florida Central securities was hypothecated to Edward Houstoun to cover a debt owed him for services rendered during 1868–70. Although they became embroiled in complicated litigation when Littlefield's personal creditors attached them in New York, none of these bonds was ever sold.[15]

Even before the bond transactions were completed the railroad had financial difficulties in Florida. News of Swepson's manipulations and Littlefield's personal extravagance brought numerous lawsuits from exasperated creditors and made businessmen in Florida reluctant to accept notes of the Jacksonville, Pensacola and Mobile. Confidence was further weakened when Franklin Dibble's Jacksonville bank closed in mid-1870. By August 1870, all construction workers had left the job and work was at a standstill. With some of the money from the bond sale, construction superintendent James G. Gibbs eventually procured enough iron and workers to complete the extension from Quincy to River Junction in March 1872, but the company never laid any rails west of the Apalachicola. A national commercial convention at Baltimore in 1871 noted that the 200 miles from Quincy to Pensacola were the only missing link in the necessary railroad from New Orleans to Jacksonville, but the line was not completed until 1883.[16]

Littlefield struggled to maintain control of the railroad but was forced out of its management in 1873. As late as 1875 he was lobbying for a new law to promote his plans for a westward road, but he failed. His home in Jacksonville was sold at a sheriff's sale in 1873, and he borrowed $100 for living expenses from Edward L'Engle in 1875. By 1872 both the Florida Central and the Jacksonville, Pensacola and Mobile were embroiled in dozens of suits by stockholders of the original roads; by first and second mortgage bondholders anxious to collect unpaid principal and interest; by equipment firms trying to obtain payment for boxcars, engines, steamships, and other equipment; and even by the Internal Improvement Fund trustees for the remainder of the original purchase price represented by Swepson's personal check.[17] The company soon defaulted on its bonds and the Dutch holders of state securities sent a commission to check on the investment.

Service on the road was generally poor. Equipment and track sometimes went without needed repairs. Passengers from Jacksonville to Savannah complained of a twenty-one hour journey, two-thirds of which was spent at Live Oak awaiting connections. An eleven hour wait was necessary at Baldwin on a trip from Jacksonville to Gainesville. In 1873 most travellers from Tallahassee northward went by way of Thomasville to avoid the long delay at Live Oak. Worst of all, there was still no railroad between the Apalachicola River and Pensacola. The 1874 legislature noted that a round-trip ticket from Pensacola to Gainesville cost $110 and the passenger was routed through Montgomery, Columbus, Macon, and Baldwin to Gainesville. In August 1873, employees of the Jacksonville, Pensacola and Mobile struck for a week until they were paid wages due them for May and June.[18] But that company and the Florida Central continued to provide at least minimal service while various court decisions placed them under one receiver after another, always treating them as two separate companies.

State policy toward railroad financing in general and the Jacksonville, Pensacola and Mobile in particular changed in 1873. The state had authorized bond exchanges with seven other companies at rates of $10,000 to $16,000 per mile of new construction.[19] Because of the unfortunate experience with the Jacksonville, Pensacola and Mobile, the 1873 legislature prohibited the use of state credit to aid private corporations and repealed all outstanding legislation which tendered such aid. At the same time the Trustees of the Internal Improvement Fund offered to exchange railroad company bonds held by the state for Florida bonds held by the Dutch investors. Attorney General William Archer Cocke assured them that their only hope to realize any return on their investment was to "return the [state] bonds and use the lien on the road as they please."[20] Not all trustees agreed. Governor Hart was enraged at Cocke's action and asked for his resignation. Hart and Stearns both contended that the state should honor its bonds, but the matter was settled in January 1876 when the state supreme court declared the entire $4 million issue unconstitutional on the ground that a railroad with terminals outside the state (Mobile) was not a "public works" within the constitutional meaning. It awarded the state's lien to the innocent Dutch bondholders. The state took over the road and operated it until it could be sold to satisfy the lien.[21]

Litigation over the Jacksonville, Pensacola and Mobile and the Florida Central continued for several more years. The Western Division of the Western North Carolina Railroad Company sued to collect some of the money embezzled by Swepson, but its case was dismissed. In 1879 the United States court agreed with the Florida supreme court that the state bond issue was null and void. It awarded the Dutch bondholders a first lien of about $315,000 against the Florida Central and a second lien of about $4,400,000 against the Jacksonville, Pensacola and Mobile. Florida Central bonds were never sold but the lien resulted from their use to pay interest on the other bonds. The state was awarded a first lien on the Jacksonville, Pensacola and Mobile for the unpaid Swepson check of 1869 and accrued interest.[22] The roads were sold at auction in 1882 for a fraction of the judgments against them. Henry Plant acquired them.

As outlined in chapter eight, the Florida Railroad Company, under the conservative management of David Yulee and Edward N. Dickerson, avoided the complicated litigation in which the other major antebellum railroads became involved. It was reorganized as the Atlantic, Gulf and West India Transit Company in 1872. The company's original charter called for a road from Fernandina to Tampa with a branch to Cedar Key, but Yulee had built only the branch line. The company still had authority to build to Tampa and the acts which extended state aid to the Jacksonville, Pensacola and Mobile made the same benefits available to the Florida Railroad. But, while urging the Florida Railroad to begin construction toward Tampa, the legislature also placed conditions on the aid it was willing to grant. An 1870 act extended the company's charter to include right-of-way to Charlotte Harbor and permitted it to create a separate company capitalized at no more than $3 million, but it stipulated that construction had to begin within one year after passage of the act and reach Ocala within two years. Failure to meet the deadlines would result in revocation of the company's right-of-way to Tampa.[23]

Yulee established the South Florida Railroad Company to build from

Waldo to Tampa and agreed with Governor Reed to accept $1 million worth of state bonds in exchange for a similar amount of the new company's securities. Some grading was done between Waldo and Ocala, and Yulee began laying track in January 1871, but he soon gave up the undertaking and never accepted delivery of the state bonds. Signed and shipped to Yulee by the governor, they lay for more than two years in the Jacksonville express office with Yulee refusing to pay the $250 charges due and the comptroller imploring him to return the unwanted bonds so they could be cancelled. In November 1871, Yulee reorganized the company and undertook completion of the line from Waldo to Ocala immediately, with plans for extending it to Tampa later. The new firm put down a few miles of track in 1871, but no railroad reached Ocala until 1880.[24]

While the Florida Railroad Company managed to clear up much of its debt with assistance from the Internal Improvement Fund and remained comparatively free of litigation during the Reconstruction era, the 1866 sale by which this was accomplished caused the trustees immense difficulties and hampered their use of public land to encourage development of the state. It will be recalled that Francis Vose, an iron manufacturer to whom Yulee's company was indebted, had refused to accept the twenty cents on the dollar offered for his Florida Railroad bonds and had sought an injunction from the federal court against the Internal Improvement Fund trustees. During both the Walker and Reed administrations the trustees repeatedly offered to compromise the issue using land as part payment, but Vose steadfastly refused to settle except for cash covering the full amount, which was about $105,000, including interest. Although he also tried to collect from the Florida Railroad Company, he was much more successful against the Internal Improvement Fund.[25]

When the legislature enacted several measures providing contingent land grants to canal, drainage, and railroad companies, Vose pursued his federal court case. In 1871 he obtained a judgment for the principal and interest and an injunction which prohibited the trustees from disposing of land for internal improvements until the Vose claim was satisfied. The land could only be sold for cash, which was to be applied against the claim. The judgment caused potential investors to doubt titles of the companies which had received conditional land grants, credit became unavailable, and their projects collapsed.[26] Vose was using the United States courts to collect from the state of Florida debts owed him by Yulee's Florida Railroad Company.

In 1872 Vose obtained an order placing the Internal Improvement Fund under a receiver for forced sale of its sinking fund which contained about $100,000 worth of state bonds. At the sale Vose bought them for $45,000 and paid with other state bonds at par. In 1872 and again in 1875 he attempted to have all the state's land—estimated at fourteen million acres or more—disposed of at a forced sale to satisfy his claim. Potential recipients of land grants argued that Vose had no claim to any state lands except the 500,000 acres Florida had owned at the time of his original transaction with Yulee. Recognizing the imperative need to settle the case, the 1875 legislature empowered Governor Stearns to work out a compromise solution. Williams, Swann and Corley—a Fernandina real estate company commissioned to sell land and pay the judgment—almost completed the sale of 1 million acres in 1877, but the terms could not be agreed upon. The state's lands remained encumbered by the Vose judgment and injunction until 1881 when Governor William D. Bloxham completed the sale of 4 million acres to Hamilton Disston and paid the Vose estate.[27]

One of the companies most adversely affected by the Vose controversy was William Gleason's Southern Inland Navigation and Improvement Company which was chartered to establish an inland waterway from Fernandina to Key West by dredging and building canals. Gleason, who had been exploring and surveying south Florida since 1865, was one of the first to realize the possibilities of the area if it were drained and made accessible by suitable transportation facilities. He hoped to acquire quantities of land in return for building the water route and draining overflowed areas. An inland passage along the Atlantic Coast had been desired for years and a company had been chartered in 1866 to complete it as far south as Indian River. A national commercial convention in 1871 endorsed an inland canal from the St. Johns River to New Orleans.[28]

Authorized a multimillion-dollar capitalization, the company planned to use its potential land grant—the Internal Improvement Fund trustees were to grant the company as much as they deemed advisable—as an inducement to suppliers to accept its securities as payment for necessary equipment. In a series of actions between February 1869 and February 1871, the trustees sold Gleason's company about 1,350,000 acres of "swamp and overflowed" land for forty dollars a section, slightly more than six cents per acre. On the basis of the grant, the company purchased materials for constructing dredges and began work on the waterway. But Vose won a decision from the federal court in 1873 directing the trustees to reclaim the land and hold it for satisfaction of his claim. Gleason complained that the decision "robs us of rights without notice" after his company had expended $60,000 for dredges and $52,000 for land. Dredging practically ceased because "contractors became timid" about accepting company bonds after the Vose decision. To salvage his operation, Gleason asked the trustees to reconvey the land already sold him. In March the board of trustees reaffirmed his title and extended the time allowed for completion of the project, but weakened their statement by the qualification that they—a new group of trustees—assumed the contracts had been legal. They later refused to convey any more land to him, alleging that the 1855 Internal Improvement Act had not authorized grants for drainage, but only for canals.[29]

In 1874 Gleason contracted with John H. Fry of New York, an enthusiastic proponent of a cross-Florida ship canal, to expand the company's capitalization to $18 million (based on its equipment and about 3,100,000 acres of land to which Gleason then claimed title), raise $6 million in gold, and build the canal. By March he had acquired more than a million acres in west Florida by purchase from the trustees. The remainder was apparently about two million acres of swamp and overflowed land belonging to the fund, which the trustees had authorized Gleason to sell on a commission basis. Of course, the grand scheme was still-born, and had he raised the money it would have been inadequate for the project. Fry continued striving for a cross-Florida canal, but Gleason concentrated on drainage of swamp lands. His company made no substantive improvements of the inland waterway, completion of which awaited the twentieth century. In 1879 the Internal Improvement Board revoked Gleason's authority to ditch and drain south Florida land on grounds that he had done no work on the project in the past ten years. He salvaged something for his efforts, however. The Southern Inland Navigation and Improvement Company sold its rights to the Atlantic and Gulf Transit Company for $150,000 cash and $1,250,000 in the new company's bonds.[30]

While Gleason was willing to improve the state's transportation system if he could, it seems that his first concern was the land development scheme made possible by the grants from the Internal Improvement Fund. His dredging work was directed at least as much toward drainage as toward clearing navigable channels.

Another project authorized by the Florida legislature with the combined purpose of land acquisition and construction of transportation facilities was the Great Southern Railway Company. With the grand purpose of connecting the "North and the tropics," the company obtained charters in 1870 from Georgia and Florida to build a railroad from Millen, Georgia, to Key West. The Florida corporation was authorized to build from King's Ferry on the St. Mary's River southward. The entire line would have been about 870 miles long. In 1874 the Florida legislature authorized the Great Southern of Florida to consolidate with its Georgia counterpart. Although nineteen men were named as incorporators—including Governor Reed, the other trustees of the Internal Improvement Fund, Senator Osborn, and the most influential state senators—the organizers were A. C. Osborn of Brooklyn, the senator's brother, and Morris H. Alberger, his personal secretary. They sought land grants from the Internal Improvement Fund as well as from the United States Congress. The charter bill simply authorized a grant of as many acres "as may hereafter be granted . . . by the United States." A bill providing land for the new company died in Congress. Nevertheless, the trustees agreed to a large conditional grant in November 1870 only to revoke it in January 1872 because it conflicted with a grant already made to the South Florida Railroad.[31]

Failure of the congressional enactment set off another intraparty fight between Florida Republicans as Reed and Osborn struggled for party supremacy. Congressman Hamilton, who was replaced in 1870 by Josiah Walls as the party's nominee for Congress, was credited with defeating the bill. When A. C. Osborn accused Hamilton of offering to support the congressional land grant in return for $1 million worth of company stock and $5,000 attorney fees, Hamilton retaliated with his own version of the episode. He said Osborn had tried to bribe him with offers of stock and a company position, but that he had refused. He substantiated his countercharges with several letters from Osborn.[32]

Nothing more was heard about the Great Southern Railway until 1873 when the company was organized with ex-Senator Osborn as president, Sherman Conant as vice-president, A. C. Osborn as treasurer, and M. H. Alberger as general superintendent. They claimed to have contracted for construction of the road between Jacksonville and Jesup, Georgia. Jesup was the junction of the Atlantic and Gulf Railroad with the Brunswick and Macon. Work was expected to begin by December 1873. About the time of this renewed activity, Alberger was arrested for the robbery of the Jacksonville post office mentioned earlier. Although they had failed to obtain a valid land grant from Florida, the incorporators were mollified by a bargain completed with the trustees on March 29, 1873. For a road between the St. Mary's River and Key West, with branches deemed necessary by the company, the trustees agreed to sell 128,000 acres for every ten miles of track. The land was to be sold for five cents an acre in lots, each time ten miles of the railroad was placed in running order. It was estimated that the sale would eventually have amounted to 6,400,000 acres, more than one-sixth of the total area of the state.[33] No track of the Great Southern was laid during the 1870s, but the incorporators kept trying for nearly twenty years.

Although Pensacola remained without rail connections to middle Florida during the Reconstruction period, there was considerable railroad activity around the town. The Alabama and Florida was sold to the Pensacola and Louisville which rebuilt the war-damaged line. The new company had financial troubles, however, and was sold in 1872 to Albert

Hyer for $66,000. Hyer re-sold it in 1877 to the Pensacola Railroad Company, owned by Daniel F. Sullivan, a Pensacola banker. In 1880 Sullivan's road became part of the Louisville and Nashville Railroad. Under the leadership of William D. Chipley, the Louisville and Nashville built eastward from Pensacola to River Junction on the Apalachicola in 1883.[34] This completed the long-awaited link in the Jacksonville to Pensacola railroad.

The Pensacola and Mobile Railroad and Manufacturing Company, chartered in 1861, built about five miles toward the Perdido River from Pensacola during the war. Torn up by retreating Confederate forces, the line became primarily a logging road. Receiving a land grant from the 1866 Florida legislature, the company languished until 1873 when it tried to rebuild with aid from the Pensacola and Louisville. It was sold along with that road in 1876 and became part of the Louisville and Nashville.[35]

While it contributed little to the statewide railroad system deemed necessary by Florida leaders, the Pensacola and Perdido Railroad was one of the few lines built during the period. Chartered in 1868, this eight-mile line between Pensacola and Perdido Bay was built to serve the lumbermen who established a new community called Millview. Richard L. Campbell was president of the railroad and O. M. Avery, former president of the Alabama and Florida, supervised construction. Completed in 1872, the line extended 2,400 feet into Pensacola Bay, enabling lumber trains to load directly on waiting schooners without the expense of using lighters to reach the deep water vessels. In 1873 the road served five lumber mills on Perdido Bay, the largest of which was the Perdido Lumber Company, capable of cutting 195,000 feet a day. C. L. Robinson and Company of Jacksonville had one mill in operation, cutting 40,000 feet a day, and another mill being prepared. Forty to seventy lumber schooners at a time were observed in Pensacola Bay in 1873, supplied by many mills in Escambia and Santa Rosa counties in addition to those at Millview. About 600 vessels a year were clearing the port with long-leaf yellow pine lumber at the time.[36]

Except for the Lake Eustis Railroad which was being graded toward Sanford by convict labor in late 1876, there was no other railroad building during the Reconstruction period, although the legislature had chartered more than twenty companies between 1866 and 1876.[37] Eight were offered financial aid by the state, others were to receive land, and some were authorized both forms of assistance. Many of the land grants were ultimately confirmed, although they were delayed until the 1880s. After the debacle resulting from the Jacksonville, Pensacola and Mobile bond transaction, the state backed away from the practice of using state credit in aiding railroads. Only the $3 million issue was sold and it was ultimately repudiated by a state supreme court decision. The $1 million worth issued in behalf of the Florida Central was not sold, but part of it was used to pay debts. The repudiation also applied to this issue. The $1 million issued to Yulee's South Florida Railroad was never taken from the packages in which it was shipped because the company defaulted on its obligations. There may have been one other issue to the Jacksonville and St. Augustine Railroad, chartered by Governor Reed, Swepson, Littlefield, and others and desperately sought by St. Augustine promoters, but nothing was done about it. By the time Fred Dockray tried to find a buyer in 1873, New York investors were aware that Florida was preparing to nullify legislation authorizing such bonds.[38]

Governor Reed and the Republican legislature tried to implement existing internal improvement legislation to solve the state's universally recognized need for transportation. The effort failed at least partially because of the machinations of Swepson and Littlefield. As the chief executive who recommended legislation to facilitate their schemes, Reed perhaps deserves criticism for misjudging the two men. But they came to him highly recommended by some of the state's most respected Conservative leaders. Reed was slow to condemn Littlefield because both he and his wife had known the charming scoundrel since their wartime days in Fernandina. The mistake was soon corrected. In mid-1870, Reed reiterated his position favoring limited aid to internal improvements, but cautioned that the legislature had gone too far. He called for repeal of some of the grants and a prohibition against future ones.[39] Instead of burdening the state with huge debts incurred by supporting unsuccessful railroad ventures, the second Republican administration obtained legislation prohibiting the loan of state credit to private companies, and the state supreme court effectively relieved the state of responsibility for the one bond issue which was sold. Florida taxpayers were never assessed a cent to pay for these bonds. Railroad taxes were paid in many counties, but they were to liquidate bonds issued long before 1868. Even the repudiation was not as disastrous to state credit as the earlier refusal of Florida to pay its territorial bonds issued in support of banking institutions, because by the mid-1870s the state was managing a bonded debt for which it accepted responsibility.

The Vose injunction which prohibited the free use of state lands by the Internal Improvement Fund resulted directly from the decision of the trustees during the Walker administration to sell the Florida Railroad according to terms prearranged with David Yulee. The purpose of the sale was to clear up the company's debts at the expense of innocent bondholders and it caused the dissatisfied investors to look for redress to the trustees instead of the Florida Railroad. The Internal Improvement Board had legal authority to do what it did, but if any blame accrues, as it has according to most historians who have dealt with the subject, it should be remembered that Conservative-Democrats, not Republicans, sat on the board of trustees in 1866.

15

A Northern City in a Southern Latitude

Florida's population was still sparse and investment capital was scarce when George F. Drew became governor, but, contrary to accepted interpretations, the state did not stagnate during the Republican era and then suddenly boom as it was "redeemed" and restored to "home rule." Northern investment capital began coming into Florida soon after the war and continued to do so throughout the 1870s. Its volume was affected more by national financial conditions than local political problems. As always, money went where profits were most likely. Thus, financing was available for hotels on the St. Johns River while increasing numbers of tourists were availing themselves of Florida's mild winter climate, but there were few buyers for middle Florida plantations when agricultural prices were falling.

Despite the societal disruptions and military casualties of the Civil War, the state's population growth was comparatively constant during the last four decades of the nineteenth century. The 140,424 Floridians of 1860 increased to 528,542 in 1900. The percentage growths during the intervening decades were 33.7 per cent, 43.5 per cent, 45.3 per cent, and 35 per cent respectively. War and depressions seem to have affected population growth at least as much as concern over whether Republicans or Democrats were in power. The total increase was accompanied by internal migration. Middle Florida, comprising most of the old plantation black-belt, was relatively static during the period. Some of its residents joined immigrants from both northern and southern states in settling the east Florida counties, especially along the St. Johns River to Orlando and the Indian River country. Florida remained rural and agricultural for many years after the Civil War, but cotton diminished in importance while citrus groves and winter vegetables increased as the population expanded into the peninsula.

Almost everyone in the state believed immigration desirable, though their reasons varied. Some landowners wanted white agricultural laborers to replace the freedmen while others were bringing hundreds of South Carolina and Georgia blacks to work in their fields. Harrison Reed appointed J. S. Adams as commissioner of lands and immigration in 1869 to induce permanent settlers to buy land and invest in other activities. Adams distributed information extolling Florida throughout the United States. J. Berrien Oliver, an old Florida newspaperman, subsequently moved to New York and published the *Florida New Yorker,* a monthly magazine which touted Florida's salubrious climate and productive soil. Samuel A. Swann and other land speculators corresponded with midwestern editors and individual citizens interested in settling Florida tracts. Former Confederates showed little animosity toward Northerners with money to invest. A. C. Clark, a Sumterville lawyer and realtor, asked to have his calling cards distributed in Jacksonville "to Yankees as I want them to bring as much money to the county as possible and . . . come out in the interior . . . and settle."[1]

In 1870 C. H. Dupont of Quincy revived the moribund Agricultural and Immigration Association, still hoping to replace Negro farm workers with European immigrants. Dupont reasoned that Europeans would be willing to work one year to pay costs of their transportation to the United States. They could be hired out at an annual rate of $120 for men and $100 for women. Thinking that many planters would hire a few such workers if they were available, he planned to form a company financed by private sources to bring the immigrants to Florida, hire them out for a year, and pocket the difference between cost of transportation and the year's wages. The scheme was not a success, but Dupont brought a few Swedish immigrants to Gadsden County. Henry Sanford helped finance the undertaking and hired several groups of Swedes to work in his orange groves and saw-mill at Sanford.[2]

A Dr. Henschen acted as Dupont's agent, contracting in Europe with the prospective immigrants and bringing them to the United States in several groups beginning in May 1871. Led by a minister named Thiemann, several of them arrived in Gadsden County in August 1871. Most were already employed by planters who had agreed in advance with Dupont. A few women were hired as domestic workers. The arrangement was unsatisfactory and nearly all the Swedes were gone from the county within a year. They arrived at the wrong time of year to benefit their employers, they were dissatisfied and homesick, and Thiemann soon became so embittered toward Dupont that the two spent most of their time abusing each other.[3]

A permanent colony near Lake Monroe eventually resulted from the Swedish labor experiment. Among those who hired the immigrants were Benjamin F. Whitner, formerly of Madison County, and Count Frederick DeBary, who was himself an immigrant from Belgium. Sanford hired fifty-three in 1871, at least seven of whom were women. He employed at least twenty more in 1873. Some of the men who came alone planned to bring their families later. Although some expressed satisfaction with the food, shelter, and working arrangements, others were discontented and several ran away from the Sanford property. DeBary had similar difficulties. Paid from $12 to $17 for field labor and $15 to $20 at the saw-mill in addition to their board, the immigrants worked from five A.M. until dark with one hour for breakfast and two hours for lunch. Most of the newcomers were skilled craftsmen unaccustomed to common labor. They complained that Henschen had promised that they would be employed at their trades. Hoping for better jobs, several stowed away on the Jacksonville steamers and others went overland to Apopka. They eventually found employment in Jacksonville or Charleston, although one shipped out as a sailor. Nearly all were arrested and were returned until it was established that the contracts made in Europe were probably invalid. After that Sanford's manager used persuasion to keep them on the job. Some were happier when he began paying extra cash for odd jobs, but most important of all was Sanford's promise of land and lumber with which to build homes at the end of the contracted term. Both Negroes and Swedes were employed on Sanford's property at the same time, but the blacks were gradually replaced by the white immigrants. When one of the Swedish women took up residence with a Negro fireman at the sawmill, he was fired and replaced by a Swede while the woman's employment was uninterrupted.[4]

By 1873 thirteen former contract laborers had taken up their own land and were building houses with lumber furnished by Sanford. With their families they constituted a colony of forty-seven. By 1876 more than 100 Swedes had settled in the Sanford area.[5]

A few immigrants of other nationalities came to Florida. Sanford hired a group of Italians in 1873, but none of them brought their families and all were gone within a few years. A German named Koch worked with Samuel A. Swann to settle a few of his countrymen in Florida. Those who came apparently purchased land which had already been cleared and improved. A small colony of Germans led by George Pfeiffer also settled at Pensacola in the early 1870s. The numerous Cubans who came to Key

West during the ten-year revolution which began in 1868 had a significant effect on that city, but only a few came to mainland Florida before the 1880s.[6]

European immigrants did not populate Florida nor did they replace Negroes as the main labor force. The few who came from Europe to live permanently were seeking a better life. Most of them acquired their own land or found more lucrative uses for their skills than were available in the cotton fields or orange groves.

The immigration which did change the composition of Florida's population and the course of its economic development came from within the United States. Private land developers and state government agencies were joined by increasing numbers of tourists and visitors in publicizing the state as a desirable place to seek health or fortune. Jacksonville's winter population was double its summer size by 1870 and hotels were built all along the St. Johns River. Tourists could find hotel accommodations of sorts as far away as Manatee County on the Gulf Coast, and "quite a colony of Downeasterners" settled at Sarasota in 1868. One observer estimated that 25,000 tourists visited Fernandina and Jacksonville in 1874 while about 50,000 went up the St. Johns and Oklawaha rivers to Silver Springs.[7] As they passed Mandarin above Jacksonville some passengers were able to see Harriet Beecher Stowe hard at work at her home near the river. Their chances of seeing the famous writer were enhanced because officials of the steamer lines had contracted with her to come out on her veranda and pose while the boats were in view. On H. L. Hart's Oklawaha River steamers most passengers were awed by the beauty of the stream while some stood near the rail and shot alligators by the hundreds until they tired of the "sport." Some of the visitors and many of their acquaintances bought Florida land. A few stayed and others returned later.

Henry Sanford had acquired about 23,000 acres near Lake Monroe. He planted extensive groves of his own but was also interested in selling land to settlers. Since most of the arable government lands available for homesteading near Sanford were taken by 1871, his sales were brisk at increasing prices during the 1870s. In 1873 he sold ten acre tracts to prospective settlers from Salem, Ohio, for $25 per acre. At the same time his land agent was receiving thirty to fifty letters per week asking about land. Property owners were incensed in 1873 when the tax assessor raised Orange County valuations by 65 per cent. The county then had about 4,000 people, nearly 3,000 of whom had recently come from other states. Seventy new settlers arrived on a single day in November 1875. General W. T. Sherman, General Orville Babcock, and Senator Henry Anthony of Rhode Island bought land near Sanford. With the area being settled rapidly in 1875, a prospective buyer thought the $75 per acre asked for Sanford area land was a fair price.[8] General Sanford realized little profit from his endeavors at Lake Monroe, but by the mid-1870s large orange groves were beginning to produce and Sanford, Enterprise, and Orlando were becoming trade centers for an increasing population.

The Florida Land Improvement Company also located settlers in Orange County around Mellonville and in other areas of the state. Advertising 160-acre tracts for $10 per acre with one-fourth down and the balance in ten annual installments at 6 per cent interest, the company boasted a close association with the Florida state government whose "cordial support" it was authorized to pledge in support of its sales.[9] Another cooperative venture was arranged between the Florida Land and Immigration Company and J. S. Adams, the commissioner of lands and immigration. Adams became the authorized agent to sell land for the company and its chief executive was made assistant commissioner of immigration. The company controlled about one million acres along the Florida Railroad from Fernandina to Cedar Key, most of which belonged to the railroad company managed by David Yulee. The joint agency announced its special interest in groups of ten or more settlers for whom it promised reduced transportation fares. C. L. Robinson of Jacksonville also organized a Florida Land Agency in 1866 which continued to sell land during the period. Williams, Swann, and Corley, with Samuel A. Swann as the leading figure, also handled large quantities of state lands. Among many other real estate agencies which advertised Florida as a place to settle were the Southern Land and Immigration Company and Ludlow, Hayes, and Hurlburt.[10]

Whether they settled on state, national, or private land, people came to Florida in increasing numbers. Although Swann referred to the land along the Florida Railroad as an "elephant" which he hoped to "unload," it sold in considerable quantities to northerners. A newcomer to Alachua County from Chicago in early 1877 wrote that he met many former acquaintances when he arrived in Gainesville. Incorporated in 1866, Gainesville boasted thirteen grocery stores by 1873, as well as fifteen dry goods stores, two drug stores, five hotels and boarding houses, two printing offices, two tailor shops, a billiard saloon, two barrooms, "sundry places dispensing tanglefoot," and "not a jail in the county."[11]

Lumber companies acquired huge tracts around Cedar Key. The largest operators included E. W. Faber, G. N. Nutter, and J. J. Philbrick. The latter was an influential Key West merchant with lumbering interests all along the Gulf Coast. Also operating on large holdings in the area was the Florida Lumber Company, a New York firm headed by Mark W. Downey, a crude and belligerent former Union officer who acquired a reputation as a duelist when he first came to Florida after the war. A few people also came to Cedar Key to fish and gather sponges while others were employed at the railroad docks where cargoes were transferred between trains and steamships. In 1874 the town had three hotels and several stores, but a resident complained that in summer "our little burg . . . is entirely void of any kind of amusement or excitement." Most of the people left during the hot season and returned when it was cooler. C. B. Rogers, who ran a general merchandise store there, complained that business was slow in 1874, yet he boasted at the same time that he often had accounts of $25,000 in New York or New Orleans and had always managed to pay them off.[12]

In Fernandina—the Atlantic terminus of the Florida Railroad—land transactions remained exceedingly hazardous because of continuing litigation over the wartime tax sales, but the city enjoyed a brisk tourist trade. Its two hotels were the Riddell House and Norwood House, both run by Northerners, with rooms available at about $3 per day. Rooming houses boarded people for $5 to $15 per week. Nearly as many Southerners as Northerners vacationed there in the summer. Because of its island location, Fernandina also boasted a mild winter climate enabling oranges to grow unharmed when cold weather damaged the mainland crop. The town suffered a severe setback when most of the business portion burned in 1875.[13]

Jacksonville was the boom town of the Reconstruction era, located at the junction of the major water route into south Florida with the railroad across the most populous portion of the state. It became a major transportation center where both passengers and merchandise were transferred from one mode of transportation to another, a tourist resort where travellers paused on their way to interior Florida or remained as winter residents, and a financial center where northern capital was more readily available than anywhere else in the state. By 1869 the city had several rooming houses and four hotels—Price House, Taylor House, St. Johns House, and the recently completed St. James. People complained that the facilities were inadequate to meet demands for accommodations and that prices were inordinate, but a local newspaper claimed that board was only $10 per week at the "first-class" hotels and $3 at the rooming houses.[14]

By 1873 Jacksonville was claiming 2,000 visitors who wintered there for health reasons and thousands of others who passed through. An aggressive board of trade was planning a state fair and the Jacksonville Trade Palace had been opened by Furchgott, Benedict, and Company. With taxable property valued at $2 million, the city tax for 1873 was fifteen mills, but the mayor predicted that debts would be liquidated and ten mills would operate the city thereafter. There were twenty saw-mills nearby whose transactions were estimated at $6,000 to $8,000 per day. Personnel of the United States land office at Tallahassee wanted to move to Jacksonville "because all immigration now or likely to come for many years is to the peninsula and . . . absolutely all immigrants go to Jacksonville." Other east Floridians joined Jacksonville citizens in suggesting that the state capital be moved there—with the state house at Tallahassee to be converted into a Negro university.[15]

By 1876 the major hotels in Jacksonville were the Grand National, St. James, Metropolitan, Waverly House, and St. Johns House. About forty smaller hotels and rooming houses were available. A traveller warned, "You don't want to stop long in Jacksonville for it will cost you about $5 per day for each member of your party." But another found accommodations at Keen's boarding house for $2 per day. Like many of the business firms in the city, most of the hotels were owned by Northerners, many of whom had made Florida their permanent residence. Since the city was a "grand depot for Florida travel," there were immense profits to be made. The St. James paid dividends of 33 per cent in 1873–74 even though the country was gripped by a financial panic.[16]

Congressman Purman regarded Jacksonville as an "enterprising Yankee town in the South" and others agreed that it was "really a Northern city in a Southern latitude." One observer found it "quite like a city" with brick and stone structures, steeples, and hotels, but "its shade trees make the place." He found "many fine stores" on Bay Street which was the main business thoroughfare, and the "city is fast building up with Northern capital." There were dissenters from this view. An 1876 visitor was disappointed with the climate which she found "so hot in summer that grass will not grow." She disliked the dry hot sand and city streets which were like country roads.[17]

St. Augustine was hampered by inadequate transportation—it was most accessible by St. Johns River steamer and an overland journey from the river—but northern investors built or renovated hotels and several handsome residences became tourist attractions. The local newspaper boasted that the city would become the "Naples of America" as the "New City" to the north of old St. Augustine built up. The three major hotels were the St. Augustine, Florida House, and Magnolia. There were smaller hotels and several wealthy Northerners leased cottages. Local boosters were elated when Isaac Stone, formerly English consul at Havana, purchased a city lot for $2,500. The city population was about 2,500 in 1876 and it enjoyed some success in attracting tourists from in and out of the state, but St. Augustine still needed railroad service which was not available until the 1880s.[18]

Palatka became an important town on the St. Johns as tourists and settlers began moving into Orange County, the Indian River country, and to Silver Springs on the Oklawaha. Hubbard L. Hart was the most important developer of Palatka. He planted groves and operated lumber mills, but was perhaps best known for his steamship lines which ran down the St. Johns to Jacksonville, Savannah, and Charleston and up the Oklawaha to Silver Springs. Brock's Line also carried passengers and freight to and from Palatka. The town was enjoying a heavy tourist business shortly after the war. A settler from Gadsden County wrote in 1868 that "Palatka is full of northerners–invalids and tourists–sail boats and pleasure parties pass daily and they often call and visit us. There is plenty of life and stir on the river." During the winter, its hotels–Putnam House, St. Johns House, Eggleston House, and Underwood House–were usually full and visitors "had to beg for a room."[19]

It was the climate and its situation on the river rather than its charm as a city which brought people to Palatka. The local newspaper complained that horses running in the street were a nuisance and dangerous to children. Another time it asked if something could not be done about the prisoners in the jail who "make that neighborhood hideous" by striking their chains on the floor, yelling, and "going on disgracefully." But the paper was also optimistic that Palatka was advancing. By 1875 the population was nearly one thousand, several new buildings were going up, two steamers a day were leaving for Silver Springs in the winter, 400 property transactions had occurred in the past year, and Putnam County's population had increased by 25 per cent to nearly 5,000.[20]

Oranges and winter vegetables were grown all along the St. Johns River after the Civil War, but the belief in easy wealth from their production brought especially rapid settlement and clearing of land around Palatka and south to Volusia and Orange counties and the Indian River country. Individuals from all over the country and several groups from the Midwest settled in the area to plant groves or winter gardens. Daytona, with about 150 people in 1876, was settled by people from Ohio. Samuel Swann's claim that "thousands are now pouring into the state" was slightly exaggerated, but he sold several large tracts to groups from Michigan and Illinois in the mid-1870s. Several families from Florida's plantation belt came to the upper St. Johns area to escape what they regarded as undesirable changes in their old homes. State newspapers applauded in late 1875 when O. E. Miller of Minnesota brought about 180 men, women, and children to settle in Florida.[21]

A freeze in 1868 destroyed most of the growing oranges but did not harm the trees. It was the first freeze damage since 1835 and did not deter enthusiasm. Land continued to be cleared at great expense and nurseries with orange trees for sale did a brisk business. Much of their rootstock came from Douglas Dummit's huge groves near Merritt Island. Labor was scarce and those able to bring in groups of workers were considered fortunate. Ross and Wingate of Daytona apparently contracted to clear future grove lands for $40 to $50 per acre. John G. Price, who lived at Bostrom's boarding house near Daytona while preparing his land, paid a Negro man $50 per acre to dig out the undergrowth and declared himself fortunate to obtain such a favorable arrangement. Another prospective grower hired workers for $1.50 per day without board to clear his land.[22] Orange production was increasing by the mid-1870s, but not until a decade later did citrus constitute a major crop. Still, oranges were declared the most important crop of the upper St. Johns area with vegetables running a close second. Groves in Hillsborough and Manatee counties on the west coast were developing at the same time. Indian River oranges were already becoming known for their excellence.

The Florida Fruit Growers' Association held a convention at Palatka in November 1874 to consider common problems and exchange useful information. P. P. Bishop of San Mateo was president and C. Codrington, editor of the *Florida Agriculturist*, was secretary. Harrison Reed took an active part in the proceedings, along with J. S. Adams and Hubbard L. Hart. High costs and poor handling of oranges by transportation companies were major complaints. The association joined other groups in demanding that the United States government dredge the bar at the St. Johns River mouth so that a direct line of steamers from Jacksonville to New York could be established. Although this specific problem was eventually solved, the fruit growers would be plagued by unsatisfactory transportation to market until the twentieth century.[23]

William H. Gleason wrote in 1867 that "Biscayne Bay is so beautiful and healthful that it must one day become the resort of the invalid, the tourist and the lover of adventure." This stocky, brown-bearded immigrant from Wisconsin tried to make his fortune by promoting development of the Miami area. W. H. Hearn planned to colonize Northerners at Fort Dallas to raise tropical fruit. About $10,000 worth of pineapples grown on the keys in 1868 attracted favorable attention. Although neither scheme succeeded, Miami was a fairly active frontier community during the Reconstruction era. Connected to the outside world primarily by boat to Key West, several families lived within a few hours ride of Brickell's store at Miami. Seminole Indians frequently visited to trade buckskin, feathers, and other wares for supplies and whiskey. They still had Negroes with them whom they were willing to hire out to the whites since they did not recognize emancipation or any other United States laws. The Indians frequently dined with the white families in the area and several of the white men enjoyed hunting parties as the Indians' guests. After one party, the Indians became inebriated and "carried on pretty well in the river shouting out all the little English they knew," but most of the whites were also drunk. "What a subject for a temperance lecture this place is," declared an amused visitor.[24]

Settlement was retarded by lack of clear land titles. Surveyors were busy in south Florida, but it was a vast area. Dozens of "squatters" had already settled and made improvements but they were anxious for some legal assurance that they would not be ousted. Gleason and his partner, William H. Hunt, had potential land grants from the state for both drainage projects and an inland waterway along the coast. They often discouraged settlers by claiming the land, even though they had not acquired title from the state. The two men were exceedingly unpopular around Miami. One property dispute with a Dr. Harris caused extreme bitterness and violence. When Hunt and Gleason tried to oust Harris from property which both sides claimed they owned, Harris threatened to shoot Hunt on sight and sought a duel with Gleason. The duel never occurred and Harris gave up the property and left, but he whipped Gleason with a cowhide strap on Key West's main street in April 1874, to the vicarious satisfaction of numerous witnesses.[25]

Key West was described as a pretty place covered with low white houses and coconut trees. As one approached the town, Fort Taylor stood out prominently and, with several gun batteries scattered around the island, gave it a somewhat formidable appearance. Several large merchandising establishments and steamship companies were influential in Key West, but the United States government was the dominant entity. Wrecking, although diminishing in importance, still kept numerous people busy. Others gathered sponges or caught turtles. Quantities of fresh fruit were sold. Producers of perishables had once been at the mercy of a buyers' monopoly, but the town had established a daily auction at which all goods were sold. The auction was more satisfactory to all concerned and produce was moved out before it spoiled.[26]

The St. James Hotel was the best place to stay at $3.50 per day, but room and board was otherwise available at $1.50. There was a skating rink and several billiard rooms. Church socials and bazaars were frequent. A large portion of Key West's population was transient, including military personnel, Cuban revolutionaries, buyers and sellers of goods, and seasonal workers. Not all Cubans were temporary residents—many came to find employment in the cigar industry as it moved out of Cuba to Key West. Vicente Martinez Ybor moved his factory to the island in 1868 primarily because of difficulties with the Cuban cigarmakers' union. *La Rosa Espanola,* Seidenberg and Company of New York, and other manufacturers followed, and by 1875 there were at least fifteen factories at Key

West, employing several hundred workers. Most of the employees were Cubans who had either followed the factories or left because of the revolution. There were about fourteen other cigar factories scattered throughout mainland Florida by the mid-1870s, most of them small and usually operated by local labor.[27]

The hundreds of Cubans who settled at Key West influenced Monroe County politics and created excitement because of their interest in the Cuban revolt. The violence between contending Cuban groups mentioned earlier caused less tension than the *Virginius* affair. The *Virginius*—formerly suspected of smuggling Negroes out of the United States to Cuba under its original name, the *Virgin*—was running guns in 1873 to the revolutionaries under the United States flag. It was captured by the Spanish on October 31, 1873, and fifty-three crew members, some of them Americans, were shot as pirates. Secretary of State Hamilton Fish settled the matter diplomatically by securing an indemnity from the Spanish government to the families of the deceased Americans, but the people of the United States were incensed over the affair and the government made preparations for hostilities. With high excitement among the Key West Cubans, many of whom wore black crepe arm bands, the decrepit United States navy stationed twenty-six warships near the island city and sent a few troops to Fort Taylor and Fort Dallas near Miami.[28]

The Pensacola naval base was re-inforced with five war vessels and 841 tons of ordnance were shipped from St. Louis. The naval commander at Pensacola negotiated with local firms to supply him coal in the event of hostilities. Railroad officials hoped the military preparedness would alleviate the depression gripping Pensacola, but it brought little relief. The excitement lasted several months, gradually subsiding in late 1874 as people became more concerned with economic depression and with the severe yellow fever epidemic which struck port cities from Key West to Pensacola.[29]

None of the ports between Key West and Pensacola attained the significance of Cedar Key during this period. Tampa had about 600 people in 1875. There were two hotels, a few boarding houses, several stores, and two churches. A few orange groves were beginning to produce in Hillsborough, Manatee, and Polk counties and several sugar plantations were prospering there, but the population was scattered and the sale of cattle and hogs to Cuba was still the most profitable activity. A stage line ran to Ocala and both scheduled and unscheduled steamers and schooners stopped at Tampa. Yet a treasury agent assured his superiors that people were leaving Tampa Bay for more desirable places and "the port must continue to go backwards for years to come." A Tampa Board of Trade, organized in the early 1870s, was unaware of the dire prediction and within fifteen years the town had a railroad and was becoming a major cigar manufacturing center.[30]

St. Marks never regained its antebellum prominence. Much of the town was swept away by a hurricane in September 1873, and only forty ships entered and cleared the port between January 1, 1873, and July 1, 1874. A few small boats engaged in fishing and oystering in the winter and sponging in summer. Apalachicola's case was similar. After a boom in 1866–67, the port lost its volume of cotton trade. Moribund for several years, the town jubilantly welcomed the Pennsylvania Tie Company which moved there in 1873. With a new chemical preservative, it planned to manufacture durable cross-ties from black cypress. The company invested about $40,000 in a mill and established a mail and passenger line to St. Marks where it was to connect with the railroad from Tallahassee. But the enterprise did not prosper and Cottrell and Ayers' existing mill closed in 1873 because its Philadelphia financial backer went bankrupt. A visitor to Apalachicola in 1876 observed only a few sponge and oyster boats operating out of the town. Nearby Carrabelle was founded in 1876 by Oliver H. Kelly, organizer of the National Patrons of Husbandry, but it attracted few settlers.[31]

Pensacola and surrounding communities were the center of a rapidly expanding lumber business. Elsewhere railroad construction in the area was discussed, especially the Pensacola and Perdido Railroad which connected the new lumber firms at Millview with docks on Pensacola Bay. Milton, in Santa Rosa County, had a population of about 2,000 and several companies were cutting timber and sawing lumber there. The largest of them was Keyser, Judah and Company, whose manager and major owner was William J. Keyser. Two miles south of Milton at Baghdad were the Simpson and Company saw-mills and the Baghdad Sash Factory. Probably the largest single operation in the Pensacola area was the Muscogee Lumber Company, but there were dozens of others operating on a large scale. In March 1873, 858,922 cubic feet of timber and 2,925,222 square feet of lumber cleared the Pensacola harbor for both domestic and foreign ports.[32]

Pensacola's lumber industry grew despite epidemics and financial depression. No port in Florida, except perhaps Key West, suffered from yellow fever as much as Pensacola did during the Reconstruction era. In 1867 the town was evacuated by everyone who could leave and activities came practically to a standstill. Dozens of lives were lost both in the town and at the naval station eight miles away. An 1873 epidemic was even more severe. By October about 1,000 people—approximately one-fourth of the population—had fled, and at least fifty-five people had died of the disease. The towns along the railroad toward Montgomery also lost heavily and one observer declared the "pineywoods" almost devoid of children because of the fever. Many Florida natives were shocked when another epidemic followed in 1874 at both Pensacola and Key West. It was the first time they could remember yellow fever striking in consecutive years. The entire state was threatened by another epidemic in 1876, but Pensacola's quarantine was effective that year and the city was spared its ravages.[33]

When the Panic of 1873 occurred, Pensacola felt a severe money shortage, business slowed drastically, and recovery was slow. Yet, in May 1874, the town was filled with people looking for places to live or establish businesses. "A hundred houses could be rented, if the foundations were laid," wrote one resident not noted for optimism. At the same time mills were under construction on the Perdido River. In early 1876 there were 216 vessels in the harbor. The 114 of foreign registry were mostly British and Norwegian. Of the American vessels, 23 were from foreign ports and 79 were in the coastal trade.[34]

Though Northerners with capital were investing in Florida land, hotels, and businesses, and settlement was scarcely interrupted along the St. Johns River during the depression beginning in 1873, there was inadequate capital in the state to supply legitimate demands and circulating medium was woefully scarce for the volume of trade. A sound state banking law was enacted in 1868, but no financial institution was organized under it before 1877. One national bank was opened in Jacksonville in 1874 with a capital of $50,000. T. W. C. Moore was its president and his father-in-law, Treasurer of the United States F. E. Spinner, was its principal advocate. The Freedmen's Savings Bank and Trust Company opened branches in Tallahassee and Jacksonville soon after the war to encourage thrift among the freedmen. Hundreds of Negroes opened savings accounts and whites of all political persuasions also availed themselves of its facilities. The Freedmen's Bank did a general banking business in the state until 1874 when the institution was liquidated.[35]

Most of the banking business of Florida during the period was done by private banks. At first most transfers of funds were carried on by the Southern Express Company and the few post offices authorized to handle money orders. A few merchants worked out arrangements with financial institutions in other cities and gradually began doing general banking business. B. C. Lewis and Son, with pre-war banking experience, was doing a deposit business in Tallahassee soon after the war. By 1870 the bank had twenty-five depositors with a total of $12,000. By May 1875 it had grown until its capital was $72,000 and average deposits $454,840. In the same city William R. Pettes opened a private bank in 1867, offering to buy and sell sight and time drafts on New York, Savannah, and New

Orleans. He also bought gold and silver and bank bills of several states.[36]

Comparable services were available in Pensacola at Hyer Brothers who opened in 1865. Ten years later they had $12,000 capital and average deposits of $15,200. F. C. Brent opened for business in 1876. William A. Mackensie and Company did a banking business for several years after 1867 in Apalachicola. W. B. C. Duryea offered similar services at Fernandina after 1870. J. J. Philbrick opened a bank at Key West in 1876, although his merchandising business had already been engaged in limited financial activities for several years.[37]

There were four private banks in Jacksonville during the Reconstruction era. Franklin Dibble began business in 1869 with financial connections to Dibble, Worth and Company of New York, partially owned by his brother. Daniel G. Ambler opened Ambler's Bank in 1868. His principal New York connection was Howes and Macy, but he could also draw on Duncan, Sherman and Company, and M. A. Wilder and Son. In 1874 he had a capital of $180,000 and average deposits in 1876 of $892,935. James H. Paine and Jonathan C. Greeley opened a private bank in 1872 which was expanded and incorporated as the Florida Savings Bank and Real Estate Exchange in 1874. Its May 1876 deposits were averaging $207,702. Denny's bank was also doing a small business with deposits averaging about $30,000 when it failed in 1874.[38]

The banks in the larger Florida towns sometimes provided service for outlying communities. For example, Henry Sanford's interests at Lake Monroe banked at Ambler's in Jacksonville, usually forwarding deposits either by registered mail or by an officer of the steamer *Darlington*. But many planters and merchants in the cotton belt continued to use credit arrangements with cotton factors in Savannah, Charleston, or New York. Falling cotton prices and partial crop failures often left them in debt at the end of the year and reduced the already sparse supply of circulating currency.

A stringent credit situation in 1870 upset the incipient banking system in Jacksonville. While planters and country merchants were struggling to stave off suits by their creditors, some northern investors were withdrawing investments in Florida. E. G. Eastman of Chicago complained that he had not received any interest on his $20,000 investment in Ambler's bank and that he could obtain 15–25 per cent on good security in the Midwest. He asked his lawyer to close out his Florida loans by compromise and send him the proceeds. "I have very gloomy accounts of business in Jacksonville this season," he concluded. Ambler survived the crisis but Franklin Dibble was less fortunate. When Dibble, Worth and Company of New York closed, they brought him down with them. Dibble left Jacksonville suddenly amid rumors that he had pocketed some of the funds. The

$77,000 worth of claims against him was paid at twenty cents on the dollar within thirty days. Creditors received a little more when liquidation was finally completed.[39]

Credit and circulating currency remained scarce after 1870. Some companies issued their own notes and the state government used scrip and treasury warrants. A multiprice system prevailed. Banks were paying 10 per cent on time deposits. Perhaps a measure of the problem was the great difficulty creditors encountered in recovering judgments in the courts. "If the Lord ever forgives us for getting ourselves into Florida law this time we promise to sin no more," wrote I. H. Cohen of Moses and Cohen in New York. But some businesses were making money. Sanford's general merchandising business sold on credit at 2 per cent interest per month, taking liens on debtors' entire crops of cotton and sugar, but never lending more than one-fifth of the estimated total value. Collections were good in 1872 and the store made $8,000 in the first nine months of the year. Jacksonville hotels were returning 33 per cent on investments after the 1873 panic occurred.[40]

The Panic of 1873 had little adverse effect on the immigration which was accelerating into east Florida in the 1870s, and it merely worsened a poor situation in the agricultural areas of the state. But the crisis seriously upset the incipient financial institutions and damaged businesses such as railroads and lumber mills. It also removed any chance which may have existed for laborers to redress their grievances against employers by concerted action.

In early 1873 Pensacola stevedores had rioted and attacked Canadians who competed for Florida jobs during the winter when it was too cold to work in the northern woods. Their militance was rewarded by a legislative enactment requiring six months residence before a person could obtain a stevedore's license. Railroad shop men struck in unison at noon on August 4, 1873, and stayed off the job a week until they were paid past-due wages for May, June, and July. But the most important strike of the year failed. The Labor League, to which most black mill workers around Jacksonville belonged, struck on June 9 after the operators rejected their demands for a ten-hour day and a wage increase to $1.50 per day. Eight sawmills were affected, about half of which were closed down. The others kept operating on a limited basis with nearly all white workers. Although strikers tried to pressure those who continued working and seven persons were tried for attacking one of them, there was comparatively little violence during the two months strike. With plenty of unskilled workers available, the strike was broken and the participants either drifted back to their jobs or went to other towns. Within a few months most of the mills were hard hit by depression rendering further strikes useless.[41]

Within days after Jay Cooke's failure on September 18, several New York firms suspended payments, including Howes and Macy. Word of their failure brought a run on Ambler's bank. Depositors withdrew $21,000 on September 24, after Ambler had already loaned the Freedmen's Bank $5,000 in currency. The Freedmen's Bank was unable to remain open and Ambler, with only about $5,000 in cash on hand, was inclined to close until several Jacksonville businessmen talked him out of it. Sherman Conant brought a little currency from Tallahassee and Alva A. Knight, Collector of Internal Revenue at Jacksonville, loaned him some cash. The following day, depositors' confidence was restored and Ambler survived the panic. Denny's small bank was at first relatively unaffected by the crisis. Jonathan C. Greeley, another local banker, accurately predicted that "the crash has so unsettled the finances of the country, I am afraid there will be very few sales here this winter." By early October, business at Sanford was "at a standstill in sympathy with the panic in New York."[42]

Across the state at Pensacola, mills north of the city were discharging their hands because of lack of greenbacks. "It is a wonderful state of things," wrote one railroad manager, "plenty of money and more pouring in from the old world, and yet greenbacks are hardly to be had."[43] By mid-November only two mills were operating near Jacksonville, the large Drew and Bucki mill in Madison County was expected to close, "and the merchants are blue."[44]

The crisis continued through 1874, but there were also encouraging signs. Several new businesses were going up in Jacksonville and people were looking for places to open stores and shops in Pensacola. The Florida Savings Bank incorporated in mid-1874 and offered depositors 7.3 per cent interest. The First National Bank of Jacksonville opened under the management of T. W. C. Moore. Ambler continued to operate on a sound basis. However, Denny finally failed in October 1874, paying about thirty-three cents on the dollar on deposits of $30,000. At Pensacola, C. L. LeBaron and Son failed, costing creditors about $70,000.[45]

The lumber industry gradually recovered but Florida generally continued in the grip of "extreme impecuniosity." Problems in the cotton country remained relatively unchanged. A typical planter-merchant wrote in 1876 from Madison County that he "made money last year, but lost all the year's work in cotton. Nothing moving in the county now." He could only collect on debts if he accepted cotton as payment and its market price was "shrinking rapidly." Yet tax collections improved and scrip sold all over the state at eighty to ninety cents on the dollar in 1875.[46]

National financial policy and the diminishing position of agriculture in an industrializing economy adversely affected Florida as political control of the state was transferred from Republicans to Democrats. The problem was worsened by the depression which followed the money panic of 1873. Yet people continued to settle in Florida during the worst of the depression and new construction was financed by money from northern sources just as it had been in the first few years after the war. The country emerged from the depression about the same time Governor William Bloxham settled the long-standing Vose claim against the Internal Improvement Fund. There followed a period of railroad building and immigration which has been applauded as a Democratic inspired boom. It should be remembered, however, that the growth rates of the seventies and eighties were almost identical, notwithstanding the depression of the earlier decade. The policies of the Republican administrations, which were practically the same as those of Drew and Bloxham, had stimulated population growth in the peninsula and attracted outside attention and capital. The internal development which occurred in the eighties was not an abrupt departure from the events of the Republican era, but a logical consequence of them.

16

Political Smoke Is Like the Pitch Pine Smoke

With their party in shambles and an unenviable record behind them, Florida Republicans approached the 1872 national and state elections with apprehension. When Governor Reed was finally returned to office in May after the last impeachment episode, the party was already planning the forthcoming nominating convention. The April convention in Jacksonville adopted a resolution endorsing Acting Governor Samuel T. Day and another castigating Reed. The state executive committee chairman predicted party success if Day remained governor and disaster if Reed were restored. Others doubted that Reed would even support the party ticket in 1872. Senator Osborn accused the governor of "stumping the state against everybody and both parties." Reed told a convocation of Negro leaders that the Republicans could carry Florida only if most of the incumbent federal officials in the state were replaced. Union League members took the statement seriously, warning William E. Chandler, national Republican party secretary, that "we may look for trouble [in Florida] unless steps are taken to avert it."[1]

Even with harmony and cooperation among the white Republican leaders, their situation would still have been precarious. Of the 187,746 Floridians reported on the 1870 census, nearly 49 per cent were Negroes. If all eligible blacks registered and voted Republican along with the approximately 2,000 whites of that party, a small majority could be expected, but there were two complications. Important Negro leaders were dissatisfied because they had received inadequate recognition within the party since 1868. At the April convention major concessions were made to placate the blacks. As a result of a new delegate apportionment formula, Negroes would have a greater voice in the nominating convention than in earlier Republican gatherings. The other problem was the physical and economic intimidation which had discouraged Negroes from voting. Threatened or actual violence at the polls in 1870 had influenced the election result and nocturnal visits to isolated tenant dwellings by regulators had been persuasive. To counteract physical intimidation, the Republicans were depending on vigorous enforcement of civil rights legislation, especially by United States Marshal Sherman Conant and District Attorney Horatio Bisbee whose past efficiency had infuriated native whites.

There were also conservative Republicans in east Florida disgusted with the party's record and anxious for improved state administration. They wanted a stable state government to facilitate economic development by attracting settlers and investors. Rallying around Henry S. Sanford, a prominent Connecticut Republican and former diplomat who was then developing extensive orange groves near Lake Monroe, Jonathan C. Greeley of Jacksonville, E. K. Foster of St. Augustine, and several sympathizers attempted a coalition between conservatives of both parties. They conferred with David Walker and other prominent Democrats, but when it became clear that the former governor envisioned their joining the Democratic party, Sanford politely declined. Agreeing that the state government needed improvement and expressing his highest regard for the Democratic leaders, Sanford still preferred Republican answers to public problems. He was expecting a diplomatic appointment if Grant remained president. Foster, who deplored the "folly of universal suffrage," campaigned actively for the Democrats in 1872 and never returned to the Republican party, but Sanford, Greeley, and most of the others refused to go that far.[2]

Disruption of the national party increased the difficulties of its Florida counterpart. Personal feuding among national leaders—combined with dissatisfaction over the Grant administration's civil service policy, continued use of martial law in the southern states, and high protective tariff—caused influential Republicans to leave the party in 1872. Forming the Liberal Republican party they met at Cincinnati, Ohio, in May and nominated Horace Greeley for president and B. Gratz Brown of Missouri for vice president. Since their hope of victory was based on anticipation of Democratic endorsement of their ticket, the Greeley nomination was surprising. As editor of the *New York Tribune* for many years he had heaped invective and satirical scorn on slaveholding Southerners and the South. Regardless of the Democratic response to Greeley, however, the Liberal Republican movement attracted dissident Florida Republicans who would never have been willing to become Democrats. Thirteen counties sent delegates to a Liberal Republican convention at Jacksonville on August 14, the same day the Conservative-Democrats met there.

The Reed-Osborn factionalism which continued during the election practically eliminated the two as contenders for re-election, but both remained influential. Reed controlled the state election machinery through his power to appoint county officials. Osborn's strength lay in his contacts with the Grant administration and the national Republican party. Both men had made enemies and numerous state partisans were anxious to take their places. John T. Sprague, the former military commander who had become a St. Augustine resident, was frequently mentioned as a gubernatorial candidate, although he was believed willing to accept either party's nomination.[3] Ossian B. Hart, associate justice of the supreme court, had strong support. A native Floridian and former slaveholder who had been a consistent wartime Unionist and later an organizer of the Jacksonville Union Republican club, Hart appealed to the southern loyalists of the party. A close friend and business associate of David Yulee, Hart had once been an extreme state rights advocate. In November 1865, he argued that the Freedmen's Bureau had no authority after the "restoration of peace." " 'Sambo' will have to rely on the good faith of the southern people. Negroes as free men are citizens and only the state authority can work on them," he said. Six months of the "Johnson government" changed his mind, and in June 1866 Hart was insisting that the Freedmen's Bureau should set aside state court decisions.[4] By 1872 he had won the respect and support of several Negro Republicans while retaining good relations with native white Conservatives.

Another gubernatorial contender was Marcellus L. Stearns, who had been a bureau agent in Gadsden County. A former Union officer with an artificial arm and a bushy beard, the thirty-four year old Stearns had opposed Governor Reed while he was speaker of the house. John Tyler, Jr., the former president's son who was active in both Florida and Virginia during the 1870s, was also interested in the nomination. Shortly before the convention he bluntly warned that he could influence federal appointments if his wishes were ignored. Tyler's claims were taken seriously since he had just become internal revenue collector, replacing William J. Purman, chairman of the state executive committee, who had been ousted without warning. Senator Osborn was incensed that he had not been told of the change. It was "exceedingly rough," he protested, to advocate the national administration in the state and at the same time have to apologize to loyal partisans for the way Washington treated them. If the president could "at least let us fight his . . . battles for him without opposition I shall be glad."[5] Purman, mistakenly believing Osborn responsible for his removal, repeatedly attacked the senator in his campaign speeches.

Destructive delegate contests occurred in several counties, but none so bitter or enduring as the one in Leon County where two gubernatorial hopefuls resided. Simon B. Conover, supported by "Bishop" Charles Pearce, and Sheriff Edmund C. Weeks, supported by Negro leader John N. Stokes, fought to a deadlock in the county convention. The Republican state convention met at Tallahassee on August 7, only a few days after the county fight and long before tempers cooled. The state central committee was able to decide all the delegate disputes except the one from Leon. It ruled that both the Pearce and Stokes delegates should be seated, with each having six and a half votes. The Pearce faction refused to sit in the convention and Conover declined to have his name offered for nomination.[6]

H. S. Harmon, a Negro from Alachua County, was named temporary chairman of the convention. John Stokes delivered an impassioned appeal to the Leon County Negroes who were boycotting the convention, but Pearce was unmoved. No one was convinced by subsequent reports that illness kept Pearce away. When Robert Meacham, Negro senator from Jefferson County, was seated as permanent chairman, nominations were opened for governor. Of the 112½ delegate votes represented, an informal ballot gave Stearns forty-four votes, Hart thirty-two, Reed thirteen, and Weeks seven.[7] On the formal ballot Hart received fifty and Stearns fifty-two. Marion County then changed six votes from Hart to Stearns, giving him a majority. Before this change was announced the Leon County delegation leader changed its six and a half votes to Stearns over the protests of some of its delegates. When Stearns was declared nominated by sixty-six and a half to forty-four, the convention broke up. Led by John R. Scott of Duval County, Negro delegates who favored Hart and disliked Stearns began leaving the convention. Stearns managed to get their attention long enough to withdraw in favor of Hart and party harmony. When order was restored, J. Willis Menard, another Duval County Negro, moved Stearns' nomination for lieutenant governor because of his selfless act. The motion was accepted and the convention turned to congressional nominations. Reapportionment after the 1870 census had given Florida a second congressional seat.

Josiah Walls of Alachua County, a Negro who had been elected to Congress in 1870 and subsequently unseated, was easily renominated but there was a contest for the second nomination. On the first ballot Robert Meacham received thirty-five votes to twenty-four for William Gleason. Meacham failed to increase his strength and a telegram was read, ostensibly from the national committee, threatening to withhold funds from the Florida campaign unless Gleason were nominated. Although it may have been a forgery, it ruined Gleason's chances and Purman was nominated. He was allegedly chosen because he was a west Floridian who would balance the ticket since Walls was from east of the Suwannee.

Noting that it would be difficult for the Republican party to win without executive support, a delegate recommended a conciliatory gesture toward Governor Reed. This was not easily achieved. Stiff opposition was raised against the resolution endorsing the governor and he twice refused to even address the convention. When Reed finally spoke just before adjournment, opposition diminished and Stearns even led three cheers for the man he had fought so hard to impeach. One resolution endorsed Reed's administration and another pledged party support for his election to the United States Senate in 1873.[8] Reed was unconvinced. He campaigned for Grant and Wilson and tried to provide for a fair election, but he remained indifferent toward the gubernatorial ticket and actively opposed Purman's election. His caustic attacks on other Republicans—"[Our] two Senators, one embicile and one knave"—were scarcely helpful to the party.[9] While failing to convince Reed, the resolutions enhanced his strength with the Republican national committee, causing serious difficulty during the campaign.

The platform promised reform of the "complications" surrounding railroad financing and protection of the state's credit in future public works programs, opposed land grants to corporations at the people's expense, and called for United States assistance to Cubans in revolt against Spain. Under Florida law, persons who had been in the state one year and their resident county for six months could vote merely by declaring their intention of becoming United States citizens. About 400 voting-age Cuban males lived at Key West. Some were exiles because of the revolution and most desired Cuban freedom. They held the balance of power in Monroe County and their support was deemed important for state as well as national candidates.[10]

Republican leaders expressed satisfaction that the convention had reconciled party differences. It probably had accomplished as much as possible toward party unity. Hart was acceptable to many Negroes and appealed to southern Republicans as a respected lawyer and native Floridian. Walls' renomination was satisfactory to the Negroes while his moderation pleased some white Republicans. Stearns and Purman had allies among the white Republicans, especially those from the North who held offices in state or national government, but they were exceedingly unpopular with Negroes, at least partially because they had helped expel "Bishop" Pearce from the state senate on bribery charges.[11] Pearce refused to coalesce with the Stokes-Weeks faction in Leon County and he headed an independent slate of legislative candidates there. His leadership of the powerful African Methodist Episcopal Church increased the significance of his defection outside Leon County. But the most anxiety resulted from uncertainty about the governor's plans.

Reporting a harmonious Florida party, Senator Osborn asked the national committee for $5,000 for the campaign. Edward M. Cheney, who managed party finances, thought $10,000 from Washington was necessary. It was difficult to raise money in the state, he said. United States officials always contributed, but he expected nothing from state officeholders, whom he believed to be with the opposition. The national committee sent $4,000 to which Osborn added $1,000. Cheney raised $850 by assessing customs officials, the Jacksonville city police, and others dependent for employment on a successful Republican campaign.[12]

The national Democratic party, anxious to defeat Grant in 1872, overlooked Horace Greeley's past and emphasized his more recent advocacy of an amicable settlement of the "Southern question." Meeting at Baltimore, they named Greeley and Brown as their standard-bearers and joined the Liberal Republicans for the campaign. The reaction of Florida Democrats was ambivalent. The Baltimore convention aroused little enthusiasm and did not cause serious disaffection. A Key West newspaper predicted the demise of the Democratic party as a consequence of the nomination, and Henry L. Mitchell of Tampa warned that a well-organized campaign would be required to counteract the resulting indifference. A few Florida Democrats, led by Circuit Judge William Archer Cocke of Jefferson County, sought funds to launch a Grant and Wilson campaign among disaffected Democrats, but they received only minor support. Cocke campaigned for Grant, however, and was appointed attorney general by Governor Hart in 1873.[13]

Most Democrats were soon praising Greeley and predicting that he would draw hundreds of blacks to their ticket. J. J. Finley of Columbia County, eyeing the United States Senate election in early 1873, said the actions of the Cincinnati and Baltimore conventions "will save our republic. . . . The election of Greeley will . . . lead us back to the old constitutional paths."[14]

The Greeley nomination and the Liberal Republican activity in Florida offered an opportunity and posed a problem for the state Democrats. It was expected that William Bloxham would be nominated for governor by the Jacksonville Democratic convention. Bloxham had maintained good relations with Leon County Negroes and thought the party should try to capitalize on their disenchantment with the regular Republicans. After a Liberal Republican policy meeting at Lake City in early July scheduled the new party's convention for Jacksonville on the same day as the Democratic convention, Bloxham urged a fusion ticket. Except for R. H. M. Davidson of Gadsden County, few Democrats agreed with him, but the Leon County Democratic convention named Isaac Warren, Henry Hicks, and at least three other Negroes as delegates to the state convention. There were also some Negro alternates.[15]

Bloxham expressed amazement at the number of east Florida Republicans who had indicated their desire to support Greeley and Brown. He wanted their cooperation but was noncommittal on their requests to have a Liberal Republican named on the Democratic ticket. Recognizing that many of his partisan supporters wanted to run a campaign aimed at "redeeming" the state from Negroes and Republicans, he merely observed that "it is a serious question and the pros and cons are very numerous. It will greatly depend on what strength they can develop."[16]

Their strength was considerable. Liberal Republican candidates for the legislature were nominated in several counties. At least four newspapers—the *Jacksonville Republican, Fernandina Observer, Lake City Herald,* and *Pensacola Express*—supported Greeley and Brown and the Democratic state ticket. Thirteen counties sent delegates to the Jacksonville convention. Some of them had been influential in the Republican party and represented more votes than their own. Calvin Robinson and A. W. Da Costa of Jacksonville had been active Unionists or Republicans since 1862. Their Duval County colleague, R. B. Van Valkenberg, was a circuit court justice soon to be elevated to the state supreme court. From Nassau County came Robert M. Smith, Liberty Billings, and David M. Hammond. As a bureau agent five years earlier, Hammond had detested Billings' role in organizing Fernandina Negroes, but the two cooperated in 1872. Billings was president pro tem of the state senate. Alachua County was represented by Lemuel Wilson, wartime Unionist and assessor of internal revenue, and William Birney, one-time commander of Union troops in east Florida and more recently a member of Reed's cabinet.[17] Wilson was removed from his revenue office when he left the regular party. Escambia County sent Lyman W. Rowley, a delegate to the 1868 constitutional convention, and Asa B. Munn, a Republican legislator.

Among the Leon County delegates were Hamilton Jay, W. E. Burleigh, John Proctor, and O. B. Armstrong. Jay was spokesman for Simon Conover who sought the gubernatorial nomination and was the prime mover behind the Liberal Republican movement. Burleigh was assistant to Secretary of State Jonathan C. Gibbs. Proctor and Armstrong were both Leon County Negro leaders. Circuit Judge John W. Price of Putnam, Frank Harris of Marion, and Alvin B. Munger, former sheriff of Leon County, attended. J. B. C. Drew, formerly Reed's attorney general, represented Florida at Cincinnati and also attended the Jacksonville convention. A strong Monroe County Liberal Republican group was headed by Customs Collector William G. Vance, a former Freedmen's Bureau agent, whose defection also cost him his office. Conover did not campaign for Greeley and Brown but his newspaper, the *Lake City Herald,* supported them.[18] Even though he did not use the appellation, Conover was regarded as a Liberal Republican during the campaign.

When the Conservative-Democrats met in Jacksonville there was strong opposition to any collaboration with Liberal Republicans or Negroes, even though there were blacks seated in the convention. Benjamin F. Wardlaw of Madison moved that a committee meet with a similar group of Liberal Republicans. Edward M. L'Engle led the opposition which favored ignoring the other convention, but Wilkinson Call supported the motion vigorously. "The assistance of such men as General Van Valkenberg is not to be coldly refused," he proclaimed. The Wardlaw motion carried and the two committees met. The Liberal Republicans wanted to join the Democrats by naming Lemuel Wilson for lieutenant governor and William Birney for Congress, but the Democrats were only willing to give them the lieutenant governorship and two presidential electors. When no agreement was reached, the Democrats nominated William Bloxham for governor, Robert W. Bullock for lieutenant governor, and Silas L. Niblack of Columbia County and Charles W. Jones of Escambia for Congress. Meanwhile, the Liberal Republicans considered naming their own ticket, consisting of Bloxham for governor, Wilson for lieutenant governor, and Birney and Jones for Congress. But Calvin Robinson, objecting that two different tickets would be confusing, moved acceptance of the entire Conservative-Democratic ticket. After heated argument, Robinson's motion carried and some delegates left the convention in disgust.[19]

With their nominations completed, the remaining Liberal Republicans adjourned and were seated in the Conservative-Democratic convention. Their officers took seats on the platform, and Robinson addressed the jointly assembled body. Having approved a straight out Democratic slate of state candidates, the consolidated convention nominated Wilkinson Call, R. H. M. Davidson, John G. McLean, and George D. Allen as presidential electors. Only Allen, a United States marshal at Key West, was a Republican. The only Negro to receive recognition was Isaac Warren of Leon County, an alternate presidential elector. When the convention adjourned, all the delegates were honored by an excursion to the St. Johns bar. Numerous spokesmen, including seven Negroes, pledged support for the Bloxham ticket. Senator Osborn chortled that the Democratic "straight out radical rebel ticket" had done more for the regular Republicans than they could have done for themselves.[20] Although the senator was too optimistic, potential Liberal Republicans were alienated by the lack of recognition afforded them by the Democrats. Still, some campaigned for Greeley and Brown and for the Bloxham ticket.

The Democrats stumped the state, and local organizations were established in most counties, but it was difficult to generate enthusiasm among voters. When Bloxham visited Jacksonville in September, few people knew he was there and he did not even make a speech. The Greeley and Brown clubs were begun enthusiastically but attendance dropped off. Worse yet, new Republican registrations were accumulating at about four for every one new Democrat. When Charles Daly, a Negro Liberal Republican from Leon County, spoke for Bloxham in Jacksonville, he was mobbed by irate blacks.[21] The Bloxham people were more successful in other areas, however, especially at Tallahassee, Cedar Key, and Key West. Unfortunately perhaps, Bloxham's plan of conciliating Negroes was ignored by most of the Democratic speakers who emphasized the necessity of overthrowing "Negro rule" and restoring government to native whites.

The Republicans sent speakers along the railroads and into out-of-the-way places to reach as many potential voters as possible. One group of Republicans touring west Florida was ambushed and three men were wounded.[22] Gubernatorial candidate O. B. Hart exhausted himself and spent the last two weeks of the campaign in bed with pneumonia.

Both sides were keenly interested in Monroe County. The Cubans there had favored the Republicans, but in 1872 they leaned to the Liberal Republican presidential candidates and the state Democrats. Because the Cubans were influenced by their local *Junta*, Monroe County Republicans, working through Secretary William E. Chandler in Washington, asked the New York *Junta* to intervene in their behalf with the Key West organization. Osborn promised to support the Cuban cause in the next senate session. The senator also spoke at Key West, but he failed to reach the doubtful voters. Bloxham retained the support of Key West Liberal Republicans, and the Democrats carried Monroe 619 votes to 287.[23]

The national and state Republican parties recognized their interdependence. In fact, one of the major issues of the presidential campaign was Grant's role in maintaining Republican administrations in southern states. But, while the judicious use of patronage by the national government could be beneficial, it was sometimes difficult for Republicans in Washington to determine which Floridians spoke for the party. Because of this problem, which is inherent in American party organization, the national administration inadvertantly contributed to the disharmony of Florida Republicans late in the campaign.

Osborn, Purman, Walls, and several others remained apprehensive about Governor Reed's plans, suspecting that he was secretly working with the Democrats.[24] Feeling his support imperative, Purman asked the national party to assure Reed of a future position. "The next administration can certainly find some nook in which to stow Harrison Reed, 'during good behaviour,' " he wrote. Others made similar suggestions. Because of these communications and the convention's endorsements, Chandler asked Reed's opinion of the Florida situation and invited him to speak in northern cities. Reed immediately responded that Florida was safe for Grant, but only if District Attorney Horatio Bisbee and Marshal Sherman Conant were removed and replaced by Charles H. Cowlan and F. B. Bassnett. Cowlan was described by Osborn as the messenger between Republican "soreheads" and Democrats. Bassnett was Wilkinson Call's law partner. Thinking the request reflected party sentiment in Florida, Chandler prevailed upon President Grant to make the changes.[25]

Reed, who wanted the Grant and Wilson ticket to win but probably had no objection to a Democratic state victory, had been told by Conservative-Democratic leaders that appointment of "honest men" in place of Bisbee and Conant would be cause enough for them to abandon the Greeley ticket and vote for Grant. He subsequently maintained that the personnel change had that precise effect, and Bloxham did run 576 votes ahead of Greeley in November.[26] But to the majority of Republican leaders the entire transaction merely proved Reed's duplicity.

A. A. Knight, a presidential elector, explained that the Republican majority in Florida was small and that the United States court was the only force which the Democrats respected. By arresting and punishing regulators, Bisbee and Conant had encouraged black and white Republicans to vote in November. Josiah Walls fumed, "leave us alone and Florida will give you a 3,000 majority." President Grant, Attorney General George H. Williams, and Secretary Chandler were deluged with protests. Charles Cowlan warned that the protests were "tricks of this crowd of thieves. They are telegraphing in names of all sorts of people all sorts of rubbish. . . . We have got the state perfectly in hand."[27]

Chandler realized the mistake and Bisbee and Conant were reinstated. Within a few days the administration was receiving thanks for its prompt action. After his removal, Cowlan campaigned for the Democrats. In the election, he received sixty write-in votes for Congress from Jonathan Gibbs and other Leon County blacks who detested Purman. Bassnett became the Republican party attorney with approval of most party leaders, although he continued briefly as Wilkinson Call's law partner. Governor Reed complained that Grant's capitulation caused state Republicans to declare open war against him. That was certainly nothing new, but Osborn supported the governor's allegation with a telegram that "Reed is out for the Democrats and has sent another agent . . . to get the appointment of marshal. Stop it, a change will ruin us."[28]

Governor Reed excoriated Purman, Osborn, and several Republicans in his speeches, but persistently praised the Grant administration. When he issued a circular calling for vigilance by election officials and concomitantly refused to replace several Democratic county commissioners, he was again assailed for party treachery. A Gadsden County Republican predicted defeat in his county unless the governor made the requested changes. Reed still refused and Gadsden returned a large Republican majority. A. A. Knight alleged that Reed had arranged Leon County polls so that only one of the sixteen had a majority of Republican inspectors and had relocated five of the ten Jefferson County precincts to please Democrats,[29] but the Republicans carried Leon 2,397 to 674 and Jefferson 2,235 to 599.

Marshal Conant appointed deputy marshals in several counties, ordering them to guard against intentional miscounting and fraud by poll inspectors as well as against physical intimidation. Without the governor's knowledge, troops were requested and the Second Infantry Regiment sent thirty-six men to Jacksonville, twenty each to Marianna and Tallahassee, twelve each to Lake City and Quincy, and five each to Monticello and Madison. Reed remarked that troops and marshals were sent only to precincts where the major legislative contests were between rival Republicans. He was referring to the continuing battle between the Pearce and Stokes factions in Leon County and several large counties where independent candidates were running against the regular Republican nominees. A notable example was H. S. Harmon's independent candidacy against Leonard G. Dennis in Alachua.[30] In all fairness, however, the governor should have recognized that these towns were the sites of most of the 1870 intimidation.

The threat of violence deterred some voters, but no major disturbances occurred at the polls on election day. There was fraudulent voting and election officials of both political affiliations acted illegally. Returns from Jefferson, Gadsden, and Jackson counties appeared to have been altered, but they were verified with corrected copies sent from the county seats before the state canvassing board counted them. Marshal Conant and his deputies arrested the Hamilton County canvassing board and several officials in Leon, Alachua, and Marion counties. All those charged were either Liberal Republicans or Democrats accused of rejecting precinct returns with large Republican majorities. The most publicized incident was the arrest of William Birney and two other members of the Alachua County canvassing board. Birney wrote that he and his colleagues had tried to impartially apply the state election laws and for this they had been arrested and indicted by a grand jury. Fearing that a fair trial could not be obtained, Birney fled the state, planning to sell his Alachua plantation. But Attorney General Williams quashed the case, and Birney returned a few weeks later.[31]

Returns came to Tallahassee slowly from the distant counties. The Democrats said a violent storm and heavy rains in south Florida had prevented some of their voters from reaching the polls, but they claimed a small majority.[32] Bloxham tried to arrange an interview with the president to "put himself in harmony with General Grant's administration."[33] Erstwhile Republican Elezear K. Foster had supported the Democrats and declared that "political smoke is like the *pitch* pine smoke, to [sic] thick to see through yet," but he thought Hart would eventually be counted in.[34]

When the state canvassing board finally sifted the returns—rejecting some as illegal and restoring others which had been thrown out by county boards—all the statewide Republican candidates were declared victorious. Grant and Wilson received 17,765 votes to 15,428 for Greeley and Brown. Hart and Stearns ran about 160 votes behind the presidential ticket but still received 1,599 more than Bloxham and Bullock. Walls and Purman were both elected over Niblack and Jones, but Niblack contested Walls' seat and later replaced him. The Republicans retained a nominal majority in both legislative houses—thirteen to eleven in the senate and twenty-nine to twenty-three in the house.[35] Republican E. T. Sturtevant of Brevard was seated over his opponent by grossly unfair methods, causing controversy during the next three years. The legislative balance was clouded by the presence in the senate of two independent Republicans and two independent Democrats. In the house there were four independent Republicans and two independent Democrats. All but one of the independent Republicans were from Leon County where the Pearce-Conover slate of candidates, including John Wallace, John Proctor, and William G. Stewart, had been elected over the Stokes-Weeks faction with major support from Conservative-Democrats who had not entered legislative candidates in the campaign.[36]

The election resulted in few surprises. The Democrats were defeated by a badly splintered Republican party which had the assistance of federal officials. Counting heavily on Republican factionalism, suppression of voters by physical and economic intimidation, and a native white population aroused and determined to overthrow the unpopular Republican regime, the Conservative-Democrats had considered the popular Bloxham's chances of election promising. But they had miscalculated badly. Republican factional bickering was intense and personal, but it drove only a few partisans into the Democratic party. Although desiring Liberal Republican support, the Democrats offered little incentive for it. The cautious effort to fuse dissatisfied blacks with Conservative-Democrats had little substance. There was small advantage in the position of alternate presidential elector, and the Democrats supported few Negroes for local offices. Although Bloxham and the *Tallahassee Floridian* reminded blacks of how little Negroes had received from the Republican party, elimination of "carpetbaggers," "scalawags," and Negro voting was their major theme.

Bisbee and Conant offset the effects of voter intimidation which many Democrats expected to reduce registration lists, but the Negroes remembered which side had inspired the night-riders. At the same time, Democratic politicians overestimated their ability to mobilize the native white voters. In several counties, potential voters were not interested enough to register. An east Floridian reflected an attitude not uncommon in his region when he declined to "go up there [to a political rally] in this sun to hear any orator that Florida possesses."[37]

A conservative east Florida Republican succinctly analyzed his party's situation: "I think Hart will make good appointments, although there is a strong influence . . . on him to continue the old order of things. If it is continued we can say good bye to Republican rule in Florida."[38] Hart never recovered from the pneumonia contracted during the campaign. Incapacitated throughout most of 1873, he died in March 1874, and Marcellus L. Stearns, a major participant in the "old order of things," became governor.

17

The Muddy Pool of Florida Politics

During its second term in power the Republican party failed to overcome the divisive factionalism which had disrupted the Reed administration. Individual Republicans continually hurled acrimonious and exaggerated epithets at each other which the Democrats gleefully collected and used for election campaign material. As a result the party failed to capitalize at the polls on what might otherwise have been recognized as a creditable legislative accomplishment.

Governor Hart's inauguration was favorably noted by Liberal Republicans and Democrats, but he soon alienated them by some of his state and local appointments. A few months after assuming office, he left the state for extended treatment at Morristown, New Jersey. He kept close correspondence with Tallahassee much of the time, but Lieutenant Governor Marcellus L. Stearns assumed the gubernatorial duties. Hart died in March 1874, and Stearns became governor for the remainder of the four-year term.[1]

The accession of their old enemy to the governorship dismayed and further alienated many Negro leaders who were still restive under the predominantly white leadership of their party. The breach between dissident Negroes and regular Republican organizations was widened in several counties. The Leon County black leaders fought Stearns throughout his administration and during his 1876 bid for re-election. "Reform" Republican organizations were formed in Jefferson and Madison counties. In Alachua County, Congressman Josiah T. Walls, H. S. Harmon, and William Birney acquired the *Gainesville New Era* through which they opposed Leonard Dennis and his *Gainesville Independent*. In the Jacksonville municipal election of 1873, dissident Republicans unsuccessfully fused with Democrats in opposition to the regular party.[2]

Despite his failure to attract Negro support, Stearns used state and county patronage effectively and exercised more influence in the party organization than Reed had. The *Tallahassee Sentinel* and *Jacksonville Florida Union* were Stearns' papers. They defended the governor and attacked his enemies.

Stearns' most prominent adversary was former State Treasurer Simon B. Conover, elected to the United States Senate as a compromise choice in January 1873, after both Democrats and Republicans failed to elect one of their own in the closely divided legislature. Neither party could control the 1873 legislature. Both Liberty Billings, the holdover president of the senate, and Conover, elected as house speaker, were Liberal Republicans. Intense interest in the senatorial election and awareness of the near balance between the parties in the legislature caused pressure on the committees on privileges and elections in both houses. The senate committee, with a Republican majority, refused to rule on some contested elections, especially the highly irregular proceeding which had sent E. T. Sturtevant to Tallahassee from the twenty-first district. The Sturtevant election remained unsettled until 1875 when it caused a parliamentary crisis. Several other state senators held federal offices. A joint resolution declaring dual officeholding illegal narrowly failed to pass the senate. Senator James W. Locke of the twenty-fourth district was also a federal judge. Since his district had gone Democratic after his election, Locke held tenaciously to his seat despite pressure from the senate judiciary committee and the United States attorney general. Locke finally resigned from the senate shortly after the senatorial election. Even with Locke and Sturtevant holding seats, few Republicans were optimistic. One partisan lamented that the Democrats would probably unite on William Bloxham and "buy" about three of the "needful" Republicans' votes to win.[3]

The Democrats were much more cohesive than the Republicans, but neither side consistently supported one man during the twenty-two ballots required to elect a senator. On a single day, fourteen different men received votes. Despite the Republican convention's promise to support Reed, he was virtually ignored, as was outgoing Senator Osborn. On the third day, Tampa Democrat John A. Henderson received thirty-one votes with thirty-nine required for election. The following day, Bloxham received thirty-four.[4] When Bloxham failed to win with nearly every Democrat supporting him, both parties switched back and forth between Conover and James D. Westcott, a Democratic supreme court justice. Westcott, a Reed appointee, received his most consistent support from the Republicans formerly identified with Senator Osborn. An indignant Liberal Republican editor condemned Westcott for besmirching his heretofore spotless record by bargaining with the "Jacksonville Ring" of federal officeholders in his "first attempt to rise to the top of the muddy pool of Florida politics."[5] Conover's strength came from Democrats, Negroes, and the few white Liberal Republicans. After five ballots on January 31, he received forty-three votes to twenty-one for Westcott. Both candidates had bipartisan support on the final ballot. That Conover ultimately received more Democratic votes than Westcott, some Democrats explained, was due to their wish to retain the latter's services on the supreme judicial bench.[6] Nevertheless, the Democrats chose Republican Conover for the United States Senate when they could have elected Westcott. Conover incurred the wrath of regular Republicans when he subsequently acknowledged his indebtedness to Democrats.

Both Liberal Republican and Democratic newspapers praised the election result. The regular Republicans were generally dissatisfied although one astute partisan advised quiet acceptance of the election since the new senator could prove useful in the future. Other less gracious losers charged that bribery had brought about Conover's election, but a legislative investigation failed to turn up any evidence. According to the *Floridian*, "those who spoke loudly on the street were unwilling to testify."[7]

In Washington, Conover first alarmed Florida Republicans by nominating William Bloxham for United States surveyor general at Tallahassee. Bloxham was not appointed because Senator Gilbert insisted that his son be given the position.[8] But the Stearns-Conover feud began in earnest when the senator obtained important federal offices for two prominent Negro leaders. John R. Scott became customs collector at Jacksonville and William G. Stewart was made Tallahassee postmaster.[9] When the *Sentinel* criticized Conover's appointive policy, John Wallace condemned the paper for opposing Negroes in high offices and praised Conover as "the only Republican who ever recognized the prominent colored men as officeholders."[10] Editor Dyke of the *Floridian* fueled the dispute by praising Conover and Congressman Walls for forcing the removal from federal offices of Horatio Bisbee, Horatio Jenkins, Jr., and Leonard G. Dennis.[11] Thus, once again the major political division was within the Republican party between factions led by the governor and a United States senator. This time, however, the Negroes were aligned with the senator, and they had learned through political experience how to bargain more effectively. As the opposition party, the Democrats continued to exacerbate Republican differences whenever possible, but their increased strength also enabled them to play a greater role in positive legislation than in the past.

The 1873 legislature enacted several important measures. A comprehensive civil rights act was finally passed with the aid of three Democratic votes in the senate.[12] It provided for equal enjoyment by all citizens of inns, common carriers, theaters, and public schools which were supported by taxation; it prohibited discrimination on juries; and it forbade discrimination through use of the word "white." Violations were made misdemeanors punishable by fines of $100 to $1,000. Aggrieved persons were to be awarded $100. However, the law did not extend to private schools, cemetaries, and institutions of learning established exclusively for "white or colored" persons and maintained by voluntary contributions. Worse yet, the positive provisions of the law were narrowly interpreted. When Negroes sued the operator of a Tallahassee skating rink for denying them entry, a black justice of the peace dismissed the suit on the ground that the rink was private property which its proprietor could use as he pleased.[13] Another law made legal process available to poor people. Justices of the peace were permitted to continue demanding fees in advance as they had always done, except when complainants were insolvent.[14]

After the immense difficulties resulting from state bond issues in support of railroad construction, the 1873 legislature prohibited the issue or endorsement of any more state bonds for that purpose and repealed all portions of laws authorizing bond issues for private corporations of any kind. For the first time taxes were levied on telegraph lines operating in Florida.[15]

In his message to the legislature, Governor Hart reiterated former Governor Reed's pleas for legislation to put the state on a cash basis. The legislators responded with an improved tax collection law, requiring tax collectors to be bonded and making their failure to settle accounts a felony. They were required to state whether the taxes they collected were in scrip or currency. The comptroller was required to report violations to the attorney general for prosecution.[16] When the legislature adjourned without passing a funding bill, Governor Hart called an immediate special session which enacted a suitable law in one day. It authorized the issue of $1 million in thirty-year coupon bonds at 6 per cent interest payable in gold. A four mill tax was levied on real and personal property to pay the interest and a sinking fund. One half of the bonds were to be exchanged by the comptroller for valid outstanding Florida bonds. All those received on exchange were to be cancelled immediately. The other half were to be sold by the governor and comptroller at no less than eighty cents on the dollar. With the proceeds the treasurer was to first redeem the bonds hypothecated in 1868 and 1869 and then pay state indebtedness accruing after July 1, 1873. An 1874 law also authorized exchange of the bonds for outstanding state warrants.[17]

The funding act and the legislation relating to tax collections brought order to Florida finances for the first time in years. Within four months Comptroller Cowgill sold $250,000 worth of the 6 per cent bonds and redeemed the hypothecated bonds of 1868 and 1869. By 1875, $900,400 worth had been sold for at least eighty cents on the dollar or exchanged for outstanding bonds. Tax collections of $320,000 in 1873 exceeded annual expenditures for the first time since the war. The legislative appropriation of $316,000 for 1873 included deficiencies for 1872 as well as special relief bills including several teachers' salaries unpaid since 1868.[18]

The 1874 and 1875 legislatures added other measures beneficial to the several classes represented by it, but the trend was toward eliminating state benefits to private corporations and forcing them to bear part of the tax burden. The people ratified two constitutional amendments prohibiting the use of state credit to aid any private individual or corporation and requiring taxation of all corporate property except that used for religious, educational, or charitable purposes. The 1873 legislature had already enacted a law denying such use of state credit and the 1874 session required all railroad companies to make annual tax returns on the total value of their property. An exception to this trend was a five year tax exemption on all goods and buildings of any manufacturing company established in Florida to process cotton, sugar, paper, or salt. Another amendment ratified by the people eliminated annual legislative sessions in favor of biennial meetings. Although it was effective in time to preclude an 1876 session, the savings resulting from this economy measure were realized about the same time the Democrats came to power in 1877, enabling them to capitalize on the change.[19]

A general incorporation law was enacted in 1874, replacing the unsatisfactory practice of passing special legislation for every group desiring incorporation.[20]

In further efforts to improve state financing, the legislature of 1874 set state taxes at eleven mills for general appropriations, schools, and debt management. It continued to permit owners to evaluate their property, but required that it be done under oath. It continued the practice of accepting comptrollers' warrants and treasury certificates for taxes at full face value, and authorized the exchange of 1873 bonds at par for these floating notes. An amendment to the school funding act permitted school boards to tax as much as fifteen mills on the assessed value of all property in the county and required them to tax at the rate of at least half the amount received from the state common school fund.[21]

In 1873 Governor Hart had called for legislation relating to the deplorable condition of public roads. The 1874 legislature charged county commissioners with responsibility for roads and highways and authorized them to appoint road supervisors and to summon all able-bodied men ages eighteen to forty-five for not more than eight days work on the roads each year.[22]

A measure designed to aid laborers declared ten hours to be a legal day's work and, in lieu of specific contract, entitled workers to an extra day's pay for work performed beyond ten hours. An 1870 law providing for licensing of stevedores was amended to require six months' residence in Florida before the license could be issued. The amendment was in response to demands from the Pensacola Workingman's Association which resented competition from Canadian laborers who had been spending their winters in Florida. "An Act to protect Laborers and Lumbermen" created a lien on all timber cut by them until they were paid for their services. An 1872 act had already given agricultural laborers such a lien. Another act prohibited garnishment of wages due laborers.[23]

In 1874 an election was held for two congressmen and a state legislature. An important consideration in the campaign was another United States Senate vacancy in 1875. Since 1872 when both congressional seats were filled at large, the state had been divided into two districts. One embraced all counties west of the Suwannee and those touching the Gulf of Mexico. East Florida constituted the second. A harmonious Democratic convention nominated John A. Henderson for west Florida congressman. Several potential candidates in east Florida were eliminated at a Jacksonville convention which nominated J. J. Finley of Columbia County. The Democratic organizations united behind their candidates and launched a campaign to overcome voter apathy. Dyke of the *Floridian* warned that many potential Democrats had sworn to eschew politics permanently and that only strong measures would "stir up the lukewarm" whose votes were necessary for victory.[24]

Republican unity was typically lacking. Purman and Walls were the likely candidates, but both men were being viciously attacked by the *Tallahassee Sentinel* and *Jacksonville Union* in 1874. John Wallace led a group of Leon County Negroes against Governor Stearns' handpicked convention delegates. He accused the governor of offering him a bribe to step aside in favor of the E. C. Weeks delegation from Leon County to the district convention. A July meeting of the state central committee degenerated into an argument between Stearns' supporters and those of Purman, Walls, and Conover. When the second district convention at Jacksonville renominated Walls, the *Union* came out for Finley, his Democratic opponent.[25]

The first district convention met in Tallahassee, where tempers were still raw over the usual Leon County delegate dispute, and resulted in a violent brawl. With backing from Governor Stearns, Negro Senator Robert Meacham contested the renomination of incumbent Congressman Purman. Returning from a recess, the Purman group found the convention completely reorganized by Stearns and Meacham. An argument ensued between Purman and Malachi Martin, a white state senator from Gadsden County and warden of the state penitentiary. Martin knocked Purman to the floor with a chair and other delegates joined in a pitched battle to the detriment of the assembly hall furniture. On orders from Governor Stearns, Adjutant General John Varnum cleared the capitol building. The Purman advocates, including a majority of the state central committee, reconvened in the street and renominated the congressman. The Stearns faction nominated Meacham.[26]

The convention imbroglio and the dual candidacy inspired Democratic confidence in John Henderson's election chances. Several Republicans confided to Democratic friends their corresponding pessimism regarding their chances. Their estimates improved somewhat in September when a reconciliation between Stearns and Purman brought about Meacham's withdrawal from the race. An embarrassed *Sentinel* was obliged to rephrase the derogatory comments it had previously made about Purman. By November most influential Republicans had been induced to support the party's candidates. The earlier factional fighting was remembered by some partisans, however, especially in east Florida where independent voting had already been encouraged by the 1872 Liberal Republican movement. Many of the whites who came to east Florida in the 1870s were longtime Republicans, but they were primarily interested in capitalistic enterprise, low taxes, and economical government. They were influenced by two independent Republican editors who advised them to vote for national Republicans and Democratic state candidates to rid the state of the destructive intraparty bickering of the past several years. This policy was advocated by both John S. Adams, editor of the *Jacksonville New South* and former immigration commissioner, and Solon Robinson, longtime agricultural editor of the *New York Tribune* who had settled in Jacksonville as editor of the *Florida Agriculturist.* An observer in 1874 reported a growing tendency among east Floridians to split the ticket.[27]

The parties again cultivated Monroe County where the number of Cuban exiles had increased since 1872. Most of the new arrivals had declared their intention of becoming citizens and were registered to vote. There were also 193 Bahama Negroes working in Key West who were registered to vote. Both parties were apprehensive over this influx of foreigners whose party affiliations were uncertain. Purman spent several days with the New York *Junta* trying to assure a solid Cuban vote for the Republican party. He was comparatively successful. When John Henderson visited Monroe in early November he could only report the Cubans as divided.[28]

The election was accompanied by fraud and intimidation, but there was comparatively little violence. A typical Democratic sympathizer reported a quiet and orderly election in Escambia County where his party carried the election "to the delight of all who are tired of negro domination for the benefit of thieves and jailbirds from the North."[29] William U. Saunders, the former Union Leaguer who was a deputy marshal during the election, allegedly interfered illegally with proceedings at an Alachua County precinct. Irregular Republican votes were allegedly cast at the Colored Academy precinct in Columbia County. A vigorous local campaign had been waged there between Democrat Francis M. Weeks and Republican Elisha G. Johnson. When a congressional investigating committee examined the second district election, Democrats charged Johnson with responsibility for the fraud. Before he could be questioned, the Republican leader was shotgunned to death from ambush by an unidentified person.[30]

The most serious election-day violence occurred at Key West where local officials had scheduled a yacht race to keep wrecking crews and sponge boats in port for the election. A labor dispute disguised as political violence caused an all-day riot in which several casualties were inflicted before United States troops restored order. Regardless of the disturbance, more than 1,300 votes were cast, an increase of 400 since 1872. The Cubans split their votes, reducing the large Democratic majority of 1872 to a mere twelve votes.[31]

Canvassing boards threw out precinct returns for alleged irregularities in several counties, notably Santa Rosa, Jefferson, and Leon. When they learned that John Wallace had been defeated for the state senate by what they believed to be unfair county canvassing board action, Leon County Negroes determined to resist the decision. They were spared the trouble, however, when the state board overruled the county decision and declared Wallace elected. Purman received 9,203 votes to 8,628 for Henderson, and Walls defeated Finley 8,349 to 8,178. Finley contested on the basis of the Colored Academy controversy, and Walls was unseated late in the term for the third successive time.[32] The state senate was tied with twelve members from each party. Democratic gains in the house gave them a majority of twenty-eight to twenty-five, although the presence of a few independents prevented a working majority.

When the 1875 legislature met in early January, the senatorial election was uppermost in the minds of most legislators. The independent Democrats played a crucial role in the election of a house speaker. William W. Hicks, recently elected as a Democrat from Monroe County, nominated Thomas Hannah, an independent Democrat from Washington County, for speaker. He was easily elected over Madison County Republican David

Montgomery, a close associate of Governor Stearns. The evenly divided senate spent ten days before electing Democrat A. L. McCaskill as its president.[33] The senatorial election began on January 26 and lasted more than two weeks. Voting was scattered among numerous candidates, but both parties displayed more unity than had been demonstrated in 1873. Democrats Wilkinson Call, David Walker, John A. Henderson, and Robert W. Bullock all came within a few votes of the thirty-nine required. During fourteen ballots, Republicans voted for Henry Sanford; Samuel Walker, the wartime Unionist at Key West who had aligned with the Leon County Negroes; and Samuel B. McLin, Stearns' secretary of state and editor of the *Tallahassee Sentinel.* Walker and McLin received the most serious consideration among the Republicans, with Hicks and the independents consistently voting for the latter. But on the fifteenth ballot, Hicks nominated Charles W. Jones, a comparatively obscure Escambia County Democratic representative who had run unsuccessfully for Congress in 1872. On that ballot Jones received thirty-four votes. For several ballots, Horatio Bisbee received most of the Republican votes while Jones competed with Bullock among the Democrats. On the twenty-fourth ballot, Hicks persuaded the independents to vote for Jones. One Republican joined them, giving Jones forty votes and the election.[34]

At a time and place where political puzzles were commonplace, William Watkins Hicks was one of the most enigmatic personalities. He was a Brooklyn minister who had spent fifteen years as a missionary in India before coming to the post–Civil War South. Until 1875 he had always been a Conservative-Democrat. After helping the Democrats organize the house in 1875, he then supported the staunch Republican McLin for the senatorship before switching to Jones. Meanwhile, he had moved from Key West to Nassau County where he became editor of the *Fernandina Observer,* which he owned jointly with Democrats Samuel Swann and David Yulee. Then, in February 1875, while Hicks was being credited with bringing about the Democratic senatorial victory, Governor Stearns appointed him state superintendent of public instruction.[35] He soon became a vitriolic opponent of the Democratic party, dissolved his partnership with Swann and Yulee, and was sued for libel by the Democratic *Jacksonville Press.* He remained a bitter opponent of his former party throughout the Stearns administration.

Just before Jones was elected, the *Floridian* had warned that it was "not a matter of who the Democrats *will* elect but who they *can* elect." Jones was not the Democrats' choice but he was acceptable to them as well as the independents. His election was hailed as a great Democratic landmark on the way toward "redemption" of the state from "carpetbaggers" and "scalawags." The independent Republican *Jacksonville New South* also accepted Jones as a competent man who would serve the state well. It called on Governor Stearns and other disgruntled Republicans to stop trying to fix the blame for defeat, which had been caused by "the years of disgraceful squabbling within the party."[36]

Every election during the 1870s was followed by contests for legislative seats in both houses. The committees on privileges and elections were kept busy investigating disputed cases and the majority party often benefited by their decisions. Although they were not strong enough to pass measures by strict party votes in 1875, the Democrats had been able to organize both houses of the legislature with independent support. In the senate there were two Republicans sitting in contested seats. The Democrats hoped to oust one of them and break the senate tie. E. T. Sturtevant, Republican incumbent from the twenty-first district, had the weakest claim to his seat. Israel Stewart had contested his election in the 1873 session, but the committee on privileges and elections—controlled by the Republicans in 1873 and 1874—had not acted. In 1875, Democratic Senate President McCaskill appointed two Democrats and one Republican to investigate the case. They recommended Sturtevant's removal.

The twenty-first district was composed of Dade and Brevard counties. The entire district had about 100 voters. Sturtevant had been an inspector at the only Dade County precinct in the 1872 election. As county judge he was also on the canvassing board which reviewed the precinct returns and reported them to the state. Thirty votes were cast in Dade County and sixty-nine in Brevard. Sturtevant received fourteen Dade votes to sixteen for Stewart. As a candidate he contested the eligibility of three voters, although as a precinct inspector he had permitted them to cast ballots. With the other county board members, he expunged the three votes so that Dade County returns showed a majority of one for himself. The Brevard returns gave Stewart thirty-nine votes while Sturtevant received none of the remaining thirty. The state canvassing board declared Sturtevant elected because the Brevard returns were received too late to be counted.[37]

The report set off an extended controversy and became a major test of party loyalty and strength in the senate. The Republicans tried to delay action while the Democrats tried to force a vote without permitting Sturtevant to participate in the decision of his case. John Wallace, the anti-Stearns Negro from Leon County, was persuaded to vote with the Democrats, but B. F. Oliveras, a St. Augustine Democrat, wavered toward the Republican side.[38]

On February 17, it briefly appeared that the Democrats had the necessary votes and the Republicans prevented action by leaving the senate chamber. The sergeant-at-arms was sent to bring in the absent members.

There had already been a shooting between an assistant sergeant-at-arms and Senator A. J. Parlin of Escambia over the issue. L. G. Dennis of Alachua County also led a boisterous street demonstration, apparently to remind any wavering Republican senators of their party duties. The missing members were brought in on February 18, but the issue was deadlocked by a vote on straight party lines and the Sturtevant case was dropped.[39]

Having acted with the Democrats at first, Wallace ultimately switched back to the Republican side. He later wrote that his vote to uphold Sturtevant was one of the two acts which he regretted, but in Tallahassee—where Negroes outnumbered whites about six to one—it was a serious matter for a black Republican to bolt the party when the public was so aroused. The case came up once more late in the session, but no decision was reached. Sturtevant was still in the senate when it adjourned.

Francis M. Weeks, a Columbia County Democrat, contested the seat of Elisha G. Johnson of the fourteenth district.[40] Johnson was accused of altering the election result by fraud committed at the Colored Academy precinct, but Weeks had not received favorable action on his complaint when the legislature adjourned in 1875.

Johnson was a prominent Republican and had been the party chieftan in his county since 1868. He had received several threatening letters signed "KKK" during the violent years between 1868 and 1871, but no attempts had been made on his life then. While walking home from his Lake City store late at night on July 21, 1875, Senator Johnson was killed by a shotgun fired from ambush. Although the reason for his assassination was never clearly established, it was a grim reminder of the many political assassinations a few years earlier. The Republicans exploited the incident, charging that the Democrats were still the party of murder and violence. Democratic newspapers deplored the murder but noted that Johnson was in office as the result of fraud and his removal gave the Democrats a senate majority.[41] One unreconstructed rebel wrote privately that "in his death is our gain, it is an ill wind that blows no one good. That gives us a clear majority without putting out Sturtevant. . . . In losing Johnson we gain a county. Who could not afford to make this sacrifice. . . . If I was on a jury of inquest I should say shot by persons unknown and served him right."[42]

Harney Richards of Alachua County was arrested for the crime on circumstantial evidence and his case became a partisan cause. Republican Judge R. B. Archibald told a congressional investigating committee that Johnson was murdered to give the Democrats a senate majority and that the state's "best citizens" tried to help the murderer escape. The Democrats in the 1877 legislature threatened to impeach Archibald for his testimony. After a lengthy controversy and extensive publicity the grand jury released Richards because he had "proved an alibi by some of the very best citizens of the state." Richards was not released until May 1876, and the assassination became an issue in the hotly fought 1876 election campaign.

18

To Give the Lost Cause a Union Flavor

Sensing the urgency which politicians of both parties attached to the approaching election, a Democratic state legislator observed in July 1875 that "the political caldron has already begun to simmer about Tallahassee for 1876."[1] The presidential election was important because the state Republican party depended on national patronage as well as enforcement of civil rights legislation by marshals and the army. Yet most Floridians regarded the national election as ancillary to the struggle for control of the state government. They had no way of knowing that the dispute over the electoral votes of Florida, Louisiana, and South Carolina would thrust their state into the center of national politics and relegate the local contest temporarily to a secondary role.

Despite the lack of cohesion within the Republican party and the refusal of Democrats to accept Negro suffrage as a legitimate addition to the political system, many elements of two-party politics were present in Florida by 1876. Fraud and intimidation were very much part of the election, but the parties minimized irregularities by watching each other closely. There had been much more violence in the 1870 election than there was in 1876 and intimidation would be more pervasive in years to come. Yet the national significance of Florida's four electoral votes, partisan diligence in uncovering irregularities, thorough news coverage, and the lengthy dispute between Republican Rutherford B. Hayes and Democrat Samuel J. Tilden over the election's result caused nearly every actual or alleged incident to be ferreted out and reported to election officials and the nation's press. Florida was linked inseparably with Louisiana and South

Carolina, where the 1876 election had been exceptionally violent and corrupt. The result was general acceptance of the belief that violence and fraud distorted the Florida election to a much greater degree than was the case. These problems were present in 1876, but to no greater degree than in the previous eight years and significantly less than in those which followed.

For the Republican incumbents the major problem in 1876 was the same as in the past. "Party unity must and shall be preserved! Just how we are not prepared to say," was the *Tallahassee Sentinel*'s blunt summation. Republican leaders ignored the warning and continued their devastating personal attacks on each other. At a congressional civil service investigation Governor Stearns and his ally, prison warden Malachi Martin, testified that Congressman Purman abused his prerogatives in federal appointments. This attack angered John Wallace of Leon County, George Witherspoon of Jefferson, and Benjamin Livingston of Jackson, all important Negro leaders whose names were besmirched by the testimony. Purman retaliated with a tirade in which he told his congressional colleagues that Stearns had been foisted upon Florida against the party will and "as South Carolina once had its Moses, and New York its Tweed, so Florida has now its Stearns."[2]

Each Republican leader was accused of collusion with Democrats, which was often true since much recent legislation and some administrative appointments had been bipartisan. But Senator Conover received the worst criticism for an alleged "Dyke-Conover Ring" in which he exchanged federal appointments for Democratic support of his gubernatorial candidacy. A letter purporting to substantiate the charge was stolen from Dyke's home and published. His Republican enemies even applauded when Conover was indicted by a grand jury in March 1876 for embezzling funds while he was state treasurer. He was arrested and released on $10,000 bond. If a conspiracy existed between Conover and the Democrats, it did not prevent Robert H. Gamble from testifying that he had turned over to Conover $40,000 of state funds for which there was no accounting. When it appeared that Gamble really did not know what had become of the money and that his own inefficiency in keeping the comptroller's accounts was the major cause of the discrepancy, he retracted his charge and declared that Conover was not responsible. The incumbent comptroller, Clayton A. Cowgill, published a statement exonerating the senator.[3] The Democrats backed away from the issue as soon as one of their own appeared responsible.

The Republican state executive committee, controlled by Governor Stearns who was seeking renomination, called a nominating convention to meet at Madison on May 31. It triggered another controversy by announcing the convention's temporary organization. Conover, who was also running for governor, refused to accept the committee action. To allay his outspoken opposition, the state central committee met at Live Oak in early April and endorsed the previous convention call including the temporary organization. Conover proponents competed in several county conventions, but most of them lost to delegates pledged to Stearns. Refusing to abide by their county conventions' decisions, contesting Conover delegations from several large counties attended the Madison meeting.[4]

Stearns' control of the temporary organization was ultimately decisive, but only after a demoralizing battle. Nine pro-Conover delegations presented their credentials. All except the one from Monroe County were turned away. Monroe Republicans were treated carefully because the nearly 1,000 Cuban voters constituted the most unpredictable group in the Florida electorate. Their votes were almost enough to swing an election in the closely divided state. F. N. Wicker had arranged the Monroe County delegation in favor of Stearns, but only by the ruse of calling the convention at one place and holding it at another. The seating committee at Madison decided in favor of the pro-Conover Monroe delegation which complained that Wicker's methods were unfair.[5]

Congressman Purman attacked Governor Stearns in an address to the convention and read a letter from Frederick Douglass, the famous Negro leader, endorsing Conover. Conover's speech was also hostile to Stearns. He was followed by John Wallace and George Witherspoon, both of whom opposed Stearns' renomination. After a recess during which Madison County Sheriff G. W. Bogue was shot in the leg while trying to separate two fighting delegates and John W. Butler of Santa Rosa County verbally abused Conover while friends held him to prevent a physical attack, the convention renominated Stearns for governor. After Horatio Bisbee, Jr., declined, David Montgomery of Madison County was nominted for lieutenant governor. Presidential electors were W. H. Holden, Charles H. "Bishop" Pearce, T. W. Long, and F. C. Humphries. Delegates were chosen for the national convention, and a platform was adopted endorsing the national party, praising the existing state administration, and calling for economy and integrity in government.[6]

The Conover delegates held their own convention in the woods near Madison. With about twenty-six counties represented, Josiah T. Walls was named chairman. Simon B. Conover was nominated for governor, and Joseph A. Lee, a southern Unionist from Sumter County, for lieutenant governor. They also elected delegates to the Cincinnati convention.[7]

"Entire unity was not secured at the convention," the *Sentinel* complained as it called on "malcontents" to return to the "charted course."

Party harmony in the state suffered another setback when the Cincinnati convention seated the Conover delegates and rejected the regular Florida representatives. Although Conover's acquaintance with national Republicans probably explains the action, it re-inforced the senator's determination to stay in the governor's race. An Ocala newspaper called it a "big button in Conover's coat."[8]

The Cincinnati convention nominated Ohio Governor Rutherford B. Hayes for president on a reform platform. William A. Wheeler of New York was his running mate. The convention selected Hayes because the scandals of Grant's administration and the economic depression since 1873 threatened the Republicans' election prospects. With strong northern sentiment against continued national governmental action in the South—especially since it had failed by 1876—Hayes' announced intention to resolve the "Southern question" was a popular position. Although they may have preferred a different nominee, Florida Republicans accepted the convention's decision and campaigned for Hayes and Wheeler.

William D. Bloxham was still the most prominent Conservative-Democratic gubernatorial hopeful, but the party was determined to win in 1876 and any southern Democrat, no matter how able or popular, had liabilities in Florida where immigration was changing the composition of the white population. George F. Drew, a conservative lumber mill owner from Ellaville, Madison County, was frequently mentioned as a suitable candidate by prominent party men as they prepared for a nominating convention at Quincy on June 7. They thought he would appeal to native white Floridians while also attracting some of the dissident Republicans who would be unwilling to vote for an ex-Confederate. Drew was born in New Hampshire but for many years before the Civil War had lived in Columbus, Georgia, where he manufactured iron and later milled lumber. He was known to have been a staunch Unionist during the war, but so had others active in the Democratic party. Unreconstructed Southerners could forgive him since he had supplied Confederate forces with bridge timbers and salt. The fact that he had left the Confederacy and joined Union forces at Savannah late in the war was not generally known in 1876.[9]

By acclamation the Quincy convention nominated Drew for governor and Noble A. Hull, a Sanford merchant, for lieutenant governor. Presidential electors were Robert W. Bullock, Wilkinson Call, Robert B. Hilton, and James Yonge. The platform condemned the incumbent Republican administration and pledged the party to reduce taxes and public offices and to expose corruption. It also called for retrenchment at both national and state levels, opposed national interference in state affairs, and extended a cordial welcome to immigrants.[10]

Drew was chosen over Bloxham because he had the best chance of winning. A pre-war Whig and wartime Unionist, he had voted for Grant in 1868 and Greeley in 1872. Along with a few other Liberal Republicans he remained with the Democrats afterward. The Republican press was furious at his nomination. "He must have been nominated to give the 'Lost Cause' a Union flavor," the *Sentinel* fumed. "His nomination is a wicked fraud to catch Union men and Northern Republicans coming into the state. We would rather have the most bitter Bourbon." Conservative-Democrat Edwin W. L'Engle believed Drew had a good chance of election but that he would be little better than a "Radical." Columbia County Democrats endorsed him even though he was "recently of the Radical party." Even the Republican *Jacksonville Sun* agreed to support him if he stayed "free of the Bourbons."[11]

Hull was a Georgia native who had spent the previous twenty-five years in Florida. Two terms in the state legislature had given him a wide acquaintance in the upper St. Johns country. R. H. M. Davidson of Gadsden County and Jesse J. Finley of Columbia County were nominated for Congress. Davidson had served in the legislature before the war and then fought for the Confederacy under General Finley. Finley had been a United States judge before becoming a Confederate general. Like Drew, all three men were former Whigs.[12]

At St. Louis the national Democrats nominated Samuel J. Tilden, the reform governor of New York, for president with Thomas A. Hendricks of Indiana for vice president. Tilden's reputation as a reformer was believed advantageous in view of Grant's sordid record. Eastern Democrats generally favored hard money policies, while Westerners wanted credit expansion. On this issue Tilden satisfied the East and Hendricks' support of an inflationary policy balanced the ticket toward the West. Tilden considered himself a Jeffersonian Democrat, emphasizing strong local government and frugality in public spending. His position would normally have been pleasing to Southerners, but in 1876 they were yearning for federally assisted internal improvements such as northern areas had been receiving since the Civil War. Still, Florida Democrats were satisfied with the national ticket because they believed Tilden would win.

Having nominated a ticket which they thought might appeal to dissident opposition voters, the Conservative-Democrats were determined to see that every potential supporter registered and cast a vote on election day. Samuel Pasco of Jefferson County headed the state executive committee which called on county committees to count all potential voters in their areas, see that they were on the registration lists, and provide transportation for them to the polls if necessary. It also suggested compiling voting lists and sending challengers to the polls to see that no illegal votes were cast. Democratic clubs were suggested as a method of keeping up enthusiasm. The *Floridian,* which had castigated apathetic citizens in the past, approved the Pasco plan but lamented that "things will soon lapse into idleness and indifference unless the County Committees are active and energetic."[13]

The Democrats held rallies and barbecues for both blacks and whites. Republicans reluctantly admitted that blacks attended them, but explained that it was only because of the food. There were both white and black "Drew and Hull" clubs and a few boasted mixed membership. John B. Gordon and Benjamin H. Hill of Georgia and Alpheus T. Baker of Alabama campaigned through Florida for the Democrats. A sensation was created when the Thomasville Cornet Band and 300 Georgians accompanied Hill and Baker to a Monticello rally. Some Democrats complained that Drew spent most of his time at his mill while others campaigned for him, but little was said about it until after the election. In the north Florida counties Democrats expressed satisfaction with the effectiveness of the campaign, but others who stumped the southern counties found the same indifference and apathy which had prevailed in earlier elections.[14]

The Republican party held separate congressional nominating conventions in August, more than two months after the Madison meeting. Both Stearns and Conover tried to win their endorsements. A jubilant Democratic press merely reprinted their assaults on each other, while the *Sentinel* warned that "Florida Republicans must 'Unite or Die!' " Both district conventions finally endorsed Stearns. Purman was renominated for Congress from the first district and made his peace with the governor. In the second district, Josiah T. Walls was passed over in favor of Horatio Bisbee. Except for "Bishop" Pearce, who was a presidential elector, there was not a Negro nominee for state or national office on the ticket. The district conventions' actions damaged Conover, but he announced that he would remain in the race.[15]

The continued factional split worried Republican leaders. There had been such divisions before but they had always been resolved before the election. The national Republicans were finally induced to intercede. Not only were there two state tickets in the field but also two electoral tickets. A disgusted Florida Republican wrote that many honest Republicans were going to vote for George F. Drew for governor, but were still willing to vote for Hayes and Wheeler if they had the opportunity. To make this possible the national committee would have to see that only one Republican electoral ticket was offered on election day. At the national committee's insistence, Conover withdrew in early September. The *Sentinel* urged its partisans to "get out in every nook and corner and get those unregistered and indifferent people."[16]

Conover did not campaign for Stearns but asked all party members to support the regular party candidates. Not everyone heeded his suggestion. John Wallace continued his attacks on Stearns in Dyke's *Floridian*. As a last-ditch demonstration of dissatisfaction, Wallace and J. Willis Menard, a Duval County Negro leader, announced their candidacies for first and second district congressional seats on a ticket with ex-Governor Harrison Reed, editor of the *Jacksonville Semi-Tropical*, for governor. William Saunders, the former Union League official, campaigned for them. Solon Robinson, editor of the *Florida Agriculturist*—which enjoyed some influence among the new settlers along the St. Johns River—called on his readers to vote a split ticket for Hayes and Drew as he intended to do. Henry Sanford, whose influence reached numerous East Florida Republicans, contributed to the Hayes and Wheeler campaign in Florida but ignored Stearns and Montgomery.[17]

Both parties carefully worked for the support of the Key West Cubans. In his address to the 1875 legislature, Stearns asked the members to make Cuba's cause their own. In early 1876, Conover, Walls, and Purman obtained the appointment of Isaac Carrillo as southern district attorney for the frankly avowed reason that he could unite the party in Monroe County. Carrillo was a Cuban native who had established residence in Florida and was influential with his countrymen. The delegation to Washington also aided Manuel Govin, a naturalized citizen of Key West who had formerly worked in the revenue department, in obtaining the highly desirable Jacksonville postmastership in July 1876, to the chagrin of powerful Duval County Republicans who coveted the job themselves. Purman also tried to obtain a revenue job for C. M. de Cespedes, who had once been involved with Govin in a questionable incident regarding government funds. When collector Alva A. Knight refused to make the appointment, Purman asked him to reconsider. "*Action* is a *political necessity*. . . . By this I will judge your friendship toward myself and vice versa."[18] All three of these men worked hard for the Republican cause at Key West, and the Spanish language newspaper *El Republicano* was revived for the campaign, but most of the Cubans favored Conover until he withdrew from the race. At one time the *Sentinel* thought so little of Stearns' chances of winning their support that it condemned the state election law which permitted aliens to vote after only one year's residence and a declaration of intention to be naturalized. The Cubans and Nassau Negroes in Key West had no right to vote in Florida elections, according to the paper.[19]

The Democrats were also busily negotiating for Cuban support and obtained endorsement from General Aldaince, president of the New York *Junta*, who suggested to his Key West associates that they form a Cuban

Democratic club. By late October the club claimed 300 members. George D. Allen, the former Liberal Republican presidential elector who had become a Democrat by 1876, thought nearly all the Cubans would have joined the Democratic club had it not been for Govin and Carrillo. But he still thought enough would vote for Tilden to give him Monroe County by 300 votes. He was too optimistic. Monroe County's electoral vote was about 1,047 for the Democrats and 980 for the Republicans.[20]

Under Florida election laws, county clerks were required to revise registration lists thirty days before the election and voters were obligated to see that they were registered at least six days before the balloting occurred. County commissioners designated enough polling places for an orderly election and posted notices of their locations at least twenty days in advance. The commissioners also appointed three inspectors who conducted the election at each poll.[21] Federal laws required supervisors to be present at each location. The inspectors opened the polls at eight o'clock and closed them at sunset with a half hour for lunch between noon and one o'clock. When the polls closed the inspectors canvassed the ballots in public without adjourning and forwarded the returns to a county canvassing board.

If a voter's name was not on the registration list, or if he was challenged for any reason, he could cast his vote by swearing that he was an eligible voter. Aliens could vote if they had lived in Florida one year and the county six months and declared their intention of becoming United States citizens. The ballot box was to be openly displayed at all times during election day. As each voter cast his ballot, one inspector received and deposited it in the box, another checked his name off the registration list, and the third added his name to the poll list.

On the sixth day after the election—or sooner if the returns were received from all precincts—the county canvassing board, composed of the county judge, county clerk, and a justice of the peace chosen by them, publicly canvassed the precinct returns and forwarded a certificate of the results by mail to the secretary of state, with a duplicate copy to the governor. The distant southern counties with scattered populations and poor communications were permitted twenty days in which to meet. On the thirty-fifth day after the election—or sooner if the returns were received from all counties—the secretary of state, attorney general, and comptroller of public accounts were to meet as a state canvassing board, count the votes returned by the counties, and declare the results.

Several loopholes in the laws, the great distances and poor communications between polling locations and the state canvassing board at Tallahassee, and mutual suspicions of fraud added to the tension which developed during the campaign. The law prescribed no uniform ballot.

Each party issued its own and they were rarely alike. The only requirement was that all candidates for which an elector voted had to appear on the same ballot. If there were more ballots in the box than the poll lists called for, an inspector could extract enough to remove the surplus. Since it was usually easy to distinguish between party ballots, the inspectors could favor their own party in the process.[22] There was no statutory provision for precinct divisions within the counties, making possible repeated voting through multiple registration or collusion with poll inspectors.

Because the governor appointed county officials and members of the state canvassing board, the Republican party had an advantage. This did not mean, as Democrats charged, that all county officials were Republicans, but the governor's party often controlled the important county commissions. Whether officials were Republicans or Democrats, they could frequently further their party's aims, but their ability to do so was curtailed by close observation from the opposition. County clerks could sometimes register ineligible voters or strike legitimate names from the lists, but it required skill to escape detection.

Republicans were accused of registering minors in Jefferson and Duval counties, but the Democratic executive committee asked its local workers to enlist the assistance of every white male over seventeen years of age. A census of voters was taken in 1875 which became the basis for a general revision of registration lists. After the corrected lists were prepared, party workers compared them to their own lists and advised unregistered persons to have their names replaced on the official rosters. On the other hand, opposition registrants were checked closely to insure that they were legally qualified. Complete lists of all registered voters were compiled and given to party workers who acted as challengers at the polls.[23]

Governor Stearns was accused of colluding to void the election in Manatee County—a large, sparsely settled south Florida county with about 2,700 whites and 100 blacks. Several weeks before the election, J. F. Bartholf, Republican county clerk, resigned. Stearns delayed appointing a successor until October 20, too late for him to prepare for the November 7 election. When Andrew Green was appointed, he refused to post bond and his commission was further delayed. Samuel Pasco paid the fees and Green was notified by telegraph to proceed with his duties, but he refused until his official commission was delivered. Since Manatee was largely Democratic, the Republican officials were believed to be abusing their official positions to nullify a quantity of opposition votes. Edgar N. Graham and other Manatee Democrats prepared for the election without the assistance of the county clerk, complying as nearly as possible with the election laws, and the election was held.[24]

Economic intimidation occurred in several forms, although the Democrats had the advantage. In the agricultural counties, they usually owned the land on which Negroes lived and the stores from which they obtained provisions on credit, but they tried to give the impression that economic intimidation originated with the Republicans. The Jacksonville, Pensacola and Mobile Railroad had been taken over by the state in early 1876 and Dyke said it was levying political assessments on those who wished to keep their jobs. He suggested that landowners follow the railroad's example. Jefferson County Democrats had not waited for the advice. In May they told Negroes either to seek their "advances" from the "Radicals" or come into the Democratic party "where the last crust shall be shared." Planters and merchants established a priority system whereby tenants who voted Democratic received first preference, those not voting at all came next, and Republican voters were last. The latter group was to be charged one-fourth more for land and goods, and one of every three would be denied employment as an example. Some Negroes abstained from voting in Jefferson County while a few voted Democratic because of the pressure.[25]

The Florida Railroad Company gave its employees numbered ballots in Nassau and Duval counties and kept lists to see that they were placed in the ballot boxes. A Key West cigar manufacturer threatened to discharge Cuban laborers who voted the Republican ticket. A few Jacksonville businessmen made similar threats. When a large Republican parade was held just before the election, the *Jacksonville Press* published names of white participants and called on its readers to show their disapproval. John H. Abbot, a wealthy Massachusetts native who had settled in Jacksonville for his health, was insulted on the street afterward. The Democratic trustees of a hospital fund withdrew $6,000 from the First National Bank because its president, J. W. C. Moore, marched in the parade.[26]

At the same time, a Key West Democrat complained that "there is but little to be expected for Tilden from colored voters, as the Negroes wanting to vote for [him] would have to encounter a very uncompromising hostility from Radical Negroes." Hayes and Wheeler clubs kept up pressure on their members to work for a solid Republican vote. Negro Democratic voters faced social ostracism as well as threats of physical harm. Negro women at several polls attacked blacks whom they believed inclined toward the Democrats.[27]

A few Democrats resorted to tactics of earlier days. In Columbia County, where there was a small majority of Negroes on the registration lists, a group of white men led by Elias Osteen and Joel Niblack tried to make Democratic voters of Joseph Sims, Joe King, and a group of other blacks on a country road near Lake City. Placing a noose on one man the regulators calmly discussed the intricacies of a proper hanging and then offered to let the Negroes go if each would withdraw from the local Republican club and campaign for the Democrats. The Negroes understandably agreed and were released. Osteen and Niblack were later arrested by the United States marshal. Columbia County elections had been turbulent in the past, but had returned Republican majorities in 1872 and 1874. In 1876 the Democrats received a majority of nearly 200 votes.[28]

While most Florida political leaders called for a peaceful election, a few thought weapons would be useful. The Jefferson Rifles were organized in April 1876 but were not prominent during the election. When Governor Daniel H. Chamberlain of South Carolina ordered the rifle clubs there disbanded, Edward L'Engle offered to buy their guns. The South Carolina clubs decided to keep their weapons in defiance of the governor, but referred L'Engle to a hardware merchant who would accommodate him. William Bloxham subsequently claimed that the Democrats had arms and ammunition in the Presbyterian Church in Tallahassee, but only for defensive use. There was no resort to arms there on election day, but white men were armed in Jackson, Monroe, and other counties, and Negroes brought guns to several Alachua County polls.[29]

During the last few days of the campaign, tension mounted as speakers warned their listeners of impending disaster if the opposite side won. Malachi Martin, Republican state executive committee chairman, added to the excitement with a circular explaining that armed Georgians were planning to invade Florida on election day. The *Thomasville Enterprise* emphatically denied the allegation and no Georgians appeared. Martin may have misunderstood an exuberant editorial which called on Thomas County citizens to accompany prominent Georgians to Monticello and Tallahassee on speaking tours. Several Leon County Democrats called on Governor Stearns to assure him that they shared his desire for a peaceful election. Since the election law permitted voters to cast ballots anywhere in a county, they also suggested that he assign specific precincts to reduce the possibility of repeated voting as well as violence resulting from overcrowding. Stearns took no action, but the parties mutually agreed to divide Jacksonville polls by race; two for whites, two for blacks, and two where the different races voted at alternate hours.[30] Some of the Jackson County polls also provided for Negro and white voting at alternate hours.

Both parties requested United States troops, and small detachments were stationed temporarily at Pensacola, Marianna, Tallahassee, Monticello, Gainesville, Tampa, St. Augustine, and Key West. Despite Democratic charges, they were not allowed to interfere with orderly voting. When ardent Republican George E. Wentworth, a deputy marshal, tried to distribute troops from the company assigned to Pensacola, the military headquarters notified him that he had no authority over troop deployment. Marshal Sherman Conant appointed temporary deputies in each county. The Democrats demanded a proportionate number of the positions, but Conant merely promised that the deputies would be neutral. Although interference by marshals at the polls had sometimes occurred in past elections, no such incidents were reported in 1876.[31]

There were numerous incidents of threatened violence, hostile verbal exchanges, fraud, and subterfuge on November 7, but no large-scale rioting and no killing. Leaders of both parties immediately declared that the election had been orderly and peaceful, but reports were soon circulating that there had been excitement at several places. Because of the national significance attached to the Florida election, most incidents were eventually reported, sometimes in exaggerated form.

At polls where officials were from the same party, opposition party challengers sometimes had difficulty. Democrats complained that their poll watchers were excluded from Jefferson County polls despite written agreements to admit them. Beasley's store was designated as a poll, but was left deserted while the election took place at Lickskillet, nearly a mile away. Because no one was present to prevent it, Republican officials permitted numerous minors and non-residents to vote. Key West precinct number three, in an overwhelmingly Democratic neighborhood, was situated on the second floor of a building and accessible only by a narrow stairway. Republicans complained that white men crowded potential voters away from the stairs. Juan M. Reyes, the only Republican inspector at the precinct, testified that he was not permitted to challenge questionable voters. Manuel Govin estimated that fifty Republicans were denied the opportunity to vote there.[32] Despite the irregularity, Democratic conduct at precinct three could not have prevented many voters from casting ballots, because precinct one was controlled by Republicans and there was mixed voting at number two, only a few hundred yards from the controversial stairway.

Republicans complained before the election and Democrats afterward that aliens from the Bahamas and Cuba voted illegally, but neither party officially contested the Monroe County returns on that point. The Republicans questioned the validity of precinct three on the technical ground that the inspectors had adjourned without completing the count immediately as required by law. The inspectors of one Hamilton County precinct also adjourned before counting the ballots. Republicans said the Democrats stole the Hamilton County returns and kept them several days until it was time for the county board to meet. The Democrats countered that their actions were necessary since they had a majority and the Republican officials were intentionally violating the law so the votes would be thrown out by the state board.[33]

At Friendship Church precinct in Jackson County, Democratic inspectors allegedly kept the ballot box in a window high above the voters' heads so that no one could see what happened to the ballots. After the polls closed they took the box to a private home about two miles away and completed the count. The inspectors at Campbellton poll, also in Jackson County, were accused of placing the ballot box in a locked store during the noon hour whereupon someone surreptitiously entered the building and withdrew Republican ballots. Democrats vehemently denied the charges that Alabama Democrats voted at Snead's store in Jackson County. Republicans alleged that Democrats fraudulently changed a normal Republican majority in Jackson County to a majority for themselves.[34]

Democratic inspectors supposedly altered ballots as fast as they were received at two Columbia County precincts. Columbia went Democratic for the first time during Reconstruction. At Richardson Schoolhouse poll in Leon County, seventy-three small Republican ballots about one and one-half inches square were found in the box. They were placed there by Joseph Bowes, a Republican inspector who had printed them at the *Tallahassee Sentinel* office. They were counted and Bowes boasted that he had elected a president since Hayes' majority in Florida was only forty-three.[35] Bowes was indicted, but he had left for Washington where he was employed in the treasury department.

More than 100 Levy County Democrats were accused of voting at Cedar Key after casting their votes elsewhere in the county. They then seized the Cedar Key ballot box and kept it until November 13, while Republican officials were "compelled to fly for safety." A Democratic railroad official sent a gang of black workers into Alabama where their train "broke down" until it was too late for them to vote in Florida. At Waldo in Alachua County, a train stopped while out-of-state passengers debarked and voted for Tilden and Hendricks. The *Jacksonville Press* denounced Republican officials for releasing prisoners from the local jail and permitting them to vote. Republicans were accused of altering the returns from Archer precinct in Alachua County by adding names to the registration lists. Green Moore, a poll inspector whose veracity was later impeached, reportedly entertained the other inspectors in the store which served as a poll while Democratic ballots were being replaced with Republican ones in a back room. The inspectors at Archer ostensibly signed blank returns which were subsequently filled in at Gainesville by Leonard G. Dennis, Alachua County Republican boss.[36]

Dennis was also accused of the ingenious ruse of dressing Negro women as men and sending them to the polls in Alachua and Bradford counties. The *Jacksonville Press* probably exaggerated its allegation that forty-two women voted at Barnes store in Alachua. "Two or three were arrested and their sex ascertained," the paper added without elaboration. Because many of their voters were illiterate, the Republicans printed a ballot with an easily distinguishable emblem on it. The Democrats printed ballots similarly emblazoned but with their own candidates listed. These ballots were then distributed to Negro voters where possible. Republican leaders who discovered the ruse watched closely, but some of the spurious ballots were cast in Jackson and Columbia counties.[37]

Both sides were equally confident of victory as soon as the election was over, although it would be days before all the returns were in. Most of the heavily populated northern counties were served by telegraph or railroads and their returns were soon available. By various combinations of actual returns and guesses based on past elections, the parties were soon demonstrating how their majorities would be compiled. Only a few persons doubted that their party had won. Republican Senator Conover thought the Democrats had a majority, but he changed his statement within a few days. Four days after the election, Democrat James D. Westcott wrote that he believed Hayes had a small majority because Solon Robinson and his east Florida followers had voted the Republican national ticket and the Democratic state one. Three days later Westcott also changed his mind.[38] The changes came as both sides realized that the national election depended on Florida's electoral votes.

19

One Might Decide the Other Way with Perfect Fairness

The national campaign of 1876 was waged by the two major parties on similar platforms. Issues before the nation included the economic depression, the Grant administration scandals and the correlative need for civil service reform, national financial policy, and the problem of continued federal intervention in the southern states. With both Republican Rutherford B. Hayes and Democrat Samuel J. Tilden running as reform candidates and neither party anxious to raise questions of monetary policy because of internal disagreements, the campaign became bitter and emotional, centering on "Grantism" and the "bloody shirt" argument about whether the Democrats could be trusted to rule the country. Racial strife in South Carolina late in the campaign focused attention on the "Southern question" which Hayes promised to resolve peacefully. When the South Carolina governor asked for assistance, President Grant sent troops to preserve order and supervise the election. Most observers expected the 1876 election to be closer than any since the Civil War, and several noted the need for acceptable methods of resolving contested elections. Hayes commented in early October that legislation was needed in advance to decide cases involving disputed electoral votes.[1] The *New York Times* remarked prophetically that a disputed election would be a misfortune because there was no method of deciding between two electoral certificates received from a state. If there were objections raised about counting the votes, the *Times* predicted, "there will immediately arise pretensions, based on plausibility which no human tribunal could decide, and if disposed of at all would require an incredible degree of forbearance on both sides."[2]

On election night many Republicans retired believing Hayes had lost the election. All the leading newspapers, except the *New York Times*, declared Tilden and Hendricks elected. The *Times* reported that Tilden had 184 electoral votes and Hayes 181, with only Florida remaining in doubt. If it went Republican as expected, Hayes would win with a majority of one. On November 9, the *Times* exulted "The Battle Won! . . . Florida is Republican."[3] Other Republican papers quickly followed the *Times* and the lines were drawn for the four-month period of uncertainty and anxiety over the disputed election.

At Republican national headquarters on election night it was noted that the outcome of elections in Louisiana, South Carolina, and Florida were undecided and that they could make the difference between victory and defeat for Hayes. Telegrams were sent to their governors telling them to be on guard against the Democrats because their electoral votes were essential to a national victory. It is immaterial whether the idea was indigenous to Republican headquarters, suggested by John C. Reid of the *New York Times*, or stimulated by the remarkable General Daniel E. Sickles, as has recently been suggested.[4] That the undertaking was a "conspiracy" to alter the popular will was a Democratic allegation resulting from Hayes' ultimate victory despite the Democrats' best efforts and Tilden's popular majority of about 250,000 votes. The authors of the telegrams were Republican partisans anxious to win the election. Their messages and the *Times* editorials following the election helped stiffen Republican resistance to Democratic claims. But whatever influence they may have had on the electoral count in Louisiana and South Carolina, it is unlikely that Florida's election would have been conceded by either side until after the official count. The election was too close for anyone to admit defeat on the basis of unofficial returns.

William E. Chandler, the astute national party secretary, left New York on November 8 for a first hand examination of affairs in the three southern states. By the time he reached Florida on November 12, both national parties had realized that only a few votes would decide the contest there. Leading politicians and several national newspapers believed that the presidential contest depended on its outcome.[5] Chandler agreed and decided to remain in Tallahassee and direct Republican strategy.

While the national parties were taking stock and formulating plans, Florida politicians were trying to establish and protect their victory claims. Returns from the larger northern counties were soon available, but those from west Florida came in slowly and, as one northern visitor complained, "Quebec was nearer in time than some of the southern counties."[6] To prevent alteration of county returns by partisan officials, both sides sent couriers to every county seat to obtain certified copies of the returns for later comparison with the official certificates. A train carrying Republican couriers to west Florida was wrecked on November 8. While some blamed the accident on the railroad's poor condition and a Democratic newspaper said "providence" had torn up the rails, Governor Stearns claimed the train was "ku-kluxed."[7] He immediately called for additional troops to preserve order until the votes were counted.

General Thomas H. Ruger was ordered to Tallahassee where he was to communicate with Governor Stearns. By November 11, twelve companies of federal troops, including an artillery unit, were on their way to the Florida capital. They were in addition to those already stationed at other communities before the election. Since there was no disorder after they arrived, the new units camped near Tallahassee and the soldiers hunted and fished while the election dispute raged.[8] After November 20, some of them were ordered to Alachua and Jackson counties to help gather information about the election contests.

As tension increased throughout the nation over the undecided election, responsible men of both parties became concerned over a decision which all sides would willingly accept. Prominent Republicans and Democrats, popularly referred to as "visiting statesmen," went to Tallahassee. In addition to Chandler, important Republican visitors included Francis C. Barlow of New York, General Lew Wallace of Indiana, John A. Kasson of Iowa, and ex-Governor Edward F. Noyes of Ohio. Among the Democrats were Manton Marble, former owner of the *New York World*, G. W. Biddle, D. W. Sellers, John F. Coyle of Pennsylvania, and ex-Governor Joseph E. Brown of Georgia. They were ostensibly sent to observe proceedings and see that the Florida count was fair, but they became intimately involved in the contest. Each considered himself a legal counsellor for his own party. They gathered testimony to support their parties' claims and then argued before the state canvassing board. Members of both parties crowded into the City Hotel which was soon overflowing. During the electoral count the hotel lobby and dining room were filled with animated discussions and hurriedly whispered conferences. Every incoming train brought other visitors representing neutral civic clubs interested in an unfettered decision.

The state canvassing board was required to meet and count the votes thirty-five days after the election, or sooner if all the county returns had been received. The board had power to "determine and declare who shall have been elected" and to exclude returns which were "irregular, false, or fraudulent."[9] According to precedent and Democratic Attorney General William Archer Cocke's opinion, the board had quasi-judicial power to examine evidence and exclude returns. Chandler looked into the situation and decided the Republicans could prove they had won the election if they had the personnel to gather evidence. He assigned the "visiting statesmen" as well as government officials specific areas where disputes had developed and instructed them to obtain information to support the party case. Florida Republicans willingly accepted Chandler's leadership and worked harmoniously with the visitors. Chandler regarded party representatives and government officials alike as partisan agents. They were not instructed to report Republican malfeasance.[10]

There were persistent rumors that Republican county officials had altered the Archer precinct returns in Alachua County by adding 219 fraudulent Republican votes.[11] Democrats were expected to show evidence to discredit the precinct's return. Francis Barlow of New York was sent to investigate and defend the Republican case at Archer precinct. He was a former Union general, and, as New York attorney general, had assisted Samuel J. Tilden in sending "Boss" William M. Tweed to jail.[12] President Grant had personally requested him to go to Florida and see that the election was free of collusion. Barlow, to the chagrin of his colleagues, interpreted the president's request literally. He soon concluded that the Democrats had a better claim in Alachua County. He confided this discovery to Chandler who hastily removed Barlow from the case and replaced him with Edward F. Noyes of Ohio. Noyes used federal troops to help obtain affidavits from hundreds of Negroes purporting to have voted at Archer.[13] Lew Wallace used troops for the same purpose in Jackson County.

Chandler was afraid that Democrats in the late-reporting counties would return fraudulent counts after it was too late to refute them. To avert this he dispatched W. J. Webster and Samuel Hamblen to check on Manatee and other distant counties. Arriving at Sumterville, Polk County, the two were stopped by armed men and told they could proceed no farther without a pass from the Democratic executive committee. The spokesman said the Democrats had a good majority in the area and would not tolerate anyone tampering with it. The two men were offered safe conduct if they were willing to follow a guide and stop only where he suggested. Unaccustomed to such frontier hospitality, the two returned to Tallahassee. On November 18, Chandler gloomily reported to Hayes that the Republicans would probably lose Florida by about 150 votes. He believed there were many Democratic frauds which could be successfully attacked, but he had neither time nor capable personnel to do it. In short, everything in Florida seemed to be against the Republicans except two-thirds of the state canvassing board's members.[14]

The Republican *New York Tribune* remarked that both parties had been claiming a Florida victory by as much as 2,000 votes when the result would ultimately be decided by fewer than 200. It agreed that the Democrats had a slightly better chance of winning. Most estimates of the election results showed Hayes running slightly ahead of Stearns in nearly every county with the greatest differences occuring in east Florida where Republicans dissatisfied with the Stearns administration had voted split tickets. Even if the Republican presidential electors won, there was a chance that the state ticket would still lose to Drew and Hull.[15]

Henry Grady, describing the Tallahassee situation for the *New York Herald,* wrote, "it is all a whisper and a wink. There is nothing frank or easy. The truth of the matter is both parties are at sea. Neither knows exactly what to do, and yet is bewildered by the fear that the other will do it first."[16] Lew Wallace of Indiana confessed that "money and intimidation can obtain the oath of white and black to any required statement. A ton of affidavits could be carted in . . . and not a word of truth in them, except the names of the parties. . . . If we win our methods are subject to impeachment for possible fraud."[17]

Joe Brown of Georgia was the first Democratic visitor to arrive. He came at the request of the Democratic national chairman to direct Florida strategy. Other visitors joined him and, together with local partisans, concentrated their efforts on proving Republican irregularities in Alachua, Jefferson, Leon, and Manatee counties and on defending themselves against charges of fraud in Jackson, Hamilton, and Monroe.

An important concern of the Democrats was possible chicanery at the capital by Republican officials. Both the secretary of state and governor received official copies of the county returns, but they adamantly refused to release any figures from the thirty-two counties which had reported. The two officials explained that the remaining unreported counties were all Democratic strongholds and if figures were released, the opposition would know how much to alter the returns to win. On the other hand, the Democrats were afraid that the Republicans had already altered the official returns and planned to wait until the last moment to publish them so there would be no opportunity to prove malfeasance. The electoral college was required to meet on December 6, twenty-nine days after the election, yet Florida law permitted the canvassing board to wait thirty-five days before convening to count the votes. Although the state Democrats wanted to await the board's action and seek redress in the courts if necessary, they deferred to their visiting colleagues' desire to force an early count so their case could be argued.

On November 17 the Democrats asked the board to begin the count to allow time for presentation of evidence. The board voted two to one against the request. The Democrats then applied to Circuit Judge Pleasant W. White for a mandamus ordering the canvassing board to convene immediately. When the judge arrived on November 23, both sides were prepared to argue before him and were ready for immediate appeal to the supreme court as soon as he decided. Governor Stearns had already asked the justices to assemble. While White was considering the case, Secretary of State Samuel B. McLin announced that the board would convene on Monday, November 27.[18]

The two Republicans and one Democrat who comprised the canvassing board had all been involved in the political struggles of the past few years and had political enemies, but they were generally regarded as men of ability and integrity by both sides. McLin, the Republican secretary of state and chairman of the board, was from Tennessee, had belonged to the Georgia bar, and had lived in Florida about twenty-two years. He had served briefly in the Confederate army before being medically discharged.[19] McLin was appointed to office by Ossian B. Hart in 1873 and had edited the *Tallahassee Sentinel* until a few days before the board convened.

Clayton A. Cowgill, the Republican comptroller, was also a Hart appointee. A doctor and former Whig from Delaware, he served in the Union army as a surgeon. In 1867 he moved to Putnam County where he cultivated oranges and held local offices until 1873. Although a pronounced Republican, Cowgill tried to be impartial as a board member. Considering himself a balance between the Democratic member and McLin, he was subjected to extreme pressures and wavered from side to side during the count. Democrats offered to continue him in Drew's cabinet if he voted for them, but Cowgill was probably more influenced by Francis Barlow's views than the Democratic promise. Cowgill admired the former New York attorney general and, when Barlow announced that he could not support the Republican case, the comptroller was profoundly impressed. The sudden decision to convene the board on November 27 was due to Cowgill's belief that the Democrats should be heard.[20]

The third member of the board, William Archer Cocke, was the Democratic attorney general and an accomplished constitutional historian. Cocke was a Virginian who came to Florida in 1863. A former Whig who became a Democrat before the war, he was appointed a circuit judge by Harrison Reed, supported Grant in 1872, and was appointed to Hart's cabinet in 1873. He had broken openly with Stearns but refused to resign the office.[21]

Convening at noon on November 27, the board had nine calendar days in which to determine the election results so the presidential electors could cast their votes on December 6. Its members assumed that their powers were quasi-judicial rather than merely ministerial, and drew up rules to govern its proceedings. Realizing the delicate situation created by the doubtful election and the "visiting statesmen" present in Tallahassee, the board permitted ten representatives of each party to attend the proceedings. The small secretary of state's office was further crowded by the presence of Governor Stearns, George F. Drew, and General John M. Brannan, who had replaced Ruger as troop commander.

Dealing solely with the presidential electors before taking up the state election, the board ruled that the secretary of state would open the returns in alphabetical order, the three members would determine immediately from their face whether they met the legal requirements, and the votes would be announced and recorded, subject to final review. As each county return was announced, anyone desiring to contest it was required to give notice. Statements were to be filed in writing as soon as possible, furnishing details and the relief requested. The board had no authority to compel witnesses, and affidavits were acceptable as evidence.

If either side wished to present oral testimony, it would first have to present a written statement naming the witnesses and the facts to be introduced. The board reserved discretion to accept or reject testimony on an individual basis. All documentary evidence was to be made available to both parties. Oral argument was ostensibly not permitted, but this rule was wholly disregarded during the first few sessions. Decisions were to be based on majority votes. The board further reserved the right to alter its rules if deemed necessary to complete the count on time.

On Tuesday morning the first returns were opened. Only Dade County was still unreported. All thirty-eight counties were contested as they were announced.[22] Samuel Pasco protested Baker County and the larger counties with Republican majorities, while Malachi Martin questioned the remaining twenty-eight. Baker was the only county whose returns surprised either party.

When McLin announced the Baker vote as 130 Republican and 89 Democratic, Pasco leaped to his feet shouting, but permitted the figures to be recorded as read subject to subsequent argument. This was a tactical error, since the Democrats suspected that McLin had conflicting Baker County returns in his possession. The initial count was completed showing 24,337 for Hayes and 24,294 for Tilden, a Republican majority of forty-three. The news was quickly circulated through the country, enhancing the Republican claim to Florida's votes.[23]

There were three Baker County returns in McLin's hands. None was completely in accord with the law, which required the return to be signed by the county judge, county clerk, and a justice of the peace chosen by them. Until three days after the election there was only one justice of the peace in Baker County. One return was dated November 10, and signed by the county clerk and justice of the peace. It included all four Baker County precincts with a total of 238 Democratic and 143 Republican votes. Another was identical to it except it was dated November 13. The third return was also dated November 13 and signed by the county judge, the sheriff, and another justice of the peace who had been appointed on November 10, three days after the election. It showed only two precincts with 130 Republican and 89 Democratic votes. Without authority to do so, the improperly constituted county board had thrown out two precincts; one because its members had *heard* that a qualified voter was prevented from voting, and the other because they *heard rumors* that seven illegal votes had been cast.[24]

The Democrats conferred at dinner about Baker County and in the evening Pasco asked if McLin had other returns from there. After a hostile exchange between them and dilatory comments from Chandler, McLin admitted he had them. When he read them, a long argument followed, but the Republicans finally agreed to count the Baker County returns according to the Democratic version. The change gave the Democrats a ninety-four majority on the initial count. Unfortunately for them, the Republican version had already been published across the nation.[25] For this significant tactical victory the national Republicans were deeply indebted to the state officials. Governor Stearns had appointed the pliable justice of the peace and McLin had suppressed the Democratic returns.

More than two days were spent on the Alachua County case. The returns from Archer ballot box number two showed 399 Republican and 136 Democratic votes. The Democrats alleged that Republicans had added 219 votes to their total and a like number of names to the registration lists. They presented testimony supporting the charge. W. H. Belton, the justice of the peace who acted as a county canvasser, refused to accept the Archer precinct return at first, but was later induced to sign the county returns which included it.[26] The Republicans answered with 317 affidavits from persons claiming to have voted at Archer precinct. But Green Moore and Floyd Dukes, two Archer poll inspectors, signed affidavits declaring the correct return to be 180 Republican and 136 Democratic votes. Later they signed others saying the first ones were erroneous. In oral testimony they both admitted accepting bribes to sign the second affidavits. Neither could remember whether the returns they originally signed were blank, but L. G. Dennis subsequently testified that they were.[27] The majority of the board, with Judge Cocke dissenting, decided there was insufficient proof to reject the return and counted Alachua County's returns as received, except for seventeen votes deleted because they had been cast by transient train passengers at Waldo.

By Friday it was clear that this procedure would extend the count far beyond the December 6 meeting of the electoral college. The board announced that its prohibition of oral argument would be enforced and both parties were to have their papers filed by Saturday, December 2. On that day the board heard remaining charges and accepted the last written information. Each party was allowed one hour on Monday for a final oral argument. The Dade County return arrived on Saturday and laughter broke the tension when McLin announced its nine Republican and five Democratic votes.

On Monday closing arguments were delivered by Edward F. Noyes for the Republicans and G. W. Biddle for the Democrats. Biddle enumerated returns which should be excluded if the board insisted on throwing out votes. His figures would have given Tilden a 1,700 majority. Despite original Democratic insistence on the board's quasi-judicial powers, Biddle said the agency's function was purely ministerial and it should simply count the returns as received, also giving Tilden a slight majority.[28]

While the board was in session both parties were accused of attempting bribes. No agreement was reached, but subsequent evidence indicated that prominent Democratic visitors tried to make an arrangement with McLin, failing only because the board decided before the transaction was completed. Manton Marble exchanged telegrams with William T. Pelton, Tilden's nephew, concerning a favorable vote for $200,000. About the same time, C. W. Woolley, a Pennsylvania Democrat in Tallahassee, wired that he could obtain the vote for $50,000. During the ensuing bargain hunt, the New York collaborators heard that Florida had gone for Tilden without a bribe and cancelled the negotiations. When they realized the mistake, it was too late. Pelton eventually admitted his role in the affair, but Marble denied any knowledge of it.[29]

During the same period the Republicans reviewed their situation. Chandler and some of his northern colleagues, primarily concerned with the presidency, thought enough returns could be thrown out on legitimate, or at least defensible, grounds to give Hayes and Wheeler a small majority. But to go beyond that and count in the Republican gubernatorial ticket, which ran several hundred votes behind the presidential electors, would necessitate procedures so doubtful that the courts might intervene and overturn the entire Republican victory. Some of the Democrats thought the Republicans would allow a Democratic victory as a concession for the presidential count, but more practical men reminded them of the interdependence of the state and national elections for the Republican party and predicted that Stearns and Montgomery would be counted in if Hayes and Wheeler received a majority. Indeed, when Chandler told him that the state ticket could not be elected, Governor Stearns replied that the loss of the governorship would destroy the Florida Republican party, which would be poor recompense for having delivered the state's electoral votes to Hayes. He left a clear impression that canvassing board members would lose interest in a victory which they did not share.[30] But when they tried to throw out enough votes to elect the Republican state ticket, the board members acted so unfairly that they invited court action against their decision.

Francis Barlow's activities troubled the Republican managers. After his refusal to defend the Alachua case, he was excluded from strategy conferences, but he further dismayed his fellow Republicans by freely discussing his views with Democrats. William M. Ampt, a Republican visitor from Ohio, compared Barlow's actions to "a lawyer confessing he had no case in the presence of the jury." Barlow's remarks about the election were widely circulated and damaged his party's case, but of more immediate significance was their influence on undecided Clayton Cowgill. After Henry Grady reminded Barlow of President Grant's admonition that he see to an impartial count, the New Yorker spoke to Cowgill, who admitted that he could not conscientiously vote for the Hayes electors. During their conversation, Governor Stearns joined them and Barlow explained their discussion to him. Aghast at what he heard, Stearns hurried Cowgill away. The two men never met again, but Cowgill later wrote Barlow a detailed explanation of his ultimate decision for Hayes. General Barlow also explained to President Grant his personal conviction that the Archer precinct vote should have been reduced by 219, but he added that "one might decide the other way with perfect fairness."[31]

With time running out the board limited its jurisdiction and narrowed the scope of its investigation by refusing to consider questions of intimidation (such as the Florida Railroad Company's use of numbered ballots to force its employees to vote as it demanded). The decision was practical because of time limitations and the inconclusive nature of the evidence, but it caused the board's decision to depend on procedural irregularities while substantive physical and economic intimidation was ignored. Overwhelmed by the huge mass of ex parte testimony presented, the board selected the counties which it intended to examine closely. Every county return had been contested by one of the parties, but twenty-six were canvassed as received without scrutiny. Five others were dispensed with after minor alterations, which added seventeen Democratic and six Republican votes to the initial totals.[32]

The six remaining counties, with Baker and Alachua, were most seriously disputed and received the closest examination. Jefferson County, with about three Negroes for each white voter, returned 2,660 Republican and 737 Democratic votes. Democrats charged that there were more votes than registered voters, juveniles had voted, and the county board was improperly constituted. The Republicans responded that the registration lists were wrong, that a few juveniles had voted but not as many as alleged, and that the improper board membership was immaterial. With Judge Cocke dissenting, the state canvassers deleted one Democratic and sixty

Republican votes cast by juveniles and accepted the remainder of the Jefferson County return. The Democrats protested Duval County because the return was improperly prepared, but McLin and Cowgill said the discrepancy was insignificant and counted the return as received. The case was similar to Baker County which had been decided for the Democrats, but Judge Cocke inconsistently dissented from the decision. The Republicans contested the Manatee returns which gave the Democrats 262 to 26 for their opponents. Chandler's argument was based on the irregular way the election had been conducted. The Democrats reminded him that it had been Republican officials who caused the difficulty, but the New Hampshire senator asked why his couriers had been stopped by armed guards on their way to Manatee if the Democrats had nothing to hide. The two Republicans voted to exclude the Manatee County return.[33]

Two Hamilton County precincts were questioned by the Republicans. White Springs had given the Democrats a majority of 83 to 58. The state board's Republican majority excluded it on a technicality no more serious than others they ignored. Jasper had returned a 323 to 185 Democratic majority. It was thrown out because the inspectors, who were Republicans, had not complied with the election laws. Campbellton and Friendship Church precincts in Jackson County had given the Democrats majorities of 291 to 77 and 145 to 44 respectively. The Republicans alleged procedural discrepancies and the board voted two to one to exclude both returns.[34] The Jackson County case was identical to that of the Archer precinct in Alachua except the parties' positions were reversed. If the rules had been equally applied, both counties would have been counted or the faulty precincts deleted in both cases. Barlow thought they should have been handled the same way and Cowgill at one time agreed with him. Cowgill ultimately joined McLin to decide both cases for their party's benefit.

Late Tuesday night, December 5, the board took up the last contested return. Monroe County's Key West precinct number three showed 401 Democratic and 59 Republican votes. The Republicans protested it because of technicalities similar to those in Jackson and Alachua counties, and a majority of the board excluded the return. Cocke first voted with the majority, but after conferring outside the room with his Democratic colleagues, he returned and told the clerk to record him as dissenting from the decision. On the following day, Cowgill also wanted to change his Monroe County vote. Governor Stearns' secretary wrote that Cowgill was "frigid with a fit of conscience or Barlow" after the electoral vote decision was announced, and was threatening to go before the world and make a fool of himself. A postscript was appended, saying that Cowgill was once more under "contract."[35]

A crowd gathered around the capitol on Tuesday evening as excitement over the impending decision mounted. A small detachment of troops moved in nearby and camped for the night. The crowd was still waiting after one o'clock in the morning when the announcement was made that Hayes and Wheeler had won by a 924 vote majority. Reporters hurried to the telegraph office only to find the wires had been cut between Tallahassee and Monticello. Several of them set out immediately for the neighboring community. By afternoon of December 6, news was spreading that Florida's electoral vote had gone to Hayes.

The final count showed 23,843 votes for the lowest Hayes elector to 22,919 for the highest Democratic one.[36] The original count from the face of the returns had given the Hayes electors 24,337 to 24,294 for Tilden. This 43 majority for Hayes was achieved by counting the fraudulent Baker County certificate, which was thrown out in favor of another from that county giving Tilden an initial majority of 94. The Republican majority of the state canvassing board threw out more than 1,800 votes to find the 924 Republican majority.

On December 6, the Republican electors met and cast their votes for Rutherford B. Hayes and William A. Wheeler. While they were assembled, attorneys for Tilden and Hendricks applied to the circuit court for a writ of quo warranto requiring the Hayes electors to show cause why they should not be replaced by their Democratic opponents. The Republican sheriff served the writ with a smile and the electors received it with laughter.[37] There was ample precedent for judicial intervention in Florida elections, but the electors felt they could depend on the federal courts even if the state supreme court accepted a case against the canvassing board. They completed their certificate and dispatched it to the president of the United States Senate. Attorney General Cocke issued a certificate of election to the Democratic electors who met on the same day, cast their votes for Tilden and Hendricks, and sent their certificates to Washington.

These duplicate returns, with similar ones from Louisiana and South Carolina, created a congressional stalemate. While congressional leaders were trying to reach an acceptable compromise, the Florida canvassing board began counting the votes for state officials. The court battle which was fought in Florida over the gubernatorial election was closely watched by national politicians who realized that the court's decision would reflect on the presidential election.

The Republican canvassing board members were severely criticized after the election. When they decided to examine evidence and rule on the validity of returns, they inevitably invited the wrath of the losing side. They had tried to make judicial decisions on evidence which was inconclusive at best. In fairness to the board members, it should be recognized that much of the information concerning the election which later became public was not available on December 5, 1876. Both houses of Congress investigated and compiled volumes of testimony. The 1878 Potter Committee obtained more testimony and confessions from prominent figures in the affair. The "visiting statesmen" not only acted as legal counsel for their respective parties, but also exerted pressure on the board members. But even with due consideration of their difficult positions, McLin's and Cowgill's actions are still questionable. They had the discretion to choose the method of testing the returns, but they were obligated to apply it equally. If the burden of proof had rested with the side attacking the returns, they should have counted Manatee County, the two Jackson County precincts, both Hamilton County precincts, Key West precinct number three, and the Archer precinct in Alachua County. If the burden had rested with the defenders of the returns, they should have rejected the returns of the Archer precinct, Campbellton and Friendship Church in Jackson, White Springs and Jasper in Hamilton, the Key West precinct in Monroe, all of Manatee, most of Jefferson, and Richardson's Schoolhouse in Leon.[38] Either method would have given the Democrats a majority. The Republican majority of the state canvassing board arbitrarily changed enough returns to show a victory for the Republican state ticket as well as the Hayes electors.

Cowgill had been uncertain all along and continued to threaten the Republican case until Hayes was inaugurated. McLin testified in 1878 that he had given the Republican party the benefit of every doubt, seeing his duties not as that of an impartial judge but a Republican partisan.[39] His belated "confession" was little more reliable than his 1876 decision, because he was then angry at having been denied a suitable federal appointment by the Hayes administration. Cocke's actions were scarcely more commendable, since he had become increasingly partisan as he saw the Democratic majority steadily dwindling. He finally endorsed the opinion that the board was a ministerial agency without power to rule on returns despite his earlier written opinions to the contrary.[40]

With the county returns showing a majority of fewer than 100 votes for either party, it was to be expected that reasonable men might disagree on the final result. It could also be anticipated that the loser would seek redress in the courts, but it is doubtful that the supreme court would have entertained the case had the canvassing board acted more judiciously. Chandler was probably correct when he argued that the board could have excluded enough votes to achieve a Hayes victory without inviting court action. The presidential election was so close that there was little the Democrats could have done about such a decision. They had been fortunate that the canvassing board decided not to consider questions of economic intimidation. But the Republican dilemma was that the political lives of the state officials who had made the Hayes victory possible depended upon a state victory as well. Since the state ticket had run well behind Hayes, a bare majority for Stearns and Montgomery necessitated an overall Republican majority of several hundred votes. When the Republicans tried to throw out enough votes to accomplish this, they applied methods so unacceptable that the entire Republican case was jeopardized. The ensuing court battles in Florida kept the presidential election in doubt for several more weeks.

20

The Matter before the Supreme Court

The duplicate electoral certificates from Florida, Louisiana, and South Carolina created a grave problem for the United States Congress. The Constitution provided that presidential electors, chosen by the states, were to cast their votes and certify the results to the president of the senate and he "shall in the presence of the Senate and House of Representatives, open all the certificates, and the Votes shall then be counted." It did not specify who was to count them. Since 1789 the two houses had usually agreed in advance on rules governing the count. There had been disputes before, but never had the outcome of the election depended on the questioned votes. Since 1865 the Congress had acted according to a joint rule that both houses must approve an electoral vote before it was accepted. But the rule had not been adopted by the Forty-fourth Congress which was sitting in 1876.

Since the Senate had a Republican majority, the Hayes forces argued that the Constitution clearly charged the president of the Senate with responsibility for counting the votes. This meant that Michigan Senator Thomas W. Ferry, a staunch Republican, would be able to decide which of the conflicting certificates he should count. But the Democrats controlled the House of Representatives and they insisted that, since no candidate had a clear majority, the lower house should decide the question according to the Constitution. With national business leaders demanding a solution of the stalemate and some Democratic governors threatening to use militia forces to seat Tilden, a joint congressional committee began working on a compromise measure. Not until late January did Congress finally enact the electoral commission bill which established a carefully constructed fifteen-member body to rule on the disputed electoral certificates.

In the interim, litigation in the Florida courts continually threatened the Republican claim to Florida's electoral votes. Although the courts were considering only the gubernatorial election, the Republican presidential victory had been achieved by the same methods which the Democrats were attacking. As a result, national political leaders watched the proceedings in Tallahassee closely for several weeks after the electoral college met on December 6.

When the canvassing board decided against the Tilden electors, most of the northern Democrats left Tallahassee, believing that Florida was lost and the case closed.[1] They had little confidence in the quo warranto proceeding against the Republican electors or the Democratic electoral certificate improperly signed by Attorney General Cocke, which had been suggested by ex-Senator David L. Yulee and Charles Gibson of Missouri. When the northern Democratic managers left, Robert B. Hilton and George P. Raney assumed the initiative on behalf of gubernatorial candidate George F. Drew. They obtained an injunction from Circuit Judge Pleasant W. White forbidding the canvassing board to count the returns except by merely totalling the votes shown on the county returns with no alterations, a procedure which would have resulted in a majority for Drew and Hull.[2] Tilden was advised of the action and its potential benefit to the Democratic presidential case, but neither he nor any of his associates showed any interest.

The Republican majority on the canvassing board ignored the injunction and on December 8 announced a majority for the Stearns and Montgomery ticket. Attorney General Cocke dissented from the decision and wrote a lengthy indictment of the entire board proceeding. Judge White cited the board for contempt and ordered a hearing for December 11. The case was postponed at the request of the Democratic lawyers.[3] The Republicans were not seriously concerned about an adverse court decision. They knew Judge White was a pronounced Democratic partisan who would give every benefit of the doubt to his side, but they served notice that any circuit court decision would be appealed to the state supreme court which was composed of two Republicans and one Democrat. All three had agreed to hold a special session on December 12 because an early resolution of the problem was important to the state and nation.[4] Chief Justice Edward M. Randall was a Republican, originally from Wisconsin, appointed by Harrison Reed in 1868. In 1876 Randall was a candidate to replace Philip Fraser, recently deceased federal judge for north Florida. Randall and Governor Stearns were personal and political enemies. Associate Justice R. B. Van Valkenberg was a New Yorker who had moved to Florida after the Civil War, participated prominently in the 1872 Liberal Republican movement, and been appointed to the court by Governor Hart. James D. Westcott, Jr., was the Democratic member. He had been appointed by Reed in 1868 after a brief term as attorney general. He had received significant Republican support for the United States Senate in 1873 and entertained hopes of filling the vacant north Florida federal judgeship.[5]

At Judge White's suggestion, Hilton, Raney, and R. L. Campbell of Pensacola, who had joined them on the case, agreed to drop the contempt case and apply to the supreme court for a writ of mandamus ordering Cowgill and McLin to perform a ministerial count.[6] Believing their chances before the court favorable, the Republican board members agreed to abide by the court's decision. The *New York Times* expressed relief that "the matter will be brought before the Supreme Court tomorrow and its decision will be respected, for it is beyond suspicion of partisan action."[7] But the paper also emphasized that the litigation pertained only to state officials and its results would not affect the presidential election.

William E. Chandler urged Governor Stearns to fight boldly in Florida because northern public opinion strongly favored the Republicans. General Lew Wallace returned to Tallahassee on December 17 to assist J. P. C. Emmons on the case. The national party also sent funds to replenish the depleted coffers of the state Republican party. Neither Tilden nor any other national Democrats showed concern for the Florida proceedings until the local party won its case. Late in December Manton Marble cautioned Tilden not to be "zealous for appeal in the Supreme Court of Florida."[8]

When Congress met in December both houses sent investigating committees to Florida and the other contested states. The Democrats desired information to strengthen their case when Congress counted the electoral votes and the Republicans were equally anxious to defend their position. The majority of each house dominated its committee and both submitted majority and minority reports depending on partisan interpretations of their work. Both committees were travelling through Florida taking sensational testimony while the court case was being argued. The publicity given the committees, together with the judicial proceedings, increased suspense and tension during December and January.

The writ of mandamus was issued by unanimous decision on December 14. Drew, claiming 24,613 votes to 24,116 for Stearns, argued that the board had usurped judicial functions and powers by going behind the county returns and accepting evidence. He said it had erred in rejecting the Manatee County return and in refusing to canvass Jackson, Monroe, and Hamilton counties according to the face of the returns. On December 16, McLin and Cowgill responded that the Manatee return was so irregular that it was impossible to determine the true vote. In Jackson, Hamilton, and Monroe, evidence had proved the returns false and fraudulent. Cocke filed a separate answer that he had voted to count the returns in question. The court refused to accept the McLin-Cowgill answer because it was "argumentive and evasive." The two were ordered to amend their answer and include specific grounds for their actions by noon of December 18.[9]

The Republican board members refused to answer, claiming the court had no jurisdiction since the board had completed its duties and ceased to exist. The Democratic attorneys argued that the board had not ceased to exist because its functions had not been performed properly. On December 22, McLin and Cowgill agreed to file an amended answer, but declined again on the following day. The court issued a peremptory writ directing them to count the votes as shown on the county returns and declare the results by December 27.[10]

The unanimous decision of the supreme court surprised the Democrats and alarmed Republicans. Uncertain as to Van Valkenberg's position, the Democrats had expected Randall to favor the Republicans. The *New York Times,* which had praised the Florida court for impartiality a few days earlier, termed the decision a "judicial crime."[11] Senator A. A. Sargent, a Republican member of the senate investigating committee in Florida, was not surprised at the decision because he had observed "rivalries and jealousies here that have too much influence even on judicial minds. . . . The state is gone and forever." Governor Stearns wrote, "This beats us in the state but we shall try to save Hayes. The opinion is a surprise to everyone here." McLin, who was also an aspirant for the federal judgeship, wrote, "Randall was only glad of an opportunity to sacrifice Stearns. The traitor would have destroyed the electoral vote if necessary to make his spite on Stearns and one or two others."[12]

Senator Sargent advised northern Republicans that the principle of the court's decision left enough discretion for the board to save the electoral votes, but that the situation would have to be watched closely. Local Republicans had lost interest after having lost their election. Worried about the quo warranto pending before Judge White against the Hayes electors, Sargent suggested providing a competent lawyer with adequate funds to try the case if it came up, because "a judgment against our electors during the next month might ruin the nation."[13]

McLin and Cowgill first decided to resist the court's order and apply to the United States court for relief if state authorities arrested them. The Democrats had been careful to avoid any reference to the presidential electors which might bring the federal courts into the affair. But McLin and Cowgill were cognizant of a similar controversy in South Carolina in late November. Federal Judge Hugh L. Bond ordered the release of South Carolina canvassing board members who had been arrested for disobeying a state court order. Bond reasoned that a federal issue was involved because part of the board's duty was to count the votes for federal officers according to a congressional law, and they had been arrested for acts committed in performing that duty.[14]

Governor Stearns announced that the court decision settled the state election and advised the board to comply with it. Cowgill agreed with Stearns and the matter seemed to be ended without anyone going to jail. McLin notified Cocke and Cowgill to meet with him on December 27 and carry out the court order. Meanwhile, Secretary Chandler and Senators Oliver P. Morton of Indiana and John Sherman of Ohio had considered the Florida court activities in light of national public opinion. They decided that even though the court was not dealing with presidential electors, the state and national Republican majorities both depended on the canvassing board's power to exclude returns. An adverse decision on the state Republican candidates would reflect on the national election. Chandler wrote Lew Wallace that the country would stand for a total disregard of the court order, but if the board once admitted that the court could direct its actions there was nothing to prevent a similar decision pertaining to the presidential election.[15]

On December 26, Chandler and his colleagues asked Lew Wallace and Governor Stearns to ignore the Florida supreme court's order. It is not clear whether Stearns acquiesced in this tactic, but McLin notified the canvassing board members not to meet according to his earlier notice because he and Cowgill were filing a motion to set aside the mandamus. George H. Williams, former attorney general in the Grant cabinet, arrived in Tallahassee on December 28 to assist in legal matters and to assure Florida Republicans of administration support. Senator Sherman telegraphed Judge William B. Woods at Montgomery, Alabama, that a federal judge was needed in Tallahassee to secure justice. At the senator's request Woods agreed to go there because the north Florida judgeship was still vacant.[16]

Attorney General Cocke disregarded McLin's notice cancelling the board meeting, appeared at the appointed time, and counted the votes alone to show a 497 majority for Drew and a 94 majority for the Tilden electors.[17] The two Republican members then decided to obey the court order under protest and gratuitously to include a recount of the electoral votes showing a Hayes majority according to the ministerial method prescribed by the court. At four o'clock, December 28, McLin and Cowgill answered the writ, protesting the court's jurisdiction over the adjourned board, but attached to it a certificate showing a majority for Drew and Hull. The vote was 24,179 to 23,984. It also showed a 208 majority for Hayes over Tilden. They had accomplished these results by counting the Republican version of the Baker County return, which the board had unanimously thrown out during the original count, and excluding the entire Clay County return, which had received scant consideration earlier, on the ground that it was irregular on its face.[18] Judge Cocke refused to join in the action pertaining to the presidential electors.

On January 1, 1877, Supreme Court Justice Westcott, speaking for a unanimous court, refused to accept the canvassing board's answer and directed strict compliance with the peremptory writ by five-thirty that same afternoon.[19] When the board corrected its answer, the court accepted it. This response to the court order elected Drew and Hull as governor and lieutenant governor. R. H. M. Davidson, Democratic candidate in the first congressional district, won over W. J. Purman, but Horatio Bisbee, Jr., the second district congressional candidate, defeated Democrat J. J. Finley. Finley contested and was later seated by the House of Representatives committee on privileges and elections. Both houses of the legislature had Democratic majorities. There was no reference to the presidential electors.[20]

All federal troops had been withdrawn from Tallahassee on December 9, except one infantry company which remained until January 18, 1877. General Thomas H. Ruger watched the Florida situation from his South Carolina headquarters, but instructed the company commander at Tallahassee not to interfere unless the civil authorities were unable to preserve order and then only on request from local officials.[21] Governor Stearns made no attempt to carry on a government in conflict with the new Democratic administration as had been rumored. Despite a large crowd of Negro and white citizens, Drew and Hull were inaugurated peacefully on January 2, 1877.[22] President Hayes' subsequent removal of troops from Louisiana and South Carolina in April, long regarded as part of the "compromise of 1877" and the "end of Reconstruction in the South," had nothing to do with Democratic accession to power in Florida. Some of the legends which still circulate in Tallahassee and elsewhere in Florida about the dramatic inauguration are embellishments of the actual event.

Drew's inauguration satisfied many members of both parties. Wilkinson Call, a Tilden elector, denounced some of his fellow Democrats as unwilling to work for Tilden's election once they had obtained the state offices.[23] This partially explained Democratic unwillingness to insist on a recount of the electoral votes under the court order. Hilton, Raney, Campbell, and probably Samuel Pasco were satisfied with the state victory regardless of the outcome of the presidential controversy. Jesse T. Bernard, a prominent Democratic merchant who had just replaced Samuel Walker as mayor of Tallahassee, wrote a Republican friend in Philadelphia that he was satisfied with Drew as governor and Hayes as president. The recipient commented on the speed with which Bernard and other southern Democrats were dropping Tilden in lieu of the governorship.[24] Governor Stearns' secretary wrote Senator Chandler, "I believe it possible to have this incoming State administration thoroughly in accord with the Hayes government."[25] The Republican *Jacksonville Florida Union* editorialized: "If we have got to have a Democratic State government, we rejoice that there is so little of the old Democracy in it."[26]

The election of Drew, who had been defeated initially by the same count which defeated Tilden, encouraged national Democrats but did nothing for their legal position. Some of them misunderstood and thought the court was ordering a recount of the entire election. R. B. Hilton cautioned Manton Marble, whose interest in the Florida case suddenly revived, that the mandamus related only to the state. The arguments which he and the Florida Democrats were pursuing for a ministerial count were contradictory to the position taken by northern Democratic counsel when Tilden's case was lost. Hilton explained that he had not insisted on correcting the board's final action because Judge Westcott advised him that nothing more could be done. He reminded Marble that the other two judges were Hayes supporters and inferred strongly that the indirect benefit for Tilden was much more than the northern lawyers had achieved. "I remind you," he concluded, "we are before an unfriendly court none of whom are men of the highest character. Our northern friends did not send *us* an ex-United States Attorney General to advise with."[27]

Wilkinson Call, Edward A. Perry of Pensacola, and Edward M. L'Engle of Jacksonville disagreed with Hilton, Raney, and Pasco. Believing the mandamus decision for Drew should be applied to the presidential case, they announced on January 2 that the matter would be taken to the supreme court.[28] But the suit was soon abandoned because the board members had gone out of office when Drew was inaugurated and everyone agreed that a court order carried out by the Democratic officials who replaced McLin and Cowgill would be of no value. After lengthy correspondence with Marble in New York, Call also abandoned plans for a quo warranto from the supreme court because that body refused to accept original jurisdiction at its forthcoming regular session beginning January 9. Call and those who agreed with him finally decided to proceed with the quo warranto in Judge White's court and concomitantly have the state legislature, a majority of which sympathized with Tilden, enact legislation providing for a new canvass of the presidential votes.[29]

While the Democrats worked through the legislature on the main floor of the capitol and in Judge White's court in the basement, the Republicans were still worried about the state supreme court justices and the vacant federal judge's office. McLin actively sought the office and was recommended by numerous Florida Republicans. The party was indebted to McLin whose political future had been ruined by the Democratic victory. The new administration was already preparing embezzlement charges against him for alleged acts committed as secretary of state. Judge Westcott proclaimed his satisfaction with the board's decision for the Democratic state ticket and Republican presidential electors, a position which retained for him Senator Conover's endorsement for the federal bench. Conover, opposed to Governor Stearns but favoring the national Republicans, was expected to have an influential voice in filling the vacancy. Chief Justice Randall, who also disliked Stearns, said he thought the presidential electors' vote was a matter beyond the court's jurisdiction.[30] As long as these men had hopes of receiving the appointment, they were not expected to interfere with the Republican electors. For this reason, Governor Stearns had advised Attorney General Alphonso Taft to hold the judicial appointment until the election excitement abated. In early January, Taft was again cautioned against filling the vacancy for a few weeks. Thomas Settle of North Carolina, to whom the party was obligated for recent election activities, was actually appointed in late December, but his name was quickly withdrawn.[31]

Lew Wallace, in Florida for the third time to defend the Republican electoral vote, was relieved when the appointment was withdrawn. He warned, "in all earnestness, if that vacancy is filled I am broken down here completely. . . . Keep that vacancy open, and the vote of Florida for Hayes is under good protection so far as the courts of the state are concerned." Meanwhile, Wallace cynically promised McLin his support for the office, explaining that nothing could be said until the electoral vote was beyond recall by the supreme court.[32]

There was little chance that any Florida Republican could have obtained the judgeship. Settle was a prominent figure who was being considered for a possible cabinet position if Hayes were seated, but he preferred the certain judicial appointment to the uncertain Washington post. He was acceptable to Conover, and Democratic Senator Charles W. Jones was opposed to any Florida Republican for the position.[33] Settle's nomination was sent to the Senate on January 26, after it was too late for adverse court action. McLin was promised a judgeship in New Mexico territory, but the Senate ultimately denied confirmation because of Conover's opposition.

In early January the joint congressional committee was still working out details of the electoral commission but the general principles of the compromise were decided. It appeared that the electoral commission would consider evidence concerning electoral certificates which were referred to it. For the first time Tilden's campaign manager, Abram S. Hewitt of New York, showed interest in the Florida controversy. He recommended that Marble and other Tilden men draft suitable legislation for passage by the Florida legislature, and asked that D. W. Sellers and G. W. Biddle return to Tallahassee and assist with the quo warranto suit before Judge White. Marble was already working on draft legislation which was subsequently enacted in Florida. The first bill was passed and signed by Governor Drew on January 18, directing a "legal canvass of the electoral vote of Florida as cast at the November election." The new canvassing board, composed of Secretary of State William D. Bloxham, Attorney General Columbus Drew, and Comptroller Walter Gwynn, all Democrats, reported a Tilden majority of about ninety-four for each elector. The legislature then passed the second bill declaring them duly elected and authorizing the governor to issue certificates of election. They met on January 26, cast their votes for Tilden and Hendricks, and forwarded a third certificate of Florida's electoral votes to the United States Senate.[34]

Marble and his associates considered the quo warranto matter important but they did not send the Philadelphia lawyers back to Tallahassee. Neither Pasco nor R. L. Campbell participated in the case. Wilkinson Call assured Marble that Edward A. Perry and Augustus E. Maxwell of Pensacola were competent to handle the case, which they argued from January 8 to January 25. Lew Wallace tried to have the case removed to the United States Circuit Court, but Judge White refused to agree to the transfer. On January 25, White declared that the Republican electors were mere usurpers of the offices to which the Democratic electors had been elected.[35] Wallace appealed the decision, but the supreme court refused to hear it until the regular June session. Rendered moot by the electoral commission, the case was dropped before the court convened in June.

Governor Stearns accepted the reality of a Republican presidential victory at the same time the state was turned over to the Democrats, but some of his associates insisted that he should apply for his own quo warranto writ against Drew. When he did not, David Montgomery accused Stearns of selling out for a federal appointment. "If Hayes is President then Stearns is governor," he wrote after the presidential inauguration.[36] Others agreed with Montgomery that Stearns should try to oust Drew. Referring to this sentiment, Stearns wrote ex-Senator Osborn that he was willing to sue but only if he obtained advance assurance that Judge Randall would uphold him. Since they were not friends, Stearns absolutely refused to go before Randall without prior guarantees. The former governor prophetically added that Hayes might withdraw support from existing Republican governments in the South rather than try establishing new ones and "we may look for the warm loving embrace of southern whites by the next administration."[37]

With the electoral count scheduled to begin on February 1 and Florida the first disputed state to be reached because of its alphabetical position, Democrats hurriedly assembled their documentary evidence in Washington. There were three certificates before Congress purporting to be the electoral vote of Florida. Only the one signed by the Republican electors and Governor Stearns on December 6 met all the legal requirements. The others were legally deficient because of improper signatures or erroneous dates. But the Democrats supported their certificates with Judge White's decision against Hayes as well as the administrative and legislative records pertaining to the second canvass which resulted in the third electoral vote. Call and Pasco went to Washington with printed copies of court records, legislative acts, and records of the new canvassing board. William D. Bloxham and former Attorney General Cocke followed with the original returns and all related papers.[38] The Democrats were prepared to present overwhelming evidence supporting their claims to Florida's vote if the commission agreed to go behind the electoral certificates and determine which was the correct one.

Congress assembled on February 1 and the count began. There were no objections until Florida's three certificates were reached. All three with accompanying documents were referred to the electoral commission. Both parties had excellent legal counsel, but little new information was introduced. The arguments of both sides had become public knowledge during the weeks following the election. The crucial question was whether the commission itself was a canvassing board with power to review evidence behind the certificates, one signed by Governor Stearns and another by Governor Drew.

The Democrats argued that Tilden had received a majority in Florida which had been changed by a dishonest canvassing board. They pointed out that every branch of Florida's government supported the Tilden electors and asked for a chance to prove it. The Republicans based their argument on the finality of the certificate which bore Stearns' signature and on the doctrine of necessity. The commission had no power to go behind the certificate signed by a state's chief executive. And, if the commission did go behind the certificates, it would have to investigate the entire record. Since there was inadequate time to do so, the commission was compelled to accept the legally executed certificate as final. The Republican argument continued that the framers of the Constitution had not intended the judiciary to have power over the election process. The court could not even correct mathematical errors or results of bribery if discovered after the electors had been certified by the governor.[39]

Argument of the Florida case ended on February 6, and three days later the fifteen-member commission, composed of eight Republicans and seven Democrats, awarded Florida's four electoral votes to Rutherford B. Hayes on the ground that it had no power to go behind the certificate of the state governor. Since the most important factor seemed to be the Republican majority of the commission, many observers believed that the Florida decision settled the election. The *New York Tribune* commented that "the decision of the Tripartite Commission in the Florida case is a great victory for . . . Governor Hayes, masked however in such a way that the Democrats . . . regard it as not quite a crushing defeat of Mr. Tilden."[40] James G. Blaine declared that the Florida decision virtually settled the contest, and William E. Chandler advised Hayes to choose his cabinet and prepare his inaugural address.[41] The Louisiana and South Carolina cases were ultimately decided according to the Florida precedent by the same eight-to-seven vote. On March 2, the count was completed and Hayes declared elected.

Democrats were incensed: the Republicans had won in Florida by advocating the canvassing board's power to accept evidence proving fraud; then, they reversed themselves and won before the electoral commission by upholding the principle that state returns could not be investigated. The Democrats had a strong case had they been able to get the commission to consider it, but the Republicans also had a good case. They had met all the forms of law and were able to prevent the Democrats from showing the circumstances by which that was accomplished. Chandler's shrewd management in Florida had conveyed the impression to the nation that the Florida canvassing board's original count showed a Hayes victory. Building on that tactical victory, he obtained the properly prepared certificate of the electoral vote and got it into the proper channels in Congress. Although the Democrats won their arguments in the Florida courts, they were unable to present a duly executed electoral certificate. Each side realized that the public would not accept a decision which flagrantly violated the forms of traditional democratic practice, and they used every available method to legitimize their arguments. While the Democrats succeeded in the courts, the Republicans were more successful in the administrative and legislative channels.

The returns sent from the Florida counties, questionable though some of them were, probably were not far from an accurate measure of the parties' relative strengths. The presidential election would have hinged on a mere handful of votes in 1876 regardless of the irregularities during the election or the canvassing activities which followed it. On the face of the returns the Democrats won the state election by several hundred votes while the difference between the presidential tickets was less than 100. The disparity was due to split-ticket voting by east Florida Republicans. Had the state canvassing board excluded the more obviously irregular returns, counted a small Hayes majority, and left the Democrats a state victory, it is unlikely that the Florida supreme court would have entertained the case against the canvassing board members. The two Republican justices were Hayes supporters and believed he had been elected. They did not think the Republicans had won the state election. Neither was friendly with Governor Stearns, which made it easier to order the board to correct an obviously unfair decision. At the same time, the two Republicans were joined by Democratic Judge Westcott in limiting their court order so that the Hayes electors would retain a majority. Westcott and Randall had personal reasons for this decision, but in such a close election, they were also reluctant to substitute a court order for the canvassing board decision.

Drew and Hull received a clear majority in the election and earned the offices which they assumed in January 1877. The outcome of the presidential contest is not as clear. It is unfortunate that the Republican canvassing board members furnished such overwhelming evidence against the Republican presidential electors by their arbitrary efforts to count in the Republican state ticket. Their action is the basis for the long-standing and widely accepted Democratic claim to the Florida electoral votes, but this contention glosses over the question of fraud and intimidation upon which the county returns were based. The election machinery was not accurate enough to resolve beyond a doubt an election as close as that between Hayes and Tilden. After both sides had exhausted all possible remedies and the inaugurations were held in Tallahassee and Washington, it was possible that an equitable resolution of the dispute had been achieved.

21

We Have Lost the State for a Long, Long Time

A few weeks after his inauguration President Hayes ordered all United States troops out of Baton Rouge and Columbia where they had been protecting the Republican governments of Louisiana and South Carolina against contesting Democratic regimes supported by local whites. The troop withdrawal and resulting collapse of the two Republican administrations symbolized the end of federal efforts to implement the Reconstruction acts of 1867. Conservative white Southerners hailed Hayes' troop removal as the "restoration of home rule" and began nullifying the actions of Republican administrations in their states. Since Florida was involved with Louisiana and South Carolina in the election dispute and proceedings of the electoral commission, it has often been linked with them in discussions of the troop withdrawal. But President Hayes' April decisions had no direct effect on Florida. Governor George F. Drew had been peacefully inaugurated on January 2, 1877, and the last troops left Tallahassee on January 18, three months before Hayes removed them from Baton Rouge and Columbia.

Clayton A. Cowgill predicted that the Republican party had "lost the state for a long, long time." "Well, we niggers is done," was the way an aging Negro evaluated Drew's inaugural ceremony.[1] The moderate Republicans who implemented the 1867 Reconstruction acts in Florida had never given Negro rights more than secondary consideration. Black voters contributed more to the Republican party than they received from it. Even their basic right to vote was diluted by provisions for disproportionate legislative representation. Yet, their situation between 1868 and 1877 was infinitely better than it was to be for the next seventy-five years.

Ill equipped as many of them were for political participation, most Negroes risked physical danger and economic pressure to exercise the franchise. Some were venal—as were some of their white counterparts—but most took pride in their right of suffrage.

With voting privileges, Florida Negroes were beginning to make some progress during Reconstruction. Leaders emerged who were learning to bargain their strength for substantive concessions. As long as their right to vote was positively protected, the blacks had a chance. In no other period has the Florida legislature been so favorable to laborers. The licensing and protection of stevedores against foreign competition, prohibition against garnishment of laborers' pay, statutory liens to protect agricultural and lumber workers in the fruits of their labor, and a ten-hour day law all were measures which benefited more blacks than whites. The 1873 civil rights act, long delayed by Democratic opposition and moderate Republican ambivalence, was enacted with bipartisan support after Negroes displayed much more political skill and versatility in the 1872 election than in earlier campaigns. It is true that the bill was limited in its application to schools and was narrowly interpreted in other areas. It did not alter an essentially segregated society which had been established by custom. But as long as it remained in the statutes, the whites who defied it were the opponents of law and order. It was decidedly preferable to the later Jim Crow legislation which legalized and required racial segregation of Florida society.

The independence of such Negro leaders as "Bishop" Pearce, John Wallace, J. Willis Menard, and H. S. Harmon indicated that they were more than mere instruments of "carpetbagger" control of the state. Had there been any alternative to the Republican party, these men might have proved the success of their political apprenticeship. Unfortunately for everyone, there was no alternative. The Conservative-Democrats had demonstrated their unwillingness to coalesce with Negroes in 1872. Despite Bloxham's cautious overtures, racial antipathy in his party rendered fusion impossible. Limited though it was, the Negroes' only hope was in the Republican party as long as it was supported from Washington. That support was withdrawn in 1877.

The native whites who formed the Conservative-Democratic party emerged from the Reconstruction era unscathed. Among them were antebellum Whigs and Democrats, Confederates who had lost the war, and Unionists who had been denied the fruits of victory by Andrew Johnson's amnesty program, but they all participated in winning the peace. Legal slavery was the only component of their antebellum institutions to fall casualty during the war. A substitute suitable to them had evolved by 1877.

Neither President Johnson's plan nor the subsequent congressional program ever threatened the supremacy of the native whites who had always dominated Florida. Moreover, the Johnson plan strengthened the Conservatives by its treatment of wartime Unionists and then gave them a moral victory when they met the president's minimum requirements and were denied readmission. When the president offered amnesty with restoration of non-slave property to ex-Confederates who swore future loyalty to the United States, he offended loyal Unionists who had suffered at the hands of the Confederate government. Many had lost property under Confederate sequestration laws and were obliged to seek repossession through expensive and lengthy litigation. Others had furnished supplies to Union troops and waited years to be partially reimbursed by a parsimonious United States claims commission. Still others had acquired formerly Confederate-owned property at wartime tax sales, only to be immediately dispossessed in favor of returning ex-Confederates. All resented being ignored while their former enemies were rewarded. When the Johnson plan failed and Congress enfranchised Negroes, many of the Unionists regarded Negro suffrage as the final affront and joined the Conservative-Democrats to resist what they regarded as an ungrateful government. At the same time, the restoration of property to former Confederates undercut the Freedmen's Bureau which had intended to use the land for distribution to Negroes.

Provisional Governor Marvin, like the president a consistent Unionist and white supremacist, told native white Floridians that they could be readmitted to the Union by meeting Johnson's mild demands and they would not be asked to consider Negro suffrage. The 1865 constitutional convention complied with the president's program, but Florida was denied readmission. Thus, people who had tried and failed to destroy the nation were permitted the luxury of believing that they had made a bargain and the United States government had broken it. With this moral boost and their state's rights convictions, Conservative Floridians watched the developing struggle between President Johnson and Congress. When Congress enacted the civil rights law and the Freedmen's Bureau extension law over executive opposition, Johnson countered with proclamations restoring civil authority in the southern states. Floridians followed the executive proclamations while military men tried to enforce congressional laws. Gradually the state officials gained the upper hand in Florida while Johnson was losing to Congress in Washington.

During 1866, bureau and military officials utterly failed to obtain justice for Negroes in the state courts. With Johnson's encouragement, all three branches of Florida government defied national laws. Governor Walker tried to cooperate with General Foster at first, but by November

1866 he also became obdurate. When Congress repudiated the Johnson policy and enacted the 1867 Reconstruction laws, white Floridians were bitter and confused, but they had successfully resisted unwelcome interference in their lives for two years. They were much more self-confident than they had been in early 1865.

The military Reconstruction program was mild enough in concept, and as implemented in Florida it posed no threat at all to the whites. Moderate Republicans whose economic ambitions and beliefs were identical to those of Conservative leaders had little use for the Florida Radicals who advocated Negro rights at the expense of native whites. The 1868 constitution permitted Conservatives to participate fully in the governing process. While they were helping write some legislation and obstructing passage of other laws in the capital, Conservative-Democrats were using physical and economic pressure in the counties to dissuade Negroes from engaging in political activity. That they were not more successful was due to the Negroes' determination and to enforcement of national laws by the United States marshals and courts.

If there was ever a chance for Negroes to find a place in Florida society in the late-nineteenth century—and without a basic change of attitude by native whites it was slight—it depended on federal protection of their right to vote over a long period of time. Even conservative General Foster warned in 1866 that "the state of feeling in this country is so much influenced by the late War that it will be necessary . . . that a strong Military Force be retained for a long time."[2] But most Americans believed Negroes inferior and were unwilling to support such a sustained effort for their protection during a period of apprentice citizenship. And without a commitment to Negro equality, the prevailing constitutional idea of dual federalism operated as a barrier against the exercise of force.[3]

The Conservative-Democrats were the principal beneficiaries of the 1868 constitution which the congressional Reconstruction committee approved over the bitter protests of Florida Radicals. Once they won the governorship, the Democrats acquired control of both state and local governments, including the election machinery. Also freed from the scrutiny of federal agencies, they destroyed the Republican party and relegated Negroes to a status much like their former situation. The Democrats took over control of a state whose financial position had improved immensely since 1868 and whose population had been growing steadily during the same period. The way had been prepared for significant economic development within a few years.

Drew was applauded for "redeeming" state administration from "carpetbaggers" whose extravagance and profligacy had plunged the state into financial chaos. Yet, in financial and economic matters he continued the policies implemented by the Republicans: responsible management of the bonded debt, refusal to lend state credit to private corporations, attempts to satisfy the Francis Vose claim and resume the use of state land to encourage internal improvements, inducement to immigrants including tax benefits to manufacturing concerns, and biennial legislative sessions. A premature tax reduction initiated during the Drew administration caused financial chaos in the late 1870s and the levy had to be raised again.

The only major policy shift between the Democratic administrations after 1876 and their Republican predecessors was in civil rights. Nearly all Conservative-Democrats agreed on opposition to Negro suffrage and equality. Having maintained their position in the face of federal laws since 1868, they acquired power to alter state policy just as the national government withdrew its support of Negro rights. Cautiously but with increasing confidence, the Democrats incorporated white supremacy into statute and constitutional law. The Republicans fought back for a while. Horatio Bisbee, Jr., won the east Florida congressional election as late as 1882, although Simon Conover was soundly defeated for governor by William D. Bloxham in 1880.

By the mid-1880s the Democrats felt secure enough to call a convention to replace the 1868 constitution. The 1885 document reduced the governor's extensive powers. Most officers were made elective, but white control of the large Negro-majority counties was assured by continuing the appointment of county commissioners by the governor. The constitution authorized a poll tax as a voting requirement. By 1890 most Negroes had ceased voting in Florida. Beginning in 1887 the state legislature enacted a series of Jim Crow laws which guaranteed separation of the races. Unlike the civil rights law of 1873 which lacked the support of the majority of whites and thus did little to alter social conduct, the Jim Crow legislation re-inforced existing social customs which had remained unchanged by post–Civil War developments. Racial slavery was abolished during the Civil War, but Reconstruction ended before Negroes secured a place in society. The problem of extending the promise of America to the newly freed blacks was deferred for later generations.

Notes

1

1. Ethelred Philips to J. J. Philips, January 12, 1865, James J. Philips Papers; John S. Sammis statement, January 8, 1873, Records of the Southern Claims Commission, Florida.

2. *Tallahassee Florida Sentinel*, September 22, 1863; C. P. Chaires to T. W. Osborn, October 28, 1865, Records of the Bureau of Refugees, Freedmen, and Abandoned Lands, Florida, hereafter cited as BRFAL. Citations refer to Florida unless otherwise stated.

3. John Milton to Patton Anderson, May 5, 1864, Patton Anderson to John Milton, May 8, 1864, John Milton Letterbook, 1863–65; *War of the Rebellion: Official Records of the Union and Confederate Armies*, series 1, vol. 53, p. 319, hereafter cited as *OR*; John E. Johns, *Florida During the Civil War*, p. 167.

4. E. Philips to J. J. Philips, January 14, 1864, Philips Papers.

5. Records of Volunteer Regiments, First and Second Florida Cavalry, War Department; Lyman Rowley to George S. Boutwell, April 2, 1869, Applications for Collector, Dept. of the Treasury.

6. E. O. Hill to J. M. Hawks, March 27, 1862, Esther and Milton Hawks Papers; *St. Augustine Examiner*, April 9, 1862.

7. *Tallahassee Florida Sentinel*, December 9, 1862.

8. Theodore Bissell to Harrison Reed, April 1, 1864, Lyman D. Stickney letter, May 6, 1864, Records of Direct Tax Commission, Dept. of the Treasury, hereafter cited as DTC.

9. Louis P. Harvey to A. Lincoln, n/d 1862, James R. Doolittle et al. to A. Lincoln, n/d, 1862, Letters of Application and Recommendation, Department of State, hereafter cited as Applications and Recommendations.

10. Florida Citizens to A. Lincoln, December 5, 1862, microfilm of Abraham Lincoln Papers; George Winston Smith, "Carpetbag Imperialism in Florida, 1862–1868," pp. 121–22.

11. Thomas Wentworth Higginson, *Army Life in a Black Regiment*, pp. 75, 95.

12. Lyman D. Stickney to Salmon P. Chase, April 27, 1863, DTC; Smith, "Carpetbag Imperialism," p. 267.

13. Austin Smith to W. P. Fessenden, July 30, 1864, DTC.

14. Lyman D. Stickney to Joseph J. Lewis, January 25, 1864, John S. Sammis to Joseph J. Lewis, January n/d, 1864, Harrison Reed to Philip Fraser, August 20, 1863, ibid.

15. Cornelius Longstreet Diary, 1864–65; H. H. Helper to W. P. Fessenden, September 22, 1864, John S. Sammis to J. J. Lewis, January 1864, Edward N. Dickerson to Green B. Raum, December 13, 1882, Harrison Reed to S. P. Chase, March 4, 1864, Eli Thayer to W. P. Fessenden, August 12, 1864, DTC.

16. L. D. Stickney to S. P. Chase, December 11, 1863, Salmon P. Chase Papers.

17. Ibid., February 24, 1864, Homer G. Plantz to S. P. Chase, November 23, 1863, ibid.

18. *Fernandina Peninsula,* December 24, 1863; L. D. Stickney to S. P. Chase, December 21, 1863, Homer G. Plantz to S. P. Chase, May 12, 1864, Chase Papers.

19. Captain Le Diable (pseud.), *Historical Sketch of the Third Annual Conquest of Florida,* p. 11.

20. William Roscoe Thayer, *The Life and Letters of John Hay,* p. 155; Smith, "Carpetbag Imperialism," p. 281.

21. A. Lincoln to Quincy A. Gillmore, January 13, 1864, Lincoln Papers.

22. L. D. Stickney to S. P. Chase, January 11, March 2, 1864, Chase Papers; Quincy A. Gillmore to A. Lincoln, January 21, 1864, Lincoln Papers.

23. L. D. Stickney to S. P. Chase, February 5, 1864, Chase Papers; Smith, "Carpetbag Imperialism," p. 283; General Order Number 16, Department of the South, January 21, 1864, Lincoln Papers.

24. L. D. Stickney to S. P. Chase, February 5, 1864, Chase Papers.

25. John Hay to A. Lincoln, February 8, 1864, Lincoln Papers.

26. L. D. Stickney to S. P. Chase, February 16, 1864, Chase Papers.

27. *Pensacola Tri-Weekly Observer,* October 29, 1868; John G. Nicolay to Theresa, February 28, 1864, John G. Nicolay Papers; U. S. Senate, *Report No. 47,* 38th Cong., 1st sess., pp. 14, 21.

28. J. G. Nicolay to Theresa, March 25, 1864, Nicolay Papers.

29. L. D. Stickney to S. P. Chase, February 24, 1864, Chase Papers.

30. Ibid., February 16, 1864; Florida Citizens in Washington to A. Lincoln, May 17, 1862, O. M. Dorman to Jesse O. Norton, January 21, 1864, Lincoln Papers; C. L. Robinson to R. L. L. Andros, September 15, 1865, Applications for Collector; Frank W. Klingberg, *The Southern Claims Commission.*

31. H. G. Plantz to S. P. Chase, November 23, December 1, 1863, January 12, 1864, Chase Papers.

32. Ibid., December 12, 1863, February 20, 1864, L. D. Stickney to Chase, October 22, 1863, ibid.

33. Samuel Walker et al., statement, April 2, 12, 1864, DTC.

34. L. D. Stickney to S. P. Chase, March 2, 1864, Chase Papers; H. G. Plantz to J. Hubley Ashton, October 5, 1864, Attorney General's Papers, hereafter cited as AGP.

35. L. D. Stickney to S. P. Chase, March 15, 1864, Chase Papers; Le Diable, *Conquest of Florida,* pp. 12–13; O. M. Dorman, Diary and Notes, 4:142.

36. C. L. Robinson to George S. Boutwell, December 5, 1870, Applications for Collector; Johns, *Florida During the Civil War,* p. 200.

37. Philip Fraser to S. P. Chase, September 30, 1864, Chase Papers; Austin Smith to W. P. Fessenden, July 30, 1864, Brief in U.S. v. Stickney, May 18, 1865, DTC.

38. J. W. Douglas, "Brief History of the Florida Railroad Case," n/d, DTC.

39. Longstreet Diary; N. C. Dennett to Milton Hawks, September 27, 1864, Hawks Papers; H. H. Helper to J. J. Lewis, October 14, 1863, Harrison Reed to J. J. Lewis, October 3, 1863, DTC.

40. *Fernandina Peninsula,* April–May 1863; School Record of Jacksonville, February 25, June 29, 1864, Hawks Papers.

2

1. Proclamation of Major General Sam Jones, Headquarters, District of Florida, April 28, 1865; F. F. L'Engle to Edward M. L'Engle, April 29, 1865, Edward M. L'Engle Papers; *Jacksonville Florida Union*, January 14, 1865.

2. A. K. Allison to D. L. Yulee, May 12, 19, 1865, David L. Yulee Papers; *OR*, series 1, vol. 47, part 3, p. 538; James H. Wilson to Edward McCook, May 16, 1865, Milton Letterbook.

3. Florida, *House Journal*, 1865–66, pp. 81, 103–5.

4. Harold D. Woodman, *King Cotton and His Retainers*, p. 237.

5. *Tallahassee Semi-Weekly Floridian*, November 24, 1865; T. W. Osborn to O. O. Howard, October 1, 1866, Jacob A. Remley to S. L. McHenry, August 31, 1866, BRFAL.

6. William Watson Davis, *Civil War and Reconstruction in Florida*, p. 324; U.S. House, *Report No. 22*, 42d Cong., 2d sess., 1:160–61.

7. James Banks to John MacRae, May 17, 1868, John MacRae Papers.

8. James L. Watkins, *King Cotton: A History and Statistical Review, 1790–1908*, p. 130.

9. E. Philips to J. J. Philips, August 2, October 24, 1865, Philips Papers.

10. Charles A. Hentz Autobiography, 1:367, Hentz Family Papers; E. Philips to J. J. Philips, June 21, 1866, Philips Papers; F. F. L'Engle to E. M. L'Engle, April 29, June 26, 1865, L'Engle Papers.

11. Articles of agreement of the Florida Emigration Society, n/d, 1865, L'Engle Papers.

12. F. F. L'Engle to E. M. L'Engle, June 13, 26, July 5, 1865, L'Engle Papers.

13. Dorman, Diary and Notes, 4:133–34; Hentz Autobiography, p. 26; *Thomasville Times*, April 4, 1874.

14. L. C. Man to A. Johnson, May 23, 1865, Andrew Johnson Papers.

15. Israel Vogdes to S. P. Chase, June 7, July 31, 1865, Chase Papers.

16. Stephen R. Mallory to Zachariah Chandler, July 20, 1865, Zachariah Chandler Papers; *Tallahassee Semi-Weekly Floridian*, September 26, 1865.

17. *Tallahassee Semi-Weekly Floridian*, September 26, 1865.

18. T. W. Osborn to O. O. Howard, November 10, 1865, BRFAL.

19. *Memoirs of Helen Moore Edwards* (privately printed, n.d., copy in possession of Michael Monroe, Gadsden County), pp. 7–8.

20. General Order No. 9, Headquarters, District of Florida, July 3, 1865, W. H. Branch Papers; T. W. Osborn to O. O. Howard, November 10, 1865, BRFAL; General Order No. 5, Headquarters, District of Florida, June 29, 1865, DTC.

21. J. G. Foster to T. W. Osborn, December 15, 1865, BRFAL.

22. D. T. Hancock to S. L. McHenry, September 17, 1865, ibid.

23. Nathaniel Usher to James Speed, August 17, 1865, AGP; Usher to Solicitor, June 5, 1865, U.S. Attorney's Reports, Records of the Solicitor of the Treasury, hereafter cited as Solicitor's Records.

24. Joseph J. Lewis to Florida DTC, May 17, 1867, DTC; C. P. Chamberlain to T. J. Coffey, April 5, 1864, Nathaniel Usher to James Speed, August 15, 1865, AGP; Nathaniel Usher to Solicitor, June 5, 1865, Solicitor's Records.

25. *Tallahassee Semi-Weekly Floridian*, April 17, 1866; Adolphus Mot to A. A. Cole, June 27, 1867, BRFAL.

26. T. W. Osborn to Joseph Remington, November 2, 1865, BRFAL.

27. Nathaniel Usher to James Speed, August 17, 1865, AGP.

28. Special Field Order No. 5, October 31, 1865, Special Orders, Florida, Applications of Sophia Lyons, J. J. Scott, and C. C. Yonge, January 3, 1866, William Fowler to T. W. Osborn, October 31, 1865, S. L. McHenry to Thomas A. Leddy, March 2, 1866, Truman Seymour to Allen Jackson, October 5, 1867, BRFAL.

29. T. W. Osborn to J. T. Sprague, January 17, 1866, Osborn to A. M. Jones, February 1, 1866, T. A. Leddy to S. L. McHenry, April 10, 1866, McHenry to Leddy, March 13, 1866, BRFAL.

30. *Tallahassee Semi-Weekly Floridian,* October 24, 1865; see also business correspondence in L'Engle and Philips papers for 1865–66.

31. F. F. L'Engle to E. M. L'Engle, June 26, 1865, Robert W. Bullock to E. M. L'Engle, December 5, 1865, L'Engle Papers; Hentz Autobiography, 1:372; S. L. Niblack to D. L. Yulee, August 18, 1865, Yulee Papers.

3

1. Rembert W. Patrick, *Reconstruction of the Nation,* pp. 29–30. For a critical account of Johnson's program see Eric L. McKitrick, *Andrew Johnson and Reconstruction.*

2. A. Mot to S. P. Chase, June 30, 1865, Chase Papers.

3. J. George Harris to A. Johnson, June 9, 1865, Harrison Reed to Montgomery Blair, June 26, 1865, S. P. Chase to A. Johnson, May 25, 1865, Johnson Papers; Davis, *Civil War and Reconstruction,* p. 371; Whitelaw Reid, *After the War: A Southern Tour,* pp. 160–61.

4. Harrison Reed to Montgomery Blair, June 9, 1865, Johnson Papers.

5. Petition from inhabitants of Hillsborough County, Florida, June, 1865, Applications and Recommendations.

6. J. George Harris to A. Johnson, June 8, 1865, Johnson Papers.

7. R. B. Marvin to William H. Seward, July 6, 1865, Applications and Recommendations; William M. Robinson, Jr., *Justices in Grey,* p. 165.

8. L. D. Stickney to Joseph Holt, July 9, 1865, Joseph Holt Papers; Davis, *Civil War and Reconstruction,* p. 355.

9. Stephen R. Mallory to William H. Seward, July 11, 1865, Applications and Recommendations; H. Reed to M. Blair, June 26, 1865, Johnson Papers.

10. W. Marvin to P. Fraser, June 27, 1865, R. B. Marvin to W. H. Seward, July 6, 1865, Johnson Papers.

11. C. L. Robinson to A. Johnson, July 3, 1865, ibid.; L. D. Stickney to J. Holt, July 9, 1865, Holt Papers; Davis, *Civil War and Reconstruction,* p. 353.

12. Raphael P. Thian, *Military Geography of the United States,* pp. 124–25; James E. Sefton, *United States Army and Reconstruction, 1865–1877,* Appendix A, p. 255; *Tallahassee Semi-Weekly Floridian,* September 26, 1865.

13. Sefton, *Army and Reconstruction,* p. 19.

14. John G. Foster to P. H. Sheridan, August 6, 1865, P. K. Yonge Library.

15. Ibid.

16. Address of William Marvin, August 3, 1865, Department of State, Provisional Government of Florida, hereafter cited as Provisional Government.

17. U.S. Senate, *Document No. 26,* 39th Cong., 1st sess., pp. 203–5.

18. Proclamations of Governor Marvin, August 26, September 11, 1865, Provisional Government.

19. *Journal of the Constitutional Convention of 1865 at Tallahassee, Florida,* p. 132.

20. *Tallahassee Semi-Weekly Floridian,* September 26, 1865.

21. Elijah Williams to Patent Office, Letters Patent, April 30, 1867; C. M. Hamilton to J. G. Foster, BRFAL; *Tallahassee Semi-Weekly Floridian,* September 26, 1865.

22. *Tallahassee Semi-Weekly Floridian,* September 26, 1865.

23. Ibid., December 12, 1865, quoting *Jacksonville Florida Times.*

24. *Journal of the Convention of 1865,* pp. 9–11.

25. Ibid., p. 14.

26. Ibid.

27. *Tallahassee Semi-Weekly Floridian*, October 27, 1865.
28. *Constitution of 1865*, Ordinance 1 and Article XVI; *Journal of the Convention of 1865*, pp. 57, 77, 103, 108–9; Davis, *Civil War and Reconstruction*, p. 363.
29. *Constitution of 1865*, Ordinance 4.
30. Ibid., Resolutions 2, 3.
31. Dorman, Diary and Notes, 4:232, 248; Kate Brandon to E. M. L'Engle, December 1, 1865, R. Bullock to E. M. L'Engle, December 5, 1865, L'Engle Papers.
32. J. G. Foster to AAG, Military Division of the Gulf, December 24, 1865, Adjutant General's Office, Records, hereafter cited as AGO.
33. O. O. Howard to T. W. Osborn, September 6, 1865, L. M. Hobbs to T. W. Osborn, December 26, 1865, BRFAL.
34. G. R. Hughes to AAG, June 30, 1866, R. Hall to T. W. Osborn, December 30, 1865, E. C. Love to T. W. Osborn, January 8, 1865, BRFAL.
35. J. G. Foster to AAG, January 1, 1866, AGO; *Tallahassee Semi-Weekly Floridian*, July 26, 1865.
36. Proclamation of Governor Marvin, November 10, 1865, Provisional Government; *Tallahassee Semi-Weekly Floridian*, November 24, 1865; J. G. Foster to E. D. Townsend, November 23, 1865, AGO; Davis, *Civil War and Reconstruction*, p. 368.
37. *Constitution of 1865*, Resolution 4; Memorandum of S. J. Douglas, November 10, 1865, Provisional Government.
38. W. Marvin to A. Johnson, November 18, 1865, Johnson Papers.
39. Florida, *House Journal*, 1866, p. 9.
40. T. W. Osborn to O. O. Howard, September 21, 1865, BRFAL.
41. *Tallahassee Semi-Weekly Floridian*, March 19, 1867; *Gainesville New Era*, June 15, 1867; T. W. Osborn to O. O. Howard, November 30, 1865, BRFAL.

4

1. Florida, *House Journal*, 1865–66, p. 8; William Marvin to A. Johnson, December 29, 1865, Johnson Papers; Davis, *Civil War and Reconstruction*, p. 366; *Tallahassee Semi-Weekly Floridian*, February 9, 1865.
2. Florida, *House Journal*, 1865–66, pp. 33–34, 41.
3. Theodore B. Wilson, *The Black Codes of the South*, pp. 13–41.
4. J. H. Durkee to T. W. Osborn, February 28, 1866, BRFAL; A. B. Hawkins to W. H. Branch, January 8, 1866, Branch Papers; E. J. Lutterloh to Dear General, January 30, 1867, W. J. Lutterloh Papers; *Tallahassee Semi-Weekly Floridian*, December 15, 19, 1865.
5. Special Order 155, Headquarters, U.S. Troops at St. Augustine, December 8, 1865, H. H. Moore to T. W. Osborn, January 11, 1866, BRFAL.
6. *Tallahassee Semi-Weekly Floridian*, November 3, December 1, 1865.
7. Florida, *House Journal*, 1865–66, p. 205.
8. *Tallahassee Semi-Weekly Floridian*, February 9, 1866.
9. Florida, *House Journal*, 1865–66, pp. 60–62, 65.
10. Florida, *Senate Journal*, 1865–66, p. 20.
11. *Laws of Florida*, 1865, p. 32; 1866, pp. 21–22; Wilson, *Black Codes*, p. 991.
12. *Laws of Florida*, 1865–66, p. 62.
13. Ibid., p. 28; Wilson, *Black Codes*, p. 99; Joe M. Richardson, "Florida Black Codes," p. 374; T. W. Osborn to O. O. Howard, February 19, 1866, S. L. McHenry to A. H. Jackson, March 26, 1866, BRFAL; *Tallahassee Semi-Weekly Floridian*, January 9, 1866.
14. *Laws of Florida*, 1865–66, pp. 25, 30, 38, 65; Richardson, "Florida Black Codes," p. 374.
15. Florida, *House Journal*, 1866, p. 15; Joe M. Richardson, *The Negro in the Reconstruction of Florida, 1865–1877*, pp. 30–31; Wilson, *Black Codes*, p. 99.

16. *Laws of Florida*, 1865–66, p. 34.

17. Florida, *House Journal*, 1865–66, pp. 59, 62–63.

18. *Laws of Florida*, 1865–66, pp. 23–25; Wilson, *Black Codes*, pp. 97–98.

19. T. W. Osborn to William Marvin, December 30, 1865, Osborn to Howard, December 30, 1865, Howard to Osborn, January 12, 1866, BRFAL.

20. D. S. Walker to T. W. Osborn, January 26, 1866, Osborn to J. H. Durkee, January 18, 1866, Osborn to O. O. Howard, May 4, 1866, S. L. McHenry to C. M. Hamilton, May 8, 1866, BRFAL.

21. *Tallahassee Semi-Weekly Floridian*, February 6, 1866.

22. A. B. Thomas to D. S. Walker, May 19, 1866, A. B. Grumwell to A. H. Jackson, February 29, 1866, J. H. Durkee to S. L. McHenry, July 13, 1866, BRFAL.

23. T. W. Osborn to O. O. Howard, April 27, 1866, J. G. Foster to O. O. Howard, November 28, 1866, BRFAL; J. G. Foster to D. S. Walker, June 12, 1866, John G. Foster Letterbook.

24. T. W. Osborn to O. O. Howard, March 2, 15, 1866, D. S. Walker to Osborn, March 30, 1866, BRFAL; Florida, *House Journal*, 1866, pp. 18–19.

25. Florida, *House Journal*, 1865–66, pp. 116–17; *Laws of Florida*, 1865–66, pp. 39–40.

26. *Tallahassee Semi-Weekly Floridian*, January 26, 1866; T. W. Osborn to O. O. Howard, January 19, 1866, Osborn to D. S. Walker, January 18, 1866, Fred M. Cole to Osborn, April 17, 1866, BRFAL; Richardson, *Negro in Reconstruction*, p. 100.

27. *Laws of Florida*, 1865–66, p. 101; Florida, *House Journal*, 1865–66, pp. 109–10, 113–15.

28. Hans L. Trefousse, *The Radical Republicans: Lincoln's Vanguard for Racial Justice*, p. 339.

5

1. *U.S. Statutes at Large*, 13:507–9; John A. Carpenter, *Sword and Olive Branch*, pp. 83, 88. For a general account of the agency see George R. Bentley, *A History of the Freedmen's Bureau*.

2. S. L. McHenry to J. T. Sprague, June 23, 1866, Special Orders 114, August 6, 1866, and 105, April 15, 1867, J. G. Foster to O. O. Howard, August 1, 1866, J. T. Sprague to O. O. Howard, October 31, 1868, O. O. Howard to G. W. Gile, March 5, 1869, BRFAL; J. G. Foster to P. H. Sheridan, November 25, 1866, J. G. Foster to O. O. Howard, November 21, 1866, Foster Letterbook; *Tallahassee Semi-Weekly Floridian*, March 2, June 1, 1866; *Jacksonville Florida Union*, November 7, December 7, 1868, April 29, 1869; *St. Augustine Examiner*, January 5, 1867; John T. Sprague, *The Origin, Progress, and Conclusion of the Florida War*, pp. xix–xx.

3. *Tallahassee Semi-Weekly Floridian*, May 25, 1866; *Laws of Florida*, 1865–66, pp. 105, 115.

4. *Tallahassee Semi-Weekly Floridian*, May 25, 1866; William S. McFeely, *Yankee Stepfather: General O. O. Howard and the Freedmen*, p. 248.

5. J. G. Foster to J. E. Quentin, July 26, 1866, Quentin to Foster, July, n/d, 1866, BRFAL; *Report of the* [U.S.] *Commissioner of Agriculture*, 1871, p. 170.

6. Rufus Saxton to N. C. Dennett, August 15, 1865, BRFAL, South Carolina; Nathaniel Usher to James Speed, August 14, 1865, AGP; J. H. Lyman to J. E. Quentin, October 30, 1865, T. W. Osborn to D. M. Hammond, September 21, 1865, BRFAL; Dorman, Diary and Notes, 4:144–45; Carpenter, *Sword and Olive Branch*, p. 107.

7. T. W. Osborn to O. O. Howard, November 10, 1865, Osborn to William Arthur, February 17, 1866, BRFAL.

8. J. G. Foster to P. H. Sheridan, October 4, 1866, Foster Letterbook; Sefton, *Army and Reconstruction*, Appendix B.

9. J. G. Foster to T. W. Osborn, December 15, 1865, Osborn to O. O. Howard, September 21, November 10, 1865, General Order 40, November 15, 1865, BRFAL; *Tallahassee Semi-Weekly Floridian*, November 21, 1865.

10. War Department Circular 22, December 22, 1865, T. W. Osborn to Henry J. Stewart, February 23, 1866, J. A. Remley to S. L. McHenry, July 31, 1866, R. W. Bullock to Remley, August 11, 1866, J. H. Durkee to Osborn, February 10, 1866, J. B. Collins to Osborn, February 22, 1866, Osborn to J. H. Durkee, January 17, 1866, M. L. Stearns to J. H. Lyman, October 22, 1866, J. G. Foster to J. A. Remley, August 16, 1866, Winer Bethel to Osborn, February 23, 1866, BRFAL.

11. J. T. Sprague to O. O. Howard, January 1, 1868, S. L. McHenry to F. W. Webster, June 23, 1866, ibid.

12. S. L. McHenry to Commanders of Posts, November 13, 1865, T. W. Osborn to O. O. Howard, November 30, 1865, Max Woodhull to Osborn, December 1, 1865, Osborn to Charles Mundee, January 15, 1866, ibid.

13. J. F. Denniston to T. W. Osborn, February 8, 1866, Osborn to O. O. Howard, February 1, 1866, Osborn to William Arthur, February 1, 1866, Osborn to C. Mundee, September 30, 1865, Osborn to Howard, September 30, 1865, Osborn to D. M. Hammond, September 30, 1865, F. J. Wheaton to Osborn, December 20, 1865, F. W. Webster to Osborn, February 7, 14, April 6, 1866, ibid.

14. Richardson, *Negro in Reconstruction*, p. 26.

15. D. M. Hammond to T. W. Osborn, October 20, 1865, Osborn to Judges of Probate, December 23, 1865, Charles Mundee to A. B. Grumwell, August 23, 1866, BRFAL.

16. T. W. Osborn to Judges of Probate, December 23, 1865, Osborn to C. Mundee, December 31, 1865, ibid.

17. T. W. Osborn to A. E. Kinne, December 31, 1866, ibid.

18. M. L. Campbell and M. T. Wilder to T. W. Osborn, February 21, 1866, ibid.; J. G. Foster to George Lee, August 28, 1866, Foster Letterbook.

19. Fred M. Cole to T. W. Osborn, March 10, 1866, W. J. Purman to E. C. Woodruff, February 28, 1867, J. H. Durkee to Osborn, February 28, 1866, F. E. Grossman to A. H. Jackson, January 5, 1868, BRFAL; Maria Baker Taylor Diary, November 2, December 16, 1867; A. B. Hawkins to William Branch, January 8, 1866, Branch Papers.

20. W. J. Purman to E. C. Woodruff, February 28, 1867, A. B. Grumwell to E. C. Woodruff, February 8, 28, 1867, Contract of A. Martin and S. C. Redrick with Phil Dupree, et al., Contract of W. S. Shuler with freedmen families, February 1867, BRFAL.

21. Charles Mundee to A. B. Grumwell, August 16, 1866, James Banks to T. W. Osborn, May, 1866, John H. Baker, to F. E. Grossman, August 6, 1867, J. F. Mowe to F. E. Grossman, August 5, 1867, ibid.

22. J. G. Foster to O. O. Howard, October 8, 1866, W. W. Armstrong to A. H. Jackson, August 3, 1866, A. B. Grumwell to E. C. Woodruff, December 31, 1866, ibid.

23. H. H. Kuhn to T. W. Osborn, May 31, 1866, ibid.

24. W. G. Vance to A. H. Jackson, October 31, 1867, ibid.

25. A. Mahoney to E. C. Woodruff, March 31, 1867, M. L. Stearns to Woodruff, April 1, 1867, A. B. Grumwell to Woodruff, January 14, 1867, J. A. Remley to J. H. Lyman, November 31, 1866, M. Martin to A. H. Jackson, October 8, 1868, M. Martin to Francis Eppes, September 29, 1868, Spencer C. Osborn to Jackson, February 16, 1867, C. M. Hamilton to Jackson, December 31, 1867, ibid.; Taylor Diary, May 30, 1867.

26. J. A. Remley to J. T. Sprague, October 2, 1867, C. M. Hamilton to A. H. Jackson, March 31, 1867, BRFAL.

27. J. T. Sprague to O. O. Howard, October 1, 1867, Confidential Letter of O. O. Howard, September 19, 1866, A. P. Ketchum to Sprague, December 19, 1866, J. H. Lyman to Paul Roemer, October 6, 1866, circular letter of assistant commissioner of Florida, January 15, 1867, ibid.

28. J. T. Sprague to O. O. Howard, Annual Report, October, 1868, J. T. Sprague to Howard, February 6, 1868, J. H. Durkee to A. H. Jackson, July 8, 1868, George B. Carse to A. H. Jackson, July 1868, ibid.

29. *Tallahassee Semi-Weekly Floridian*, November 6, July 26, 1866; *St. Augustine Examiner*, February 16, 1867; J. T. Sprague to O. O. Howard, January 10, 1868, BRFAL.

30. Carpenter, *Sword and Olive Branch,* p. 114; Richardson, *Negro in Florida Reconstruction,* p. 73; J. T. Sprague to O. O. Howard, May 18, 1867, BRFAL.

31. *Tallahassee Semi-Weekly Floridian,* January 11, 29, 1867; *St. Augustine Examiner,* January 26, February 16, 1867; J. H. Durkee to AAAG, January 1, 1877, Statement of Thomas Harley et al., September 17, 1866, M. L. Stearns to E. C. Woodruff, December 31, 1866, BRFAL; J. G. Foster to G. L. Hartsuff, September 20, 1866, Foster Letterbook.

32. Homestead records of Tallahassee Land Office, Ozias Morgan to Joseph Wilson, May 30, 1867, Ralph Ely to Morgan, October 15, 1867, Morgan to Commissioner Wilson, December 23, 1867, Records of General Land Office, hereafter cited as GLO; A. H. Jackson to A. B. Stonelake, January 15, 1867, BRFAL.

33. T. W. Osborn to H. H. Moore, January 31, 1867, Osborn to W. W. Marple, January 31, 1866, L. M. Hobbs to Osborn, January 29, 1866, BRFAL.

34. *Tallahassee Semi-Weekly Floridian,* February 1, 1867; J. T. Sprague to Charles F. Hopkins, February 7, 1867, ibid.

35. E. C. Woodruff to W. J. Purman, March 4, 1867, Purman to Woodruff, April 13, 1867, ibid.; Purman to Mrs. Dr. Hawks, May 13, 1867, Hawks Papers.

36. J. T. Sprague to O. O. Howard, February 28, 1867, Charles F. Hopkins to Sprague, February 27, 1867, BRFAL.

37. J. M. Hawks to T. W. Osborn, January 19, April 11, 1866, ibid.; Alfred Jackson Hanna, *Florida's Golden Sands,* p. 87.

38. James C. Beecher to Esther Hawks, September 29, 1864, Hawks Papers; Richardson, *Negro in Florida Reconstruction,* p. 99.

39. A. Mahoney to S. L. McHenry, March 31, 1866, F. E. Grossman to McHenry, August 12, 1866, BRFAL.

40. T. W. Osborn to Lyman Abbott, April 23, 1866, Osborn to David S. Walker, January 18, 1866, ibid.

41. *Tallahassee Semi-Weekly Floridian,* January 26, 1866; Perry G. Wall to J. T. Sprague, July 31, 1867, J. G. Foster to O. O. Howard, December 3, 1866, F. E. Grossman to E. C. Woodruff, April 6, 1867, BRFAL; P. A. Meline to J. T. Sprague, August 15, 1867, Third Military District Records, hereafter cited as 3MD; Foster to Howard, November 21, 1866, Foster Letterbook.

42. *Tallahassee Semi-Weekly Floridian,* January 25, 1866; S. L. McHenry to H. H. Moore, March 5, 1866, A. P. Ketchum to J. T. Sprague, May 10, 1867, Sprague to O. O. Howard, April 9, 1868, A. H. Jackson to C. Thurston Chase, August 5, 1867, BRFAL.

43. *Gainesville New Era,* March 2, 1867.

44. J. H. Durkee to T. W. Osborn, May 1, 1866, C. M. Hamilton to A. H. Jackson, May 31, 1867, W. J. Purman to Jackson, July 31, 1867, C. M. Hamilton to S. L. McHenry, April 30, 1866, Hamilton to E. C. Woodruff, December 31, 1866, BRFAL.

45. Ednah D. Cheney to Mrs. E. Hawks, October 22, 1867, Hawks Papers; John Wallace, *Carpetbag Rule in Florida,* pp. xxiii–xxiv.

46. E. B. Duncan to G. H. Braman, June 4, 22, 1866, Special Order of C. M. Hamilton, July 5, 1866, W. J. Purman to Hamilton, May 31, 1866, BRFAL.

47. Jacob F. Chur to William G. Cox, March 15, 1869, ibid.

48. G. W. Gile to H. B. Stowe, June 14, 1869, Gile to Whittlesey, May 19, 1869, ibid.

49. G. W. Gile to C. Thurston Chase, June 7, 1869, Gile to J. Q. Dickinson, March 4, June 10, 1870, Dickinson to Gile, February 24, 1870, ibid.

50. G. W. Gile to Whittlesey, June 30, December 31, 1869, July 6, 1870, ibid.

51. Ibid., December 31, 1869.

52. Ibid.

53. T. W. Osborn to O. O. Howard, April 18, 1866, Osborn to Charles Mundee, November 29, 1865, S. L. McHenry to Chloe Merrick, November 28, 1865, J. T. Sprague to Howard, April 2, 1868, Sprague to David S. Walker, September 12, 1867, F. G. Shaw to Freedmen's Bureau, July 25, 1867, Sprague to Howard, January 21, 1868, ibid.; *St. Augustine Examiner,* June 27, 1867.

54. T. W. Osborn to O. O. Howard, November 30, 1865, Osborn to E. C. Woodruff, March 2, 1866, A. H. Jackson to J. E. Quentin, February 27, 1868, S. L. McHenry to A. B. Grumwell, June 13, 1866, J. T. Sprague to Harrison Reed, October 19, 1868, BRFAL.

55. Florida, *House Journal*, 1865, p. 179; J. C. Braynard to E. C. Love, April 23, 1866, T. A. Leddy to S. L. McHenry, April 5, 1866, D. M. Hammond to A. H. Jackson, August 10, 1867, BRFAL; *Tallahassee Semi-Weekly Floridian*, January 5, 1866.

56. R. H. Gamble to T. W. Osborn, January 13, 1866, T. A. Leddy to S. L. McHenry, April 5, 1866, W. T. Purman to A. H. Jackson, September 30, 1867, A. Mahoney to J. H. Lyman, October 2, 1866, BRFAL.

6

1. J. G. Foster to G. L. Hartsuff, April 11, 1866, Foster to Lorenzo Thomas, April 22, 1866, Foster to Clayborn and Cunningham, April 19, 1866, Foster Letterbook.

2. J. G. Foster to James Tucker, April 29, 1866, ibid.

3. *Tallahassee Semi-Weekly Floridian*, February 6, 1866; *Gainesville New Era*, February 23, 1867.

4. *Tallahessee Semi-Weekly Floridian*, April 13, 1866; Many Colored Citizens of Franklin County to T. W. Osborn, February 23, 1866, BRFAL; J. G. Foster to D. S. Walker, September 29, 1866, Foster to W. P. Dockray, October 19, 1866, Foster Letterbook.

5. J. E. Quentin to Charles Mundee, August 1, 1866, BRFAL.

6. Catherine R. Bent and Harriet R. Barnes to T. W. Osborn, March 14, 1866, J. H. Durkee to Osborn, January 26, 1866, ibid.

7. *Tallahassee Semi-Weekly Floridian*, March 23, May 1, 1866; S. L. McHenry to W. G. Vance, May 25, 1866, BRFAL.

8. E. D. Townsend to J. G. Foster, April 9, 1866, Foster to AAG, June 19, 1866, Foster Letterbook; Townsend to Assistant Commissioner, April 9, 1866, AGP; *Tallahassee Semi-Weekly Floridian*, April 17, 1866; Nathaniel Usher to Edward Jordan, November 15, 1866, Solicitor's Records; Foster to James Speed, June 13, 1866, AGP.

9. J. G. Foster to George Lee, July 26, 1866, Foster to G. L. Hartsuff, June 15, 1866, Wilkinson Call to U. S. Grant, June 9, 1866, Foster Letterbook.

10. J. A. Remley to S. L. McHenry, July 31, 1866, W. W. Moore to A. Mahoney, April 4, 1866, McHenry to Mahoney, April 11, 1866, Mahoney to McHenry, May 1, 1866, BRFAL.

11. S. L. McHenry to A. B. Grumwell, June 25, 1866, D. S. Walker to T. W. Osborn, May 22, 1866, Thomas Chase to D. S. Walker, June 27, 1866, ibid.; Charles Mundee to L. L. Lulansky, April 11, 1866, Foster Letterbook.

12. A. B. Grumwell to S. L. McHenry, June 30, 1866, C. M. Hamilton to S. L. McHenry, March 31, 1866, BRFAL.

13. W. G. Vance to T. W. Osborn, May 1, 1866, S. L. McHenry to Vance, May 8, 1866, F. E. Grossman to J. H. Lyman, October 19, 1866, ibid.

14. J. H. Durkee to S. L. McHenry, June 18, July 1, 1866, James Banks to T. W. Osborn, May, 1866, ibid.

15. W. L. Apthorp to S. L. McHenry, May 29, 1866, A. Mahoney to McHenry, May 1, 1866, ibid.; *Tallahassee Semi-Weekly Floridian*, June 25, 1866.

16. J. H. Durkee to T. W. Osborn, May 1, 1866, J. A. Remley to A. H. Jackson, May 31, 1867, BRFAL.

17. J. H. Durkee to S. L. McHenry, July 20, 1866, D. S. Walker to J. G. Foster, August 3, 1866, ibid.

18. J. G. Foster to Commander, Department of South Carolina, April 28, 1866, Foster to Nathaniel Usher, April 29, 1866, Foster to D. S. Walker, May 19, 1866, Foster to W. P. Dockray, October 19, 1866, Foster Letterbook; J. E. Quentin to J. H. Lyman, October 17, 1866, BRFAL.

19. J. G. Foster to D. S. Walker, June 12, 1866, Foster Letterbook.

20. D. S. Walker to Joseph Tilman, June 13, 1866, BRFAL; U.S., House, *Executive Document No. 57*, 40th Cong., 2d sess., p. 11.

21. J. G. Foster to D. S. Walker, June 27, 1866, A. B. Grumwell to Charles Mundee, September 29, 1866, BRFAL.

22. C. N. Jordan to D. S. Walker, June 26, 1866, A. C. Blount to Jordan, June 26, 1866, Walker to J. G. Foster, July 9, 1866, ibid.; Robert Garrett claim, Southern Claims Commission.

23. D. S. Walker to J. G. Foster, July 25, 1866, BRFAL.

24. *Tallahassee Semi-Weekly Floridian*, July 26, 1866; W. G. Vance to E. C. Woodruff, October 5, 1866, BRFAL.

25. J. G. Foster to D. S. Walker, May 7, 1866, Foster to J. T. Sprague, May 10, 1866, Foster to Lorenzo Thomas, May 10, 1866, Foster Letterbook.

26. E. Philips to J. J. Philips, July 2, 1866, Philips Papers; J. G. Foster to W. H. Kimball, July 6, 1866, Foster Letterbook; C. M. Hamilton to Charles Mundee, June 24, 1866, Hamilton to S. L. McHenry, July 5, 1866, BRFAL.

27. Amos Whitehead to W. H. Branch, August 16, 1866, Branch Papers; D. M. Hammond to A. H. Jackson, October 7, 1867, BRFAL.

28. Patrick, *Reconstruction of the Nation*, p. 86; *Tallahassee Semi-Weekly Floridian*, July 23, August 30, 1866.

29. *St. Augustine Examiner*, September 15, October 13, 1866; *Tallahassee Semi-Weekly Floridian*, August 23, 1866.

30. J. G. Foster to George Lee, September 11, 1866, Foster Letterbook.

31. *Tallahassee Semi-Weekly Floridian*, December 11, 12, 1866.

32. J. G. Foster to Francis Eppes, September 11, 1866, Foster to D. S. Walker, September 11, 1866, D. P. Hogue to Foster, September 14, 1866, Foster to Hogue, September 15, 1866, Foster to G. L. Hartsuff, September 17, 1866, Foster Letterbook; *St. Augustine Examiner*, October 6, 1866; Francis Eppes to Walker, September 15, 1866, BRFAL.

33. P. H. Sheridan to J. G. Foster, October 8, 1866, Foster to Francis Eppes, September 12, 1866, Foster Letterbook; *Tallahassee Semi-Weekly Floridian*, October 19, 1866.

34. M. H. Strain to A. B. Grumwell, November 9, 1866, W. G. Vance to J. T. Sprague, October 21, 1866, BRFAL.

35. W. J. Purman to C. M. Hamilton, September 29, 1866, ibid.

36. M. L. Stearns to J. G. Foster, October 5, 1866, Foster Letterbook; C. A. Hentz Autobiography, 2:22, Hentz Papers.

37. E. B. Duncan to J. G. Foster, September 21, 1866, BRFAL.

38. T. A. Leddy to S. L. McHenry, August 1, 1866, M. L. Stearns to J. H. Lyman, October 22, 1866, J. G. Foster to J. H. Durkee, October 17, 1866, J. T. Sprague to O. O. Howard, December 12, 1866, ibid.; *St. Augustine Examiner*, February 2, 1867; *Tallahassee Semi-Weekly Floridian*, February 12, 1867.

39. A. Mahoney to Charles Mundee, September 2, 1866, BRFAL.

40. E. C. Woodruff to Commander, Port of Tampa, April 22, 1866, P. G. Wall to T. W. Osborn, June 5, 1866, W. G. Vance to Osborn, June 20, 1866, ibid.

41. J. G. Foster to D. S. Walker, October 12, 1866, Foster to W. P. Dockray, October 19, 1866, Foster Letterbook; Foster to W. G. Vance, October 13, 1866, Foster to O. O. Howard, December 3, 1866, BRFAL.

42. Confidential letter of O. O. Howard, September 19, 1866, A. P. Ketchum to E. C. Woodruff, December 19, 1866, W. G. Vance to J. T. Sprague, October 21, 1866, BRFAL; *Tallahassee Semi-Weekly Floridian*, November 6, 1866.

43. F. E. Grossman to J. H. Lyman, October 27, November 10, 1866, BRFAL.

44. J. T. Sprague to O. O. Howard, February 28, 1867, ibid.

45. War Department Circular Number 20, November 20, 1865, ibid.; J. W. Barlow to Florida DTC, April 10, 1866, Tax Commission to Barlow, April 10, 1866, DTC; J. G. Foster to D. S. Walker, April 14, 1866, Foster Letterbook.

46. J. G. Foster to D. S. Walker, May 12, 1866, Charles Mundee to J. T. Sprague, May 7, 1866, Foster Letterbook.

47. J. G. Foster to Lorenzo Thomas, May 12, 1866, Foster to D. S. Walker, May 19, June 26, 1866, Foster to O. O. Howard, June 26, July 6, 1866, ibid.; *Tallahassee Semi-Weekly Floridian*, May 18, 1866.

48. George Lee to J. G. Foster, August 19, 1866, Foster Letterbook.

49. J. G. Foster to Mrs. S. N. Freeman, October 6, 1866, Foster to Colonel Barlow, October 6, 1866, Foster to J. T. Sprague, October 6, 1866, ibid.

50. D. S. Walker to J. G. Foster, October 18, 1866, ibid.

51. J. G. Foster to D. S. Walker, October 19, 1866, ibid.

52. J. G. Foster to G. L. Hartsuff, October 6, 1866, ibid.

53. J. G. Foster to O. O. Howard, November 21, 1866, ibid.

54. J. G. Foster to George L. Hartsuff, November 19, 1866, ibid.; *Tallahassee Semi-Weekly Floridian*, November 16, 1866; Florida, *House Journal*, 1866, pp. 128–29.

55. J. G. Foster to O. O. Howard, November 18, 21, 1866, Foster to P. H. Sheridan, November 25, 1866, Foster Letterbook; Daniel Richards to Elihu B. Washburne, November 23, 1866, Elihu B. Washburne Papers.

56. *Tallahassee Semi-Weekly Floridian*, November 16, 1866; Florida, *House Journal*, 1866, pp. 25, 43.

57. *Tallahassee Semi-Weekly Floridian*, October 30, November 6, 13, 1866; Florida, *House Journal*, 1866, pp. 75–81.

58. *Gainesville New Era*, April 20, 1867.

59. P. A. Meline to D. S. Walker, November 21, 1867, 3MD.

60. W. G. Vance to A. H. Jackson, September 25, 1867, J. A. Remley to Jackson, October 31, 1868, BRFAL.

61. A. B. Grumwell to A. H. Jackson, July 31, 1867, W. G. Vance to Jackson, July 31, 1867, W. J. Purman to Jackson, November 12, 1867, C. M. Hamilton to E. C. Woodruff, February 4, 1867, J. A. Remley to Jackson, July 31, 1867, Jackson to R. Comba, March 10, 1868, ibid.

62. J. A. Remley to A. H. Jackson, July 31, 1867, ibid.

63. J. E. Quentin to A. H. Jackson, December 1, 16, 1867, F. F. Flint to A. B. Grumwell, August 8, 1867, W. J. Purman to Jackson, September 30, 1867, Grumwell to Jackson, June 12, 1867, ibid.

64. J. E. Quentin to E. C. Woodruff, March 29, 1867, Woodruff to Quentin, April 4, 1867, ibid.; *Tallahassee Semi-Weekly Floridian*, April 2, 1867; *Gainesville New Era*, April 20, 1867.

65. J. C. Emerson to D. Richards, January 11, 1867, William Pitt Fessenden Papers.

66. *Tallahassee Semi-Weekly Floridian*, November 6, 1866.

7

1. Paul E. Fenlon, "The Florida, Atlantic and Gulf Central Railroad: The First Railroad in Jacksonville," pp. 73–76.

2. A. R. Meek to Sanderson and L'Engle, April 20, 1870, L'Engle Papers; *Tallahassee Semi-Weekly Floridian*, February 26, 1867; *St. Augustine Examiner*, June 19, 1869; J. R. Hawley to C. G. Halpine, March 5, 1863, Marshall O. Roberts to E. M. Stanton, March 11, 1869, AGO.

3. George W. Pettingill, Jr., *The Story of Florida Railroads*, pp. 24–26.

4. *Tallahassee Semi-Weekly Floridian*, March 9, 1866.

5. T. W. Osborn to C. Mundee, Osborn to W. L. Apthorp, October 2, 1865, BRFAL; General Israel Vogdes to AAG, Department of the South, May 27, 1865, Yulee Papers.

6. Alexander Bliss to Maxwell Woodhull, October 27, 1865, BRFAL; Samuel A. Swann to D. L. Yulee, July 8, 1865, Yulee Papers.

7. Nathaniel Usher to James Speed, August 17, 1865, J. G. Foster to Speed, July 9, 1866, AGO; Nathaniel Usher to Solicitor, July 5, 1867, Solicitor's Records; E. G. Campbell, "Indebted Railroads: A Problem of Reconstruction," pp. 168–69.

8. George Lee to J. G. Foster, November 6, 1865, Foster Letterbook.

9. A. R. Meek to Sanderson and L'Engle, April 20, 1870, William H. Whitner to Sanderson, April 1, 1869, L'Engle Papers; *Tallahassee Semi-Weekly Floridian*, October 9, 1866, January 22, 1867; A. B. Stonelake to Joseph Wilson, January 22, 1867, GLO.

10. Thomas B. Coddington v. Pensacola and Georgia Railroad and Internal Improvement Fund Trustees, U.S. Circuit Court Cases; Marshall O. Roberts to E. M. Stanton, March 11, 1863, AGO; *St. Augustine Examiner*, June 19, 1869; Nathaniel Usher to Solicitor, June 5, 1866, Solicitor's Records; David S. Walker to James Speed, June 18, 1866, AGP; F. F. L'Engle to E. M. L'Engle, June 26, 1865, L'Engle Papers; *Tallahassee Semi-Weekly Floridian*, November 7, 10, 1865.

11. *Tallahassee Semi-Weekly Floridian*, November 7, 10, 1865.

12. Ibid., March 9, 1866.

13. Ibid., November 17, 1865, July 5, 1866.

14. *Thomasville Southern Enterprise*, June 20, 1866; *Tallahassee Semi-Weekly Floridian*, June 21, 25, July 12, August 27, October 9, 19, 1866.

15. Ethelred Philips to J. J. Philips, December 19, 1866, Philips Papers.

16. *Tallahassee Semi-Weekly Floridian*, June 7, 11, August 22, 1867; *Thomasville Southern Enterprise*, August 30, October 25, December 6, 1866; *Jacksonville Florida Union*, July 15, 1869.

17. *Minutes of the Proceedings of the Board of Trustees of the Internal Improvement Fund*, pp. 293–94 (hereafter cited as *Minutes of the IIF*); Harrison Reed to Pensacola and Georgia Board of Directors, February 23, 1869, Pensacola and Georgia Railroad Directors Minute Book.

18. *St. Augustine Examiner*, June 29, 1867; J. G. Foster to S. L. Niblack, Foster to N. Usher, April 24, 1866, Foster Letterbook; *Minutes of the IIF*, pp. 293–94, 305–21; *Gainesville New Era*, August 31, 1867; Paul E. Fenlon, "The Notorious Swepson-Littlefield Fraud," p. 237.

19. Pettingill, *Florida Railroads*, p. 39; Pensacola and Georgia Railroad Directors Minute Book, March 19, 1869.

20. *Jacksonville Mercury and Floridian*, January 16, March 13, 1869.

21. Marshall O. Roberts to E. M. Stanton, March 11, 1863, AGO; Dudley S. Johnson, "The Railroads of Florida, 1865–1900," p. 79; *St. Augustine Examiner*, September 8, 1866; Samuel A. Swann to Singletary, May 3, 1866, Swann Papers; *Tallahassee Semi-Weekly Floridian*, February 22, 1867; D. M. Hammond to A. H. Jackson, September 10, 1868, BRFAL; *Gainesville New Era*, March 9, 1867; F. C. Barrett to D. L. Yulee, July 11, 1865, Yulee Papers.

22. *Minutes of the IIF*, pp. 287–90; Swann to Singletary, May 3, 1866, Swann Papers.

23. *Minutes of the IIF*, p. 293; Magrath to Sanderson and L'Engle, July 10, 1869, W. R. Rembert to E. M. L'Engle, February 25, 1870, L'Engle Papers; *Jacksonville New South*, June 2, 1875; *St. Augustine Examiner*, June 29, 1869.

24. *Tallahassee Semi-Weekly Floridian*, November 13, 1866, March 15, 1867.

25. Johnson, "Railroads of Florida," pp. 75–76; Charles Murphy to M. R. Emery, April 24, 1882, Commissioner of Internal Revenue, Records.

26. J. H. Jenks to N. Sargent, September 9, 1868, M. H. Hale to George S. Boutwell, March 2, 1870, Special Agents' Reports, Department of the Treasury; C. B. Rogers to W. J. Lutterloh, December 7, 1869, January 5, 22, June 6, 1870, Lutterloh Papers.

27. Johnson, "Railroads of Florida," p. 80.

28. O. M. Avery to General E. S. Canby, May 15, 1865, Microfilm 619, File 30T66, AGO.

29. O. M. Avery to General Charles R. Woods, December 18, 1865, George H. Thomas to Quartermaster General, January 31, 1866, General Richard Delafield to War Department, February 6, 1866, ibid.

30. Warren Q. Dow Diary, February 14, 1868; Minute Book, U.S. District Court, Northern District of Florida; *Tallahassee Semi-Weekly Floridian*, February 26, 1867.

31. *Tallahassee Semi-Weekly Floridian*, March 25, 1868; *Laws of Florida*, 1868, p. 133; *Brief of Pensacola and Louisville Railroad in Matter of the Alabama and Florida Railroad* (Washington, 1869), pp. 5–6, PKY; *Pensacola Tri-Weekly Observer*, October 19, 1868; *Pensacola Commercial*, February 26, 1868.

32. *Minutes of the IIF*, pp. 308, 313, 317, 345–46; F. T. Smith, ed., *Florida and Texas, A Series of Letters*, p. 40; Florida Merchant Marine Survey, WPA Writers' Project, manuscript.

33. *Minutes of the IIF*, p. 299; *Tallahassee Semi-Weekly Floridian*, April 9, 1867.

34. T. W. Osborn to O. O. Howard, January 25, 1866, BRFAL.

35. Samuel A. Swann to Rafael Perez, August 5, 1865, Swann Papers.

36. *St. Augustine Examiner*, November 17, 1866; Smith, *Florida and Texas*, p. 40; *Tallahassee Semi-Weekly Floridian*, June 8, 1866; Florida Merchant Marine Survey.

37. *Tallahassee Semi-Weekly Floridian*, March 9, 1866.

38. S. C. Osborn to A. H. Jackson, February 14, 1867, BRFAL; *Tallahassee Semi-Weekly Floridian*, February 12, 1866, February 5, 1867.

39. *Tallahassee Semi-Weekly Floridian*, January 25, 1867; *Jacksonville Florida Union*, October 22, 1868; W. G. Vance to George S. Boutwell, September 21, 1869, Applications for Collector; W. L. Apthorp to A. H. Jackson, February 15, 1868, BRFAL.

40. D. M. Hammond to A. H. Jackson, October 2, November 3, 1868, BRFAL; C. H. Mallory to George S. Boutwell, June 30, 1871, William P. Clyde to Boutwell, June 30, 1871, Applications for Collector.

41. *Report of Secretary of Treasury, Commerce and Navigation*, 1866–68.

42. Frank N. Wicker to George S. Boutwell, November 25, 1870, Special Agents' Reports.

43. S. A. Swann to W. H. Stringfellow, September 21, 1868, Swann Papers.

44. *Jacksonville Florida Union*, October 1, 1868; *St. Augustine Examiner*, June 19, 1869; D. E. Maxwell et al. to Secretary of the Treasury, May 1, 1866, Applications for Collector.

45. J. S. Fullerton to T. W. Osborn, October 1, 1865, BRFAL; Israel Vogdes to AAG, May 27, 1865, Yulee Papers; Florida, *House Journal*, 1865–66, pp. 131–32; J. G. Foster to N. L. Delafield, October 21, 1866, Foster Letterbook.

46. *Gainesville New Era*, August 17, 1867; *St. Augustine Examiner*, December 7, 1867; Smith et al. Brief, April 16, 1869, Agreement between Florida Railroad Company and Peninsular Telegraph Company, March 26, 1867, Articles of Incorporation, October 29, 1866, L'Engle Papers.

47. C. A. Hentz Autobiography, 1:367, Hentz Papers; E. Philips to J. J. Philips, October 24, 1866, Philips Papers.

48. Florida, *House Journal*, 1865–66, p. 143; E. Philips to J. J. Philips, July 2, 1866, Philips Papers; *Tallahassee Semi-Weekly Floridian*, July 14, April 13, November 23, 1866, January 29, 1867; *St. Augustine Examiner*, March 30, 1867.

8

1. *Eighth Census*, 2:195, 225; *Ninth Census*, 1:728, 760, 3:348.

2. *Tallahassee Semi-Weekly Floridian*, October 24, 1865.

3. Joseph J. O'Toole to John C. Breckinridge, April 24, 1869, copy in possession of the author.

4. M. L. Campbell and M. T. Wilder to T. W. Osborn, February 21, 1866, E. M. West to J. T. Sprague, March, 1867, J. W. Childs to A. H. Jackson, July 21, 1868, J. E. Quentin to C. Mundee, August 1, 1866, BRFAL.

5. *Gainesville New Era*, December 14, 1867.

6. A. K. Allison to D. L. Yulee, March 22, 1866, Yulee Papers.

7. *Tallahassee Semi-Weekly Floridian,* December 15, 1865, January 11, 26, 1867; *Thomasville Southern Enterprise,* January 25, 1867; *St. Augustine Examiner,* January 26, February 16, 1867; A. B. Grumwell to E. C. Woodruff, January 14, 1867, J. A. Remley to E. C. Woodruff, December 31, 1867, J. H. Durkee to O. O. Howard, November 26, 1866, J. H. Durkee to AAAG, January 1, 1867, BRFAL.

8. *Tallahassee Semi-Weekly Floridian,* November 30, 1866, March 3, 1867; *St. Augustine Examiner,* June 1, 1867.

9. Minute Book 27, U.S. Bankruptcy Court.

10. S. D. McConnell to E. M. L'Engle, August 9, September 11, October 2, 1867, March 2, April 20, 1868, E. M. L'Engle to Cohen, Henckel and Co., December 24, 1868, L'Engle Papers.

11. Maria Baker Taylor Diary, November 8, 1867.

12. S. A. McDowell to Sanderson and L'Engle, November 10, 1870, L'Engle Papers; Maria Baker Taylor Diary, December 1867.

13. S. S. Alderman to E. S. Jaffray and Co., November 27, 1868, Carter, Kirkland and Co., to E. M. L'Engle, October 19, 1867, Simon Katzenberg to E. M. L'Engle, August 10, 1867, Vann and Whitner to E. M. L'Engle, August 13, 1867, Katzenberg to E. M. L'Engle, November 23, 1867, L'Engle Papers.

14. Henderson and Henderson to E. M. L'Engle, October 25, 1868, A. C. Clark to E. M. L'Engle, December 31, 1867, ibid.; W. G. Vance to A. H. Jackson, December 2, 1867, J. E. Quentin to A. H. Jackson, January 1, 1868, BRFAL.

15. J. T. Sprague to O. O. Howard, January 10, 1868, BRFAL; J. P. Bouse to E. M. L'Engle, April 14, 1868, L'Engle Papers.

16. E. Philips to J. J. Philips, December 19, 1866, Philips Papers; T. A. Leddy to E. C. Woodruff, January 1, 1867, J. H. Durkee to AAAG, October 1, 1867, J. E. Quentin to A. H. Jackson, November 2, 1867, A. B. Grumwell to A. H. Jackson, February 29, 1868, BRFAL.

17. M. L. Stearns to A. H. Jackson, July 1, 1867, J. T. Sprague to O. O. Howard, October 31, 1867, A. B. Grumwell to A. H. Jackson, February 29, 1868, BRFAL.

18. A. W. DaCosta to A. Mahoney, June 28, 1867, ibid.; E. Philips to J. J. Philips, December 19, 1866, Philips Papers; *Tallahassee Semi-Weekly Floridian,* February 1, 1867.

19. W. G. Vance to T. W. Osborn, March 31, 1866, J. E. Quentin to A. H. Jackson, October 1, 1867, Petition of Jefferson County planters, March 5, 1868, Order of A. B. Grumwell, March 24, 1868, T. A. Leddy to S. L. McHenry, March 31, 1868, D. M. Hammond to A. H. Jackson, October 2, 1868, BRFAL; E. Philips to J. J. Philips, December 19, 1866, Philips Papers; *Laws of Florida,* 1877, p. 57.

20. G. B. Carse to A. H. Jackson, August 15, 1868, BRFAL.

21. *Tallahassee Semi-Weekly Floridian,* December 1, 1865, October 19, 1866.

22. A. B. Stonelake to Joseph Wilson, July 31, 1867, GLO; *Tallahassee Semi-Weekly Floridian,* February 12, 1867 J. E. Quentin to A. H. Jackson, July 12, 1867, BRFAL.

23. Maria Baker Taylor Diary, October 21, November 2, 27, 1867; J. A. Remley to A. H. Jackson, October 31, 1867; C. M. Hamilton to A. H. Jackson, December 31, 1867, W. J. Purman to A. H. Jackson, January 4, 1868, BRFAL.

24. J. A. Remley to A. H. Jackson, January 30, 1868, BRFAL; Agricultural and Immigration Association of Florida, *Florida, Its Soil, Climate, and Production*; *Jacksonville Florida Union,* November 26, 1868.

25. *Report of the Commissioner of Agriculture,* 1867, p. 105; Walter N. Hart to Ma, January 15, 1867, Microfilm of Walter N. Hart Letters.

26. *St. Augustine Examiner,* March 16, 1867; C. A. Hentz Autobiography, 2:31–32, 43, Hentz Papers; *Jacksonville Florida Union,* October 1, 1868; *Minutes of the IIF,* 1:296; *Pensacola Tri-Weekly Observer,* October 6, 1868; *Tallahassee Semi-Weekly Floridian,* February 19, 1867.

27. E. R. Ames to AAAG, May 6, 1868, BRFAL.

28. E. Philips to J. J. Philips, August 23, 1867, Philips Papers; McIntosh and

Osborn to W. H. Branch, February 9, 1867, Branch Papers; *Tallahassee Semi-Weekly Floridian*, January 26, August 20, 1866; *Tallahassee Sentinel*, December 10, 1868; Leon County Deed Record Books: N, 596; P, 386; U, 363.

29. J. G. Foster to O. O. Howard, September 14, 1866, J. H. Durkee to S. L. McHenry, August 15, 1866, BRFAL; *Tallahassee Semi-Weekly Floridian*, November 24, December 19, 1865.

30. F. E. Grossman to A. H. Jackson, January 5, 1868, J. A. Remley to A. H. Jackson, July 31, 1867, January 30, 1868, R. Comba to E. C. Woodruff, January 23, 1867, BRFAL.

31. *Laws of Florida*, 1865–66, p. 62; M. Martin to A. H. Jackson, September 10, 1868, E. R. Ames to AAAG, May 6, 1868, BRFAL.

32. *Report of the Commissioner of Agriculture*, 1868, p. 465; Records of the Tallahassee Office, GLO.

33. *Tallahassee Semi-Weekly Floridian*, December 15, 1867; M. L. Stearns to C. Mundee, August 31, 1866, S. F. Halliday to Jacob F. Chur, April 19, 1869, George D. Robinson to J. H. Durkee, February 25, 1868, A. B. Grumwell to A. H. Jackson, March 31, 1868, J. T. Sprague to O. O. Howard, October 1868, George B. Carse to A. H. Jackson, June 1, 1868, S. F. Halliday to A. H. Jackson, October 21, 1867, J. Reyes to A. H. Jackson, January 5, 1868, George F. Lippert to A. H. Jackson, July 25, 1868, W. L. Apthorp Report, July 3, 1867, J. L. Husband to A. H. Jackson, September 30, 1867, BRFAL.

34. J. E. Quentin to J. G. Foster, October 1, November 18, 1866, Quentin to Denniston, November 13, 1866, A. B. Stonelake to Joseph Wilson, October 5, 1866, Stonelake to Timothy Welsh, July 23, 1867, A. B. Grumwell to C. F. Larrabee, June 1, 1867, J. G. Foster to O. O. Howard, October 8, 1866, Foster to Nathaniel Usher, May 25, 1866, Foster to T. W. Osborn, May 25, 1866, ibid.

35. Richardson, *Negro in Florida Reconstruction*, p. 79.

36. T. W. Osborn to O. O. Howard, January 25, 1868, BRFAL; *St. Augustine Examiner*, February 16, 1867.

37. J. G. Foster to G. L. Hartsuff, March 6, 1866, AGO; J. Harry Jenks to N. Sargent, April 1, 1867, Special Agents' Reports; Florida Merchant Marine Survey.

38. *Tallahassee Semi-Weekly Floridian*, October 12, 1866; C. A. Hentz Autobiography, 1:368–69, Hentz Papers; *St. Augustine Examiner*, December 11, 1869.

39. *Palatka Herald*, September 25, 1875; M. H. Hale to George S. Boutwell, December 24, 1872, F. N. Wicker to Boutwell, March 14, August 8, 1872, George D. Allen to George H. Williams, July 31, 1873, Harry Jenks to N. Sargent, October 11, 1868, Special Agents' Reports; R. W. Bullock to E. M. L'Engle, January 24, 1870, A. H. Cole to E. M. L'Engle, June 28, 1870, L'Engle Papers; Frederick Tench Townsend, *Wild Life in Florida*, p. 146.

40. F. N. Wicker to George S. Boutwell, August 8, 1872, Special Agents' Reports; George H. Dacy, *Four Centuries of Florida Ranching*, pp. 57–58; J. W. Tucker to H. Sanford, November 9, 1870, Henry S. Sanford Papers.

41. *Tallahassee Semi-Weekly Floridian*, March 19, 1867; *Report of the Commissioner of Agriculture*, 1866, p. 491, 1868, p. 449, 1871, p. 163; C. M. Hamilton to G. S. Boutwell, Applications for Collector; *Reports of the Secretary of Treasury, Commerce and Navigation*, 1866–68; Charles Black to W. L. Crigler, October 13, 1868, W. L. Crigler Papers; Samuel A. Swann to Rafael Perez, August 5, 1865, Swann to Robert Erwin, June 10, 1868, Swann Papers; E. J. Lutterloh to D. L. Yulee, September 20, 1865, Yulee Papers; A. H. Jackson to A. B. Grumwell, August 21, 1868, BRFAL; F. F. L'Engle to E. M. L'Engle, June 26, 1865, L'Engle Papers.

42. A. Mahoney to E. C. Woodruff, January 18, 1867, A. Mahoney to T. W. Osborn, March 1, 1866, January 18, 1867, W. G. Vance to Osborn, March 31, 1866, H. H. Kuhn to Osborn, May 31, 1866, W. J. Purman to A. H. Jackson, June 7, 1867, BRFAL; *Ninth Census*, 1:728; *Tallahassee Semi-Weekly Floridian*, March 19, 1867.

43. T. W. Osborn to O. O. Howard, June 1, 1866, George E. Wentworth to A. H.

Jackson, December 31, 1867, J. A. Remley to Jackson, June 22, 1867, BRFAL; Letters Patent 97, 112, November 23, 1869, U.S. Patent Office Records; William H. Racy to E. M. L'Engle, July 13, 1866, L'Engle Papers; Lemuel Wilson and Robert Meacham to Commissioner, September 15, 1871, GLO.

44. M. L. Stearns to C. Mundee, August 3, 1866, BRFAL.

45. *St. Augustine Examiner*, February 16, 1867; *Tallahassee Semi-Weekly Floridian*, April 24, 1866, February 12, 22, 1867; Dorman, Diary and Notes, 4:312; *Ninth Census*, 1:728; D. M. Hammond to Lt. Sanno, March 1, 1866, D. M. Hammond to A. H. Jackson, March 2, 1868, BRFAL; S. A. Swann to W. H. Stringfellow, September 21, 1868, Swann Papers; S. D. McConnell to E. M. L'Engle, April 13, 1868, L'Engle Papers; A. M. Reed Diary, November 11, 26, 1867; Signature Books, Tallahassee Branch, Freedmen's Savings and Trust Company.

46. *Ninth Census*, 1:728; *Gainesville New Era*, August 31, 1867; D. M. Hammond to A. H. Jackson, March 2, October 2, 1868, W. G. Vance to Jackson, October 31, 1867, BRFAL.

47. Friend R. to Mrs. Hawks, August 3, 1867, Hawks Papers; *Jacksonville Florida Union*, April 29, 1869; *Pensacola Observer*, December 24, 1868; D. M. Hammond to A. H. Jackson, October 2, 1868, J. E. Quentin to E. C. Woodruff, February 25, 1867, W. J. Purman to A. H. Jackson, June 7, 1867, BRFAL.

48. W. J. Purman to A. H. Jackson, June 7, 1867, Petition to T. W. Osborn, April 5, 1866, Robert Hall to Osborn, December 30, 1865, Osborn to McKibben, February 27, 1866, BRFAL; Ledyard Bill, *A Winter in Florida*, pp. 84–85.

49. C. M. Hamilton to J. G. Foster, May 31, 1867, BRFAL.

9

1. W. J. Purman to E. C. Woodruff, February 28, 1867, BRFAL; *Memoirs of Helen Moore Edwards.*

2. Susan Bradford Eppes, *Through Some Eventful Years*, p. 307.

3. Ibid., pp. 308–11.

4. *Tallahassee Weekly Floridian*, February 23, October 12, 30, December 4, 7, 1866, January 15, February 5, 12, 1867; Eppes, *Through Some Eventful Years*, pp. 363–65.

5. T. A. Leddy to S. L. McHenry, April 10, 1866, J. T. Sprague to T. W. Osborn, April 30, 1866, Wilkinson Call to O. O. Howard, May 14, 1866, BRFAL.

6. *Tallahassee Weekly Floridian*, January 28, 1873; Simon P. Richardson, *Lights and Shadows of an Itinerant Life*, p. 181; Charles T. Thrift, *Trail of the Florida Circuit Rider*, p. 95; *Tallahassee Sentinel*, May 1, 1869; *Jacksonville Florida Union*, January 21, 1869.

7. Thrift, *Circuit Rider*, p. 113; *Jacksonville Florida Union*, January 21, 1869.

8. Charles Sumner Long, *History of the AME Church in Florida*, pp. 10, 52, 55–57, 64, 77–78; *Gainesville New Era*, June 22, 1867; Richardson, *Negro in Florida Reconstruction*, p. 85.

9. J. A. Remley to A. H. Jackson, January 30, 1868, Spencer Curtis to T. W. Osborn, April 16, 1866, J. B. Collins to Osborn, May 8, 1866, A. B. Grumwell to E. C. Woodruff, December 31, 1866, M. L. Stearns to Woodruff, December 31, 1866, BRFAL; *Gainesville New Era*, June 22, 1867.

10. Long, *AME Church*, pp. 80–84; *Laws of Florida*, 1872, p. 68, 1873, p. 26; *Jacksonville Tri-Weekly Florida Union*, April 15, 1873.

11. John L. Rosser, *A History of the Florida Baptists*, p. 20; J. T. Sprague to O. O. Howard, October 1, 1867, BRFAL; *Jacksonville Florida Union*, October 14, 1869.

12. Maria Baker Taylor Diary, July 28, 1867.

13. Joseph D. Cushman, *A Goodly Heritage*, pp. 78, 147; Edgar Legare Pennington, "The Episcopal Church in Florida, 1763–1892," p. 56.

14. Cushman, *Goodly Heritage*, p. 66; Warren Q. Dow Diary, March 26, 1868; *Pensacola West Florida Commercial*, June 15, 1869.

15. Cushman, *Goodly Heritage*, pp. 88–90; P. S. Croom to John P. Sanderson, July 12, 1869, A. Marvin to E. M. L'Engle, August 21, 1873, L'Engle Papers.

16. H. A. L'Engle to E. M. L'Engle, January 19, 1869, L'Engle Papers; *Gainesville New Era*, March 22, 1873.

17. Cooper C. Kirk, "A History of the Southern Presbyterian Church in Florida, 1821–1891," pp. 251–60, 266–67, 269–71.

18. Ibid., pp. 267–68, 275; *Gainesville New Era*, March 16, 1867.

19. Michael V. Gannon, *The Cross in the Sand*, p. 182.

20. *St. Augustine Examiner*, September 8, 1866; Gannon, *Cross in the Sand*, p. 184.

21. *St. Augustine Examiner*, January 12, February 9, 1867.

22. J. G. Foster to A. Verot, June 18, 1866, Foster Letterbook; *St. Augustine Examiner*, October 3, 1868; *Jacksonville Florida Republican*, February 5, 1873; Gannon, *Cross in the Sand*, p. 187.

23. J. E. Quentin to E. C. Woodruff, March 7, 1867, BRFAL.

24. A. Mahoney to J. H. Lyman, October 2, 1866, A. B. Grumwell to S. L. McHenry, July 30, 1866, C. M. Hamilton to A. H. Jackson, May 31, 1867, W. G. Vance to A. H. Jackson, September 25, December 2, 1867, J. T. Sprague to Harrison Reed, October 19, 1868, ibid.

25. Signature Book, Freedmen's Savings and Trust Company; *Laws of Florida*, 1869, p. 39; Florida, *Senate Journal*, 1875, p. 297; *Tallahassee Weekly Floridian*, January 28, 1873.

26. *St. Augustine Examiner*, July 24, 1869; *Jacksonville Florida Union*, October 14, 1869; *Live Oak Times*, March 22, 1876; *Quincy Journal*, January 31, 1873; *Jacksonville Florida Republican*, February 5, 1873.

27. *Tallahassee Weekly Floridian*, September 2, 1873; *Laws of Florida*, 1873, p. 37; J. H. Fowler, *Orange Culture in Florida*; S. D. McConnell to E. M. L'Engle, August 29, 1870, L'Engle Papers; *Key West Dispatch*, January 4, 1873.

28. *Jacksonville Florida Union*, January 21, 1869; *Jacksonville Florida Republican*, February 5, 1873; Robert B. Beath, *History of the Grand Army of the Republic*, p. 637.

29. *Tallahassee Weekly Floridian*, September 2, 1873; *Lake City Weekly Reporter*, August 14, 1873.

30. *Tallahassee Weekly Floridian*, July 30, October 12, 16, 1866, August 24, 1869, May 27, September 2, 1873; *Jacksonville Florida Republican*, February 5, 1873; T. W. Osborn to John Pope, June 25, 1867, 3MD.

31. Florida, *Senate Journal*, 1870, *Report of the Superintendent of Public Instruction*, p. 57.

32. A. W. Leonard to H. S. Sanford, August 1, 1872, J. W. DeForest to Sanford, July 7, 1872, Sanford Papers; *Key West Dispatch*, January 4, 1873; Richardson, *Negro in Florida Reconstruction*, p. 115.

33. *St. Augustine Examiner*, September 25, 1869.

34. Nita K. Pyburn, *The History of the Development of a Single System of Education in Florida, 1822–1903*, pp. 93–95.

35. Florida, *Senate Journal*, 1870, *Superintendent's Report*, pp. 55–57, 1872, pp. 57–58, 1874, p. 7; Pyburn, *Education in Florida*, p. 111.

36. Richardson, *Negro in Florida Reconstruction*, p. 122; Pyburn, *Education in Florida*, pp. 113–14; *Tallahassee Sentinel*, May 13, 1876.

37. Florida, *Senate Journal*, 1877, *Superintendent's Report*, p. 94; *Tallahassee Semi-Weekly Floridian*, February 26, October 19, 1866, January 15, 1867; *Gainesville New Era*, February 23, 1867.

38. Florida, *Senate Journal*, 1870, *Superintendent's Report*, pp. 62–63; Pyburn, *Education in Florida*, pp. 109–10.

39. *Report of the Commissioner of Agriculture*, 1873, p. 326, 1874, p. 319, 1875, pp. 473–74, 1876, pp. 329–30; *Jacksonville Tri-Weekly Union*, April 15, 1873.

40. Pyburn, *Education in Florida*, p. 110; "Negro Education in the Cities," Federal Writers' Project Manuscript; Richardson, *Negro in Florida Reconstruction*, p. 121.

41. *Tallahassee Semi-Weekly Floridian*, November 21, 1865, November 16, 30, 1866, September 24, November 5, 1872; W. H. Davidson Diary, December 12, 1873.

42. *Jacksonville Florida Union*, October 14, 1869; A. B. Grumwell to E. C. Woodruff, February 28, 1867, BRFAL; C. A. Hentz, Autobiography, 2:103, Hentz Papers; *Tallahassee Weekly Floridian*, November 26, 1872.

43. William G. Dodd, "Ring Tournaments in Tallahassee"; *Gainesville New Era*, March 22, 1873; *St. Augustine Examiner*, July 31, 1869; Warren Q. Dow Diary, March 26, 1868.

44. *Tallahassee Weekly Floridian*, January 14, March 4, 11, 18, September 2, 1873; *St. Augustine Examiner*, July 3, 24, September 18, 1869; *Gainesville Alachua Citizen*, May 15, 1875; *Gainesville Independent*, May 10, 1873.

45. *Tallahassee Semi-Weekly Floridian*, February 8, 1867; *Thomasville Times*, July 26, 1873; *Jacksonville New South*, August 17, 1874; *Gainesville Alachua Citizen*, February 12, 1876.

46. *Tallahassee Semi-Weekly Floridian*, June 25, 1866, April 9, 1867; George Ledman to N. P. Banks, February 22, 1868, Nathaniel P. Banks Papers; J. A. Remley to A. H. Jackson, July 31, 1867, BRFAL.

47. *Tallahassee Weekly Floridian*, January 7, 1873; *Fernandina Observer*, February 5, 1876.

48. Horace I. Smith to Ellen Call Long, March 8, 1873, Mrs. E. D. Gillespie to Mrs. Long, November 15, 1873, Richard Keith Call Papers; Ellen Call Long, *Florida Breezes*, with an introduction by Margaret Louise Chapman, p. xiii.

49. J. B. Browne to Mrs. Long, January 13, 1876, M. Martin to Mrs. Long, November 19, 1874, Emma Westcott to Mrs. Long, February 21, March 1, 1876, Call Papers.

50. Jesse T. Bernard to Mrs. Long, November 23, 1874, M. S. Girardeau to Mrs. Long, December 20, 1874, Minnie White to Mrs. Long, January 27, 1875, Rebecca White to Mrs. Long, April 4, 1875, E. A. Perry to Mrs. Long, December 15, 1875, ibid.

51. Ida Wood to Mrs. Long, April 8, 1872, ibid.

10

1. David H. Donald, *The Politics of Reconstruction, 1863–1867*, pp. 77–82. In demonstrating that the legislation was the result of compromise, Donald revises Howard K. Beale's older but still useful *Critical Year: A Study of Andrew Johnson and Reconstruction*, which emphasizes economic motives on the part of a comparatively unified group of Radicals which overcame a well-meaning President Johnson and fastened on the South a program whose purpose was primarily to protect powerful northern economic interests by perpetuating Republican ascendancy. Another recent challenger of the Beale thesis is Stanley Coben, "Northeastern Business and Radical Reconstruction, A Reexamination," which shows that businessmen differed on most economic questions of the period. *In Politics, Principle, and Prejudice, 1865–1866*, LaWanda and John H. Cox show that many supporters of congressional Reconstruction were motivated by belief in the principles of civil rights and voted their convictions in the face of opposition from their constituencies. In *The Radical Republicans*, Trefousse argues that the Radicals were more successful in agitating for a policy than in executing one.

2. *Tallahassee Semi-Weekly Floridian*, January 15, 25, 1867; Edwin M. Stanton to Henry Stanberry, January 25, 1867, AGO.

3. Jonathan F. Turner to D. Richards, January 12, 1867, C. L. Robinson to D. Richards, January 8, 1867, O. B. Hart to D. Richards, January 8, 1867, Fessenden Papers; J. T. Sprague to O. O. Howard, February 28, 1867, BRFAL.

4. Patrick, *Reconstruction of the Nation*, pp. 97–99.

5. *Gainesville New Era*, March 9, 1867; *St. Augustine Examiner*, March 9, 1867; S. D. McConnell to Edward M. L'Engle, March 9, 1867, L'Engle Papers.

6. *Tallahassee Semi-Weekly Floridian*, March 1, 1867.

7. Sefton, *Army and Reconstruction*, p. 113.

8. J. T. Sprague to O. O. Howard, March 31, 1867, BRFAL; *Tallahassee Semi-Weekly Floridian*, March 19, 1867.

9. *Gainesville New Era*, April 20, 1867.

10. *St. Augustine Examiner*, April 20, July 20, 1867.

11. *Tallahassee Semi-Weekly Floridian*, March 26, 1867.

12. *St. Augustine Examiner*, March 30, April 2, 6, 13, 1867; E. A. Stanley to C. H. Howard, n/d 1867, Edward McPherson Papers.

13. *Gainesville New Era*, April 6, 1867; Third Military District Orders, May 22, August 24, September 6, November 2, 1867, January 1, March 12, 13, May 22, 1868, G. Troup Maxwell to General John Pope, October 17, 1867, D. S. Walker to Pope, November 9, 22, 1867, J. T. Sprague to Pope, November 13, 1867, 3MD.

14. *Gainesville New Era*, April 13, 1867, Third Military District Order, February 25, 1868, 3MD; U.S. House, *Executive Document No. 1*, 40th Cong., 2d sess., p. 80.

15. *Executive Document No. 1*, p. 24; J. A. Remley to A. H. Jackson, November 30, 1867, BRFAL; J. T. Sprague to John Pope, December 22, 1867, 3MD.

16. *Tallahassee Semi-Weekly Floridian*, April 9, 1867; Third Military District Order, August 12, 1867; *Executive Document No. 1*, p. 24.

17. U.S. House, *Executive Document No. 342*, 40th Cong., 2d sess., pp. 102–7.

18. Davis, *Civil War and Reconstruction in Florida*, p. 466; *Gainesville New Era*, June 29, 1867; *St. Augustine Examiner*, July 6, 1867.

19. Sefton, *Army and Reconstruction*, pp. 130–32; *Executive Document No. 342*, pp. 106–7.

20. John M. Taylor to AAAG, September 28, 1867, AGP; P. A. Melino to J. T. Sprague, July 2, 1867, 3MD; Florida Superintendent of Registration Circular No. 5, September 9, 1867, BRFAL; Third Military District Order, October 5, 1867, Andrew Johnson Papers; *Executive Document No. 1*, p. 25; *Jacksonville Florida Union*, October 12, 1867. Figures vary slightly in different sources.

21. W. H. Nelson to A. B. Grumwell, November 11, 1867, Third Military District Order, October 4, 1867, BRFAL; Third Military District Order, October 5, 1867, Andrew Johnson Papers; P. A. Melino to O. B. Hart, September 3, 1867, William Marvin to Commander, January 17, 1868, 3MD; Wilkinson Call to Edward M. L'Engle, November 3, 1867, L'Engle Papers; *Gainesville New Era*, October 19, 1867.

22. Proceedings, Union Republican Club of Jacksonville.

23. Harrison Reed to D. L. Yulee, April 18, 1867, Platform of April 1867, D. L. Yulee to Philip Fraser, May 17, 1867, Yulee Papers.

24. J. C. Greeley to S. N. Williams, May 7, 1867, ibid.; Proceedings, Union Republican Club, pp. 14–23; Constitution of Union Republican Club of Jacksonville.

25. David S. Walker to D. L. Yulee, May 6, 1867, Charles E. Dyke to Yulee, July 22, 1867, Yulee Papers.

26. John T. Shuften, *A Colored Man's Exposition of the Acts and Doings of the Radical Party South, From 1865 to 1876 and Its Probable Overthrow by President Hayes' Southern Policy*, p. 8; J. A. Remley to E. C. Woodruff, February 28, 1867, BRFAL.

27. J. A. Remley to A. H. Jackson, May 31, 1867, A. B. Grumwell to Jackson, June 29, 1867, Third Military District Order, June 27, 1867, BRFAL.

28. Wallace, *Carpetbag Rule*, p. 44.

29. D. M. Hammond to A. H. Jackson, November 4, 1867, W. G. Vance to Jackson, July 31, 1867, A. B. Grumwell to Jackson, October 3, 1867, BRFAL; *Gainesville New Era*, May 4, 1867; *St. Augustine Examiner*, May 25, 1867.

30. J. H. Durkee to AAAG, October 1, 1867, Lieutenant Sanno to A. H. Jackson, September 29, 1867, BRFAL.

31. *St. Augustine Examiner*, April 27, 1867; W. J. Purman to Jackson, July 1, 1867, J. H. Durkee to AAAG, November 3, 1867, J. E. Quentin to Jackson, July 1, 1867, BRFAL.

32. J. E. Quentin to A. H. Jackson, June 20, July 1, 30, 1867, A. B. Grumwell to Jackson, August 31, September 30, 1867, W. J. Purman to Jackson, July 31, 1867, BRFAL; *Tallahassee Semi-Weekly Floridian,* March 19, 1867; *Thomasville Times,* April 4, 1874.

33. *St. Augustine Examiner,* July 27, September 7, October 5, 12, 1867; Beath, *Grand Army of the Republic,* p. 637.

34. *St. Augustine Examiner,* October 12, 1867.

35. Wilkinson Call to Edward M. L'Engle, November 3, 1867, L'Engle to D. L. Yulee, November 5, 1867, L'Engle Papers; *Gainesville New Era,* June 29, August 31, 1867.

36. Maria Baker Taylor Diary, November 24, 1867; S. D. McConnell to Edward M. L'Engle, September 18, 1867, L'Engle Papers; *Jacksonville Florida Union,* October 1, 1868.

37. Samuel Walker to Thaddeus Stevens, August 21, 1866, Thaddeus Stevens Papers.

38. William H. Christy to Edward McPherson, May 21, 1868, McPherson Papers; G. W. Atwood to Henry S. Sanford, January 29, 1872, Sanford Papers.

39. Minute Book 3, United States District Court, Northern District of Florida.

40. *Gainesville New Era,* June 1, July 18, 20, 1867; *St. Augustine Examiner,* July 27, 1867.

41. *St. Augustine Examiner,* July 27, 1867.

42. J. A. Remley to A. H. Jackson, July 31, 1867, BRFAL; *St. Augustine Examiner,* August 10, 1867. Richards later obtained an injunction staying tax collections in Nassau County but Judge Fraser dissolved it after about ten days.

43. Friend R. to Mrs. Hawks, August 3, 1867, Hawks Papers.

44. C. D. Lincoln to William P. Fessenden, September 20, 1867, Fessenden Papers.

45. J. H. Durkee to AAAG, November 3, 1867, A. B. Grumwell to A. H. Jackson, October 31, 1867, BRFAL; *St. Augustine Examiner,* November 2, 1867.

46. John Allen Meador, "Florida Political Parties, 1865–1877," pp. 78–79.

47. Daniel Richards to E. B. Washburne, November 13, 1867, Washburne Papers.

48. M. L. Stearns to A. H. Jackson, November 1, 1867, BRFAL.

49. G. G. Meade to Adjutant General, February 10, 1868, AGO; J. A. Remley to A. H. Jackson, November 30, 1867, BRFAL; Edward M. L'Engle to D. L. Yulee, November 15, 1867, L'Engle Papers.

50. Daniel Richards to E. B. Washburne, November 19, 1867, Washburne Papers.

11

1. William Marvin to Commander, January 17, 1868, 3MD; Alexander Magruder to Attorney General, January 6, 1868, AGP.

2. Daniel Richards to G. W. Atwood, January 13, 1868, D. Richards to E. B. Washburne, November 19, 1867, February 2, 1868, Washburne Papers.

3. Harrison Reed to John Pope, December 21, 1867, 3MD.

4. L. H. Pelouze to Adjutant General, July 27, 1867, AGO; E. M. Cheney to Edward McPherson, May 13, 1867, W. P. Dockray to McPherson, December 28, 1867, McPherson Papers.

5. *Journal of the Proceedings of the Constitutional Convention Begun January 20, 1868,* pp. 3–5; D. Richards to Washburne, February 2, 1868, Washburne Papers.

6. Wallace, *Carpetbag Rule,* pp. 53–57; Davis, *Civil War and Reconstruction in Florida,* p. 497; *New York Tribune,* February 5–8, 1868.

7. *New York Tribune,* February 10, 1868.

8. Third Military District Order, January 29, 1868, AGO; G. G. Meade to C. H. Austin, January 29, 1868, 3MD.

9. *Pensacola West Florida Commercial,* January 28, 1868; Philip D. Ackerman,

"Florida Reconstruction from Walker through Reed, 1865–1873," p. 112; G. G. Meade to J. T. Sprague, January 26, 1868, 3MD; *New York Tribune*, February 8, 1868.

10. *New York Tribune*, February 8, 1868.

11. *Journal of the Convention of 1868*, p. 30; *New York Times*, February 2, 1868.

12. *Jacksonville Florida Union*, February 8, 1868; *St. Augustine Examiner*, February 8, 15, 1868; *New York Times*, February 7, 1868.

13. U.S. House, *Miscellaneous Document No. 109*, p. 2, and *No. 114*, p. 3, 40th Cong., 2d sess.; *St. Augustine Examiner*, March 7, 1868.

14. *Journal of the Convention of 1868*, pp. 42–47.

15. *New York Tribune*, February 17, 1868; *Pensacola West Florida Commercial*, February 18, 1868; G. G. Meade to O. B. Hart, February 7, 1868, Meade to H. Jenkins, February 11, 1868, Meade to F. F. Flint, February 16, 18, 1868, 3MD.

16. Wallace, *Carpetbag Rule*, pp. 371–74; *Jacksonville Florida Union*, February 28, 1868; U.S. House, *Miscellaneous Document No. 109*, pp. 21–24.

17. *Journal of the Convention of 1868*, pp. 34, 48–49.

18. Ibid., pp. 130–32; *St. Augustine Examiner*, February 22, 1868; H. Reed to D. L. Yulee, February 16, 1868, Yulee Papers.

19. Wallace, *Carpetbag Rule*, pp. 350–58, 362, 393–94; Jack B. Scroggs, "Carpetbagger Constitutional Reform in the South Atlantic States, 1867–1868," p. 492.

20. Wallace, *Carpetbag Rule*, p. 362; Scroggs, "Constitutional Reform," p. 489.

21. U.S. House, *Miscellaneous Document No. 109*; E. B. Washburne to W. E. Chandler, December 17, 1866, DTC; C. B. Wilder to E. B. Washburne, June 10, 1868, Washburne Papers; H. Reed to D. L. Yulee, May 29, 1868, Yulee Papers; C. L. Robinson to George S. Boutwell, December 5, 1870, Applications for Collector.

22. W. H. Gleason to Benjamin F. Butler, December 28, 1868, H. Jenkins to Butler, March 26, 1868, Butler to H. Jenkins, April 8, 1868, John W. Butler to Benjamin F. Butler, April 13, 1868, Benjamin F. Butler to J. W. Butler, April 20, 1868, Benjamin F. Butler Papers; Louis P. Harvey to A. Lincoln, n/d 1862, James R. Doolittle et al., n/d 1862, Applications and Recommendations. In an impressive essay derived perhaps as much from having lived in the 1960s as having studied the 1860s, C. Vann Woodward argues convincingly that congressional members and their northern constituencies were race conscious and just as concerned with keeping Negroes out of the North as with giving them equal status in society. In commenting on Woodward's essay, Russell B. Nye shows that it was easy, within the context of reform movements of the period, for northern reformers to abandon the Negroes in their quest for civil rights after having passionately insisted on their freedom from slavery. See Harold M. Hyman, ed., *New Frontiers of the American Reconstruction*, pp. 125–56. A comprehensive consideration of the same problem is W. R. Brock, *An American Crisis: Congress and Reconstruction, 1865–1867*.

23. W. E. B. DuBois, *Black Reconstruction*, pp. 514–16.

24. *Jacksonville East Floridian*, March 5, 1868; Wallace, *Carpetbag Rule*, pp. 57–58.

25. *New York Tribune*, February 12, 1868; *Washington Weekly Chronicle*, March 28, 1868.

26. *Jacksonville Florida Union*, April 11, 1868; D. Richards to E. B. Washburne, April 8, 1868, D. Richards to G. W. Atwood, June 8, 1868, Washburne Papers; J. T. Sprague to O. O. Howard, March 31, April 30, 1868, BRFAL.

27. J. T. Sprague to G. G. Meade, May 8, 1868, Meade to Sprague, May 29, 1868, Sprague to Meade, July 1, 1868, 3MD; *Jacksonville Florida Union*, April 4, 11, October 1, 1868; B. F. Butler to H. Jenkins, March 26, 1868, Butler Papers; A. B. Grumwell to A. H. Jackson, April 13, 1868, BRFAL.

28. W. H. Christy to Edward McPherson, May 21, 1868, McPherson Papers; D. Richards to E. B. Washburne, April 8, 1868, Washburne Papers; H. Reed to D. L. Yulee, May 29, 1868, Yulee Papers.

29. *Jacksonville Florida Union*, March 7, 1868, quoting *Jacksonville Mercury*, and

March 21, 1868, quoting *Pensacola West Florida Commercial; Pensacola West Florida Commercial,* March 10, 1868; *St. Augustine Examiner,* March 28, 1868.

30. D. S. Walker to D. L. Yulee, February 24, 1868, Yulee Papers.

31. C. E. Dyke to E. M. L'Engle, March 16, 23, 1868, L'Engle Papers.

32. M. D. Papy to E. M. L'Engle, March 10, 1868, Mallory, Maxwell, and Miller to J. P. Sanderson et al., March 26, 1868, J. R. Harris to J. P. Sanderson et al., March 21, 1868, B. A. Putnam to E. M. L'Engle, April 6, 1868, J. M. Palmer to E. M. L'Engle, March 28, 1868, ibid.

33. J. C. McLean to E. M. L'Engle, March 29, 1868, W. D. Barnes to E. M. L'Engle, March 29, 1868, St. George Rogers et al. to J. P. Sanderson et al., March 17, 1868, Joseph Finegan to E. M. L'Engle, March 26, 1868, John A. Handerson to E. M. L'Engle, March 27, 1868, ibid.

34. *Jacksonville Florida Union,* April 23, 1868; *St. Augustine Examiner,* April 11, 1868; E. M. L'Engle to C. E. Dyke, April 10, 1868, John Friend tò J. B. Oliver et al., April 9, 1868, J. B. Oliver to E. M. L'Engle, April 2, 1868, L'Engle Papers.

35. *St. Augustine Examiner,* April 11, 1868; Warren Q. Dow Diary, April 24, 1868; G. G. Meade to J. T. Sprague, April 27, March 10, 12, 1868, 3MD; E. M. L'Engle to W. D. Bloxham, April 7, 1868, G. W. Scott to E. M. L'Engle, April 27, 1868, L'Engle Papers.

36. D. Richards to E. B. Washburne, April 14, 20, May 6, 1868, Washburne Papers.

37. D. M. Hammond to A. H. Jackson, April 1, May 7, 1868, G. B. Carse to A. H. Jackson, April 13, 1868, J. A. Remley to A. H. Jackson, May 1, 31, 1868, BRFAL; S. D. McConnell to E. M. L'Engle, April 13, 1868, L'Engle Papers.

38. A. B. Grumwell to A. H. Jackson, April 30, May 1, 1868, BRFAL; Warren Q. Dow Diary, May 7, 11, 12, 13, 1868.

39. W. J. Purman to A. H. Jackson, May 7, 1868, A. B. Grumwell to Jackson, May 30, 1868, BRFAL; Samuel Walker to E. B. Washburne, June 12, 1868, Washburne Papers; *American Annual Cyclopedia and Register of Important Events* (1868), p. 270.

40. A. Mot to Salmon P. Chase, June 17, 1868, Chase Manuscripts; *Jacksonville Florida Union,* March 7, 1868.

41. B. A. Putnam to E. M. L'Engle, June 4, 1868, L'Engle Papers; G. G. Meade to D. S. Walker, June 3, 1868, 3MD.

42. *St. Augustine Examiner,* August 21, 1869.

43. *Congressional Globe,* 40th Cong., 2d sess., pp. 3607, 3672; U. S. Grant to G. G. Meade, June 27, 1868, Meade to Grant, July 8, 1868, Microfilm 619, File 375A, 1868, AGO.

44. J. T. Sprague to O. O. Howard, June 30, 1868, J. A. Remley to A. H. Jackson, August 31, 1868, BRFAL.

45. G. G. Meade to John M. Schofield, August 2, 1868, Microfilm 619, File 375A, 1868, AGO.

46. *Jacksonville Florida Union,* May 20, 1869.

47. In "The [Florida] Constitution of 1868," pp. 367, 373–74, I implied that the committee's decision against the advocates of Negro rights in Florida was based primarily on the ground that the Monticello draft met all procedural requirements while the Radical draft did not. Since that decision virtually assured the control of Florida by white men, the racial attitudes discussed by C. Vann Woodward in the essay cited in note 22 seem to have been an important factor.

48. Hilary A. Herbert, *Why the Solid South?,* pp. 140–42; E. C. Weeks to H. Reed, September 30, 1868, D. Montgomery to J. C. Gibbs, March 17, 1870, John L. Crawford to Reed, May 13, 1872, Proclamation of Governor Reed, November 6, 1871, Files of the Secretary of State of Florida.

49. E. J. Vann to D. H. Hamilton, January 19, 1869, Ruffin-Roulhac-Hamilton Collection.

12

1. Daniel Richards to E. B. Washburne, January 6, 1869, Washburne Papers.

2. *St. Augustine Examiner,* December 16, 1871; *Laws of Florida,* 1871, pp. 30–31; Florida, *House Journal,* 1872, Governor's Message, p. 31.

3. Florida, *House Journal,* 1868, p. 76; Edward Haslewood to W. H. Gleason, November 17, 1870, William H. Gleason Papers; William A. Scott, *The Repudiation of State Debts,* p. 54; Reginald C. McGrane, *Foreign Bondholders and American State Debts,* p. 298.

4. *Tallahassee Sentinel,* July 3, 1869; Ackerman, "Florida Reconstruction," pp. 164–65; Florida, *House Journal,* 1872, Governor's Message, p. 33.

5. *St. Augustine Examiner,* June 26, 1869; Letter of E. N. Dickerson, June 15, 1870, Yulee Papers.

6. *Jacksonville Florida Union,* February 4, 1869.

7. *Tallahassee Sentinel,* January 8, 1876; *St. Augustine Examiner,* July 3, 1869; *Jacksonville Florida Union,* July 1, 1869.

8. Florida, *House Journal,* 1868, p. 73; H. L. Hart to H. S. Sanford, March 26, 1870, Sanford Papers; *Jacksonville Florida Union,* October 22, 1868; *St. Augustine Examiner,* October 23, August 15, 1868.

9. M. H. Hale to George S. Boutwell, May 6, 1870, Special Agents' Reports.

10. Proclamation of Governor Reed, November 6, 1871, Files of Secretary of State of Florida.

11. *Tallahassee Weekly Floridian,* September 20, 1870.

12. Samuel A. Swann to D. L. Yulee, September 20, October 9, 20, 1871, Swann Papers.

13. Florida Commission of Lands and Immigration, *Florida: Its Climate, Soil and Production,* p. 2.

14. Edward C. Williamson, "Florida's First Reconstruction Legislature," pp. 41–43; M. Martin to A. H. Jackson, October 22, 1868, BRFAL.

15. *St. Augustine Examiner,* August 15, 29, 1868; *Tallahassee Weekly Floridian,* August 11, 1868; *Laws of Florida,* 1868, pp. 166–67. Contrary to Otis A. Singletary's assertion in *Negro Militia and Reconstruction,* p. 36, "military preparedness" of the Reed administration had nothing to do with Florida's electoral votes being cast for Grant and Colfax in 1868.

16. Proclamation of Election, October 28, 1868, Files of Secretary of State of Florida.

17. Florida, *Senate Journal,* Extra Session, 1868, p. 23; Florida, *House Journal,* Extra Session, 1868, pp. 41–42.

18. *St. Augustine Examiner,* November 14, 1868; C. M. Hamilton to George S. Boutwell, December 20, 1869, Applications for Collector.

19. George W. Gile to George B. Carse, November 12, 1868, A. B. Grumwell to A. H. Jackson, November 30, 1868, BRFAL; *St. Augustine Examiner,* November 28, 1868; *Tampa True Southerner,* December 3, 1868.

20. *Jacksonville Florida Union,* December 3, 1868; *Tallahassee Weekly Floridian,* December 1, 15, 1868; *Tallahassee Sentinel,* December 10, 1868; State v. George B. Carse, May 12, 1869, Leon County Circuit Court Records.

21. *Pensacola West Florida Commercial,* December 8, 17, 1868; *Tallahassee Sentinel,* December 10, 24, 1868; 12 *Florida Reports* 259–67; *Jacksonville Florida Union,* December 31, 1868, January 7, 21, 1869.

22. *Jacksonville Florida Union,* January 14, February 4, 1869; Florida, *House Journal,* 1869, pp. 4–6; C. M. Hamilton to George S. Boutwell, December 20, 1869, Applications for Collector.

23. *Pensacola West Florida Commercial*, January 14, 1869; *Jacksonville Mercury and Floridian*, January 10, 1869.

24. *Tallahassee Sentinel*, January 30, 1869.

25. H. Reed to U. S. Grant, January 24, 1870, Source-Chronological Files, Department of Justice, hereafter cited as S-C Files.

26. *Tallahassee Sentinel*, February 6, 13, 1869; *Jacksonville Florida Union*, February 11, 1869; H. Reed to Columbus Delano, December 4, 1869, Applications for Collector.

27. W. H. Gleason to B. F. Butler, December 28, 1868, Butler to Gleason, January 4, 1869, Butler Papers; D. Richards to E. B. Washburne, January 6, 1869, Washburne Papers; U.S. Senate, *Report No. 101*, and *Miscellaneous Document No. 102*, 41st Cong., 2d sess.

28. *Jacksonville Florida Union*, January 28, 1869; *Pensacola Semi-Weekly Commercial*, June 8, 1869; *Palatka Herald*, June 2, 1869, quoting Dyke.

29. *Jacksonville Florida Union*, June 17, 1869; *St. Augustine Examiner*, July 3, 1869; Jonathan C. Gibbs to Edward McPherson, June 17, 1869, McPherson Papers.

30. *Jacksonville Florida Union*, June 17, 24, 1869; C. T. Chase to G. W. Gile, June 9, 1869, BRFAL; Florida, *House Journal*, Extra Session, 1869, p. 32; Derrell Roberts, "Social Legislation in Reconstruction Florida," p. 359.

31. Margaret C. Fairlie, "The Jacksonville Yellow Fever Epidemic."

32. *Jacksonville Florida Union*, June 17, 1869.

33. Ibid., June 17, 24, 1869.

34. Edward M. L'Engle to John P. Sanderson, August 19, 1870, L'Engle Papers.

35. *Laws of Florida*, Extra Session, 1869, pp. 25–36, 40–42; M. S. Littlefield to D. L. Yulee, June 12, 1869, Yulee Papers; *St. Augustine Examiner*, June 19, 1869.

36. *Laws of Florida*, Extra Session, 1869, p. 36.

37. *Jacksonville Florida Union*, July 22, 1869; Fenlon, "Swepson-Littlefield Fraud," p. 246; *Minutes of the IIF*, 1:388.

38. *Laws of Florida*, 1870, pp. 10–13.

39. *Tallahassee Weekly Floridian*, May 31, 1870.

40. C. M. Hamilton to George S. Boutwell, December 20, 1869, J. S. Adams to George S. Boutwell, January 21, 1870, Applications for Collector; Abijah Gilbert to U. S. Grant, January 29, 1870, S-C Files.

41. E. M. Cheney to C. M. Hamilton, January 24, 1870, AGP.

42. G. W. Swepson to H. Reed, May 31, 1869, in Wallace, *Carpetbag Rule*, p. 119; Investigation into the Conduct, Acts, and Doings of H. Reed, Governor of Florida, by a Committee of the Assembly, 1870.

43. *Tallahassee Weekly Floridian*, February 15, 1870; Investigation of Governor Reed.

44. Stephen R. Mallory to E. M. L'Engle, February 19, 1870, L'Engle Papers; Cortez A. M. Ewing, "Florida Reconstruction Impeachments," pp. 315–16.

45. Wallace, *Carpetbag Rule*, p. 105; State v. Milton S. Littlefield, cases 30 and 31; State v. C. H. Pearce, case 27; State v. J. N. Krimminger, case 33, Fall Term, 1870, and State v. J. N. Krimminger, case 43, Spring Term, 1871, Leon County Circuit Court Records; Dorothy Dodd, "'Bishop' Pearce and the Reconstruction of Leon County," p. 9; U.S. House, *Report No. 22*, part 13, pp. 177–79.

46. State v. Krimminger, case 33, Leon County Circuit Court Records.

47. D. S. Walker to D. L. Yulee, June 9, 1870, Yulee Papers.

48. G. E. Wentworth to T. W. Osborn, October 7, 1870, Wentworth to A. T. Ackerman, December 15, 1870, AGP.

49. District Attorney to Solicitor, July 29, 1872, Solicitor's Records; Ralph L. Peek, "The Election of 1870 and the End of Reconstruction in Florida," p. 359.

50. *Tallahassee Weekly Floridian*, August 27, 1872; U.S. House, *Report No. 22*, p. 87; Peek, "Election of 1870," pp. 357–58; Northern District Marshal's Office, Circular No. 1, October 18, 1872, S-C Files; U.S. v. Arthur Macon, February 13, 1872, U.S. Circuit Court Cases.

51. S. L. Niblack to E. M. L'Engle, November 18, 1870, L'Engle Papers.

52. U.S. Circuit Court Cases; *Quitman* [Georgia] *Banner*, January 6, 1871; *Laws of Florida*, 1871, pp. 24–25; State ex rel Bloxham v. Board of State Canvassers, 13 Florida 55, pp. 76–77 (1871); Wallace, *Carpetbag Rule*, p. 209; *Jacksonville Weekly Republican*, February 5, 1873; O. M. Dorman, Diary and Notes, 6:587; *Tallahassee Weekly Floridian*, January 10, 24, February 7, 1871.

53. C. O. Howe to President Grant, June 23, 1871, Applications for Collector.

54. Ibid.; A. M. Soteldo, Jr., to U. S. Grant, April 10, 1871, ibid.

55. Harrison Reed to Commissioner of Internal Revenue, March 4, 1871, T. W. Osborn to A. Pleasanton, April 22, 1871, H. Jenkins to Osborn, April 19, 1871, ibid.

56. N. Gordon Carper, "The Convict-Lease System in Florida, 1866–1923," pp. 15–16, 25–26.

57. Florida, *House Journal*, 1872, Governor's Message, p. 30.

58. Ibid., Extra Session, 1870, pp. 7–8; *Laws of Florida*, 1871, p. 13.

59. Florida, *House Journal*, 1872, Governor's Message, p. 24.

60. Ibid., p. 26.

61. Ibid., p. 9.

62. *Tallahassee Weekly Floridian*, August 1, 1871.

63. Florida, *House Journal*, 1872, pp. 16, 71.

64. Ibid., pp. 257–63; Ewing, "Florida Reconstruction Impeachments," pp. 306–7; Wallace, *Carpetbag Rule*, pp. 160–65.

65. Florida, *House Journal*, 1872, p. 263; J. P. C. Emmons to Edward M. L'Engle, February 9, 1872, George P. Raney to L'Engle, February 8, 1872, L'Engle Papers.

66. M. H. Clay to D. L. Yulee, February 16, 1872, Yulee Papers.

67. Agreement between Harrison Reed and C. T. Chase and F. H. Flagg of the JPMRRCO, and D. L. Yulee of the Florida Railroad Company, January 13, 1872, Yulee Papers.

68. Florida, *Senate Journal*, 1869, p. 320.

69. Wallace, *Carpetbag Rule*, p. 180.

70. *Pensacola Weekly Express*, April 20, 1872.

71. *14 Florida Reports* 303–7.

72. Florida, *Senate Journal*, Extra Session, 1872, p. 68.

73. Herbert, *Why the Solid South?*, p. 159.

74. *Jacksonville Weekly Republican*, February 5, 1872.

75. J. C. Greeley to H. S. Sanford, December 7, 1872, Sanford Papers; A. A. Knight to W. E. Chandler, November 24, 1872, William E. Chandler Papers; J. S. Adams to Horace Porter, October 5, 1872, AGP.

13

1. A. B. Grumwell to A. H. Jackson, August 11, 1868, BRFAL.

2. Florida, *House Journal*, 1868, p. 75; Harrison Reed to Andrew Johnson, July 13, 1865, Andrew Johnson Papers.

3. *St. Augustine Examiner*, August 8, November 14, 1868; *Quitman* [Georgia] *Banner*, September 18, 1868; *Tampa True Southerner*, November 19, 1868.

4. George G. Meade to John M. Schofield, August 2, 1868, Meade to John A. Rawlins, October 14, 1868, AGO; George W. Gile to F. D. Sewell, November 30, 1868, BRFAL; Sefton, *Army and Reconstruction*, Appendix B, p. 262.

5. U.S. House, *Report No. 22*, part 13, pp. 13, 167; Ralph L. Peek, "Lawlessness in Florida, 1868–1871."

6. *Tallahassee Weekly Floridian*, November 7, 1871; Francis P. Fleming, "Reconstruction," microfilm of manuscript.

7. U.S. House, *Report No. 22*, passim.

8. J. E. Quentin to A. H. Jackson, June 1, July 1, July 7, 1868, Edward C. Henry

to A. B. Grumwell, June 17, 1868, S. F. Halliday to A. H. Jackson, September 15, 1868, BRFAL; U.S. House, *Report No. 22*, pp. 13, 114, 127, 135.

9. H. C. Whitley to A. T. Ackerman, September 29, 1871, S-C Files; U.S. Circuit Court Cases.

10. *Tallahassee Sentinel*, April 3, 1869; U.S. House, *Report No. 22*, pp. 166, 264; Richardson, *Negro in Florida Reconstruction*, p. 168.

11. A. A. Knight to G. H. Williams, March 12, 25, 1873, S-C Files; Samuel T. Day to W. A. Richardson, June 18, 1873, C. R. King Deposition, July 15, 1873, W. W. Moore to George S. Boutwell, July 27, 1873, Applications for Collector; T. Pearson to W. A. Richardson, October 6, 1873, Special Agents' Reports; U.S. Circuit Court Cases; *Thomasville Times*, March 22, 1871.

12. J. A. Remley to A. H. Jackson, May 1, September 30, October 31, November 30, 1868, BRFAL.

13. S. D. McConnell to E. M. L'Engle, September 28, 1868, L'Engle Papers; J. A. Remley to A. H. Jackson, September 30, 1868, BRFAL.

14. Robert Bullock to E. M. L'Engle, September 11, 1869, January 24, 1870, L'Engle Papers.

15. U.S. Attorney's Report, March 18, 1874, Solicitor's Records; U.S. Circuit Court Cases; Sherman Conant to A. T. Ackerman, October 23, 1871, S-C Files; Ralph L. Peek, "Lawlessness and the Restoration of Order in Florida, 1868–1871," p. 199.

16. U.S. House, *Report No. 22*, p. 185.

17. A. M. Reed Diary, February 23, 1868; *Tallahassee Sentinel*, March 6, 1869; Peek, "Lawlessness and Restoration of Order," p. 124; *Jacksonville Florida Union*, July 15, 1869.

18. U.S. House, *Report No. 22*, pp. 177–80.

19. E. Philips to J. J. Philips, July 2, 1866, Philips Papers.

20. U.S. House, *Report No. 22*, p. 147.

21. W. J. Purman to A. H. Jackson, June 30, 1868, BRFAL; Wallace, *Carpetbag Rule*, p. 109.

22. *Tallahassee Sentinel*, March 6, 13, 1869; Proclamation of Governor, March 4, 1869, Files of Secretary of State of Florida.

23. *Jacksonville Florida Union*, October 14, 1869; Peek, "Lawlessness in Florida," pp. 178–80.

24. *Tallahassee Weekly Floridian*, November 2, 1868.

25. U.S. House, *Report No. 22*, p. 148; *Tallahassee Weekly Floridian*, May 2, 16, 1871.

26. U.S. House, *Report No. 22*, pp. 89, 165.

27. Richard Pooser et al. to U. S. Grant, November 18, 1871, S-C Files; Daniel Gillis to Uncle, December 10, 1871, Robert Bigelow Burton Papers.

28. District Attorneys' Reports for 1872, 1873, 1874, S-C Files.

29. Warren Q. Dow Diary, September 25, 1868; Stephen R. Mallory to A. F. Mallory, October 3, 1868, Stephen R. Mallory Papers; H. H. Kuhn to J. G. Foster, October 28, 1866, BRFAL; I. Blumenthal to W. R. Anno, August 9, 1875, Coulter and Lutterloh to E. Pierrepont, January 8, 1876, George P. Fowler to E. Pierrepont, November 23, 1865, S-C Files.

30. J. T. Sprague to O. O. Howard, July 31, 1868, BRFAL; *Gainesville Alachua Citizen*, January 1, 1875; Richardson, *Negro in Florida Reconstruction*, pp. 173–74.

31. S. D. McConnell to E. M. L'Engle, September 28, 1868, L'Engle Papers.

32. J. W. Tucker to H. S. Sanford, November 9, 1870, Whitner and Marks to Sanford, September 13, 1870, DeForest to Sanford, June 10, 25, July 14, 1872, E. K. Foster to H. L. DeForest, July 1, 1872, Foster to Sanford, July 21, 1872, Sanford Papers.

33. E. Yulee to E. M. L'Engle, March 8, 1872, L'Engle Papers.

34. Sherman Conant to E. Pierrepont, January 24, 1876, John B. Stickney to Pierrepont, March 16, 1876, S-C Files.

35. W. H. Davison Diary, April 9, 1870.

36. *Tallahassee Weekly Floridian*, January 14, 1873, W. K. Hyer to J. J. Midland, January 8, 1873, State Dept., Notes from British Legation.

37. Hamilton Fish to Edwards Thornton, January 24, 1873, State Dept., Notes to Foreign Legations in the U.S.; A. A. Knight to G. H. Williams, February 26, March 3, 1873, S-C Files.

38. George W. Parsons Diary, 1874, 2:149.

39. A. Leib to N. Sargent, March 4, 1869, Leib to George S. Boutwell, July 20, 1869, Charles S. Park to M. H. Hale, April 4, 1872, Special Agents' Reports.

40. T. Pearson to Secretary of the Treasury, October 4, 1872, Leib to Sargent, March 14, 1868, F. N. Wicker to G. S. Boutwell, October 26, 1870, Special Agents' Reports.

41. A. Leib to N. Sargent, March 14, 1868, M. H. Hale to G. S. Boutwell, September 28, 1872, F. N. Wicker to Madge, October 11, 1872, C. S. Parks to Henry Johnson, August 11, 1874, Special Agents' Reports.

42. W. H. Heiss to E. M. L'Engle, February 8, 1873, L'Engle Papers.

43. Horatio Bisbee to E. C. Banfield, January 5, 1869, U.S. Attorneys' Reports; M. H. Hale to George S. Boutwell, March 2, 1870, January 31, August 8, December 9, 1871, Special Agents' Reports; John Henry Norton, *Jacksonville Trade Circular and Real Estate Advertiser*, p. 6.

44. M. H. Hale to George S. Boutwell, October 17, 1870, T. Pearson to W. A. Richardson, January 3, 1874, A. Huling to G. H. Williams, December 7, 1874, Special Agents' Reports; Sherman Conant to E. Pierrepont, October 5, 1875, S-C Files.

45. A. C. Huling to H. S. Sanford, July 18, 1873, Sanford Papers; Sherman Conant to G. H. Williams, May 22, 1873, S-C Files; John E. Walker to Chairman, Senate Judiciary Committee, January 24, 1874, Papers of the U.S. Senate.

46. G. D. Allen to Edward Jordan, September 15, 1868; U.S. Attorneys' Reports, March 18, 1874; F. N. Wicker to George S. Boutwell, September 24, 1872, Special Agents' Reports; *Marianna Courier*, March 18, 1874.

47. *Jacksonville Florida Union*, October 14, 1869; *Marianna Courier*, March 18, 1873; *St. Augustine Examiner*, October 16, 1869; H. Bisbee to E. C. Banfield, July 10, 1869, G. E. Wentworth to E. R. Hoar, January 17, 1870, AGP.

48. G. D. Allen to E. R. Hoar, October 18, 1869, AGP; J. B. Chinn to Joseph H. Taylor, February 1, 1870, AGO 94; C. R. Mobley to B. H. Bristow, November 21, 1871, S-C Files.

49. F. N. Wicker to G. S. Boutwell, November 25, 1870, Special Agents' Reports; George W. Parsons Diary, November 20, 1874.

50. Lemuel Wilson and Robert Meacham to Commissioner, General Land Office, September 15, 1871, GLO.

51. John S. Banks and S. F. Halliday to Willis Drummond, June 18, 1873, ibid.

52. Banks and Halliday to Willis Drummond, June 17, July 19, 1873, H. S. Harmon to Banks and Halliday, July 19, 1873, ibid.

53. Banks and Halliday to Commissioner, August 27, 1873, Banks and Halliday to Drummond, August 28, 1873, T. A. Leddy to John S. Banks, July 23, 1873, George J. Alden to Register and Receiver, July 12, 1873, J. A. Lee and S. F. Halliday to S. S. Burdett, June 16, 1874, ibid.

54. Davis, *Civil War and Reconstruction in Florida*, p. 586.

14

1. E. Houstoun to J. P. Sanderson, February 3, 1869, L'Engle Papers.

2. C. K. Brown, "The Florida Investments of George W. Swepson," p. 276; Fenlon, "The Notorious Swepson-Littlefield Fraud," p. 238; Pensacola and Georgia Minute Book.

3. Brown, "Florida Investments of Swepson," p. 276; *Jacksonville Mercury and Floridian*, March 27, 1869; *Minutes of the IIF*, 1:370–72.

4. Paul E. Fenlon, "The Struggle for Control of the Florida Central Railroad," pp. 70–72, 88.

5. A. R. Meek to J. P. Sanderson, January 17, April 20, 1870, William H. Whitner to Sanderson, April 1869, L'Engle Papers; *Jacksonville Florida Union*, September 23, October 14, 1869; H. Bisbee to E. C. Banfield, July 16, October 1, 29, 1869, March 28, 1870, Solicitor's Records.

6. Dibble's bankruptcy in 1870 bears out Sanderson's contention.

7. *Jacksonville Florida Union*, October 14, 1869.

8. Ibid.

9. See pp. 209–11.

10. *Tallahassee Weekly Floridian*, May 17, 24, 1870.

11. D. L. Yulee to C. E. Dyke, July 15, 1870, Yulee Papers; Fenlon, "Swepson-Littlefield Fraud," p. 255.

12. Brown, "Florida Investments of Swepson," p. 276; Jonathan Daniels, *Prince of Carpetbaggers*, p. 225.

13. S. W. Hopkins to Milton S. Littlefield, September 6, 7, 1870, E. M. L'Engle to J. P. Sanderson, August 19, 1870, L'Engle Papers.

14. Brown, "Florida Investments of Swepson," p. 282; Johnson, "The Railroads of Florida, 1865–1900," p. 56; Daniels, *Prince of Carpetbaggers*, pp. 259–61; *Tallahassee Weekly Floridian*, October 24, 1871.

15. *Tallahassee Weekly Floridian*, April 20, 1875; E. Houstoun to J. P. Sanderson, November 10, 1870, L'Engle Papers.

16. E. M. Cheney to J. P. Sanderson, August 29, 1870, E. M. L'Engle to Sanderson, August 19, 1870, L'Engle Papers; James G. Gibbs to U. S. Grant, May 2, 1875, Applications for Collector; Pettingill, *The Story of the Florida Railroads*, p. 36; *Report of the Commissioner of Agriculture*, 1871, p. 165.

17. A. Marvin to E. M. L'Engle, July 10, 1873, M. S. Littlefield to L'Engle, June 9, 1875, Henry Elliott to L'Engle, February 22, 1875, Brief of March, 1872, A. Huling to Littlefield, April 15, 1871, M. D. Papy to L'Engle, May 28, 1872, F. B. Papy to L'Engle, August 29, 1873, L'Engle Papers; M. S. Littlefield to W. H. Gleason, April 26, 1875, Gleason Papers; Holland v. Littlefield, April 8, 1871, U.S. Circuit Court Cases; *Tallahassee Weekly Floridian*, October 8, 1872, July 8, 15, 1873.

18. *Gainesville Independent*, May 10, 1873; *Tallahassee Weekly Floridian*, March 25, July 8, 1873; *Laws of Florida*, 1874, p. 108; F. B. Papy to E. M. L'Engle, August 14, 1873, L'Engle Papers.

19. *Tallahassee Weekly Floridian*, June 14, 1870; McGrane, *Foreign Bondholders and American State Debts*, p. 301.

20. W. A. Cocke to Henry S. Sanford, July 18, 1873, Sanford Papers.

21. *15 Florida Reports 533* (1876); *Fernandina Observer*, January 1, 1876; *Tallahassee Sentinel*, January 22, 1876; George P. Raney to E. M. L'Engle, January 21, 23, 1876, L'Engle Papers; 103 *U.S. Reports* 335.

22. Western Division of Western North Carolina Railroad Company v. Jacksonville, Pensacola and Mobile Railroad Company et al., April 13, 1877, U.S. Circuit Court Cases; 103 *U.S. Reports* 333; Johnson, "Railroads of Florida," p. 64.

23. *Laws of Florida*, 1870, p. 111.

24. *Minutes of the IIF*, 1:402; G. W. Means to E. M. L'Engle, January 27, 1871, L'Engle Papers; Agreement between H. Reed and . . . D. L. Yulee, January 16, 1872, Clayton A. Cowgill to D. L. Yulee, August 30, September 10, 1873, May 23, 1874, Yulee Papers; Florida, *House Journal*, 1872, p. 50; Johnson, "Railroads of Florida," p. 81.

25. *St. Augustine Examiner*, June 19, 1869; *Jacksonville Florida Union*, June 8, 1869; Francis Vose v. Florida Railroad Company, October 25, 1876, U.S. Circuit Court Cases.

26. *Jacksonville New South*, June 2, 1875; W. H. Gleason to Trustees of the IIF, n/d, Petition of Southern Inland Navigation and Improvement Company in Vose v. Trustees of the IIF, May 18, 1875, Gleason Papers.

27. Williams, Swann, and Corley to William H. Ludlow, n/d, 6:141–44, and to

Francis Vose, January 23, 1875, 6:6, Swann to Vose, 6:441, 590, Swann Papers.

28. *Laws of Florida,* 1866, p. 37, 1868, p. 139; *Jacksonville Mercury and Floridian,* February 27, 1869; M. L. Stearns to Joseph Wilson, February 26, GLO; *Tallahassee Semi-Weekly Floridian,* April 9, 1867; *Report of the Commissioner of Agriculture,* 1871, p. 165.

29. Contract between Southern Inland . . . Company and Trustees of the IIF, n/d, Bill of Complaint, Gleason v. Southern Inland . . . Company, October, 1883, N. H. Moragne to S. B. Conover, February 7, 1871, Memorandum to Trustees of the IIF, Gleason Papers; *Minutes of the IIF,* 2:8, 93–94.

30. *Minutes of the IIF,* 2:61–63, 482–83, 298–99; Deed of Southern Inland . . . Company to Atlantic and Gulf Transit Company, n/d, Gleason Papers.

31. *Great Southern Railway,* preface; *Laws of Florida,* Extra Session, 1870, p. 54, and 1874, p. 75; *Tallahassee Weekly Floridian,* April 15, 1873; *Minutes of the IIF,* 2:444–45, 469–70.

32. A. C. Osborn to M. H. Alberger, February 19, 1871, S-C Files; *Tallahassee Weekly Floridian,* April 15, 1873.

33. *Tallahassee Weekly Floridian,* April 15, August 19, 1873; *Minutes of the IIF,* 2:13–14.

34. *Tallahassee Weekly Floridian,* August 20, 1872; Johnson, "Railroads of Florida," p. 114.

35. Prospectus of the Pensacola and Mobile Railroad and Manufacturing Company, n/d, 1873; W. H. Davison Diary, November 11, 1872; Johnson, "Railroads of Florida," p. 113.

36. W. H. Davison Diary, September 4, 1868; *Tallahassee Weekly Floridian,* November 5, 1872, July 1, 1873; Prospectus of Pensacola and Mobile Railroad and Manufacturing Company, p. 4.

37. *Jacksonville Weekly Florida Union,* December 16, 1876.

38. *St. Augustine Examiner,* August 29, 1868; *Thomasville Times,* July 26, 1873.

39. *Tallahassee Weekly Floridian,* May 31, 1870.

15

1. Edward King, "Pictures from Florida"; Samuel A. Swann to J. M. Wing and Company, March 5, 1875, Swann Papers; A. C. Clark to E. M. L'Engle, May 23, 1870, L'Engle Papers.

2. *Florida, Its Climate, Soil and Productions . . . A Manual . . . to Immigrants;* C. H. Dupont to H. S. Sanford, June 19, 1870, Joseph Finegan to Sanford, June 16, 1871, Sanford Papers.

3. C. H. Dupont to E. M. L'Engle, March 28, May 17, 1871, L'Engle Papers; C. A. Hentz Autobiography, 2:91–92.

4. B. F. Whitner to H. S. Sanford, November 1, 1870, H. L. DeForest to Sanford, April 11, June 7, 17, July 19, 23, 1871, January 11, March 4, 28, April 1, 15, May 6, June 17, 1872, September 22, 1873, Sanford Papers.

5. H. L. DeForest to H. S. Sanford, April 15, 1872, September 22, 1873, ibid.

6. H. L. DeForest to H. S. Sanford, January 14, 23, 1873, ibid.; Samuel A. Swann to D. L. Yulee, August 2, 1871, Swann Papers; W. H. Davison Diary, November 3, 1873; *Jacksonville Florida Union,* September 16, 1869; *Pensacola West Florida Commercial,* February 18, 1869.

7. *Pensacola Tri-Weekly Observer,* October 6, 1868; Derrell C. Roberts, "Joseph E. Brown and Florida's New South Economy," p. 53.

8. Richard J. Amundson, "The Florida Land and Colonization Company," p. 153; Thomas Haigh to H. S. Sanford, April 29, 1871, H. L. DeForest to Sanford, March 11, 1873, A. W. Leonard to Sanford, October 9, 1873, Sanford Papers; *Palatka Eastern Herald,* April 13, 1874, November 20, 1875; George W. Parsons Diary, May 21, 1875.

9. Thomas Haigh to H. S. Sanford, April 29, 1871, Sanford Papers; Florida Commission of Lands and Immigration, *Florida: Its Climate, Soil and Production.*

10. Central Florida Land Agency, *Florida: Its Climate, Soil and Productions*; Fowler, *Orange Culture in Florida*; S. A. Swann to D. L. Yulee, August 28, 1875, Swann Papers.

11. Samuel A. Swann to D. L. Yulee, August 28, 1875, Swann Papers; Diary of Erastus Hill, January 1877; *Tallahassee Weekly Floridian,* April 8, 1873.

12. Samuel A. Swann to Sanderson and L'Engle, November 29, 1870, Felix Livingston to Sanderson and L'Engle, March 8, 1871, L'Engle Papers; George W. Parsons Diary, September 11, 1873; C. B. Rogers to W. J. Lutterloh, June 25, 1874, July 23, 1877, W. J. Lutterloh Papers.

13. *Fernandina Observer,* June 28, 1873, December 19, 1874; George W. Parsons Diary, September 8, 1873; Samuel A. Swann to B. H. Gurganus, March 24, 1875, Swann Papers; Daniel H. Jacques, *Florida as a Permanent Home.*

14. *Jacksonville Mercury and Floridian,* January 10, 1869; *Jacksonville Florida Union,* May 20, 1869.

15. *Jacksonville Weekly Republican,* April 15, 1873; *Tallahassee Weekly Floridian,* September 2, 1873; *Gainesville New Era,* March 22, 1873; *Jacksonville Florida News,* May 4, 1873; *Jacksonville Tri-Weekly Republican,* April 15, 1873; Leroy D. Ball to J. A. Williamson, GLO; *Fernandina Observer,* January 1, 1876.

16. *Tallahassee Weekly Floridian,* March 25, 1873; Norton, *Jacksonville Trade Circular and Real Estate Advertiser,* p. 6; T. C. Rigbey, *Dr. Rigbey's Papers on Florida,* p. 56; William Watts to Menifie Huston, March 20, 1874, D. L. Huston to Menifie Huston, March 17, 1874, Menifie Huston Papers; George W. Parsons Diary, May 29, 1875.

17. W. J. Purman to W. J. Douglass, November 19, 1874, Applications for Collector; George W. Parsons Diary, May 29, June 2, 1875; H. A. Lilly to Dear Friend, March 5, 1876, Miscellaneous Letters, SHC.

18. *St. Augustine Examiner,* June 27, December 11, 1869; *Jacksonville Florida Union,* January 21, 1869; Rigbey, *Rigbey's Papers,* p. 58.

19. C. A. Hentz to Brother, February 23, 1868, Hentz Papers; Walter N. Hart to Ma, January 15, 1867, Hart Letters; L. D. Huston to Menifie Huston, March 17, 1874, Huston Papers.

20. *Palatka Eastern Herald,* September 11, November 6, 20, 1875.

21. L. D. Huston to Menifie Huston, March 17, 1874, Huston Papers; Samuel A. Swann to J. M. Wing and Co., March 5, 1875, Swann Papers; *Palatka Eastern Herald,* November 6, 1871.

22. John G. Price to Daughter, February 10, March 26, 1876, C. G. Simrall Papers; Bill, *A Winter in Florida,* p. 112; A. M. Reed Diary, December 26, 1868; *Jacksonville Weekly Republican,* February 5, 1873.

23. *Gainesville Alachua Citizen,* January 1, 1875; *Report of the Commissioner of Agriculture,* 1874; *Proceedings of the Florida Fruit Growers Convention, 1874,* p. 7.

24. *St. Augustine Examiner,* February 2, 12, 16, 1867; *Tallahassee Semi-Weekly Floridian,* February 12, 1867; George W. Parsons Diary, January 22, 25, 1874.

25. M. A. Williams to W. H. Gleason, July 22, 1870, W. H. Hunt to Gleason, May 15, 1871, Gleason Papers; George W. Parsons Diary, December 3, 1873, May 3, November 2, 1874; M. L. Stearns to Willis Drummond, July 28, 1871, Stearns to Joseph Wilson, July 24, November 8, 1869, GLO.

26. George W. Parsons Diary, November 8, 1873, July 25, 1874.

27. Assessment Lists, Solicitor's Records; "Cubans in Florida," Federal Writers' Project manuscript.

28. George W. Parsons Diary, November 15, 1873, January 31, 1874.

29. W. H. Davison Diary, November 29, December 1, 2, 15, 1873; George W. Parsons Diary, June 17, 1874.

30. Townsend, *Wild Life in Florida,* p. 47; George W. Wells, *Facts for Immigrants,* pp. 9–10; W. W. Van Ness to H. S. Sanford, September 22, 1871, Sanford Papers; T.

Pearson to H. C. Johnson, May 3, 1875, Special Agents' Reports; *Tampa Florida Peninsular*, February 5, 1873.

31. Charles S. Park to Henry C. Johnson, August 10, 1874, Park to Buford Wilson, April 28, 1876, Special Agents' Reports; *Tallahassee Weekly Floridian*, January 14, February 18, May 20, 1873; *Fernandina Observer*, June 28, 1873; Saunders B. Garwood, "Florida State Grange," p. 175.

32. E. B. Duncan to J. T. Sprague, May 17, 1867, W. J. Purman to A. H. Jackson, June 7, 1867, BRFAL; William J. Keyser Memorandum, November 28, 1870, William J. Keyser Papers; W. H. Davison Diary, October 10, 1874, September 10, 1876; *Tallahassee Weekly Floridian*, April 22, 1873.

33. S. R. Mallory to Philip Phillips, October 3, 1867, Phillips-Myers Papers; W. H. Davison Diary, October 8, 14, 1873, August 30, 1874, June 2–7, 1876; George W. Parsons Diary, September 5, 1874; Edwin W. L'Engle to E. M. L'Engle, October 13, 1876, L'Engle Papers.

34. W. H. Davison Diary, May 13, 1874; *Fernandina Observer*, February 5, 1876.

35. J. E. Dovell, *History of Banking in Florida, 1828–1954*, pp. 64–66; *St. Augustine Examiner*, May 23, 1874; Signature Book, Freedmen's Savings and Trust Company, Tallahassee; M. S. Littlefield to E. M. L'Engle, January 12, 1871, L'Engle Papers.

36. *Tallahassee Semi-Weekly Floridian*, July 14, 1866, January 8, March 12, 1867; Dovell, *Banking in Florida*, p. 61; Assessment Lists, Florida, Solicitor's Records.

37. Dovell, *Banking in Florida*, p. 61; Assessment Lists, Solicitor's Records.

38. Assessment Lists, Solicitor's Records; J. C. Greeley to H. S. Sanford, April 12, 1876, Sanford Papers; A. Marvin to E. M. L'Engle, October 30, 1874, L'Engle Papers.

39. E. G. Eastman to E. M. L'Engle, February 3, 1870, E. G. Johnson to McKesson and Robbins, September 2, 1870, William P. Marshall to Cohen, Henckel and Co., April 1, 1870, S. D. McConnell to E. M. L'Engle, August 29, 1870, F. Lueders to Coffin and Brothers, September 28, 1870, L'Engle Papers; Whitner and Marks to Sanford, September 13, 1870, Sanford Papers.

40. D. G. Ambler to E. M. L'Engle, January 29, 1872, Moses and Cohen to E. M. L'Engle, December 1, 1871, I. H. Moses to E. M. L'Engle, May 7, 1872, January 29, 1873, L'Engle Papers; H. L. DeForest to H. S. Sanford, April 1, May 27, June 25, September 30, 1872, Sanford Papers.

41. H. Fish to Edwards Thornton, January 24, 1873, State Dept., Notes to Foreign Legations; *Laws of Florida*, 1874, p. 103; *Tallahassee Weekly Floridian*, May 27, June 3, 10, 24, July 1, August 5, 1873; F. B. Papy to E. M. L'Engle, August 14, 27, 1873, L'Engle Papers.

42. M. D. Papy to E. M. L'Engle, September 24, 1873, John C. L'Engle to E. M. L'Engle, September 24, 1873, L'Engle Papers; *Tallahassee Weekly Floridian*, September 30, 1873; *St. Augustine Examiner*, October 4, 1873; A. W. Leonard to H. S. Sanford, October 9, 1873, Sanford Papers.

43. W. H. Davison Diary, October 13, 14, 1874.

44. F. B. Papy to E. M. L'Engle, November 13, 1873, A. Marvin to E. M. L'Engle, November 17, 1873, L'Engle Papers.

45. Aaron Marvin to E. M. L'Engle, October 30, 1874, ibid.; Fowler, *Orange Culture in Florida*; W. H. Davison Diary, December 15, 1874.

46. A. Livingston to E. M. L'Engle, June 20, 1876, Edwin W. L'Engle to E. M. L'Engle, November 23, 1875, Henry Elliott to E. M. L'Engle, November 25, 1875, G. P. Raney to E. M. L'Engle, May 27, 1875, L'Engle Papers.

16

1. William J. Purman to W. E. Chandler, April 25, 1872, T. W. Osborn to Chandler, July 11, 1872, Thomas F. Baker to Chandler, May 23, 1872, Chandler Papers.

2. W. W. Van Ness to H. S. Sanford, January 12, 1872, Sanford to J. J. Daniel, n/d

1872, E. K. Foster to Sanford, June 22, 1872, H. L. DeForest to Sanford, September 24, 1872, Sanford Papers.

3. J. C. Greeley to H. S. Sanford, June 22, 1872, ibid.

4. O. B. Hart to T. W. Osborn, November 24, 1865, Hart to Perry G. Wall, June 14, 1866, BRFAL; Hart to D. L. Yulee, July 15, 1868, Yulee Papers.

5. T. W. Osborn to W. E. Chandler, August 5, 1872, Chandler Papers.

6. *Tallahassee Weekly Floridian*, August 13, 1872.

7. Ibid.

8. E. K. Foster to H. S. Sanford, August 27, 1872, Sanford Papers; W. J. Purman to W. E. Chandler, August 22, 1872, Chandler Papers; Wallace, *Carpetbag Rule*, p. 215.

9. H. Reed to U. S. Grant, June 25, 1872, Miscellaneous Collection of Yulee Letters, in Yulee Papers.

10. *Laws of Florida*, 1868, p. 3; James O. Knauss, "Growth of Florida's Election Laws," p. 12; J. W. Locke to T. W. Osborn, October 1, 1872, Chandler Papers.

11. *Tallahassee Weekly Floridian*, August 20, 1872.

12. E. M. Cheney to W. E. Chandler, August 26, 1872, Chandler Papers; E. M. Cheney to O. B. Hart, October 12, 1872, Sanford Papers; A. C. Fisher to U. S. Grant, March 27, 1873, Applications for Collector; *Tallahassee Weekly Floridian*, September 24, 1872.

13. *Key West Dispatch*, July 13, 1872; H. L. Mitchell to E. M. L'Engle, July 25, 1872, L'Engle Papers; *Tallahassee Sentinel*, November 30, 1872; H. C. Page to E. D. Morgan, October 14, 1872, Chandler Papers; *New York Herald*, November 20, 1876.

14. *Tallahassee Weekly Floridian*, August 6, 1872; J. J. Finley to A. L. Smith, July 31, 1872.

15. W. D. Bloxham to R. H. M. Davidson, July 30, 1872, PKY; *Tallahassee Weekly Floridian*, August 6, 1872.

16. W. D. Bloxham to R. H. M. Davidson, July 30, 1872.

17. Florida, *Senate Journal*, Extra Session, 1872, p. 12; O. M. Dorman, Diary and Notes, 4:19–20.

18. *Tallahassee Weekly Floridian*, August 13, 27, October 15, 1872; Abijah Gilbert to Senate Judiciary Committee, n/d, Papers Relating to Presidential Nominations, Senate Papers; J. J. Philbrick to U. S. Grant, March 11, 1872, Eldridge L. Ware et al. to Grant, n/d 1872, F. N. Wicker to George S. Boutwell, August 13, 1872, Applications for Collector; Simon B. Conover to Samuel B. McLin, August 10, 1872, John A. Sherman Papers.

19. *Tallahassee Weekly Floridian*, August 20, 27, 1872.

20. Ibid., August 20, 1872; T. W. Osborn to W. E. Chandler, August 17, 1872, Chandler Papers.

21. C. H. Summers to E. M. L'Engle, August 29, 1872, L'Engle Papers; *Tallahassee Weekly Floridian*, October 15, 1872.

22. A. A. Knight to W. E. Chandler, October 6, 1872, Chandler Papers.

23. W. H. Gleason to W. E. Chandler, September 18, 1872, J. W. Locke to T. W. Osborn, October 1, 1872, Osborn to Chandler, October 2, 1872, Chandler Papers; U.S. Senate, *Report No. 611*, Part 2, 44th Cong., 2d sess., p. 17.

24. T. W. Osborn to W. E. Chandler, October 18, 1872, Josiah T. Walls to Chandler, October 16, 1872, Chandler Papers.

25. W. J. Purman to W. E. Chandler, August 22, 1872, W. E. Chandler to H. Reed, September 15, 1872, H. Reed to Chandler, September 18, 19, 1872, T. W. Osborn to Chandler, August 27, 1872, Chandler Papers; J. O. Townsend to George H. Williams, October 7, 1872, Chandler to U. S. Grant, September 24, 1872, AGO.

26. H. Reed to U. S. Grant, November 4, 1872, Miscellaneous Collection of Yulee Letters; *Tallahassee Weekly Floridian*, October 8, 1872.

27. A. A. Knight to W. E. Chandler, October 6, 1872, Charles H. Cowlan to Chandler, October 8, 1872, Chandler Papers; H. Bisbee to H. S. Sanford, October 9, 1872, Sanford Papers; Josiah T. Walls to Chandler, October 16, 1872, AGP.

28. *Tallahassee Weekly Floridian*, November 5, 1872; T. W. Osborn to W. E. Chandler, November 10, 1872, H. Reed to Chandler, October 24, 1872, T. W. Osborn to Chandler, October 25, 1872, Chandler Papers.

29. A. C. Lightberry to J. C. Gibbs, October 7, 1872, Files of Secretary of State of Florida; A. A. Knight to W. E. Chandler, November 4, 1872, Chandler Papers.

30. Circular No. 1, Marshal's Office, Northern District of Florida, October 18, 1872, S-C Files; *Tallahassee Weekly Floridian*, October 8, November 5, 1872.

31. William Birney to George H. Williams, December 23, 1872, S-C Files; E. K. Foster to H. S. Sanford, November 24, 1872, Sanford Papers; U.S. Circuit Court Cases.

32. R. Bullock to E. M. L'Engle, November 10, 1872, L'Engle Papers; *Tallahassee Weekly Floridian*, November 5, 1872; Wallace, *Carpetbag Rule*, p. 219; Florida, *Senate Journal*, 1935, Bloxham Memorial Service, p. 15.

33. D. L. Yulee to H. G. Stebbins, November 28, 1872, Yulee Papers.

34. E. K. Foster to H. S. Sanford, November 24, 1872, Sanford Papers.

35. Election Returns, 1862–87, Files of Secretary of State of Florida; U.S. House, *Document No. 510*, 56th Cong., 2d sess., p. 282; *Tallahassee Weekly Floridian*, December 17, 1872.

36. *Tallahassee Weekly Floridian*, July 22, 1873.

37. Edmund H. Hart to Walter N. Hart, August 29, 1872, Hart Letters.

38. J. C. Greeley to H. S. Sanford, December 7, 1872, Sanford Papers.

17

1. *Tallahassee Weekly Floridian*, June 17, 1873; *Biographical Sketch of Ossian B. Hart*, pp. 1–7.

2. *Gainesville New Era*, August 30, 1873; *Tallahassee Weekly Floridian*, September 2, 9, 1873; John R. R. Polk to Thomas F. Bayard, April 2, 1873, Thomas F. Bayard Papers.

3. Florida, *Senate Journal*, 1873, pp. 12, 18; *Tallahassee Weekly Floridian*, February 11, 1873, F. N. Wicker to General F. F. Dent, AGP; J. C. Greeley to H. S. Sanford, December 7, 1872, Sanford Papers.

4. *Jacksonville Weekly Republican*, February 5, 1873; Florida, *Senate Journal*, 1873, p. 70.

5. *Jacksonville Weekly Republican*, February 5, 1873.

6. Florida, *Senate Journal*, 1873, p. 97; *Tallahassee Weekly Floridian*, February 18, 1873.

7. *Jacksonville Weekly Republican*, February 5, 1873; *Tallahassee Weekly Floridian*, February 4, 18, 1873; A. A. Knight to H. S. Sanford, February 9, 1873, Sanford Papers.

8. *Tallahassee Weekly Floridian*, March 18, 1873; Simon B. Conover, *Speech of Personal Vindication at Mass Meeting on Capitol Square, City of Tallahassee, November 8, 1873*, p. 3.

9. *Tallahassee Weekly Floridian*, July 15, 1873; William P. Dockray to E. O. Graves, May 28, 1873, Applications for Collector.

10. *Tallahassee Weekly Floridian*, July 15, 1873.

11. Ibid., July 22, 1873.

12. *Laws of Florida*, 1873, p. 25; Florida, *Senate Journal*, 1873, pp. 52–53.

13. *Marianna Courier*, March 18, 1873.

14. *Laws of Florida*, 1873, p. 26.

15. Ibid., pp. 23–24, 30–31.

16. Ibid., pp. 9–11.

17. Ibid., pp. 12–14; *Tallahassee Sentinel*, February 22, 1873.

18. *Tallahassee Weekly Floridian*, April 1, June 3, July 8, 1873; *Laws of Florida*, 1873, p. 34, and 1874, pp. 126–28; Florida, *Senate Journal*, 1877, Comptroller's Report, p. 5; *American Annual Cyclopedia*, 1873, p. 293.

19. *Laws of Florida*, 1874, pp. 21, 116, 104, and 1875, p. 50; *American Annual Cyclopedia*, 1874, p. 308.

20. *Laws of Florida*, 1874, p. 41.

21. Ibid., pp. 16–17, 20, 23.

22. Ibid., pp. 76–82.

23. Ibid., pp. 57–58, 103, 1872, p. 54, and 1875, pp. 68–69.

24. *Jacksonville New South*, September 19, 1874; Henry A. L'Engle to E. M. L'Engle, August 2, 1874, L'Engle Papers; *Bronson* [Levy County, Florida] *Weekly Artery*, October 24, 1874, quoting the *Floridian*.

25. *Jacksonville New South*, August 1, July 15, 1874; A. Marvin to E. M. L'Engle, October 30, 1874, L'Engle Papers.

26. *Jacksonville New South*, July 15, 18, August 15, 17, 1874.

27. Henry A. L'Engle to E. M. L'Engle, August 2, 1874, L'Engle Papers; W. J. Purman to B. H. Bristow, September 15, 1874, Applications for Collector; King, "Pictures from Florida," p. 30; Edward King, *The Southern States of North America*, p. 419.

28. *Tallahassee Weekly Floridian*, November 3, 17, 1874.

29. W. H. Davison Diary, November 3, 5, 1874.

30. U.S. House, *Miscellaneous Document No. 58*, 44th Cong., 1st sess., pp. 57–58, 77, 82–83, 305–6.

31. George W. Parsons Diary, 1874, 2:147–49; U.S. Senate, *Report No. 611*, Part 2, p. 20; *Tallahassee Weekly Floridian*, November 24, 1874.

32. U.S. Senate, *Report No. 611*, Part 2, p. 20; U.S. House, *Document No. 510*, pp. 305–6.

33. Florida, *House Journal*, 1875, p. 9; Florida, *Senate Journal*, 1875, p. 19.

34. *Tallahassee Weekly Floridian*, February 16, 1875; *Jacksonville New South*, February 23, 1875; Florida, *House Journal*, 1875, p. 240.

35. Samuel A. Swann to D. L. Yulee, May 22, 1875, Agreement between Hicks, Swann, and Yulee, n/d, 1875, Swann to Yulee, August 28, September 3, 1875, Swann Papers; *Tallahassee Weekly Floridian*, March 2, 1875; Florida, *Senate Journal*, 1875, p. 406.

36. *Tallahassee Weekly Floridian*, February 9, 1875; *Thomasville Times*, February 27, 1875; *Jacksonville New South*, February 10, 13, 1875.

37. Florida, *Senate Journal*, 1875, pp. 262–63; *Tallahassee Weekly Floridian*, February 2, 1875.

38. Henry Elliott to E. M. L'Engle, February 18, 20, 1875, L'Engle Papers; Florida, *Senate Journal*, 1875, p. 357.

39. *Tallahassee Weekly Floridian*, February 2, 1875; Henry A. L'Engle to E. M. L'Engle, July 23, 1875, L'Engle Papers; Wallace, *Carpetbag Rule*, pp. 315–16; Florida, *Senate Journal*, 1875, p. 286.

40. *Tallahassee Weekly Floridian*, February 16, 1875; Florida, *Senate Journal*, 1875, pp. 228–29.

41. *Tallahassee Weekly Floridian*, July 27, August 3, 10, September 7, 1875.

42. Henry A. L.'Engle to E. M. L'Engle, July 23, 1875, L'Engle Papers.

43. *Jacksonville Florida Sun*, January 16, 1877; Florida, *House Journal*, 1877, p. 89; *Thomasville Times*, November 6, 1875; *Palatka Eastern Herald*, September 25, 1875; *Jacksonville Tri-Weekly Sun*, May 6, 1876.

18

1. D. L. McKinnon to J. G. McLean, July 31, 1875, Robert Bigelow Burton Papers.

2. *Tallahassee Sentinel*, May 13, 27, 1875.

3. *Fernandina Observer*, January 1, 1876; *Jacksonville Tri-Weekly Sun*, March 30, 1876; *Tallahassee Sentinel*, April 1, 1876; *Tallahassee Weekly Floridian*, April 4, 1876.

4. *Tallahassee Weekly Floridian*, June 6, 1876.

5. *Key West Key of the Gulf*, May 13, 1876.

6. *Quitman* [Georgia] *Reporter*, June 8, 1876; *Tallahassee Weekly Floridian*, June 6, 1876; *Tallahassee Sentinel*, June 3, 1876; *Appleton's Annual Cyclopedia*, 1876, pp. 294–95.
7. *Tallahassee Weekly Floridian*, June 6, 1876.
8. *Ocala East Florida Banner*, June 24, 1876.
9. *Quitman* [Georgia] *Reporter*, June 8, 1876; File GJ 3309, Records of the Court of Claims, Record Group 123, Federal Records Center, Suitland, Md.
10. *Ocala East Florida Banner*, June 10, 1876; *Key West Key of the Gulf*, July 1, 1876; *Appleton's Annual Cyclopedia*, 1876, pp. 295–96; *Tallahassee Weekly Floridian*, June 13, 1876.
11. *Tallahassee Sentinel*, June 10, 24, 1876; Edwin W. L'Engle to Edward M. L'Engle, May 19, 1876, L'Engle Papers; *Savannah Morning News*, May 27, 1876; *Tallahassee Weekly Floridian*, August 22, 1876.
12. *Tallahassee Weekly Floridian*, June 13, 20, 1876; *Tallahassee Sentinel*, August 5, 1876.
13. Conservative Democratic Party, *Plan of Organization for the Campaign of 1876*, pp. 3–4; *Tallahassee Weekly Floridian*, May 30, 1876.
14. *Savannah Morning News*, July 6, 1876; *Tallahassee Weekly Floridian*, June 27, August 8, 1876; *Thomasville Times*, August 26, October 28, 1876; *Quitman* [Georgia] *Reporter*, October 12, 1876; R. B. Hilton to George McWhorter, May, 1880, PKY; Samuel A. Swann to J. J. Finley, July 15, 1876, Swann Papers; John Bradford to William H. Branch, October 17, 1876, Branch Papers; Report of Edwin A. L'Engle and O. A. Myers, n/d, 1876, L'Engle Papers.
15. *Tallahassee Sentinel*, July 15, 1876; *Quincy Journal*, August 4, 1876; *Tallahassee Weekly Floridian*, August 29, 1876; Wallace, *Carpetbag Rule*, p. 333.
16. John F. Rollins to W. E. Chandler, August 9, 1876, Chandler Papers; *Jacksonville Daily Florida Union*, August 24, September 8, 1876; *Tallahassee Sentinel*, September 16, 1876.
17. Note from Harrison Reed, October 6, 1876, L'Engle Papers; *Tallahassee Sentinel*, September 16, 1876; H. S. Sanford to John Friend, December 31, 1877, Sanford Papers.
18. Florida, *Assembly Journal*, 1875, p. 68; S. B. Conover et al., to E. Pierrepont, January 7, 1876, AGP; John F. Rollins to W. E. Chandler, August 9, 1876, Chandler Papers; W. H. Gleason to B. H. Bristow, March 4, 1876, W. J. Purman to A. A. Knight, July 12, 1876, Applications for Collector.
19. *Key West Key of the Gulf*, July 1, 1876, quoting the *Sentinel*.
20. George D. Allen to George M. Lapham, October 26, 1876, Samuel J. Tilden Papers; U.S. Senate, *Report No. 611*, Part 2, p. 17.
21. *Laws of Florida*, 1868, p. 207, and 1872, p. 19.
22. Knauss, "The Growth of Florida's Election Laws," pp. 9–10.
23. *Tallahassee Weekly Floridian*, October 31, November 7, 1876; Conservative Democratic Party, *Plan of Organization*, p. 4; George P. Raney to E. M. L'Engle, October 2, 1876, L'Engle Papers.
24. George D. Allen to George M. Lapham, October 26, 1876, Tilden Papers; U.S. House, *Miscellaneous Document No. 35*, Part 1, 44th Cong., 2d sess., p. 97.
25. *Quitman* [Georgia] *Reporter*, September 14, October 12, 1876; *Tallahassee Weekly Floridian*, October 10, 1876; *Savannah Morning News*, May 24, 1876, quoting *Monticello Constitution*; U.S. Senate, *Report No. 611*, pp. 342–45.
26. *Jacksonville Daily Florida Union*, November 14, 1876; Senate, *Report No. 611*, pp. 299–306, 370.
27. George D. Allen to George M. Lapham, October 26, 1876, Tilden Papers; *New York Tribune*, November 11, 1876; *New York World*, November 11, 1876.
28. *Jacksonville Daily Florida Union*, November 11, 1876; Senate, *Report No. 611*, pp. 12, 241.
29. *Thomasville Times*, April 1, 1876; Edward McCrady to E. M. L'Engle, October 11, 1876, L'Engle Papers; Albert Hubbard Roberts, "Florida and Leon County in the

Election of 1876," p. 90; *Tallahassee Weekly Floridian*, December 5, 1876; Senate, *Report No. 611*, p. 322.

30. *Tallahassee Sentinel*, October 28, 1876; *Tallahassee Weekly Floridian*, November 7, 1876; *Jacksonville Daily Florida Union*, November 6, 7, 1876.

31. *Savannah Morning News*, September 21, 1876; *Tallahassee Weekly Floridian*, September 19, 1876; Headquarters, Department of the South to George F. Drew, November 5, 1876, and to George E. Wentworth, November 3, 1876, RG 393.

32. *Tallahassee Weekly Floridian*, November 14, 1876; *New York World*, November 11, 1876; Senate, *Report No. 611*, pp. 370, 379.

33. *St. Louis Dispatch*, November 14, 15, 1876; *New York Herald*, November 14, 1876; *Tallahassee Weekly Floridian*, December 12, 1876.

34. *Tallahassee Weekly Floridian*, November 21, 1876; Senate, *Report No. 611*, Documentary Evidence, pp. 165–66; John Friend to John A. Sherman, November 15, 1876, Sherman Papers.

35. *Rome* [Georgia] *Courier*, December 6, 1876; *Tallahassee Weekly Floridian*, November 14, 1876, December 19, 1876; *Jacksonville Daily Florida Union*, November 9, 1876; *Washington Sentinel*, December 23, 1876; *Nation*, 27 (July 4, 1878):9.

36. *Jacksonville Daily Florida Union*, November 11, 13, 14, 18, 1876; *Cincinnati Commercial*, November 15, 1876; Davis, *Civil War and Reconstruction*, p. 708; *New York Tribune*, November 25, 1876; *Chicago Daily Tribune*, January 30, 1877.

37. *Quitman* [Georgia] *Reporter*, November 16, 1876; *Savannah Morning News*, November 16, 1876; *Jacksonville Daily Florida Union*, November 18, 1876; Senate, *Report No. 611*, p. 321; John Friend to John A. Sherman, November 15, 1876, Sherman Papers.

38. L. P. Bayne to Samuel J. Tilden, November 11, 1876, Tilden Papers; *Tallahassee Weekly Floridian*, November 14, 1876.

19

1. Charles R. Williams, *Diary and Letters of Rutherford B. Hayes*, 3:370. Portions of this chapter appeared in different form in Shofner, "Florida in the Balance: The Electoral Count of 1876."

2. *New York Times*, October 27, 1876.

3. Ibid., November 8, 9, 1876.

4. Jerome L. Sternstein, "The Sickles Memorandum: Another Look at the Hayes-Tilden Election-Night Conspiracy."

5. *New York Tribune*, November 16, 1876; *Cincinnati Commercial*, November 19, 1876; *St. Louis Dispatch*, November 22, 1876; J. N. Tyner to M. C. Comly, November 14, 16, 1876, Alphonso Taft to M. C. Comly, November 17, 1876, W. A. Knapp to M. C. Comly, November 18, 1876, Microfilm of Rutherford B. Hayes Papers relating to the election of 1876.

6. *New York World*, January 17, 1878.

7. *Savannah Morning News*, November 9, 1876; *Chicago Times*, December 4, 1876; *New York Times*, November 11, 1876.

8. *New York Herald*, November 20, 1876.

9. *Laws of Florida*, 1872, p. 19.

10. House Committee to Investigate Alleged Presidential Election Frauds, *Testimony of William E. Chandler* (Pamphlet in PKY), p. 16.

11. *Tallahassee Weekly Floridian*, November 14, 1876; William R. Stewart to William Wellhouse, November 20, 1876, Tilden Papers.

12. E. H. Abbott, "Francis Channing Barlow," p. 539.

13. *Concord* [New Hampshire] *Republican Statesman*, January 11, 18, 1877; *New York Herald*, November 20, 1876.

14. *New York Times*, November 25, 26, 1876; *New York Daily Tribune*, November 28, 1876; U.S. Senate, *Report No. 611*, Part 2, p. 364; W. E. Chandler to R. B. Hayes, November 18, 1876, Hayes Papers.

15. *New York Daily Tribune,* November 24, 1876; Senate, *Report No. 611,* p. 17.

16. *New York Herald,* November 20, 1876; Raymond B. Nixon, *Henry W. Grady: Spokesman of the New South,* pp. 130–31.

17. Lew Wallace, *Autobiography,* 2:901–2.

18. William Archer Cocke to Samuel Pasco, November 18, 1876, Special Collections, Florida State University; *Augusta Chronicle and Sentinel,* November 19, 1876; *Thomasville Times,* November 25, 1876; *Macon* [Georgia] *Weekly Telegraph and Journal and Messenger,* December 1, 1876; *New York Herald,* November 26, 28, 1876; *Atlanta Daily Constitution,* November 26, 1876.

19. *Tallahassee Sentinel,* November 25, 1876.

20. John Bigelow, *Retrospections of an Active Life,* 5:285–87; *Washington National Republican,* November 22, 1876; *Atlanta Daily Constitution,* November 28, 1876.

21. *Tallahassee Sentinel,* November 25, 1876.

22. Senate, *Report No. 611,* Part 2, pp. 11–12.

23. *New York Herald,* November 29, 1876; *New York Times,* November 29, 1876.

24. U.S. House, *Miscellaneous Document No. 35,* pp. 294–96; *Document No. 143,* Part 1, pp. 3–5.

25. Manton Marble to W. T. Pelton, November 28, 1876, Tilden Papers; *Washington National Republican,* November 29, 1876.

26. Senate, *Report No. 611,* Documentary Evidence, p. 10; U.S. House, *Miscellaneous Document No. 31,* 45th Cong., 3d sess., pp. 492–95; *Tallahassee Weekly Floridian,* November 14, 21, 1876.

27. Senate, *Report No. 611,* Part 2, 431–37; *Rome* [Georgia] *Courier,* December 6, 1876; *Atlanta Daily Constitution,* December 1, 1876; Manton Marble to W. T. Pelton, November 30, 1876, Tilden Papers; House, *Miscellaneous Document No. 31,* Part 1, pp. 494–95; *New York Daily Tribune,* November 30, 1876.

28. *Tallahassee Weekly Floridian,* December 5, 1876; *New York Daily Tribune,* December 2, 1876.

29. *New York Times,* October 12, 1878; Manton Marble, *A Secret Chapter of Political History,* pp. 3–4; Clayton A. Cowgill to W. E. Chandler, February 11, 1879, Chandler Papers. Marble's papers in the Library of Congress have been carefully screened for any information on his Florida activities. See Mary Cortona Phelan, *Manton Marble of the New York World,* p. 93.

30. *Chicago Times,* November 28, December 7, 1876; *Washington Sentinel,* January 13, 1877.

31. William M. Ampt to R. B. Hayes, December 22, 1876, Hayes Papers; *New York Times,* December 12, 1876.

32. Senate, *Report No. 611,* Part 2, pp. 17, 20, 28–29, 389.

33. Ibid., p. 1; *New York Daily Tribune,* December 12, 1876.

34. Senate, *Report No. 611,* Part 2, pp. 5, 7, 41; *Congressional Record,* 50th Cong., 1st sess., vol. 19, part 9, 8290.

35. F. B. Sherwin to W. E. Chandler, December 8, 1876, Chandler Papers.

36. *Election Returns, 1862–1887,* Files of Secretary of State of Florida.

37. *Tallahassee Weekly Floridian,* January 23, 1877; *Jacksonville Weekly Florida Union,* December 16, 1876.

38. Involving the seventy-three Republican miniature ballots placed in the box by Joseph Bowes. See chap. 19.

39. U.S. House, *Miscellaneous Document No. 31,* Part 2, pp. 98–100.

40. William Archer Cocke to Samuel Pasco, November 18, 1876, Special Collections, Florida State University.

20

1. S. G. Thompson to Manton Marble, December 12, 1876, John R. Read to Marble,

December 15, 1876, Manton Marble Papers. Portions of this chapter appeared in different form in Shofner, "Florida Courts and the Disputed Election of 1876."

2. David L. Yulee to R. B. Hilton, November 27, 1876, Yulee Papers.

3. *New York Herald*, December 12, 1876; *Augusta* [Georgia] *Chronicle and Sentinel*, December 12, 1876; Marcellus L. Stearns to W. E. Chandler, December 9, 1876, Chandler Papers.

4. *Atlanta Daily Constitution*, December 12, 1876.

5. *Macon* [Georgia] *Weekly Telegraph and Journal and Messenger*, December 11, 1876.

6. Pleasant W. White to Francis P. Fleming, July 23, 1901, Manuscript Box 28, PKY.

7. *New York Times*, December 12, 1876.

8. M. L. Stearns to W. E. Chandler, December 11, 13, 1876, F. B. Sherwin to Chandler, December 14, 1876, M. Martin to Chandler, December 21, 1876, Stearns to Chandler, December 22, 1876, Chandler Papers; *Atlanta Daily Constitution*, December 19, 1876; Manton Marble to Samuel J. Tilden, December 24, 1876, Marble Papers.

9. *16 Florida Reports 19–20, 27, 29* (1876); *Washington National Republican*, December 18, 1876; *New York Daily Tribune*, December 18, 1876.

10. *16 Florida Reports 52* (1876); *New York Times*, December 24, 1876; *Atlanta Daily Constitution*, December 23, 1876; *New York World*, December 23, 1876.

11. *New York Times*, December 29, 1876; R. B. Hilton to Manton Marble, December 23, 1876, Marble Papers.

12. Aaron A. Sargent to Oliver P. Morton, December 22, 1876, M. L. Stearns to W. E. Chandler, Samuel B. McLin to Chandler, December 24, 1876, Chandler Papers.

13. A. A. Sargent to O. P. Morton, December 22, 1876, ibid.

14. *Washington National Republican*, December 23, 1876; R. B. Hilton to Manton Marble, December 31, 1876, Tilden Papers; Francis Butler Simkins and Robert H. Woody, *South Carolina During Reconstruction*, pp. 521–22.

15. *Atlanta Daily Constitution*, December 27, 1876; *New York Daily Tribune*, December 27, 1876; *Cincinnati Commercial*, December 27, 1876; *Washington National Republican*, December 27, 1876; *Savannah Morning News*, January 1, 1877; *16 Florida Reports 52–54* (1876); W. E. Chandler to Lew Wallace, December 25, 1876, Chandler Papers.

16. *New York Daily Tribune*, December 27, 1876; *New York Herald*, December 26, 1876; *Augusta Chronicle and Sentinel*, December 28, 1876; *Atlanta Daily Constitution*, December 28, 1876; William B. Woods to John A. Sherman, January 1, 1877, Sherman Papers.

17. *Tallahassee Weekly Floridian*, January 2, 1877; *New Orleans Daily Picayune*, January 4, 1877; *Savannah Morning News*, January 1, 1877; William B. Woods to John Sherman, January 8, 1877, Sherman Papers.

18. *16 Florida Reports 63* (1876); *New York Daily Tribune*, December 28, 1876; *Thomasville Times*, December 30, 1876; *New York World*, January 18, 1877.

19. *16 Florida Reports 63* (1876).

20. U.S. House, *Document No. 510*, p. 326; A. B. Hawkins to Matt W. Ransom, February 21, 1877, Matt W. Ransom Papers; E. I. Alexander to Patterson Sanders, February 13, 1877, W. Carlton Smith Collection; Lew Wallace to W. E. Chandler, January 1, 1877, Chandler Papers.

21. *New York Herald*, December 9, 1876; *Jacksonville Daily Florida Union*, January 20, 1877; Adjutant General to Captain Mills, December 20, 1876, Thomas H. Ruger to M. L. Stearns, December 22, 1876, Adjutant General to Captain Mills, December 30, 1876, Ruger to Mills, January 2, 1877, Department of the South Records; *Washington National Republican*, January 3, 1877.

22. *St. Louis Dispatch*, January 3, 1877; *New York Times*, January 4, 1877; James E. Yonge to Samuel J. Tilden, January 2, 1877, Tilden Papers.

23. Wilkinson Call to Manton Marble, January 5, 7, 1877, Tilden Papers.

24. Thomas Donaldson to R. B. Hayes, December 18, 1876, Microfilm of Hayes Papers.

25. F. G. Sherwin to W. E. Chandler, January 3, 1877, Chandler Papers.

26. *Jacksonville Daily Florida Union,* January 5, 1877.

27. R. B. Hilton to Manton Marble, December 27, 1876, January 4, 7, 1877, Tilden Papers.

28. *New York Times,* January 4, 1877; W. Call to Manton Marble, Marble to Call, January 5, 1877, Call to Marble, January 6, 1877, Marble to Call, January 7, 1877, Tilden Papers.

29. W. Call to Manton Marble, January 7, 8, 1877, R. B. Hilton to Marble, January 4, 1877, Samuel Pasco to Marble, January 8, 1877, Edward A. Perry to Clarkson N. Potter, January 22, 1877, Tilden Papers; *New York Daily Tribune,* January 12, 1877.

30. Samuel B. McLin to W. E. Chandler, December 24, 1876, January 2, 5, 1877, Charles H. Pearce to Chandler, January 11, 1877, W. W. Hicks to Chandler, January 25, 1877, Lew Wallace to Chandler, January 15, 1877, Chandler Papers; Indictment, State v. McLin, Fall Term, 1877, Leon County Circuit Court Records.

31. M. L. Stearns to Alphonso Taft, December 3, 1876, Horatio Bisbee, Jr., to Taft, January 4, 1877, AGP; S. B. McLin to W. E. Chandler, January 2, 1877, Lew Wallace to Chandler, January 15, 1877, Chandler Papers.

32. Lew Wallace to W. E. Chandler, January 15, 1877, S. B. McLin to Chandler, January 16, 1877, Chandler Papers.

33. Thomas Settle letter, January 27, 1877, Thomas Settle Papers; C. W. Jones to E. M. L'Engle, January 17, 1877, L'Engle Papers.

34. Abram S. Hewitt to S. J. Tilden, January 8, 1877, Manton Marble to W. Call, January 12, 1877, Call to Marble, January 19, 1877, Tilden Papers; George F. Drew Letterbook, January 18, 1877; *Tallahassee Weekly Floridian,* January 23, 1877; Florida, *House Journal,* 1877, p. 123; *Jacksonville Florida Sun,* January 20, 1877.

35. W. Call to Manton Marble, January 10, 12, 18, 1877, Clarkson N. Potter to S. J. Tilden, January 26, 1877, Tilden Papers; Lew Wallace to W. E. Chandler, January 15, 1877, Chandler Papers; State of Florida *ex rel* Call, Bullock, Hilton, Yonge v. Pearce, Humphries, Holden, Long, Official Documents Pertaining to Election of 1876 in Florida, PKY.

36. W. Call to Manton Marble, January 18, 1877, Tilden Papers; M. L. Stearns to W. E. Chandler, May 4, 1877, Chandler to Horatio Bisbee, May 29, 1877, David Montgomery to Chandler, March 25, 1877, Chandler Papers; *Augusta Chronicle and Sentinel,* January 19, 1877.

37. M. L. Stearns to T. W. Osborn, February 21, 1877, Chandler Papers.

38. *Atlanta Daily Constitution,* February 1, 1877; William D. Bloxham to Manton Marble and Samuel Pasco, February 5, 1877, W. Call to Marble, February 12, 1877, Tilden Papers.

39. Chester L. Barrows, *William M. Evarts,* p. 303; Frederick T. Hill, "Decisive Battles of the Law," p. 563.

40. *New York Daily Tribune,* February 8, 1877.

41. James G. Blaine to R. B. Hayes, February 14, 1877, Hayes Papers.

21

1. Clayton A. Cowgill to W. E. Chandler, December 30, 1876, Chandler Papers; *Jacksonville Florida Sun,* January 4, 1877.

2. John G. Foster to G. L. Hartsuff, October 6, 1866, Foster Letterbook.

3. Brock, *An American Crisis: Congress and Reconstruction, 1865–1877*; C. Vann Woodward, ed., *The Comparative Approach to American History,* p. 155.

Bibliography

Locations of manuscript collections:
Federal Records Centers, East Point, Ga., and Suitland, Md.
Florida State Library, Tallahassee, Fla.
Florida State University Library, Tallahassee, Fla.
Flowers Collection, Duke University, Durham, N.C.
Leon County Court House, Tallahassee, Fla.
Library of Congress, Washington, D.C.
National Archives, Washington, D.C.
Pennsylvania Historical Society, Philadelphia, Pa.
P. K. Yonge Library, University of Florida, Gainesville, Fla.
Southern Historical Collection, University of North Carolina, Chapel Hill, N.C.

Adjutant General's Office. Records. Record Group 94, National Archives.

Attorney General's Office. Papers. Record Group 60, National Archives.

Banks, Nathaniel P. Papers. Library of Congress.

Bayard, Thomas F. Papers. Library of Congress.

Branch, William H. Papers. Southern Historical Collection.

Bureau of Refugees, Freedmen, and Abandoned Lands. Records, Florida. Record Group 105, National Archives.

Burton, Robert Bigelow. Papers. P. K. Yonge Library.

Butler, Benjamin F. Papers. Library of Congress.

Call, Richard Keith. Papers. Southern Historical Collection.

Chandler, William E. Papers. Library of Congress.

Chandler, Zachariah. Papers. Library of Congress.

Chase, Salmon P. Manuscripts. Pennsylvania Historical Society.

Chase, Salmon P. Papers. Library of Congress.

Cocke, William A., to Samuel Pasco, November 18, 1876. Special Collections, Florida State University.

Commissioner of Internal Revenue. Records. Record Group 58, National Archives.

Crigler, W. L. Papers. Southern Historical Collection.

Crittenden, J. J. Papers. Microfilm, P. K. Yonge Library.

"Cubans in Florida." Federal Writers' Project. Manuscript, Special Collections, Florida State University.

Davison, W. H. Diary, 1870–76. P. K. Yonge Library.

Department of Agriculture. Reports of Commissioner. Washington: Government Printing Office, 1867–76.

Department of Justice. U.S. Attorneys' Reports. Record Group 206, National Archives.

Department of Justice. Source-Chronological Files. Record Group 60, National Archives.

Department of the South. Records, Army Commands. Record Group 393, National Archives.

Department of State. Applications and Recommendations. Record Group 59, National Archives.

Department of State. Letters of Application and Recommendation. Record Group 50, National Archives.

Department of State. Notes to and from Foreign Legations. Record Group 59, National Archives.

Department of State. Volume on Provisional Government of Florida. Record Group 59, National Archives.

Department of the Treasury. Applications for Collector. Record Group 56, National Archives.

Department of the Treasury. Records of the Direct Tax Commission. Record Group 58, National Archives.

Department of the Treasury. Records of the Solicitor. Record Group 206, National Archives.

Department of the Treasury. Reports of Special Agents. Record Group 36, National Archives.

Department of the Treasury. Reports of the Secretary of Commerce and Navigation. Washington: Government Printing Office, 1866–76.

Dorman, Orloff M. Diary and Notes. Library of Congress.

Dow, Warren Q. Diary, 1868. P. K. Yonge Library.

Drew, George F. Letterbook. Florida State Library.

Fessenden, William Pitt. Papers. Library of Congress.

Finley, J. J., to A. L. Smith, July 31, 1872. Manuscript Collection, P. K. Yonge Library.

Fleming, Francis P. "Reconstruction." Typescript, P. K. Yonge Library.

Florida. *Constitution of 1865*.

Florida. *House Journal*, 1865–77.

Florida. *Laws of Florida*, 1865–77.

Florida. *Reports*, 1869–76.

Florida. *Senate Journal*, 1868–77.

Florida, Internal Improvement Trust Fund. *Minutes of the Proceedings of the Board of Trustees*. Vol. 1. Tallahassee, 1902.

Florida, Secretary of State. Election Returns, 1862–87. Files of the Secretary of State of Florida, Tallahassee.

Florida, Secretary of State. Files. Department of Archives, History, and Record Management, Tallahassee.

Florida Merchant Marine Survey. Federal Writers' Project. Manuscript, P. K. Yonge Library.

Foster, John G. Letterbook. Miscellaneous Military Papers, Library of Congress.

Foster, John G., to P. H. Sheridan, August 6, 1865. P. K. Yonge Library.

Freedmen's Savings and Trust Company, Tallahassee Office. Signature Book. Record Group 101, National Archives.

General Land Office. Records of Register and Receiver. Record Group 49, National Archives.

Gleason, William H. Papers. P. K. Yonge Library.

Hart, Walter N. Letters. Microfilm, P. K. Yonge Library.

Hawks, Esther and Milton. Papers. Library of Congress.

Hayes, Rutherford B. Papers Relating to the Election of 1876. Microfilm, Library of Congress.

Hill, Erastus. Diary. P. K. Yonge Library.

Hentz Family. Papers. Southern Historical Collection.

Holt, Joseph. Papers. Microfilm, P. K. Yonge Library.

Huston, Menefie. Papers. P. K. Yonge Library.

Investigation into the Conduct, Acts, and Doings of H. Reed, Governor of Florida, by a Committee of the Assembly, 1870. Microfilm, P. K. Yonge Library.

Johnson, Andrew. Papers. Microfilm, Florida State University Library.

Journal of the Constitutional Convention of 1865 at Tallahassee, Florida. Microfilm, Florida State University Library.

Journal of the Proceedings of the Convention Begun January 20, 1868, Tallahassee, Florida. Microfilm, Florida State University Library.

Keyser, William J. Papers. Flowers Collection, Duke University.

L'Engle, Edward M. Papers. Southern Historical Collection.

Leon County. Circuit Court Records. Leon County Court House.

Leon County. Deed Record Books. Leon County Court House.

Lilly, H. A., to Dear Friend, March 5, 1876. Miscellaneous Letters, Southern Historical Collection.

Lincoln, Abraham. Papers. Microfilm, Library of Congress.

Longstreet, Cornelius. Diary. Typescript, P. K. Yonge Library.

Lutterloh, W. J. Papers. Southern Historical Collection.

McPherson, Edward. Papers. Library of Congress.

MacRae, John. Papers. Southern Historical Collection.

Mallory, Stephen R. Papers. Southern Historical Collection.

Marble, Manton. Papers. Library of Congress.

Milton, John. Letterbooks. Florida State Library.

"Negro Education in the Cities." Federal Writers' Project. Manuscript, P. K. Yonge Library.

Nicolay, John G. Papers. Library of Congress.

O'Toole, J. J., to John C. Breckinridge, April 24, 1869. Copy in possession of author.

Parsons, George W. Diary, 1873–74. P. K. Yonge Library.

Pensacola and Georgia Railroad Company. Minute Book, Board of Directors. Microfilm, P. K. Yonge Library.

Pensacola and Mobile Railroad and Manufacturing Company. Prospectus, 1873. P. K. Yonge Library.

Pensacola and Perdido Railroad Company. Annual Report, March 31, 1876. P. K. Yonge Library.

Philips, James J. Papers. Southern Historical Collection.

Phillips-Myers. Papers. Southern Historical Collection.

Ransom, Matt W. Papers. Southern Historical Collection.

Reed, A. M. Diary, 1869. P. K. Yonge Library.

Ruffin-Roulhac-Hamilton Collection. Southern Historical Collection.

Sanford, Henry S. Papers. Microfilm, P. K. Yonge Library.

Settle, Thomas. Papers. Southern Historical Collection.

Sherman, John A. Papers. Library of Congress.

Smith, W. Carleton. Collection. Madison, Florida.

Southern Claims Commission. Records, Florida. Record Group 217, National Archives.

Stevens, Thaddeus. Papers. Library of Congress.

Swann, Samuel A. Papers. P. K. Yonge Library.

Taylor, Maria Baker. Diary. P. K. Yonge Library.

Third Military District. Records, Army Commands. Record Group 393, National Archives.

Tilden, Samuel J. Papers. New York Public Library.

Union Republican Club. Proceedings. Typescript, P. K. Yonge Library.

United States. *Statutes at Large,* 1865.

United States Bankruptcy Court. Minute Book. Record Group 21, Federal Records Center, East Point, Georgia.

United States Circuit Court. Cases, 1871–78. Record Group 21, Federal Records Center, East Point, Georgia.

United States Congress. House. *Executive Document No. 57.* 40th Cong., 2d sess.

———. *Executive Document No. 1.* 40th Cong., 2d sess.

———. *Executive Document No. 342.* 40th Cong., 2d sess.

———. *Miscellaneous Document No. 109.* 40th Cong., 2d sess.

———. *Miscellaneous Document No. 114.* 40th Cong., 2d sess.

———. *Miscellaneous Document No. 58.* 44th Cong., 1st sess.

———. *Miscellaneous Document No. 35.* 44th Cong., 2d sess.

———. *Document No. 143.* 44th Cong., 2d sess.

———. *Miscellaneous Document No. 31.* 45th Cong., 3d sess.

———. *Document No. 510.* 56th Cong., 2d sess.

United States Congress. Senate. *Report No. 47.* 38th Cong., 1st sess.

———. *Document No. 26.* 39th Cong., 1st sess.

———. *Miscellaneous Document No. 102.* 41st Cong., 2d sess.

———. *Report No. 101.* 41st Cong., 2d sess.

———. *Report No. 611.* 44th Cong., 2d sess.

———. *Papers.* Record Group 46, National Archives.

U.S. Court of Claims. Records. Record Group 123, Federal Records Center, Suitland, Maryland.

United States District Court, Northern District of Florida. Records. Record Group 21, Federal Records Center, East Point, Georgia.

United States Patent Office. Records. Record Group 241, National Archives.

United States Supreme Court. *Reports.*

War Department. Volunteer Regiments, Records, First and Second Florida Cavalry. Record Group 94, National Archives.

War of the Rebellion: A Compilation of the Official Records of the Union and Confederate Armies. Washington, 1880–1901.

Washburne, Elihu B. Papers. Library of Congress.

Yulee, David L. Papers. P. K. Yonge Library.

Atlanta Daily Constitution, 1876.

Augusta Daily Chronicle and Sentinel, 1876.

Bronson Weekly Artery, 1874.

Chicago Daily Tribune, 1876.

Chicago Times, 1876.

Cincinnati Commercial, 1876.

Fernandina Observer, 1873–76.

Fernandina Peninsula, 1863–66.

Gainesville Alachua Citizen, 1875.

Gainesville Cotton States, 1864.

Gainesville Independent, 1873.

Gainesville New Era, 1867–73.

Jacksonville East Floridian, 1868.

Jacksonville Florida Republican, 1873.

Jacksonville Florida Sun, 1876–77.

Jacksonville Florida Union, 1865–77.

Jacksonville Mercury and Floridian, 1869.

Jacksonville New South, 1874–75.

Key West Dispatch, 1872–76.

Key West Key of the Gulf, 1876.

Lake City Reporter, 1873.
Live Oak Times, 1876.
Macon [Georgia] *Weekly Telegraph and Journal and Messenger*, 1876.
Marianna Courier, 1873.
New Orleans Daily Picayune, 1876.
New York Herald, 1864–76.
New York Times, 1868–76.
New York Tribune, 1868–76.
New York World, 1876.
Ocala East Florida Banner, 1876.
Palatka Eastern Herald, 1869–75.
Pensacola Weekly Express, 1872.
Pensacola Tri-Weekly Observer, 1868.
Pensacola West Florida Commercial, 1868.
Quincy Journal, 1873–76.
Quitman [Georgia] *Banner*, 1871.
Quitman [Georgia] *Reporter*, 1876.
Rome [Georgia] *Courier*, 1876.
Savannah Morning News, 1876.
St. Augustine Examiner, 1862–74.
St. Louis Dispatch, 1876.
Tallahassee Florida Sentinel, 1863.
Tallahassee Semi-Weekly Floridian, 1865.
Tallahassee Sentinel, 1868–76.
Tallahassee Floridian, 1865–76.
Tampa True Southerner, 1868.
Thomasville Southern Enterprise, 1866–67.
Thomasville Times, 1874.
Washington Weekly Chronicle, 1868.
Washington National Republican, 1876.
Washington Sentinel, 1876.

Agricultural and Immigration Association of Florida. *Florida, Its Soil, Climate, and Production*. New York, 1868.

American Annual Cyclopedia and Register of Important Events. 1868–76.

Barrows, Chester L. *William M. Evarts*. Chapel Hill, 1941.

Beale, Howard K. *The Critical Year: A Study of Andrew Johnson and Reconstruction*. New York, 1930.

Beath, Robert B. *History of the Grand Army of the Republic*. New York, 1889.

Bentley, George R. *A History of the Freedmen's Bureau*. Philadelphia, 1955.

Bigelow, John. *Retrospections of an Active Life*, vol. 5. Garden City, N.Y., 1913.

Bill, Ledyard, *A Winter in Florida*. New York, 1870.

Biographical Sketch of Ossian B. Hart. New York, 1901.

Brock, W. R. *An American Crisis: Congress and Reconstruction, 1865-1867*. London, 1963.

Carpenter, John A. *Sword and Olive Branch*. Pittsburgh, 1964.

Central Florida Land Agency, comp. *Florida: Its Climate, Soil and Productions*. Jacksonville, 1871.

Conover, Simon B. *Speech of Personal Vindication at Mass Meeting on Capitol Square, City of Tallahassee, November 8, 1873*. Privately printed.

Conservative Democratic Party. *Plan of Organization for the Campaign of 1876*. Jacksonville, 1876.

Cox, LaWanda, and Cox, John H. *Principles, Politics, and Prejudice, 1865–1866*. New York, 1963.

Cushman, Joseph D. *A Goodly Heritage*. Gainesville, 1965.

Dacy, George H. *Four Centuries of Florida Ranching*. St. Louis, 1940.

Daniels, Jonathan. *Prince of Carpetbaggers*. Philadelphia and New York, 1958.

Davis, William Watson. *Civil War and Reconstruction in Florida*. Gainesville, 1964.

Donald, David H. *The Politics of Reconstruction, 1863–1867*. Baton Rouge, 1965.

Dovell, J. E. *History of Banking in Florida, 1828–1954*. Orlando, 1955.

Dubois, W. E. B. *Black Reconstruction*. Philadelphia, 1935.

Edwards, Helen Moore. *Memoirs*. Privately printed, n.d.

Eppes, Susan Bradford. *Through Some Eventful Years*. Macon, 1926.

Florida, Its Climate, Soil and Production . . . A Manual . . . to Immigrants. Jacksonville, 1868.

Florida Commission of Lands and Immigration. *Florida: Its Climate, Soil and Production*. New York, 1869.

Fowler, J. H. *Orange Culture in Florida*. Jacksonville, 1874.

Gannon, Michael V. *The Cross in the Sand*. Gainesville, 1965.

Great Southern Railway. New York, 1878.

Hanna, Alfred Jackson. *Florida's Golden Sands*. Indianapolis, 1950.

Higginson, Thomas Wentworth. *Army Life in a Black Regiment*. East Lansing, Mich., 1960.

Herbert, Hilary A. *Why the Solid South?* Baltimore, 1890.

Hyman, Harold M., ed. *New Frontiers of the American Reconstruction*. Urbana, Ill., 1966.

Jacques, Daniel H. *Florida as a Permanent Home*. Jacksonville, 1877.

Johns, John E. *Florida During the Civil War*. Gainesville, 1963.

Klingberg, Frank W. *The Southern Claims Commission*. Berkeley, 1955.

King, Edward. *The Southern States of North America*. London, 1875.

Le Diable (pseud.). *Historical Sketch of the Third Annual Conquest of Florida*. Port Royal, 1864.

Long, Charles Sumner. *History of the AME Church in Florida*. Philadelphia, 1939.

Long, Ellen Call. *Florida Breezes*. Gainesville, 1962.

Marble, Manton. *A Secret Chapter of Political History*. Pamphlet reprinted from the *New York Sun*, August 3, 1878.

McFeely, William S. *Yankee Stepfather: General O. O. Howard and the Freedmen*. New York, 1968.

McGrane, Reginald C. *Foreign Bondholders and American State Debts*. New York, 1935.

McKitrick, Eric L. *Andrew Johnson and Reconstruction*. Chicago, 1960.

Nixon, Raymond B. *Henry W. Grady: Spokesman of the New South*. New York, 1943.

Norton, John Henry. *Jacksonville Trade Circular and Real Estate Advertiser*. Jacksonville, 1871.

Patrick, Rembert W. *Reconstruction of the Nation*. Oxford, 1967.

Pettingill, George W., Jr. *The Story of Florida Railroads*. Boston, 1952.

Phelan, Mary Cortona. *Manton Marble of the New York World*. Washington, 1957.

Proceedings of the Florida Fruitgrowers' Convention, 1874. Jacksonville, 1874.

Pyburn, Nita K. *The History of the Development of a Single System of Education in Florida, 1822–1903*. Tallahassee, 1954.

Reid, Whitelaw. *After the War: A Southern Tour*. Cincinnati, 1866.

Rigbey, T. C. *Dr. Rigbey's Papers on Florida*. Cincinnati, 1876.

Richardson, Joe M. *The Negro in the Reconstruction of Florida, 1865–1877*. Tallahassee, 1965.

Richardson, Simon P. *Lights and Shadows of an Itinerant Life*. Nashville, 1900.

Robinson, William M., Jr. *Justice in Grey: A History of the Judicial System of the Confederate States of America*. Cambridge, 1941.

Rosser, John L. *A History of the Florida Baptists*. Nashville, 1949.

Sefton, James E. *The United States Army and Reconstruction, 1865–1877*. Baton Rouge, 1967.

Scott, William A. *The Repudiation of State Debts*. New York, 1893.

Shuften, John T. *A Colored Man's Exposition of the Acts and Doings of the Radical Party South, From 1865 to 1876 and Its Probable Overthrow by President Hayes' Southern Policy*. Jacksonville, 1877.

Simkins, Francis Butler, and Woody, Robert H. *South Carolina During Reconstruction*. Chapel Hill, 1932.

Singletary, Otis A. *Negro Militia and Reconstruction*. Austin, 1957.

Smith, F. T., ed. *Florida and Texas, A Series of Letters*. Ocala, 1866.

Sprague, John T. *The Origin, Progress, and Conclusion of the Florida War*. Gainesville, 1964.

Thayer, William Roscoe. *The Life and Letters of John Hay*, vol. 1. Boston, 1920.

Thian, Raphael P. *Military Geography of the United States*. Washington, 1881.

Thrift, Charles T. *Trail of the Florida Circuit Rider*. Lakeland, 1944.

Townsend, Frederick Tench. *Wild Life in Florida*. London, 1875.

Trefousse, Hans L. *The Radical Republicans: Lincoln's Vanguard for Racial Justice*. New York, 1969.

Wallace, John. *Carpetbag Rule in Florida*. Gainesville, 1964.

Wallace, Lew. *Autobiography*, vol. 2. New York, 1906.

Watkins, James L. *King Cotton: A History and Statistical Review, 1790–1908*. New York, 1908.

Wells, George W. *Facts for Immigrants*. Jacksonville, 1877.

Williams, Charles R. *Diary and Letters of Rutherford B. Hayes*. Columbus, 1924.

Wilson, Theodore B. *The Black Codes of the South*. Tuscaloosa, 1965.

Woodman, Harold D. *King Cotton and His Retainers*. Lexington, Ky., 1968.

Woodward, C. Vann, ed. *The Comparative Approach to American History*. New York, 1968.

Abbott, E. H. "Francis Channing Barlow." *Harvard Graduates Magazine* 4 (1896):526–42.

Amundson, Richard J. "The Florida Land and Colonization Company." *Florida Historical Quarterly* 43 (January 1966):153–68.

Brown, C. K. "The Florida Investments of George W. Swepson." *North Carolina Historical Review* 5 (July 1928):275–88.

Campbell, E. G. "Indebted Railroads: A Problem of Reconstruction." *Journal of Southern History* 6 (1940):167–88.

Coben, Stanley. "Northeastern Business and Radical Reconstruction, A Reexamination." *Mississippi Valley Historical Review* 56 (1959–60):69–90.

Dodd, Dorothy. "'Bishop' Pearce and the Reconstruction of Leon County." *Apalachee* (Tallahassee, 1946), pp. 5–12.

Dodd, William G. "Ring Tournaments in Tallahassee." *Apalachee* (Tallahassee, 1950), pp. 55–70.

Ewing, Cortez A. M. "Florida Reconstruction Impeachments." *Florida Historical Quarterly* 36 (1958):299–318.

Fairlie, Margaret C. "The Jacksonville Yellow Fever Epidemic." *Florida Historical Quarterly* 19 (1940):95–108.

Fenlon, Paul E. "The Florida, Atlantic and Gulf Central Railroad: The First Railroad in Jacksonville." *Florida Historical Quarterly* 32 (1953):71–80.

———. "The Notorious Swepson-Littlefield Fraud: Railroad Financing in Florida, 1868–1871." *Florida Historical Quarterly* 32 (1954):231–61.

Garwood, Saunders B. "Florida State Grange." *Florida Historical Quarterly* 47 (1968): 165–79.

Hill, Frederick T. "Decisive Battles of the Law." *Harper's Monthly Magazine*, March 1907, pp. 557–67.

King, Edward. "Pictures from Florida." *Scribners' Monthly* 9 (November 1874):1–31.

Knauss, James O. "Growth of Florida's Election Laws." *Florida Historical Quarterly* 5 (1926):3–17.

Nation, July 4, 1878.

Peek, Ralph L. "Lawlessness in Florida, 1868–1871." *Florida Historical Quarterly* 40 (1961):164–85.

———. "The Election of 1870 and the End of Reconstruction in Florida." *Florida Historical Quarterly* 45 (1966–67):352–68.

Pennington, Edgar Legare. "The Episcopal Church in Florida, 1763–1892." *Historical Magazine of the Protestant Episcopal Church* 7 (March 1938):3–77.

Richardson, Joe M. "Florida Black Codes." *Florida Historical Quarterly* 47 (1969):365–79.

Roberts, Albert Hubbard. "Florida and Leon County in the Election of 1876." *Tallahassee Historical Society Annual* 4 (1939):88–96.

Roberts, Derrell C. "Joseph E. Brown and Florida's New South Economy." *Florida Historical Quarterly* 45 (July 1967):53–57.

———. "Social Legislation in Reconstruction Florida." *Florida Historical Quarterly* 43 (1964–65):352–68.

Scroggs, Jack B. "Carpetbagger Constitutional Reform in the South Atlantic States, 1867–1868." *Journal of Southern History* 27 (November 1961):299–318.

Shofner, Jerrell H. "Florida Courts and the Disputed Election of 1876." *Florida Historical Quarterly* 48 (1969):26–46.

———. "Florida in the Balance: The Electoral Count of 1876." *Florida Historical Quarterly* 47 (1968):122–50.

———. "The Constitution of 1868." *Florida Historical Quarterly* 40 (1962):356–74.

Smith, George Winston. "Carpetbag Imperialism in Florida, 1862–1868." *Florida Historical Quarterly* 27 (1948):99–156, 260–99.

Sternstein, Jerome L. "The Sickles Memorandum: Another Look at the Hayes-Tilden Election-Night Conspiracy." *Journal of Southern History* 32 (1966):342–57.

Williamson, Edward C. "Florida's First Reconstruction Legislature." *Florida Historical Quarterly* 32 (July 1953)):41–43.

Ackerman, Philip D. "Florida Reconstruction from Walker through Reed, 1865–1873." Master's thesis, University of Florida, 1948.

Carper, N. Gordon. "The Convict-Lease System in Florida, 1866-1923." Ph.D. dissertation, Florida State University, 1964.

Fenlon, Paul E. "The Struggle for Control of the Florida Central Railroad." Ph.D. dissertation, University of Florida, 1955.

Johnson, Dudley S. "The Railroads of Florida, 1865–1900." Ph.D. dissertation, Florida State University, 1965.

Kirk, Cooper C. "A History of the Southern Presbyterian Church in Florida, 1821–1891." Ph.D. dissertation, Florida State University, 1966.

Meador, John A. "Florida Political Parties, 1865–1877." Ph.D. dissertation, University of Florida, 1964.

Peek, Ralph L. "Lawlessness and the Restoration of Order in Florida, 1868–1871." Ph.D. dissertation, University of Florida, 1964.

Index

Abbott, John H., 309
Adams, John S.: encourages immigration, 202; criticizes Republican officials, 223; immigration commissioner, 259; mentioned, 211, 234, 262, 266, 294
Aetna Steam Fire Company of Jacksonville, 150
African Methodist Episcopal Church: joined by blacks, 143; used brush arbors, 144; establishes schools, 152; Florida Conference of, 187; minister shot, 229; convention of, 233–34; mentioned, 146, 280
African Methodist Episcopal Zion Church: joined by blacks, 143
Agricultural and Immigration Association, 259
Agricultural college: plans for, 217
Alabama and Florida Railroad: rails removed from, 111; sold, 117; mentioned, 110, 116, 254, 255
Alachua County: opposition to Negro schools in, 75; courts in, 87; martial law in, 90; blacks recruited in, 125; northern buyers in, 133; homesteads in, 134; lumbering in, 137; mentioned, 63, 69, 71, 72, 83, 88, 129, 132, 147, 152, 170, 174, 175, 213, 216, 228, 240, 262, 278, 281, 285, 288, 295, 298, 310, 312, 316, 317, 318, 321, 323, 324, 326
Alberger, Morris H., 238, 254
Aldaince, General: of New York *Junta*, 306
Alden, George J.: 1868 convention delegate, 181; mentioned, 182
Alderman, William, 136
Allen, B. F.: elected, 46
Allen, George D., 282, 307
Alliance Line: railroad connection with, 116; known as Florida Mail Line, 119
Allison, Abraham K.: acting governor, 18; release from prison asked, 42; interferes in election, 214; convicted, 230
Alsop, William, 8, 14
Ambler, Daniel G.: property seized, 27; mentioned, 271
Ambler's Bank, 271, 273
AME Church, 143, 144
Amelia Island, evacuated, 4
Amelia River, 118, 243
American Missionary Association, 73
Ames, Captain E. R., 168
Amnesty oath, 37, 38
Amnesty, Lincoln's Proclamation of, 8
Ampt, William M., 323
Anderson, J. Patton, 57
Anderson, Judge John, 105
Annexation of west Florida, 207
Anthony, Senator Henry B., 261
Apalachicola: occupied by Union, 3; decline of, 20; revival of trade at, 29; murder at, 90; steamers to, 119; trade in, 126; decline of, 269; mentioned, 28, 120
Apalachicola River, 17, 69, 113, 121, 147, 148, 245, 246, 248, 249, 255, 271

Apopka, 260
Apprenticeship: by Freedmen's Bureau agents, 63
Apprenticeship law, 53
Apthorp, William L., 88
Archer: violence at, 84; election violations at, 312; precinct returns of, 317; ballot box at, 321; mentioned, 324, 326
Archibald, R. B., 298
Armstrong, O. B., 175, 281
Atlanta, Georgia, 182
Atlantic, Gulf and West India Transit Railroad Company, 116, 250
Atlantic and Gulf Railroad: from Savannah, 110; connection with, 112; discussed, 112–13; reaches Bainbridge, 119; mentioned, 209, 254
Atlantic and Gulf Transit Company, 253
Attaway's boarding house, 232
Atwood, George W., 172, 173
Atwood, Mrs. George W., 155
Austin, C. H., 46
Avery, O. M., 117, 255

Babcock, Orville, 261
Baghdad Sash Factory, 269
Bahamas: shipments to, 136; aliens from, 311; mentioned, 236
Bahamians, at Key West, 294
Bailey, General William, 142
Bainbridge, Georgia, 113, 119
Bainbridge Female College, 142
Baker, Alpheus T., 305
Baker, J. Wales, 21
Baker, James M., 246
Baker, Mary Jane, 95
Baker County, 230, 320, 321, 323, 324, 325, 333
Baldwin, 10, 109, 115, 121, 137, 249
Baldwin, Abraham S., 27, 109
Ball, Leroy, 205, 206
Baltimore, Maryland: convention at, 14, 280; mentioned, 102
Baltzell, Judge Thomas, 39
Baptists, 29, 144–45
Bardwell, F. W., 173, 175
Barlow, Francis C., 316, 317, 319, 323, 324
Barnes, William D., 190, 205
Barnett, Aaron, 220
Barnhill, Gilbert H., 137
Bartholf, J. F., 308
Bartow, 136, 154
Baskins, Daniel, 83
Bass, A. G., 175, 180
Bassnett, F. B., 284
Bates, John, 87
Bayport, 97
B. C. Lewis and Son, 270
Beasley's Store, 311
Beaufort, South Carolina, 6, 7
Bellamy, James, 231
Belton, W. H., 321
Benevolent associations, 72, 75, 150
Bernard, Jesse T.: forms immigration company, 131; mentioned, 155, 334
Bethel Baptist Church, 144
Bethlehem Baptist Association, 145
Bethune-Cookman College, 153
Bettelini, Pedro, 237, 238
Biddle, G. W., 316, 322, 336
Billings, Liberty: Radical leader, 169; parliamentary victory of, 182; nominated for governor, 183; president of senate, 220; mentioned, 172, 174, 175, 176, 178, 180, 181, 187, 188, 189, 191, 281, 289
Bird, William, 214, 215
Birney, William, 281, 282, 285, 288
Bisbee, Horatio, Jr., 174, 241, 276, 284, 287, 290, 302, 305, 333, 344
Biscayne Bay, 243, 266
Bishop, P. P., 266
Black code, 42, 50
Black code of Florida: committee responsible for, 51; discussed, 51–56; mentioned, 58
Blaine, James G., 338
Blair, Montgomery: Reed reports to, 33; appoints Reed, 121; mentioned, 35, 165
Blake, E. L. T., 88
"Bloody shirt," 314
Blount, Alexander C., 91
Bloxham, William D.: sues for office, 222; urges fusion ticket, 281; mentioned, 214, 215, 216, 252, 274, 280, 282, 283, 284, 286, 287, 289, 290, 303, 304, 310, 336, 337, 344
Blumenthal, Isadore, 234–35
Board of Hope, 148
Board of Trade of Tampa, 268
Bogue, G. W., 302
Bond, Judge Hugh L., 332
Bostrom's boarding house, 266
Bowes, Joseph, 312
Boynton, William J., 13
Bradford County: courts in, 87; lumbering, 137; mentioned, 98, 312
Bradford Institute at Jacksonville, 146
Bradwell, William: Union-Republican Club member, 166; Radical affiliation of, 172; mentioned, 173, 180, 186
Braman, George H., 76
Branch, William H., 133
Brannan, John M., 320

Brazil: planned emigration to, 21, 22, 170; lumber shipped to, 137
Breniza Ferry, 136
Brent, F. C., 271
Brevard County: agricultural school in, 152; mentioned, 286, 297
Brickell's store, 266
British Honduras: threatened emigration to, 170
Brock's line: railroad connections with, 114; mentioned, 265
Brooksville, 97, 103, 120, 168
Brown, B. Gratz, 276
Brown, John M., 143
Brown, Joseph E., 316, 318
Browne, Joseph B., 155
Brown's Theological Institute, 144
Brown's University, 144, 152
Bruce, Morgan and Company, 29
Brunswick and Macon Railroad, 254
Bryan, Homer, 233, 234
Buckman, J. E., 21
Bullock, Robert W.: in mercantile business, 30; as Freedmen's Bureau agent, 63; praised for fairness, 86; Democratic presidential elector, 303; mentioned, 136, 190, 229, 230, 282, 296
Bureau Courts. *See* Freedmen's Bureau
Burleigh, W. E., 281
Burritt, S. L., 12
Busby, Milton, 88
Bush, Warren S., 229
Butler, Benjamin F., 186, 188
Butler, John W., 182, 186, 204, 302

Calhoun County, 70
Call, Henry, 143
Call, Richard Keith, 1
Call, Wilkinson: elected to U.S. Senate, 57; complains of military power, 86; railroad attorney, 114; on military bill, 160; Democratic presidential elector, 303; mentioned, 172, 246, 247, 282, 284, 296, 333, 334, 336, 337
Callahan: Pensacola labor leader, 236
Caloosahatchie River, 118, 136
Campbell, John L., 183
Campbell, Richard L., 255, 330, 333, 336
Campbellton, 76, 312, 324, 326
Capital: scarcity of, 126
Capitation tax, 52
Carrabelle, 269
Carrillo, Isaac, 306, 307
Carruth, Rev. Thomas A., 149
Carse, George B., 174, 204, 205
Carter, F. M. G., 234
Carter, Kirkland and Company, 128
Case, Howard S., 133
Castanon, Don Gonzalo, 239
Cedar Key: occupied by Union, 3; destruction at, 20; timber cutting at, 30; Negro timber workers at, 68; railroad facilities at, 115; lumbering at, 137; violence at, 234; election irregularities at, 312; mentioned, 2, 27, 116, 118, 120, 229, 235, 237, 239, 241, 250, 262, 263, 268, 283
Cessna, W. K.: 1868 convention delegate, 181; seeks impeachment of Reed, 219; mentioned, 175, 220
Chaires, C. P., 2, 30
Chaires, Green A., 171
Chamberlain, D. H.: South Carolina governor, 310
Chandler, William E., 275, 283, 284, 315, 316, 317, 322, 324, 326, 330, 332, 338
Charleston, South Carolina: steamers to, 118, 119; trade with, 126; mentioned, 108, 127, 260, 265, 271
Charlotte Harbor, 209, 243, 250
Chase, C. Thurston, 75
Chase, Salmon P.: voids tax sale, 7; presidential plans of, 8; assists Stickney, 8; supported by Stickney, 9; re-assured by Stickney, 10; abandons presidential plans, 12; visits Fernandina, 173; mentioned, 4, 6, 14, 22, 32, 33
Chattahoochee: firearms seized at, 43; U.S. arsenal at, 55; arsenal made into prison, 208; prison at, 217; mentioned, 119, 155, 230
Cheatham, Frank, 89
Chemonie Plantation, 133
Cheney, Edward M.: Republican editor, 178; explains factionalism, 212; mentioned, 211, 280
Chicago, settlers from, 262
Chinese labor, 124
Chipley, William D., 255
C. H. Mallory and Company, 120
Christmas revolt: rumors of, 42, 55
Christy, William H.: land sale by, 132; Radical Republican, 172; editor of *Florida Times*, 173; mentioned, 188
Church Aid Society, 148
Churches: racial segregation of, 142
Cincinnati convention, 280, 281, 302, 303
City Hotel in Tallahassee, 205–6, 316
City Point, steamer, 119
Civil courts: failure of justice in, 69
Civil Rights Act of 1866, 84, 92, 100, 106
Civil rights law of 1873: by Florida, 291, 341, 344
Clark, A. C., 259

Clay County, 212, 230, 240
Clearwater, 147
Clifton, Daniel, 235
C. L. Lebaron and Son, 273
Clouts, M. A., 144, 229
C. L. Robinson and Company, 255
Clyde Line, 120
Cocke, William Archer, 171, 196, 249, 250, 280, 316, 319, 321, 323, 324, 325, 326, 329, 331, 332, 333, 337
Codrington, C., 266
Cohen, Henckel and Company, 127
Cohen, I. H., 272
Coker, James, 214, 215, 231
Cole, Archibald H., 27
Colfax, Schuyler, 204
Collins, J. B.: as bureau agent, 64
Colored Academy, 295, 298
Colored Methodist Episcopal Church, 143
Columbia County: courts in, 88; blacks recruited in, 125; violence in, 214; mentioned, 171, 174, 180, 201, 215, 227, 228, 246, 280, 282, 293, 295, 298, 304, 309, 312, 313
Columbus, Georgia, 303
Conant, Sherman, 174, 206, 230, 235, 254, 276, 284, 285, 287, 311
Cone, R. W., 230
Cone, William R., 104, 180
Confederacy: support of, 1; activities of, 2; arrests innocent civilians, 2
Confederate prisoners, 10
Confederate property, 19
Confederates, 3, 6
Confiscation: by Confederacy, 1
Confiscation acts, 5, 15, 23, 28
Congressional Radicals: on Thayer plan, 5; conflict with president, 81
Conover, Simon B.: donates to Negro education, 144; 1868 convention delegate, 181; wants army to stay, 225; gubernatorial candidate, 302; convention delegates of, 303; mentioned, 278, 281, 282, 286, 289, 290, 293, 305, 306, 313, 335, 344
Constitutional convention: of 1865, 39; of 1868, 178; of 1885, 344
Constitutional Union Party, 171
Contract system, 128, 139
Convict leasing, 217
Conway, General Thomas, 178
Cooke, Jay, 273
Cookman Institute, 153
Cooper, James, 104
Corporal punishment: disapproved by Osborn, 50; provided for, 54; prohibited, 55; resisted by Freedmen's Bureau, 63, 83; failure of repeal, 102
Cotten, Frederick R., 43, 133, 171
Cottondale: AME Church founded at, 143
Cotton tax, 20, 126, 171
Cottrell and Ayers sawmill, 269
County criminal courts: defended, 91
Cowgill, Clayton A., 165, 292, 301, 319, 323, 324, 326, 330, 331, 332, 334
Cowlan, Charles H., 284
Coyle, John F., 316
Crawford, John A., 222
Credit arrangements in 1866, 126
Credit buying, 67
Credit system: adversity of, 125; criticized, 129
Crichton, F., 97
Cricket, steamer, 121
Croom, George A., 21
Crop lien law, 52, 139
Cuba: cattle shipped to, 135; lumber shipped to, 137; aliens from, 311; mentioned, 237, 238, 239
Cuban Democratic Club of Key West, 306–7
Cuban revolution: of 1868, 238
Cubans, 268, 283, 294, 295, 302
Cuba Tie Company, 240
Curry, William, 136

DaCosta, A. W., 130, 281
Dade County, 185, 297, 320, 322
Daly, Charles, 283
Dan Castello's Great Show and Exhibition, 153
Danforth, Jack, 104
Daniel, J. J., 21, 22
Darlington, steamer, 271
Darnell, Samuel, 153
Davidson, Green, 180, 181
Davidson, J. E. A., 183
Davidson, R. H. M., 281, 282, 304, 333
Davis, William Watson, 241
Day, Samuel T., 213, 216, 221, 222
Daytona, 153, 265, 266
Deadfalls, 130
DeBary, Count Frederick W., 260
De Cespedes, C. M., 306
Dennett, N. C., 15, 62, 165, 175, 182
Denney's bank, 271, 273
Dennis, Leonard G.: invests in land, 133; moderate Republican, 174; mentioned, 216, 221, 222, 285, 290, 298, 312, 321
Denton, James, 88, 104
Department of Florida: in Division of the Gulf, 36

Deserters from Confederate army, 2
Dewey, S. F., 165
Dewitt, Mrs. James, 95
Dibble, Calvin, 209
Dibble, Franklin: railroad affairs of, 113, 114; bank failure of, 248; mentioned, 137, 209, 245, 246, 271
Dibble, Worth and Company, 271
Dickerson, Edward N., 115, 200, 250
Dickinson, J. Q., 233
Dickison, J. J., 43, 91, 95, 215
Dickson, Jesse, 95
Dictator, steamer, 118, 119
Dilworth, William S., 90, 103, 147
Diocese of St. Augustine, 148
Direct tax act, 4, 5, 28
Direct tax commission, 4, 5, 32, 121
Direct tax sale, 26, 115
Disston, Hamilton, 252
District of Florida, commander of, 161
Division of the Gulf, 36
Dockray, Fred A., 172, 173, 178, 206, 211, 216, 220, 238, 256
Dockray, William P., 173
Donald, James, 231
Doolittle, Senator James R., 5, 93, 186
Dorman, Orloff M., 12, 14
Dow, Warren Q., 117
Downey, Mark W., 262
Dozier, Albert, 21
Drew, George F., 137, 258, 303, 305, 320, 329, 332, 333, 334, 336, 337, 339, 340, 343, 344
Drew, J. B. C., 238, 281
Drew and Bucki Lumber Company, 201, 240, 273
Drew and Hull clubs, 305
Dry Tortugas, 36, 63, 194
DuBose, John, 147
Dukes, Floyd, 321
Dummit, Douglas, 132, 266
Duncan, E. B., 76
Duncan, Sherman and Company, 271
Dunham, D. R., 8
Dupont, 260
Dupont, Charles H., 44, 51, 131, 259
Dupree, Jess, 229, 235
Durkee, J. H., 168, 169, 174
Durr, R. E., 21
Duryea, J. B. C., 271
Dutton, Andrew, 84
Duval County: lumbering in, 137; Union-Republican Club of, 171; mentioned, 148, 175, 183, 189, 201, 215, 240, 278, 281, 308, 309
Duval Graded High School, 152
Dyke, Charles E.: on Marvin's speeches, 39; on Philadelphia convention, 93; attacks Reed administration, 219; mentioned, 167, 170, 184–85, 188, 189, 199, 227, 247, 290, 293, 301, 309
"Dyke-Conover Ring," 301

Earle, Elias, 88–89
East Florida Presbytery, 147
East Florida Seminary, 147, 152
Eastman, E. G., 271
Eau Gallie, 152, 153
Edward Waters College, 144
Eggleston House at Palatka, 265
Eichelberger, Adam L., 126, 127, 128
El Destino Mills, 133
Election districts, 163
Election laws, 215, 307–8
Election results: of 1872, 286; of 1876, 325
Electoral college, 318, 328
Electoral commission, 329, 338
Electoral count, 337
Ellaville, 137, 303, 340
El Republicano, 306
Ely, John R., 233
Ely, Ralph, 71–72
Emerson, J. C., 172
Emmons, J. P. C., 220, 221, 330
Employment, 138
Enforcement Acts, 229, 234
England: lumber shipped to, 137
Enterprise, 136, 262
Epidemics, 208
Episcopal Church, 29, 142, 146
Episcopalians, 142
Eppes, Mayor Francis, 94–95, 145
Eppes, Rev. William, 21
Escambia County: martial law in, 90; lumbering in, 137; mentioned, 181, 255, 281, 282, 295, 296, 298
E. Simpson and Company, 127
Europe: lumber shipped to, 137
European labor, 124
Evans, John, 4
Everglades, 118
Ex Parte Milligan, 157

Faber, E. W., 262
Fairbanks, George R., 27
Fall of the Confederacy, 142
Fernandina: occupied, 3; Unionists in, 4; Stickney's plans for, 6; tax commission arrives at, 6; military forces at, 10; difficulty of travel to, 13; Negroes emigrating to, 15; tax sale at, 15; Freedmen's Bureau at, 25; Negroes at, 26;

Chase at, 33; second tax sale at, 38; rations issued at, 65; schools at, 73; military-civil clash at, 99; showdown at, 100; military activities at, 102; lumber shipped to, 137; bricks made at, 138; fire damages at, 150; Radical leaders at, 168; mentioned, 2, 12, 27, 29, 52, 63, 68, 92, 108, 109, 110, 115, 116, 119, 120, 139, 146, 148, 167, 173, 175, 181, 191, 209, 226, 239, 243, 250, 252, 256, 261, 262, 263
Fernandina Observer, 281
Fernandina Peninsula, 16
Ferry, Thomas W., 328
Fifteenth Amendment, 208
Finegan, Joseph, 7, 10, 11, 27, 46, 73, 78, 190
Finlayson, John L., 79, 232
Finley, J. J.: nominated for U.S. Senate, 57; nominated for Congress, 304; mentioned, 280, 293, 295, 333
Finley, S. Y., 97
Firearms law, 56
First National Bank of Jacksonville, 273, 309
First Reconstruction Act, 157, 158
Fish, Hamilton, 236, 268
Fleishman, Samuel, 232
Fleming, Francis P., 227
Fleming, Lewis I., 21, 27, 246
Fletcher Institute, 142
Flint, Colonel F. F., 104, 167, 184, 195
Flint River, 119
Florida, Atlantic and Gulf Central Railroad: resists Freedmen's Bureau agent, 68; built to Lake City, 109; damaged by U.S. troops, 111; unable to recover from war damage, 113; telegraph line on, 121; mentioned, 110, 114, 218, 245
Florida Agriculturist, 150, 266, 294, 306
Florida Canal and Inland Transportation Company, 118
Florida Central Railroad Company, 114, 220, 244, 245, 246, 247, 248, 249, 250, 256
Florida Collegiate and Military Institute, 152
Florida Emigration Society, 21
Florida Fruit Growers' Association, 266
Florida House in St. Augustine, 264
Florida Land Agency, 262
Florida Land and Immigration Company, 262
Florida Land and Lumber Company, 72, 125
Florida Land Improvement Company, 262
Florida Line, 119
Florida Lumber Company, 262
Florida Mail Line, 119–20
Florida Mutual Relief Company, 148
Florida New Yorker, 259
Florida Railroad Company: as landowner, 6, 27; built from Fernandina, 109; destroyed by Union raids, 111; track removed from, 112; claims against, 115; bonds of, 116; telegraph line on, 121; lumber hauling on, 137; offers land for school, 152; agents of in smuggling ring, 237; issues numbered ballots, 309; mentioned, 115, 118, 120, 122, 200, 201, 210, 220, 239, 250, 251, 256, 257, 262, 263, 323
Florida Savings Bank, 273
Florida Savings Bank and Real Estate Exchange, 271
Florida Union Cavalry, 133
Foreclosures, 128
Fort Barrancas, 192
Fort Dallas, 266, 268
Fort Marion, 188
Fort Myers, 154
Fort Pickens, 90
Fort Pulaski, Georgia, 18, 35
Fort Taylor, 239, 267, 268
Fortune, Emanuel, 180, 206
Fortune, T. Thomas, 180
Foster, Eleazer K., 173, 175, 276, 286
Foster, General John G.: labor policy of, 26; assumes command of Florida, 36; assists Governor Marvin, 37, 49; approves white militia, 43; offers arsenal to state, 55–56; assumes command of Freedmen's Bureau, 60; and labor contracts, 63; applauds school law, 74; conflict with governor, 82, 88; pleased with civil government, 86; encourages state initiative, 87; resumes martial law, 90; approves parade, 92; reviews bureau court actions, 98; orders protection of Unionists, 99, 100; asked to explain Fernandina situation, 101; comments on Walker speech, 102; furnishes transportation for civilian officials, 111; charters steamer, 119; soldiers of, 141; resigns command, 158; mentioned, 70, 80, 81, 84, 85, 89, 91, 93–94, 97, 106, 146, 171, 342, 343
Fourteenth Amendment, 14, 102, 107, 158, 163, 190
France: lumber shipped to, 137
Franklin County, 84
Fraser, Philip: Unionist at Jacksonville,

4; delegate to Republican convention, 14; absent from state, 89; urges approval of Fourteenth Amendment, 102; mentioned, 8, 28, 35, 85, 165, 186, 329
Freedmen's Aid Society, 73, 153
Freedmen's Bureau: supervises labor contracts, 26, 124, 125; manages land, 28; vagrancy policy of, 52; life of extended, 60; powers of, 62; judicial role of disapproved, 63; size of, 63; resented by planters, 68; educational efforts of, 72, 74, 150; cooperates with Walker, 75; maintains welfare agencies, 78; political activities of, 79; evaluated, 80; control of epidemics by, 82; prohibits sale of loose cotton, 130; headquarters moved, 161; agents on election boards, 163; mentioned, 15, 25, 43, 51, 64, 83, 91, 100, 106, 113, 118, 128, 134, 135, 145, 148, 179, 193, 203, 226, 229, 277, 342
Freedmen's Relief Commission, 74
Freedmen's Savings Bank, 62, 71, 148, 213, 270, 273
Freedmen's Union Commission, 78
Friend, John, 190, 191
Friendship Church, 312, 324, 326
Friends of Temperance, 149
Frierson, Adeline, 104
Fry, John H., 253
Funding bill: of 1871, 218; of 1873, 291
Furchgott, Benedict and Company, 263

Gadsden County: opposition to homesteaders in, 70; thievery in, 129; mentioned, 64, 154, 174, 175, 180, 181, 183, 190, 214, 230, 259, 265, 277, 281, 285, 294, 304
Gainesville: citizens arrested at, 88; Presbyterians at, 147; East Florida Seminary at, 147; land office at, 241; troops at, 310; mentioned, 46, 84, 96, 118, 121, 152, 168, 192, 226, 249, 262
Gainesville Alachua Citizen, 154
Gainesville Independent, 289
Gainesville New Era, 158, 288
Galbraith, John B., 46, 56, 83–84, 87, 91
Galveston, Texas, 110, 120
Gamble, Robert H., 196, 200, 215, 301
Gardner, J. C., 63–64
Garnishment of wages, 293
Gee, John H., 18
General incorporation law, 292
General Land Office, 71, 240
Germania Company of Pensacola, 150
Gibbons, James, 104
Gibbs, James C., 248
Gibbs, Jonathan C.: Presbyterian minister, 147; on education, 151; of Union-Republican Club, 166; Radical Republican, 172; 1878 convention delegate, 180; nominated for Congress, 183; supports Reed, 213; estimates murders, 234; mentioned, 173, 174, 181, 188, 191, 204, 206, 215, 281, 284
Gibson, Charles, 329
Gilbert, Abijah, 206, 207, 211
Gile, George W., 77, 78, 226
Gillis, Daniel, 234
Gillmore, General Quincy A., 7, 8–9, 10, 11, 17, 18, 25
Girardeau, W. O., 24
Gleason, William H.: state aid to, 118; explores South Florida, 135; donates to Negro education, 144; develops town, 152; nominated for lieutenant governor, 187; mentioned, 173, 184, 186, 194, 196, 203, 204, 205, 207, 238, 252, 253, 266, 267, 278, 279
Goodwood Plantation, 141
Gordon, John, 175, 305
Goss, Jesse H., 145, 172, 180, 181, 188, 191, 195
Governor Marvin, steamer, 30, 119, 136, 237
Govin, Manuel, 306, 307, 311
Grady, Henry, 318, 323
Graham, Edgar N., 308
Granberry, Oscar, 232
Grand Army of the Republic, 149, 171
"Grand Callico Ball" at Key West, 155
Grand National Hotel: in Jacksonville, 264
Grant, General U. S.: proposes combining Freedmen's Bureau and military, 60; orders quarantine, 82; supports Foster, 99; asked for instructions, 100; on voter eligibility, 163; in 1872 campaign, 283; cabinet of, 332; mentioned, 86, 204, 217, 276, 280, 284
"Grantism," 314
Great Eastern Circus, 153
Great Southern Railway Company, 253, 254
Greeley, Horace, 276, 280
Greeley, Jonathan C., 166, 222, 271, 273, 276
Green, Andrew, 308
Green, James D., 47, 206
Green Cove Springs, 155
Greenwood, 76
Grossman, F. E., 98

Grumwell, A. B.: controversial bureau agent, 61, 62; impounds cotton, 68; reports on violence, 87; complains to mayor, 95; reprimanded, 104; comments on thievery, 129; on opposition to Reconstruction, 170; on law enforcement, 225; mentioned, 129, 130, 192
Gulf-to-Atlantic trade, 116
Gwynn, Walter, 336

Hale, M. H., 238
Halifax River, 240
Hall, James W., 117, 191
Hall, Robert, 43
Halleck, General Henry W., 9
Halliday, Solomon F., 70–71, 147, 228
Hamilton, Charles M.: denounces white teacher, 76; denounced by local citizens, 92; bureau agent in politics, 168; nominated for Congress, 187; congressman, 254; mentioned, 149, 174, 183, 205, 211, 213, 214, 237
Hamilton County, 128, 228, 240, 285, 311, 318, 324, 326, 331
Hammond, D. M., 92, 168, 174, 191, 281
Hampton, A. T., 89
Hampton, Eliza, 89
Hampton, J. J., 89
Hampton, Jim, 89
Hampton plantation, 89
Hannah, Thomas, 295
Harger, David, 133
Harmon, Henry S., 206, 240, 278, 285, 288, 341
Harris, Doctor, 267
Harris, J. George, 33–34
Harrison, Ned, 228
Hart, Hubbard L., 117, 119, 261, 265, 266
Hart, Ossian B.: 1868 convention delegate, 93; favors Negro suffrage, 158; supervisor of registration, 163; tries for coalition with Conservatives, 166; law partner of Goss, 172; disagrees with Reed, 222; nominated for governor, 278; mentioned, 165, 173, 174, 175, 183, 191, 194, 196, 207, 250, 277, 279, 280, 283, 286, 287, 288, 291, 292, 319
Hartridge, Theodore, 27
Harvey, Governor Louis P., 5
Hauptman, Bob, 103
Havana, Cuba: cattle trade to, 30; cable service to, 121; mentioned, 13, 116, 119, 264
Havana Voz de Cuba, 239
Hawkins, D. C., 43
Hawks, Esther, 16, 73
Hawks, John Milton, 72, 125
Hay, John, 9, 10, 11
Hayes, Rutherford B.: election dispute of, 300; nominated for president, 303; votes received, 320; removes troops, 340; mentioned, 314, 315, 318, 322, 325, 326, 328, 331, 333, 334, 337, 338
Hayes and Wheeler clubs, 309
Hearn, W. H., 266
Helper, H. H., 7, 15
Henderson, John A., 136, 190, 203, 219, 222, 240, 293, 294, 295, 296
Hendricks, Thomas A., 304, 315, 325, 336
Hendry, F. A., 136
Henry, E. C., 228
Henry Burden: steamer, 238
Henschen, Doctor, 259, 260
Hentz, Charles A., 96, 132
Hernando County, 87, 95, 97, 104, 128, 134
Hewitt, Abram S., 336
Hicks, Henry, 281
Hicks, William Watkins, 295, 296
Higginson, Thomas W., 5, 6
Hill, Benjamin H., 305
Hill, Frederick T., 180, 213
Hill, General D. H., 142
Hill, Professor A. G., 153
Hillsborough County: petition from, 33; rations issued in, 65; antipathy toward Unionists in, 96; homesteads in, 134; lumbering in, 137; mentioned, 266, 268
Hillsborough River: timber poaching on, 240
Hilton, R. B., 303, 329, 330, 333, 334
Hilton Head, South Carolina, 6, 10, 12, 13, 17, 78
Hobbs, L. M., 42–43, 56, 75
Hogue, D. P., 39, 160
Holden, W. H.: Florida Republican presidential elector, 302
Holden, William H.: provisional governor of North Carolina, 32; mentioned, 35
Holmes, John, 125
Homestead Act of 1866, 65, 70, 125, 134, 135, 171
Hope, J. David, 103
Hope Hook and Ladder Company, 150
Hopkins, Arvah, 141
Hopkins, Edward, 57
Hopkins, S. W., 248
House, E. D., 181
Houstoun, Edward: built railroad, 110; seeks loan, 112; sale arranged by, 113; state funds held by, 218; mentioned, 114, 244, 245, 246, 247
Howard, General O. O.: authorizes use of

churches, 29; suggests extra patrols, 42; opinion asked, 55; commissioner of Freedmen's Bureau, 59; selects assistants, 60; land policy of, 62; views on homesteading, 70; beliefs about education, 72; cooperates with benevolent associations, 74; establishes bureau courts, 97–98; mentioned, 63, 64, 83, 107, 148, 160, 193
Howe, Charles, 8
Howes and Macy, 271, 273
Hubbard, John, 100
Hull, Noble A., 303, 304, 329, 333, 339
Humphries, F. C., 302
Hunt, William H., 239, 267
Hunter, Archibald, 104
Hunter, General David, 6, 34, 36
Hyer, Albert, 254–55
Hyer Brothers, 271

Immigrant labor, 131
Immigration commission, 217
Impeachment of Reed, 220–22
Indian River country, 259, 265, 266
Indigent aged persons, 56
Inside Line, 119
Internal Improvement Act, 117
Internal Improvement Board, 113, 114, 115, 116, 118, 122, 245, 253, 257
Internal Improvement Fund, 109, 111, 117–18, 209, 244, 249, 251, 252, 254, 256, 274
International Ocean Telegraph Company, 121
Irwin, John M., 76
Ives, E. R., 86

Jackson, Alec, 88
Jackson, William E., 114
Jackson County: desertion in, 2; people of, 21; opposition to Negro schools in, 76; school funds for, 77; violence at, 87; summary justice in, 130; farmers' meetings in, 131; resistance to Negro settlers in, 134; black skilled workers in, 140; emigration from, 170; mentioned, 69, 95, 104, 128, 129, 174, 179, 180, 181, 190, 192, 209, 214, 216, 231, 233, 234, 285, 301, 310, 312, 313, 316, 317, 318, 324, 326, 330, 331
Jacksonville: occupied, 3; U.S. policy in, 3; raided, 6; military expedition to, 9; Union forces arrive at, 10; Negroes emigrating to, 15; school opens at, 16; destruction at, 20; Freedmen's Bureau at, 25; trade in, 29; lumber from, 30; hunger in, 64; labor shortage near, 65; schools at, 73, 146; hospital at, 78; takes over epidemic control, 82; militia desired by citizens of, 91; railroad from desired, 109; railroad service to, 114; lumber shipped to, 137; bricks made at, 138; churches at, 148; fires in, 150; baseball team, 154; state fair at, 155; Union-Republican Club of, 165; Republican executive meeting at, 221; railroad to St. Augustine from, 256; tourism in, 261; mills at, 273; mentioned, passim
Jacksonville, Pensacola and Mobile Railroad Company, 207, 210, 211, 212, 219, 220, 238, 243, 247, 248, 249, 250, 255, 309
Jacksonville Board of Trade, 246
Jacksonville Democratic Convention, 1872, 280, 281
Jacksonville East Floridian, 189
Jacksonville Florida Times, 39, 173, 178, 188
Jacksonville Florida Union, 173, 178, 182, 211, 246, 289, 293, 334
Jacksonville Mercury, 188
Jacksonville New South, 294, 296
Jacksonville Press, 296, 309, 312
Jacksonville Republican, 281
"Jacksonville Ring," 290
Jacksonville Semi-Tropical, 306
Jacksonville Trade Palace, 263
James Robinson's Mammoth Circus, 153
Jasper, 324, 326
Jay, Hamilton, 281
Jefferson, Alfred, 87, 98
Jefferson County: emancipation in, 25; mass meeting in, 49; schools in, 78; recruits black laborers, 125; economic intimidation in, 309; election complaints in, 311; mentioned, 64, 90, 95, 129, 130, 154, 155, 171, 175, 180, 192, 207, 214, 228, 246, 278, 280, 285, 288, 295, 301, 304, 308, 318, 323, 324, 326
Jefferson Rifles, 310
Jenkins, Horatio, 149, 174, 175, 181, 183, 184, 186, 188, 191, 196, 204, 206, 216–17, 220, 221, 222, 290
Jenks, Harry, 237
Jesup, Georgia, 254
Jim Crow legislation, 341, 344
J. L. Smallwood, steamer, 119
Johnson, Andrew: assumes presidency, 18, 31; attitude of, 22; issues proclamations, 31, 32, 42, 47, 49, 57, 73, 177, 231, 342; policy approved by Reed, 33; appoints Marvin, 35; identifies with white Southerners, 60; ordered Steed-

man-Fullerton investigation, 61; amnesty plan, 62; disapproves bureau courts, 63, 69; difficulties with Congress, 81, 157; proclamations of, 82, 85, 88, 93, 101; opponents denied justice, 96; countermands Howard's order, 98; asked to intervene in Fernandina, 100; recommends rejection of Fourteenth Amendment, 102–3; on states' rights, 165; influences Reconstruction, 178; denounced by Richards, 179; mentioned, 12, 42, 90, 99, 105–6, 277
Johnson, Elisha G., 227, 228, 295, 298
Johnson, Isham, 97
Joint Committee of Fifteen on Reconstruction, 57
Jones, Charles W., 282, 296, 297, 335
Jones, General Sam, 17
Jones, George Noble, 133
Jordan, Charles N., 91
Judicial system, failure of, 91
Jupiter Inlet, 118
Jurisdictional dispute in Florida: removed by military bill, 103

Kasson, John A., 316
Kate, steamer, 118, 119
Katzenberg, Simon, 128, 213, 228
Keene, O. L., 4
Keen's boarding house in Jacksonville, 264
Kelley, Oliver H., 269
Kelley, W. W. J., 46
Kent, Robert, 171
Keyser, Judah and Company, 269
Keyser, William J., 269
Key West: held by Union, 3; Unionists in, 12; isolation of, 13; yellow fever at, 14, 82, 237; description of, 23; placed in Florida district, 36; troops at, 63, 310; cable service to, 121; AME Church at, 143; missions at, 145; Japanese jugglers at, 154; Negroes at, 236; counterfeit money at, 238; Cubans at, 260–61, 306; cigar factories at, 267–68; election complaints at, 311; mentioned, passim
Key West, steamer, 119
Key West Dispatch, 149
Key West District, 161
Kielmansegge, Lt. Col. Eugene, 3
Kimball, W. H., 92
King, Joe, 309
King, Ziba, 136
King's Ferry, 253
Kirk, William, 192
Kissimmee Valley, 136
Knight, Alva A., 173, 174, 222, 246, 273, 284, 285, 306
Knight, Joel, 136
Koch, Mr., 260
Krimminger, John N., 180, 206, 213, 231
Ku Klux Klan, 227

Labelle, 136
Labor contracts, 26, 67, 69, 126
Labor League: of Jacksonville, 272
Labor shortage: in Florida, 125
Ladd, Daniel, 21, 119
Lafayette County: guerillas in, 2; resistance to blacks in, 70; gun licenses illegally required, 84; antipathy toward Unionists in, 96; violence in, 217; mentioned, 180, 206, 213, 230
Lake City: battle site, 11; prosperity returning to, 30; unpopularity of northern school teachers at, 73; transportation resumed, 112; telegraph service to, 121; school moved to, 153; mentioned, 22, 86, 147, 215, 228, 229, 230, 280, 285, 298, 309
Lake City Herald, 281, 282
"Lake City Outrage," 229
Lake City Press, 168
Lake Eustis Railroad, 255
Lake George, 235
Lake Iamonia, 43, 133
Lake Jesup, 132
Lake Monroe, 260, 261, 262, 271, 276
Lake Okeechobee, 118
Lake Washington, 153
Land values depreciated, 132
Larceny of livestock, 129
La Rosa Espanola, 267
Latta, L. M., 165
Leddy, Captain Thomas, 29
Lee, Dennis, 192, 229
Lee, Joseph A., 302
Legislature of 1873: prohibits use of state credit by private companies, 291
Le Havre, France, 238
Leib, A., 237
L'Engle, Edward M., 21, 114, 171, 172, 189, 220, 246, 249, 282, 310, 334
L'Engle, Edwin W., 304
L'Engle, F. F., 21, 22, 30
L'Engle, John A., 17, 21
Leon County: resistance to Negroes settling in, 134; segregated schools in, 151; Conservative convention in, 170, 171; apportionment of, 185; mentioned, passim
Le Puy, France, 147

Levy County: guerillas in, 2; martial law in, 90; homesteads in, 134; lumbering in, 137; election irregularities in, 312
Liberal Republican movement, 294, 330
Liberal Republicans: Cincinnati convention of, 276; Jacksonville convention of, 277; in legislature, 289, 290; mentioned, 280, 281, 282, 286
Lickskillet, 311
Lien to protect lumber workers, 293
Lillian, steamer, 238, 239
Lincoln, Abraham: interested in Florida restoration, 8, 9; ten per cent plan of, 31–32; portrait of, 92; Hart works for, 165; mentioned, 5, 10, 11, 12, 14, 18, 21
Lincoln, C. D., 175
Lincoln Academy of Tallahassee, 152
Lincoln Brotherhood, 167, 168, 169, 174
Lincoln Temperance Societies, 148
Linda, steamer, 119
Lindley, Doctor, 235
Littlefield, Milton S.: donates to Negro education, 144; financial difficulties of, 249; mentioned, 191, 209, 210, 213, 220, 244, 247, 248, 256
Live Oak: cotton tax collected at, 126; Negro college at, 144; temperance meeting at, 149; violence at, 230; mentioned, 249, 302
Live Oak to Lawton connector, 112, 115
Liverpool, 29–30, 126
Livestock killing, 130
Livingston, Benjamin, 301
Lizzie Baker, steamer, 119
Locating agents of Freedmen's Bureau, 70, 71
Locke, James W., 289
Lollie Boy, steamer, 118
Long, Ellen Call, 155, 156
Long, Thomas T., 86, 196
Long, Thomas W., 143, 302
Louisville and Nashville Railroad, 255
Love, E. C., 43, 64, 96
Ludlow, Hayes and Hurburt, 262
Lulansky, Colonel L. L., 87
Lumber industry, 136–38

McCaskill, Alexander L., 221, 296
McClellan, James F., 232
McClellan, Maggie, 232
McConnell, S. D., 149, 162, 190, 229
McCook, General Edward, 17, 18, 22, 30, 36
McCormick, William J., 147
McDonell, Thaddeus A., 46
McDowell, S. A., 128
McGehee, John C., 21
McIntosh, McQueen, 45, 160, 166, 167, 185
McKay, John, 30, 119, 136, 237
McLean, John G., 190, 282
McLeod, Ferdinand, 46, 57, 113, 147
McLin, Samuel B., 296, 319, 321, 322, 324, 326, 330, 331, 332, 334, 335
McPherson, Edward, 178
Madison: Republican convention at, 302, 305; mentioned, 21, 22, 61, 62, 154, 285
Madison County: court injustices in, 89; military-civil conflict in, 89, 91; martial law in, 90; murder in, 104; lumbering in, 137; freedmen organized in, 170; arms destroyed in, 225; mentioned, 84, 90, 128, 129, 130, 149, 196, 201, 213, 215, 227, 228, 240, 260, 273, 282, 288, 295
Madison Messenger, 105
Magbee, Judge J. T., 212
Magnolia Hospital, 78, 79
Magnolia Hotel: in St. Augustine, 264
Magruder, Alexander, 177
Mahoney, Andrew, 174, 229
Mallory, Stephen R.: imprisoned, 18; attitude of, 24; endorses Marvin, 35; release from prison requested, 42; advocates moderation, 160; mentioned, 192
Man, L. C.: describes Key West, 23
Manatee County: rations issued in, 65; antipathy toward Unionists in, 96; mentioned, 206, 261, 266, 268, 308, 318, 324, 326, 330, 331
Mandarin, 77
Manufacturing: employees in, 137
Marble, Manton, 316, 322, 330, 334, 336
Marianna: Marvin speaks at, 38; Negro citizen of, 39; racial difficulties in, 76, 77, 131; anticipates railroad service, 113; 1864 raid on, 231; violence near, 232; troops at, 310; mentioned, 20, 79, 92, 128, 205, 226, 233, 234, 285
Marianna Courier, 207
Marion County: lawyers refuse to practice in, 103; transportation to, 118; blacks recruited in, 125; immigration meetings in, 131; Germans hired in, 131; Negroes buy plantation in, 133; northern buyers in, 133; homesteads in, 134; Negro entrepreneurs in, 137; sheriff of, 144; judicial stalemate at, 162; mentioned, 63, 69, 72, 86, 95, 124, 126, 127, 155, 172, 176, 180, 190, 192, 229, 278, 285
Marks, S. N., 237

Marriage laws, 53, 84
Martin, Malachi, 155, 174, 203, 230, 294, 301, 310, 320
Martin, Robert, 228
Marvin, William: resigns judicial position, 13; candidate for provisional governor, 34; goes to Florida, 36, 62; assisted by military, 37, 111; speaks to Negroes, 38; addresses convention, 41; calls for white militia, 43; praises constitutional convention, 44; relations with military, 49; senator-elect, 50; cautions Floridians, 51; elected, 57; as provisional governor, 58; mentioned, 7, 35, 47, 51, 55, 81, 342
Masonic Order, Grand Lodge of, 149
"Masterly activity," 159
M. A. Wilder and Son, 271
Maxwell, Augustus E., 117, 190, 336
Maxwell, G. Troup, 39, 50
Meacham, Robert: church built by, 144; 1868 convention delegate, 180; mentioned, 175, 214, 278, 293, 294
Meade, George G.: replaces Pope, 177; defends troop withdrawal, 226; mentioned, 181, 182, 183, 184, 185, 186, 191, 193, 194, 195
Mechanics and Steam Fire Engine Company of Jacksonville, 150
Meek, A. R., 215
Mellonville, 147, 262
Memorial associations, 142
Menard, J. Willis, 278, 341
Merrick, Chloe, 7, 15, 73, 78
Merritt Island, 266
Methodist Episcopal Church, South, 143, 144, 153
Methodists, 29
Metropolitan Hotel: in Jacksonville, 264
Miami, 239, 266, 268
Miami River, 238
Mickler, Myron S., 96
Middle Florida, 258
Midway, 146
"Military bill," 157
Military commissions, 85
Military forces, 68
Militia, 217
Millen, Georgia, 253
Miller, O. E., 265
Mills, Anthony, 175
Millview, 255, 269
Milton, 30, 138, 269
Milton, Governor John, 2, 18, 21
Mississippi convention, 32
Mitchell, Doctor, 170
Mitchell, Henry L., 280
Mobile Bay, 117
Molino Mills, 117
Monroe County, 180, 268, 279, 282, 283, 294, 295, 302, 306, 310, 318, 324, 326, 330, 331
Montgomery, David, 228, 295–96, 302, 306, 322, 327, 336
Montgomery, Alabama, 116, 117, 207, 269
Monticello: Negroes refuse to work at, 52; violence at, 87; Negro boy assaulted at, 95; disturbance at, 104; planters convention at, 131; Presbyterians at, 147; fires at, 150; exhibit censored at, 153; baseball team at, 154; citizens alarmed at, 167; opposition to Reconstruction at, 170; convention delegates remove to, 182; rally at, 305; troops at, 310; mentioned, 61, 62, 103, 113, 142, 145, 154, 168, 171, 183, 184, 185, 186, 187, 192, 214, 215, 285, 325
Monticello Family Friend, 49
Moody, Paran, 4, 14, 165
Moore, Green, 312, 321
Moore, H. H., 71, 73
Moore, T. W. C., 270, 273, 309
Moore, W. W., 229
Morgan, Ozias, 213
Morrill, W. C., 8
Morris, Thomas, 89
Morton, Senator Oliver P., 332
Moses and Cohen, 272
Mosquito Inlet, 120
Mot, Adolphus, 32, 33, 172, 173, 192
Mundee, Charles, 149, 171
Munger, Sheriff Alvin B., 20, 133, 281
Munn, Asa B., 281
Murat, Madame, 142
Muscogee Lumber Company, 269

Nassau, Bahamas, 13
Nassau County: Negroes cutting timber in, 68; antipathy toward Unionists in, 96; Negro constable in, 130; northern buyers in, 133; lumbering in, 137; mentioned, 171–72, 174, 175, 190, 240, 296, 309
National Freedmen's Relief Association, 16, 73
National Union Convention, 92–93
Negro colonization, 72
Negro education, 72
Negro grocers, 139
Negro labor: efforts to replace, 131
Negro soldiers, 19, 20, 36, 38, 42, 91
Negro Sunday school, 144
Negro voting: in 1865, 33
Negro women, leaving the fields, 125

New England Freedmen's Union Commission, 73
Newnansville, 71, 228
New Orleans: trade with, 29, 126; mentioned, 108, 110, 116, 119, 120, 209, 249, 252, 263, 270–71
New Orleans, Florida and Havana Steamship Company, 237
Newport: decline of, 20; resort at, 155; mentioned, 21, 119
New Smyrna: colonizing at, 72; settlement at, 132; mentioned, 136
Newton, General John, 26, 36, 66
New York: Florida Unionists at, 4; trade with, 29, 126; investors of, 112; mentioned, 13, 30, 34, 108, 117, 119, 120, 121, 127, 128, 132, 136, 170, 173, 239, 245, 247, 248, 253, 262, 263, 266, 270, 271, 272, 273, 316, 334
New York and Indian River Preserving Company, 138
New York and Key West Steamship Line, 120
New York Herald, 11, 200, 318
New York *Junta*, 283, 294, 306
New York Steamship Company, 120
New York Times, 183, 314, 315, 330, 331
New York Tribune, 179, 184, 276, 294, 317, 338
New York World, 200, 247, 316
Niblack, Joel, 309, 310
Niblack, Silas L., 113, 214, 215, 216, 282
Nichols, Matt, 232
Nick King, steamer, 119
Nicolay, John G., 11
Northern Presbyterian Church, 146, 147
Norwood House in Fernandina, 263
Noyes, ex-Governor Edward F., 316, 317, 322
Nutter, George F., and Brother, 240
Nutter, G. N., 262

Oates, Joseph, 175, 180
Ocala: atrocities at, 19; business revives at, 30; failure of justice at, 104; resistance at, 162; mentioned, 126, 127, 136, 144, 145, 152, 154, 159, 167, 172, 191, 194, 230, 235, 250, 251, 268, 303
Ocala Banner, 193
Oklawaha River, 117, 118, 139, 261, 265
Old Town Hammock, 70
Oliver, J. Berrien, 184, 191, 259, 297
Oliveras, Bartolo, 8
Olustee, Battle of, 11, 13
Orange County, 134, 185, 235, 261, 262, 265
Orange Hill, 234
Orange Springs, 104, 155
Orlando, 136, 147, 258, 262
Osborn, A. C., 253, 254
Osborn, Thomas W.: on rumors of revolt, 42; on attitudes of Floridians, 44–45; relations with Marvin, 49; disagrees with legislature, 50; orders blacks to work, 52; protests discrimination, 55, 56; appointed to head Freedmen's Bureau, 60; assumes bureau duties, 62; policy on rations, 64–65; policy on aged and infirm, 78; protests state legislation, 83; helps organize Republican party, 166; organizes secret society, 167; lacks Negro support, 168; moderate Republican, 174, 181; opposes Reed, 200, 221; mentioned, 63, 64, 73, 74, 79, 80, 83, 84, 175, 182, 184, 187, 193, 194, 199, 206, 211, 212, 230, 238, 253, 254, 275, 277, 280, 282, 285, 289, 290, 336
Osteen, Elias, 309, 310
Outside Line, 119

Paine, James H., 271
Palatka, 88, 117, 118, 119, 142, 148, 264, 265, 266
Panic of 1873, 270, 272, 274
Papy, G. N., 8
Papy, Mariano D., 44, 51, 160, 211, 247
Parker, Hugh, 105
Parker, William, 95
Parkhill, G. W., 133
Parlin, A. J., 298
Pasco, Samuel, 222, 304, 308, 320, 321, 334, 336, 337
Patrons of Husbandry, National Grange of, 149, 269
Peabody Fund, 151
Pearce, "Bishop" Charles H.: arrives in Florida, 14; home burned, 144; Radical Republican, 172; in 1868 convention, 179, 180; convicted of bribery, 213; presidential elector, 302; only Negro on ticket, 305; mentioned, 173, 175, 181, 183, 186, 203, 227, 278, 279, 285, 286, 341
Peck, George, 165
Peeler, Anderson J., 44, 51, 160, 170
Peeler-Dupont report, 83
Pelton, William T., 322
Peninsular Telegraph Company, 121
Pennsylvania Tie Company, 269
Penny, William, 138
Pensacola: occupied by Union, 3; nontaxable property at, 29; timber cutting at, 30; troops at, 63, 310; railroad affairs at, 109, 110; lumber shipped to,

137; bricks made at, 138; labor union at, 139; school at, 146; Catholics at, 147; fires at, 150; circus on way to, 153; meeting at, 160; election at, 161; yellow fever at, 208; constable shot at, 234; stevedores riot at, 272; mentioned, 29, 46, 91, 116, 117, 146, 190, 191, 193, 194, 206, 209, 235, 236, 243, 245, 248, 249, 254, 255, 260, 268, 269, 270, 271, 273, 330, 334
Pensacola and Georgia Railroad: supplies for, 22, 30; financing sought for, 112; connected with Atlantic and Gulf, 112; competition of, 113; consolidated, 114; Gulf outlet sought, 121; excursion rates of, 154; mentioned, 109–10, 209, 211, 218, 244, 245, 246
Pensacola and Louisville Railroad, 254
Pensacola and Mobile Railroad and Manufacturing Company, 255
Pensacola and Perdido Railroad, 255, 269
Pensacola Bay, 269
Pensacola Express, 281
Pensacola Observer, 192
Pensacola Railroad Company, 255
Pensacola West Florida Commercial, 188, 207
Pensacola Workingman's Association, 293
Perdido Lumber Company, 255
Perdido River, 255, 270
Perry, Edward A., 256, 334, 336
Pettes, William R., 270
Pettus, J. J., 68
Pfeiffer, George, 260
Philadelphia: convention at, 92–93; Centennial Exposition at, 155
Philbrick, J. J., 240, 262, 271
Philips, Ethelred, 1, 20, 21, 92
Picolata, 119, 121
"Pine Tucky," 25
Pitts, John, 232
Plant, Henry B., 250
Planters Hotel in Tallahassee, 150
Plantz, Homer G., 8, 12, 13, 14
Polk County, 268
Pollard, Alabama, 116
Poll tax, 344
Pooser, Richard, 234
Pope, Frank, 104–5
Pope, General John, 103, 158, 161, 162, 163, 164, 165, 167, 168, 176, 177, 179, 181
Population: in 1860, 19; in 1860 and 1870, 123; in 1870, 275
Porter, Doctor Watson, 79
Port Orange, 72, 132
Potter, Hiram, 206, 211, 216
Potter Committee of 1878, 326
Powell, John W., 175
Praetorius and Clark, 153
Presbyterian Church, 29, 142, 146–47, 156, 310
Presidential proclamation: of August 20, 1866, 98
Prevention of epidemics, 79
Price, John G., 266
Price, John W., 4, 14, 281
Price House in Jacksonville, 263
Proctor, John, 281, 286
Protestant Episcopal Church, 145
Provost and Company, 138
Public accommodations bill, 203, 208
Punishment for crimes: enumerated, 54
Punta Rassa, 121, 136
Purman, William J.: investigates bureau activities, 71–72; bureau agent in politics, 168; delays convention, 179; demands martial law, 233; attacks Stearns, 302; mentioned, 174, 181, 182, 209, 216, 222, 231, 232, 264, 277, 279, 283, 284, 285, 293, 294, 295, 301, 306, 333
Putnam, Benjamin A., 88
Putnam County, 181, 190, 281, 319
Pyles, L. G., 46
Pyles, S. M., 170

Quentin, J. E., 61, 89, 91, 228
Quincy: Negro store closed at, 43; shooting at, 95; transportation resumed, 112; railroad service to, 113, 114; Negro saloon owner at, 139; fires in, 150; Japanese jugglers at, 154; Democratic convention at, 303; mentioned, 21, 96, 119, 121, 131, 132, 156, 190, 210, 211, 213, 245, 246, 247, 248, 259, 285
Quincy Commonwealth, 188

Radical Republicans: conflict with president, 102–3; mentioned, 31
Railroad construction, 217
Railroad legislation, 210
Randall, Alexander W., 178
Randall, Edward M., 196, 222, 329, 331, 335, 337, 339
Randel, Vans, 21
Raney, George P., 220, 329, 330, 333, 334
Rations issued by Freedmen's Bureau: in 1868, 130; denounced as "Radical" plan, 134
Reconstruction Act of March 2, 1867, 99

Reed, Harrison: opposes Stickney, 4; at tax sale, 6; defends role in tax sale, 7; removed from office, 12; provoked by Stickney, 33; supports Johnson Reconstruction policy, 35; approves Conservative convention delegates, 39; railroad affairs of, 113, 114, 166, 207; mail agent, 121, 122; Union-Republican Club member, 165; denounced by Conservatives, 167; condemned by Radicals, 174; receives financial aid, 178; lobbyist at convention, 182, 186; in 1868 constitutional struggle, 185; nominated for governor, 188; supported by Conservative press, 188; includes Conservatives in administration, 191; assumes control of state affairs, 193; defines his Republicanism, 195; administrative problems of, 199–200; calls special session, 204, 208; fights impeachment, 205; exonerated of charges, 206; addresses session, 207–9; refuses to exchange bonds, 210; doubts about bond issue, 211; accused of bribery, 212, 213; struggles with Osborn, 216; addresses legislature, 217; condemns opponents, 218; impeachment investigation of, 219; in 1872 election, 219, 283, 284, 285; charges against, 220; removed from governorship, 221; bipartisan support of, 222; favors civil rights, 223; U.S. military asked to stay, 225; difficulty of law and order, 226, 232, 233; fiscal conservative, 243; active in fruit growers' association, 266; continued factionalism with Osborn, 277; announces candidacy, 306; mentioned, 14, 40, 75, 173, 189, 192, 194, 196, 198, 201, 202, 203, 214, 224, 228, 230, 231, 234, 238, 244, 248, 251, 253, 254, 256, 259, 275, 278, 281, 288, 289, 329
"Reform" Republicans, 288
Reid, John C., 315
Remington, Joseph, 27, 29
Remley, Jacob A., 86, 104, 131, 167, 191, 229
Republican party platform: of 1872, 279
Reyes, Juan M., 311
Reynolds, John C., 68
Reynolds Gymnasium, 153
Richards, Daniel: Radical leader, 169; introduces resolution, 174; on Reed, 198; mentioned, 172, 175, 176, 177, 178, 180, 181, 182, 183, 184, 185, 186, 187, 188, 191, 196, 206, 207
Richards, Harney, 298, 299
Richardson, Martha, 95
Richardson, Simon P., 143
Richardson schoolhouse, 312, 326
Riddell House in Fernandina, 263
Ring tournaments, 154
Rio de Janeiro, 30
River Junction, 246, 248, 255
Road maintenance law: of 1874, 292
Roberts, Isaac K., 115, 220
Roberts, Marshall O., 6, 114–15
Robertson, William F., 24
Robinson, Calvin L., 4, 8, 12, 14, 35, 157, 165, 186, 262, 281, 282
Robinson, Solon, 179, 182, 184, 187, 294, 306, 313
Robinson, W. Howell, 170, 171
Rogers, C. B., 263
Rogers, Calvin, 232
Rogers, Samuel St. George, 149, 190, 191
Rogers, Washington, 183, 238
Roman Catholics, 147–48
Ross and Wingate, 266
Roulhac, Joseph B., 2
Rountree, Doc, 230
Rowley, Lyman, 181, 281
Royal Rangers, 2
Ruger, Thomas H., 316, 333
Ruter, Millington and Company, 117
Rutledge, Bishop Francis, 145
Rye, Henry, 228

St. Andrews Bay, 113
St. Augustine: occupied by Union, 3; Union meeting at, 8; convention called at, 8; difficulty of travel to, 13; tax sale at, 15; school open at, 15, 73; Freedmen's Bureau at, 35; racial segregation at, 49; military headquarters at, 61, 161; rations issued at, 65; assumes epidemic control, 82; navigation to, 121; church fair at, 146; debating society at, 149; "frolic" at, 154; popular resort, 155; integrated jury at, 162; Union Club at, 170; convention at, 170; troops at, 310; mentioned, 2, 12, 119, 142, 147, 148, 193, 194, 209, 226, 256, 264, 276, 277, 297
St. Augustine Examiner, 159, 160, 161, 189, 226
St. Augustine Hotel, 146
St. James Hotel: in Jacksonville, 146, 263, 264; at Key West, 267
St. Johns bar, 120
St. Johns Church, 146
St. Johns County: homesteads in, 134;

Conservative convention in, 170; mentioned, 171, 173, 175
St. Johns House: in Palatka, 263, 265; in Jacksonville, 264
St. John's Male Academy: at Jacksonville, 146
St. Johns River: lumbering near, 68, 137; land sales near, 132; timber poaching on, 240; hotel development on, 258, 261; new settlers along, 306; mentioned, 110, 118, 119, 132, 136, 139, 252, 264, 270
St. Marks: decline of, 20, 126, 269; steamer connections at, 114; mentioned, 3, 110, 113, 119, 120, 121
St. Mary, steamer, 119
St. Mary's Academy, 147
St. Mary's Priory, 146
St. Marys River, 6, 254
Salvador, steamer, 238
Sammis, John S.: opposed secession, 1; Unionist in Jacksonville, 4; direct tax commissioner, 5, 6; criticizes Reed, 7; removed from tax commission, 12; delegate to Republican convention, 14; tax sale difficulties of, 15; mentioned, 165
Sanderson, John P.: property seized, 27; railroad affairs of, 109, 110; sold plantation, 132; mentioned, 114, 143, 211, 244, 246, 247
Sanford, Henry S.: brings Swedish settlers, 259; acquires land, 261; mentioned, 262, 271, 276, 306
Sanford: violence at, 235; mentioned, 255, 259, 260, 273
San Mateo, 266
Sanno, W. R., 169–70
Santa Rosa County: martial law in, 90; lumbering in, 137; mentioned, 182, 204, 255, 295, 302
Sarasota, 261
Saratoga: Floridians vacation at, 154
Sargent, Senator A. A., 331
Satterwhite, Hayes, 160
Saunders, William U.: Radical leader, 169; 1868 convention delegate, 180; campaigns for splinter ticket, 306; mentioned, 172, 175, 176, 178, 179, 181, 183, 184, 186, 191, 195, 205, 295
Savannah, 108, 110, 112, 119, 120, 126, 129, 136, 147, 209, 246, 265, 270, 271
Savannah News and Herald, 112
Saxton, General Rufus, 5, 6, 15, 60
Schofield, General John M., 194
School funding act, 292
School law, 53, 151, 217
Scott, George W., 171, 190
Scott, John R., 278, 290
Scott, Rev. J. J., 145
Screven, John, 110, 112, 209
Scribner, George, 88
Scrip, 218
Scull, William D., 145, 146
Scurlock, Wyatt, 232
Second Infantry Regiment, 285
Second Reconstruction Act, 159, 163
Secret meetings of blacks, 167
Segregated schools: encouraged by bureau, 74
Seidenberg and Company, 267
Sellers, D. W., 316, 336
Seminole Indians, 266
Sequestration law: of Confederacy, 342
Settle, Thomas, 335
Seventh U.S. Infantry: band, 141; redeployed, 226
Seward, William H., 35
Seymour, General Truman, 10, 11, 12, 29
Seymour, Horatio, 203
Shade, John, 86
Sharecropping, 124, 125
Sheridan, General Philip H., 36, 92, 94
Sherman, General William T., 59, 261
Sherman, John, 157, 332
Ship canal: cross-Florida, 253
Sickles, Daniel E., 315
Silver Spring, steamer, 118
Silver Springs, 261, 265
Simmons, Ben, 83
Sims, Joseph, 309
Sisters' Beneficent Society, 148
Sisters of Mercy, 147, 148
Sisters of Protection, 148
Sisters of St. Joseph, 147
Sisters of the Holy Cross, 147
Slave code, 48
Smith, Austin, 7, 14
Smith, Buckingham, 14, 148
Smith, Robert M., 281
Smith, Thomas, 104
Smuggling, 236–37
Snead's Point, 136
Snead's store, 312
Sons and Daughters of Bethlehem, 148
Sons of Temperance, Grand Division of, 149
South, Department of: commander, 17
South America: threatened immigration to, 124
Southern Export and Import Company, 29

Southern Express Company, 270
Southern Inland Navigation and Improvement Company, 252, 253
Southern Land and Immigration Company, 131, 262
Southern Loyalists Convention, 93
Southern Presbyterian Church, 146
"Southern Question," 280, 303, 314
Southern Star, steamer, 136
South Florida Railroad Company, 210, 221, 250, 254, 256
Spanish Hole, 121
Spinner, F. E., 270
Split ticket voting, 306, 339
Sprague, John T.: assumes command of Florida, 61, 98, 103; comments on hunger, 64; authorizes rations, 69; observations of, 70, 78, 129, 158, 160, 161; angered by injustice, 96; praised by local press, 168; censured by Radicals, 174; mentioned, 71, 80, 145, 159, 163, 164, 188, 191, 193, 195, 277
Spray, steamer, 119
SS *Alliance*, 120
Stanberry, Henry, 163, 164
Stanley, J. S., 87–88
Stanton, Edwin M., 9, 101
Stanton Institute of Jacksonville, 152
State Agricultural College, 152
State canvassing board, 308, 323, 325
State credit, 291, 292
State Seminary West of the Suwannee, 147, 152
Stay law, 174, 199
Stearns, Marcellus L.: Freedmen's Bureau agent, 64; comment on shooting, 96; catches Negro thieves, 129; bureau agent in politics, 168; supports Osborn faction, 174; angered by Radicals, 175; seated in 1868 convention, 183; favors Reed impeachment, 205, 212, 220; on Gadsden County trouble, 233; empowered to compromise Vose claim, 252; gubernatorial candidacy of, 277; nominated for lieutenant governor, 278; votes received, 287; becomes governor, 288; opposed by Conover, 289, 290; in 1874 convention, 294; denounced by Purman, 301; attacked by Republicans, 306; attacked by John Wallace, 306; accused of collusion, 308; attends vote count, 320; aids in Hayes victory, 321; angered by national Republicans, 322; enemy of Judge Randall, 329; votes received, 330; on Drew court victory, 331, 332; mentioned, 250, 279, 293, 297, 302, 305, 316, 323, 324, 327, 335, 336, 337, 339
Steedman-Fullerton report, 60, 61
Steele, Mayor Holmes, 161
Stern, S., 213
Stevens, Thaddeus, 27, 157, 194
Stewart, Israel, 297
Stewart, William G., 143, 286, 290
Stickney, Lyman D.: proponent of Chase, 4, 33; on Thayer plan, 5; visits Jacksonville, 6; protests tax sale, 6; critics of, 7; plans convention, 7–8; adapts to Lincoln plan, 8; influences Hay, 10; accepts Olustee setback, 11; dilemma of, 12; dissolves partnership, 14; indicted, 15; enemy of Marvin, 34; mentioned, 8, 13, 35, 172
Stokes, John N., 278, 285
Stonelake, A. B., 71, 131, 135
Stowe, Calvin E., 147
Stowe, Harriet Beecher, 77, 147, 261
Strain, M. H., 95
Strickland, W. W., 2
Sturtevant, E. T., 286, 289, 297, 298
Sullivan, Columbus, 232
Sullivan, Daniel F., 255
Summerlin, Jacob, 136
Sumner, Charles, 46, 47, 50
Sumter County, 64, 95, 147, 235, 302
"Sunset to sunrise" law, 130
Suwannee County, 230, 240
Suwannee River: lumbering near, 137, 240
Swann, Samuel, 118, 259, 260, 262, 265, 296
Swepson, George W., 113, 114, 209, 210, 211, 212, 244, 245, 246, 247, 248, 249, 250, 256
Swepson-Littlefield fraud, 243, 244
S. W. Hopkins and Company, 247
Sylvan Shore, steamer, 82, 119

Tabernacle Baptists, 145
Taft, Alphonso, 335
Tallahassee: Confederate stockade at, 2; surrender at, 17; military headquarters at, 27; Stickney reports from, 34; delegates to convention at, 39; railroad service from, 113; trade at, 126; land office at, 135; seminary in, 147; fires in, 150; ring tournaments at, 154; military headquarters moved from, 161; troops at, 310; mentioned, passim
Tallahassee Floridian: applauds Marvin,

39, 41; rebuts Sumner, 46; applauds vagrancy law, 52; boasts of Florida education law, 56, 74; on Osborn-Walker compromise, 83; publishes attorney general's opinion, 94; comments on Fernandina, 99; deprecates Fourteenth Amendment, 102; announces railroad to Savannah reopened, 112; approved of Reed, 122; on thievery, 130; on schools, 151; on "military bill," 159; on race relations, 160; on Jackson County, 233; calls for action, 305; mentioned, 107, 189, 202, 207, 211, 227, 247, 287, 290, 293, 296
Tallahassee Ladies' Memorial Association, 142
Tallahassee Land Office, 71
Tallahassee Railroad, 110, 209, 210, 245, 247
Tallahassee Sentinel: on Drew nomination, 304; warns Republicans, 305; condemns election laws, 306; mentioned, 184, 191, 201, 206, 289, 293, 294, 296, 301, 302, 312, 319
Tampa: cattle trade at, 30, 136; AME Church at, 143; smuggling at, 237; troops at, 310; mentioned, 119, 120, 128, 130, 136, 172, 190, 194, 203, 211, 240, 243, 250, 251, 268, 280, 289
Tampa Bay, 3, 116, 137, 209
Tatum, T. P., 153
Tax collection law, 291
Tax commission, 15, 16
Tax rate set, 292
Tax sale, 14, 15, 28, 38, 62, 342
Tax sale cases, 99, 100
Tax sale purchasers, 99–100
Tax system, 208
Taylor, Charles U., 87
Taylor, John, 127, 128
Taylor, Moses, 218
Taylor County, 2, 96, 217
Taylor House in Jacksonville, 263
Temperance Saloon, 149
Templeton's Opera Troup, 154
Tenant system, 139
Ten-hour day law, 293
Ten per cent plan, 11
Thackera, Owen P., 146
Thayer, Eli, 5, 7, 71
The Land We Love, 142
Thiemann, Mr., 259, 260
Third Military District, 103, 158, 161, 188
Third Reconstruction Act, 164
Third U.S. Colored Troops, 50
Thirteenth Amendment, 32, 40, 57
Thomas, Allen, 87, 98
Thomas, Edward, 88
Thomas County, Georgia, 310
Thomasville, Georgia, 110, 113, 143, 249
Thomasville Cornet Band, 305
Thomasville Enterprise, 310
Thompson, Colonel George F., 118, 135
Thompson, Edward, 228
Tidwell, B. F., 228
Tilden, Samuel J., 300, 304, 309, 315, 320, 322, 325, 328, 330, 332, 333, 334, 336, 337, 339
Tillman, Sam, 228
Tilman, Judge, 90
Titus, Henry T., 96, 138
Titusville, 145
Togni, John B., 237, 238
Tracy, E. D., 39
Traders' Hill, Georgia, 130
Tucker, Captain James W., 82, 119
Tullock, Thomas L., 178
Tutson, Hannah, 230
Tutson, Samuel, 230
Tyler, John, Jr., 277

Underwood House: in Palatka, 265
Union blockaders, 2
Union cavalry: of Florida, 3, 19
Union Club: in Fernandina, 169; in St. Augustine, 170
Union coastal blockade, 3
Unionists: during Civil War, 1; in occupied towns, 3
Union League: organized in Florida, 168; members blackballed by planters, 170; support of, 178; mentioned, 169, 172, 174, 180, 275
Union-Republican Club of Jacksonville, 165, 173, 277
Union-Republican Convention of 1864, 14, 35
Union troops, 3, 6
United States Claims Commission, 342
United States Mail Telegraph, 121
Usher, Nathaniel, 29, 89

Vance, William G., 68, 87, 97, 103, 168, 282
Vanderbilt, Cornelius, 117
Vann, Enoch J., 196
Van Ness, W. W., 170, 171
Van Valkenberg, R. B., 281, 282, 330, 331
Van Valkenberg, Mrs. R. B., 155
Varnum, John, 294
Verot, Bishop Augustin, 147, 148
Veterans Reserve Corps, 64

Vigilant Fire Company, 150
Virginius affair, 268
"Visiting statesmen," 316, 317, 319, 326
Vogdes, General Israel, 17, 22–24, 25, 27, 30, 36
Volusia County, 71, 132, 144, 185, 235, 240, 265
Vose, Francis, 115, 251, 344
Vose claim, 274
Vose heirs, 116
Vose injunction, 122, 256
Voter registration, 38, 164

Wages, 66
Wakulla County, 129, 155, 171
Wakulla Springs, 155
Waldo, 251, 312, 321
Walker, George W., 182
Walker, Gilbert, 104
Walker, Governor David S.: opposed secession, 1; on use of militia, 43; relations with president, 44; elected governor, 46, 81; speaks of freedman, 47; relations with military, 49; recommends repeal of marriage law, 53; agrees to use arsenal as prison, 56; asks attorney general's opinion, 56; appoints school superintendent, 75; cooperates with military, 75, 86, 106; conflict with military, 82, 88, 99, 100; pleased by president's proclamation, 85; admonishes local justices, 87; angered by Madison County officials, 90; defends courts, 91; on militia law, 92; appoints convention delegates, 93; Unionists during administration of, 96; amnesty statement of, 96; wins victory over military, 101; recommends rejection of Fourteenth Amendment, 102–3; retains office under military bill, 103; uncertain authority of, 105, 161; in railroad affairs, 115, 244; administration of, 118, 122, 173, 208, 218; forms immigration company, 131; cooperates with moderate Republicans, 170; obtains guard for convention, 183; opposes Reed, 199, 214, 220; opposes Negro suffrage, 224; attempts to settle Vose claim, 251; senatorial candidacy of, 296; mentioned, 35, 71, 78, 84, 89, 94, 97, 160, 167, 184, 195, 217, 276, 342
Walker, Samuel, 2, 8, 13, 172, 188, 192, 296
Wall, Perry G., 96–97
Wallace, General Lew, 316, 317, 318, 332, 335, 336
Wallace, John: as school teacher, 76; page at convention, 179; attacks Stearns, 306; mentioned, 212, 213, 219, 286, 290, 293, 295, 297, 298, 301, 341
Walls, Josiah T.: 1868 convention delegate, 175, 180; nominated for Congress, 213, 223, 278, 279; declared elected, 216; replaces Charles Hamilton, 254; acquires *Gainesville New Era*, 288; attacked by Republican papers, 293; wins over Democratic opponent, 295; heads Conover convention at Madison, 302; loses congressional nomination, 305; mentioned, 283, 284, 290, 306
Ward, Thomas D., 143
Wardlaw, Benjamin F., 149, 282
Ware, Eldridge L., 172, 180
Warren, Isaac, 281, 282
Warren, Simon, 89
Washburne, Elihu B., 186, 196
Washington, D.C.: Florida Unionists at, 4; commission dispatched to, 18; mentioned, passim
Washington County, 4
Waukeenah, 95, 170
Waverly House: in Jacksonville, 264
Weeks, Francis M., 295, 298
Weeks, Major Edmund C., 3, 133, 278, 293
Welch, Adonijah S., 165, 193, 206, 207
Wells, Richard, 183
Wentworth, George E., 214, 220, 222, 310
West, James, 91
West, Thomas, 233
Westcott, James D., 196, 215, 222, 289, 290, 313, 330, 333, 334, 339
Westcott, John, 138, 234
Western North Carolina Railroad Company, Western Division of, 210, 247
Western Union, 121
West Florida, 68, 207
Wheeler, William A., 322, 325
Whitaker, William, 136
White, Pleasant W., 196, 213, 216, 318, 329, 330, 331, 334, 335, 337
White, Thomas W., 190
White, W. B., 212
Whitehead, Amos, 92
White opposition to Negro schools, 75
White Springs, 324, 326
White Sulphur Springs, Virginia, 154
Whitley, H. C., 228
Whitner, Benjamin F., 21, 22, 260
Wicker, Frank N., 302
Widden, John, 136
Wiggins, James M., 162

William A. Mackensie and Company, 271
Williams, Elijah: Negro inventor, 39
Williams, Emanuel, 228
Williams, George H., 284, 286, 332
Williams, S. N., 165, 246
Williams, Swann and Corley, 252, 262
Wilson, General James H., 17, 18
Wilson, Lemuel, 96, 126, 211, 281, 282
Wilson, William R., 133
Witherspoon, George W., 301, 302
Wolfe, J. D., 160
Wood, Ida, 156
Wood, Lot, 231
Woodfin, N. W., 247, 248
Woods, Judge William B., 332
Woolley, C. W., 322
Workingman's Aid Society of Duval County, 148
Workingman's Association of Pensacola, 139, 236
Wrecking: at Key West, 267
Wright, Benjamin D., 57
Wyatt, John, 175, 180

Ybor, Vicente Martinez, 267
Yellow Bluff, 215
Yonge, James, 303
Young, Bob, 229
Young, John Freeman, 145, 146
Young, Michael, 84
Young Men's Democratic Club, 227
Yulee, David L.: railroad affairs of, 6, 108–9, 110, 112, 114, 115, 166; imprisoned, 18; property seized, 27; released from prison, 42; land dealings of, 116, 262; cooperates with moderate Republicans, 185, 195, 210; accused of involvement in misuse of bonds, 220, 221; attacks bond issue, 247; Vose claim against, 251, 252; mentioned, 170, 243, 250, 256, 277, 296, 329
Yulee, Elias, 235